SPORTS

ON NEW YORK RADIO

A PLAY-BY-PLAY
HISTORY

DAVID J. HALBERSTAM

MASTERS PRESS

NTC/Contemporary Publishing Group

Library of Congress Cataloging-in-Publication Data

Halberstam, David J.
    Sports on New York radio / David J. Halberstam.
        p.   cm.
    Includes bibliographical references.
    ISBN 1-57028-197-1
        1. Radio broadcasting of sports—New York (State)—New York—
    History.   2. Radio broadcasting of sports—United States—History.
    3. Radio broadcasters—United States.   I. Title.
    GV742.3.H35   1999
    070.4'49796'097471—dc21   98-46621
                                                                                CIP

Interior design by Kim Heusel

Published by Masters Press
A division of NTC/Contemporary Publishing Group, Inc.
4255 West Touhy Avenue, Lincolnwood (Chicago), Illinois 60646-1975 U.S.A.
Printed in the United States of America
International Standard Book Number: 1-57028-197-1
99 00 01 02 03 04 LB 19 18 17 16 15 14 13 12 11 10 9 8 7 6 5 4 3 2 1

CONTENTS

INTRODUCTION

It was carefully instilled by my older cousins—root for the underdog. And the Yankees in those days were hardly ever underdogs. The '61 team of Mickey Mantle, Roger Maris, and Whitey Ford was being compared to the great '27 team of Babe Ruth and Lou Gehrig. Detroit was putting up a pretty good fight. The Tigers, led by Norm Cash and Al Kaline, actually had a chance going into the Labor Day weekend of 1961. As a boy of not quite 10 and in little control of my recreational schedule, I found myself in the Catskill Mountains, where my parents decided to spend summer's traditional last weekend. From what I remember, Detroit and the Yankees were tied at the time for first place. Young, naive, and full of fresh untainted enthusiasm, I really believed the Tigers might dethrone the perennial winners.

There was actually a television set in our hotel. There wasn't one in each room, but there was a fairly big set in the lobby, and most men congregated around it. No matter which team these men rooted for, each experienced exasperating frustration. Describing the picture as hazy would be generous. The black-and-white picture was fidgety. The images had shadows and the signal was jittery. Antsy viewers poked around with the lousy rabbit-ear antenna. It was to no avail and many gave up.

"Give me a darn radio," I thought. But there wasn't a radio in our room. Never shy, I convinced this one docile, cigar-clutching fellow, who was also frustrated by the stubborn television reception, to take me into his automobile. In the car, I was pained to discover that AM signals also fade a hundred miles from home. Radio's technical limitations could even overpower Mel Allen. The voice of the stentorian crackled on the car radio outside the Pioneer Country Club.

Albeit on a feeble, unstable, and distant signal, the radio was mesmerizing. The roar of the crowd was exhilarating. Like a man finding his love, I knew then that radio was for me. It fostered a kinship that put me behind home plate and never talked back. The flickering voice of Mel was mellifluous. Phil Rizzuto was the soothing nice guy next door, and Red Barber was detached but fatherly.

The Yankees dominated Detroit that weekend and eventually won the World Series. The pennant race became secondary, and Roger Maris became primary. As he raced to set the all-time single-season home run record, Mel was unrestrained while Red would never raise his voice. Red was Red. He insisted upon pronouncing *Los Angeles* with a hard *G*, the Hispanic way. I was only a kid then, I couldn't figure it out. He pronounced the *G* in *Los Angeles* like the *G* in the word great. He was impervious to convention. The world, of course, pronounced the *G* in *Los Angeles* like the *G* in the word *generation*.

At the barbershop, the Chinese laundry, or on the Sixteenth Avenue bus in Brooklyn, the game on radio was seemingly always on, especially baseball. After all, back then, football and basketball were just ways to fill time between baseball seasons. Radio has been a wonderful lifelong companion, producing compelling, illuminating, and unforgettable theater.

At first, any announcer sounded good. Then I went through a discriminating phase of judgment and taste. Glickman was inspiring, Marv Albert was galvanizing, and Spencer Ross was invigorating. After graduating from college, I committed my professional life to radio and to learning every aspect of it. I had fallen in love with basketball as a teenager and wanted to announce the sport myself. So I moonlighted calling college games while embarking upon a sales career in radio.

I was fascinated by the history of radio sports, and beginning in the 1970s I kept copious notes on the subject. There was little written, but the old-timers were always ready to tell stories, whether of their pasts or their memories of radio in general.

In the summer of 1986 Dave Sims hosted a talk show on WNBC Radio. He knew of my love of the history of radio sports and invited me to be a guest on his program. We talked about everything, beginning with Harold Arlin's first baseball broadcast in Pittsburgh in 1921 to fond memories of Barber and Allen. We had calls from listeners, and I was in my glory. Time passed too quickly. What could be better than a public forum of an esoteric subject I love most?

"Dick from Corona" phoned in to the show. I learned that he was blind, and radio was his world. One brief conversation and it was obvious that he was a treasure. I had the producer of the show give him my number, and beginning the very next day he started to fill the many undocumented blanks. He was and is a fountain of historical data.

Since our first conversation, Dick Barhold has shared an inexhaustible wealth of information on the subject. He is blessed with a genius-like memory. I have never met anyone as brilliantly gifted for instant recall of dates and facts. For starters, give Dick a date, any date, any year. He'll tell you the day of the week it fell. He will probably also be able to tell you what he was doing that day. Beginning with the early 1940s, his mind is encyclopedic. He can jump from one year to another, relating data from one decade to the next, and he's implausibly accurate. Year by year, team by team, station by station, Dick spews out data with the flawless precision of a computer.

Also about that time, autobiographies of sportscasters started sprouting. Lindsey Nelson, Jack Brickhouse, and Ernie Harwell were among those who penned books which shed more light on a subject that had little written on it. Curt Smith had just released his priceless tome on the history of baseball broadcasting, *Voices of the Game*. Red Barber, the most prolific author of all sports announcers, had written several publications including *The Broadcasters*, which addressed the history of radio sports and its pioneers. Red's work, however, was slanted to his many likes and dislikes.

By the summer of 1996 I had hundreds and hundreds of pages of anecdotal information, notes, and data. I had a couple of off-seasons left on my contract with the Miami Heat and decided to spend this precious free time writing a book on the history of radio sports. Through the patience of my wife, Donna, and our three lovely children, I was able to immerse myself sufficiently, to assimilate the information I had collected throughout a score of years, to organize the indispensable data that Dick Barhold had shared, complete the interviews with many aging broadcasters, and, most importantly, take time to research the roots of the pioneers and retrace their wonderful steps of the '20s and '30s.

In doing so, I reacquainted myself with the wonderful resources of America's libraries. The New York Public Library offers an abundant supply of microfilm of the daily press in its halcyon years, the first half of the 20th century when the choice of metropolitan area newspapers was endless. The Library of Congress was marvelous. Dave Kelly willingly helps sports researchers. The Washington-based house of record-keeping has newspapers from the beginning of time, from major cities all over our great land. The folks at the Miami Public Library were wonderful. They were generous with their time and publications, and when I needed help out of town trying to track down obscure facts, the people at the Newark Public Library and Norfolk Public Library helped with alacrity.

I'm forever thankful to my editors, Ken Samelson and Kim Heusel. Ken is a gem who grew up listening to many of the men covered in the text and has had a great passion for the project. Kim has helped me tighten direction and steer the project to a successful conclusion. John Halligan of the National Hockey League and Gordon Hastings of the Broadcast Pioneers have also been wonderful.

Completing the book has given me an overwhelming sense of fulfillment. More than anything else, the book is meant as a tribute to the founding fathers, the ones who paved the way for and influenced generations. It's a thank-you for years of free and pulsating entertainment. It's a token of appreciation for triggering the imagination, for painting an unforgettable word picture, for making miles of freeway enjoyable and hours of red lights bearable. For a group of people that has touched millions and affected generations, these great sports communicators and pioneers have not been paid their just due. Inexorably, they are being ignored by history. In my mind, it is sad.

In some ways, radio is only getting better. The Internet is a godsend. At virtually any time, you can find any game, anywhere.

Let's not forget how we got here. Let's remember our roots.

1

BOXING

THE PUGILISTIC ROOTS
OF RADIO

Radio's roots were in the boxing ring. To review the history of sports on radio without detailing the enormous impact of boxing would be the equivalent of listing the all-time great baseball players and skipping Babe Ruth. Boxing is not only the root of sports on radio but it is the very root of all of radio.

Indeed it goes back to the very beginning. Radio was actually tested before radio stations were licensed in the early 1920s and sporting events were a part of the experiment. At the turn of the century, radio was referred to as "wireless telegraphy." From a steamship off the New York Harbor, Guglielmo Marconi broadcast an immensely popular event at the time, the America's Cup. On shore, under the sponsorship of the *New York Herald*, eager fans were able to follow the progress of the race in front of the newspaper's building at Herald Square on 34th Street. There was such a rush of people that the crowds blocked traffic.

Once the technology was in place to beam a human voice into the air and have it picked up by receivers over a vast area of land, one of the companies that manufactured receivers, Radio Corporation of America, wanted to create demand to have consumers buy their contraption. RCA's general manager was David Sarnoff. He had been with the American Marconi Company, the forerunner to RCA, which among other things was in the business of ship-to-shore transmission. As early as 1915, when he was just 24, Sarnoff suggested to the Marconi board of directors that it send entertainment and information over the air. He envisioned the public owning what he referred to as "music boxes." Sarnoff's board didn't take him seriously and turned him down.

1

By 1921 Sarnoff was in a position of authority and at the urging of Major J. Andrew White, he approved a promotional undertaking which would give radio the ultimate visibility it needed. White, at the time, worked for Sarnoff as editor of *Wireless Age*, a house organ for RCA that promoted "wireless telegraphy," the company's core business. Sarnoff approved a $1,500 budget of RCA funds for White to arrange for the live transmission of a tremendously promoted heavyweight championship fight between title holder Jack Dempsey and the French champion, Georges Carpentier.

In the early 1920s boxing dominated the sports pages, and coverage of a heavyweight title fight rivaled that of a world war. The World Series and college football, the closest events in popularity, couldn't compare in sheer public interest. Mainstream America was so consumed with boxing that even the exalted *New York Times* would dedicate half its front page to the fight. Before radio, live event coverage was nonexistent. Newspapers owned an exclusive so folks would run to the newsstands to await the arrival of the delivery trucks. A newspaper was the closest definition of immediacy.

There were problems in accomplishing this lofty mission. To begin with, much of the public didn't have receivers, RCA didn't have a license to transmit nor the equipment with which to do so and it didn't have the permission to run the fight, which was scheduled for July 2, 1921, in Jersey City, New Jersey. White worked cleverly, creatively, and cogently. Tex Rickard, Madison Square Garden's promoter, was in charge of the fight. White convinced him that since 91,000 seats had already been sold and in view of the fact that all of the nation and Europe were hungry for the fight, radio coverage would satiate public thirst. He then sold the Lackawanna Railroad on the idea of using one of its radio towers and the Navy on borrowing one of its transmitters. Next was the major issue of receivers which the general public didn't own yet. So the energetic White convinced theater mogul Marcus Loew and other operators to place receivers in their facilities. Additionally, some manufactured receivers were already in public circulation as well as some homemade sets that were made by amateurs in garages all over the country. Between the receivers the public had and the theater deals in many cities, much of eastern America could get the fight. RCA also petitioned and received approval for a one-day license to transmit. The call letters assigned were WJY. The Major attempted to get newspapers to promote the broadcast but only the *New York Times* obliged.

White apparently had some P. T. Barnum in him. To gain public support, White took part of the proceeds from ticket revenue at the theaters and earmarked it for two charities, the Navy Club and the American Committee for Devastated France. (This was just after World War I.) This way there was public sentiment in support of the project.

White and the engineering people overcame all the bureaucratic red tape and he was ready to broadcast the fight. One other problem, White had never described a fight. How would he do blow-by-blow? He had participated in some amateur boxing as a youngster, so he prepared for the broadcast by "shadowboxing in front of a mirror and singing out each move," as he would say later. "It soon became apparent to me that no one could accurately describe every blow, so I adopted the scheme of 'collecting' punches which is still in use."

July 2 was a rainy day and the main event was delayed. As such, when Major White started his historic broadcast at the pronounced time, a preliminary bout was being waged by two great bantamweights, Frankie Burns and Packy O'Gatty. White started with the undercard and announced that rain or shine the Carpentier-Dempsey heavyweight tussle would begin at 3 P.M.

The broadcast was transmitted over WJY and the fight was heard over a powerful signal that traveled for thousands of miles through the country and Europe. White and Sarnoff were congratulated by telegram the next day from virtually everywhere, including London where RCA's president was vacationing.

The experiment was such a smashing success and showcased radio in such a glittering and indispensable light that it resulted in a proliferation of radio stations and in spiraling consumption of radio receivers. New York's first station was WJZ, now WABC (770). It started broadcasting in October 1921. WEAF, now WFAN (660), and WOR, still retaining its original call letters, and other facilities began broadcasting in 1922. FM was invented in the late 1920s by Edwin W. Armstrong but was hardly a factor until the late 1960s. Westinghouse experimented with radio in Pittsburgh in November 1920 by transmitting the results of the Harding-Cox presidential election on KDKA. On April 11 KDKA took a boxing report from Florent Gibson, a *Pittsburgh Post* writer who was stationed at the Pittsburgh Motor Square Garden and put it on the air.

Major J. Andrew White will forever be enshrined as America's first sportscaster. His pioneering on-air work continued through the 1920s before he left radio in 1930. Through it all, the young medium of radio benefited by his pertinacity.

WJZ, owned by RCA, amounted to little until its dedication on May 15, 1923. Meanwhile, WEAF went on the air in 1922 under the ownership of AT&T. The telephone company entered the broadcast business hoping to lower the cost of long-distance connections. WOR was based in Newark, New Jersey, where it was owned by Bamberger's Department Store and operated in the basement of its store.

At first, WJZ was run as a noncommercial station. Sarnoff projected RCA's revenue to be generated from receiver sales. He envisioned WJZ to be supported by 2 percent of the gross radio receiver sales. In fact, for several years, he publicly advocated the endowment of stations by philanthropists. Sarnoff projected $22.5 million in receiver sales by 1923. He was right on target.

WEAF did sell commercial blocks of time to sponsors and in 1925 already showed an operating profit of $150,000. Meanwhile, WJZ was losing about $100,000 a year.

Because it was fearful of potential governmental regulation and because it didn't want to get into the entertainment business, AT&T sold WEAF to RCA on July 1, 1926. Sarnoff, now controlling both WJZ and WEAF, formed the National Broadcasting Company on November 15, 1926. Within just a couple of months, NBC broke it down to two programming networks. NBC Red was transmitted over WEAF and NBC Blue over WJZ. By the time that NBC was formed, 5 million homes were equipped with radios and NBC began signing up stations for its network.

White remained with RCA in various capacities including sports broadcaster for WJZ. However, he had been beaten out by Charles Popenoe for the

Courtesy Blair White

Radio pioneer Major J. Andrew White at ringside.

program manager's job and was growing restless. He then focused his attention on forming his own network. With the help of a concert manager and a catch-as-catch-can promoter, White formed the United Independent Broadcasters and signed up 16 stations. The Columbia Phonograph Company shortly thereafter bought into the network and its name was changed to the Columbia Phonograph Broadcasting System.

On September 18, 1927, the new network was born that would eventually compete with NBC. Andrew White was its first president. Losing about $100,000 a month, the network was in desperate need of an infusion of cash. A Philadelphia millionaire invested in the network, but by 1928, still on the verge of bankruptcy, the company was sold to the family of William Paley who dropped "Phonograph" from the company's name. Paley became chief executive of Columbia. But at that point, the Columbia network didn't own a radio station, so until it purchased its own station, WABC (860), now WCBS (880), the network leased time on WOR.

By 1934 the Kunsky-Trendle Corporation, which owned radio station WXYZ in Detroit, was hoping to syndicate its locally produced program, *The Lone Ranger*. NBC and CBS had turned it down. So WXYZ made arrangements for it to be carried on powerful outlets, WGN in Chicago, WOR in New York, and WLW in Cincinnati. This foursome formed the beginnings of the Mutual Broadcasting System at the end of 1934.

ABC was really a result of a government edict. The Federal Communications Commission ruled that no company could operate more than one network. NBC, owning two networks, the Red and the Blue, sold the Blue to the American Broadcasting System in 1943. Its first owner was Edward J. Noble, the Life Savers Company millionaire. With the purchase came ownership of New York's WJZ.

Since radio's beginnings, most New York stations have had their frequencies, wattage, and call letters changed. In fact, much has changed since the early days of radio when the medium came under the rule of the Department of Commerce. Later it came under the jurisdiction of the Federal Radio Commission, now called the Federal Communications Commission.

With the advent of television in the 1940s doomsayers were predicting the death of radio. But even with the spiraling growth of cable television, the little "music box," as Sarnoff referred to radio in 1915, is booming. Despite enormous competition from traditional and nontraditional media, radio is alive and well in the 1990s.

On July 4, 1923, Dempsey defended his title, defeating Tom Gibbons. The fight was held in Shelby, Montana. WOR provided radio coverage in New York through direct communication with Shelby from its Newark, New Jersey, studio. Its studio announcer, G. A. Frazier, gave a detailed story immediately after the last blow was struck.

Meanwhile at WJZ, White presided over a variety of broadcasts. He covered the 1924 national convention and presidential election, the play-by-play of weekly college football games and occasionally baseball. In 1923 White did the blow-by-blow of the Jack Dempsey–Luis Firpo heavyweight championship fight over a string of stations that included WJZ.

The Major did his homework before broadcasting the brawl. He spent some time at Dempsey's training headquarters at White Sulphur Springs. Again, interest in the title tussle was overwhelming. Receivers were now more common and those who couldn't access the fight on radio went to the theater where it was run on loudspeakers. After the scrap, one magazine wrote, "Argentina heard and the whole United States listened, at home, in the streets and in theaters for five epochal minutes." The battle was savage and the first round memorable. Both pugilists knocked down their opponents more than once. But the Argentinean whacked the American flat out of the ring. Dempsey was pushed back in with the help of the scribes sitting in press row alongside. Both survived being beaten to virtual pulps before they were saved by the bell at the end of the first round.

The minute's rest before the second round served Jack well. He knocked Firpo out in the first minute of the second round to defend his title. One critic later lauded the broadcast of the Major, "who was able to make vivid to the listening millions the things which were occurring with lightning-like rapidity. He is the pioneer, and still the peer of broadcasters."

Don Dunphy, who would become boxing's most prominent announcer, was a kid that September 14 night listening in his Manhattan home to the Major's broadcast from the Polo Grounds. Don recalled a lot of confusion on the broadcast. Remember that the first round was chaotic and that each fighter was knocked to the canvass several times. "'He's up! He's down! He's up! He's down!' White shouted. This would go on and on. White wouldn't say who was up and who was down," Dunphy recalled.

Graham McNamee, a rival of White's at WEAF, later made reference to the Major's confusing description in his 1926 autobiography, *You're on the Air*. Describing his own baseball broadcast style McNamee wrote, "But there was not so much raw drama, swift action, and suspense as in the ring, where often all the poor announcer can say is, 'he's up, he's down; he's down, he's up,'" an obvious shot at White.

A radio in the mid-1920s was hardly the little transistor headsets we use today when we jog around town. Nor by any means was it a transistor that can be placed on a table. Most early radio sets were of the crystal variety. Dunphy described the radio that he used that night to listen to White's call. "It was a wallet-size instrument that looked like a billfold when closed. When opened, it consisted of a coil of wire and a very thin piece of wire called a cat's whisker, touching a small piece of crystal. When this little wire was manipulated to touch different parts of the crystal, it would get different stations. Every so often, the wire would annoyingly slip off the crystal or onto a dead spot. Then a pair of earphones would connect to the set and that would amplify the sound."

In other words, as a kid Dunphy tuned in to the fight and on earphones related the developments to his entire household. It was his blow-by-blow debut. Radios with speakers weren't popular till later, and early on, the speakers were huge. Many were placed on legs so that someone small could fit underneath the set. It was a great hiding place for kids. Vin Scully remembers how as a child he would cuddle on a pillow under the radio, listening to Ted Husing on college football. The youngster was enthralled by the roar of the crowd.

Getting back to White, William Paley in his autobiography, *As it Happened*, described him "as a good broadcaster, who was known around town for his natty dress which included a prince-nez with a ribbon and a white carnation in his lapel. He had style. He asked me once for an advance of $500 and, when I gave him the money, he said, 'Thanks, it's going for a second-hand Rolls-Royce.'"

In 1926 one of the most popular single sporting events in the history of the land took place in Philadelphia. It was the first of two magnificent heavyweight title fights between Gene Tunney and Jack Dempsey. The buildup was at unprecedented heights. It was absolutely enormous. Everyone, man, woman, and child awaited the battle between these two titans. At the time, America was a country consumed by boxing, so when a formidable contender was about to challenge the champion Dempsey, the country put everything aside to follow this mammoth event. The most conservative gauge to measure the magnitude of interest is the *New York Times*. Sports are not generally the priority of its coverage. Eight-column, three-line headlines are usually reserved for war, election, and assassinations.

On the morning following the big skirmish, the *Times* headline was just that: top of the front page, the width of the page, and three bold and pervasive lines. And from the top to the bottom of page one, six of the eight columns were dedicated to coverage of this enormous event.

September 23, 1926, was another huge night for radio. The *Daily News* reported that 20 million fans from coast to coast were estimated to have listened to the fight and the *New York Times* ran a verbatim text of the blow-by-blow broadcast the following morning, using a relay team of three shorthand experts to record the quick-paced commentary.

While the country's population at the time was some 125 million, only about 5 million families had radio sets. Thus, if every set in existence was tuned to the fight, an average of four people were listening to every set. Another New York newspaper reported that the blow-by-blow coverage on radio was heard by 25 million. Either way, the numbers were immense and intense. The radio listeners were a lot more comfortable than the 132,000 who attended the championship in Philadelphia where it rained. In New York alone, it was estimated that 2 million listened to the description.

Fans gathered on Broadway, at Union Square, at Madison Square Garden, and at hundreds of shops and other spots where loudspeakers were installed. Knots of fight fans took their places as early as an hour or two before the fight to get a good spot near loudspeakers. Those in Greenwich Village celebrated the victory of Tunney, their native son and intelligent prizefighter, by shouting joyfully and thrashing tin cans while gluing their ears to the radio.

Although it was a couple of months before the NBC Network was officially started, RCA already owned both WEAF and WJZ at the time of the fight. A network of 33 stations was organized to carry the broadcast. Major White was WJZ's top sports announcer and Graham McNamee was WEAF's. In view of this, these two men, who would turn out to be pioneers of sports broadcasting, would call the fight together splitting the blow-by-blow, color, and between-rounds analysis. It was the only major sporting event that these two radio giants would work together. By 1927, of course, White had organized the network that would eventually be CBS so the two men were with competing networks.

McNamee received a letter from Texas congratulating him on a fabulous broadcast. The listener, an appreciative farmer, wondered whether the sponsor of the broadcast, The Royal Typewriter Company, also sold shovels.

McNamee was brutally honest with his listeners. At the end of the eighth round, he announced that the fight was getting "a little boresome." As the fight progressed, McNamee was frank, "Jack Dempsey is only the hollow shell of his former self."

White's description was on target, too, as the fight wound down. The Major:

Jack's left eye is tightly closed now. He is fighting with one eye. His face is all red. He is cut over the eye. Tunney lands a right on Jack's eye again.

The rain is pouring down and making it more difficult to see what is going on.

Jack lands a right hook on Gene's jaw, but it was not a stiff one. Gene was not even staggered by it. It looks as if we are going to have a new champion. Jack is unable to rally.

7

The transcript of the broadcast indicates that McNamee's style was in the past tense:

Dempsey elects to go in and did manage to deliver his left. It traveled about four inches and caught Gene clean. Gene has just caught Dempsey a hard overhand right on the ear.

White and McNamee were rivals indeed. Although they worked this gigantic event together, the two men went up against one another that fall with different football schedules.

For Major Andrew White, it was the last heavyweight championship fight he would call on network radio. Dempsey and Tunney would meet in a rematch the following September at Soldier Field in Chicago. But what resulted permanently changed the American broadcast sports landscape.

There was fantastic anticipation. Tunney-Dempsey II was being built into a spectacle. The country was again enthralled. The battle of the gladiators was seemingly on everyone's mind.

As arrangements were being made for this fighting phenomenon, the Major had already organized Columbia. He had signed his first group of stations for the new web and for the first time in its very short history NBC had competition.

In anticipation, NBC alertly signed a contract with Madison Square Garden's Tex Rickard, promoter of the fight, for exclusive coverage. But Rickard included a provision that allowed WMAQ, the Columbia outlet in Chicago, to broadcast the fight locally. White in fact was to do the blow-by-blow for WMAQ.

White, president and announcer of what was then the forerunner to CBS, announced that it, too, would make the fight available over its entire network. An incensed M. H. Aylesworth, NBC's president, reiterated that it had exclusive coverage, presenting a contract that he and Rickard had signed. Rickard was adamant that NBC had an exclusive.

But in view of the fact though that Rickard was allowing WMAQ to transmit a description of the fight and that WMAQ was a Columbia affiliate, it was White's plan to pick up WMAQ's feed via AT&T lines and make it available to the entire network. While it sounded coy, White contended that once the signal leaves Soldier Field, Rickard had no jurisdiction over it.

White seemed to be getting little support for his plan even from his Chicago Columbia affiliate. The WMAQ manager, Judith Waller, washed her hands clean of White's networking plan. "We will handle the fight ourselves with Major White at the microphone unless something unforeseen may come up that will reverse Rickard's decision," she said.

White, though, remained steadfast and bold, knowing the value of carrying this huge event on his fledgling network.

Some five days before the huge September 22 melee, AT&T said it stood ready to install the necessary lines if Columbia wanted the service and could remove itself of any legal obstacles that may be encountered. There was also speculation that should Columbia be prevented from carrying the fight, White would enter proceedings to prevent any broadcasting at all.

In the days leading up to the fight, Rickard, NBC, and Columbia all remained unwavering. Rickard and NBC insisted upon the exclusive and Columbia went ahead promoting its fight coverage, listing 15 stations it planned to feed. WOR was to be the New York outlet.

On the morning of the fight, White left for Chicago by airplane at 6 A.M. and the New York papers had both networks covering the fight, the new Columbia and NBC which at that point had 56 outlets. In fact, the *New York World* reported that fans were perplexed over the situation. "There were several fist fights over whether WEAF (NBC) or WOR (CBS) should be patronized."

What transpired at that point is unclear. Did White get cold feet? Was pressure brought forth by WMAQ? Did AT&T run into installation hassles at Soldiers Field by the fight organizers? One thing is clear. On the day of the big rematch, Columbia went to an Illinois circuit court seeking an injunction to restrain the promoters from giving NBC an exclusive broadcast right.

The court ruled that since NBC had contracted for the exclusive right, it was the most interested party other than the complainants and that it would be unfair to interfere with NBC's privilege or pass judgment on the validity of the contract without giving NBC a chance to be heard. The presiding judge dismissed the Columbia petition for want of equity.

It was the first-ever battle between two broadcasters for rights to a sporting event and a judge characterized an exclusive rights contract as "equity." The episode was a setback to Columbia. Other than in Chicago, NBC had an exclusive. It was a landmark development that would rule sports and dictate billions of network dollars through to the 21st century.

Other than Chicago, McNamee had the country to himself and opened the broadcast poetically, "All is darkness in the muttering mass of crowd beyond the light. It's like the Roman Coliseum." And through the American landscape, folks huddled around loudspeakers on the street or families gathered around the radio, hanging on every one of Mac's words.

The heavyweight tilt turned into a royal battle, one of the most controversial in boxing history. Tunney retained his crown but not before a mammoth and historical seventh-round occurrence, known to fight fans as "the long count." After being peppered by Tunney, Dempsey courageously charged the champion and knocked him to the canvas. Tunney lay clutching blindly for the elusive helping rope. By all counts, he was there for some 15 seconds. But Illinois rules required the fighter to move back to the neutral corner during the count and apparently Jack did not do that immediately. It delayed the count and Tunney not only got up, he regained enough strength to win the fight and retain his crown.

In its bold three-line, top-of- and width-of-the-page headline, the *New York Times*, heralding the result of the championship fight, included MILLIONS LISTEN ON RADIO. The numerical estimates had the listenership at 50 million. While convicts in Sing-Sing were permitted to listen to the fight, including those on death row, 10 people in the New York area alone actually died of heart attacks while following the rumble on radio.

The morning after the heavyweight tilt, the *Daily News* reported that McNamee's call was thrilling and called the evening one of "triumph for WEAF, WJZ, and the other stations of the National Broadcasting Company hookup," adding that on the other hand, "it was one of defeat for the newly organized Columbia broadcasting chain which until a few hours before the battle promised it would also give details of the contest but was prevented because of NBC." It went on to chastise Columbia "for making a false start in promising something it

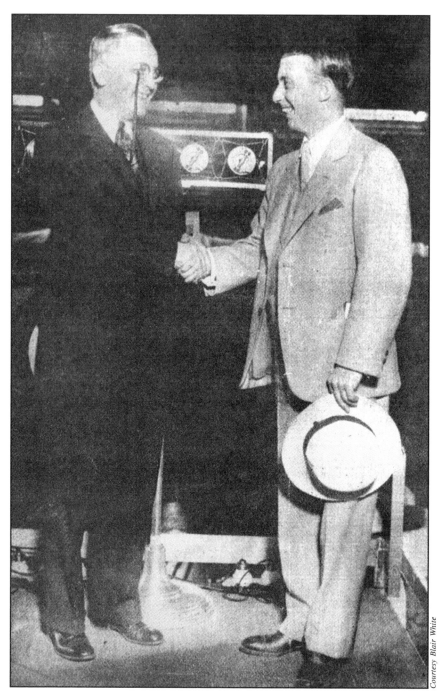

In what may be the only time Major Andrew White, left, and Graham McNamee ever shook hands, the pair meet before the second Dempsey-Tunney fight.

could not give." The *News* concluded its comments by lauding NBC: "The vast radio audience was more than satisfied with the colorful McNamee descriptions." No other heavyweight championship fight was on any other network until Gillette and Mutual assumed control in 1941.

McNamee was joined on coverage of the Dempsey-Tunney II by Phillips Carlin. Together, they were known as the "radio twins" because they worked together often and had similar voices. Carlin and McNamee would do boxing, football, and baseball together in the early 1920s for NBC. They would also work from the studio every weeknight from 4 to 10 P.M. Carlin would eventually go into management at both NBC and Mutual. He died in 1971 at the age of 77.

Meanwhile, White's role at CBS diminished once Paley took control of the company. Paley addressed White in his autobiography, *As It Happened*, referring to the Major as the nominal head of the network when he took control in 1928. "Major White understood radio at the microphone. But the business of radio or radio operations were not his talent or even within his knowledge." White would continue to broadcast sports and handle some programming responsibilities, but he no longer had a significant hand in running the company he helped found.

Just a short while before Paley's arrival in the fall, White would make a monumental contribution that would serve Columbia for almost a score of years. He hired the gifted Ted Husing who would dominate broadcast sports until after World War II. White took the young Husing under his tutelage the way Marty Glickman would do with Marv Albert 30 years later. The Major became his mentor and guided Ted through the early years of his glittering career.

By 1930 White, restless and promotionally shackled, resigned. On April 23 Paley sent a memo notifying the Columbia staff that "it is with exceeding regret that I have to report that Major White has asked to be relieved of his official connections." Some 65 years later, Major White's son, Blair, said, "Paley thought CBS history started with him and didn't want any part of my dad. Shortly after he left, my dad sold all his CBS stock. Otherwise, I would have a butler."

After trying his hand in several related and unrelated businesses, Major White moved to California in 1940 where he earned a doctorate, was a full-time psychologist and taught at the University of Southern California. He did maintain a friendship with his protégé, Husing, with whom he would occasionally get together in the 1950s and 1960s in Los Angeles. White and Husing both spent their final years in Southern California. The Major, America's first sportscaster, died in 1966 at the age of 76. Radio is forever indebted to this man of vision, passion, and energy.

When White's mission was radio, it was his imperturbable focus. Sports were no more than a means to an end. On the other hand, Graham McNamee was committed to the microphone through his entire broadcast career. He was not an administrator and never had any managerial aspirations.

Mac, as he was known to his friends, was a generalist. He would work out of the studio, hosting entertainment programs or be out on site, covering political conventions. McNamee would also do anything from a jubilee celebrating the creation of light to reporting on Lindbergh's return from his historic flight across the Atlantic. It took confidence, personality, and versatility. McNamee had these qualities and was America's first popular announcer.

Courtesy Blair White

Late in their lives, Major Andrew White, left, and Ted Husing chat in White's office.

From the start of his radio career in 1923 through the mid-1930s, if there was a big event, Graham McNamee was there. His very presence was almost an endorsement of the prominence of the event itself. He was the unquestionable signature voice of NBC and to a point the indomitable signature of radio.

By 1935 the gregarious McNamee would cover 12 World Series, 8 heavyweight title fights, and 3 Rose Bowls. No one would ever again dominate radio sports the way he did. He prided himself on his ability to cover 10 different sporting events at the drop of a hat. The popular sports were one thing but Graham would do swimming, tennis, and regattas on radio, too. The amazing element was his charm, spontaneity, and creativity. His style couldn't be characterized as derivative because no one had done it before.

Graham McNamee was born in 1888 in Washington, D.C., and grew up in St. Paul, Minnesota. His dad, a legal adviser to members of the cabinet, wanted him to become a lawyer. His mom wanted the boy to have a musical career.

As a young adult, he pursued a singing profession but concert work for a young artist wasn't very profitable. Looking to put some meals on his table, Graham took a job as a meat salesman but didn't find the work fulfilling and came to New York in the 1920s.

In 1923 he walked into radio station WEAF, then owned by AT&T. Blessed with a fine singing voice, he was hired as a staff announcer and assigned to the studio. Mac always had an interest in sports so when the station needed an announcer to describe the Harry Grebb–Jimmy Wilson fight in 1923, he was selected. That fall it was on to the World Series, followed by football and more. His list of sportscasting firsts is long and includes the first-ever national broadcast of a National Football League game, a Thanksgiving Day game in Detroit in 1934.

McNamee's voice might have been heard by more persons than any other living man at the time. No matter the subject, Mac was America's announcer. His signature greeting, "Good evening, ladies and gentleman of the radio audience," was as familiar to Americans as the voice of their president.

The great New York journalist of the time, Heywood Broun, paid McNamee the greatest praise. "Mr. McNamee has justified the whole activity of radio broadcasting. He has been able to take a new medium of expression and through it, vividly transmit a sense of movement and of feeling. Of such is the kingdom of art."

One writer of the time attributed his enormous popularity to his upbeat style and because his broadcasts generally seemed tinged with hysteria. In the 1920s and 1930s, America wasn't exactly on the verge of a nervous breakdown, but because its pace had quickened, just a smidgen of hysteria seemed appropriate.

His sports philosophy was simple. "The average fan wants excitement. Enthusiasm has to be contagious." Mac provided plenty of it. Fans adored him. To many, he was their only link to the sporting events they would only hear on the radio and never see live. Baseball as an example was in only 10 markets and most of the big fights were only in New York. Major college football programs were limited to a mere handful and the NFL was sputtering. Red Barber, a taskmaster, was profuse in his praise of McNamee, describing the relationship that he had with his audience as an "adulatory following."

Part of his preparation regimen was to literally force himself into a state of excitement or frenzy before every game broadcast. His ebullient personality always manifested itself and characterized his air work. He articulated the spirit of events, making them come alive on the radio by emphasizing emotion and color. McNamee, though, never perfected the technical precision of play calling. This would be done in following years by the likes of Sam Taub in boxing, Ted Husing in football, Red Barber in baseball, and Marty Glickman in basketball.

Ben Gross, the longtime radio critic for the *New York Daily News*, had recollections of Graham in his 1954 book, *I Looked and I Listened*: "Graham was not faking, he did not mean to deceive his listeners. But he was such an enthusiast, such an instinctive showman that before his eyes any action per se became a thrilling, spine-tingling drama."

The singer-turned-radio-announcer did not deny his philosophy. "The listeners are interested in the essential drama of the situation and the sidelights, as much as they are in the matters of how many balls and strikes have been called and how many yards have been gained."

When he had time to prepare his script, he was golden. His description of the environment at the ring was rich. "The fierce lights under their inverted cones are beating down on the contestants in the ring." McNamee also painted a colorful word picture of the fighters themselves. "Their pink and white bodies are glistening with sweat or flecked with blood." And the pioneer also did his homework, visiting the fighters in training camp, interviewing them, taking copious notes, and sharing snippets of their comments between rounds. Back then, of course, if the broadcast was sponsored, it had only one, not the laundry list of today. This in itself afforded broadcasters more time for editorial analysis and an opportunity to share some of their personality.

Graham's blow-by-blow coverage was hardly facile or fluid. It was rather uneven. He was prone to mistakes, having to correct himself too often. There were lulls followed by an avalanche of almost delirium. The southpaw didn't devise a rich nomenclature, either, and the number of his descriptive phrases was impoverished by today's standards. Often, when the action was fast and furious and required him to extemporize, he was tentative or would fluster.

One of the oldest radio sports recordings is of the Jack Sharkey–Max Schmeling heavyweight championship fight on June 21, 1932, in New York. McNamee split the blow-by-blow of the broadcast with Charles Francis Coe, a short-story writer and boxing authority. Coe sounded smoother, and more polished than McNamee. A listener to the tape today might wonder who really was the lead announcer that night.

Graham had charm, though. On June 14, 1934, Max Baer used profanity in the ring as he trash talked the champ, Primo Carnera. The ring was amply miked and McNamee was concerned that perhaps the dirty language was audible on the air. Alertly, Mac blurted, "I don't know exactly what Baer said but maybe it's better that way," and delicately moved along with his blow-by-blow description.

The broadcast of the fight was sponsored by Lucky Strike cigarettes and the sign of the time is best reflected in the between-rounds live exchange of the two commentators. They both described how men ringside and in the stands were reaching for a Lucky Strike during the pause in the proceedings.

Another commercial sign of the time was the advertising copy on a later fight for sponsor, Goodrich Tire. Every other word was *men*. "Men, when you drive this summer." "Men, the worst thing while driving is when you suffer a flat on the road." "Men, have you ever suffered a blowout on the road?" "Men, remember when you drive this July Fourth weekend . . . " This commercial was obviously written a couple of generations before political correctness was in vogue or before it was the norm to see women behind the wheel.

In 1930 McNamee covered the National Air Races in Cleveland and was on the telephone communicating with New York when his partner suddenly threw it back to him. Mac wasn't paying attention to his partner and didn't know he was on the air. He was talking angrily to the New York studio, shouting, "No station break now. We're in the middle of a race. Tell 'em to go ——— themselves." Luckily, the engineer used good judgment. Seeing that Mac was hot headed and perhaps not paying attention, he had shut his microphone off.

In Cleveland, too, on another occasion in the early 1930s, the beloved NBC veteran was working with Tom Manning, doing a heavyweight elimination fight between Max Baer and Johnny Risko. An invasion of bugs, attracted by the bright floodlights of the boxing ring, made it virtually impossible to see the action. Mac kept batting at them with a newspaper so that he can see. Finally, he blew up. "You listeners will have to read about this fight in tomorrow's paper. I'm only 10 feet away but I can't see the fighters because of these damned bugs." Mac, of course, finished the broadcast and the fans loved it.

Criticism of McNamee started to surface in the early 1930s. Radio required more precision. The influential writer Ring Lardner had written of Mac, "I don't know which game to write about—the one I saw today or the one that I heard Graham McNamee announce as I sat next to him." Not to say that Lardner was wrong but certain things never change. There is much jealousy between scribe and broadcaster.

Tom Manning was a fairly good blow-by-blow announcer himself and with swelling complaints of McNamee, NBC wanted to use him to call the Primo Carnera–Max Baer heavyweight championship fight in 1934. Manning, loyal to McNamee, insisted that NBC stick with its veteran. It did, but not for much longer.

McNamee was doing everything. He continued to team with an early radio personality, comedian Ed Wynn. The time demands on him were endless and the pressure he was under was enormous. Graham's strength, his chatty style, needed tightening. Commercials were all read live then and the timing had to be precise. Broadcasters couldn't be quite as unwieldy. Reports had to be accurate.

Pressure continued to mount in 1935 after McNamee called his last heavyweight championship fight, James Braddock's defeat of Baer, and NBC made a change. His role on football and baseball had been diminishing, and he was injured in an accident while covering the Soap Box Derby in Akron, Ohio. He was knocked unconscious by a racer and was confined to a hospital for three nights.

The critics were chirping, too. In 1935 *Literary Digest* wrote, "Radio fight fans have criticized bitterly the announcing of major fights." McNamee, of course, was NBC's centerpiece. Earlier, in 1934, the *New York Telegram*'s Alton Cook wrote, "If they don't like McNamee's description of fights, listeners can put on the fight in Spanish or Italian on shortwave."

There might have been other factors as well. By 1935 there was a fecundity of sports announcers. Ted Husing was setting loftier standards for sports broadcasting, presenting play-by-play accurately on rival CBS. In fact, at that point, Husing might have already surpassed Mac in popularity. Bill Stern had already done some work for the web and would eventually dominate NBC's sports coverage for 15 years. Stern was biting at the bit to do more. Bill Slater had come along for NBC in 1934 and by all accounts sparkled doing football.

By the end of 1935 the great Graham McNamee was put out to pasture. He was still in studio and a front man for the network but no longer its dominant talent.

He was employed by NBC until his death shortly before his 54th birthday in 1942. "He died, burned out," broadcaster Lindsey Nelson would say later.

Ben Gross visited Mac in his later years in his Manhattan apartment. "He spoke with affection of some of his famous radio broadcasts. Suddenly, he banged a fist into a palm and frowned. 'They don't want me anymore,' he said sadly."

The folks who worked with McNamee flocked to Campbell's Funeral Home in Manhattan on May 12. His pallbearers were a veritable list of who's who in broadcasting, including broadcast partners Phillips Carlin and Tom Manning, Tommy Cowan, who did the first World Series in 1921 as one of radio's first announcers, and Milton Cross. He left an estate that was valued at $137,707, roughly what a network announcer might make today for doing an event or two.

His influence was far-reaching, particularly on boxing, the rage of the generation. It's best summed up by Lindsey Nelson who was assigned his very first heavyweight championship fight in 1957 on NBC, Floyd Patterson and Hurricane Jackson at the Polo Grounds. "I don't think I ever had an assignment that excited me so much as this one. It all went back to those days of

Clem McCarthy wanted to be a horse race jockey, but when he became too tall he turned to calling the races instead. He later rose to prominence as a boxing announcer in the mid-1930s.

Courtesy Ted Patterson

sitting on the living room rug and listening to Graham McNamee do Dempsey-Tunney."

History has paid homage to McNamee, treating him with deserved reverence and veneration. Major White was the first broadcaster to call a sporting event but his prominence was a flash in the pan. He moved on to more global areas of interest. Graham McNamee persevered. He was the first to broadcast sports regularly. He did it for the first 12 years of radio's existence, making an indelible impact by hopping from one event to another and from one sport to another. Successors have perfected where he lacked technically. But few, if any, have had his impact. Interest in sports increased dramatically during the time Mac was dominant on the airwaves. The galvanizing effect that he had on the American sports scene is in itself a testimony to his fabulous contribution, let alone the trailblazing effect that he had on sports broadcasting. And unlike later when a Vin Scully sat by Red Barber's knee or Marv Albert listened assiduously to Marty Glickman, McNamee flew by the seat of his pants. There was no teacher, no textbook, and no school.

Those whom we think of as sports announcers in the early years of radio all were called upon to do some general assignment work or entertainment, too. From Ted Husing to Bill Stern to Red Barber and even Mel Allen, they all were capable of broadcasting programming other than sports. The process was slow before the networks hired full-time sportscasters. It was, in fact, done earlier locally. One reason was the sponsor tie-ins that each of these gentlemen had.

Red, as an example, did many sporting events for Old Gold, a Brooklyn Dodgers sponsor. As such, when Old Gold put a variety show on the air, it would request Red's involvement.

Clem McCarthy rose to boxing prominence in the mid-1930s when he started being assigned fights by NBC. He eventually took over, albeit briefly, for Graham McNamee on heavyweight title matches in 1937. Clem, though, was and will always be identified first with horse racing. He was the pioneer, setting the stage for so many who followed, from Fred Capossela to Cawood Ledford to Dave Johnson.

McCarthy was born in 1882, the son of a horse dealer, and spent his boyhood at tracks throughout the country. He attended his first Kentucky Derby in 1892. When he grew too tall to become a jockey, he went to San Diego and became a track reporter. In 1927, when Arlington Park opened in Chicago, it was the first track to install a public address system and Clem became its race caller. In 1928 he did the stride-for-stride of the Kentucky Derby for a local Louisville station. By 1929 he was already so prominent that NBC hired him to call the Derby on the network. He did every Derby through 1950 when, oddly enough, he referred to the winner as Middleburg instead of Middleground. Mistakes, though, were aberrant through his glorious career. He had the gift, the blarney, and spoke the language of the track.

He was born in Rochester, New York, but there was a brogue to his speech. When the action was dramatic, it was as though he was reading a child a scary fairy tale, speaking deliberately and stretching words for emphasis. There was theater but it wasn't fabricated. Clem was truly thrilling. Yet he built his reputation on painting an impeccably accurate mind-picture. His voice was so distinct it was almost indescribable. On the one hand it was gravelly, but on the other hand it was mellifluous. There was almost a whiskey tenor to it. If you heard it, you would never misidentify it.

The stories of him at the track are part of broadcast lore. To begin with, Clem would actually talk to the horses on the air. "Get your head straight or you'll be caught napping, boy," he would tell a horse as the starting gate was being filled. "He's got plenty of horse left in him," he would say, when he felt the leader of the pack had enough to win a race.

In 1947, with the whole nation glued to the radio and many with some hard dollars resting on the outcome, Clem made the error of his life misidentifying the winner of the Preakness. He was already 64, but McCarthy would be ribbed for the mistake his remaining 15 years on earth.

The normally faultless McCarthy apparently had his view obscured when Faultless leaped out of the middle of the pack to overtake Jet Pilot on the far turn. The jockeys of the two horses were wearing silks of similar colors. When the horses reappeared into his view, the veteran race caller mistook Faultless for Jet Pilot who at that point had fallen out of the money and was all but through.

When he exclaimed Jet Pilot the winner and realized his grave error, he admitted it immediately, corrected himself, felt terrible, apologized profusely on the air and said, "Ladies and gentleman, I missed. Babe Ruth struck out, too. So I might as well get in famous company."

Bill Stern was McCarthy's partner on many of the Triple Crown broadcasts. He would do the prerace color and interviews. Stern was a household name among sports fans in the 1940s. He turned drama into melodrama.

Stern's football calls were riveting but they were mistake-filled. If he noticed that he had misidentified the ball carrier, Stern would fabricate lateral passes in the middle of a run to have the right fellow with the ball. "Smith laterals to Jones who goes in for the touchdown." Stern would say. In actuality, Smith never had it, Jones had it all the time. That's how Stern would cover up his blunders and sound like he never missed a beat. For the most part, television was nonexistent then. And no one listening to the radio knew the difference. So when Stern ribbed McCarthy for his celebrated racing boo-boo, Clem aptly quipped, "You can't lateral a horse, Bill."

McCarthy worked through all sorts of adversity in his colorful broadcasting career including a 1935 incident when he was almost killed by the winner, Azucar, in the winner's circle at Santa Anita.

Clem McCarthy

© National Sportscasters and Sportswriters Assn.

Three years later in 1938, War Admiral and Seabiscuit went at it in a match the entire sports world eagerly anticipated. The nation was obsessed. Even President Franklin Roosevelt cut short a press conference to tune in the race on the radio. Yet this race call which fans would later say "was the most exciting race report they ever heard" almost failed to get on the air. Clem himself would say that it was one of the high points of his picturesque career.

Before the race, McCarthy strolled out of the broadcast booth down to the paddock, expecting to return immediately. "But I couldn't make it," he said later. "The crowd was so great. I elbowed, fought and pleaded but there was a solid wall of humanity before, behind and all about me. I was panicky. NBC had an exclusive. It was an historic race. The whole world would be listening and I wouldn't be there."

He was able to make eye contact with the broadcast director up in the broadcast booth who motioned to him to pick up a nearby mike at the railing. A microphone had been installed there to interview the eventual winner of the race (Seabiscuit). McCarthy did just that. He leaped to the top of the railing, with the mike in one hand and his glasses in another, got his cue to start from the broadcast booth when the director lowered his handkerchief. When he got the signal, McCarthy unflinchingly shouted his famous, "They're off!" The broadcast that Clem almost failed to make, ended up being one of his best. It was intense, breathless, and one of his most famous. Many of those who heard it said that it was the greatest piece of race calling ever.

As a race caller, McCarthy was peerless. In February 1938 he called the Santa Anita Derby over NBC, aired by WEAF in New York. WOR picked up the call of Joe Hernandez on Mutual. The next morning, the *Daily News*'s Sid Shalit was unequivocal in his analysis, "McCarthy wins vocal honors in a walk."

Getting back to boxing, Max Baer fought Joe Louis in a heavyweight elimination match at Yankee Stadium in 1935. With criticism of McNamee growing, NBC started auditioning potential replacements on nontitle fights it was covering. Clem was assigned the blow-by-blow job. He was teamed with Edwin C. Hill, one of the country's great newsmen at the time. McCarthy was propped up on a typewriter so that he could be chin level with the ring.

It was a fight with social implications. Black communities around the country were rooting hard for Louis, the man dubbed the "brown bomber." In Harlem, when Louis triumphed, people surged through the neighborhood and blew horns in celebration.

Meanwhile, McCarthy's broadcast boxing debut was a smashing success. The *World Telegram* wrote: "Clem McCarthy did a graphic, crisp, thoroughly satisfactory job. Apparently the tribulations of radio fight fans are over. No more NBC experiments with fight announcers will be needed." NBC concurred. McCarthy was assigned the next heavyweight championship fight, the one when Joe Louis earned the title beating James Braddock in Chicago in 1937. The affable announcer proved that he was equally as stylized ringside as he was trackside. His intensity was captivating but not overbearing. And that voice, it was precious.

Red Barber once described it to be "as though he were grinding rocks together at the same time he was talking."

In 1938 when Joe Louis met Max Schmeling for the heavyweight title, both radio and boxing were in their golden ages. Schmeling had defeated Louis in a heavyweight elimination battle in 1936 and the world was about to come to a standstill to follow this mammoth of mammoth bouts. Can the German beat the black fighter again?

A record 146 NBC stations were lined up to pick up the fight. Behind the microphone at ringside, McCarthy was brilliant. "Schmeling is down; Schmeling is down" was his throaty and almost exulting call. When the fight was over, the peppy little Irishman jumped into the ring, hoping to interview the participants. He attempted in vain to snatch Schmeling. "Max, come over here; bring him over; Officer, get Max Schmeling." This was a point in time when the on-air commentary evidently wasn't the only thing that was done extemporaneously. The production was, too. Schmeling managed to elude McCarthy but perhaps not the wrath of Hitler. The German, the man of the master race, had been beaten by a black man. It didn't sit well with the Fuhrer.

The next morning the *Daily News* wrote of McCarthy's broadcast, "an apter choice could not have been made. Clem's vivid, staccato style—accurate, yet highly dramatic—transports the listener to the ring itself." It was the zenith of Clem's on-air boxing career and maybe heavyweight boxing overall, too.

In 1962, just after Clem passed on, the talented and longtime *New York Post* columnist Milton Gross wrote that McCarthy was "the most exciting voice of sports in a day when radio was the thing." Gross reminisced about the time that he appeared on Clem's show and was misidentified by the broadcaster as the famous cartoonist. After the show ended, Gross politely corrected McCarthy. "You should have corrected me on the air," Clem said unhesitatingly. Gross told him that he didn't want to embarrass him. "If a man can't take embarrassment," McCarthy said, "he has no right to be talking to all these people who hear him."

McCarthy's years were well before the years announcers made big money. Unfortunately Clem was wiped out financially by an auto accident and a series of illnesses in the 1950s. A humble and weakened McCarthy had to acquiesce to a fund-raiser by fellow broadcasters and writers to pay for his medical expenses.

He died penniless and lonely. But for a quarter of a century, sports fans who enjoyed his work were richer for it.

During the early 1930s there was a little man who probably wondered why NBC wasn't choosing him for the most cherished of assignments, calling a heavyweight title fight across the country. After all, he was the "voice of boxing" in New York, a true pioneer. Sam Taub had given boxing its language on radio. If Red Barber, Mel Allen, Phil Rizzuto, and Bob Murphy were baseball later, Taub was boxing then.

He was a contemporary of White, McNamee, Husing, and McCarthy. But White was a dreamer, McNamee a generalist, Husing primarily a football play-by-play announcer, and McCarthy a horse-racing announcer. Taub, though, was boxing!

He wrote the fight game, occasionally refereed it, ran training camps, and later handled boxing public relations and did gratis speaking engagements, promoting the sport he loved most. He started broadcasting fights locally in New York in 1926 when Madison Square Garden put WMSG on the air. He would do three or four fights a week and later as many as five or six. If the Garden didn't have a fight scheduled, there was the Coliseum in the Bronx, the Olympic Club, St. Nicholas Arena, or the Ridgewood Grove. The wrecking ball might have long since taken care of these assemblages but it couldn't expunge the pioneering broadcast contributions that Taub made in them. If there was a scrap, Taub was there. It didn't matter what the weight classifications of the fighters were, Sam called the fight.

He had no aspirations to do baseball or college football. It started and ended at ringside. He never attended college and would hardly be confused as a master of the king's lexicons but Sam Taub constructed the verbal framework of radio blow-by-blow description. He had a thick New York accent and would swallow the ends of words, at a time when radio was very sensitive to voice quality and enunciation. When Taub was still with the *Telegraph*, before he entered broadcasting, Ben Gross wrote that "he spoke so rapidly that one had difficulty understanding him." Marty Glickman described Sam as "a lovely guy, a little round man who was very New York. He had little command of grammar and it could be pretty funny." Perhaps Marty was remembering the day that an excited Taub said, "He hit him in a neutral corner where it doesn't hurt."

It may have taken time for Taub to break in nationally but the native of the Lower East Side was a household name among fight fans in New York through the 1920s and 1930s. And even after his broadcast career ended, Taub loved the ring too much to simply ease into retirement. As late as 1959, when Sam was about 70 years old, he would work as a ring announcer. Howard Cosell was on ABC Radio covering the Floyd Patterson and Ingemar Johansson heavyweight title fight. Howard sent it ringside to Sam Taub for the introduction of the fighters. Taub was flawless and ebullient, and the strong familiar voice was in fine fettle. He was where he felt most comfortable, at a boxing match.

His husky voice belied his diminutive 5-foot, 2-inch build. He started as an assistant and later as a writer for the real Bat Masterson who was sports editor of the *New York Telegraph*. Masterson was of course later portrayed by Gene Barry in the television program that beared his name. Sam would always later say that Barry was nothing like the real Bat Masterson.

Taub's first heavyweight championship fight on network radio wasn't until 1938 but it hardly mattered to those in the know or to the New York fight fans who were weaned on his knowledgeable and engrossing broadcasts. Networks and sponsors have their own reasons for doing things and selecting talent. Too often, though, decisions aren't based on talent alone. Name a sport today. Many network announcers couldn't shine the local announcers' shoes. But who says life is fair? Sam Taub was the founding father of boxing on radio. The fights came to life on the radio through Sam Taub!

It started just after the birth of WMSG in 1926. He was asked to broadcast fights on this curious new medium of radio. "I accepted the opportunity irrespective of the fact that there was no pay. The idea of being a regular broadcaster apparently overawed me," he would say some 50 years later. The New York State Athletic Commission, which once requested Graham McNamee to refrain from editorial comments when doing blow-by-blow, finally got involved. "They forced WMSG to pay me $25 a fight." Before long, the fights were being carried on WMCA and WEAF (now WFAN). In the '30s, there were weeks that he worked five or six nights a week of boxing on radio. In addition, he also started hosting a popular program on WHN, *The Hour of Champions*. It ran for 24 years and guests were the likes of Joe DiMaggio and Jack Dempsey. They would appear happily and without being paid. Adam Hats, a staple of Sam's programs, was one of the show's sponsors.

Sam worked with many partners including the top names of radio. "In 1933, I worked a fight in Newark, New Jersey, with Ted Husing. A welterweight, Lou Halper, was fighting another guy. It's in the middle of the scrap and five fights break out in the stands. The guys in the ring stop fighting to watch. I think fast, turn around and describe the fights in the stands."

"If it was Sam, he could make you see it," the great columnist Red Smith once wrote of Taub, describing the boxing legend known for "his reedy, staccato voice, redolent of the New York streets." Smith wrote of Taub's contagious energy, "One night he was doing a fight from the Bronx Coliseum and lending an Armageddon touch to the ten-round feature until the seventh round, when the referee threw both bums out for not trying."

Taub was the first to incorporate the lingo of the fight scribes and the pugilists themselves. "The third man in the ring." "He crowded him into the ropes." "He lunges out with a long right high to his head." Some also credit Taub with the phrase "an overhand right uppercut." Others attribute it to McNamee.

Later broadcasters might have been smoother and more cultured. But Taub was the guy down the block and he was loved by fight fans the way Phil Rizzuto and Red Barber would later be adored by Yankees and Dodgers fans. Sam was unshakable behind the microphone, intense yet soothing.

While Taub and frequent partner Angelo Palange did the Primo Carnera–Tommy Loughran heavyweight championship tussle locally on WMCA in 1934, it was only because the networks had turned down the opportunity to broadcast the fight.

NBC, which then owned virtually every major fight, finally started using Taub in the 1930s. The network apparently used him reluctantly at first and certainly not on the glamour heavyweight tilts. In fact, when Sam was assigned the Tommy Farr–Lou Nova battle on December 16, 1938, the *Telegram* wrote

Boxer Max Baer jokes with announcer Sam Taub. Taub was a household name in New York during the 1920s and 1930s before rising to prominence on the national level.

rather mockingly, "His account, accent and all, will be short-waved to England." In those years, NBC did fights of all weight classifications, not only title bouts but elimination matches as well.

It was probably at the urging of Joe Louis's promoter, Mike Jacobs, who was close to Taub, that NBC finally moved him up the broadcast depth chart. On February 23, 1938, he handled the network blow-by-blow of the Louis-Mann heavyweight tilt, his first on network radio.

But when the true Armageddon between Joe Louis and Max Schmeling was held on June 22, 1938, pressure was brought forth by sponsors and NBC to have a network name. Not only was the broadcast scheduled to blanket an eager nation, it was also being fed to many parts of the world. Taub wasn't selected.

Clem McCarthy was and he was paired with Ed Thorgersen, the voice of the newsreels. Before television brought news into living rooms, Americans had to pay their way into movie houses to watch footage of world news. It was there that Thorgersen narrated the film.

Taub's partner for most network fights was the dramatic raconteur, Bill Stern, who would do prefight color and between-round analysis and commercials. Stern, himself, did the blow-by-blow of the Louis-Galento heavyweight match in June 1939, but his role on fight broadcasts was generally as host, interviewer, and between-rounds analyst. The Taub-Stern team did 10 heavyweight title tilts, all involving Joe Louis.

During that span, Louis successfully defended his title, beating Jack Roper in Los Angeles. NBC carried the fight at 1 A.M. New York time but didn't ship Taub and Stern to California. Instead, NBC picked up Mark Kelly, a Los Angeles sportswriter to do the blow-by-blow and Bing Crosby handled color. The crooner by all accounts did fairly well, noting before the fight began that Mrs. Roper "can always tell right after the first round whether her husband is going to win or lose." The psychic gift was useless in this case. Roper was knocked out in the first round. Crosby would later occasionally sit in with the baseball regulars, doing some play-by-play too. He seemed pretty comfortable in the role.

The sponsors held the broadcast rights back then and for years, the fights were under the aegis of Adam Hats. Taub was so closely identified with the sponsor that he was known as the "Adam Hat Man." When Adam and NBC lost the rights to the bouts in 1941, the winds of change blew through the broadcast booth. Taub was out.

In its obituary, the *New York Times* reported that Sam Taub also did the first-ever telecast of a boxing match when Lou Nova knocked out Max Baer at the Garden on April 4, 1941. *Variety* magazine had a review of boxing bouts televised from the Ridgewood Grove in Brooklyn on October 21, 1939. Sam Taub did the blow-by-blow and the reviewer liked his work, particularly his transition from radio to the then embryonic television. "Taub spoke in measured tones and permitted the onlooker to see for himself what went on," according to *Variety*.

Taub continued to do some television through 1947 when he called the Rocky Graziano–Tony Zale tilt, then moved back to some radio for an ad-hoc network, the long since gone Associated Broadcast Corporation. It had a familiar sponsor, Adam Hats. WMCA was the outlet for many of the Taub-called broadcasts. By the late 1940s, the true founding father of radio boxing left the blow-by-blow business. He stayed in the fight game though, doing some writing, public relations, and management. Sam Taub lived to the ripe age of 92, passing away in 1979. He witnessed an estimated 10,000 fights and broadcast some 7,500.

In 1941 a decision monumental to the broadcast of boxing was made. The Gillette Company added boxing to its cavalcade of sports sponsorship, offering $5,000 an event to the promoter which was 10 times the amount of incumbent Adam Hats. Taub and Stern, so closely identified with Adam, were replaced. Gillette naturally wanted to establish a fresh name and identity.

Gillette switched the broadcasts from NBC to Mutual, which made sense. Gillette and Mutual were already involved with baseball broadcasts, a marriage

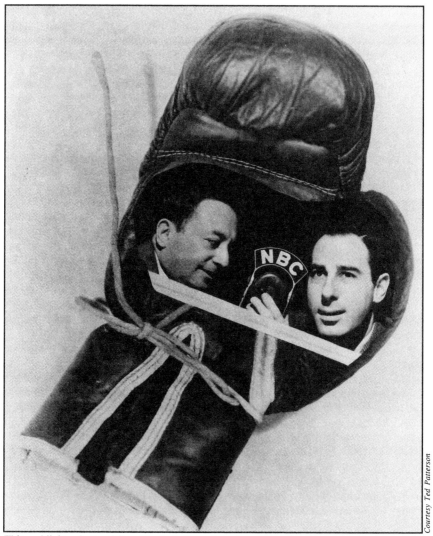

Courtesy Ted Patterson

This publicity photo of Sam Taub, left, and partner Bill Stern was taken in 1940, just a year before a change in sponsors resulted in their replacement on national boxing broadcasts.

that was formed two years earlier. NBC, the first network to do boxing, lost the major fights for the first time ever.

Gillette had its sights set on Ted Husing, then America's most popular sportscaster. Husing was an institution at CBS but Gillette carried sufficient weight to have CBS acquiesce to allow Ted to do the fights on Mutual. CBS was prepared to agree, but just then a totally unrelated dispute developed between Mutual and CBS. It was over differences regarding musical union affiliations. The two networks were feuding and CBS wasn't in a mood to cooperate. Husing wasn't allowed to do the Gillette-Mutual broadcasts. Time was a big factor.

There was only about a month before Gillette's first fight and it was a block-buster. Joe Louis and Billy Conn were to meet for the heavyweight champion-ship and Gillette had no announcers. Conn was considered the best contender for Louis since Schmeling.

The interest in the fight game was still surging when Gillette organized an audition of broadcasters for this fantastically visible position. The winner would in essence be the "voice of boxing," America's highest-rated broadcast sport.

On the night of May 22, 1941, a light heavyweight championship fight was scheduled at Madison Square Garden. The participants' names weren't ex-actly Smith and Jones. They were broadcasters' nightmares, Anton Christoforidis and Gus Lesnivich. Those who auditioned included Mel Allen, Paul Douglas (who later gained fame as an actor), Bert Lee, and others. Each announcer audi-tioning would work one round.

There was one other—Don Dunphy. He was hardly a household name. Just 32, Dunphy was sports director at WINS and his experience broadcasting fights was limited. He started at the station working for sports director Earl Harper, doing a variety of events and studio shows. But he was hardly promi-nent at the time. Dunphy had done an occasional college football game, a basket-ball game, or a track meet plus the usual daily sports reports and interviews. He had done a couple of years of amateur fights, the Diamond Belts and the Golden Gloves, and some professional fights from the Queensboro Arena. But Dunphy had never done major bouts.

He fortunately had befriended the people in Mike Jacobs's promotional office and they urged Gillette to include him in the audition. Working smartly, Dunphy won the announcers' square-off. While the others staggered through names that were tongue twisters, Don was smooth as silk, using first names only. During the flurry of his blow-by-blow, he smartly didn't risk stammering by referring to the fighters' multisyllabic last names. It was clever and it paid off. The former Manhattan College track star was teamed with Bill Corum, a well-known columnist at the time with the *New York Journal American*. Gillette waited until just a couple of weeks before the fight to make the decision.

His big national debut was the much-anticipated showdown between Billy Conn and Joe Louis. It was the fight in which Louis eventually defended his heavyweight title for an unprecedented 18th time. A crowd of 55,000 was gath-ering at the Polo Grounds ready to scream themselves hoarse. The main event was scheduled for 10 P.M.

Cec Hackett, general manager of WINS, invited Dunphy to have dinner with him and his wife at their East Side apartment and they would then all drive up to the Polo Grounds. Dunphy thought it would be prudent to accept. "I had no appetite, all I was thinking of was the fight. We left the East Side with time to spare. But traffic near the stadium was at an absolute standstill. And once we finally got there, the maze to get to the ring itself was impassable. I just made it, arriving minutes before air time. Craig Smith, the Gillette people and the Mutual folks all breathed a sigh of relief when they saw my face."

Dunphy got rave reviews from *Newsweek* shortly after the big bout. It wrote that "His rapid-fire delivery, vibrant voice and vivid style of emphasizing only the important punches thrilled millions who heard the broadcast."

From that point forward, Dunphy *was* boxing! Gillette owned the package and he was their man. (In fact, he would be assigned some nonboxing by Gillette, too. In 1959, for instance, he did the NBA All-Star Game on radio.)

Dunphy was the smoothest but the least emotional of the blow-by-blow men to that point. He was quick, crisp, and hardly ever made a mistake. Don was the perfect network guy, sensitive, politically correct, almost never critical, and always polite. There might not have been the passion of McCarthy in his voice and unlike Taub, boxing wasn't always in his blood, but he developed a conviction for his work out of pragmatism. The football and baseball gigs were out of reach, so he was relishing his role. As for Taub, Dunphy says that despite the fact that he unseated his predecessor as the "voice of boxing," the two remained friends.

Boxing's dominance is best underscored by the radio ratings it got in the '30s, '40s, and into

© *National Sportscasters and Sportswriters Assn.*

Don Dunphy

the '50s. The numbers paint an appreciation of its dynamism. The September 20, 1939, fight between Joe Louis and Bob Pastor in Detroit resulted in a mind-boggling rating of 47.6. To translate, almost half the country was tuned in to the scuffle. The World Series that season did just a 21.3 while the 1939 college football season averaged a 33.0. In other words, heavyweight boxing was the most popular sport by far, followed by college football and baseball. Basketball and hockey were barely blips on the radio radar screen at that point.

Europe was also at war then and the United States was at the brink of World War II. Americans were listening carefully to every one of President Roosevelt's words when he addressed the nation. The Louis-Pastor fight was only on one network, one of the president's important speeches on the issue was on all four (NBC Red and NBC Blue, CBS, and Mutual) and did only a 45.5, less than the boxing match. Today, the Super Bowl on television hardly garners these ratings. In 1938 the tremendous interest in the Louis-Schmeling showdown turned into a whopping 63.6. Think of it for a moment. Sixty-three percent of the United States was tuned in to Clem McCarthy's call.

Gillette would move the bouts from Mutual to ABC in 1946, but Dunphy would stay. From 1941 to 1964, the Manhattan native would dominate any major broadcast from the ring. On radio, he would do 22 heavyweight championship fights and 25 more on television or other forms of media. He made a successful transition from radio to TV in 1960 when he was assigned ABC's Fight of the Week. It had originated on television with Jack Drees. These television fights are not to be confused with the Gillette Cavalcade of Sports, a series of

Friday Night Fights on NBC Television which ran from 1948 through 1960. The *Friday Night Fights* were hosted by Jimmy Powers.

Dunphy did many of the same fights for Gillette on radio that Powers was doing on television. "Don Dunphy was as good a boxing announcer on radio as it was possible to be," Marty Glickman would say, adding, "boxing is the most difficult of sports to do on radio. It's almost impossible. But when Dunphy did fights that people could see on TV, it would be laughable. There was little relation between what Don was saying and what was happening in the fight."

Many of Dunphy's televised fights involved Emile Griffith. In 1962 Dunphy called one of the most tragic fights in boxing history when Griffith knocked Benny Paret unconscious, killing him. What was eerie was that just that week, ABC, which was carrying the fights, introduced the instant replay. Dunphy later said, "It turned out to be a tragic beginning. The replays showed the beating Paret was taking. Over and over they were repeated."

Paret's death brought upon a call for boxing reform and an investigation into the fighting game. Eventually ABC and Gillette dropped out in 1964. Dunphy would return for a handful of radio appearances, not all heard in the United States and the cordial veteran would also continue to do fights for closed circuit audiences and other television. But the glory years of boxing on radio were over. In 1973 Don King Productions had him do a closed circuit telecast of the Joe Frazier–George Foreman heavyweight title fight in Kingston, Jamaica. Never at a loss for some ringside promotion, King paired Dunphy with Pearl Bailey. "Pearl stood up and started cheering for Foreman on-air and she was supposed to be a commentator. People behind us started screaming, 'Sit down, Pearl.' As Foreman floored Frazier, Pearl celebrated by whacking me on the back in a way she thought was playful. It knocked me over and all of my papers went flying."

In the 1950s many of the fights were under the aegis of Pabst and the announcers started fluctuating. Russ Hodges began broadcasting bouts. Russ was one of the more versatile announcers in the business. He was proficient at many sports and covered baseball, football, and basketball. He did five heavyweight title matches on radio and was quite competent. The one fight that stands out is the 1965 Cassius Clay-Sonny Liston rematch in Lewiston, Maine, on Mutual. Many claim that Liston took a dive. The fight was over in the first round. Russ, probably a bit frustrated, blurted, "I came all the way from San Francisco for this!" Russ, of course, was the "voice of the San Francisco Giants" at the time and it's a long way between Maine and California. Hodges' commitment to baseball would occasionally result in Chicago-based Jack Drees giving the call. Drees's broadcasting career was dominated by horse racing.

One of Russ's partners on his boxing broadcasts was Steve Ellis, a former Giants baseball announcer. He was at the Polo Grounds while Russ was still with Mel Allen at Yankee Stadium. Ellis did some blow-by-blow, splitting the Archie Moore–Rocky Marciano fight with Hodges in 1955 and he did all the blow-by-blow of the Joe Walcott–Ezzard Charles encounter in 1951 with the late Lester Bromberg, one of boxing's all-time great writers.

Ellis got his boxing broadcast start working with Don Dunphy at the old Queensboro Arena in 1940. He had another name then, his real name, Armand Yussem and it was the sobriquet he used on WINS working with Dunphy.

Decisions in the sports broadcast business don't always make sense. Ellis was hardly in Dunphy's blow-by-blow class but after Don was anointed "voice

Courtesy Sheila Dunphy

Don Dunphy, second from right, is joined by fellow announcers (from left) Mel Allen, Bill Corum, Jim Britt, and Clem McCarthy.

of boxing" and had done some of the biggest fights in the country, he and Ellis did a local package for WHN from St. Nick's Arena in the mid-1940s. Guess who was assigned blow-by-blow? Yussem or Ellis, take your pick. In his autobiography, *Don Dunphy at Ringside*, the author, who couldn't have been too happy to play second fiddle to his understudy, accused Ellis of conflict of interest. Apparently, according to Dunphy, Ellis was managing some of the fighters whom he was covering on the air.

The early years of Cassius Clay/Muhammad Ali's dominance were the twilight years of boxing's coverage on radio. Selling tickets to closed-circuit coverage became paramount to the economics of boxing just as pay-per-view would some 15 years later.

Boxing had established its right to prohibit radio stations from doing live blow-by-blow when in 1953, New York station WOV sought the right to broadcast the Rocky Marciano–Roland LaStarza fight. It took the issue to court where Supreme Court Justice Irving Levey ruled that it can only do résumés after each round but prohibited the station from doing blow-by-blow or simulating the bout. It was the beginning of the end.

Clay's first stab at the heavyweight championship was against Sonny Liston in a celebrated match in Miami Beach on February 25, 1964. The world was waiting to see if indeed the cocky-sounding challenger had the goods to beat the formidable Liston. The lead in the front-page story of the *New York Times* the next morning read, "Incredibly, the loud-mouthed bragging, insulting youngster had been telling the truth all along. Cassius Clay won the world heavyweight title."

While Steve Ellis called the match on closed-circuit television, the radio microphones were manned by Les Keiter, Howard Cosell, and football legend Jim Brown. Occasionally prone to hyperbole, Keiter's blow-by-blow cadence was tickerlike and pulsating. Listening to him was just wonderful. His baritone had a nasal twang. There was an Orson Welles World War III quality to his delivery. The very sound was magnetizing.

Although his nemesis Marty Glickman chastised him for using too many clichés, Keiter was a master at painting a word picture of ring developments. "The fighter backpedals, bounces off the ropes; now he's back at the center of the ring, bobbing and weaving, always moving, never in the same spot for more than a second or two. Now he's got his chin tucked between his gloves in that peekaboo style." Many say Keiter might have been the best ever. "He's on one knee, his legs are rubbery, he's holding the middle strand." Keiter's style was idiosyncratic but his mark on broadcast sports was indelible.

"I remember Ali being introduced in the ring before the second Liston-Patterson fight in Las Vegas. He pointed to the champ, Liston, and said 'I want to rumble with you, I'm going to get you, you big ugly bear.' No one knew what to make of him," Les reminisced in his autobiography, *Fifty Years Behind the Microphone*. Now Les was in Miami Beach on the fateful night that the boxing world would give birth to the Clay era. Keiter opened the broadcast predicting "a great extravaganza in boxing" and proceeded to describe six riveting rounds.

While it's usually the blow-by-blow announcer who describes the winning moment and reveals the winner, such wasn't the case that night. Coming out of the break of the sixth round, Howard Cosell did his analytical shtick and said, "They're about to begin the seventh round and here's Les. Wait a minute; Sonny Liston is not coming out. Liston is not coming out. Cassius Clay is the new heavyweight champion of the world!" Cosell wasn't looking to steal Keiter's thunder. Color commentators don't usually blurt out the winner, even Howard. But then again, basketball, hockey, or football games are not won during time-outs. At that moment, Liston claimed that his shoulder was injured and Cosell simply and properly reacted to the imperatives of broadcast immediacy.

Remembering Liston's claim, Les would later say, "It was another delusion of a bizarre night. X-rays showed no fractures and Liston threw his best punches in the sixth round."

Five years earlier in 1959, Cosell and Keiter both called their first-ever heavyweight championship fight. It was carried by ABC Radio and it matched champion Floyd Patterson and challenger Ingemar Johansson. The network was running a novel promotion during the broadcast. The fight was sponsored by United Artists which was promoting its about-to-be-released flick, *The Horse Soldiers*.

ABC had the stars of the flick, John Wayne and William Holden, join Howard and Les between rounds. In other words, all four were sitting ringside doing the fight commentary on radio. Keiter would do the blow-by-blow and Cosell would be on between rounds, occasionally eliciting the opinions of the two movie stars.

Howard's commentary on the broadcast that night was the incipience of the Cosell seal. After the Swede KO'd the champ, Cosell went into the ring and took control. No one listening that night would have misidentified Howard as a rookie fight broadcaster. He grabbed the non-American winner and asked, "Did you realize that Floyd was vulnerable to your right hand?" We'll never know whether Howard ever stopped to wonder whether Johansson knew what the word *vulnerable* meant but that didn't stop him. Then at the top of his lungs, Howard shouted several times, "We'll cross the ring to the Patterson corner."

Then in the bedlam of the ring, Cosell took charge, pulling Cus D'Amato, Patterson's trainer and manager, to the microphone. As usual, there was rhetoric

Actor John Wayne, left, joined Howard Cosell, right, and Les Keiter between rounds of the Floyd Patterson–Ingemar Johansson heavyweight title fight in 1959. Wayne and fellow actor William Holden were promoting the film The Horse Soldiers.

and bluster when Howard pulled the mike from Cus in midsentence. "You just heard Cus D'Amato predict that Patterson will be the first heavyweight to regain the title," Howard declared.

The "vulnerable" comment was topped the time Howard asked Muhammad Ali if he was "truculent" by nature. Having no idea what the word meant, Ali said, "If it's good, that's me."

In 1959 Cosell had been on the air all of four years but he was hardly a callow announcer. Listeners learned quickly that Howard Cosell was not one to shy away from strong statements. Just as the tumult of the ring quieted sufficiently, Howard made exalting comparisons, "We might have just witnessed one of the truly great rounds in heavyweight championship history. Not since the first round of the Dempsey-Firpo fight on September 14, 1923, have there been this many knockdowns in one round," referring to the third round when Patterson went down seven times.

Wayne, trying to top Howard with more than just the inane, adds, "I wish we would have known about this beforehand. This way Bill (Holden) and I would have put up some money for our next picture." Holden, in a prefight interview, showed some good reporterlike instincts, asking Patterson why he doesn't believe in studying tapes of his opponent.

Floyd told him that this way he's prepared for anything. It was a memorable broadcast, Keiter's infectious excitement, early Cosell, and star-studded names John Wayne and William Holden. Years later and off the air, Cosell, not one to praise often, would say of his colleague, "If you want excitement, it's Keiter."

Cosell didn't need anyone else when it came to excitement. In fact, he didn't need anyone else period. Seven years later in London in 1966, Keiter was working radio of the Clay–Brian London fight and on the other side of the ring, he saw Howard. At this point, Cosell had graduated to television and was working the fight alone, blow-by-blow, color, and all. This, of course, before he eschewed boxing all together, disparaging the sport. In his final television years, he wouldn't cover professional boxing, only amateur bouts.

There was only one Howard Cosell and his roots were radio. He graduated New York University Law School but didn't enter radio until the relatively late age of 35 in 1953. It was the same year ABC changed the call letters of its New York station from WJZ to WABC. Cosell entered radio in somewhat of an oblique way. His law practice included sports clients, one of whom was Willie Mays. He sold the station on the idea of a radio program on which Little Leaguers would interview Major Leaguers. Cosell later described the twice-a-week show as a cross between *Juvenile Jury* and *Meet the Press*. It gained attention mainly because the questions that were posed were Cosell's. One of the panelists on the show was a young man from Brooklyn named Marvin Aufrichtig. Sports fans today know him as Marv Albert.

Later, Cosell himself did a Sunday night hour-long interview-type show on WABC, beginning in 1955. Players such as Frank Gifford would drop by after games and talk football. Cosell repaid Frank handsomely years later, calling him everything but inept for his performance on *Monday Night Football*.

Cosell later parlayed his weekend program into a nightly gig and on January 10, 1965, Cosell started his long-running program that eventually aired on the ABC Radio Network, *Speaking of Everything*. His first two guests the very first half-hour of his first show were Sonny Werblin, owner of the Jets, and Joe Garagiola who would become a Yankees broadcaster that coming spring. The second half-hour he had Metropolitan Opera star Robert Merrill, later a good friend of Yankee owner George Steinbrenner. Cosell and George were later friends, too, a rather strange couple, given Howard's vilification of baseball.

Shortly thereafter, Cosell started *Speaking of Sports*, a five-minute show each day in morning-drive on the *Harry Harrison Show*. Rick Sklar programmed WABC in its heyday and watched Cosell do the show. "Howard often worked without a script. Throwing a cue to the recording engineer, he would speak into the microphone without as much as a cue card. It was an astonishing process to witness."

Sklar says that Cosell always had to have the edge at the station. "He would hardly ever acknowledge the lesser functionaries. Upper-echelon types were regularly accosted by Cosell, whose verbal zingers probed their insecurities and made light of their accomplishments.

"He also loved playing liar's poker with the folks at the station. Howard would pull in dollar bills as he won hand after hand, or enjoy a free lunch on the hapless loser who had challenged a Cosell call," Sklar wrote in his book, *Rocking America*. Everyone on the air at WABC was a member of AFTRA (American Federation of Television and Radio Artists). When there was an AFTRA performer's strike, Cosell was ordered by the union to walk the picket line outside the ABC building. "This was a terrible task for Cosell, torn between his friendship for Leonard Goldenson and Si Siegel and his contractual union obligations to picket," Sklar remembered.

Howard redefined the sports broadcast business and it started on radio. Many newspaper columnists feuded with Cosell as though he stole their turf. Larry Merchant once wrote, "Cosell makes the world of fun and games sound like the Nuremberg trials." Like him or not, radio sports journalists today owe much to their trailblazing founding father, Howard Cosell.

With pay-per-view, the radio fights have become a thing of the past. Radio is seen as a deterrent to the potential video customer. There have been only a handful of fight broadcasts on radio since the 1970s. WFAN, at one early point in its history, experimented with a fight package from the Garden. But it lasted less than a year. Maybe they'll come back on the Internet one day. Who knows? History has a way of repeating itself.

In the late 1960s a Miami man, Murry Woromer, used a computer to concoct all sorts of dream boxing matches, producing a short-lived radio series that was narrated by Guy LeBow. It had a bit of the old re-creation touch to it. *Time* magazine described the sound as one "with taped sound effects, and a breathless, leather swinging commentary." It didn't last very long but newspapers ran accounts of the fights and Las Vegas even posted weekly odds. Some sore loser even accused the computer of taking a dive when one week it had Rocky Marciano knock out Jack Dempsey.

In their book written in the late 1920s, *Broadcasting, Its New Day*, Samuel Rothafel and Raymond Francis Yates eloquently sum up radio's impact on sports. "If the growth of sports has been brought about through communication, we may expect that radio will bring with it a revival that will end, no one knows where. It has already created a stir. People who never before took an interest in sports have found them to be exhilarating. They tasted a little of it, liked it and had more. It was radio that first actually brought them into contact with clean sport. Many of them never knew what they had been missing until the voice in the loudspeaker brought to them a mind picture of a great contest, brought to them the living voices and actions of the players as well as the spectators. Thousands awoke to find that they had a new form of recreation."

And the fights were just the beginning.

2

COLLEGE
FOOTBALL

GRAPHIC COMMUNICATORS
OF THE GRIDIRON

Radio was in an embryonic state. Stations were starting to mushroom. Sales of radio receivers took off the way spaceships did 50 years later. It was the fall of 1922. On October 29 the front sports page of the *New York Times* painted a dominating picture of college football's grip on the New York sports landscape. Each of the eight columns across and down the familiar *Times* format contained a story of college football. In fact, the *Times* had 16 separate stories this particular Sunday on the front of its sports page. All but one, a tiny box on a high school soccer match, covered games played on the college gridiron. There weren't any off-the-field baseball stories, although the World Series had been played earlier that month. There wasn't a word on professional basketball or professional hockey, either. And for good reason. The NHL wouldn't come to New York until 1925 and the birth of the Knicks was still more than 20 years away.

College football didn't have to contend with pro football yet. The National Football League was alive but barely breathing. In fact, it would be 1925 before Billy Gibson and Tim Mara would pay all of $500 for the expansion New York Giants franchise.

Columbia University of Morningside Heights—yes, the Lions—would win the 1934 Rose Bowl. The Fordham Rams of the Bronx would have the famed

"Seven Blocks of Granite" and, eventually, a team that would play in the 1941 Cotton Bowl. Others had football teams of interest, too, including Manhattan and New York University. City College would play in historic Lewisohn Stadium. And within a long field goal of the city borders were powerhouses Army, Yale, and Cornell, as well as Syracuse and Pennsylvania.

Historically, the football "broadcast firsts" were accomplished outside New York City. The first one hardly qualifies. It was November 25, 1920. WTAW of College Station, Texas, ran a game between the two schools that are now called the University of Texas and Texas A&M. The station was then operating on an experimental license, transmitting in code with no human voice. But in the fall of 1921, Harold Arlin, using his own voice, reported on the Pittsburgh–West Virginia game over America's first radio station, KDKA in Pittsburgh.

The marriage of football and radio was natural. Stations were sprouting in the 1920s and were starving for programming. In New York, Major J. Andrew White started piping football onto the airwaves over WJZ and Graham McNamee over WEAF. Other local stations followed in the mid-1920s. Eventually WEAF and WJZ came under the dual ownership of RCA. NBC was born shortly thereafter and it immediately formed two networks, NBC Red and NBC Blue. They would syndicate the broadcasts of major college games involving the prominent national programs. The web of stations was small in number at the beginning but NBC nonetheless programmed two broadcasts each Saturday, one for each of its networks. McNamee would do one game and Phillips Carlin would do the other. In 1927, when Major White started the Columbia Network, college football was an integral piece of its Saturday programming, with himself at the mike.

If this wasn't enough, every station in New York seemed to want to cash in on local football which was flourishing. There was interest in Columbia, Fordham, Manhattan, and CCNY, and stations wanted to have a piece of it. From the top of the dial to the bottom, the airwaves on Saturdays were filled with college football. Oftentimes in the 1930s, there would be as many as 9 or 10 games aired at the same time. The broadcasts were being fed by the networks, NBC Red, NBC Blue, and later CBS and Mutual, while nonaffiliated stations carried local college clashes.

McNamee, Carlin, and White would be the "name trio" identified with broadcast football through the late 1920s. Carlin was one of the medium's first announcers before moving into the executive suite. He was paired with McNamee in the mid-1920s on several baseball and boxing broadcasts. A busy man, Carlin was appointed WEAF's program director in 1925 but nonetheless continued doing nightly studio work with McNamee. In the early years of radio, this wasn't uncommon. Sports broadcasting was just one of many responsibilities for the on-air talent. There would be administrative work and other announcing chores.

The broadcast conditions were horrible. Many of the stadia did not have broadcast booths. Announcers and engineers had to withstand the elements, a driving rainstorm or, later in the season, heavy snows. In Philadelphia, at historic Franklin Field, the broadcasters were placed on a scaffold. A tarpaulin that was tossed over the upright corner beams served as a flimsy roof. Water seeped through everywhere. Ty Tyson, the legendary Detroit broadcaster who called Michigan football as early as 1924, said, "We all used to huddle through drenching rains and blanketing snow storms."

Major J. Andrew White in 1927 at the age of 38, the year he helped start the Columbia Network.

Courtesy Blair White

Ted Husing broke in under White and gave sportscasting an element of science with his prescribed preparatory formula and innovative working gadgetry. As a young staff announcer at WJZ, Husing once accompanied the Major to Philadelphia for a football broadcast. Ted opened the show, setting the scene.

"I introduced him and leaned back, exhausted," Husing wrote in his 1959 autobiography, *My Eyes Are in My Heart*. "I'll never forget his broadcast. I still marvel at it. He just marched in cold, picked up the microphone and the river of words began flowing. A masterpiece was winging through the air."

The immediacy of radio play-by-play required the announcer to identify yard markers at first glance. To accomplish this, the markings on the field had to be made bigger and brighter. Signals from the officials on the field also had to be clearer and had to be made in a flash. Referees had to cooperate. Broadcasters could not have their audiences wait. Developments on the field had to be communicated to the press box instantly and intelligibly. Indeed, the early broadcasters successfully impressed upon the referees and athletic officials the importance of streamlining the game so that it was more radio friendly. Gradually there was progress.

In 1929 Husing shared the plight of radio announcers with Ellwood Geiges, one of the country's top officials of the day. He and his officiating cohorts devised four signals still used today, offside, holding, illegal shift, and time-out.

© National Baseball Hall of Fame Library, Cooperstown, N.Y.

Graham McNamee was a leader in the broadcast of all sports when radio emerged as an important and necessary medium.

When McNamee started in 1923, he really needed even more help. By today's requirements, the pioneer announcer would be deemed incapable of handling the play-by-play role. An "associate" would sit a few feet away and talk to him in low tones so that his voice was not picked up by the microphone. The associate would be giving Mac all sorts of rudimentary information. Other assistants would be situated elsewhere, their voices never heard. They would be referred to as outpost reporters. In essence, they would relay elementary information. Was the pass complete? Who was the back carrying the ball or did he get it over the goal line? Was it a touchdown?

Things would change, of course. Over the next 50 years, the broadcast booth would employ a battery of spotters and statisticians. But the announcer still has to be adequate enough to give all the pertinent details of each play himself. He shouldn't need extra pairs of eyes for this elementary requirement.

To Graham McNamee, America's first announcer, it was the intensity of the atmosphere or the essential of the drama. He once wrote, "Before the year is over, I'll be carried away with the spectacle before me and make a hundred or more mistakes, but who cares about mere details."

McNamee wrote of his dilemma in an article for *Radio Daily*:

The Red team is up against its own goal posts. The blue team is marching steadily down the field reeling off gain after gain. Third down and two yards to go. The ball snaps back, a few bewildering gestures with it to confuse the Red players and then a plunging mass of tangled arms and legs. The ball is nowhere in sight. Is it a touchdown? Or did they just fall short of that last white stripe?

Go ahead, tell 'em about it. Out there at the loudspeakers millions of rabid fans are agonizing over the delay. You can almost hear their thoughts screaming in your ears, "Come on, what happened?

Those are the seconds that are years long for the announcer. You can sense the impatience of the listeners but you can't do anything about it until you see what happened. Perhaps five or six seconds elapse before you can tell about it. To the announcer it seems like five or six minutes and to the average listener—according to letters—it seems like five or six hours.

But I still think honest enthusiasm and the general picture are what the audience wants. And that is what I intend to give them because that is the way I feel.

In 1927 NBC secured the rights to the Rose Bowl, called by McNamee. To comprehend the importance of the "granddaddy of 'em all," bear in mind that the other bowls were not born yet. The next wave, the Cotton, Sugar, and Orange Bowls would be founded in the mid-1930s. There was no Super Bowl in 1927. The giant events were big heavyweight championship fights, the World Series and the Rose Bowl. In importance, the Rose Bowl was the equivalent of today's Super Bowl.

When Graham McNamee ventured to California on behalf of NBC, it was the first-ever coast-to-coast hookup. Broadcast history was in the making. More than 20,000 miles of wire were used to transmit nationally. It was a historic football broadcast. McNamee did the play-by-play again in 1928. But two specific comments would cause his eventual banishment from the Rose Bowl broadcast booth.

McNamee would often digress, "Ah, the sun shining on those California hills is a wonderful sight, I tell you!" That's fine but the proud citizenry of Pasadena was slighted when the esteemed McNamee misidentified the neighboring San Gabriel Mountains for the Sierra Madre Range. Worse, as part of the rights agreement with NBC, the Rose Bowl Committee insisted that Pasadena be portrayed glowingly. The Pasadena Chamber of Commerce, as sponsors of the game itself, prepared copy for McNamee to read.

It prepared copy that painted the elements and atmosphere on a sunlit day. McNamee was to read it verbatim. He did. There was only one problem. He did so on a day when it was raining hard and coming down steadily. McNamee was disparaged for it by newspaper writers.

The Rose Bowl asked for changes. After just two Rose Bowl games, McNamee was relegated to color in 1929. Carl Haverlin and Bill Munday were

Courtesy Ted Patterson

Bill Munday, right, shares the mike with another legend, Ernie Harwell. Munday got his start as a sportswriter when he was 15 years old and quickly made his way into radio. He was at the mike for the 1929 Rose Bowl when Roy Reigels ran the ball to his own goal line.

brought in to share the play-by-play. Thereafter, Graham wasn't assigned the Rose Bowl game. For that matter eastern announcers were not approved by the committee at all. McNamee did return to the Rose Bowl in 1941, but simply to receive a plaque commemorating NBC's 15th Rose Bowl broadcast.

With Carlin in management and out of the on-air picture and White out of the business, McNamee was still one of the big three football announcers in 1930, along with the quick-rising Ted Husing at CBS and Munday.

Bill Munday exploded onto the scene in 1929 to almost immediate stardom. But in a matter of four or so years the bottle had gotten the better of him and he slipped to near anonymity. Future stars such as Red Barber, Ernie Harwell, and Lindsey Nelson would never forget him. To these three Southerners, Munday, a Georgian, was somewhat of a hero.

Bill Munday was precocious. In 1918 at the age of 15, he began reporting sports for the *Atlanta Journal*. He then became an accomplished athlete at the University of Georgia, an ace southpaw pitcher, who also played football and basketball. Then he graduated from law school. In 1930 the *New York World* reported that he was the youngest person ever admitted to the bar in the state of Georgia.

It wasn't uncommon then for stations to recruit announcers from the sports desks of the metropolitan newspapers. Sam Taub, Clem McCarthy, Don Dunphy, Stan Lomax, and others all started on the print side. While working for the *Atlanta Journal*, Munday was asked by sister radio station WSB to broadcast the

Southern Conference basketball tournament. Furman Bisher, the accomplished Atlanta columnist referred to basketball back then as a "marathon of dribbling and center jumping." Back then, of course, there was a center jump after every made field goal. Munday, nonetheless, was terrific and before long became the sports "voice of the South."

Carlin discovered Munday when he was in Georgia in 1928 for a Yale-Georgia game. He invited Munday to give a game summary at halftime. Summaries, interestingly, back then, were often referred to as résumés. Munday did brilliantly so Carlin told McNamee about the prodigy. When Graham did a subsequent Georgia Tech game, Munday was used again and was fabulous again.

After the season, the Jackets were invited to play in college football's only bowl game, the Rose, in January 1929. Lambdin Kay, general manager of WSB, an NBC affiliate and pioneer radio station in the South, convinced NBC to include Munday on the Bowl broadcast team. Kay told Bisher, "I got Bill assigned to help Graham McNamee with the broadcast."

Munday was asked to share the Rose Bowl play-by-play with Haverlin. McNamee did color. Bill's homespun commentary flowed and the colorful phrases charmed. His call was refreshing and spiriting. He described the huddle as "that crap shooter's formation."

Much of the nation was spellbound, spending its New Year's Day listening to the radio, engrossed by one of the most memorable football games in history. The '29 Rose Bowl will always be remembered as the game in which Roy Reigels of the University of California ran the wrong way. A Tech back fumbled the ball on a run, and Reigels, a member of the Bears defensive team, picked it up alertly. Confused, he was enticed by a clear path of some 65 yards toward his own goal line. He then started sprinting the wrong way before a teammate grabbed him by the arm and spun him around so that his body wouldn't fall into the end zone. Then pinned against its own goal line, Cal was scored upon by Tech on a safety. The bizarre and implausible development cost the Bears the game. Tech won, 8–7. Munday was brilliant calling the play-by-play and the wild dash the wrong way. He used descriptions never heard before, referring to the end zone as the "land of milk and honey" or "the promised land,"phrases still popular today.

Upon the death of Munday in 1965, Bisher helped explain the country's infatuation with Bill after the historic 1929 broadcast. "The Southern accent had captivated the people who heard it. You must remember that there had been little exchange of colloquial dialects in those days because there had been no previous means of reaching the masses."

The Rose Bowl broadcast was critically acclaimed. Editors hailed Munday's work. Listeners sang his praises. The next season, Carlin, now in management, needed a replacement for himself. He selected Munday. McNamee and Munday were now NBC's show on the highly popular Saturday football broadcasts.

Munday's reputation was ballooning. He was assigned boxing for NBC and more. His exposure started growing, too. As early as July 29, 1929, the *Daily News*'s Paul Gallico wrote, "Suddenly from the loudspeaker comes a fresh new voice, a voice for all its Southern cadences and rhythmics is letting fly a bristling, rapid-fire of description, couched in a new and gay phraseology, teeming with good humor and enthusiasm, and demonstrating without ostentation how sports on radio should be spoken."

In an unprecedented way, too, Munday helped integrate the broadcast booth. In the early 1930s he was in Pittsburgh for an NBC broadcast of a Nebraska-Pitt game. When he couldn't find a spotter, Bill went to the black porter who worked the Pullman car of the train which transported the Nebraska team. Munday asked the porter to work with him in the broadcast booth.

But there was a price to pay for the glory and for Munday it was too overbearing. The fast living of the big time was his greatest challenge. He started drinking heavily. "Several times McNamee and I would work games together," he once told Bisher. "When we would get back to the room, there was always a bottle there. First, it was a nip or two, and then it was a slug or two. I noticed that I was doing all the drinking and McNamee was watching but I thought he was just being nice to me."

The word in broadcast circles later was that announcers were pushing whiskey in front of a susceptible Munday. These "colleagues" were clearly not benefiting from Bill's high stock and golden boy status at NBC. The booze affected his work. By 1934 his name started disappearing from NBC's weekly listings of football announcers. Slowly, he was relieved of his responsibilities. He tried to straighten out a number of times but it never lasted long.

NBC boss Niles Trammel once gave Munday another chance, assigning him to an Alabama–Georgia Tech game in Birmingham. He had obviously had a few when he opened the broadcast destructively, "How do you do ladies 'n gentlemen. This is Bill Munday from Legion Field in Birmingham, a town of hard drinkers and fast women." NBC pulled the plug on him immediately.

Now his life was sinking. He moved from one job to another. It turned into misery. He found himself drifting into the streets where he became a pan-handler, begging for loose change. His redeeming asset was his wife who stuck with him throughout.

In the mid- to the late 1940s Bill Munday found religion and got off the stuff for good. In 1948, when Atlanta sports broadcast legend Al Ciraldo was getting ready to enter a small high school stadium to do a football game, Munday approached him at the gate. He asked Al, "Can you get me into the stadium?" Al did and gave him the microphone at halftime.

"He had the drunklike walk even though he was sober. His mind was brilliant," the longtime "voice of the Georgia Tech Yellow Jackets" said.

Red Barber later gave him a break, having Munday participate on his weekly *Football Roundup* over the CBS Radio Network. It could have been quite embarrassing for the fastidious Red had Munday not been emotionally ready. It turned out fine. "His voice was vibrant and sure," Red would say later. Bill became a model spokesman for Alcoholics Anonymous, traveling the country and spreading the word of the evils of liquor.

In the 1950s Tom Gallery, NBC Television's director of sports, invited the Southerner to do color and a little play-by-play with Lindsey Nelson on a college football game. "Television had been invented while he was drunk. Now he loved it. Those eyes sparkled and those creased old cheeks broke into a smile." Lindsey Nelson would say later in his autobiography, *Hello Everybody, I'm Lindsey Nelson*.

Munday remained on the wagon until his death in 1965. "All of us South-erners have some Bill Munday in us, consciously or subconsciously," said fellow Georgian, Ernie Harwell, echoing what I imagine was the sentiment of Barber and Nelson.

McNamee's stock as a sports announcer was dropping slowly in the early 1930s. He was kept on some glamour assignments through the mid-1930s and would maintain a presence on the World Series broadcasts and heavyweight title fights but he was no longer NBC's lead sports announcer.

With Munday undependable and McNamee's sports role diminished, NBC built a stable of football announcers to dip into for its Saturdays of doubleheaders. In the 1930s folks such as Bill Slater, Don Wilson, Jack Ingersall, Ford Bond, Halsey Hall, Fort Pearson, and Tom Manning would be assigned by the older and bigger network. The local football broadcasts on the nonaffiliated stations were manned by Dick Fishel, one of the early names in local New York sportscasting; Ward Wilson, who was later involved in Rangers hockey broadcasts; Stan Lomax, the WOR broadcast legend; and Ford Frick, a scribe and part-time broadcaster who would eventually become commissioner of baseball.

Meanwhile, radio was booming and the prices of receivers were dropping. In 1930 the average radio was $103, down from $136 in 1929. A small AM transistor radio in the mid-1990s was about $8 at a tourist-trap shop in Times Square.

In 1934 the Columbia University Lions made their famous trip to the Rose Bowl, and the *Los Angeles Times* did a short story on NBC's broadcast plans to use Ken Carpenter and Don Thompson. They also took a shot at McNamee, ridiculing his history-making 1927 broadcast. "Graham McNamee was brought out from the East to handle the assignment. Graham glorified the purple hills of the Arroyo Seco, Southern California's climate, the orange blossoms, and did just about everything but let the fans in on what was happening on the gridiron where Alabama was holding Stanford to a tie."

Ben Gross, in a review of a 1938 Saturday when the radio "was raining football again," wrote, "This year, our announcers seem to have the tricks of the game well in hand and most of them have been turning out fast, accurate accounts. It makes for crisp, informative reporting, even if some of the exuberance of the time when Graham McNamee was exciting the listeners is lacking. On the whole, you hear a better brand of pigskin reporting over the air today."

Through the 1930s the Rose Bowl used announcers who were assigned both the annual football game and the Rose Parade. Carpenter, Thompson, and Wilson would dominate the booth during this span. "Hefty Don Wilson" as he was sometimes referred to, was the announcer on the *Jack Benny Show*, first on radio and later on television. Carpenter did the same for the *Bing Crosby Show*. Apparently, Hollywood had quite a bit of say on the broadcasters. Thompson was a San Francisco–based announcer.

The review of their play-by-play was hardly sterling, though. Gross didn't hold back on January 2, 1932. "The Tulane–Southern Cal game was exciting. But the announcing of the two Dons, Wilson and Thompson, was not what it should have been. They were so confusing that even several football experts sitting beside my loudspeaker could not follow the ball."

At halftime of the '32 Rose Bowl broadcast, Pop Warner was put on the NBC airwaves to answer a series of questions about football. It sounds as though he would have been a better help to listeners during the play-by-play. In 1937 Wilson and Ken Carpenter teamed for the Rose and again Gross carped, "Don was vivid, excited, even if at times confused."

On the day of the 1932 Rose Bowl, CBS celebrated its 90th affiliated station when WMBD, Peoria, signed on. But it would be five years before Paley's network would have a Bowl of its own, the Orange. Ted Husing was the first and longtime "voice of the Orange Bowl." One of his greatest regrets was that he never had an opportunity to "voice a Rose Bowl." When CBS got the rights for three years beginning in 1949, he had already left the network. Peoria, meanwhile, would develop a reputation as a spawning ground of fine sportscasters, including Jack Brickhouse, Chick Hearn, and Bill King.

In 1934, when the Columbia University Lions went to Pasadena, so did Husing, but not to broadcast. A one-time Lions mascot as a 15-year-old, Ted couldn't miss the opportunity. It was a busman's holiday but hardly a vacation because it rained for seven straight days. On game day, Ted drifted into NBC's broadcast booth and listened to Carpenter and Thompson "sweat to identify the twenty-two mud-spattered players."

Not all were fun and games, though, on January 1, 1934, even on the sports pages. There was a hint of Germany's scourge. Adolph Hitler had prohibited German boxer Max Schmeling from fighting King Levinsky on February 16, 1934, at Chicago Stadium. Hitler wouldn't allow Schmeling to fight a Jew. It was an augury to the Holocaust.

The august Rose Bowl and the Pasadena parade were the places to be on New Year's Day. This was the game and the parade was the event. It had the tradition and was looked upon with awe not only in the college football world but throughout the sports world.

Broadcasters fantasized over a Rose Bowl assignment. Lindsey Nelson recalls a day in Los Angeles in December 1961 when he was told that he was hired by the Mets. He and his wife were so delighted that they took a leisurely meandering drive. Before long, they found themselves on a freeway to Pasadena, heading to the Rose Bowl. The stadium was empty. They walked into the old stadium and looked around. Lindsey said to his better half, "One day, I'll get the chance!" Lindsey fulfilled that lifelong dream when he was asked to do the 1964 Rose Bowl on television.

The Rose Bowl was not only the first-ever coast-to-coast radio hookup. In 1952, with Mel Allen and Jack Brickhouse behind the mike, it was the first-ever coast-to-coast telecast and in 1962 the first remote football color telecast.

The list of those who have worked the Rose Bowl reads like a who's who of sports announcing. Marty Glickman was a man in his late 60s when he was asked to do it in the mid-1980s. A former football star himself, Marty went with alacrity. The enthusiasm and crispness of his Rose Bowl broadcast were reminiscent of his early years with the New York Giants when he was at the top of his game. There was always a palpable quiver, too, in Curt Gowdy's voice when he opened up all those Rose Bowls in the 1970s. This wasn't an ordinary assignment.

Later when Bob Costas called a Rose Bowl on radio, he paused to pay homage to the tradition of the Rose Bowl booth. He gushed with appreciation of having had the privilege to sit in the same chair as the legendary names of the past. In addition to McNamee, Munday, Gowdy, and Glickman, Bill Stern, Red Barber, Al Helfer, Mel Allen, and Chick Hearn all did Rose Bowls on radio.

While teaching and coaching sports in Minneapolis, Bill Slater, a West Point man by education and posture, was urged by his students to broadcast

Bill Slater, right, is joined by Byrum Saam during a 1944 picture-taking session for announcers on the Football Network of the Atlantic Refining Company.

football. He was bright, had graduated from the U.S. Military Academy at age 21, was quick and verbally gifted. Before long, he was doing football for the decorated WCCO, the city's leading radio station. In late 1933 the networks beckoned. Herbert Glover at CBS called upon Bill Slater to join Ted Husing on the big Army-Navy broadcast.

Slater's reviews were so stellar that within a few days after the big battle of the two service academies, he was assigned the Princeton-Yale matchup. Despite the rave reviews of his 1933 work, Slater was not asked back by CBS the following season. Red Barber says the reason was Ted Husing, whom he decries in his book, *The Broadcasters.* "Ted shared nothing with anybody for any longer than he had to," Barber says with a tinge of anger in his reference to Slater's fleeting stay at CBS.

This was nonetheless the beginning of a successful and versatile career for Slater who would transcend radio and television. NBC picked up Slater immediately and viewed him as a potential successor to McNamee and Munday. Slater would indeed bridge the gap of one radio legend, McNamee, and the start of another, Stern.

Starting in 1934, Bill Slater sparkled for the peacock network for three years. In 1936, Slater went to Berlin as NBC's man at the Olympics, competing with CBS's Husing. When he got back though, Bill Stern was skyrocketing to the top at NBC as number one sports dog. By the end of 1936, Slater's tenure at NBC was over. In his autobiography, *The Taste of Ashes*, Stern blames

NBC's loss of Slater on a dispute with John Royal over Bill's Olympics expense account. There were those who wondered whether Stern had his fingerprints on Slater's back. At that point, the two of them were vying for the top sports spot at the network.

Slater took his verbal wares and parked them at Mutual, which, as the upstart web then, was looking for good talent. He later also did gridiron work for independent packagers.

Through many of his years on radio, Slater continued his pedagogy at Adelphi Academy in Brooklyn where he was Head Master. His last radio play-by-play broadcast was the December 2, 1950, Army-Navy game.

Before, during, and after World War II, Bill Slater was a household name. When he died in 1965 at the age of 61, his obituary would highlight his work as an announcer of local major-league baseball, the World Series, the Olympics, CBS, NBC, and Mutual.

It was also fitting that this military-man-turned-announcer was on radio at the Polo Grounds, both on the eve of the war and at the end of the war. On December 7, 1941, Slater did the Dodgers-Giants football game, (the NFL had another New York team then, the Brooklyn Dodgers). On V-J Day Slater was in the booth behind home plate, broadcasting a Dodgers-Giants baseball game. He then gazed out at the aperture inside the outfield scoreboard where he had called the football game almost four terrible years earlier. During the war he had been recalled to active duty as a major. He remembered and reminisced, sharing an emotional thought with his audience. The war was over. His broadcast partner, Al Helfer, a Navy man, echoed tersely, "Thank God."

When television emerged, Slater was one of the new medium's pioneer announcers, including the first televised World Series in 1947 which alternated coverage over three networks. Television was in its infancy and the series aired only on the East Coast. The classy cadet later hosted a variety of television quiz shows such as *Twenty Questions* and *Charade Quiz*. Slater was not flamboyant. He carried his barrel chest with class and dignity and walked with the expected, erect pride of one drilled at West Point.

Bill had a good reputation for his football work and Barber concurred, "football best and track well." Barber continues unrestrained, "He had brains, he had clear eyes. He was like a beautifully trained tenor with what they call a 'white' voice. He was almost without color or warmth."

When Slater left NBC in 1936, Ted Husing was established at CBS and NBC became the exclusive sports domain of Bill Stern. By the late 1930s, Stern's stock had risen so that he and Husing were running neck and neck on top of the popularity polls.

Bill Stern and Ted Husing, NBC and CBS, respectively, were as known then as Dick Enberg and Pat Summerall would be 50 years later. But unlike the gentlemanly rivalries of today, Stern and Husing would compete bitterly in ways never seen before or since. It was war. Stern was colorful and controversial. Husing had presence and a command.

Ted Husing influenced a generation of America's best sports announcers in every corner of the country. He had the vocal tools, the great command of the language, enunciated perfectly and most importantly, was always ready. Graham McNamee was America's first popular announcer who did sports. Husing was America's first sports announcer. Ernie Harwell best described the

When Bill Slater left in 1936, NBC became the exclusive sports domain of Bill Stern.

Courtesy Ted Patterson

impact of Ted Husing. "When Husing came along the entire concept of sports announcing changed."

Any budding sports announcer in the 1930s and 1940s dreamt of living the career of Ted Husing. Jack Brickhouse was the "voice of Chicago sports" for decades and writes of Husing's play-by-play of the final couple of minutes of the classic 1935 Ohio State–Notre Dame football game, a contest that Husing himself said was the most thrilling he's ever called. "The game was one of the most exciting in NCAA history with Notre Dame coming back in the final moments with two touchdowns. Husing's description is absolute 'must listening' for any aspiring broadcast student." Chicago's Bob Elson, a contemporary of Husing, also spoke of the baritone in exalting terms. "He was the best football announcer I ever heard."

Mel Allen lionized Ted, serving as his understudy at CBS, and Don Dunphy would walk the streets of Manhattan on fall Sunday mornings, imitating Husing's call of the previous Saturday's football game. Bill Mazer, an announcer whose voice reminds Marty Glickman of Husing's, can't stop singing Ted's praises. "His pattern of speaking was what you would hear in a Broadway theater. Each syllable of every word was perfectly pronounced. He had the best command of language and best voice of any sportscaster I ever heard. 'On a windswept afternoon in Ann Arbor.' The words might as well have been coming from the stage of a theater, not a stadium broadcast booth," Mazer extolled.

Even the great Vin Scully who by design didn't listen to other announcers was inspired as a kid by Husing's football broadcasts. A young Vin would crawl under the radio and listen to Husing and the roar of the crowds. Husing was the king and for the most part lionized by his own colleagues. His contemporaries viewed him the way a musician would Louie Armstrong, as a jazzman's jazzman.

Born on Thanksgiving Day of 1901 and raised in New York, Edward Britt Husing became America's most successful and durable sports announcer over the first 30 years of the medium's history. During that span, Ted Husing, the name he used on the air and off, would be synonymous with the very acronym CBS. In essence, Husing was CBS, the network's voice of sports and more. He had many likes and dislikes and was not afraid to state his opinion. Speaking his mind got him in trouble a couple of times during his glittering career.

It started in 1924, on the train returning to New York from his Florida honeymoon, Husing picked up a newspaper during a train stop in Washington, D.C. As usual, he gravitated to the sports pages, absorbing every last word. He then thumbed through the rest of the paper when his eye caught a fine-print ad for a radio announcer. He answered the ad and was one of 600 applicants for a $45-a-week job at WJZ, RCA's radio station. He won the audition and the job.

Major White was already established at WJZ and became Ted's "tutor, idol, and father-confessor." White suggested he play football, have his nose broken to get a feel for the game. Ted did play some semipro football and had his antrums widened to improve his resonance. A determined Husing also started memorizing the dictionary and thesaurus.

By the fall of 1924 Ted started assisting White on sports broadcasts. After a while, RCA sent Ted to its Washington station for further seasoning before he was brought back. At that point, WJZ was a 50,000-watt powerhouse and Husing continued in his role as staff announcer. There would be musical programs and all sorts of specials. Through it all, Ted was enjoying the good life and frequenting the entertainment belt. He was never a big drinker but during Prohibition, he became familiar with the speakeasies, especially the landmark, "21."

When a poll was released by a publication showing Husing to be the seventh-most popular announcer on radio, he brazenly walked into the office of the station's program director, Charles Popenoe, and demanded a raise. When it was refused, he quit angrily.

Within a week Husing landed a job with WBET, a start-up station in Boston. He convinced the Braves to allow the station to carry their games which he announced. The Husing stay in Boston didn't last long. New York beckoned. His mentor, Major White was organizing CBS and he asked Husing to be a freelance sports broadcaster. In the fall of 1927 he was back home.

At the same time, Husing made a deal with WHN to broadcast Columbia University football games. The *New York American* newspaper sponsored the broadcasts and promoted them amply. The paper urged its readers to tune in the Lions' games with Husing, "the greatest sportscaster of all time." In 1927 the

© National Baseball Hall of Fame Library, Cooperstown, N.Y.

Ted Husing influenced a generation of America's best sports announcers in every corner of the country.

Herald Tribune reviewer wrote, "Husing has been consistently better than the more famous Graham McNamee and Phillips Carlin."

On Christmas Day 1927 Husing joined CBS full time as White's assistant and office manager. Over the course of the next year until Bill Paley's purchase of the company bailed out Columbia from potential bankruptcy and possible extinction, the network operated on a fraying shoestring. Husing did all sorts of work, from covering the funeral of war hero Floyd Bennett, to President Herbert Hoover's acceptance speech, to a tragic inferno at an Ohio penitentiary.

When Paley arrived in 1928, White was chief cook and bottle washer. He was president and still doing sports. One day, White was ill and scheduled to travel to Chicago to broadcast a football game. Paley called for Husing to fill in. "As a result I lost an impossible office manager and gained the best and most famous sportscaster in the country," Paley said. By 1930 White left CBS and it was Ted Husing's show.

In 1929 Husing built CBS's stable of sports, launching radio coverage of such social sports as international polo or tennis. In 1929 Ted called the World Series by himself, the Army-Navy football game, and the Kentucky Derby. Ted continued the good life, too, during his rise to stardom. His CBS paycheck would vanish, "like the American buffalo."

Husing preferred working alone. One year, both networks, NBC and CBS, covered the Kentucky Derby. NBC sent a large crew. Husing went alone. It was Husing against the country's best race caller, Clem McCarthy. NBC attempted a sophisticated production. McCarthy was to call the race until the finish line when he would turn it over to a reporter at the finish line. This way NBC was assured of calling the right winner.

Husing admittedly knew little about racing but Paley had confidence in him to do virtually everything. In fact, on the day of the race, Paley was entertaining some friends and had two speakers on in his office, one tuned to Ted and one to the NBC broadcast. It was a tight race and Husing declared "Clyde Van Dusen wins the Derby." The NBC call had Blue Larkspur winning. Paley and friends listening in New York started laughing. Paley wired Husing in Louisville. "Sorry about the finish, you did a swell job, kid, up to that point." NBC then corrected itself. Indeed, Husing working alone had the right winner the whole time. From then on NBC smartly let McCarthy call races himself.

47

Husing also competed hard with Graham McNamee even in nonsports. In 1929 one big event was the Golden Jubilee of Light, the 50th anniversary of Thomas Edison's invention. It was scheduled for Detroit and President Hoover was to partake in the event. NBC had it all tied up through the event's sponsor, General Electric which owned NBC's Schenectady affiliate, WGY. It also had an in with the host of the Jubilee, Henry Ford, because the Ford Motor Company sponsored many NBC programs. Husing and the upstarts at CBS were being shut out.

It didn't discourage Husing, who effectively pulled off the ambush coverage. Ted saw to it that a ladder was run up the exterior of the building. Peering through an open window, Husing described the proceedings for the CBS audience. Ted had copped NBC's log and had all the times of the proceedings. It worked out perfectly. CBS was able to pick up President Hoover's remarks live at that magical moment when a switch was activated and the room was awash in light.

Red Barber, who was hardly charitable in his comments for Husing, claimed that Ted was obsessed with McNamee. "He always wanted to outdo McNamee." By the mid-1930s Husing had conquered McNamee. Ted was the number one sportscaster in the country. It had to make Ted feel especially good because, among other things, he and McNamee lived in the same Manhattan apartment building and would cross paths.

While the New York–reared voice was the first to make football broadcasts a science, Husing was smooth and lightning quick in his rich description of other sports, too. He covered golf and track, lugging pounds and pounds of heavy equipment on his back roaming around golf courses and track-and-field stadia. His accounts were thorough and flawless. Even his tennis description (yes, tennis on radio) was perfectly painted. He was crisp and made tennis come alive on the radio. He did many U.S. Opens. "It was beautiful, he didn't miss a let, a backhand, or a forehand. He was mesmerizing," says Bill Mazer. "He had a brilliant mind for his work."

Marty Glickman, who was one of the first rapid-fire announcers in the country, still shakes his head when thinking back to the day that tennis was attempted on radio, adding though with a taut smile of amazement, "He did it quite well."

Husing was constantly being written about, his picture was everywhere, and his distinguished voice was potent. His football work was so celebrated it was featured in magazine and newspaper articles. As early as 1930 Husing, writing a guest column in the *New York Telegram*, described his streamlined system of doing football play-by-play. The system of "outpost reporters," used by McNamee, was inefficient and outdated. "Having helpers whisper in an announcer's ear is disruptive and breaks a train of thought."

Instead of relying on others to communicate with him verbally on air, Husing and his assistant, Jimmy Dolan, concocted an organizing device, called a spotter board. Today it is an indispensable tool for any football announcer. Husing, Dolan, and the CBS engineers actually developed it into an electrical spotter. It was colored, green for one team and red for another. This way the 11 men on the field for each team were lit up on the board. The observer had to do no more than point to the tackler to help Husing identify the right player. Husing called his invention "annunciators" and said it took the "guesswork" out of calling a game.

The *New York Times* praised the innovation, referring to it as an "illuminated indicator board." Imitation is the best form of flattery and football broadcasters were then all devising their own spotter boards. In 1940 *Popular Science* featured the electrical board constructed for the WHO announcers in Des Moines.

In an article in *Literary Digest*, Husing said that the best tip he got in broadcasting football came from the legendary coach, Knute Rockne, who told him that the eye of the broadcaster and the fan takes the "road of least resistance." They look at the backfield on offense and the line on defense. Rockne's eyes did just the opposite.

The funniest thing Husing witnessed was in a Dartmouth-Princeton game when Ivy League football was on top of the world. Dartmouth was getting whipped. On a play at the goal line and in a tight formation, a Dartmouth fan, Mike Mesco, dove into the play to help his poor team. It gained him fame for a week but hardly helped Dartmouth. Princeton won the game, big.

The 12th man on the field might have gotten a chuckle from Husing but a 1931 incident involving Harvard didn't. For that matter, it got him into some trouble. Husing was obviously always thoroughly prepared. The spotter boards were just the start. Ted was meticulous about attending practice and getting a list of the plays that each team would run. Given the fact that he promised not to divulge them until broadcast time and in view of his national stature, coaches would generally oblige.

The announcer had asked Harvard coach Eddie Casey for the plays his team would run and was turned down. When asked for permission to attend practice, it was refused, too. Through the course of the Dartmouth-Harvard broadcast, Husing was critical of Harvard, perhaps overly critical, irritating Harvard fans and alumni. Barry Wood was the Harvard quarterback and apparently Husing was not very charitable in his assessment of the playmaker's performance. Ted described Wood's play as "putrid." (Funny, on the very next play, Wood arched a marvelous pass that sailed right into the hands of a Crimson receiver.) Today, few would bat an eyelash at a comment of this sort but, back then it wasn't fashionable to be critical of players. How things have changed.

CBS received a flood of protest mail from listeners. William Bingham, the school's director of athletics, barred him from Harvard Stadium and sent a letter of protest to CBS head William Paley. Bingham had to take action to back Wood for many reasons, none bigger than the fact that Wood's dad was a trustee of the distinguished school. It was an embarrassing development for all parties. Husing claimed his comment was not intended to disparage Wood, rather to describe his poor play against Dartmouth compared to his sparkling performance in an earlier contest against Army. Husing later said he eliminated the word "putrid" from his vocabulary.

Paley called Husing into his office and Ted was prepared for the worst. Paley, though, was apparently quite understanding and reassuring, and told him not to worry. The CBS boss then addressed the press where he backed his announcer and told the assembled writers, "How many of you have said 'no' when you meant 'yes'?" Westbrook Pegler, Bill Corum, and Heywood Broun, the leading columnists of the day, were all in Husing's corner, too.

For all his successes, his well-rounded knowledge, and great command of the language, Husing never attended college. When he applied for his first announcing job, he doctored his résumé, claiming he was a college graduate. Harvard, Husing would say later, made him feel his inadequacies the most.

The interesting sequel is the fact that the popular broadcaster voted Wood to his all-radio team at the end of the 1931 season. All was forgiven a couple of years later when Harvard also invited Husing back to its stadium.

One of Husing's gifts was his picture-painting that placed the listener right alongside him in the booth. He would describe the stadium, its environs and the city, the setting and, when applicable, the gorgeous campuses. His love of the English language would occasionally draw the wrath of media critics, too. In 1937 Ted, calling a Baylor-Texas contest referred to a player's ears as his "auricular appendages."

Lester Smith, the longtime WOR broadcaster, remembers a game that Husing called from Holy Cross in Worcester, Massachusetts. "On his way to the game, Husing's eye caught a series of impressive red brick buildings nestled on a hill. He was told it was an extension of the campus. So he raved about the place on the broadcast, gushing over the serenity and beauty. When he finished his broadcast, a listener rushed up to him. 'Mr. Husing, there's hardly any serenity in the brick buildings you were talking about. That's the Massachusetts State Hospital of the Insane.'" Smith says that there was quite a fuss over the faux pas.

Husing was a man on the move in the 1930s, covering almost 70 remote sporting events a year alone, including a parachute-jumping contest. He would travel more than 30,000 miles a year before plane travel was routine. His football broadcasts drew many millions of listeners each week. It wasn't unusual for games to get ratings of close to an incredible 40. Pro football doesn't do as much today on television. And these were pretelevision days when fans were hanging on every one of the announcer's words.

For many reasons, Husing's work was on the cutting edge of football broadcasting. The creative spotting board that he popularized was just the beginning. Most importantly, it was his preparation. He spent considerable time each week with both coaches and studied films of both teams. The baritone was also the first to incorporate the language of the game, applying basic coach's lingo and explaining the terminology in layman's terms.

When he set up in the booth, the spotter board, or the "annunciator" as Husing called it, wasn't the only automated aide that he had in front of him. Husing's assistants in the booth, Les Quailey and later Jimmy Dolan, constantly updated another mechanical board that was always right in front of Ted's nose. This device had all the basics that the listener demanded immediately, the score, the time remaining, and the down and distance. These were numbers, but basic numbers, easily digestible by the radio listener. Just as Red Barber had his egg timer in front of him as a reminder not to go more than three minutes without giving the baseball score, Husing knew that giving these elementary details regularly was imperative.

At kickoff, he was ready. Nothing got past him or the listener. Before every play was run from scrimmage, the master would religiously describe the look of the formation, picturesquely and informatively. Ted's staccato was perfectly cadenced for the rhythm of the game. He pitched his voice perfectly and appropriately. Each play had a punch line and the listener was able to sense the tension in his voice.

The announcing legend preferred working alone and generally didn't have a color commentator with him. His two assistants, Quailey and Dolan, would occasionally go on the air but it was hardly as though they were salient on-air participants. A score here or there, some special player profile was the extent of it. When Quailey and Dolan moved on, Walter Kennedy became Ted's assistant. He did get more air time. The future NBA commissioner worked with Husing on Army football broadcasts after the war.

The two devised another unique approach. Husing concentrated on offense and Kennedy on defense. Husing called it a "two-platooning idea." The identification would be so indelible that Kennedy would later sign letters to Husing, "Defense."

When he left CBS, Les Quailey went to work for ad agency, N.W. Ayer which ran all the college football broadcasts sponsored by Atlantic Richfield. And there were quite a few. In 1939 Quailey streamlined the coverage of broadcast football further. Ordinary sideline markers were too small to be seen immediately by announcers. He impressed upon many schools to paint a diamond midway between the sidelines on the 20-yard line, a cross on each 40-yard line, and a large circle in the middle of the field. Drawings have been embellished since but credit Quailey for these essential improvements.

Jimmy Dolan was once asked what set Ted apart from other sports announcers. "He could bring you to the edge of your chair without screaming. He had a sense of pacing. He loved the language, the sound of it and the flow of it." Ted's sound was indeed mellifluous and it had a trace of New York accent to it.

To appreciate Husing's popularity in New York, remember that Major League Baseball broadcasts were banned by the three teams. It wasn't until 1939 that Red Barber and Mel Allen came along. So Husing really owned the turf. The interest in the NFL then was minimal and NHL hockey in New York was still relatively young and, like today, esoteric to many. College football was it, supreme even in 1939 when ratings dipped from 1938, from 35 to 33.9.

The only local play-by-play announcer in New York in the 1930s was Earl Harper, who voiced the football Giants, college basketball, and Newark Bears baseball. Sports on New York radio in the 1930s was dominated by the networks.

The impact that Husing had on the Orange Bowl was enormous. NBC was locked into the Rose Bowl and in the mid-1930s the Sugar Bowl. The Orange Bowl which started in 1933 as the Palm Festival needed a jolt. It had little national visibility. The economics of sport were quite different then. Rights fees were a thing of the future.

Desperate, the Orange Bowl Committee convinced Husing and CBS to broadcast the game and, for that matter, paid the network $500 for line costs. In 1937 CBS started its Orange Bowl tradition. Leading into it, throughout the fall of 1936, Husing promoted the Miami game, each Saturday of the regular college football season and Monday to Friday on his daily shows. It was just what the Orange Bowl needed. The charismatic Husing was cogent. He gave the event credibility.

When Husing broadcast his first Orange Bowl, the seating capacity at the stadium was 22,000 and the seats were secondhand bleachers which were purchased from the American Legion. Over the next 10 years, all of which time Husing was its radio voice, the Orange Bowl gained national acceptance. Improvements were made to the stadium, the seating capacity was increased, and the committee was able to attract teams that were more prominent nationally. Duquesne and Mississippi State played in Ted's first Orange Bowl broadcast in 1937. But by 1939 the Orange Bowl featured powerhouses Tennessee and Oklahoma, two undefeated teams. Ted was the voice of the first 10 Orange Bowls.

Many big-name broadcasters followed Ted. Red Barber, Mel Allen, Jack Brickhouse, and Jim McKay all called the Miami game. The Mets' Bob Murphy did a couple of Orange Bowls for NBC in the late 1980s. A voice synonymous with broken bats was describing broken tackles. Even as he talked about the quarterback "fading" to throw, Murph's very voice conjured warm thoughts of summer.

Not one afraid to speak his mind, Ted Husing engaged in a debate at Town Hall on March 22, 1945. The question was "Should Organized Sports Be Abolished for the Duration of World War II?" He and Larry MacPhail, the president of the Yankees, argued that sports should continue. Stanley Frank and John Tunis dissented, stating that organized sports be canceled in deference to the soldiers. The veteran announcer argued that the United States would become "completely regimented" should sports and all nonessential industries be closed down. "The majority rules and the majority has demonstrated it wants sports continued," Husing argued.

A year after Husing was a prominent protagonist in Town Hall, extolling the virtues of organized sports in the day-to-day life of millions of Americans, he himself moved to greener pastures, away from sports. In 1946, after almost 18 years with CBS, a network he helped build, Husing resigned.

The chill started when television was born in 1941. Husing did the blow-by-blow of the Joe Louis–Billy Conn heavyweight title bout at the Polo Grounds on TV. Husing felt that he "fitted like a perfectly tailored suit into the new medium." He wanted more money.

But with the advent of television, CBS was no longer an intimate company. It was now a corporation that had structure and hierarchy. There were others between Paley and Husing. Ted started negotiating a raise with a Paley underling who was placed in charge. Husing's request was turned down. Dissatisfied and disappointed, he quit. At that point, one would assume that a man of his success and esteem would have had enough saved for a rainy day or two. But through all the years of being in great demand and of earning high wages, Husing had virtually nothing tucked away. By his own admission, he "invested his money in life."

After brief employment with a Philadelphia radio station covering racing from Garden State Park in Philadelphia, Husing hit a gold mine. Bert Lebhar was running WHN, one of Ted's alma maters. Bert asked Ted to do a daily music show. Husing hesitated at first. But once wages were discussed, he accepted. In 1946, the year that Jackie Robinson revolutionized baseball, Husing revolutionized radio-listening habits. A man identified with sports for so long was moving to music. There was now a daily program called, *Ted Husing's Bandstand*.

Sports fans never quite got used to it. The very open, the very jingle to his new show, was an aberration. His pay was tied to advertising sales. Lebhar estimated that his pay would be at about $100,000 a year, a significant fortune in 1946. In reality, Husing's income was said to be $250,000 annually. He never did better financially in his life. To appreciate the impact of an income of that size, the cost of a New York subway token didn't increase from a nickel to a dime until 1948.

While Husing was no longer doing play-by-play for CBS, he did continue to do football for other networks such as Mutual. This itself resulted in a funny mix-up one Saturday during his first football season away from CBS. On November 2, 1946, CBS and Mutual were both covering the Alabama-Georgia game. Maury Farrell was doing the play-by-play for CBS and Husing for Mutual.

The telephone installer at the stadium would routinely stay at the stadium during the game broadcast to make sure that broadcast transmissions go smoothly. He fed the two broadcasts leading into his mainframe to their respective networks. This telephone man, working instinctively, sent Farrell's feed to Mutual and Husing's to CBS. He went with his inclination. After all, Husing's voice was connected for 18 seasons with CBS.

So here was Husing back on CBS, the network from which he resigned over a pay dispute, courtesy of an error by the local telephone man, who was overpowered by his tendency. It took several minutes until the problem was corrected and the men were on their assigned networks.

From 1947–49 Ted did the Baltimore Colts games of the All-America Conference. Their quarterback was a man named Y. A. Tittle. That's when Husing crossed paths with Bill Mazer who was doing the Buffalo Bills games. "I idolized the man to begin with and had him on at halftime. That was a thrill. But that electrical spotter board, I will never forget it," Mazer said some 50 years later with a heave of amazement as though it was fitting for the best to have the best. Ted would later say that his heart was never in the pro assignment. It was collegiate ball that was his first love. The Colts' 1-11 record in 1949 could hardly have stimulated his enthusiasm, either.

Although he did do the Giants in 1950 for WMGM, Husing's connection with football after leaving CBS was primarily with Army, where he would do games for Mutual from 1947–53. His last year of play-by-play was 1953.

Some will say he could be quite arrogant. Ernie Harwell tells the story of the young announcer who eagerly wanted to show him a picture of his newborn child. Husing looked at the announcer with lofty contempt, telling him that all babies look alike and just walked on.

Lindsey Nelson describes the way Husing carried himself. The inference is that his very gait and demeanor rendered him supercilious. Arriving at a stadium in a chauffeur-driven Cadillac and dressed to the hilt, Husing wore alligator shoes and a beret. He sauntered in with a cigarette in a long holder. As he strode down a ramp toward the entrance, Husing, according to Lindsey, was impervious to cries for his autograph.

In 1954 the great Husing suffered a brain tumor, could no longer work, and moved to Pasadena where he lived under the care of his mother. Ted had one annulment, then two marriages and two divorces. Out of money, his bills were footed by Paley, the owners of "21" in New York, and other friends. California physicians provided many of their services gratis. Ralph Edwards re-created Ted's life on his NBC television series, *This is Your Life*. In California, the once-powerful broadcaster attempted a comeback as a sports commentator on a local station for $150 a week, but it was canceled after just a short period of time. Ted could hardly walk, his memory was shot, and he was going blind. The mighty man of sports broadcasting died in California on August 10, 1962, just shy of his 61st birthday.

The great Red Smith wrote, "The reason he has been the best is that he has been the most painstaking and accurate and knowledgeable reporter of facts covering sports on the air. Nobody ever worked harder at learning the game he was broadcasting."

From the time that Slater left NBC in 1936, Bill Stern dominated the peacock network and warred with Husing as though each was bloodthirsty. Today the battles seem almost comedic but back then they were ferocious.

Bill Stern was born Bill Sterngold in Rochester, New York, in 1907. His father was a well-to-do businessman who would later lose his bundle. But times were good in Bill's youth and his dad had him attend prep schools and eventually the Pennsylvania Military College where he graduated in 1930. Bill's interest gravitated to theater and New York. When Radio City was built, it was to house NBC and two theaters. Bill Stern got a job there as a stage manager in 1932.

After a while, Stern wondered what it would be like to be a radio announcer. He met and "haunted" NBC vice president of programming John Royal. He had no radio experience but a strong, vibrant, magnetic, and cogent voice.

Stern had always had an interest in sports and he kept nudging Royal for a chance. This was 1934 and NBC started spreading its football work around. Royal acquiesced and convinced McNamee to let Stern "hang himself" by allowing him to do two minutes of the Navy–William and Mary game.

It was a rather dull contest and McNamee didn't let Stern get his hands on the mike until the very end. Navy was marching down the field and it wound up being the only stretch of excitement, albeit a short stretch. Navy scored and Stern described it. When he returned to New York, Royal complimented him on a good job and Nick Kenny of the *New York Mirror* referred to Stern as an "ace football announcer."

Saturday was football day on the radio. Only the very small stations didn't broadcast football. In fact, Kenny wrote, "As far as radio is concerned, football is more important than the president of the United States. Football is accorded more hours on more stations at any time than anything else on the air today."

Royal then assigned Stern one quarter of a game a week later, Army against Illinois. Stern, so eager to impress Royal, pulled a fast one that backfired on him. About four or five days before this assignment, he called friends and family, suggesting that they send letters complimentary of his performance. Eager to please, they obliged. There was one problem. The telegrams were sent immediately. By Thursday, Royal was getting correspondence saying Stern did a great job on a game that hadn't been played yet. An incensed Royal called Stern into his office and fired him on the spot.

Now that he had a taste of it, Stern wanted to continue. When nothing surfaced immediately, he went to work for a friend of the family who owned a clothier with stores in several cities. He was assigned to Schenectady, New York, where he became a suit salesman. Several months went by when the clothier called Stern in to tell him that its Shreveport, Louisiana, store had purchased a sponsorship of the Centenary College football games. As was often the case then, the sponsor was responsible for producing the broadcasts and hiring the announcer. Stern was told to head south.

The games were carried on KWKH. Stern was the play-by-play announcer and Jack Gelzer of the station's staff handled color. The first broadcast went splendidly. The second game of the season was in Austin, Texas, where Centenary would play the University of Texas. The two men made the long drive through the Texas flatlands and the broadcast went smoothly. A day after the game on October 20, 1935, Bill Stern's life would change forever. Driving back to Shreveport on a sun-washed and clear day, Stern and Gelzer were sailing through the limitless stretch of prairie.

About 20 miles from the cosmopolitan metropolis of Teague, Texas, Stern's car collided with another. His vehicle overturned and the area was littered with glass and oil. There were also fuel odors. Gelzer was able to get out unscathed. Stern's legs, though, were pinned under the car. With Gelzer pushing and manipulating the car, Stern was able to wriggle free.

He was put in a facility labeled a hospital in Teague. But in reality it was no more than a small-town doctor's home, office, and occasional hospital. The foot, though, got badly infected, and the pain was excruciating. The doctor administered painkillers. The pain was intractable and after a couple of days, Stern was taken by ambulance to Palestine, Texas, where he was given another painkilling injection and put on a train to New York. On the train ride back, he was told that he was given enough morphine to kill him.

In New York, Stern was taken to the Hospital for Joint Diseases. These were prepenicillin days and the practice then was to insert maggots to fight infection. The procedure didn't work and finally, after several days, physicians were left with no option other than amputating his left leg just above the knee.

Stern was horrified and shocked when doctors told him that they had to amputate his leg. He was in a virtual state of disbelief. When reality set in, Stern told his mother that he would be better off dead and wished that he would have died on the operating table.

Word had gotten back to Royal of what had happened. Bright and early one morning with Stern in his hospital bed and hardly eating, the NBC programming boss walked in and unceremoniously shoved Stern's breakfast tray under his nose and demanded to know "How will you get well and broadcast for NBC if you don't eat?" Royal's visit and apparent promise to give him work again lifted Stern's spirits.

When Stern mastered his artificial leg in August 1936, he went up to NBC to see Royal, who kept his promise. Stern was hired on a freelance basis to do football in the fall of 1936. To make a real living, Bill kept an affiliation with the Stein Stores, the clothier for whom he had worked earlier. His stock shot up at NBC. On November 22, 1936, Jim Farley of the *New York Daily News* praised Stern for his work on the Princeton-Dartmouth contest and suggested that he is a "potential rival of Ted Husing." He added. "Though lacking Ted's cool, almost blasé delivery, Stern packs a dramatic wallop in his descriptions."

Of course, this was just the beginning of both Stern's celebrated rivalry with Husing and his "dramatic wallop." Bill will not be remembered for accurate play-by-play. When it was possible to correct himself smoothly and in a way that he felt was innocuous, he would do just that. He would admit freely that if he had

Army's Doc Blanchard running all by himself when he noticed it was Glenn Davis, he would snap, "And he laterals off to Glenn Davis."

Stern justified his practice by claiming that listeners would rather hear a smooth description. He felt that if an announcer starts calling attention to his own blunders, fans lose faith in his call. Many of Stern's critics, and there were quite a few who lambasted him, felt that the argument was rather specious.

Stern's lack of integrity wasn't limited to the football field. Ernie Harwell was hired by Stern to cover a hole at the Masters which Stern was anchoring. Ernie was stationed at the second hole and action had moved on to the third. Unaware, Stern called in Ernie who told the audience that the golfers had passed. Stern later told Harwell, "You should have faked it. This is showbiz." Jack Brickhouse summarized it, "Stern had everything but integrity."

By 1937 Bill Slater was out and NBC hired Stern full time at $75 a week. Later, some said that it was more than an expense account dispute that doomed Slater's NBC career. Stern was lurking and manipulating.

Meanwhile, pain persisted from his leg and Stern got hooked on sleeping medication and painkillers. He got addicted on morphine and Demerol. Whenever he got the urge, Stern faked illness and doctors administered an injection. Stern also seemed to get chronic bouts with kidney stones and it exacerbated the situation.

Stern was the lead play-by-play announcer on the 1938 Sugar Bowl and by that point, *Radio Daily*'s top three national sports announcers were Husing first, Clem McCarthy, the race caller and boxing announcer second, and Stern third.

In 1939 the Rose Bowl finally relaxed its ban on eastern announcers and Stern started a 10-year run as "voice of the Rose Bowl." It was a huge break for the melodramatic Stern. The Rose Bowl was still the premier football event of the year. There was no television then. Radio was it and folks planned their New Year's Day around the radio schedule. There were years when half the country was listening to Stern's broadcast. His very first Rose was fantastic. In the final minutes of a riveting 1939 classic, Southern California beat previously undefeated and unscored-upon Duke to win.

The Rose Bowl Committee and NBC agreed that Stern be paired with Ken Carpenter, which he was, through 1944. One of the eeriest Rose Bowls that the two covered was in 1942. The war wasn't quite a month old and the country's spirits were sagged. The game was shifted to North Carolina. During the broadcast, Stern, alone in the stadium, switched to Carpenter in the empty Rose Bowl for a report of what it was like to be in a building that on the first of January usually had more than 100,000 folks screaming and yelling.

Stern's popularity exploded. By 1940 Stern leaped to number one in *Radio Daily*'s popularity poll, ahead of Husing. He would remain the country's most popular sports voice the next 13 years. Everything was going perfectly. Later that year, America's most popular sports announcer was featured in *Variety*, detailing the service requirements of a football announcer. Stern listed seven:

1. Advance information, specifying broadcast location to facilitate installation
2. An alphabetical and numerical list of players
3. Players' weights and nationality
4. A spotter

5. An opportunity to watch practice or motion pictures of the plays and players in previous games

6. A reliable list of musical tunes so that the announcer can talk over any restricted number

7. Seven tickets to the game for the announcer, the home team's spotter, the visiting team's spotter, two engineers, and a Western Union telegraph operator to keep the announcer informed of scores of other important games of the day.

In 1946 *Life* magazine did a pictorial on a Saturday in the booth with Stern. There was a field engineer, a Western Union ticker, and boom microphones rigged up everywhere in the stadium. Stern was surrounded in the booth by a horde of assistants. The booth was festooned with notes of papers. He had different synonyms listed. One read, "passes, tosses, throws, pitches, rifles." As he would use these words, he would cross them off one at a time.

In the 1940s organized sports were not yet marketing savvy. Yet there were Bill Stern games, books, and endorsements. There was not a sports fan in America who didn't know his name.

As enormously popular as he was through his football work, Bill Stern will always be remembered for the dramatic and fabricated stories that he told on his long-running weekly program called *Bill Stern's Colgate Sports Newsreel.*

The Colgate show started in 1939 and ended in 1951. Listeners sat ensconced and enraptured as he would tell one emotional, gripping tale after another. He would tell stories with an "O'Henry twist." They were set to music and by Stern's admission, fableized and dramatized to appeal to the housewife. These melodramatic vignettes were an immediate hit and a smashing success. They made Stern tons of money. Colgate paid him up to $2,500 each week. It was an enormous amount, considering that in 1939 he was still earning just $75 a week from NBC.

In its obituary of Stern, the *New York Times* recounted a couple of the anecdotes Stern would tell. One explained that Thomas Edison's deafness came about when he was beaned in a baseball game by Jesse James. Another told of the origin of baseball. According to Stern's story on the Colgate show, Abraham Lincoln's dying words to Abner Doubleday inspired the latter to create the game. The venerable San Francisco broadcaster, Bill King, remembers growing up in the Midwest where kids shared their Stern experiences each Saturday morning, "'Hey, did you hear his story about Lou Gehrig yesterday?' It was that kind of wild stuff."

Bill Mazer added, "He couldn't shine Husing's shoes doing football but Stern was the greatest sports storyteller ever."

The program was widely criticized, but Stern maintained that the show was entertainment just as Jack Benny's or others were. It didn't appear as though Stern ever tried to defend the stories but admitted that he was "miserably upset" by all the criticism. Yet one wonders how there was no sense of responsibility, given the fact that Stern is introduced on the show as "the Colgate man who shows the dope he really knows."

One incident in particular embroiled Stern with writers. In September 1944 the St. Louis Browns were on their way to the American League pennant. They were in first place but were going through a slump. A Chicago turf paper, *Collyer's*

Eye, inferred that the club was losing on purpose because baseball had more to gain in receipts should New York or Detroit advance to the World Series.

Stern was in Detroit getting set to do a Michigan football game when the story broke. It was a Friday and he decided to go with the story on his popular Friday show. That night Stern made the most of shock radio. He opened his show with an almost alarming lead.

"Attention America. If the St. Louis Browns blow the American League pennant, there will be a baseball investigation, according to *Collyer's Eye*, the publication that broke the 1919 Black Sox scandal."

There was blistering criticism of Stern all around the country and demands that he apologize. He refused to until organized baseball and others put sufficient pressure on him to do so. He later admitted that it was a mistake but not before he was blasted by many, including *New York Telegram* sports columnist Joe Williams, who did so scathingly.

During that rough week, the beleaguered Stern got a call from arch rival Ted Husing, certainly no close friend. Husing told him to hang in and reminded his NBC nemesis that he went through something similar some 12 years earlier when he referred to Harvard quarterback, Barry Wood, as "putrid."

Husing and Stern were like oil and water. The core to the problem was duplicate coverage. Until 1939, when Gillette bought the rights to the World Series and awarded exclusive coverage to Mutual, baseball had as many as four different networks covering its Fall Classic. And while the Bowls did grant exclusives for the most part, regular-season games were basically open to any network. Each network wanted the top game each week. Ben Gross in the *Daily News* gave a review of Saturday's football broadcasts on November 20, 1938, and it was typical. "The eagerly observed battle between Notre Dame and Northwestern was brought to tense listeners by WABC (CBS) and WJZ (NBC) with Ted Husing and Bill Stern, respectively, giving two of the best accounts of the day."

Husing and Stern would be broadcasting the same contest for so many weeks that animosity grew. If each could make life more difficult for one another, he would. And it's amazing because these two weren't kids. They were the top two personalities in broadcast sports when there wasn't the plethora of outlets that there are today. These two were as big as they come. Anyone who remembers will tell you. Husing and Stern were eye-popping and awe-inspiring names.

But all's fair in love and war. It started with a little ribbing. They were both standing in the South Bend train station after a Notre Dame football game, waiting for the train back to New York. Stern admired the jacket that the impeccably dressed Husing was wearing. "That's a beautiful jacket. Where did you get it?" Husing responded "My god, Stern, now you are going to start copying my clothes, too?"

Stern was asked to do a horse race that Husing was also doing. Bill asked Ted for a tip on how to do it, since he never had. Knowing Stern's reputation for constantly having to correct himself on football by using the escapable lateral pass, Husing suggested that Stern simply guess and correct himself once the leaders cross the finish line.

Unfortunately, while the stories sound amusing, one was truly trying to inflict damage on the other. Stern once arrived in Champaign, Illinois for an Army-Illinois football game. The NBC and CBS booths were side by side on the top of a triple-deck stadium. The cables and transmission lines ran along a narrow ledge. Stern took a pair of pliers from his engineer's bag and crawled precariously on the narrow ledge. Remember that Stern was lame. This was dangerous.

He then snipped what he thought were Husing's lines. These guys weren't kidding. There had to be some real hatred. Stern would say that he sat in his booth "waiting with satanic delight." Both networks were to go on the air at the same appointed time. Sitting in adjacent booths, the two could dimly hear one another. Airtime comes and there's no cue for Stern to start. Meanwhile, Stern hears Husing opening the broadcast. In a panic, Stern turns to his infuriated engineer who starts hollering at him, "You genius, you cut our lines."

On one occasion in Nashville, a menace got both of them. The booths were next to each other so he painted one door "men" and the other "women." Bathroom seekers poked their heads in the broadcast booths all afternoon.

In July 1937 the two got into another celebrated case. This one wasn't sabotage, rather bootlegging. NBC had purchased the exclusive broadcast rights to the Senior National AAU Track and Field meet in Milwaukee. CBS, trying to avoid being shut out, broadcast from an adjacent roof, said to be the spire of a church. The spot on the roof provided a clear vantage point. Stern wanted to blind Husing's vision by shining a bright light in his eyes. But he didn't have to resort to it because he discovered that Husing had to contend with one natural blind spot, a piece of the track hidden by a tree.

As the race progressed, one runner took a tumble and Husing reported it immediately on CBS. NBC claimed that Husing and associate Jimmy Dolan were monitoring Stern's NBC broadcast and got the otherwise unobtainable information. Stern was screaming "bootleg," claiming Husing couldn't possibly have seen the spill without having him tuned in.

One year, when CBS had an exclusive for the prestigious Poughkeepsie Regatta, Stern stationed himself on a building along the Hudson River. However, he couldn't see the race sufficiently to call it. According to Stern, he listened to Husing's call and "dressed it up." But it was to no avail. Husing had the wrong winner that day. They both looked bad. In this sense, Husing and Stern were incorrigible.

Variety referred to the ongoing shenanigans as "dog-fight tactics." It would go on at any wide-open facility where the entrance couldn't be policed or a neighboring vantage point could be accessed. At times, when one suspected the other of bootlegging, he would purposely make mistakes to see if the other would repeat them. If he did, it proved that the other is culpable. What a world! This went on constantly. The fact that giant networks CBS and NBC were engaged in this chicanery is hardly imaginable today.

Unfortunately, Stern was getting hooked on painkillers. This adult man was sadly becoming a drug addict, popping sleeping pills and regularly visiting doctors for morphine. There were nights that he admitted taking up to 16 sleeping pills. Stern had kidney problems which needed attention on a weekly basis. He had to be in a hospital overnight, giving him an excuse to get a shot of morphine or Demerol. When he was on the road, he would often summon the hotel doctor, feign illness, and get the hotel doctor to provide the addicted shot.

By the 1950s he started acting strangely and people suspected something might be seriously wrong. They knew he wasn't a serious drinker. The drug addiction was becoming apparent. In 1952 in the NBC offices, there was a constellation of symptoms suggesting addiction. Finally, in 1956, there was an on-air paroxysm which basically wrecked his career.

The addiction was overbearing and the pressure was intense. His condition was exacerbated by the fact that the Colgate show was dumped in 1951 after ratings had dropped badly. At the same time, Tom Gallery had been installed as NBC's sports director in January 1952. It usurped Bill's power. He now only had a talent contract and reported to Gallery. NBC didn't want its on-air talent administering radio and a growing television department. CBS would do the same in 1955.

In June 1952 Gallery walked into Stern's office and observed a sickly almost incoherent Stern lying on a couch in his office. Stern was on the verge of a breakdown. Gallery had to call Bill's wife to have him taken home.

Gallery knew what was going on. He was tipped off by one of Stern's doctors, Dr. Herman Tarnower, that the announcer was getting more and more addicted to drugs. Tarnower had suggested to Stern that he enter rehabilitation. Stern told Tarnower he feared losing his income stream during the rehabilitation period. Hearing this from the doctor, Gallery saw to it that Stern's salary continue while he spent time in a sanitarium. If the name Herman Tarnower rings a bell, it should. He was the well-known Scarsdale Diet inventor who was later killed mysteriously by Jean Harris.

Later that summer, with Stern off injections but still taking painkillers, Gallery informed him that he would not be doing the college football television package which NBC purchased. It went to Mel Allen and Russ Hodges. Stern was terribly dejected and that night rediscovered his friendly physician who administered the injection. Over the next three years, the buildup of injections was to the point where he needed them twice a week. Drugs were dominating his life.

To Gallery, the Stern situation was a nightmare. He didn't buy into the announcer's argument that the drugs were to ease pain for the amputated leg. It was an excuse according to Gallery, who remembers Stern locking himself into a hotel room and getting drugged up.

In 1953, under the aegis of megasponsor Anheuser-Busch, Stern moved to ABC Television where he did studio programming and play-by-play. On January 2, 1956, his addiction hit the fan. ABC assigned him to do the telecast of the Sugar Bowl in New Orleans between Pittsburgh and Georgia Tech. On the night before the event, the addict, Bill Stern, overdosed. He cajoled a local doctor into a strong injection and later swallowed more sleeping pills.

The next morning, the day of the game, he got up dazed. He summoned the local doctor one more time and convinced him to administer one more shot to get him through the day.

When the doctor left the room early in the morning, Stern passed out completely. He did manage to awake and get over to the stadium. He arrived minutes before kickoff, bedraggled and in a drug stupor.

He struggled to open the show: stumbling, stammering, and stuttering. He could hardly identify the two opponents and couldn't get through the first verse of the opening lineups. Ray Scott was scheduled to assist him that day. It was obvious something was terribly wrong with the renowned Bill Stern. Billy Whitehouse, ABC's sports director, was ordered by New York to take Stern off the air.

Word spread quickly. When, in an adjoining broadcast booth, Al Ciraldo, "voice of the Jackets," found out, there was no sympathy. Bill Munday had told him about the days when Stern would rat on him to the NBC brass, telling management "Munday's drunk." On this day in New Orleans, Ciraldo had the feeling that it served Stern right.

After the horror show on national television, the world knew that sportscasting superstar Bill Stern had problems. He later acknowledged it in his autobiography, *The Taste of Ashes*. While it was a terribly dark day for Stern, it was a sparkling start for Ray Scott whose career rocketed after that Sugar Bowl performance.

Stern was undergoing rehabilitation again in the fall of 1956 when *Variety* printed a brief story, noting that football season will begin without four of the all-time standout announcers. Ted Husing and Bill Slater were gravely ill and Bill Stern was in a sanitarium. Graham McNamee, it was pointed out, had died several years back.

In February 1957 Stern managed to get back on the air doing morning drives on WINS. Stern was on 7-10 A.M. His producer was Rick Sklar. "Stern had private numbers of celebrities he wanted to interview. The problem was that some were on the West Coast where it was the middle of the night. We would wake them up and they would hang up on us. When they did, Stern would explode. He would rip the receiver out of the phone and throw it against a wall. I began to dread the sound of his arrival." Sklar reported.

Later Stern was invited to do a nightly sports show for Mutual. He was back on network radio, doing sports and doing it where he craved, nationally. Stern got back into the play-by-play business in the late 1950s when Mutual picked up a service academy package. At first, the athletic directors of the academies objected to Stern doing the games but later acquiesced. He did his last game in 1960 and died in 1971. Bill Stern, one of the most famous, most controversial, and most colorful sports announcers in American history, was dead at 64.

Jack Ingersoll occasionally broadcast football for NBC in the 1930s. In 1937 he was doing Holy Cross football when he suffered a nervous breakdown. Al Helfer had to replace him. Gene Kelly, a Phillies baseball announcer, also suffered a breakdown prior to a Notre Dame broadcast.

After Stern left NBC and after the Rose Bowl had gone to CBS for three years, Al Helfer took over as principle announcer, broadcasting "the granddaddy" for seven years. The Bowl was sponsored by Gillette which suggested that he do the game. The one who pays the fiddler usually calls the tune. Helfer had been around. Baseball, football, political conventions. He had worked baseball with Red Barber in Cincinnati and later in Brooklyn. In 1937 *Variety* reviewed a Notre Dame game he broadcast for WLW, Cincinnati. It said he "was crowding in too many words, causing fast-talking incessantly. It is a Helfer error that makes it stiff for auditors." Critics could be brutal back then.

Dual coverage started in the late 1920s. It continued all the way into the late 1940s and early 1950s when schools finally sold rights on an exclusive basis. In these pretelevision days, not only were fans being cheated from being unable to watch games, they couldn't even listen to a variety of them.

During the height of play-by-play duplicity, Husing and Stern were the sports directors of their respective networks. They chose the games that they would call and that their networks would run. If there were half a dozen attractive matchups, each of the networks would settle for nothing but the best, not to be outdone by the competition.

NBC had two networks and would often run games on both. The table below depicts the CBS and NBC schedules in 1940.

Date	Networks	Game(s)	Announcers
September 28	CBS	Minnesota-Washington	Ted Husing
	NBC	Minnesota-Washingon	Bill Stern
October 5	CBS	Duke-Tennessee	Ted Husing
	NBC	Duke-Tennessee	Bill Stern
October 12	CBS	Notre Dame–Georgia Tech	Ted Husing
	NBC	Notre Dame–Georgia Tech	Fort Pearson
	NBC	USC-Illinois	Bill Stern
October 19	CBS	Minnesota–Ohio State	Ted Husing
	NBC	Minnesota–Ohio State	Bill Stern
October 26	CBS	Pennsylvania-Michigan	Ted Husing
	NBC	Pennsylvania-Michigan	Bill Stern
November 2	CBS	Army–Notre Dame	Ted Husing
	NBC	Army–Notre Dame	Fort Pearson
	NBC	Northwestern-Minnesota	Bill Stern
November 9	CBS	Michigan-Minnesota	Ted Husing
	NBC	Michigan-Minnesota	Fort Pearson
	NBC	Texas A&M–SMU	Bill Stern
November 16	CBS	Princeton-Yale	Ted Husing
	NBC	Michigan-Northwestern	Fort Pearson
	NBC	Columbia-Navy	Bill Stern
November 23	CBS	Penn-Cornell	Ted Husing
	NBC	Penn-Cornell	Fort Pearson
	NBC	Notre Dame–Northwestern	Bill Stern
November 30	CBS	Army-Navy	Ted Husing
	NBC	Army-Navy	Bill Stern

It hardly mattered that fans had an insatiable appetite for football. The duplicity was maddening. Often, Mutual and other independent networks would take a third and fourth booth in the same stadium. Listeners wanted as much as they could get. But on many Saturdays, even though there was a game on virtually every station, there would be two and three and sometimes four stations running the same one.

Fans were being cheated by the jealousy of the lead announcers who would generally select their games at the beginning of the preceding week. If NBC got wind of the fact that CBS was to schedule the game from Notre Dame, it would do the same. No one wanted to be scooped. This was all at the expense of the public.

By 1946, after cutting each other's throats for almost 10 years, Stern and Husing, the bitter antagonists behind the CBS-NBC rivalry were apart. The most colorful and perhaps the ugliest chapter in American broadcast sports history was over. It would be a number of years though before the network rivalry would completely subside.

When Red Barber succeeded Ted Husing at CBS in 1946, one of the goals he set was to end the duplication of football broadcasts. The season didn't start as though much progress was made. Three of the first four Saturdays Barber and Stern covered the same games. This was the fall in which both the CBS and NBC affiliates in New York changed call letters. During the first weekend of November, CBS changed its New York calls from WABC to WCBS and NBC changed its call signs from WEAF to WNBC. (When Paley bought WABC in 1928, the acronym was for the Atlantic Broadcasting Company. It had nothing to do with the American Broadcasting Company.)

On November 23, 1946, Barber experimented with a change. He took a different approach. NBC and Mutual took a Big Ten game with Rose Bowl implications, Northwestern and Illinois. Stern worked for NBC and old friend Husing then freelanced for Mutual.

Red Barber was a step ahead. He convinced CBS management to situate on-air personnel at both the Illinois contest and the Michigan–Ohio State showdown. The outcome of both games impacted the Rose Bowl. One game started at 2 P.M. and the other at 2:30 P.M. eastern time. The papers that Saturday morning listed CBS to have "intermittent coverage." It worked. During his second football season with the network, 1947, CBS Radio did this for two weekends instead of committing itself to just one game from kickoff to the final gun.

By the 1948 college football season, Barber was ready to institute an expanded approach to "intermittent coverage" and do it full time each Saturday. Announcers would be assigned to more than just two venues, perhaps as many as six. Barber would anchor at the studio and hop around the country getting updates. When a game was of interest and competitive, he might switch there for live coverage. It might have been a bit more expensive to have folks stationed all over the country but it gave CBS a niche that caught on with listeners. He called it the *CBS Football Roundup* and it became a full-time thing.

Barber may not have realized it then but he was making history. Years later, many radio networks would run a similar format. Barber avoided being locked into one game which could wind up a dud and no other game to which to escape. According to Barber, the impetus was Stern who misled him during the first weekend of the 1948 football season. Wanting to avoid duplication, he called Stern at NBC early in the week before the first Saturday of the season and asked him to pick a game. Stern assured Barber that he would not select the Army-Illinois contest. When Barber showed up for CBS, guess who was also there? Stern for NBC.

Barber left CBS in 1955, and the *Roundup* ended the same year. The network then used a television approach to radio, feeding games regionally with folks such as John MacLean and Gene Kelly behind the microphone. Once Stern left NBC in 1952, the network forged along with football broadcasts using Curt Gowdy and Mel Allen. By the mid-1950s, though, NBC Radio was out of the Saturday football business. The great CBS-NBC wars were over. Television was broadcasting games nationally and the bigger schools expanded their individual networks.

Army continued to have a national package and Husing was its voice from 1947–53. The Cadets national network coverage ended in the early 1970s when its football program declined in prominence. Notre Dame has been the only school to continue to air its games across the country. Established voices such as Joe Boland, Van Patrick, Al Wester, and Tony Roberts have done the play-by-play. In 1956 there was also an interesting broadcast tandem that worked a season of Army games together—Marty Glickman and longtime quiz show host Bill Cullen.

Wester has a call that's in the Pro Football Hall of Fame. In 1970, as "voice of the New Orleans Saints," Wester described Tom Dempsey's record-setting 63-yard field goal that beat the Detroit Lions. Dempsey was born without a right hand and without toes on his right foot and was an erratic kicker. Wester was on 50,000-watt WWL. Minutes before the miraculous game-winning kick, the station had technical problems at its transmitter and was knocked off the air. Television blackouts were still in effect, so fans in New Orleans couldn't even listen live to this spine-tingling finish on radio. Even though WWL was off the air, Wester continued to call the game down the line. The studio taped it and later replayed it. It's now featured in the Hall of Fame in Canton.

Patrick enjoyed a prominent career in sports broadcasting as the man behind the mike for the Detroit Tigers and Lions. Patrick was also the first "voice of *Monday Night Football*" on Mutual. His love for Notre Dame was boundless. Suffering terribly from cancer, he continued to broadcast Irish football until just a couple of days before his death in September 1974.

Van had his detractors. One particular fan in Detroit kept writing the local newspaper letters, critical of Patrick's work. The newspaper kept printing them. Annoyed and frustrated, Patrick gave the chronic letter writer the treatment. He saw to it that coal was delivered to the complainer's house. Then it was a house full of lumber. When the complainer persisted, Patrick had a young lady call the complainer's house. When his wife answered the telephone, this sexy voice asked if her husband was home.

3

HOCKEY

RADIO ON ICE

It would be an injustice not to begin a history of hockey broadcasting with Foster Hewitt, the longtime "voice of the Toronto Maple Leafs" and the progenitor of hockey on radio. After all, the game is Canadian and his pioneering work was so revered that he became one of the most famous men in Canada in the 1930s. Many Canadians went as far as to say that his broadcasts galvanized the country's population and served as a unifying force in the country north of the border. Foster was so popular that he received as many as 90,000 letters a year from his fans.

As was the case with some of the early baseball and boxing broadcasters in the United States, Foster Hewitt started on the newspaper side. He was an employee of the *Toronto Star* when he did his first hockey broadcast on March 23, 1923. It was an intermediate-level hockey match that was done out of a glass booth. The booth had no holes in it and Hewitt almost suffocated. In fact, the glass kept fogging up, so he kept wiping it. He felt as though he was broadcasting in a haze. Yet it was that very first night that he blurted out in his falsetto, "he shoots, he scores." It would turn out to be the legend's trademark call forever. But after this terribly unsettling and uncomfortable experience, Hewitt swore that it would be his last. The response from fans was so overwhelming, however, that Foster stayed on. With the NHL established in Toronto in 1926, Hewitt started doing the play-by-play.

The influence that Foster Hewitt had on broadcasters of a variety of sports was immeasurable. New York's first true basketball broadcaster, Marty Glickman, has said that the geography Hewitt gave hockey on radio offered great illumination on his approach to the game played on the hardwood. Terms such as "along

This famous Franklin Arbuckle painting of Foster Hewitt calling Toronto Maple Leafs games graced the cover of Liberty *magazine in the 1950s. It was a gift from the artist to Hewitt. From his perch high in the rafters of Maple Leaf Gardens, Hewitt became known as the "voice of hockey" for his six decades of work behind the mike.*

the boards," "crosses the blue line," or "moves it into the Leafs' zone," all had basketball equivalents that helped steer Glickman in developing the nomenclature for his groundbreaking basketball work.

In his autobiography, Conn Smythe, hockey legend and longtime head of the Leafs and the Maple Leaf Gardens, says that he had a great deal to do with Hewitt's broadcasts. Apparently in the late 1920s there were those who were opposed to coverage of Leafs games on the radio. "There were some Leaf directors who thought that we shouldn't broadcast games because it would hurt seat sales. I knew we should broadcast. People who were interested enough to listen to our games on the radio were going to buy tickets sometime, although I didn't realize that some in years later would travel clear across the country (Canada) to buy tickets for a team they had never seen but felt they knew through Foster's broadcasts."

Smythe had so much respect for Hewitt and treasured the importance of his broadcasts to the point where he allowed him to design his own broadcast booth. "I told him to tell the designers exactly where his broadcast gondola should be. He went to a tall building that had windows overlooking the street. He walked from floor to floor, looking at people on the street below, until he decided that the fifth-floor height, 56 feet, was best, and that's the height at which his gondola was built." When Maple Leaf Gardens opened in 1931, Foster Hewitt worked the games from that perch. In 1932, when the National Hockey League expanded from a 44- to a 48-game schedule, the Leafs won the Stanley Cup. By 1933, Hewitt's work became so popular that his hockey broadcasts were heard on some 20 stations across Canada.

The always prodding Smythe, apparently half-kidding, once suggested to Hewitt that he expand his goal call beyond his popular signature, "he shoots, he scores." But that would be just like telling Mel Allen not to use "going, going, gone" on a home run. Hewitt broadcast the games for nearly 50 years and was revered for almost half a century. Hewitt's son, Bill, followed in his dad's footsteps in Toronto and was a terrific hockey broadcaster himself. His grandson, Bruce, abdicated the Hewitt legacy and went into the farming business in Ontario.

The Foster Hewitt Award, initiated by the Hall of Fame, is given annually to a distinguished hockey broadcaster. The only inductee who traces his roots through New York is Jiggs McDonald, the ex-longtime Islanders broadcaster. Other great American broadcasters who have been enshrined are Lloyd Pettit, the one-time Blackhawks announcer; Dan Kelly, the late baritone of the Blues; plus Bob Wilson and Fred Cusick, both of whom retired recently after many years as the radio and television voices, respectively, of the Bruins.

Among the many letters that Foster Hewitt would receive, there would occasionally be one with a tirade against his grammar. Hewitt's broadcast style was described as "common-man in approach" and he staunchly defended it. "There are terms and expressions used in sports that are quite different from what you find in a dictionary. When you're describing an event, you have to speak the fan's language."

Was Hewitt popular? During World War II the officer commanding the Royal Regiment of Canada told a wartime audience, "More than anything else, the men in England want the hockey broadcasts, then cigarettes, then your parcels."

Hewitt grew less ebullient for hockey in his later years. While Foster himself was a bidder for the Vancouver franchise when the NHL first broadened from the original six teams in 1967, he was quoted to be vehemently against expansion. "Moving from six teams to twelve (which the league did for the 1967–68 season) is regrettable. They're taking too big a bite out of the cherry."

American hockey broadcasters were greatly influenced by the Canadian broadcast legend. Gene Hart, who spent 28 years calling the Philadelphia Flyers games and was the voice associated with the Broad Street Bullies, grew up in Manhattan and picked up Hewitt's broadcasts.

"Foster was first. He had the vocabulary and the flair. The excitement wasn't manufactured. He was crisp, had the voice intonations and the drama.

My greatest thrill the first year I covered the Flyers was meeting the legendary Foster Hewitt." There were others. Doug Smith in Montreal, and later Danny Gallivan, but Hewitt was the dean. In the words of the great number nine of the Chicago Blackhawks, Bobby Hull, "When I met him, it was like meeting God." However, Jim Gordon, who spent many years broadcasting Rangers games on both television and radio, put the accolades in a tempered perspective. "It didn't take much to be good back then. We were a primitive business. By today's standards, he was awful."

Hewitt was at Madison Square Garden in the late 1940s to broadcast a game on radio. He spotted Win Elliot doing the same game on television. In the infancy of the visual medium, Elliot was the first to announce an NHL game on television. The legendary Hewitt approached Elliot and asked if he could observe his work to get a feel for how hockey is done on television. Elliot naturally obliged and later recounted what a great thrill it was to have the father of hockey broadcasting "want to watch me." Hewitt would, of course, later go on to become revered for his early television coverage of hockey as well.

The New York Americans were the first National Hockey League team in New York. They arrived in 1925 and were followed a year later by the New York Rangers. The Rangers and the Americans coexisted at Madison Square Garden until the Americans folded following the 1941 season. Bill Chadwick, a native New Yorker, longtime member of the Rangers broadcast team and Hall of Fame referee, remembers the early years. "It was a theater crowd. The men came in black ties and the ladies in their evening dresses. The games would start at 8:45. It was an opportunity to have a night out on the town. It was dinner and the game." The esteemed, late Stan Lomax went further. "People would attend games, dress in tuxedos, have no idea how the game was played or why players were fighting on the ice."

Hockey broadcasts were scant in the early years but they did exist. When the Americans opened on February 13, 1926, the *Tribune* reported that Garden boss Tex Rickard allowed the opening Americans game to be broadcast. "The broadcaster (Jack Filman) described the hockey plays in detail, and the wireless waves also carried into thousands of homes the wild cheering of the spectators, the blare of the bands and the other noises incidental to the fray, bringing a genuine thrill to radio owners tuning in and creating an intense desire to see a game of hockey played." The newspaper reported that since that opening-night hockey broadcast, hockey at times outdrew boxing "in the amount of box office receipts for a given week."

The broadcast certainly was not presented the way it is today. Until 1939, the occasional broadcast would begin for the most part at 10 P.M. and sometimes go for a half an hour or an hour. It might include some play-by-play followed by a wrapup. Records don't indicate any consistency to the broadcast schedule. Some seasons the games were on, some seasons they weren't. Some seasons there were more games on, some seasons less.

In the mid-1920s there was much debate as to the effect of radio broadcasts on the sports gate, particularly with regard to boxing. Rickard determined that it was best for Madison Square Garden to have its own radio station. The Garden bought radio station WWGL in 1926, situated at 1420 on the AM dial, and appropriately assigned it the call letters of WMSG. The station was to carry virtually every event taking place inside the Garden.

From the author's collection

John H. Filman, known as Jack when on the air, is considered the founding father of hockey on New York radio.

The founding father of hockey on radio in New York was John H. Filman, known on air as Jack Filman. He began broadcasting hockey games the same time that pioneer Sam Taub started his illustrious career calling prizefights. They were both on WMSG. Filman called the home games of both Garden-based clubs, the Rangers and the Americans.

Before coming to New York, Filman, a native of Hamilton, Ontario, coached both hockey and lacrosse and was considered an authority on both sports. Filman not only covered hockey games live, referred to then as skate-by-skate, he also wrote quite a bit about the sport. In the mid-1930s, Filman also did a general nightly sports show on WOR and WINS.

Filman's distinction was his ability to talk at a rapid pace. The *Times* compared the speed of his delivery to the legendary Floyd Gibbons, a popular news broadcaster for CBS in the 1930s. Gibbons spewed exciting stories of his own World War I experiences and pioneered on-the-spot remote broadcasting. He was said to be able to talk a mile a minute. Filman himself was said to be able to speak extemporaneously at the rate of almost 500 words a minute. He once challenged Gibbons to a "radio word duel." It was to cover spontaneous description of any event. The match, though, never eventuated.

Because he was the voice of both teams, one wonders where Filman's heart was when he called a classic third game of the best-of-three playoff match between the Americans and the Rangers in 1938. It went three overtimes before the Americans eliminated the Rangers. "I recall listening to him a bit that night but because of the late start, I had to go to sleep," said longtime hockey scribe Ben Olan.

John H. Filman died a young man in 1940 at the age of 43, the first "voice of the NHL" in New York. In its obituary, the *New York Times* said that Filman broadcast hockey from the Garden for 14 years ending in 1939 but listings don't substantiate each season. The *Herald Tribune* claimed that Filman's hockey broadcasts were heard at intervals over radio station WMCA from 1925 to 1939 and the *Journal American* says his hockey broadcasts were heard at intervals over WINS, WMCA, and WMSG.

In the Rangers' game program for the 1926–27 season, there's a picture of the trailblazing Filman talking into a WMSG microphone. The quarter-page advertisement simply reads, "Hello Folks. Tex Rickard and Colonel Hammond wish to thank our many radio fans for their letters of appreciation of the Garden's policy to broadcast the National Hockey League, the fastest game in the world."

At right is a copy of an ad that appeared in the 1926-27 New York Rangers' game program promoting Jack Filman and his hockey broadcasts.

"HELLO FOLKS—TEX RICKARD and COLONEL HAMMOND *wish to thank our many radio fans for their letters of appreciaton of the* Garden's policy to broadcast National League Hockey, the Fastest Game in the World."

JACK FILMAN

Editor of Programs, Manager of Amateur Hockey and Official Broadcaster of all hockey games over Station WMSG

Courtesy Madison Square Garden

It was signed Jack Filman, Editor of Programs, Manager of Amateur Hockey, and official broadcaster of all hockey games over station WMSG.

But WMSG had an inferior signal and after about a year the Garden sued the Federal Radio Commission, testing the existing radio laws and the Commission's jurisdiction. Within the roughly four-year or so span of the Garden's ownership of WMSG, it moved frequencies from 1410 to 990 to 1070 and to 1270. Even the Radio Association of Reliable Merchants in Richmond Hill, Queens, started a campaign to get WMSG a better wavelength. The merchants claimed to have trouble selling radio sets because they were unable to guarantee reception of Garden events. The suit was to no avail.

Garden management also squabbled with its partners, and shortly after Rickard, the protagonist of radio ownership, died in 1929, the Garden gave up its stake in the facility. Madison Square Garden then moved the Rangers to WMCA, but it was a difficult year-to-year task to find the hockey broadcasts a home every year.

It was different elsewhere. In the 1930s in Detroit, as an example, WJBK ran all home and away games and paid the Red Wings a $10,000 rights fee. Al Nagler was the announcer. He did home games live and re-created road games.

There were other New York hockey broadcasts in the 1920s and the 1930s but they were rare and they covered games of the amateur variety or semipro. In

1925, WEAF (now WFAN) ran a U.S.–Canada amateur game from New England. Bob Elson, the distinguished "voice of Chicago sports" for many decades would cover the Blackhawks for WGN in the mid-1930s. His hockey broadcasts would occasionally be picked up on WGN's sister station in New York, WOR. New York radio rolls back then lists the Elson pickups for a 10 P.M. start and they would run a half hour or an hour. Today, of course, stations are prohibited from picking up team's out-of-town broadcasts. But radio coverage was sparse back then and there were no rules.

The legendary Don Dunphy told a great early hockey radio story. As a stringer for the old *New York American*, Dunphy was at the New York Coliseum (then located in the Bronx) to cover a hockey game. The Coliseum would host amateur hockey games with teams representing the New York Athletic Club or other city-based clubs. Minor-league farm teams of NHL franchises would also play there from time to time. In the same building as the Coliseum was a Bronx-based radio station, WBNX, which would run quite a few of the Coliseum events. One of the station's aggressive salesmen sold the minor-league game to a sponsor. The salesman himself was the play-by-play announcer. According to Dunphy, one night this announcer/salesperson took air for a hockey match scheduled to begin at 8 P.M. When the contest didn't begin on time and the players were just warming up on their ends of the ice, this announcer created his own game and according to Don, "he had teams flying up and down the ice, executing well-planned plays." Just prior to the real game at the arena, the national anthem was played. "Without missing a beat," Don said, "this unflappable fellow announced, 'Ladies and gentlemen, we must pause. The District Attorney has just arrived and they're playing *The Star-Spangled Banner.*'"

It wasn't until the 1939–40 season that Rangers hockey was given a strong and consistent identity on radio. For the first time, the Rangers and the Americans were covered from face-off to the final horn. It was then that WHN started carrying Madison Square Garden games regularly. It was the beginning of the Bert Lee era and the beginning of a couple of decades of great sports coverage on WHN. Bud Greenspan, the marvelous Olympian archivist, was then the sports director of the station. Through the 1950s, the station was to the New York sports fan what ESPN is today to the American sports fan. It was the source. It had the personalities and the teams. Lee, Glickman, Ward Wilson, Sam Taub, and more, the Dodgers, Giants, Rangers, and later the Knicks. WHN *was* sports!

And Lee was the catalyst. Bertram Lebhar Jr., known to his listeners as Bert Lee, a New York native and Cornell graduate, entered the world of radio in the early 1930s working for WOR and later WMCA in various sales capacities. By 1939 he was a vice president of sales for WMCA before moving over to WHN that same year. He pinch hit, doing an occasional sportscast on WMCA in the late 1930s but didn't emerge into any on-air prominence until his arrival at WHN. It was said that Lee, himself, did not plan to go on the air but those who initially auditioned were unsatisfactory to sponsors, at which point Lee, the ultimate salesman, stepped up to the mike.

While many will remember Lee for his work with many of the pre- and postgame programs around Brooklyn Dodgers broadcasts, he also called NHL hockey on WHN from 1939 through 1954. He later returned for one campaign on WINS in 1955–56. Lee was the Rangers' voice for 16 seasons, including his first when the Rangers won the coveted Stanley Cup. Goff Lebhar, Bert's son and a successful broadcast executive himself for many years in Washington, would say, "My dad wasn't a broadcaster, he was a fan on the air. He and his partner, Wilson, would enjoy an occasional cocktail on the air."

Gene Hart, who grew up listening to Lee said, "He had nothing to go by. They (Lee and his colormen Dick Fishell, later Marty Glickman and Ward Wilson) flew by the seats of their pants. Yet they were more controlled than the guys today. They screamed less. They were reportorial," leading him to lament over the style of many of today's young announcers. "They're too mechanical, like a teletype machine."

Bert Lee

Courtesy Goff Lebhar

When raising the name Bert Lee, fans will nostalgically and instantly recall the "Pabst Automatic Goal Judge." There was a horn connected to the booth and it would blare each time the Rangers scored, playing the first few notes of *How Dry I Am*. Glickman, who started as a go-fer for Lee and Fishell in 1939–40, had the task of stocking the booth with bottles of Pabst for the sponsor and its guests. Lee was also the station's sales manager. When Pabst didn't renew, Schaefer bought the package and the naming rights to the horn.

"Bert Lee got me hooked on hockey," said Sal Messina, who's been the Rangers' color commentator for a quarter of a century. "In our neighborhood in Astoria, kids grew up baseball and basketball fans. I would roller-skate. It was hard to get ice time. Lee was theater. I envisioned the NHL by listening to his broadcasts. He really started me on hockey."

Glickman, who did two years of hockey color with Lee, also filled in doing play-by-play occasionally in his career. While he did a credible job, Marty would be the first to admit that he was more adept at basketball.

Stan Fischler, a prolific author and hockey historian, won't forget Bert Lee's Rangers broadcasts. "He wasn't the ultimate stylist because he had no rhythm. Bert was the ultimate homer who had priceless expressions. 'It's a capacity crowd, they're standing on every shelf.' After a near goal, 'It missed the net by inches only.' The Rangers were once down 15–0 and Lee, the ultimate optimist, told his color commentator, Ward Wilson, 'Ward, time enough for one goal, time enough for twenty!' Bert Lee was unforgettable," Fischler gushed. "Lee might have gotten complaints one night when there was a tremendous free-for-all and he blurted, 'There's a riot! There's a riot! There's a riot!' Listeners took cover."

Wilson, Lee's Rangers partner on the radio for 12 years was a vaudevillian who worked with Morey Amsterdam on *Can You Top This?* on both television and radio. Wilson also participated in some of the early, popular pre- and postgame Dodger programs on WHN.

Although he only did New York Rangers hockey on radio for four years, Win Elliot made his mark. Here he broadcasts a game with Detroit in October 1964.

Lee had a unique way of responding to complaints by listeners. Bertram Lebhar, executive, wrote back apologizing for Bert Lee, sportscaster. Lee also was a champion in the world of tournament bridge, founding the Greater New York Bridge Association. He would miss an occasional broadcast to partake in a bridge tournament.

While Filman was a hockey devotee and unquestionably the sport's first voice in New York, radio was primitive in the '20s and '30s. The Rangers and Americans lacked the gumption and sponsorship support to put a whole game on the air, let alone a full schedule. Filman, though, had the credentials, knowledge of the game, education, and ability to be clear and rapid-fire. Yet it was Lee's emotional broadcasts and more importantly, his sales spirit and business vision, that gave the Rangers a real radio presence in 1939.

Lee and Wilson were in Toronto in 1940 describing the Rangers' third-ever Stanley Cup, a championship-round victory over the Leafs, capped by Bryan Hextall's overtime goal in game six. Little did they realize that it would be 54 years until the team would repeat. It would even take 10 years before the broadcast pair would announce the team's first regular-season road game in 1950.

When Lee left WHN and later when the Garden package moved to WINS, Win Elliot arrived behind the radio microphone. There are many who believe that Elliot might have been the best radio broadcaster the Rangers ever had. He didn't do radio very long, only some four seasons, but his work was memorable. Unlike any play-by-play man the Rangers have ever had, Elliot played the game in college. He was a goalie at the University of Michigan, where he majored in zoology.

Courtesy New York Rangers

As the father of 10, Elliot could also have had his own hockey, baseball, or basketball team. Blessed with a great set of pipes and a wonderful ability to paint a colorful word picture, Elliot's broadcasts were riveting. Andy Bathgate, their great goal-scorer, not withstanding, the Rangers finished near the bottom in each of Win's years at a time when the league was only six deep and didn't extend farther west than Chicago.

There are many who believe that Win Elliot might have been the best radio broadcaster the New York Rangers ever had.

Win Elliot did a variety of sports, including horse racing, where he worked on several occasions with the legendary Clem McCarthy; and boxing, where he covered heavyweight titles with Mr. Boxing, Don Dunphy. While he spent only four years with the Rangers on radio, Win did several years on television for the *Schaefer Circle of Sports* where he was equally as entertaining. For years, and as late as the 1980s, Elliot was the anchor of the *CBS Weekend Sports Roundup* where he would creatively and humorously mix his skillful voice inflections and disarming quips with sobering taped actualities from sports newsmakers in winning and losing locker rooms.

In the long run, the move to WINS in 1955 resulted in more unsettling broadcast years. One year, it was a partial schedule, the next year a handful of broadcasts. In 1958–59, for the first time ever, the Rangers ran their entire schedule on radio (not all live). But in 1960–61, the club wasn't on at all again. It was usually dictated by the ability to secure one meager sponsor.

During the WINS days, Bud Palmer, an original Knicks player (1946–49), tried his hand in play-by-play of hockey. It's not a common transition. Through all these years of NBA basketball, there has been only one ex-NBA player who has flourished as a radio play-by-play announcer. It's the capable Hot Rod Hundley, the only play-by-play voice in the history of the Jazz, both in New Orleans and later in Utah. Many baseball players have become very proficient in the booth but hockey and basketball usually demand a skill that must be developed and sharpened at an early age. For that matter, there aren't any National Hockey League or National Football League radio booths where the play-by-play voice is an ex-league player.

© Jerry Pinkus

Jim Gordon became one of the principal play-by-play men for the Rangers and later spent 11 years as the team's lead voice on TV.

Les Keiter was sports director of WINS when it was running the Rangers games for an off-and-on span of seven years, from 1955–62. Hockey was certainly not in Les's blood and when given the task of calling an occasional hockey game, Les writes, "Frankly, I hardly knew the game at all. I was on a train to Detroit, poring over the NHL rule book along with the help of a grade-school primer on the sport. I felt that I knew enough not to embarrass myself or insult my listeners."

Jim Gordon also served as one of the principal play-by-play men. He later spent 11 years as the team's lead voice on television. After his long on-air hockey career, which also included NHL work for the CBS Television Network, it's hard to believe that Gordon says "the first game I ever broadcast was the first I ever saw."

"I would always try to be ahead of the play and not be afraid to make mistakes. I wanted to beat the crowd's roar. That's fundamental." It wouldn't bother him if he blurted "save" and the puck trickled in. "Sometimes, while anticipating, I may be wrong. But I would rather be into the game than overly prudent and mechanical. I'd have fun with a mistake. The great Mel Allen and Red Barber would make occasional mistakes, too, and they would have fun with their mistakes.

"I filled in for Marty Glickman in those early years. Many others did, too, including those who went on to have great broadcast careers such as Curt Gowdy, Johnny Most and Chris Schenkel. Later, I was asked to do more Knicks games because Bert Lee Jr. was thrown out of the Garden by Ned Irish for screaming at the officials," Gordon said. "I was offered $75 a game. It's more than I had in the bank. I was living with my wife and kids in the basement of my parents' home in Rego Park. We were all looking to feed our family."

Gordon's partner during the 1959–60 season might be the most popular of all the Rangers announcers ever. And it wasn't his Rangers radio work that gave him his instant public recognition throughout the country. Anybody who would give away cash, furniture, vacations, and other valuable commodities had to be loved. "I think we paid him $75 a game. He was a Canadian and had a pretty good feel for hockey. He was always talking about television ideas, about a talk show or about a game on TV with a big Monopoly board." Gordon was referring to Monty Hall, the legendary host of the network game *Let's Make A Deal*. The program ran from 1963 through 1985, primarily on NBC and later ABC television. Hall developed and produced the show, handled the contestants amicably and was a skillful, clever, and warm host. Gordon says that Hall "was a spectacular color man. He was an analyst before there were analysts." As for Keiter with whom Gordon shared assignments, Gordon chuckled, "Les was a real radio man, a great salesman, a real talent, and he created popular clichés."

By the 1962–63 season, the Garden teams were on WCBS Radio. It was the first of four straight seasons when the Rangers would finish last or next to last. It was also when Marv Albert called his first Rangers game. After a successful debut on January 27 filling in for Marty Glickman on a Knicks broadcast, Marv was assigned his first hockey broadcast, March 13, against the Red Wings in Detroit. And it wasn't an easy assignment. The Olympia arena was old and decrepit, and the only view of the scoreboard was behind the broadcasters. To enable the announcers to see the time and score, a mirror was placed in front of them and they would have to read numbers backward. Marv passed the test with flying colors.

Monty Hall, known for his popular TV show Let's Make A Deal, *served as a color commentator for one season of Rangers hockey.*

How did Gordon feel about Albert? "Marv was a terrific young man. I had no compunctions when Marty took him under his wings, gave him jobs, and recommended him for other assignments. But remember that no one cared about basketball and hockey on radio then. Everything was baseball and football. In the early 1960s pro football was just beginning to evolve. The big names were associated with baseball. Mel Allen and Red Barber, they were the kings."

In 1963–64 the Rangers had an abbreviated schedule of games at the end of the season that were carried on WCBS, and in 1964–65 another partial schedule on WCBS. It was then that the Knicks and Rangers split stations for the first time. The Knicks could only get a Saturday night schedule on WOR.

It was a mess. Both teams were scrambling for radio coverage. Stations were hardly excited about carrying either team and it wasn't a case of greed. There simply was very little interest. In those years AM radio stations were still carrying music and long-form magazine programming with which they were afraid to tinker. WNEW, as an example, featured big names such as William B. Williams, Gene Klavan, and Ted Brown. It was one of the highest-rated radio stations in America and wouldn't dare touch hockey or basketball. The station did take the football Giants in 1961, but the consistency of once-a-week programming was hardly a disruption of its format. And the Giants, who were blacked out on television, were the darlings of Madison Avenue.

It didn't get easier to clear stations. By 1965 WINS, once a sports player, was no longer an option. It had become New York's first all-news radio station, establishing an uninterrupted format of updated information 24 hours a day. After years of rock 'n roll and big-name disc jockeys such as Alan Freed and Murray the K, Westinghouse, owner of the property, committed to a risky and pioneering all-news format. The financial commitment to an all-news radio station is enormous. It's a very labor-intensive format, given the payroll of personnel and other costly services. Radio prognosticators at the time didn't give all-news WINS a chance to succeed. WOR was considered the news leader, programming 15 minutes of news at the top of every hour, unleashing a team of reporters on the street when necessary and even sending a team of newspeople to political conventions. Other stations, such as WNEW and WCBS, also had a presence in the news venue. It's also quite expensive for a station to advertise and promote any format change. Changing people's habits is difficult, risky, and time consuming.

But the risk was worth it. Westinghouse was patient and WINS hit the jackpot. It was helped by a number of developments in its early years. In November 1965 the city was hit by a blackout. Amidst the bedlam, battery-operated portable radios proved handy if not indispensable. In 1966 New York was crippled by a subway and bus strike. WINS was there to provide immediate news and traffic reports as folks ventured in and out of the city. In 1967 the six-day war in the Mideast left many starved for the latest news. It was before the immediacy of satellite pictures and any wild dreams of all-news cable formats like CNN. During any catastrophe, people turned on their radios first.

While the format wouldn't allow play-by-play, there was good news for the sports fan. Sports updates were now aired every half hour, day and night. For the first time, fans were able to get the latest scores and developments twice an hour, 24 hours a day. It was a new and free luxury.

By 1967 WCBS, a middle-of-the-road format to that point, decided to compete against WINS and also program 24 hours of news. So now there was yet another option for the sports fan. In the early years, WCBS would do sports at 10 minutes after and 20 minutes before the hour, when WINS was 15 before and 15 after. It gave the listener four options an hour to get the latest scores and sports news.

Through the years for a number of reasons, WINS has generally been the ratings leader among the two all-news stations. To begin with, WINS has a better urban signal where the population is the most dense. Second, WINS gears its news to items of local interests, mostly crimes and fires. WCBS is tied to the CBS radio format and other national features. Third, WINS was the first to program news, building a loyal following and establishing indelible "brand" call letters synonymous with news.

It's amazing that today there are nine professional teams in town and each has a radio home. In the '60s there were only six and the Knicks and Rangers weren't always successful landing a station.

FM stations remained generally uncultivated in the 1960s. It wasn't until the early 1970s that FM receivers became popular in automobiles and stereo reception caught on in homes. FM ratings were nonexistent in the 1960s and as such, license holders viewed their FM signals as an encumbrance. To cut costs, they would either simulcast their AM programming on their FM stations or run inexpensive prepackaged music to keep costs down. Because FM was hardly an alternative for the listener then, music was the precious property of AM radio. The AM stations didn't want to tinker with their music to carry play-by-play.

By the mid-1960s the Rangers were averaging no more than 20 wins a season, and going into the 1965–66 season they faced yet another uncertain radio year. Enter WHN again. In 1964 it had picked up the Mets from WABC and management at the time attempted to lure Marty Glickman back as its sports director. The station must have come close to a deal because Marty himself recorded spots that ran on the station promoting his return on March 2, 1964. But as it turned out he would never again be heard on WHN. It was embarrassing.

It was his protégé, Marv Albert, who was hired as sports director. He had completed his schooling at NYU and undertook a full-time position with WHN. Initially he didn't do any play-by-play, sticking only to sports reports and some pre- and postgame shows around the Mets.

WHN was still essentially a music station in 1965 and indisposed to run hockey and basketball games. But the Rangers were desperate in 1965–66 and reluctantly agreed to a package that regressed their radio coverage to the sporadic days of Jack Filman in the 1930s.

On games played on Sunday nights only, Albert would be allowed to pick up the last five minutes of the first two periods and the whole third period. Marv was persistent with station management. It was always, "let's do more." But it wasn't until the Garden beefed up its broadcast department under Jack Price that it would all pay off.

By 1966–67 WHN agreed to carry a complete Knicks and Rangers package, not all games, but a sizable schedule of both teams. Don Criqui was hired as Knicks radio and television voice. Virtually all home games were on radio and many road games were on WOR-TV. Marv was assigned to the Rangers' radio package.

It was no easy task. Marv worked all alone. He did so with verve, spirit, and vitality. If the listener did not have a passion for hockey itself, it was easy to develop a romance for Marv's melodic hockey broadcasts. Albert brought gusto, preparation, and an inimitable style, characterized by symphonic stop 'n go intonations that mirrored the action on the ice. There weren't any lulls in his rhythmic delivery. His voice would perfectly echo the activity on the ice. When play was in the neutral zone and less intense, there was a calmness and steadiness in his delivery. His voice would pick up when a team would initiate an attack into the opponent's zone and it would escalate to a controlled frenzy when action was frenetic in front of the goal. Marv gave hockey a system on radio, not missing a beat when lines were changed on the fly. It demands impeccable memorization and imperturbable concentration. Marv Albert was a star!

As a kid in Brooklyn, Marv certainly heard plenty of Glickman and Keiter on basketball, but his hockey style was influenced by the many hours he tuned in to Canadiens broadcaster Danny Gallivan. "He captured the excitement of those great Canadien teams," Marv would say. When Albert was young, he had hockey aficionado Fischler listen to his tapes. Stan would suggest that he listen to progenitor Hewitt. "You can get him between WOR and WABC," the scribe would say. But Marv told Fischler he wasn't electrified by Hewitt.

Because hockey is played in an open rink and skaters weave constantly in various directions, most good hockey play-by-play broadcasters will always give their listeners the location of the puck by identifying the puck handler, the zone in which the puck is, the direction of the goal, right or left, at which each team is

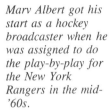

Marv Albert got his start as a hockey broadcaster when he was assigned to do the play-by-play for the New York Rangers in the mid-'60s.

Courtesy Madison Square Garden

shooting, and the offensive lines on the ice for each team. Most important, unlike basketball where points are scored every few moments, hockey can go periods without a change in score. Therefore, it's essential that the score and time of game is given repeatedly. In baseball, Red Barber would have an egg timer serve as a reminder.

In his 1979 book *Yesss!*, Albert suggests that it's virtually impossible to describe everything going on. He feels it's better to talk in terms of patterns, otherwise it's easy to fall behind. It's only once the puck is in the offensive zone that every pass is paramount. Albert's patented line in hockey usually followed a flurry and a great save by the goalie. With typical Albert flair, it was "stick save and a beauty!" Of all the rapid-fire broadcasters on New York radio through the years, the closest to flawless has been Marv Albert. Marv would usually wait that extra second to be perfectly sure, not to risk a mistake.

Gene Hart is less effusive about Marv's hockey. Now retired after years in Philadelphia, Hart feels that, "It's a matter of taste. To me, Marv was a clinician. He's like a great doctor. He'll do a great job but I get the feeling that he doesn't get the goose bumps. He's very proficient, a great technician but his broadcasts were not memorable, he didn't have the artistic flavor."

From the very beginning, Marv knew that he had to be careful of every word he uttered on the radio. In one of those early years, he returned from a broadcast in Detroit only to receive a phone call the next day at WHN from book contributor Dick Barhold. "Did they change the side from which you broadcast last night?" Dick asked a stunned Marv. "How did you know?" Marv responded. "Well, last year, the Rangers moved left to right in the first period, this year they

This ad appeared in a 1968 New York Rangers game program.

went right to left." A radio announcer's best critics are sightless, which Dick is. Those who are vision-impaired depend completely upon the word picture painted by the radio announcer.

Hockey players are generally more approachable than basketball. Many are pranksters and love to fool around. One time Ranger Nick Fotiu locked Marv in the toilet on an airplane. I can just imagine Patrick Ewing doing the same. Hardly! In fact, the Knicks' announcers aren't allowed on the team charters.

By 1967–68 the Rangers were coming off their first playoff appearance in five years, and Emile Francis was at the helm of the organization. It was obvious that the franchise had turned the corner and would become a contender. The same year, the NHL doubled in size, from 6 to 12 teams and the Rangers were to move into the new Garden in February 1968. It was time for Marv to get a partner.

Emile asked ex-referee Bill Chadwick to be Marv's color commentator. The "Big Whistle" as he was known, was bold, personable, and a fabulous raconteur. Having him alongside really enhanced and popularized the broadcasts, not to mention that the Rangers finished with at least 90 points in each of the five years of the Albert-Chadwick marriage.

National Hockey League

Bill Chadwick

What makes hockey broadcasts so unique is that on one hand, it's probably the most difficult of the four major sports to visualize on radio because the action is so helter-skelter. And no matter how skillful and gifted the play-by-play announcer is, much gets lost in translation. Yet the lulls after a whistle for a penalty or an icing create a natural pause, long enough for an insightful comment without being obtrusive or overbearing.

Chadwick's warmth and wealth of experience made for great stories. He had been around hockey forever, was arguably the best official in the history of the game, and developed many of the signals used by referees on the ice today. Imagine, Chadwick officiated the seventh game of 10 Stanley Cup finals.

He went back to the days when the Rangers practiced at the Brooklyn Ice Palace, which had four pillars in the middle of the ice. Bill himself lost one eye playing hockey in 1935. Undaunted, he continued with only one eye before he "wised up and gave it up for officiating." The New York–raised Chadwick refereed when the Americans went into financial default and had to be taken over by the league. When he was officiating, zealous fans would call him "a blind bastard." Once in a while, he would turn around and tell them "you're half right."

"We had a nice ride," Bill said, referring to his five years with Marv. "He told the audience what and I told them why." Albert told them what and Chadwick why when the Rangers played their last game at the old Madison Square Garden on February 11, 1968, and when they played their first one in the new one a week later. Cable coverage was limited and die-hard fans listened to Marv and Bill assiduously on radio.

In 1972 Chadwick was promoted to television, where he worked for nine years before retiring after the 1980–81 season. Other than the first year when he worked with Sal Marchiano, Chadwick teamed with Gordon for eight seasons on television. "Jim was the ultimate pro, the show was first."

When Chadwick shifted to television, Gene Stuart became Marv's side-kick. Gene was amazing, a broadcaster with a golden voice who had worked as a disc jockey at various radio stations. Unfortunately he had the use of only one arm, but it wouldn't deter him from playing hockey or traveling. Somehow, Gene managed to light a match without any help. Stuart though didn't light a fire with his employers, lasting just one Rangers season. The New York Golden Blades of the World Hockey Association hired him the following season and he worked with Barry Landers.

A few months into the season, the Blades left Madison Square Garden and finished the campaign in a minor-league facility in Cherry Hill, New Jersey.

Before the team vacated the Garden and New York, Stuart looked at the schedule. Gene's immediate response was, "Have bags, will travel!" Often, when I found the arduous rigors of the NBA schedule a drag, I thought of the late Gene Stuart. One arm and all, he would improvise enthusiastically.

In those years, while the entire schedule wasn't on radio, the Garden attempted to at least put all home games on radio and virtually all road games on television. Those road contests not televised would be aired on radio. So if the Rangers had a five-game road trip out West and one of those games was on radio and the rest on television, the television crew, already traveling, would be assigned to radio play-by-play. During that 1972–73 campaign, Sal Marchiano and Bill Chadwick worked a radio game that was being picked up on what was then WNBC-FM. WNBC-AM had a Knicks game that night. The FM station ran a beautiful-music format.

When Marchiano and Chadwick took their seats at their broadcast location about an hour before the game, the engineer was trying to make contact with the station. That's fine except neither the engineer at the studio nor Sal and Bill realized that everything they mumbled was going out on the air, right over the music. It was funny.

In 1973, at the recommendation of Chadwick, Sal Messina was put in the color commentator's chair replacing Stuart. In the quarter century since, Sal hasn't let go.

Marv Albert missed more games than he made. It has resulted in Sal having survived engagements with both of Marv's brothers, Al and Steve, in addition to his son, Kenny. A good-humored sort, Sal's measure of survival has been his ability to endure being the butt of Marv's wry and disparaging wit. But at a serious moment, Marv will be the first to say that "over the years Sal has been vastly underrated. He is one of hockey's most incisive color commentators." But Marv couldn't stop. His inveterate dry humor adding "his accomplishments are particularly remarkable when you consider how he has overcome a series of personality disorders."

Marv's disparaging sense of humor started with Sal, the sort who's an easy target. Marv nicknamed Sal "Red Light," and the label has stuck. Marv says Sal deserved it "in honor of the many glorious goals he gave up"(as a budding goalie). He couldn't have pulled the deprecating shtick on the more feisty Chadwick. Messina was just happy to be there even if it meant he was Marv's foil. At the same time, Marv's career and confidence were swelling like a sponge in water.

A fixture in the Garden booth, Messina has been the ultimate employee, handling production chores and whatever else was asked of him. The Rangers became the last NHL team to run their entire schedule live on radio when a deal was struck late in the summer of 1987. To that point, only a limited number of road games were carried on radio. It was already September. But without a whimper, Messina made all necessary preparations to be able to travel and be away from his full-time job as a sales manager for an airplane parts company.

Great Rangers of the past have retired. Potentially, many have been attractive booth mates for the hockey play-by-play announcer. Yet the Garden continues to feature Messina on radio color. Sal is New York. He's New York hockey. He grew up in Queens and still lives on Long Island. He played for the

Courtesy Madison Square Garden

Sal Messina

minor-league Long Island Ducks, held an emergency backup role with the Rangers to goalie Jacques Plante, then became an off-ice official at the Garden. Hockey is in his blood, he knows the sport and his on-air comments gush with an unmatched love for a game that has been a part of his entire life.

Rangers radio hasn't been helped by the fact that the broadcasts have been spread over eight different outlets through the years and the fact that Sal has worked with 18 different play-by-play people. Thus, there's an immeasurable value to the constancy that Sal brings.

In 1973 Marv was appointed the "voice of the football Giants." He would arrive at many Sunday night games in the middle of the first period. He was probably cringing in the car listening to Sal fill in on play-by-play. It was comical, but Sal pulled it off with unrestrained emotion.

Through the 1980s and 1990s, Marv turned into no more than a voice emeritus on the Rangers' radio broadcasts. He was a victim of his own success. The Giants were followed by work for NBC, including college basketball. His increasing absences were exacerbated by a mushrooming of assignments. By 1979 Marv took over the Knicks' telecasts. This meant that he was now doing virtually every road game, and it cut down drastically on his availability for the Rangers. When NBC got the NBA rights, his handful of annual Rangers radio appearances became almost amusing. Yet Marv's very affiliation with the Rangers still helped in selling radio sponsorships. His name was very well respected in the advertising community, particularly in the New York area. Additionally, the Garden took Marv's "backup" position seriously, looking beyond the run-of-the-mill. Since the early 1980s, the Rangers' "backup" radio announcer has been compensated handsomely and treated as full-time help.

Once Marv's schedule reached the point where it required the Garden to appoint a semipermanent replacement, the Rangers had some winners. Spencer Ross was the first. Hockey wasn't in his native tongue but a very curious type by nature, he learned quickly. In some ways, Ross was a throwback to the old-time versatile broadcaster, one with an ability to do virtually anything, including anchoring the news out of the studio.

Sam Rosen was another. A City College graduate whose first Garden work was as a statistician for Ross on the Knicks Radio Network in 1972, Sam has filled in on both Rangers and Knicks games on radio. Now the proficient television "voice of the Rangers," known for his impassioned call "it's a power play goal!," Rosen will occasionally be called upon to do the NHL playoffs on a syndicated radio network.

The best of the lot technically has been Mike Emrick, an eloquent hockey essayist whose colorful and masterful descriptions have delighted listeners and viewers of the sport since the 1980s. If hockey has a Vin Scully version, it's Emrick. And it's not because he has a Ph.D., it's because he's a great student of the game, he's glib, has a powerful command of the language, and knows anything there is to know about the league. After getting his doctorate from Bowling Green University, he did an apprenticeship at almost every level, starting with Port Huron in the International Hockey League in 1973. He's done more than 2,000 hockey matches and probably most of them impeccably. It's no coincidence that Mike has been selected to do hockey at its very highest level, on network television, as "voice of the NHL" on the Fox Network.

When he did the Rangers on radio, there was an unquestionable bond, an unmatched passion that Emrick had for hockey. But was there a passion for the Rangers? Unlike Marv Albert, there was no time-in-grade, no link or real attachment to the zealous fans or to Rangers clubs of the past. Mike hasn't been with any one team very long, unlike Danny Gallavin in Montreal or Dan Kelly in St. Louis. Fans didn't grow up with Emrick as their hometown announcer, usually a requirement to gain legendary status. He is now affiliated with the New Jersey Devils as their television voice.

If there was Rosen and Ross, there had to be Rose. And how could the Rangers not have had Howie Rose? He had the natural credentials. As a kid growing up in Queens, he loved hockey, was an ardent Rangers fan, and was more than just a fan of Rangers voice Marv Albert. As a teenager, Howie actually started the Marv Albert Fan Club. He had all the credentials to broadcast the games very emotionally. And being a Marv fan, it was no surprise. There were derivatives of Marv in Howie's pitch, inflection, and pausing. He would open the broadcast exactly the way his mentor did. "The officials have hit the ice, the goalies are . . . we'll be back with the face-off after this."

Starting at the Queens College radio station in the 1970s, Howie paid his dues, including broadcasting a football game gratis between two unordinary opponents. It was the New York City Police Department against the Atlanta Police Department, and it was aired on city-owned radio station WNYC. And it wasn't just a case of traveling to Atlanta to broadcast the game. The broadcast was carried on a tape-delayed basis and Howie actually had to schlepp the reel-to-reel tape by subway to the WNYC studios in the Municipal Building.

When he was on that subway in 1976, not in his wildest dream could he imagine calling the Rangers' Stanley Cup playoff championship series 18 years later. Yet that's exactly what happened in 1994. Marv still had precedence on the play-by-play, and although he had made only sparse appearances in the Rangers' booth that year, he wasn't about to miss the Cup-clinching game at the Garden. Marv was thoughtful, though. He invited Howie to do the second period to feel part of that historic broadcast.

Bright, opinionated, articulate, and informed, Rose could do virtually anything in sports, anchor reports, and do a frank sports talk show. Not many can make a successful transition from talk to play-by-play and Rose has. Before delving into play-by-play full time, Rose did a popular sports talk show on WFAN, taking shots at the Mets and whoever else deserved it in his opinion. When he

Courtesy Madison Square Garden

Ken Albert

left WFAN and the Rangers' broadcasts for SportsChannel, radio lost a gifted talent.

Kenny Albert followed Rose into the Rangers' booth in 1995. A Vancouver Canuck fan as a kid, Marv's son had hockey in his blood early. And like his dad, he attended New York University. He broadcast Violets basketball for the noncommercial student radio station where he once had his dad split a game with him. "He was delighted," Marv would say later, "until I asked for the appropriate fee."

Both precocious and connected, the likable Kenny is now also a telecaster on Fox covering football and hockey. The younger Albert brings his dad's work ethic and much of his style to the booth. While his dad's flair for the craft douses the listener, Kenny's encyclopedic hockey knowledge and precise information permeates Rangers fans immediately. It's hard not to root for Kenny, who wasn't raised with a silver spoon, is pleasant to be around and quite humble.

The Islanders came into being in 1972, a year after the co-owned Nets moved to WHN. Al Albert, the middle Albert brother, got the call. "Al never had enough of the sport. He was a fanatical goaltender," Marv would say in *Yesss!* Al got a tryout with the Rangers, attended training camp, and played briefly in a minor league. He then spent a couple of years in Toledo as radio "voice of the Blades" in the International Hockey League.

Although the Islanders gig was right up his alley, he made his broadcast name in basketball with the Nets and later with the Denver Nuggets. Al is also a prominent boxing blow-by-blow announcer, where he hosted a weekly series for many years on the USA Network.

Bill Mazer participated in the Islanders' broadcasts for a while. He had done some Rangers color on WOR television in the 1970s. When he did, there was an entertaining incident in Chicago one night. He was down on the ice, ready to interview Stan Mikita. Everything was set. The cameraman was down on the bench when, as the story goes, Hawks coach Billy Reay wouldn't allow Mikita to come out. At that point, Mazer used some ingenuity. He did a make-believe interview with Mikita, asking him questions and answering them the way he thought Stan would. "So, Stan how did your line play tonight?" Then Mazer would impersonate Mikita. "Well, Bill, I thought that we . . . " It was humorous.

After a year of Dom Valentino's rasp on WMCA in 1974–75, the Islanders were covered by John Sterling, who had little schooling in the fundamentals and howled a choppy play-by-play. He would empty his lungs on each Islanders goal, blurting "Islanders goal . . . Islanders goal . . . Islanders goal!"

By 1978–79 the Nets and Islanders were under separate ownership and the package split. The Nets moved to WVNJ and the Islanders stayed on WMCA. Each team now ran all of its games on radio for the first time. The Isles simulcast their games the first year and simulcast part of their games the following year.

Steve Albert and Tim Ryan were among the simulcasters. Ryan had more than a passing interest in hockey. Many will say that it's his best sport. For years, Ryan was the television "voice of the Rangers" and at one time, he worked for Charles Finley, doing the California Golden Seals, one of the six new teams in the NHL in 1967.

Bob Lawrence was a Long Island radio man by way of central Pennsylvania. He did some Nets basketball, had a wonderful voice, was the program director at WGBB, did that station's morning show, and hooked on with the Islanders in the mid- to late 1970s, working between periods with Sterling. In 1979 he was assigned some play-by-play responsibilities. It turned out to be a pretty good year to get the job. Whenever there's a clip of Bobby Nystrom's magical overtime goal that gave the Long Islanders their first-ever Stanley Cup, the voice belongs to Lawrence.

The next year, the Islanders' second consecutive chance to win the Cup, it was back to a simulcast before radio got its individual due again in 1981–82. Basketball has done simulcasts for years. They're a disservice to both radio listeners and television viewers. Radio doesn't get enough description and television gets too much. If there's a sport where it could work it might be hockey, which needs so much identification and elaboration on television, anyhow.

For 16 of the first full 25 years of the Islanders' existence, their play-by-play broadcaster on radio was Barry Landers, shortened from Friedlander. Jovial and stocky with a sweet and smooth voice, Barry paid his dues. Raised in the Bronx, he studied at City College and later earned his master's degree from Ohio State University. Untiring and diligent, Landers was one of the first to run an industrious "stringing" service which has become a means of income for many around the country. After sporting events, he would churn into dressing rooms with a cassette-tape recorder, popping questions on players and coaches. He would then sell these actualities at $20 or $25 apiece. The buyers would be all-news stations or talk shows and the national radio networks.

Like most sportscasters, Barry had play-by-play on his mind. His idol had always been Win Elliot, whose hockey style he embraced. Barry went to work on Long Island doing anything it took to make a go of it. He landed a job as radio "voice of the Long Island Ducks" of the Eastern League. To land the job, he had to do an audition tape at the Island Arena. "The smoke in the building was so thick I could barely see the ice. I was awful. I'd say things like, there goes number twenty-one up the wing. It was horrible . . . The owner leans over, I think he had been drinking, and tells me I had the job."

As it turned out, the station, WGLI, was also an affiliate of the Mets Radio Network when the team's flagship was weak-signaled WJRZ. It gave Landers exposure to baseball, then certainly radio's top-rated sport. During that same period, when the Nets games were on competitor WGBB, he was asked one night to fill in for Spencer Ross. He did. But affiliated with WGLI, he was forced to use an assumed name. That night Barry Friedlander-turned–Barry Landers became Jim Barry.

In 1973 New York's World Hockey Association franchise was about to begin its second season and under a new ownership and management. The games were to be carried by WRVR, then a remote jazz FM station at 106.7. Hockey and jazz, what a combination. A listener really had to go out of his way to the end of the rarely used FM dial to get the now New York Golden Blades.

Courtesy New York Raiders

John Sterling

(They were the Raiders the year before, with John Sterling on WMCA. Sterling's partner was Yankees pitcher Fritz Peterson.)

Landers heard about the Blades opening and might have been the only applicant. He and his partners, Gary Peters and Gene Stuart, called the fledgling team's games as long as they were around. Within a couple of months the owners went bust and the Blades were shipped to Cherry Hill, New Jersey. Landers then bounced around but always made a living. It was anchoring sports reports on WINS one day, WCBS the next, a high school game in Northport, Long Island, a lacrosse match at Hofstra, stringing at a Yankees game, and an occasional fill-in assignment to do the Rangers on radio. One night he filled in on a Rangers preseason game on radio, going up against the World Series. What a night to showcase your wares!

By 1981 the Islanders were growing in stature. They were on their way to their second Cup and simulcasting their broadcasts. Art Adler, one of the great catalysts on the business side of radio sports, took over, built a stable of sponsors, and turned the Islanders' package quite profitable. So by the time the playoffs rolled around, Landers was doing the radio games and the simulcasters were left with television. He was paired with ex-defenseman Jean Potvin, and by the next season the two were a permanent team.

The Islanders' broadcasts hit their peak in 1983 when WOR surprised the radio community committing to Islanders broadcasts for five seasons. Landers and Potvin were retained. Why would a powerful and prestigious station such as 50,000-watt WOR run the Islanders? After all, there were no financial guarantees. The team wasn't buying the time and hockey's listenership isn't vast, particularly the Islanders, whose constituency is limited.

Bob Biernacki was WOR's general manager at the time and he explained that the station had great audience numbers in New Jersey. This was an opportunity, he said, to establish a presence on Long Island. He left out one important factor. He and Bill Torrey, the Isles' president and architect of the Stanley Cup teams, were college classmates. Biernacki also made a deal to cover the Generals of the now defunct United States Football League.

But over a course of time, after winning four straight Cups, the Islanders lost their luster. Attendance started to dip and the club lost its allure. After the 1987–88 season when the five-year deal expired, WOR had no interest in renewing its Islanders contract. The team then went to WEVD which, when the 1988–89 season started, was on the FM dial.

By midseason, WEVD took over the 1050 facility on AM and the Isles were back on a 50,000-watt property. To explain, Emmis Broadcasting had owned WHN at 1050 and in 1987 turned it into WFAN. In 1988 Emmis bought the now defunct WNBC at 660 and moved WFAN there. In a complicated deal, Emmis sold the 1050 signal to a Spanish broadcaster, who in turn traded it several months later for WEVD's FM signal. WEVD wound up with the 1050 facility. Sound convoluted? Radio often is.

The Islanders were purchasing the time, and advertising revenue was beginning to decline. By the second season, Jean Potvin did only home games, shying away from traveling so that he could tend to his brokerage business. On the road, Landers would pick up color men locally. Anybody means anyone. Whether it's a parent who coaches community hockey at a dilapidated rink, some part-time hockey writer with a weekly newspaper, or the uncle of a minor official in a junior league, Barry was always generous. He always made these hangers-on sound great, introducing them in exalting fashion. The way Barry would build their credentials, the listener thought he was having the opportunity to listen to the next Scotty Bowman. But truth be known, the whole setup was an embarrassment.

When WEVD teamed up with Madison Sqaure Garden in 1991 to run overlap games of the Knicks, Rangers, and St. John's, the Islanders were dropped. The team could then do no better than WPAT, a New Jersey station that sadly could not be heard in the Nassau Coliseum parking lot. Islanders radio was beginning to unravel. With the exodus of broadcast sponsors, the Islanders were off New York City radio by the end of the 1993–94 season. At that point, they settled for WLIR, a Long Island FM rock station. The economics of the entire package changed. The station couldn't generate the necessary revenue to operate Islanders radio in a big-league manner. So after a number of years, Barry Landers was broadcasting in anonymity. By the end of the 1996–97 season he was told that he was through, dumped unceremoniously after almost 17 dedicated seasons. He was replaced by Jim Cerny.

The Devils, meanwhile, showcase their radio with the hope of having it enhance their image. Their initial voice their first four years was Larry Hirsch who was teamed with an esteemed coach, the late Fred Shero. Hirsch was a colorful cheerleader who hardly took himself seriously. Hirsch also did some baseball for the Astros when the Devils and Houston team were co-owned by John McMullen. After the Devils, he drifted to Tampa where he is a popular "voice of the Lightning."

Hirsch wore his emotions on his sleeve. Following a Devils win, it wasn't unusual for him to celebrate by dancing on top of the broadcast table situated in the middle of the stands in the lower tier. After a Devils goal, Larry would exchange the high five with whoever would extend a hand. He was a character, a piece of work who rooted openly. Others, concerned about the repercussions by media critics, would rather get ulcers by hiding their feelings. Hirsch was honest with the fans. When the Devils were faltering, Hirsch would not sugarcoat it. In many ways, he was Phil Rizzuto in Phil's early years, prepared, descriptive, down-to-earth, and on top of the action. And listeners knew where his heart was. It was with them.

He would perspire profusely, almost as though it was he who was on the ice. Why not? Emotionally, he was. He broadcast as though he was playing. One night in Buffalo, three periods of tense and frenetic regulation play ended in a tie. Hirsch, sweating bullets, had obviously just gone through an emotional grinder. All the listener heard at the horn were groans, "ah, ah . . . I'm drained!" The cry and the two words by Hirsch painted a great picture.

Marv Albert's body shakes to tighten his concentration; Hirsch is constantly contorting his body in unrestrained emotion, thrusting his arm or pounding his fist. Or as one Tampa-area critic put it, "Larry Hirsch uses two languages at the same time, English and body English."

Larry was once asked what would happen if his hands were tied behind his back. "It would be like putting a blindfold on me," he would say in a somewhat hoarse tone but with an accent, unquestionably New York.

In New Jersey, he was vilified by the media critics. In Tampa, fans heap their adulation by, among other things, bringing radios to the home games and wearing T-shirts with his trademark goal-scoring call "Yessir, Yessir, Yessir."

Hirsch was followed by Dale Arnold, an upbeat, rarely hoarse, always smooth play-by-player. If he did emote, it probably sounded like a whimper after Hirsch, so who could tell? Arnold went to New England after his couple of years with the Devils, where he did a talk show and Patriots football for a year.

Lou Lamoriello runs the Devils and he does so with an iron fist. He's a shrewd no-nonsense executive who's a savvy deal maker. But he'll pay whatever it takes to get on a major radio station. For the 1988–89 season, the Devils made a deal with WABC, paying an exorbitant amount of money to have the 50,000-watt powerhouse run their hockey games. The dollars are huge but the radio persona it authors is immense. The Yankees preempt the Devils broadcasts and when the Devils won the Cup in 1995, contests during the playoff drive got knocked off to remote stations. What does that say about the team's popularity?

Gene Hart once gave this analogy when asked what it's like to be an NHL television play-by-play announcer for a local team. The TV announcer called every regular-season game. But when the Stanley Cup comes around, he's asked to step aside for the network telecasters. His comments apply to the Devils getting bumped during the pivotal Cup contests. "It's like paying for your kids four years of college, but you're not allowed at graduation."

Hart had a definite opinion on Arnold's replacement in 1988 on WABC. "It's a TV call," referring to the style of Chris Moore who got his NHL break with the Devils. Chris spent four seasons in New Jersey, a period in which he did a good job of breaking in a woman color commentator, Sherry Ross. Moore's easy-going conversational style was quite disarming, enabling Ross to feel comfortable behind the microphone. Sherry, a one-time reporter returned to the newspaper side after four years. Unlike Suzyn Waldman, who's done some color, Sherry was not quite as emotional or vehement in her on-air opinions.

While Moore was criticized for a nonradio, nondescriptive style, he knew hockey and would make bold comments that other play-by-play people would be afraid to make.

"If they continue this open style, they won't win." This one sentence is quite redeeming and captures a thousand words. When Moore wasn't renewed in New Jersey in 1993, he was hired by the expansion Florida Panthers and has enjoyed a successful career as play-by-play man and talk-show host in South Florida.

Mike Miller, a solid, technically accurate announcer more in the mold of Arnold, followed Moore at the Meadowlands.

Some 250 games are broadcast on radio live each year. Hockey has come a long way since Jack Filman sporadically hit the airwaves with some third-period skate-by-skate, as it was referred to then in the 1920s.

4

PROFESSIONAL FOOTBALL

FALL SUNDAYS OF INDISPENSABLE THEATER

The National Football League has become a part of the American tapestry. Fall Sundays in many American homes are scheduled around professional football. In many homes, families watch games together. In others, men seem to be impervious to the cries of their left-out wives and unfortunately marriages end in divorce. Everything about the support and the economics of the game dictates dominance. The ratings are outstanding. The dollars wagered each weekend can probably support a Third World nation. Stadiums brim with fans who've elbowed their way in. Sponsorship commitment is in the billions each year. Everybody seems to love the NFL; fans, corporations, and the media. It appeals to white collar America and blue collar America, to those who appreciate caviar and those who overindulge in sausages, to those arriving in limousines and to those who lumber into parking lots in their pickup trucks, ready for a couple of hours of tailgating.

It wasn't always this way, even in New York. Through the 1930s and 1940s, Fordham, Columbia, and even New York University garnered more attention than the pro game. The colleges got steady radio and newspaper coverage and the professional game didn't. The Giants started drawing crowds in the late 1930s but their following was hardly what it was starting in 1956 when they moved from the Polo Grounds to Yankee Stadium.

Professional football was fragmented and fragile in the early 20th century. There were teams that weren't all members of the same league. The competition generated dramatically rising salaries and players jumping from one team to another. College players were also being used by these clubs.

A union was needed to simply make pro football viable. In 1920, the American Professional Football Association was formed, made up of teams in small and large Midwest cities, and Rochester and Buffalo, New York. On June 24, 1922, the circuit was renamed the National Football League and when it was, New York City did not have a franchise yet.

In 1925 the NFL awarded New York a franchise. Tim Mara and Billy Gibson purchased it for $500 and their club, the Giants, played at the Polo Grounds. At the end of the college football schedule that season, the great galloping ghost, Red Grange, a national phenom, signed with the Chicago Bears. In December, Grange and the Bears drew 73,000 fans against the first-year Giants at the Polo Grounds.

In 1926 Grange and his agent, C. C. Pyle, requested of the NFL that they be given a New York franchise of their own. When Tim Mara refused to give up territorial rights and the league turned them down, Pyle started a competing league, the American Football League. They awarded themselves their own franchise, the New York Yankees, playing at Yankee Stadium. The league folded after one year and the lone survivor, the Yankees, joined the NFL in 1927. Grange injured a knee and retired from pro football after the 1928 season.

Through the years, there were other NFL teams in New York City, including the Staten Island Stapletons which suspended operations after the 1932 season. From 1933–43 there were two franchises in New York, the Giants and the Brooklyn Dodgers. It was a period when the Giants dominated not only New York but the NFL.

The league started a championship game in 1933 when the Bears defeated the Giants, 23–21. Five of the first seven title contests involved the Giants. In 1926 the NFL was made up of an unwieldy 26 teams. By 1935 the league was made up of a more manageable nine. But pro football was suffering terrible growing pains. It was a distant second in popularity to college football, which was still the focus of attention.

While the networks—NBC, CBS, and later Mutual—would all knock the doors down to get a broadcast booth at the same major college game, they weren't batting an eyelash at pro football. Finally, in 1934, the Lions played the Chicago Bears in a Thanksgiving Day game. NBC, with the dean, Graham McNamee, and Don Wilson behind the mikes, broadcast the first-ever NFL game on network radio. It was a one-time broadcast.

In the 1930s Mutual did broadcast NFL title games, which ran on WOR in New York.

In 1936 the Boston Redskins qualified for the title game but abandoned their hometown for lack of interest. The team's owner, George Preston Marshall, moved the championship contest to a neutral site, the Polo Grounds. With 29,543 on hand, Green Bay won 21–6. Cas Adams, who did occasional football for NBC, handled the play-by-play.

In 1937 the Redskins moved to Washington and lost the NFL championship showdown in Chicago to the Bears, 28–21. The game was again on WOR, with Tony Wakeman. Wakeman was the first radio "voice of the 'Skins" when they moved to the nation's capital. He also seemed to be a pretty feisty individual. In 1944 he was involved in an incident which would have made the front page of today's tabloids. The sportscaster was on the air when he was struck over the head with the leg of a piano by a fellow station announcer. Wakeman and the announcer, Sam Brown, had apparently gotten into it earlier when Wakeman objected to Brown giving sports results on the show that preceded his.

In 1940 Red Barber did the play-by-play for Mutual on a coast-to-coast hookup of the title game.

Locally, radio listings in the 1920s indicate that there might have been parts of professional football games broadcast on remote stations. In 1928, for instance, portions of a New York Yankees contest were on the air. There just wasn't the compelling interest. For that matter, at that time, no one team in any sport had all its games on radio. A series perhaps, but no network or station would carry every contest.

Research indicates that the Giants finally put together a sustained package in 1934. WINS, hardly the ratings winner it is today and hardly broadcasting with the same 50,000 watts of power, carried the schedule. Earl Harper, an Alabama-born and highly visible New York sports announcer in the 1930s, did the play-by-play. He was also the "voice of the Newark Bears" baseball team when the three major-league New York clubs basically banned broadcasts. Harper also announced college basketball games from Madison Square Garden.

Before World War II the suburbs of New York did not extend far. As such, many more AM signals deemed inadequate today were sufficient then.

Harper, who was described by *Daily News* radio critic Ben Gross as having a high-pitched voice, was born on a cotton plantation in Alabama. He had worked in New Orleans before arriving in the big city. In 1934 Harper also did a package of Manhattan College games on WINS. A young Don Dunphy, later a legendary boxing broadcaster but at that time a young announcer looking for a break, became Harper's assistant the same year. The tie was natural. Dunphy was a Manhattan College alumus and he began spotting for Harper at the Jaspers' games.

The Giants advanced to the NFL championship game in 1934. It was the second-ever title game and the Giants would win their first before a crowd of 35,059, significantly short of a sellout. The New Yorkers battled the Chicago Bears in the championship game as they had the previous season. It was a memorable contest, one that will always be remembered as the "sneaker game." Overnight rain and freezing temperatures caused the Polo Grounds turf to be frozen solid. Neither team had any traction. Players were skidding and sliding during the first half. The Giants were down at halftime, 10–3.

These were the days before the pro football clubs had big bucks to spend on a medical staff. The Giants and Manhattan College shared the same doctor and trainer. The two men had a thought at halftime. They rushed by car from the Polo Grounds to Manhattan College in Riverdale and grabbed as many sneakers as they could find on the campus. These were preplatooning times. There were fewer players, and they played on both sides of the football. In the second half, New York outscored Chicago 27–3 and won its first NFL championship, 30–13. Dunphy said later, "Millions must have been listening to Harper that day." The Giants had a tremendous and versatile star from New York University, Ken Strong. He could do it all—kick, run, block, and tackle. On the broadcast following a Strong romp, the listener might hear the public address announcer in the background, "That's Strong and that's all!"

There was another NFL team in town then, the Brooklyn Dodgers. They appropriately played at Ebbets Field and had a following of sorts, too. The next year, Harper, New York's king of play-by-play at the time, expanded WINS programming. The station picked up a schedule of both Brooklyn Dodgers and New York Giants games.

By 1936 WOR got in the act, doing 9 of the 12 Giants games that season. Stan Lomax, a better than 40-year fixture at 710 AM, was the announcer. Stan did the Giants two seasons, continuing through 1937. Lomax, who started in the business as a writer for the *New York Journal*, seemed to be better in the studio than at a remote where he called the live action.

Variety reviewed a Lomax performance and was hardly charitable. The newspapers didn't pay much attention then to pro football broadcasts in New York City, but occasionally the Giants would play a college all-star team for charity or promotion. The entertainment weekly said that Lomax "spoke slowly and left frequent blanks in the narration." Going up against Bill Stern and Dick Fishell, all broadcasting the same game for different stations, Lomax, it was said by *Variety*, "was behind the other two on calling 'em, lacked detail of his rivals and was guilty of stumbling on occasion." The *Variety* reviewer describes his experience of listening to all three broadcasters at the same time. "Frequently all three spielers would say a different player carried the ball, made the tackle, caught the pass or fell on the fumble, indicating some frantic guessing in the broadcast booths." And we think today's media critics are harsh!

In those early years, newspapers were referring to pro football as "the melting pot of punch-silly bone twisters." In 1938, though, the league was making strides. NFL president Joseph Carr told reporters that there were 1.2 million paying customers, an increase of 20 percent over 1937.

In the Midwest, Chicago Cardinals games were carried on radio and were fully sponsored. WIND carried the games, broadcasting all home contests live and re-creating all road games except the one in nearby Milwaukee which was done live. Russ Hodges was the play-by-play announcer.

Hodges had his problems with the one live road broadcast in Milwaukee. Listeners couldn't hear his live spots for Chevrolet because the public address announcements in the stadium were sponsored by Economy Markets and Hodges couldn't outshout the blaring loudspeakers. Russ let the public address have it on-air. He would have been better off re-creating the game.

The relationship between automobile manufacturers and the eventual long-time "voice of the baseball Giants" was not made in heaven. Lindsey Nelson told the story about the early years of television when Hodges was part of NBC's NCAA football announcing crew. It was 1952 and Russ was in the studio to do spots for sponsor General Motors.

"There he was with a big smile, welcoming the audience on behalf of General Motors. The people in Detroit, seeing the spot for the first time nearly fainted. Back then, of course, all spots were live. The problem was that Russ looked exactly like GM adversary, Walter Reuther, the union leader."

By the next week, Russ was in the booth doing commentary with Mel Allen. Lindsey joked, "He may have looked like Reuther but he didn't sound like him." GM brought in a commercial announcer to do the spots.

Variety assessed Hodges as follows, "He has a Midwest rep for his play-by-play in baseball, football, hockey and other games. Style is forceful, full of action and without the usual stumbles of overexcited spielers."

The New Yorkers proceeded to win their second NFL championship in 1938, beating Green Bay, 23–17. The Polo Grounds attracted 48,120 to the title game, a 37 percent increase over the 1934 championship contest at the same venue. Despite the apparent jump in interest, there weren't any hints of Giants broadcasts that season. For that matter, even the title game was not listed for radio coverage.

New York was behind the Midwest in broadcasting football, baseball, and other sports. In the Big Apple, when it came to pro football, there was apparent apathy by stations and sponsors. In baseball, it was simply a fear for attendance. That wasn't the case in Chicago. Baseball was carried in Chicago beginning in the 1920s and pro football was ensconced on radio in the 1930s.

The 1938 calendar year also brought some legal problems to the Giants' front offices. Just a few days before defeating Green Bay at the Polo Grounds, the Giants' offices were seized by three members of the Internal Revenue Service. Two Giants employees, one of whom was the niece of team owner Tim Mara, were arrested on price gouging charges.

During the 1939 season the Giants and Dodgers football teams jumped from station to station, week to week. WABC, WHN, and WOR all got in the mix carrying both. Announcers changed game to game and there wasn't any consistency. The play-by-players included Mel Allen, Red Barber, and Dick Fishell.

Fishell, a New York radio fixture in the 1930s and 1940s, started at WMCA and moved over to WHN in 1938. He was associated with the Giants' football broadcasts and pre- and post-Brooklyn Dodgers baseball programming. Fishell was hardly in the class of a Husing, who the *Daily News* called "the vanguard of football announcers." He was hardly as quick or as seasoned as Stern, but *Variety* nonetheless critiqued him to be "accurate, a straight reporter minus the dramatics."

Allen, the legendary Yankees voice, had football in his blood. He was a native of Alabama who first made his broadcast mark as a gridiron announcer. In 1936 a young Melvin Israel, as he was known on-air at the time, broadcast college football in his home state. When he arrived in New York in 1937, he changed his name to Mel Allen for concern of discrimination. Allen was quick to point out, though, that the local head of the Ku Klux Klan in Alabama was also named Israel.

In 1936 *Variety*, which was fairly harsh in its critiques, dubbed him, "the find of the year." Mel was also given high marks by the publication for his newscasts in Alabama. He re-created a football game between Auburn and Tulane and it was deemed "exceptional." The weekly magazine went on, "Israel nonetheless turned in a clear-cut job, and it was hard to detect that it wasn't the real McCoy. And, of course, there were no errors; the ticker doesn't get nervous."

It didn't take much for Allen to make the jump to New York. He was getting rave reviews in *Variety*, a national publication based in New York City. But football was his ticket to New York, not baseball. Coach Frank Thomas and Birmingham writer Bill Lumpkin held the young man in high esteem and had connections in the big city. By November 1937 the respected Ben Gross of the

New York Daily News gave Mel, now Allen, stellar reviews. The deep-voiced announcer was doing a package of Fordham and Manhattan games on WINS and Gross, not known for hyperbole, made it clear, "Allen is one of the most promising of the young announcers in New York."

Therein lie the beginnings of Melvin Israel Allen. He covered a lot of football, mostly the college game, headed up by Rose Bowls on radio and television. In 1960 Mel did the Giants on radio and was later the first "voice of the Dolphins" in Miami.

Because of all his football work in the fall and his national television appearances in the 1950s on the World Series, Allen was considered America's most popular announcer. He was more than just New York. What constituted network television then anyhow? It was college football and the World Series.

Red Barber, New York's first true baseball broadcaster, was a prominent football announcer in the 1940s and 1950s. He covered many bowl games, the Rose, Cotton, and Sugar, in his illustrious career plus the Giants from 1942–46. Allen Hale was his first Giants partner followed by Connie Desmond. In the 1940s Red would do three of the four quarters of the game and Connie the third quarter.

His network football was first heard on Mutual and later CBS. *Variety* said that he did a "swell job." In an interview one day with Bill Mazer, Red told the audience that his goal doing football was the same as baseball, "Be objective and be accurate."

Red's on-air warmth and soft drawl were more suited for baseball which he carefully crafted and the sport in which he gilded his legend. His football, by all accounts, was satisfactory. When I visited Barber in his Tallahassee home in the mid-1980s, he told me that the key to any performance was "preparation and execution." Red obviously gave football much thought and devoted a chapter to the sport in his critically acclaimed book, *The Broadcasters*.

It wasn't Red's first love. He even referred to it as "organized confusion," a phrase he would deem blasphemous in describing his revered baseball. Barber feels that while baseball is a more difficult sport to broadcast, it becomes easier through experience. Football becomes no less easier through the years because identifying players is the most difficult challenge each week.

The "Ol' Redhead" felt that for a pro game, a broadcaster could work without the help of a spotter but needed two, one for each team, at a college game. Broadcasting different college games each week as he did often in his days with the networks, presented the greatest challenge of learn, forget, and learn again. That's the way it was in the days that announcers saw two new squads each week.

Working for Mutual, Barber actually made quite a mistake in what might have been the game of the decade in the 1930s. Notre Dame beat Ohio State in 1935 on the very last play. Ted Husing announced it on CBS and Jack Brickhouse refers to his call as a must-listen for budding sports announcers.

Quarterback Bill Shakespeare connected with end Wayne Milner on the last down to give the Irish the come-from-behind victory. Barber's Notre Dame spotter was so overjoyed by the catch that he stormed out of the booth without assisting Red with identification. Barber took an educated guess but was wrong. He called Peters. Barber was "abashed by it."

Mel Allen   *Red Barber*

In his later years Red was critical of the preponderance of ex-athletes in the booth and the battle for airtime. "At times, there is much more of a contest in the announcer's booth between the two announcers than there is on the field itself." The baseball Hall of Famer said that the "expert" shouldn't say something after every play, only when "there's a genuine need to comment."

Red makes a lasting comment concerning radio football. "The radio listener needs a little quiet to mentally visualize the game. The incessant chatter shuts out the imagination of the audience and the possible participation from the listener."

Barber could be quite obstinate and stiff-necked. It basically cost him his job on three occasions in baseball. The first when he held firm on fees which cost him the opportunity to do the 1953 World Series; the second, a brazen approach with his employer Walter O'Malley, which caused the baseball Dodgers not to renew him for the 1954 season; and finally, the Yankees gig in 1966 when he feuded with his fellow announcers.

In 1941 Barber was scheduled to be the radio chronicler of Brooklyn Dodgers football on WOR Radio. The franchise was then part of the NFL. Red insisted that he negotiated a deal with the station that enabled him to miss the game at Green Bay because of a conflict with the Princeton schedule he was also doing.

The station, nonetheless, assured Dodgers owner Dan Topping that Barber would call the Green Bay game. When Topping heard that Barber couldn't make the trip, he said, "If Barber isn't on the train with us to Green Bay, he is off the broadcasts." As Red said later, "The train left while I was at Princeton." Topping was furious and Barber never did do the play-by-play. What might have infuriated Topping was the fact that Red had already missed the first two games because of World Series conflicts, and Al Helfer had to substitute. Bill Slater replaced him and that might have wrinkled the relationship between the two big-name broadcasters.

Since its inception the National Football League has endured and survived competition. First it was the one-year existence of the American Football League in 1926. Later in the 1940s, it was the All-America Football Conference. Another American Football League started up in 1960 that eventually merged with the NFL. And then there were the futile attempts of the World Football League in the 1970s and the United States Football League in the 1980s.

The Giants' local competition going into World War II was the Brooklyn franchise which played at Ebbets Field. The Dodgers, though, were rechristened the Tigers in 1944 and didn't win a game all year, going 0–10, and by 1945 the Brooklyn team merged with the Boston Yanks. Such was the twisted nature then of what is now an esteemed National Football League. Yes, there were many painful growing years. In fact, during the war, the NFL lost many players to military service and seriously considered suspending operations until the conflict ended.

Franchises started folding and moving like musical chairs. In a shocking development in December 1945, Dan Topping, owner of the Brooklyn franchise, took his team and jumped to the newly established All-America Conference.

From 1946–48 there were three pro teams in New York, the Giants and two AAFC clubs, the Dodgers and Yankees. By the end of the 1948 season the Dodgers, playing in anonymity at Ebbets Field, folded and merged with the Yankees. Meanwhile in the NFL, the Boston franchise moved to New York and was named the Bulldogs. So in 1949 there were still three New York clubs, the AAFC Yankees and the NFL Bulldogs and Giants. At the end of 1949 the AAFC folded. Three teams were absorbed into the established NFL, the Baltimore Colts, the San Francisco 49ers, and the Cleveland Browns. With the AAFC Yankees dead, the NFL Bulldogs became the Yanks. The chart at the top of the next page shows how the interesting and complicated sequence of events broke down on radio.

The unsettling years of shifting teams, different leagues, nickname changes, and folding franchises included zany broadcast twists, too. First of all, bear in mind that the franchise name of the second NFL team in town was not Yankees. It was Yanks. Dan Topping, owner of the Yankees baseball team, wouldn't allow the football owner the use of the name. The Giants might have been the team that has outsurvived a lot of competition through the years, but in 1951 the Yanks, who couldn't draw at the gate, were on national radio. "The Old Scotchman," Gordon McLendon, who ran the Liberty Network, did the announcing and would proudly tell his WINS audience and the rest of the country that the Yanks were on the air in all 48 states.

In 1951 McLendon took some time off after a long season of baseball coverage on Liberty. So Lindsey Nelson did most of the games, making his New York debut on October 8. It was a little later, in December 1951, when New Yorkers heard the first of Bob Murphy. The future Mets broadcaster and Nelson partner covered an Oklahoma basketball game on Liberty. It was heard on WMGM.

Topping and Mara were both pretty competitive as far as their football teams were concerned. Topping was pretty committed. In 1946 for instance, with both the Yankees baseball and football teams on WINS, he preempted Mel Allen and the second game of a baseball doubleheader to go to Russ Hodges in San Francisco for a football game. In those days, there were no alternate sta-

Team	League	Home	Station	Announcers
1944				
NY Giants	NFL	Polo Grounds	WHN	Red Barber/Connie Desmond
Bk Tigers	NFL	Ebbets Field	WINS	Stan Lomax/Don Dunphy
1945				
NY Giants	NFL	Polo Grounds	WHN	Red Barber/Connie Desmond
1946				
NY Giants	NFL	Polo Grounds	WHN	Red Barber/Connie Desmond
Bk Dodgers	AAFC	Ebbets Field	WMCA/ WBYN	Stan Lomax/Ernie Stone
NY Yankees	AAFC	Yankee Stdm	WINS	Mel Allen/Russ Hodges
1947				
NY Giants	NFL	Polo Grounds	WHN	Connie Desmond/Stan Lomax
Bk Dodgers	AAFC	Ebbets Fields	WMCA	Joe O'Brien/Ernie Stone
NY Yankees	AAFC	Yankee Stdm	WINS	Mel Allen/Russ Hodges
1948				
NY Giants	NFL	Polo Grounds	WMGM	Connie Desmond/Bert Lee
Bk Dodgers	AAFC	Ebbets Field	WNEW	Ernie Harwell/Jimmy Dolan
NY Yankees	AAFC	Yankee Stdm	WINS	Mel Allen/Russ Hodges
1949				
NY Giants	NFL	Polo Grounds	WMGM	Marty Glickman/Harold Holtz
NY Bulldogs	NFL	Polo Grounds	WMCA	Russ Hodges/Steve Ellis
NY Yankees	AAFC	Yankee Stdm	WINS	Mel Allen/Curt Gowdy
1950				
NY Giants	NFL	Polo Grounds	WMGM	Ted Husing/Marty Glickman
NY Yanks	NFL	Yankee Stdm	WINS	Gordon McLendon
1951				
NY Giants	NFL	Polo Grounds	WMGM	M Glickman/Ernie Harwell
NY Yanks	NFL	Yankee Stdm	WMCA	G. McLendon/Lindsey Nelson
1952				
NY Giants	NFL	Polo Grounds	WMGM	M.Glickman/Chris Schenkel
NY Yanks	NFL	transferred to Dallas and ceased operation		

tions. The baseball game was just not carried, period. Mara, meanwhile, in 1951 didn't allow his sister New York NFL team to do its broadcast from the Polo Grounds. Successful people do what it takes, including being obstinate.

With Barber's responsibilities swelling at CBS, where he was appointed sports director in 1946, Stan Lomax joined play-by-player Connie Desmond in the Giants' booth in 1947. In 1948 Desmond did the games with Bert Lee, the Rangers' radio voice. Goff Lebhar, Bert's son, a youngster then, fondly remembers that season even though the club went just 4–8. The young Lebhar sat near his father in the cramped Polo Grounds broadcast booth. Between plays he shouted at the top of his lungs, "Daddy, I have to make a wee-wee." The cute little remark went out over the air and broke up the announcers. And it wasn't easy getting out of the antiquated broadcast quarters. To begin with, the announcers were situated inside the baseball scoreboard in the outfield. One of the numerical slots was opened to create an aperture. The commentators would then cramp in, one at a time. The first one to go in was the last one to go out. Bert must have had a devilish time getting his kid to the bathroom.

Because of a sponsor conflict in 1949, Desmond no longer broadcast Giants football.

Pabst entered the Giants' picture a year after the baseball Dodgers came under the aegis of Schaefer. It was an either-or situation for Connie who continued with Barber at Ebbets Field.

Marty Glickman arrived in the Giants' booth full time in 1949. It was the start of a memorable association of team, announcer, and fan. If Mel Allen will always be linked to the Yankees and Red Barber to the Dodgers, then Marty Glickman will always be remembered for gripping Giants broadcasts that punctuated New York autumns. It started on WMGM in 1949 with seven seasons at the Polo Grounds (all play-by-play except 1950 when he did color). But it was his second tenure of duty with which Glickman is most often identified. The latter stint started in 1961 on WNEW when the Giants' home was Yankee Stadium and a ticket was an impossible commodity to obtain. Games were being blacked out on television, the club was winning, and the football Giants had become the darlings of the business community. Still, one way or another, Glickman and the Giants were together for 19 seasons. (In the interest of accuracy, Marty did fill in doing color on a game in 1942 and did his first play-by-play on October 17, 1948, substituting for Connie Desmond. And that was some indoctrination. The Giants were rocked by the Chicago Cardinals 63–35.)

The Giants-Glickman affiliation actually took root on the field in 1939 when the ex-star out of Syracuse University played for the Giants' farm team at Jersey City. This Giants team was coached by Bill Owen, the younger brother of Giants head coach Steve Owen. Marty made $50 a week. In those days, pro football players made a pittance compared to today. So although he was invited back for another season by owner Wellington Mara, he pursued the broadcasting business and gave up playing football.

When he finally did get the much-coveted broadcast football gig, the college game was still king. The Husings and Sterns were the gridiron voices of Saturday. Army and Notre Dame were still grabbing the highlights. The pro game had its place but its spurt was yet to come. While the early popularity of college football was a result in large part to radio, professional football's growth coincided with that of television in the mid- to late 1950s.

Glickman initially would have preferred to announce football but because the jobs were taken by the big names he smartly settled on basketball. And hoop fans were better off for it. Yet he turned into a fabulous football announcer. New York's first glimpse of his football greatness was his 1949 work when the Giants went 6–6. At the time Glickman must have thought he had the world over a barrel. He was just 32 years old and he was the "voice of the Knicks" and the Giants, and detailed the huge Madison Square Garden college basketball games.

Radio was king and if television was to grow as expected, he would surely be a part of it. In fact, in 1949 when Chesterfield, sponsor of the baseball Giants, was looking for a partner for Russ Hodges, it wanted Marty. "The dollars were just not there. I wanted twenty thousand dollars and Chesterfield offered fifteen. If I would have taken the baseball, I would have had to give up the basketball which was sponsored by Old Gold." Marty paused when he told the story, wondering where his career would have headed had he pursued baseball. Back then, baseball was the radio sport.

Courtesy Marty Glickman

Marty Glickman, far left, spent 19 seasons broadcasting New York Giants football games. Here he shares the booth with, from left, producer Nat Asch, analyst Kyle Rote, and analyst Al DeRogatis.

Allie Sherman joined the Giants in 1948 assisting head coach Steve Owen, working with quarterback Charlie Conerly. Marty would occasionally work out with the team, not formally but would catch some passes. Glickman and Sherman got close. In fact, Marge, Marty's wife, introduced Allie to his future wife. Marty was best man at his wedding and Marge matron of honor.

Just as he thought he latched on to a football job, there was a change in 1950. WMGM had Ted Husing on its staff, doing a very successful disc-jockey show. Husing had done the broadcasts of the Baltimore Colts of the All-American Football Conference, which folded at the end of the 1949 season. At that point Husing was considered by most as the best football announcer ever. He was still doing Army football but could work pro games on Sunday. It only made sense that WMGM, given the opportunity to use a man of this stature, do so. Marty, still offered the color slot, smartly stayed on. "I did it because it was the great Husing, I worked for the station and I had fostered a relationship with the Giants." So in 1950 it was Husing on the play-by-play and Glickman on color. Marty did fill in for one game when Ted was on the West Coast doing Army-Stanford. Then there was another occasion when Ted let Marty describe one kick. That's how Major White had broken Husing in. Meanwhile, the team cooperated. The Giants went a healthy 10–2, but lost to Cleveland in a playoff.

When listening to Glickman and to old tapes of the master, Husing, there's no question that some of Marty's voice cadence and intonations were of a derivative nature. But Marty denies patterning himself after Husing and in fact wasn't all that effusive in his assessment of football's broadcast progenitor. "I learned what not do. He didn't know the game. He would say things that didn't make sense. I had played the game in high school and college and knew football."

Marty had no problems with Husing the broadcaster. "His voice was beautiful and his delivery was melodious, the best I ever heard. But he would describe things that were not happening.

"I remember driving back from an Army game after leaving early with a buddy. We listened to Husing call the finish. We agreed. The words flowed smoothly but it wasn't football. When I was doing his color on the Giants, he couldn't recognize a double-wing after Steve Owen tipped us off that he would use it."

Marty had gotten to know the legend just after he entered the broadcast business. As an ex-track star, Glickman was assigned to assist Husing. "He came to my farewell party when I was headed overseas with the Marines. I remember that my parents were impressed that the great Husing showed up."

Pro football, though, was never Husing's real cup of tea. He admitted that he preferred the college game. Doing Army on Saturday, the Giants on Sunday, and a disc-jockey show all week was just a bit too much. He kept what was the best of the football assignments, Army. He quit the Giants after just one campaign. According to Marty, Husing was simply not renewed.

Either way, in 1951 Glickman was again at the helm in the booth. He had been given a five-year contract by Miller Beer, which hired him and sponsored the broadcasts. His partner that first season was Ernie Harwell. The mellifluous longtime baseball voice worked quite a bit of football and was familiar with the game. After all, he was a Southerner.

Ernie tells a funny story. Miller's ad agency wanted Ernie to interview Fred Miller, the president of the brewery, at halftime. "The ad people were apparently so paranoid about how it would go that they gave me a script of questions. They also gave Miller a script for answers. It was the only time I interviewed with a script."

Glickman and Harwell witnessed a Giants team that went 9–2. "I remember calling something special. Emlen Tunnell of the Giants returned a kickoff one hundred yards. On the ensuing kickoff, Buddy Young of the Yanks caught the ball at the ten and ran it back ninety yards. Runbacks of that magnitude are exciting to call."

The following season, 1952, a young man with a pencil-thin mustache arrived to team with Glickman. Chris Schenkel had worked in Providence. "He had done horse racing among other things, up there," Marty remembered.

"The Maras were conservatives. We were flying out to the Midwest to training camp. I remember suggesting to him that he shave the facial hair." Back then, only hip folks had a mustache.

It didn't take long for Schenkel to excel. By 1953 television beckoned. And it was right in front of Marty's eyes where he had to have aspirations himself. In those years, the NFL didn't sell its package as a group of teams. Each team sold its television independently. That's the way it was until the 1960s.

Harry Wismer was the telecaster in 1953 and had to miss the Giants' first game in Los Angeles because of a bad throat. Schenkel, scheduled to work with Glickman on radio, was asked to do TV. Out west, Glickman interviewed his old mentor, Dick Fishell, at halftime. Fishell had left the business and was working in Hollywood. The next week, October 3, at Forbes Field in Pittsburgh, Wismer gave it a try. But his throat was stubborn. By halftime, Schenkel had to leave the radio booth and take over television. Had Wismer's throat been in fine fettle, who knows what would have happened?

But by 1954 what did happen was Schenkel got the TV gig and was associated with the Giants as TV announcer through the 1964 season. The Indiana

© National Sportscasters and Sportswriters Assn.

Chris Schenkel

native was the TV announcer for 11 seasons, 9 of them with CBS beginning in 1956. One man who was no longer associated with the Giants was Steve Owen. He had been the team's coach for 24 years. Jim Lee Howell, who played with the team in the 1930s, was appointed the head man.

Glickman and Schenkel became very good friends. Their families were fairly tight. In fact, Chris got married in Glickman's house. But the relationship soured. Marty's son, Johnny, flew helicopters in Vietnam and was returning to the States. He needed help pursuing a career in aeronautical engineering. Marty bumped into Schenkel and mentioned it to him.

Chris was from Indiana and was well connected with the Chancellor of Purdue University. He volunteered to intervene on Johnny Glickman's behalf. After a couple of weeks went by and Marty didn't hear from Schenkel, Glickman called. "His wife, Fran, answered and assured me that Chris would get back to me. He didn't. I kept calling and he never got back to me. After all, it was my son."

When ABC Television got the rights to the NBA games in 1965, Marty Glickman was one of those considered to get the play-by-play assignment. One day, Roone Arledge called Marty and told him that the job was given to Schenkel. Here was this guy who worked under Marty in the Giants' radio booth excelling on network television. Schenkel, in Marty's view and in many others, wasn't a trailblazing basketball play-by-play man.

Johnny Most, the basketball Hall of Famer and longtime "voice of the Celtics," was Marty's partner in the Polo Grounds in 1954 and 1955. Johnny came to the Giants the same year as Vince Lombardi arrived to run the offense. The taskmaster implemented the power sweep.

Most was already affiliated with Red Auerbach's hoopsters but rasped color with Marty. Marty had a great deal of influence on Most, who was from the Bronx and whose real name was Moskowitz. The stories about Johnny are endless.

Many of them are indeed funny. He smoked a million cigarettes and more than once put himself on fire while calling games. A number of years ago at NBA broadcast meetings, a tape of Johnny was played. He was in the twilight of his career and the Celtics were playing in the McDonald's Preseason Classic in Paris. Boston was playing a French team and none of the foreign players was familiar to even the ardent Celtics follower. Johnny did something smart that was totally misunderstood by the attenders at the meeting. While they broke up in laughter, it was pretty astute of the ragged and wrinkled Johnny.

Instead of identifying unfamiliar and unknown names back home, he said, "Now the French team has the ball. The redhead has it. He passes to the right side to the baldheaded guy, crosscourt to the little lefty." Quite frankly, it painted a more descriptive picture than strange names. The folks laughed because they thought Johnny was out of it and could get away with rasping anything he liked.

After the 1955 campaign Glickman's station, WMGM, lost the radio rights to the Giants. WINS was in the hunt. It already had the Yankees, Rangers, and Knicks. On August 14, 1956, WINS sports director Les Keiter announced proudly that the station had acquired the rights to the football broadcasts. It was Marty's 39th birthday, but it was hardly a birthday present.

The year produced bizarre radio. It was the Giants' first year in Yankee Stadium, leaving the Polo Grounds for the first time since they were born in 1925. First there's the story of the announcers. Keiter was the station's sports director and claimed that he wanted Glickman as his partner. "Marty Glickman doesn't do color with anybody. Either I'm number one or I'm not on at all," is what Keiter claims Marty told him. Glickman will admit that Les wasn't his favorite guy but denies being so cold or brash. The first broadcast was an exhibition game in Massachusetts on August 20. Keiter and Glickman did the contest together. The broadcast was sustained, which in broadcast lingo means unsponsored.

When the regular season arrived, the Giants were scheduled to open in San Francisco. The game began and there was no WINS play-by-play. Where was Keiter? The proud man, who effusively announced in August the Giants were coming, didn't say a word. The game was not on television, either, marking the last time that a Giants game was not on either TV or radio. The next week at Chicago against the Cardinals, there was again no radio broadcast. Luckily for the fans this time, the Chicago game was televised live.

On October 7, 1956, a day that shall live in ignominy in WINS lore, an embarrassed Keiter went on-air and explained that the station was having problems finding sponsors. "If any of our listeners know of any sponsors, you can call me at the station." Somehow, I can't see Glickman, Barber, Allen, or Albert doing the same. But so it was.

In the week leading up to the third game, a road game at Cleveland, a sponsor came to the rescue. The *New York Times*, with "all the news that's fit to print," became the sole sponsor. It really wasn't until the 1970s that play-by-play broadcasts were sponsored by more than just two or three marketers. Now it's a laundry list as sports marketing has exploded. But back then, stations often had problems finding just one advertiser to pay the freight.

Keiter scrambled around and got the old vaudevillian Ward Wilson to work with him that October 14. By the following week, Keiter got a full-time partner to do color, ex-Yankee outfielder Tommy Henrich. "Old Reliable" was successful in the beer business in the Midwest and was just having some fun. But on November 25, 1956, Henrich had to go back home to help his parents celebrate their 50th wedding anniversary. Working with Keiter that day at the Stadium was Yankee infielder Jerry Coleman. It was against the Bears on a football broadcast that he made his radio debut. "Keiter paid me $50 for my effort," remembers Coleman, who has had a long career as a baseball announcer.

The Giants' first year at Yankee Stadium was successful. In fact, it could hardly have been any better. The club went 8–3, tops in the East and played the Chicago Bears, 9–2 and tops in the West, for the NFL championship. On December 30, 1956, the two traditional clubs met for the league title in icy Yankee

Stadium. A throng of 56,836 shoved into the Stadium. Jim Lee Howell's New Yorkers stole a page out of their 1934 brethren's playbook. They wore sneakers for better traction and slaughtered the Monsters of the Midway, 47–7.

Up in the radio booth, there was yet another twist in a strange broadcast season and in the festering Keiter-Glickman rivalry. Marty Glickman got the last laugh. A sponsor conflict had arisen. Les did a television sports show on Wednesday nights for Channel 7 which was sponsored by Chrysler. Pontiac was the national sponsor involved in the NFL title game. Keiter was associated with Chrysler and couldn't work the WINS broadcast. Marty got assigned to the title game on WINS.

What a strange year it had been for Keiter. First, it was words with Glickman, then they split an exhibition game and probably didn't go to dinner together after the game. Then the station couldn't secure sponsors and the first two games weren't broadcast. He had three different color commentators, two of them baseball players. Now this. Keiter couldn't work the game after doing them virtually all season. Glickman basked in the glory as the Giants routed the Bears for the NFL title.

During the 1950s, there wasn't a legitimate New York sports fan who didn't know the names Glickman and Keiter. They both did rapid-fire sports on competitive stations. They had styles that were totally different and both very effective in their own way. Keiter had more shtick. And neither liked the other. It was that simple.

By 1957 WINS was a colorful radio station. To begin with, there was Keiter, a voluble sports director; Bill Stern, the melodramatic morning man; and two legendary disc jockeys, Murray the K and Alan Freed. WINS was among the top-rated stations in the country. Freed eventually got involved in a payola scandal. But he was one of the first on-air music hosts to introduce black music on mainstream radio stations.

In addition, the baseball personalities on WINS in 1957 were the trio of Mel Allen, Phil Rizzuto, and Red Barber, and the station also had the Knicks and Rangers. Furthermore, the programming department had a rising star in Rick Sklar, who in the 1960s would mastermind the ascension of WABC to the top rock 'n roll radio station in America. It was truly a group of who's who.

John Condon, who was Madison Square Garden's public address voice for basketball and at one time president of MSG Boxing, also had a radio stint. The man who so many New Yorkers heard say with an unmistakable ring, "That was Walt Frazier," was Les's color announcer in 1957. He even got himself caught doing some play-by-play one late-season day in Pittsburgh. Keiter was in Cincinnati for a Knicks game the night before and arrived in Pittsburgh late so Condon did the start of the game. At the end of two wild seasons on WINS, the Giants left the station. The end of 1957 was not good for 1010 AM. It lost both the Yankees and the football Giants.

The next three years were unusual for New York's football team. The package went to WCBS Radio. But more often than not, the broadcasts were carried on the entire CBS network. First off, Keiter campaigned to be a part of the broadcast crew and succeeded. So over the next couple of years, he did events on both WINS and WCBS; a Knicks game on 1010 and a Giants game on 880.

The way Les tells the story, the order came from the boss himself. When the announcement was first made that the broadcasts were moving to WCBS,

Les Keiter stand outside his current home, Aloha Stadium in Honolulu, Hawaii.

Jimmy Dolan, CBS's sports director called Keiter to tell him he wouldn't be sought for the job. Then, according to Keiter, the commissioner, Bert Bell, called him and said, "You're our man in New York." When the gravel-voiced Seattle man told the commish that Dolan had already told him that he wasn't getting the job, Bell said, "I'll take care of him." Within an hour, Dolan called Les again and said, "We've changed our minds, we would like to have you do the games. Let's get together tomorrow to work out a contract."

The 1958 lineup was unusual. When the Giants' games went out over the entire CBS network, Jack Drees was brought in to do play-by-play and Les would assist him. When it was aired on 880 alone, Les would do the play-by-play. Drees, a Chicago-based broadcaster, once said, "This is hard to believe but it's unbelievable!"

No matter who did what in the radio booth, it was what occurred on the field that made the 1958 season so special. First, the Giants pulled out the last two regular-season games to tie the Cleveland Browns for the Eastern crown. Then, in the snow at the Stadium, Pat Summerall hit a 49-yard field goal to win a playoff game with the Browns. The Giants were now matched up with the Baltimore Colts for the NFL championship.

Football historians say that it was the December 28 battle that won-over millions of fans and television executives. It was a breakthrough day for the National Football League. The league had installed an overtime rule in 1955 and it was implemented memorably that afternoon. The Colts tied the game on a Steve Myhra field goal with seven seconds remaining in regulation. In the NFL's first-ever sudden death overtime, Baltimore scored after some eight minutes of play on an Alan Ameche plunge from the one-yard line. It was one of those games that had fans talking forever. Pro football had arrived.

By 1959 Tom Dowd, an ex-official and traveling secretary for the Boston Red Sox, was Keiter's color man. But by 1960, the Giants' last year on WCBS, Keiter was gone. He had extricated himself from his contract and bolted for the newly formed American Football League. According to Keiter, one of the architects of the league, longtime football broadcaster Harry Wismer loved Les's work and pushed ABC Television to hire him as the lead man on its network telecasts. Wismer would eventually own the New York franchise the Titans. ABC's Chet Simmons wanted Jim Simpson but the league cajoled the network into going with the raspy Keiter. They felt that his excitement was infectious and that he would help sell the league. But Keiter had no real TV play-by-play experience. He was a radio man at heart and ABC dropped him after just one season.

Keiter's radio football was exciting. The game was a war. He was a master at getting the fans to listen assiduously, to have their pulses quickened with his fevered presentation. Dan Parker, in the now defunct *New York Mirror*, paid homage to Les. "I'm not aiming to undermine the Giants' box office when I say that listening to Les Keiter's version of the game is better than seeing the original. I am merely stating a fact which will be borne out by most of his ten million fans."

Keiter's stock line for most touchdown runs was "5," pause, "4," pause, "3," pause, "2," pause, "1," pause, "touchdown!" Those last five yards took forever to let Keiter squeeze every last second of drama from it. Another Keiterism was, "He zigged when he should have zagged. And he zagged when he should have zigged."

Meanwhile, the Giants' games on WCBS were still going out over the entire CBS Radio Network. Mel Allen was brought in. He had done some Giants broadcasts in 1939. But because Allen was busy with baseball in 1960, Marty Glickman was brought in for a couple of preseason broadcasts at Jersey City and at New Haven. When Mel would take over, he would primarily work alone but occasionally bring in Jimmy Dolan or, believe it or not, his brother for commentary. One constant was Ballantine. Mel was a great on-air beer salesperson for his sponsor. If the baseball connection was a "Ballantine blast," the football link was, "He got a first down by the length of a bottle of Ballantine."

By 1961 things were changing. John F. Kennedy moved into the White House. The Yankees fielded what many said was baseball's best team ever. WCBS got the Yankees' baseball rights. The Mets were planning for their debut in 1962. The Knicks and Rangers were coming off another season of not being on radio and the football Giants were about to make a station move. This one would be almost permanent. The fall denizens of Yankee Stadium shifted to WNEW, and the two grew into an old couple. They were together for an unprecedented 32 years. It's the longest association between a radio station and professional team in New York.

WNEW was a very successful radio station at the time. It's not often that a time-buyer at an advertising agency has to be nice to a salesperson at a radio station. It's usually the other way around. But through the 1950s and into the 1960s, WNEW was so successful and running so tight with its advertising inventory that the station had the pick of the lot. Media department heads at the major agencies told their time-buyers to "be nice to your WNEW salesperson so our spots will get cleared on the air." The music format in the pre-FM days had wonderful tradition and overpowering ratings. There was Gene Klavan, Ted Brown, William B. Williams, and the Milkman's Matinee. The Giants were Madison Avenue. Tickets were now almost impossible to get. The home games were blacked out on television and the games ran just once a week. The broadcasts didn't really disrupt the format of mighty WNEW very much.

Jack Sullivan, formally John Van Buren Sullivan, was WNEW's general manager. He was a radio man's radio man. The man loved to sell, wine and dine, promote, talk the medium, and talk up his beloved station. The Giants were the perfect fit. Indeed, time would prove that the match was lasting.

Sullivan started to think about talent. Joe Hasel had been around the station. He had done various packages in the 1930s and 1940s, including Army football on WNYC. When the preseason schedule started, Hasel was calling the plays. It really wasn't his thing. He hadn't done it in a while and would never really do it again. In those years, the regular season consisted of 14 games and the preseason of 6 games. In 1961 the Giants played the exhibition schedule out West. Hasel would pick up partners city by city.

Marty Glickman had talked to WNEW. Other than a couple of fill-in games, Glickman hadn't done the Giants since 1955. During the exhibition game broadcasts Marty must have listened and cringed, wondering why he wasn't getting the gig.

After each of Hasel's performances in August and into September, Marty said to himself, "Sullivan will call me on Monday. He can't let this go on." A number of Mondays came and went without Sullivan phoning. The Giants played their last formal dress rehearsal at the Yale Bowl. "I remember walking out of the stadium with Allie Sherman. He told me he thinks he will have a good ballclub." By then Sherman was the head coach. This time, too, Glickman was convinced that Sullivan could not let this continue. "He'll call me on Monday."

This Monday, Sullivan did indeed call. Glickman was hired and Hasel was eventually relegated to host. The WNEW general manager also hired former defensive tackle Al DeRogatis to do color, a move that was truly groundbreaking. "DeRo," as he was often called, was a true analyst. To that point, color commentators would do no more than describe the weather, the field conditions, run through the lineups, give some basic statistics, talk little during the action, and read commercials at time-outs. Al DeRogatis did little of that, he just assessed the game. And he was the first to do so on the radio.

The confluence of talent on the field and in the booth made for a great show. The home games were not on local television, the Giants were contenders, WNEW was an excellent radio station, Marty Glickman was a fabulous football play-by-play announcer, and DeRogatis told the listeners not only why but what might happen next.

The ruddy-faced Jack Sullivan, complimented so often for his hire of the popular duo, loved to tell the story of what it was like to be in the booth during some of the early broadcasts. "I would stand behind Marty and Al. Marty kept talking between plays. Back then, the announcers didn't use headset mikes. The stick mikes were fixed on the desk. Al would lean back on his chair and whisper to me, 'Watch Tittle throw to Gifford.' I pointed to the mike and said, 'tell them.' He was so reticent at the beginning."

Eventually, DeRo loosened up. The commentary flowed. And the predictions to the unaware listener were mind-boggling. More often than not, he

Courtesy New York Giants

Al DeRogatis

was right. If he would say, "Watch Y.A. throw right to Del Shofner," that's exactly what would happen. There's no question that he had a brilliant mind. He went to Duke, knew his football, and did his preparation. But it was the fact that both he and Glickman had such a close relationship with Sherman and the Giants coaching staff that they were allowed in the chalk talk and were privileged to confidential information.

When he died at the young age of 68, around Christmas of 1995, the *New York Times* wrote of him, "He spent many of his autumn and winter Sundays in the broadcast booth, shrewdly explaining why this play worked and that play misfired." The newspaper also complimented the longtime vice president of Prudential as "considerably popular through his keen analysis of pro football."

Until the Giants bottomed out in the mid-1960s, Sunday broadcasts from the Stadium weren't complete until Marty proclaimed, "They're working it toward the open end of Yankee Stadium." Marty's descriptions were simply vivid. He would put listeners right alongside him in the booth. Each possession was a plot. Each down was a subplot. He was brilliant and had an absorbing and rich voice. The broadcasts were simply mesmerizing. If budding announcers imitated Ted Husing in the 1930s and 1940s, they would do the same with Glickman in the 1960s.

The club went 10–3–1 in 1961 but lost the championship game at Green Bay, 37–0. After going 12–2 in 1962, the Packers won the title game again, this time at Yankee Stadium, 16–7. After finishing the 1963 regular season with an 11–3 record, the Bears beat the Giants at Wrigley Field, 14–10, to win the crown. By 1964, after three straight appearances in the title game, the Giants' dynasty crashed to 2–10–2.

The 1962 championship game was a triple dose of trouble for Giants fans. The game was blacked out on television, the Giants lost, and they couldn't even listen to Marty. An IBEW engineering strike at WNEW and a picket outside the stadium forced the cancellation of the local broadcast. Marty doesn't remember it but such was the case. Kyle Rote did a pregame show from the studio and then explained the situation to WNEW's listening audience, suggesting, in fact, that they tune in WNBC for the network play-by-play. Marty's wife, Marge, listening to this story some 35 years later, interrupted, "Hey, I remember that game. It was so cold that we left at halftime to listen to Marty do the second half in the parking lot on the car radio." Marge may have been nice and warm in the running automobile. But if she listened to the game, it was on WNBC which had the NBC national broadcast with Ken Coleman and Ted Moore. It wasn't Marty.

The league has come a long way financially since 1962. A crowd of some 65,000 was at Yankee Stadium. The gate receipts for the day were just $600,000 and the television-radio revenue $615,000.

In 1963 league commissioner Pete Rozelle made a decision he later gravely regretted. On November 24, 1963, just two days following the tragic assassination of President Kennedy, he proceeded with the NFL schedule. The country was in mourning but the tackles and passes continued on the gridiron. The Giants were at home against the St. Louis Cardinals. Marty called the game but WNEW decided to run it on tape Tuesday night, a day after Kennedy's funeral.

In 1964 WNEW started a three-man booth, bringing in ex-Giant star Kyle Rote to work with DeRo and Marty. Rote did local television, worked for the network, and spent three years in the booth with Glickman and DeRogatis. Marty thought that Kyle would eventually have a fabulous broadcast career because he was funny and glib and was a good storyteller. But Glickman points out that Rote didn't work at it, didn't prepare, and faded out of the business.

In 1967 Chip Cipolla came along. Chip was a broadcaster, hardly an analyst. The broadcast was fine as long as DeRogatis remained. But once DeRo left in 1968, chasing the pursuits of network television, the loss created an unfilled void. There was a one-year experience with ex-quarterback Charlie Conerly, but it was fleeting.

When three in the booth was deemed too much, Cipolla and Glickman worked as a duo for three years. Without a real analyst in the booth, Marty used Chip the way Husing had used Walter Kennedy on Army broadcasts. He had Chip concentrate on defense while he looked after the offense. Chip was a competent announcer, a broadcaster, not an analyst. New Yorkers, though, had already come to enjoy DeRogatis for his insight and accurate play forecasting. In fairness to Cipolla, he had big shoes to fill. Marty did the best he could with him.

In 1972 Sam Huff arrived, bringing with him a crumbly voice, an irreverent style, and the blarney of a salesman. He gave the booth a little more electricity. He had a little self-disparaging humor to him. Huff actually does sales for the Marriott Hotel chain and has been there for quite a while. When his work led him to Washington in the mid-1970s, he joined the 'Skins' radio booth where he continues to entertain fans in the nation's capital.

When Glickman broadcast a game, he felt as though he himself was playing. When the quarterback dropped back to throw, he was down on the field emotionally, throwing the football. It pulled the listener closer to the stadium. At the end of a game, Marty would sometimes just sit there as exhausted as some of the players.

When that football was sailing in the air, Marty didn't miss a trick. The ball wasn't only kicked. It was "end-over-end" or a "spiral." Backs didn't just run right, they ran "off right tackle" or "right guard." And when a ball carrier was tackled to the turf, "he was pulled down by the right side of the defense." Painting pictures is what it was all about, transporting the listener closer to the stadium is what Glickman was all about. "The Giants' helmets gleaming under the bright sunshine." If Mel Allen's classic home-run description was "going, going, gone," Marty's field-goal call was his stamp on the broadcast. "It's high enough, it's deep enough, it's through there, it's through there!"

In those great years when the television was a no-no for home games, Marty brought tension, emotion, and romance. And if a listener didn't feel guilty enough that he missed much of the game when he tuned him in late, Marty would welcome him or her. "Two minutes to go, it's been a wonderful game; if you've just joined us, where have you been?" And on those special occasions, "If you're driving, pull to the side of the road." And at Yankee Stadium in the 1960s, the radios were blasting, echoing Marty's voice in the "House that Ruth Built." And keep a dictionary handy because you never know when you will hear the words *torpid*, *desultory*, or *phlegmatic*.

A student of broadcasting picks up so much from listening to the master.

1. Statistics are boring. "They drive me nuts." Don't say "he's a sixth-round pick. How important is it?"

2. Describe what you see.

3. Every play is a story with a punch line. The storyteller's voice inflections should reflect it.

4. Give down and distance on every play.

5. Don't read notes verbatim.

6. The game is first.

7. Describe players' physiques. Marty would have no qualms about detailing a player's complexion, "a pale-faced 6 feet, 2 inches" or "a swarthy 6-5." He also seriously considered doing the same with black players, "a coffee-colored 6-9." He decided against it but New York might have been ready for it.

8. A Marty quirk: "Don't say 'we're tied.' Say 'the game is tied.' We're nothing," he will tell you.

9. Most important, the pause. "The ball is in the air (a slight pause) it's caught." Marty will tell his students to create a sense of urgency. No one did it better than he did.

10. If your team is getting blown out, instead of belaboring your team's ineptitude, focus on the opponent's impressive showing. Talk about what has made their play strong.

Marty has dealt with blowouts in his days including in college. In the 1980s, Marty was not broadcasting either the Giants or Jets. He was keeping current and entertaining New England, calling the games of the University of Connecticut football and basketball teams. At the time, Joe Tait, the splendid "voice of the Cleveland Cavaliers" was broadcasting Nets games and was on his way to New England one Saturday. He'll never forget Glickman's brilliant picture painting of a sailboat visible in the water off to the side of the stadium. Marty chuckled when reminded. "The stadium at the University of Rhode Island was open-ended. The wind was whistling through the stadium and off to the corner of the lake, my eye caught a sailboat in the wind. Being a sailor myself, it drew my attention. I was really with him as I described this fellow getting knocked down and then trying to scramble back up." Tait: "He's the best. I was mesmerized. It was great radio."

Marty never shared his secret of how he handled human nature's call during long football broadcasts. In 1971 I did see Marty drink a lot of water to keep his voice in order at Three Rivers Stadium in Pittsburgh. A number of times, he would lift himself off the seat of his chair and squat awkwardly. There was an audible grunt but I didn't have the chutzpah to ask.

Glickman did have the chutzpah to do something in the 1960s which drew attention. The Giants and the Jets were crosstown rivals. The Jets thought that they were making strides against the established team, winning new fans. According to Marty, Wel Mara wanted Jets fans at Shea Stadium to openly root for the Giants to sort of stick it to Jets ownership.

Many of them couldn't get Giants tickets so they bought Jets tickets. One day the Giants were in need of a big drive against Pittsburgh at Yankee Stadium when the Jets were playing at the same time at Shea Stadium. At that point, Marty remembered his conversation with Mara and spontaneously intoned, "OK Giants fans, all together now, 'Go, Giants, Go.'" The Yankee Stadium crowd responded verbally and rhythmically, "Go, Giants, Go." Giants fans at the Jets' game did the same, "Go, Giants, Go." The power of Marty and the power of the transistor radio were formidable.

In 1973, after 11 straight years with the Giants, there were changes at WNEW. Jack Sullivan wasn't running the show anymore, the station wasn't dominant anymore, and station management didn't respond quickly enough to Marty's renewal. WOR, which acquired the Jets, made an attractive offer. Glickman did the prudent thing. He went with the only offer he had at the time. Glickman ended his long association with the Giants, a team with which he was so closely identified.

This was news even before the tabloids had sports broadcast critics. It was the equivalent of Red Barber going from the Dodgers to the Yankees. Glickman, the man whose charisma got Jets fans at Shea to shout "Go, Giants, Go" was bolting for the hated enemy, for the crosstown rival.

The home-game TV blackouts were under scrutiny. Congress determined that beginning in 1973, blackouts were to be lifted if a stadium was sold out three days in advance of a game. When blackouts were in effect, many fans would ride to Connecticut where the game was shown on local television. Many would also pack their radios so that they could turn the sound down on the TV and listen to Marty. Radio football would lose some of its luster with the end of the blackout. Radio would no longer be indispensable. It was a fitting time for Marty to make the move.

"I spoke to business manager Ray Walsh. He tried to intervene with WNEW. But it didn't work out. Once it was all done, I didn't have the heart to call Wel Mara. It was a mistake," Glickman remembered 25 years later. The days of Glickman on Channel 11 each fall Saturday doing a high school football game and on radio each fall Sunday with the Giants were over. Nothing is forever.

It took some 20 years, the subway token would increase from 35 cents to $1.25, before Glickman was welcomed back by the Giants. In 1992 Wellington Mara invited Glickman to accompany the club to Berlin for a preseason exhibition game. Marty knew the stadium. He had been stymied in it. It was where the '36 Olympic Games were held, where Marty's hope of participating as a member of the U.S. Olympic Track team was dashed for concerns of embarrassing Adolph Hitler.

In 1973 WNEW pushed the Giants to approve the Bronx-born and melodious-sounding Cipolla to get the job. The Giants squawked. They wanted a "name" play-by-play man. After all, the team was replacing a legend in the booth. They

Courtesy Madison Square Garden

Marv Albert

were planning to leave Yankee Stadium and open their own building in the Meadowlands.

The station and team agreed upon Marv Albert. Just 32 at the time, he did his first Giants game in San Diego, an exhibition with the Chargers in August 1973. The game started at 11 P.M. on a Saturday, hardly prime time. If he was to make rookie mistakes, this was the time to do it.

Football didn't come naturally to Marv Albert. The Glickman protégé had made his mark with the Knicks and Rangers. His first love was basketball, his niche was hockey, and now he was doing the Giants. Maybe he didn't pound the walls out of elation when he got the job, which was the case when he got the Knicks. Yet he was smart enough to realize the importance of doing football, of doing the Giants. A sports broadcaster doesn't grow without feeling comfortable in the football broadcast booth. But with a so-so team and the blackout lifted, the halcyon days of radio were not about to be re-created. And immediately he was thrown into the fire, a three-man booth.

When Marv was first assigned to do football, his mentor, Marty Glickman, had to teach him the elementary. "I was doing the races at Yonkers Raceway. He would come up and we would go over the rudimentary between races. Marv was simply not familiar with the lingo of the game. He never played it. I would go through fundamental terms, a slot back, a trap play, etc. Marv's bright and he picked things up quickly."

Marv had done some football on radio. In the early 1970s he did an Army package with one of his Giants partners-to-be, Dick Lynch. Some years earlier, he had done local high school football. It's the way to learn, the hard way.

Information is hard to come by at the high school level. And it's not always accurate, as Marv found out. In the early 1960s he prepared for a New Jersey high school game on a Thanksgiving Day. When he arrived at the field, he discovered that many numbers had been changed. It was impossible to identify one player from another. He said that he was rather uncertain and tentative during the game, and that the broadcast was a complete disaster. When he left the game, he couldn't look at anyone straight in the eye. He thought everybody must have heard him embarrass himself.

Teacher Marty heard part of the broadcast and didn't think Marv's career was dead yet. To Marty, it didn't sound as bad as Marv thought. His first suggestion was to go right at it again.

Albert also learned that doing football on radio requires a different voice cadence than basketball or hockey. Plays start and stop. Pause, start and stop.

Football play-by-play is basically a succession of quick spurts. Basketball and hockey can often result in endless trips up and down the court or ice.

When he did the Giants, Marv made the best of the week between games. In the pro game, there's film and a plethora of information. It must have seemed like a piece of cake compared to the high school game on that Thanksgiving Day. By Sunday, everything is ingrained. And numbers just don't change at the drop of a hat.

No one on the broadcast circuit works harder preparing for a game than Albert. He's not been spoiled by years of experience and success. If it's a Rangers broadcast on radio or the NBA finals on NBC, his material was carefully and painstakingly prepared. If it's just good habits, insecurity, or both, the Brooklyn boy has not been spoiled by success.

There were some occurrences that won't be forgotten from those mid-1970s Giants days. At the Yale Bowl, which the Giants called home temporarily while the Meadowlands was being built, Sam Huff got into it with fans. He had a sarcastic sense of humor and while fans were listening to him during the game broadcast, they suddenly starting pelting him with snowballs. He didn't let up and neither did they.

Then there was the unforgettable moment at the Yale Bowl when Cipolla, who wore a hairpiece, was seconds away from taking air. He was leaning against the wall of the decrepit booth when the engineer counted down, "ten seconds, Chip." Cipolla sprung toward his seat and as he did a protruding nail caught Chip's hairpiece and yanked it off his pate. He had no time to deal with it immediately. So there was Chip behind the mike greeting listeners, and his hairpiece dangling from a rusty nail on the wall. By 1976 Cipolla was gone and Marv had Dick Lynch all to himself. It was just the two of them in the booth. Marv left after that season but vehemently denied that it was having to work all alone with Lynch.

The Giants gave Albert no material with which to work. The four years he did their games can be summarized as follows, 2–11, 2–12, 5–9, and 3–11. In Marv's four years, there were three coaches, Alex Webster, Bill Arnsparger, and John McVay, and four different homes, Yankee Stadium, Yale Bowl, Shea Stadium, and finally the Meadowlands. Marty might have said to himself, "Thank God, I'm out of there."

Marv will never be remembered for his Giants years the way Glickman was. Yet why complain? The next year, 1977, he was doing football for NBC Television.

As strongly as Glickman is connected with the Giants, even nostalgically today, no single play-by-play announcer had the successive time in grade with the club as Jim Gordon. When Marv left, the Giants' rights were still ensconced at WNEW. The station's news director was Jim Gordon. He was at the right spot at the right time. Glickman, of course, had influence on his immediate successor, Marv Albert, whom he brought along like a son, since his own blood offspring abdicated the potential crown. But he also had influence on Gordon, whom he brought to New York from Syracuse to do all sorts of fill-in work in the 1950s. Jim was a native New Yorker who was also busy doing Rangers hockey telecasts at the time.

Now Gordon had his biggest radio gig at a time when the club was hoping to turn around its fortunes. But it took a while. In 1981 the Giants finally had a better-than-.500 year, 9–7 under Ray Perkins. It ended eight straight years of losing seasons and marked their first playoff appearance since 1963.

Gordon had not done football in a while and it showed when he became Giants play-by-play man in 1977. He was rusty. It was a forgettable year, not only for the ball club, 5–9, but for him, too. "He runs to the 45, 50, and he's down at the 55-yard line." That's enough to shake up more than just one listener, who either thought they may have had one too many or tuned in the Canadian Football League.

"I hadn't done it in a while and the first year was difficult," Gordon, now retired, said 20 years later. "I thought about giving it up. Things like down and distance, the basics, didn't come back to me automatically. I struggled.

"But I hung in there for a couple of reasons. [General Manager] Ray Walsh, was behind me. He was very understanding. But I wasn't proud of my own work. You get embarrassed once, then it's pride."

Although he started feeling more comfortable the following season, Gordon made mistakes that some fans found annoying. "I tried to beat the roar of the crowd." There were calls that sounded like this. "He throwwwwws . . . complete . . . no, incomplete! . . . [Lynch]: Intercepted, Jim!" Sometimes it was quite entertaining.

Gordon's style and his cadence of speech were different than Glickman's or even Marv Albert's. There wasn't the sharp staccato to his delivery. There wasn't the silent pause to heighten tension between a throw and a potential completion or a kick and a potential split of the uprights. Lynch didn't help. Dick would interrupt and confuse the listener. Marty Glickman would say, "He's saddled with Lynch."

Dick Lynch hails from the New York area, played at Notre Dame, and was a very popular member of the Giants. A good-looking 6-foot, 1-inch defensive back, Lynch was a member of the Giants from 1959–66. He was friendly, talkative, and around the Giants' scene. During the off-season, when playing, Lynch worked for a printing company and then got involved on Wall Street. He worked Army football with Marv Albert in the early 1970s and was thrown into the Giants' booth in 1975 when Sam Huff left for Washington.

He had befriended one of the Giants' owners, Tim Mara. The two were buddies. Mara was an important ally even when WNEW wanted to make changes. Mara had battles with Glickman, once forcibly keeping him out of the Giants' locker room after a game.

"Lynch was hurt immediately because he was compared to Al DeRogatis," Gordon said. Al defined the role of the radio football analyst with Glickman in the 1960s before moving into the television booth. Al deciphered plays intelligently, and clairvoyantly broke down options on almost every play. The cards weren't stacked evenly, though. DeRogatis, Glickman, and coach Allie Sherman were friends and the two broadcasters were often allowed in team meetings. Lynch was not.

Lynch, on the other hand, was hardly as eloquent as the Duke-schooled DeRo and rarely as prophetic. When the WNEW salespeople positioned Lynch to potential sponsors, they would say, "he's our Phil Rizzuto." Lynch was hardly Rizzuto. When Phil was broadcasting for the Yankees, he saw everything on the field, Lynch did not. One ex-sponsor said, "Rizzuto, who are they kidding? That's a poor excuse. Phil was the warm guy next door. This guy came off as a buffoon." So why buy the Giants' package? "It was the only way to get tickets to all home games. The Giants were sold out and the tickets came with the radio sponsorship package."

Gordon, who worked with Lynch for 18 seasons, said he's bright and has a good feel for the game. "His speech was affected by all the hits he took on the football field. No matter how keen a football mind he had, he didn't have the sharp, quick delivery."

Sam DeLuca, a heady analyst in his day covering the Jets and later on network television, said he thought Lynch has improved. "What I like is that he doesn't try to sugarcoat everything. He would criticize. He would make his comment and move on. He wouldn't belabor the criticism."

The newspaper critics were merciless on the Gordon and Lynch duo even when the club was winning. One New York critic wrote that they lacked fundamentals. That hurts. "The critics don't understand, never did and never will," Gordon, a one-time Putnam County politician said.

The Giants, of course, won two titles, one in 1987 in Pasadena where Gordon described his broadcast position: "Most of the field is to our right." The Giants also did most of the scoring, whipping the Denver Broncos 39–10.

They won another in 1991. The silver anniversary Super Bowl game in Tampa was golden for the Giants, defeating Buffalo, 20–19. That day, Gordon made what was arguably New York radio's most dramatic sports call ever. Scott Norwood missed a 47–yard field-goal attempt which would have won the Super Bowl for the Bills. The kick sailed wide right, as Giants fans will remember forever. Gordon exulted in the booth. It was football's version of Bobby Thomson.

Gordon, like many football announcers, always worked in the booth with the window open to get a better feel for the environment, the sights and sounds of the field. Friends would kid him. No matter the conditions, snow, wind, or a bone-chilling rain, Jim would open the broadcast, "It's a beautiful day for football."

There were times that Jim's commitment to the Rangers had him running thin. On one occasion, a game was running long and he had to make a flight to get to a Rangers telecast. He left early, leaving Lynch to call the rest of the game!

In 1988 Karl Nelson, who had to quit his playing career because of Hodgkin's Disease, joined Gordon and Lynch in the booth. He was all business, worked at his craft but eventually got let go. Somehow the Giants always protected Lynch. Amazingly, after more than 20 years in the radio booth, not many have warmed up to the cigar-puffing Lynch. Most complain that, at best, he is the master of the obvious.

In 1992 when WNEW changed hands and changed call letters to WBBR, the broadcasts shifted to WOR. It ended a 32-year relationship with 1130 AM. WOR was hoping it could at least break even on the package but it took a financial bath. It slowly took cost-cutting measures to save cash and when that wasn't enough, it subcontracted the package to WFAN in 1996.

Gordon was livid in 1994. When he turned ill and was forced to miss a number of games, his WOR paycheck was reduced on a prorated basis. He was fuming. He had a good and long relationship with WNEW. "WOR was awful. When my contract ended, I had to hear from a third party that it wasn't going to be renewed. The business can be downright cold."

Player photo courtesy New York Giants; inset © Jerry Pinkus

Dick Lynch was a popular player for the New York Giants from 1959–66. He teamed with Jim Gordon in the broadcast booth for 18 seasons.

After a successful 45-year broadcast career, Jim Gordon had some thoughts about today's young play-by-play men. "Technically they're wonderful. But they don't have any role models. We all grew up influenced by a Husing, Stern, an Allen or a Barber. The young guys today call the game flawlessly but they lack description of surroundings or capture the emotions, the elements that develop a fan's romance with the sport. They just don't have the warmth." And two color analysts at the same time: "The three-man booth can't work on radio. There's no time for personality or for the audience to pause. There's just too much for the listener to digest. Everybody's trying to cram things in. It's just too much."

Gordon had personality and warmth on-air and did one thing when he did television that was a nice touch. When the telecast was over, he would always go into the truck and say good night to the crew. He genuinely cared.

117

After a successful 45-year career, Jim Gordon (left) says of today's young broadcasters: "Technically they're wonderful. But they don't have any role models . . . They just don't have the warmth."

Bob Papa, a technically accurate broadcaster who portrays Jim's description, filled in for Gordon when the veteran got ill. Papa had been the morning sportscaster on the long-running WOR show, *Rambling with Gambling*. The Fordham alum had also filled in on Nets games and eventually got the full-time basketball gig. He was well schooled to become the Giants' announcer when the opportunity arose, and was also at the right place at the right time. Whether or not he develops the finer talents Gordon alluded to and whether or not fans warm up to him will tell over time.

While the Giants enjoyed relative stability through three decades of radio broadcasts, the Jets went through announcers and radio stations the way they did coaches, often! Management seemed to put greater emphasis on rights fees than on consistency or announcer loyalty. The Giants would instinctively protect their play-by-play and color team in station negotiations. The Jets, though, said to their incumbent announcers eager to retain their jobs, "we won't get involved." Under the Steve Gutman regime in particular, the Jets didn't seem eager to reciprocate their announcers' loyalty. Take the money and run. As a result, the Jets have wobbled from one radio station to another and from one play-by-play man to the next. There's been little identity.

They weren't always the Jets, not when they started. It was 1960 and the start of the old American Football League. Again the National Football League was being challenged. Harry Wismer owned the New York franchise and it was to play in the Giants' old home, the Polo Grounds. The team was then known as the Titans.

Wismer came out of the broadcast booth to own a sports franchise. He was one of the big-name network sportscasters in the 1940s and 1950s. Harry also broadcast the Redskins' games from 1943 through 1950. His love was always football and in fact he wrote a book about the sport. Earl Gillespie, who was the "voice of University of Wisconsin football" for 31 years, said, "When he did those Army-Navy games, you would have to tackle the lamps in our house. He was incredibly dramatic." Among the many great traditional service academy matchups that he did was the celebrated 1946 game when the Cadets held off the Midshipmen on their final drive of the game to maintain an undefeated season.

An athlete at Michigan State, Wismer had the blarney and the salesmanship to get into the broadcast business. Harry did a lot of college football for Mutual and ABC Radio, where he was the network's first sports director. The aggressive Wismer called 9 straight Sugar Bowls, 11 straight NFL championship contests, and many big regular-season matchups of the collegians. He is really considered the first national "voice of the National Football League." While he dabbled in track, basketball, and studio shows, his union was football.

Wismer bumped into Red Barber on the eve of an NFL championship game. Barber was scheduled to work the game alone and was having dinner with Skins owner George Preston Marshall. Wismer, uninvited, joined the dinner table and asked Red in front of Marshall if he could do one quarter. Now that's chutzpah.

Marty Glickman refers to Wismer as a self-important bozo. "He would mention friends who were at the game. It didn't matter if they were there or not. I was once sitting with Giants owner T. J. Mara listening to Wismer call a game. Suddenly, Wismer said, 'there's my friend T. J. Mara.' We just started laughing. That's Harry." Glickman also recalls a basketball game Wismer did. It was a Holy Cross game. He had six men on the floor at the same time."

At least Marty heard him do a game when he showed up. Stan Lomax's son tells a story about Harry that tops them all. "My dad was supposed to do his color one night at a basketball game from the Garden. The game was being carried on Mutual and it was about to begin and there's no Harry. My father opened the broadcast, started to call the game and after a while, just gave up on him. The next thing you know, I'm doing color for my dad," Charles Lomax said.

Harry also called the first-ever NFL championship game on network television. It was simulcast on radio. His color man was the Galloping Ghost, the great Red Grange.

Wismer married into money, one of the heirs to the Ford fortune. He eventually divorced but had apparently put away enough to talk himself into owning the New York franchise of the new league. He was in pretty big company. One of the franchise owners was Lamar Hunt, one of the wealthiest men in the world. Could Harry play with the big boys?

He certainly did his best to cultivate relationships. Contemporaries would say that if there was a sponsor or anyone in a position to help, Wismer would mention him on the air. All references started with congratulations. "On the way in to the stadium today, I bumped into Craig Smith of Gillette. Congratulations, Craig, you're looking great, just great." Harry also liked traveling in first-class circles. In 1942, while broadcasting an NFL championship game, Wismer made sure to interview pioneering film star Al Jolson.

Courtesy Ted Patterson

Harry Wismer, considered the first national voice of the National Football League, later came out of the broadcast booth to own a franchise.

Harry was dramatic and had a feel for football, a game that he had played and loved. But he didn't chronicle it sequentially the way Husing did or Glickman would later. The latter two started their description when the huddle disengaged. They would paint a picture of the formation, count down the quarterback's signals, and describe the play step-by-step. Fans felt part of the play.

One of the most dramatic calls Wismer ever made came in the final seconds of the '46 Army-Navy game. The last pivotal play just erupted out of Harry's mouth, suddenly and without warning. Before the listener knew it, the game was over.

When the new league started, Wismer pushed Les Keiter to pursue the AFL lead play-by-play job on television. Harry kept telling Les, "You're the next Harry Wismer. You'll be great for this league. We'll grow together." Keiter gave up his Giants radio gig when the ABC network reluctantly agreed to hire him. But Les's radio style didn't sit well with the television people. When he tempered his style to be more television friendly, Wismer would call Les and say, "What happened to that exciting Keiter I know?" Keiter was in a no-win situation.

Conditions were terrible. Wismer's Titans played before invisible crowds at the Polo Grounds, although the attendance numbers were almost always inflated in the morning paper. Players weren't fitted for shoulder pads. They just started passing them around in the locker room and players picked sizes that fit best. By 1963 Wismer declared bankruptcy and the team was purchased by Sonny Werblin.

Wismer died in 1967 at the age of 56. The cause of death was a fall that caused a fractured skull. There were those who said it was a mob hit because Harry was fooling around with the girlfriend of one of the mob members. He was described in an obituary as a "short, plump man with a mercurial temper."

The Titans' first year on the radio didn't take off smoothly. One of the preseason games was aired on an ad-hoc network and carried locally over WINS with Bud Foster and Tony Rizzo. WINS then promoted the first regular-season game, a 10:45 broadcast from Oakland. The Oakland game came and went. It was not broadcast. No sponsor, no broadcast. Finally, five games were carried on WMGM (1050). Tom Moorehead, a Philadelphia-based broadcaster, joined former Notre Dame coach Frank Leahy on the broadcasts, four of which were at home and one was away.

After the 1961 schedule wasn't carried on radio at all, a man who will always be remembered for baseball in New York became the last "voice of the Titans" and the first "voice of the Jets." Bob Murphy brought his usual enthusiasm to the broadcasts in 1962 on WABC and in 1963 on WHN. When they were the Titans, Murph's partner was Jim Crowley, one of the great four horsemen at Notre Dame. When they became the Jets, it was the former Giants baseball player, Monte Irvin. The connection was Rheingold. The brewery sponsored the Mets and was now sponsoring the Jets. Irvin did work in the community on behalf of the brewery.

"Yeah, Monte Irvin," Bob Murphy said 35 years later with the familiar hearty laugh, "What a guy. He might have been the first black analyst ever."

The Polo Grounds football broadcast location was inside the outfield baseball scoreboard. It was hardly ideal. There was nowhere to place notes or spotting charts, and remember that the first one in the booth was the last one out. The scoreboard wasn't electronic. If you can imagine a nine-inning baseball scoreboard, each half-inning had a cutout to place the number of runs scored in the frame. A number of these cutouts were opened for football and that's where the announcers sat. Irvin, whether it was a case of a paucity of football knowledge or whether he was simply in a hurry, would more often than not make the laconic comment, "right Bob." Murph also had a surprise partner a couple of weeks the club was out on the West Coast. A surprise but not a stranger, Ralph Kiner worked with Bob Murphy on the radio in chilly autumn. On the broadcast from San Diego's Balboa Stadium, Kiner told Murph that he played both baseball and football there as a youngster.

There was hardly anything right about the Jets. Bulldog Turner's team went 5–9 in 1962 and even under Weeb Ewbank, who would coach the club to a Super Bowl title in 1969, the Jets were an identical 5–8–1 in 1963, 1964, and 1965.

After four years of popping around the dial or not being on at all, as was the case in 1961, the Jets were about to build some stability on the field and on the air. They were growing into a Super Bowl team and a merger with the established National Football League.

In 1964 WABC, a powerhouse of a facility, was the home of the Jets. The station would rocket to number one in the market. The rock 'n roll was blasting, the British invasion was overpowering, and a generation of New Yorkers would grow up with the city's oldest radio station. AM was still king and FM was still a nuisance to most radio operators. Only esoteric programming such as educational or jazz was played on FM.

WABC disc jockeys Harry Harrison, Dan Ingram, Cousin Brucie, and Ron Lundy would become household names. If these names weren't enough to illuminate the environment, hated colorful rivals Howard Cosell and *Daily News* columnist Dick Young were both connected with the Jets' broadcasts. And if the growing number of listeners weren't sure what station was carrying the games, Merle Harmon, the play-by-play announcer reminded them resoundingly, "Your dial is Jet set!"

"I was in my hotel room in St. Louis getting ready to do a Braves-Cardinals game in 1964 when the phone rang," Merle Harmon reflected from his Texas home where he lives in retirement after a highly visible and successful sports announcing career. "It was the sports director of WABC, Howard Cosell. He said, 'You have been selected to call Jets games on our station.'" Harmon had done work for ABC Television doing studio scoreboard shows and play-by-play. His 1964 start marked the beginning of the longest consecutive stretch of seasons any play-by-play announcer would have with the Jets. Jim Gordon would eventually do 18 with the Giants (1977–94) and Marty Glickman had 12 with the Giants (1961–72). But nine for the Jets is a lot and it was Merle Harmon on the mike from 1964–72.

Harmon had a self-described Illinois-Missouri twang. He was a wonderful broadcaster in New York albeit his style was redolent of his Midwestern roots. The differences between him and his Giants counterpart Glickman were twofold. Merle put more emphasis on being upbeat, dynamic, and energetic than descriptive and sequential in narrative. This is not to say that Harmon's broadcasts lacked essential detail. It was easy to follow the downs on his calls and his enthusiasm was infectious. But unlike Glickman, Harmon's voice inflection didn't reflect the subplot of each play. Harmon's voice cadence was steadier.

Secondly, the audience sensed that Glickman was playing the game while broadcasting for the Giants and Harmon was rooting while broadcasting for the Jets. When Marty described Tittle fading back to pass, the listener sensed that the broadcaster was almost stretching up his arm to throw. When Harmon had Matt Snell running with the ball, the audience had a sense that he himself was hoping for a big gainer with vein-bulging excitement.

The overlapping years of Harmon and Glickman were New York's best and most enjoyable in radio pro football history. Many will say that the two were the best one-two punch the Giants and Jets have ever had. It was, of course, also a time when the games were blacked out. Radio, if not indispensable, was at least mandatory in following the two local football clubs.

Otto Graham, a great star at Ohio State, was Merle's sidekick his first couple of seasons. By 1966, though, Graham was in Washington coaching with the

Merle Harmon's Illinois-Missouri twang gave away his Midwestern roots, but his voice cadence was steady and his enthusiasm was infectious.

Courtesy Milwaukee Brewers

Redskins. The controversial and popular columnist, Dick Young, joined Harmon. But Young wouldn't get there until the World Series was completed each year. Baseball was still his priority. An injured player, Sam DeLuca, was healthy enough to make it to the booth, where he filled in during 1967. By 1998 no announcer would have more seasons in grade with the Jets than DeLuca, 13 full campaigns.

On October 1, 1967, the WABC engineers were on strike. Their union was NABET. The announcers would not cross the picket line. As such, Harmon stayed home. DeLuca was still a player and not part of AFTRA's union, so he filled in. The play-by-play was done by the station's general manager, Wally Schwartz, who described the Jets' 29–7 victory over the Miami Dolphins.

Meanwhile, when the World Series and the engineering strike ended, Young and Harmon were together again. Dick gave the Jets credibility. He was New York's top columnist. Having him identified with the Jets added to the club's stature. But Young had an ongoing feud with Cosell. In fact, Cosell would tape a pregame show and end it by saying, "Stay tuned for the game with Merle Harmon," conveniently ignoring his nemesis Young. Dick, on the other hand would refer to Howard in the *Daily News* as Howie. Cosell would constantly disparage many writers, notably Young. It made life interesting in New York.

By 1968 Merle Harmon had a new full-time partner, Sam DeLuca. "He prepared!" Harmon remembers. "I got scared when I saw him walk into the booth for the first broadcast. He had pages of single-lined notes. We did the game and I thought he did a fine job. I looked at him afterward and he didn't

An injury during the 1967 season helped get Sam DeLuca, an offensive guard for the New York Jets, into the broadcast booth. He later made it a permanent home.

Courtesy New York Jets

look too satisfied. I said, 'good job, Sam.' But he looked unhappy and proceeds to tell me that he got to only 10 percent of his notes. I told him that notes are only a tool if the game's dull and you're running out of material."

His predecessor, Young, would tell many aspiring writers, "Don't feel compelled to cram all your quotes or notes into a single story. Tomorrow is another day. Your knowledge will go to good use down the road."

"When I broadcast, I had an agenda based on the way I thought a game could go. As a result, I may have been a bit pedantic," DeLuca said. "If I started all over, I would just react and be myself. I was looking for things to be informative rather than interesting." And this from a man whose early years with Harmon on WABC were so impressive that he was hired by NBC Television to do games for the network. DeLuca was an astute analyst even if a lot of his commentary started with the offensive line. After all, he was an ex-lineman himself.

The former Lafayette High School star didn't do much preparation by watching film or talking to players. "I liked talking with the coaches. They had the knowledge and the insight. Players' answers were predictable and as I got older, I couldn't relate to them any more."

In the early years DeLuca was working in the off-season to supplement his income. He taught school and then was an advertising salesperson for the ABC

Radio Network. "My office was right around the corner from Howard Cosell's. In fact, I got so friendly with his secretary, Denise, that I married her." Sam must have figured that if Denise could put up with Howard, she could put up with anybody.

"I quickly learned that it wasn't what you said but how you said it." Sam said, referring to Cosell's sharp-tongued, often blistering and brash, commentary. "His intellect was his greatest strength.

"He was always pumping me for information. He would say, 'you don't have Frank Gifford's looks so it's what you say that counts.'"

Cosell's relationship with the Jets soured to the point that even during the season leading up to the 1969 Super Bowl, few players would oblige him for interview requests. Therefore, DeLuca was Cosell's pregame guest more often than not. "He wangled me into saying something one day that I regret to this day. I got coaxed into implying that Weeb was a wishy-washy coach. Cosell would do that. You had to be on your toes with him." Sam though summed up Cosell, "In many ways he was all bluster. Believe it or not, he was so insecure, he had little confidence in himself." Talking of pregame shows, "It seemed that every year we would get to Miami, Larry King would have me on. Heck, their lead-in programming down there would go all morning. King was scrambling around for guests. And he didn't need too many excuses. We went to the same high school in Brooklyn."

A one-time draft choice of the New York Giants, DeLuca worked with four different Jets radio play-by-play announcers: Harmon, Spencer Ross, Charley Steiner, and Steve Albert. One thing DeLuca's partners had to be cognizant of was that he was exclusively a football guy. He had no interest in other sports. Charlie Jones, on NBC Television one day, learned the hard way. Jones made a reference to a fairly well-known baseball player and DeLuca had never heard of him. But Sam DeLuca was a student of football and still appreciates the game today. "The players are bigger and stronger. It's a pleasure to watch them. I would just love to see more creativity in areas of skills. You don't see the linemen, for instance, employ any subtle techniques that we undersized guys were taught and forced to learn."

DeLuca and partner Harmon had all those years of Jets growth while the blackout was in effect. "I had a lot of recognition then, more so than in the later years when the blackout was lifted."

They were also together for what were arguably the two most famous games in Jets history, the 1969 Super Bowl and a game a couple of months earlier in Oakland, on November 17, 1968, the "Heidi" game. NBC decided to cut away from the Jets-Raiders game at 7 P.M. sharp to present the famous kids movie. The Jets were up at the time 32–29 with a couple of minutes left. Oakland scored twice in the final moments to win 43–32. "We had no idea what happened. In those days, to begin with, I would leave the booth early to get down to the locker room to do the live interviews. I, like the viewers, assumed the Jets won. Then I saw a forlorn Dave Herman storm in. When he smacked his helmet against the wall, I asked him what's the matter. I found out!" DeLuca said some 28 years later.

Harmon remembers how Ewbank's wife was so certain that the Jets won that she called the locker room to congratulate her husband. "Then, of course, later, we heard how NBC's switchboards in New York, Chicago and elsewhere were flooded. They never pulled that one again."

Courtesy Sam DeLuca

Sam DeLuca, right, shares the podium with one of his broadcast partners through the years, Spencer Ross.

"Obviously the Super Bowl experience was great. But the only thing I remember about it is the frustration of trying to get into the locker room to do the postgame show. Security was very tight. Finally, Kyle Rote, working for NBC at the time, came by and convinced the guard that I was OK. Then, after all that, I remember that we had technical trouble and we had to cut the show short," Sam added.

Between radio and television, the soft-spoken ex-broadcaster worked games for 21 years, but was disappointed when WCBS didn't hire him in 1988 when it got the rights again. "I did a good job for them when they had the rights earlier, I thought they would have me back." How about the team? "They didn't want to get involved. I know that infuriated Dave Herman in 1979 when the club didn't go to bat for him when the rights shifted from WOR."

DeLuca was a heck of a planner at an early age. He could see something like this coming. "As I looked around, I noticed that there were few older play-by-play and color commentators. I was in radio advertising sales and noticed the same thing there, too. So I looked around and got into business."

He first bought a McDonald's franchise in the Bronx, expanded, sold them, and then got into the loft storage business in Manhattan and Westchester. "Broadcasting was always an avocation to me," said the man whose preparation and analysis were meticulous.

Merle Harmon was a commuter. Through all the seasons that he did the Jets, he never lived in New York. He would fly to the ball games, often arriving in the nick of time.

Mr. Positive, Harmon, was hopping from one assignment to the next. "One day, the Jets had an exhibition game in Mobile, Alabama, on a Saturday night. I had a baseball game in Minneapolis. The Twins allowed me six absences a year. But one inning constituted an appearance. So I left after one inning on a Saturday afternoon and I flew to Washington where an ABC private jet met me. We landed at the Mobile airport. A police car whistled me over to the stadium.

"I'm running for my life because the game is about to begin. I take the elevator to the press box. Then I had to run up a flight of stairs to the broadcast booth. When I got up there, the official was about to give his signal to start play. Dick Young was working with me, I thought he would have a nervous breakdown. When he saw me, he was relieved. He was a heck of a writer but I don't think he ever did play-by-play.

"And don't think that's the end of the story. I'm out of breath when the Patriots take the kickoff. And would you believe, they run it back for a touchdown on the very first play. I'm dying and now the Jets get the ball for the first time. Now they run it back all the way to the 10-yard line. Luckily, I got saved by a commercial at that point and caught my breath."

This would go on constantly. "One day, the Jets are playing in Winston-Salem and as our plane lands in the small airport, I could look down and see the teams getting set for the opening kickoff." This was 1968 and WABC was ready. It had the longtime "voice of the Tar Heels," Woody Durham, standing by. He did the first quarter.

On October 5, 1969, Harmon was with the Twins who were in the playoffs against the Orioles. So fellow ABC employee Keith Jackson filled in. Jackson would go through something similar on October 7, 1978. ABC Television had him doing the Texas-Oklahoma football game from Dallas one Saturday afternoon. They then flew him to New York on a private jet where he was scheduled to work the Kansas City–Yankees playoff game. To get through the New York traffic mess ABC transported him from the airport to the ballpark by ambulance. For having had to endure the strident sound of a siren for a good hour, Jackson was cool and collected and didn't miss a beat.

When the Jets left WABC, a station that Harmon would occasionally refer to as "the tower of power," the Jets went to WOR. That was 1971. But Merle still used his signature line, "your dial is Jets set." And Harmon and DeLuca remained together there for a couple of seasons before Marty Glickman did the blasphemous, leaving the Giants. This is what transpired.

Through all his years with the Giants in the 1960s, Glickman worked for WNEW on a handshake relationship. In fact, Glickman didn't have a written contract with the radio station until 1971, when his play-by-play responsibilities were expanded to include a late-night sports talk show. In 1972 he was earning $50,000 a year.

By early 1973 WNEW didn't feel that the nonplay-by-play sports programming was working as it had hoped. George Duncan was general manager of the radio station and Gary McDowell was the operations manager. Unsure how to handle Glickman, it did nothing and paid for it. It was the responsibility of the station to hire the announcers. The Giants' management had its hands tied. While Ray Walsh, the club's business manager, kept prodding the station to act, it didn't.

WOR had a management team with strong New York roots. WNEW did not and it apparently had little passion with regard to the Giants. While WNEW's management approached Glickman with laconic indifference, WOR was ready to pounce on opportunity.

Herb Salzman was WOR's general manager and Nat Asch was involved on the operations side. Nat and Marty were good friends; the two had worked together at WHN and WNEW. WOR wanted its Jets play-by-play man to have a greater New York identity. Merle Harmon was commuting from the Midwest. He was unavailable during the off-season for promotional and sales activity. As good a job as Harmon was doing, he was hardly as identified with New York as Glickman.

Salzman, a sales-savvy general manager, knew that Marty's connection would produce additional revenue. As such, WOR was eager to make a deal. It made an attractive offer, one that would free up Glickman to do virtually anything else when the Jets were not playing.

Glickman kept phoning WNEW wondering when a renewal offer would be forthcoming. Even when he spelled it out, making it clear there was a sense of urgency to act, WNEW seemed unconcerned. By the time McDowell was informed that WOR had made a deal with Glickman, he made lame corporate excuses about having problems contacting in-house attorneys to make a contract offer to Glickman. "We couldn't get our signals straight," McDowell said at the time, admitting WNEW was late in meeting a deadline.

Marty accepted WOR's offer and Salzman was delighted. These were days before play-by-play announcers made the newspapers every day, before the New York newspapers had sports media critics covering the sports announcers' beat a number of times each week. The Glickman story, though, was big and the *Post* featured the change on its back sports page and there was a lengthy article inside the sports pages.

Marty psyched himself for the change but wasn't quite sure how the Jets' coaching staff and others would react to him. To his surprise and delight, coach Weeb Ewbank and staff welcomed him with open arms. He was immediately accepted as part of the family.

Glickman recalls his first game in Houston. "I was proud of myself. Not once did I refer to the Jets as the Giants. I felt good. When I left the booth, though and needed direction to the locker room, I instinctively asked security, 'where's the Giants' dressing room?'"

Initially, DeLuca was to remain on color but the networks came calling and Sam sought greener pastures. So Marty's first couple of Jets partners were ex-Jets Larry Grantham, who was with him just one season, and then Dave Herman, who was with him five years. Herman was so intense that Marty used to have concerns that he would fall out of the booth. He really got involved. Herman went on to become a successful broadcast sales executive.

Marty had some back surgery early in his tenure with the Jets. WOR used its veteran newsman, Lester Smith, to fill in for three games. But Marty was back shortly, describing the Jets' uniforms "as a rhapsody of green." And the commercials were done with such heart by one of the few sportscasters who used

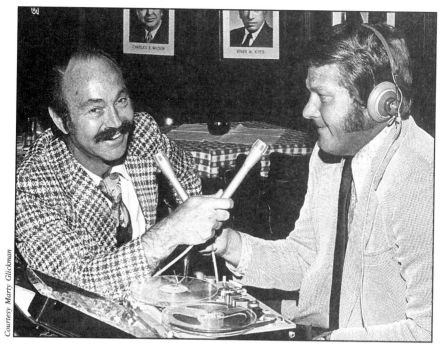

Courtesy Marty Glickman

Marty Glickman, left, moved from the Giants' to the Jets' radio booth in 1973, where he teamed with ex-Jet Larry Grantham in that first season.

his voice properly, speaking right from the diaphragm. "Jets football is sponsored by Hess, for quality gasoline and service, you'll like them for the little things they do!" Glickman was so convincing, listeners would be tempted to drive to Hess at halftime.

At the end of the 1978 season WOR lost the Jets' rights. The new station would be Newsradio 88, WCBS. Glickman wanted to make the move but he never had a chance. For whatever reason, Lou Adler, the man in charge, had no interest in Marty. "I wouldn't hire him on a bet," Adler was heard to say shockingly one day.

Spencer Ross was the station's afternoon drive sports anchor. He wanted the play-by-play job and got it. He beat his mentor Glickman for it. Ross, still close with Marty, admitted owing much to him. "Growing up in New York, there was no better play-by-play man. If it wasn't for Glickman, I wouldn't be here today. He was the inspiration for me to get into the business. In fact, when WCBS was first looking, I told everybody that Glickman should get the job. But the station made it clear that it wasn't going in that direction. When I eventually got it, I felt strange. In fact, I remember one conversation at the time that I had with Marty. He said 'what will I do now on Sundays?'" The Brooklyn-born Ross paused. "The toughest thing for me was replacing a legend."

WCBS now had to put its Jets team together. Sports director and morning sports anchor Ed Ingles was assigned the job as host and Sam DeLuca reentered the radio picture as color commentator. DeLuca had been with NBC Television. Network announcers have shelf lives, some are longer and some are shorter.

Spencer Ross, left, with ex-Jets quarterback Joe Namath, replaced Marty Glickman in the Jets' radio booth in the 1979 season. Saying it was tough replacing a legend like Glickman, Ross added, "If it wasn't for Glickman, I wouldn't be here today."

Sam lasted four years. One of his partners, Charlie Jones, has survived at NBC for 30. His stock went up and down but he played his cards right, was good at what he did, and made no waves.

DeLuca was happy to be in radio again and he did his usually good informative job with Ross. "Football play-by-play men have a prescribed job. There are holes each of us fits. I worked with many partners on radio and television. They were generally all professionals and easy to work with." Initially, Ingles provided commentary that was apparently viewed as extraneous or excessive. His in-game role was quickly reduced to reporting scores and providing prominent numbers. Once these quirks were worked out, the threesome enjoyed five good seasons together. Ross developed into a solid football play-by-player.

In 1984 the Jets, impervious to history, were out seeking the highest bidder again. Despite the fact that WCBS was highly successful and a prestigious all-news station, and had served the Jets and their fans well for five years, Steve Gutman was out to squeeze the old buck. After all, Mr. Hess needed each last one that he could get. While word on the street was that it was a forgone conclusion WCBS and the Jets would re-sign, change was about to occur. One evening Jim Haviland, the general manager of WABC Radio, walked into a media hangout and told folks he thought WCBS would re-up.

Two days later, word was out. Haviland signed the Jets to a WABC contract. The Jets were moving. If they didn't have enough of a public relations challenge competing with the darling Giants, how about an inexplicable move to a station that will bump 7 or so of the 20 games scheduled because of Yankees commitments? If Larry MacPhail made the best of radio when he ran the Brooklyn Dodgers, Steve Gutman might have made the worst of it running the Jets. Loyalty and consistency meant nothing.

Haviland searched around for a play-by-play announcer. His number one sports talent was talk-show host Art Rust Jr. He was opinionated, provocative, and highly rated. In fact, he was then basically it in New York because WFAN didn't hit the air until 1987. Rust endorsed Glickman, who interviewed with Haviland. Jim was a Midwesterner. He didn't grow up with Marty. He wondered whether the veteran was "current." By hiring Ross, it seems he wasn't convinced. DeLuca was brought over for color and the third man in the booth was ex-Jet Randy Rasmussen.

Ross and DeLuca had a funny exchange one day. There was a group in Buffalo that would wear tuxedos to the games every week and serve in a cheerleading capacity. They were colorful. Ross would see them around on the Jets' annual trips to Buffalo but had no idea what they were called. Suddenly, in the middle of a broadcast, DeLuca, who was all business and spoke in an even tone, blurted out, "Hey, Spencer, did you see 'Knox's nuts?'" Ross's eyes popped. "I thought to myself, has he gone nuts? Where's Sam going with this? Is he wondering whether I saw coach Chuck Knox's nuts? I gave him a pleading look. So when he explained that the group in tuxedos was named for coach Chuck Knox, we cracked up so hard, I couldn't go on." Spencer remembered.

When Ross made the move to WABC from WCBS, you knew it would happen. At least twice in the first broadcast, he said, "Spencer Ross, Sam DeLuca and Ed Ingles back at Giants Stadium." The inclination was apparently as overpowering as calling the Los Angeles Raiders the Oakland Raiders when they first moved to Southern California in the 1980s. The rookie broadcaster Randy Rasmussen must have sat there wondering, "Do they want me here?"

Rasmussen got the last laugh, though. Cost-cutting measures resulted in DeLuca losing his job after the 1986 season. The booth was reduced to two announcers. WABC was losing money on the Jets package and dropped the team after the 1987 campaign. Ross lasted just one year on WABC. He moved to baseball in 1985 and Steve Albert was brought in to do morning sports and Jets play-by-play. Albert has earned a distinction of doing all four sports locally on radio, the Mets, Jets, Islanders, and Nets twice. When Albert left for Channel 9 sports, the sepulchral Charley Steiner spent a couple of years on Jets play-by-play.

When the United States Football League was introduced in 1983, the New Jersey Generals were the local franchise. Donald Trump eventually owned the team. WOR carried the games and Steiner called them. The third year, WMCA was the Generals' station and Steiner made the shift. There was no fourth year, of course, because there was no longer a USFL. When the World Football League attempted to rival the National Football League in 1974, the New York Stars lasted only part of the season. The team played at decrepit Downing Stadium on Randall's Island. It was John Sterling on play-by-play and Matt Snell on color over WMCA.

Ed Kiernan was brought in to run WCBS in the late 1980s. Ed loved sports and got the rights back to the Jets in 1988. I was broadcasting St. John's basketball on the station at the time. He called me in and asked me who I felt he should hire. I was flattered that he asked me but I didn't hesitate telling him Marty Glickman. Kiernan didn't hesitate agreeing with me. Glickman was back calling pro football. This was 1988. Marty had been away from the Jets since 1978. He had done two separate stints with the Giants. Now he was about to begin his second tenure covering the Jets. He was 71 years young at the time.

Marty had not been away from football. Through much of the 1980s he called University of Connecticut football and the pro game is easier to do. He had also done some network NFL games the couple of years that NBC Radio held the rights in the mid-1980s. When he returned to the Jets, he allayed any of Haviland's fears. Glickman was current.

Dave Jennings, a former Giants and Jets punter, was hired to do color. He had done some work on radio with WNEW. DeLuca was disappointed that he wasn't selected. Sports director Ed Ingles had endorsed him but Kiernan had his own thoughts. "I was a little peeved. I had done a good job for them in the past and thought I would get it. But I was so immersed in my own business, I just moved on," said DeLuca.

Jennings was a good hire. He was well-spoken, astute, and thoroughly prepared. "There wasn't a rule he wouldn't know. We would sit on planes and he would be studying this tome, the NFL rule book. And it's been a great help," Glickman, the professor, would say. Marty did actually spend a good number of years coaching the NBC Television sports announcers. He still works with the student announcers at Fordham University's campus radio station WFUV. Glickman may yet mold another Vin Scully.

The NFL was a bit different when Marty returned in the late 1980s. "There was a greater distance between many coaches and players and the media. I don't remember it being that way in the early years," Glickman, now enjoying retirement in Manhattan, reflected. "I wasn't close to Bruce Coslet, the Jets' coach. Coslet wouldn't let any media people get close to him. I accepted it and worked under this condition."

Any memories of his second tour with the Jets? There was no hesitation in Glickman's answer, "Dennis Byrd, it was frightening." Byrd, a Jets defensive end, broke his neck at the Meadowlands in November 1992 colliding with a teammate, Scott Mersereau. It just so happened it was one of the last games Glickman would call before retiring. "Apprehension built when he lay motionless on the field. Trainers and doctors ran out and circled him. Later I found out that many were praying for him.

"It reminded me of a 1960 game at Yankee Stadium when Frank Gifford was flattened by Chuck Bednarik. That was stunning because unlike Byrd, Gifford got hurt out in the open. Frank was out for the year but came back the next." Byrd, of course, made a remarkable recovery from a paralyzing injury. It was spectacular. As dispiriting as the moment of the injury was, the recovery was equally heartwarming.

Dave Jennings said that he and Marty enjoyed five wonderful years together. "I was the student. He was the teacher but we worked on an equal basis. He would say to me, 'The game is the important thing, you want the listener to be able to talk about the game the next day.' He would tell me not to get too technical and that if I made reference to a technical term, explain it. If I said they are playing a 4–6 defense, explain it.

"The best thing about working with Marty was listening to his descriptions. When he would open the broadcast, I would lean back, close my eyes and listen. He could make the concrete of the stadium come alive on the radio."

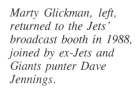

Marty Glickman, left, returned to the Jets' broadcast booth in 1988, joined by ex-Jets and Giants punter Dave Jennings.

Courtesy Marty Glickman

Jennings was asked about all the losing years with the Jets. "I often dream of what it would be like to broadcast six months instead of five, of working into January instead of quitting after December."

Glickman waited until the end of his career before making an inevitable blunder. Now he might smile about it. When he made it, he was severely criticized. It was the last game of the 1991 season. The Jets were playing the Miami Dolphins and needed a win to make it into the playoffs. The Jets led through much of the game. In the final minute Dan Marino threw a touchdown to give the Dolphins a three-point lead. Glickman said, "This game is over." If so, the season was, too.

Yet the Jets marched down the field and Raul Allegre kicked a game-tying field goal. The Jets won in overtime. The media critics blasted the great broadcast veteran. Dave Jennings remembers the incident well.

"I interrupted Marty immediately and declared that the Jets had a chance. But I know where he was coming from. He reacted to the emotions of the players and coaches on the field. He looked at their sagged bodies and went with his feelings. The guys looked defeated at that moment. Having played the game in the NFL, I thought like a player. You never give up."

The last year of WCBS's Jets contract was 1992. Glickman announced prior to the season that it would be his last. As the preseason started, he turned 75 on August 14. "I prepared as hard for the last as I did for my first. I didn't say much about it on the air. The television people put the camera on me during a timeout. My closing comments were brief. 'My heart goes out to Dennis Byrd, Mike Utley and Darryl Stingley.' These three, of course, suffered paralyzing injuries. Byrd recovered."

A class finish for a class guy!

George Vecsey, the versatile and gifted columnist, did an eloquent piece in the *New York Times* when Marty retired. "The very best way to enjoy this sport (football) has never been in the stadium or in front of the tube, but rather raking leaves or taking a walk or going for a long drive in the country with the radio on. His voice is a Brooklyn Bridge of grace and strength."

Gutman and the Jets were on the move again after the season. This time it was 1993 and the station was WFAN. The station smartly signed Jennings to do color and hired Paul Olden for play-by-play. Olden became the first black to do radio play-by-play in New York on any sport other than baseball. The Yankees had broken the color barrier in 1971 when they hired Bill White.

Olden had done the Cleveland Indians, UCLA football, and basketball among other events. He was a disciple of Vin Scully but there was more Dick Enberg to his style. Olden and Jennings spent four years together. A melodious voice, Paul Olden was an easy listen.

When WFAN had a Mets game, the Jets went to FM and when Olden wasn't rehired after the 1996 season, Ian Eagle was. Eagle transcends both—he's a talk-show host on the all-sports station and does play-by-play. Another Syracuse alum, Eagle has successfully shown his play-by-play wares. He was hired to do Nets radio with limited play-by-play experience. He did so nicely that he was hired to do television. He has gotten good TV reviews resulting in additional assignments. Before getting the Jets' play-by-play gig, he hosted WFAN's Jets pre- and postgame shows. Eagle left the Jets for a television football assignment with CBS in 1998.

Before *Monday Night Football* came along, national radio broadcasts of the NFL were essentially limited to championship games. Mutual started in 1936 and they've been on radio pretty much every year since. But it was really in response to the controversial Howard Cosell on television that radio found its niche with regular-season game-of-the-week type broadcasts.

It was Mutual again that jumped on the opportunity in the 1970s. The enthusiastic and big-voiced Van Patrick called the action the first couple of years of the package, 1972 and 1973, before his untimely death. The broadcasts were heard primarily on WMCA. The radio backlash to Cosell got quite a bit of attention from the press in the 1970s including an unlikely source, *The Wall Street Journal*. This was when Cosell could be at his obnoxious best. Like being an anti-Yankee fan in the 1950s, it was a practice of many to watch *Monday Night Football* with the sound down.

Lindsey Nelson did four years of *Monday Night Football* for Mutual, beginning in 1974 and continuing through 1977. While Lindsey did so much baseball in New York, he was a football man at heart. He grew up around college football in Tennessee under coach Bob Neyland and even did the NFL as early as 1951 for the old Liberty Network.

Lindsey Nelson did many, many things very well, but one thing he did as well as anybody was create an environment of infectious enthusiasm. The audience always had the feeling that there was nowhere in the world Lindsey Nelson would rather be at that moment than at the ballpark.

Years later Nelson would do NFL football for CBS Radio. "Wherever you went around San Francisco this morning, the subject of conversation was this football game. Whether it was the hostess turning over the tables at the restaurant, the cab driver or the doorman, everyone wanted to talk about Joe Montana

© National Sportscasters and Sportswriters Assn.

Lindsey Nelson

and these San Francisco Forty-Niners." Sitting around with his mentor, Bill Stern, painting a dramatic scene became second nature to the man who covered the Mets for 17 years.

Early in his career, *Variety* wrote of Nelson's football: "Lindsey Nelson has been touted for many years as one of the tip-top grid casters on the national scene. Precise, methodical, and efficient, he may not have the color of Bill Stern, the heartiness of Mel Allen, the analytic powers of Red Barber or the glamour of Ted Husing, but as an information purveyor who's right on top of the play. He is almost prescient, the peer of any and the superior of many." Lindsey had a sing-song delivery perfectly suited for football.

When CBS got the radio rights to NFL *Monday Night Football* in 1978, it appointed Jack Buck to call the games. His longtime partner, Hank Stram, came along a year later. Glickman once described Buck as "slick." Marty meant it positively. Buck rarely made a mistake. He was on the play but he didn't jump to conclusions. Buck wasn't going to guess and look bad. If he couldn't identify the ball carrier, it was "Handoff, handoff to the second man through who plows down to the 30-yard line. That was a nice run, Hank, by Smith." He was great at buying time in midsentence. Often Hank would jump in, "they're going to run right, Jack."

A classic Buck call would be, "Pass into the end zone, caught, caught, touchdown San Francisco, touchdown Forty-Niners. Taylor the touchdown. John Taylor, the catch, touchdown, San Francisco." Buck was smooth and dramatic. He reported to his audience the most important development, the big catch and the score. But why risk a mistake? In his prime, he called a down with the subplot cadence of the best of them. The punch line unfolded dramatically and perfectly. Telling a story is also a Buck specialty. He's a very popular after-dinner speaker.

In 1986 and 1987 the package went to NBC Radio before it returned to CBS. Don Criqui did play-by-play and Bob Trumpy did color. *Sports Illustrated* at the time described the Cincinnati-based Trumpy "as irreverent, candid, shoot-from-the-hip." NBC did do one thing a bit differently. After the game, the duo hosted a national call-in show. Paying $11 million at the time for two years, NBC Radio took a financial hit. It was a long way from the $13,000 a year Mutual paid in 1972. The same magazine described Criqui as "perfectly groomed, a good nuts-and-bolts announcer but lacking warmth and as colorless as Cream of Wheat."

Stram and Buck developed a nice rapport. "We just clicked." Buck said. "We prepared well but never rehearsed. I trusted him and he trusted me. Our work was all spontaneous." And they did it so long that after a while their very voices on the radio in September were a sign that autumn had arrived. Jack's voice sounded as though he got out of a deep sleep. He would open the show with his deliberate greeting and would welcome Stram. "All right, Henry, welcome to another *Monday Night Football* game." Hank: "Yes, it's great to be here in Pittsburgh, Jack, and it's always nice to see Chuck Noll. I remember when he broke into football, Jack." Stram, an astute analyst had hearing problems, particularly in his later years. There were times he couldn't hear a word Jack was saying. Buck would ask one thing and Stram would answer another. It got humorous after a while.

Jack Buck

Buck's voice problems accelerated, and he and Stram were retired unceremoniously after the 1995 season. Neither was happy about it. Buck had worked for the network for many years, doing radio and television, baseball, football, and more. One of the games that Buck worked for CBS Television was the famous ice bowl in Green Bay, the 1967 NFL championship game between the Packers and the Cowboys. "It was an open booth. I spent the whole game drinking coffee spiced with vodka. I also borrowed a stocking cap to keep my head warm."

When Buck and Stram were relieved, CBS hired Howard David and Matt Millen. Matt was an opinionated, provocative, no-nonsense guy. He wasn't going to allow David to rib him. You don't fool around with Millen. David, on the other hand, is one who feels it's mandatory to spice humor into the call of each down. David was also hired by the Jets to replace Ian Eagle in 1998.

5

THE WORLD
SERIES

THE FALL CLASSIC ON THE AIR

Until the advent of radio, baseball fans waiting for word on the World Series had little choice but to await the arrival of the evening newspaper at the neighborhood newsstand. The paper might have had nothing more than a partial score but it was better than nothing.

If a fan couldn't attend a game, the next best thing might be getting a vantage point near the newspapers' headquarters. Many papers would have prominent Play-O-Graph boards that portrayed the Series. They would invite fans to gather in front of the outer facade of their headquarters, and on the outer wall a huge scoreboard would be set up. It had each team's scoring production inning by inning and the running totals of runs, hits, and errors. Many also graphically depicted a diamond that displayed base runners, if any, the outs, and the count on the batter. Huge crowds would assemble and cheer as the news from the ballpark came in. Many fans at these locations could occasionally get boisterous, particularly when two New York teams would be playing one another.

In the early 1920s, while radio was in a nascent state, these Play-O-Graph boards were still popular because not everybody could afford a radio. So "scoreboard watching" was well attended right through the Roaring '20s. Some newspapers that were equipped accordingly might even amplify the radio call through a loudspeaker and into the throng. This way fans had the visual benefit of the scoreboard to supplement the radio.

137

Those unable to get to newspaper offices might go to the bigger pool houses where updates were being received as well. Theaters might also announce scores after every inning, as a public service.

Even in 1924 hundreds of thousands caught the glad tidings of the New York Giants' victory in the first game of the World Series in Washington. In front of the *New York Sun* building on Chambers Street in lower Manhattan, the crowd was so enormous there was a hurried call for police to handle the jam. Mounted police appeared quickly to keep the street open to traffic. And it wasn't just men. There were women and girls. Every key play was greeted wildly. Every vantage point where the scoreboard was visible, whether it was City Hall Park, roofs or windows, was filled to capacity. The *New York Times* compared the scene to the picture presented when the first American troops returned from France at the end of World War I. Street cars coming down Park Row and Broadway slowed or stopped to catch a glimpse of the scoreboard.

When radio was born in New York in 1921 it needed programming. Baseball was coming off the 1919 Black Sox scandal (in which eight White Sox players were banned from baseball for allegedly fixing the World Series) and it needed an uplifting promotional boost. The match of the two was made in heaven. Radio and baseball—it was love at first sight. Like Fred Astaire and Ginger Rogers, what would one do without the other?

Baseball, it was learned quickly, can be visualized graphically by the radio listener. The scoreboards and the Play-O-Graph boards would become obsolete. Appetites were now being satiated by radio. Just as there would be a fascination later with television, cable, and the Internet, radio changed the lives of Americans. It changed the way they were informed, the way they were entertained, and the way they followed sports. Radio led the 1920s into the golden decade of sports.

Major League Baseball was only played in the Northeast and parts of the Midwest. Many cities, including some very large ones, had no baseball. Radio spread interest across the land. Radio made it possible for millions to immediately follow the World Series in a way they never knew before! It wasn't just reading a newspaper account and imagining what it would be like. Now fans were able to hear the roar of the crowd, the crack of the bat, and the cry of the vendors. They were given a seat alongside the announcer, upstairs behind home plate. They were right inside the Polo Grounds, Yankee Stadium, or other venerable ballparks.

Like a good marriage, baseball and radio would enjoy a lasting relationship. Like a happy partner still madly in love with his spouse, there was still passion for baseball on radio at the end of the 20th century. The names have changed but the elements have remained the same. The play-by-play announcers are still lionized and the players are treated as heroes. In the 1920s it might have been Graham McNamee and Babe Ruth. As baseball and radio approach the 21st century, it is Vin Scully and Mark McGwire.

Baseball's first-ever broadcast was aired on the country's first-ever radio station, KDKA in Pittsburgh. On August 5, 1921, announcer Harold Arlin ventured to Forbes Field and reported on the Philadelphia Phillies–Pittsburgh Pirates contest. Arlin later did tennis, boxing, and football on KDKA. New York's first taste of World Series coverage came to pass in 1921. It was a hit-and-miss experiment, one of trial and error.

Two of the truly great men in their fields, baseball's Babe Ruth, left, sits down with radio's Graham McNamee for a World Series interview.

The first organized and publicized broadcast wasn't until 1922. It was an all–New York Series in 1921 and Tommy Cowan was working for WJZ Radio. He was a staff announcer and was stationed in a shack on top of the Westinghouse plant in Newark. It was that fall that WJZ officially went on the air. The station's first words were uttered by Cowan, "You are listening to the radio telephone broadcasting station, WJZ in Newark, New Jersey." He repeated the message several times, but admitted later he doubted anyone was listening.

The account of the Series was being relayed to him by reporter Sandy Hunt at the ballpark. Cowan then proceeded to describe or repeat what he heard. It was hardly Red Barber but it established the first-ever live report of a World Series game on the air. Cowan left WJZ in 1925 and joined WNYC, the city-owned station, where he spent the bulk of his career.

There were few radio sets in 1921. The newspapers didn't promote Cowan's broadcast. It was only about three months after Major J. Andrew White put the Dempsey-Carpentier fight on the air and when the majority of the listeners heard the fight by either attending the theater where receivers were placed or tuned in on amateur-built receivers. There were few mass-produced radios in the marketplace in the fall of 1921.

The first concerted effort to put every game of the World Series on radio and promote it effectively was undertaken in 1922. It took synergy. Radio station WJZ, now with a full year under its belt; the *New York Tribune*, an established daily newspaper; and other cooperative parties made it possible. The '22 Fall Classic was baseball's answer to boxing's Dempsey-Carpentier fight. Radio was hoping to cash in on the popularity of another major sporting event, a rematch of the Yankees and Giants. This is what was done:

1. Grantland Rice, an esteemed scribe of the day with the *Tribune*, broadcast the 1922 play-by-play.
2. WJZ, owned at the time by a combination of Westinghouse, General Electric, and RCA, took out advertisements, including a sizable one in the *New York Times*, promoting the broadcasts. The big print at the top of the ad was "Hear the Crowd Roar!" Of course, RCA had much to gain. It was selling radio receivers and, as the ad said, "There's an RCA for every home and every purse . . . owners of RCA sets are sure of broadcasting results from the World Series . . . Prepare for the event by buying your RCA set from your nearest dealer and ask him for the Radiola Score Sheet." RCA apparently had some promotional and entrepreneurial savvy to lure customers. WJZ was a noncommercial station at the time so the broadcast wasn't sponsored.
3. Leading into and throughout the World Series of 1922, the *Tribune*, on its front page, not its front sports page, ran a salient box publicizing the broadcast every day.
4. Believe it or not, just to be sure there was no interference with WJZ's signal, no station went on the air while the World Series was being run on WJZ. This assured the broadcast of being available within an 800-mile radius. WHN and the other handful of stations went completely off the air during the broadcasts so that WJZ's airing would be impeccably clean.
5. Tickets to the Series were sold out and the *Tribune* expected 1 million listeners. As such, the New York teams allowed the station to air the games.

The morning after the first game, the *Tribune* reported that the station was inundated with calls from all over including out-of-town places such as Syracuse where the signal was coming in clear as a bell. The newspaper called the achievement an "epoch-making event."

Certain things don't change. When Grantland Rice was asked what it was like to talk to a million people, the gifted writer said that he approached it the way he would talk to one person. That's probably the best way to approach a broadcast even today. "At least no one cut in or talked back," he said. Rice described the notables who entered the stadium, Commissioner Landis, General Pershing, Christy Mathewson, and Jack Dempsey. The writer told the audience that baseball comedian Nick Altrock "was doing his stuff in slow motion in the middle of the diamond" before the game.

Whether it was an engineering problem of mixing crowd noise or Rice's lack of experience in doing play-by-play, one listener called to say, "I would hear the crowd let out a terrific roar, and it seemed ages before I knew whether it was a single or a three-bagger." But generally listeners were just happy to get the game. It was a novel experience.

Radio receivers drew attention everywhere. One man in Hackensack, New Jersey, reported that there were more than 2,000 persons listening to his loudspeaker. In New York City, where radio stores had sprouted, listeners jammed around doors to listen to Rice's call on loudspeakers. In Newark, the situation got so bad, traffic was congested.

While the popularity of portable radios was still something of the future, there were fans who took shelter on top of a building near the Polo Grounds. They saw the game from the roof and listened simultaneously to Rice's account.

© National Sportscasters and Sportswriters Assn.

Grantland Rice

One way or another, it seemed that 1922 was a breakthrough year for radio baseball in New York. The concerted effort of all parties had worked.

On October 6, 1923, Judge Kenesaw Landis, commissioner of baseball, granted permission to both top radio outlets in New York City, WJZ and WEAF, to broadcast the Series. WEAF, the AT&T station, had another well-known writer, Bill McGeehan, scheduled to work the Series. But McGeehan became the first play-by-play announcer to quit on the job. He was apparently more facile at writing and in the middle of the Series he repaired to the typewriter. Graham McNamee, who had gone to work for WEAF earlier in the year, took over and did the play-by-play. WEAF, with AT&T supporting its transmission needs, set up the first World Series network in 1923, feeding stations WMAF in South Dartmouth, Massachusetts, and WCAP in Washington.

For the great Grantland Rice, his first year of World Series play-by-play was also his last. He apparently felt more comfortable in his newspaper role than he did in the broadcasting booth. In 1923 America's dean of sports announcing, J. Andrew White, did the play-by-play on WJZ and Rice just "provided summaries" after each inning. White was well known for broadcasting many events including heavyweight championship fights. So for the Giants-Yankees fall battle, these two broadcast giants, McNamee and White, sat side by side broadcasting from the Polo Grounds and the new Yankee Stadium on their respective stations.

But something unfair was going on. Transmission and line quality was a problem for WJZ, but not for WEAF which was owned by AT&T. The telephone company saw to it that WJZ's transmission was of inferior quality to WEAF's. It was so bad that WJZ had to relegate itself to Western Union reports by 1924, but White made the best of it. Ted Husing was assisting White at the time of the Series and remembers, "We sent a man to the park, a middleman. He flashed us by ticker a description of the action, every ball, every strike, every hit. Major White masterfully re-created the game."

The telephone company connection gave WEAF a forced exclusive. In 1924 it put together an expanded World Series network. It strung together seven stations in the Northeast Corridor, from Boston to Washington. The Washington Senators beat the Giants in seven games, but game two of the Series was bumped off powerful flagship WEAF. It was only on WNYC because a religious address took precedence. Dr. Parkes Cadman, president of the Federal Council of Churches, was on WEAF doing an interdenominational service. But WEAF was back on for game three from the Polo Grounds.

The *Herald Tribune* called McNamee's play-by-play "an excellent piece of broadcasting" while decrying the preemption as "one of the mysteries of broadcasting." Unlike WJZ, WEAF sold its time commercially. The World Series was not sponsored, while perhaps the Federal Council bought its block of time for hard cash. Thus, the game was shipped to the New York City–owned radio station. WEAF may have been at its beginnings but the station was already in the football business in 1924. McNamee's later partner, Phillips Carlin, called a Columbia-Wesleyan game just after the Series.

Quinn Ryan, the one-time *Chicago Tribune* writer and WGN commentator, joined McNamee for the 1925 Pittsburgh-Washington championship. It was another pulsating match. The Pirates knocked off the Senators in seven games and McNamee received more than 50,000 letters from appreciative fans. The *Daily News* was impressed, too. "The cheering of the crowds and the blare of the bands provided plenty of atmosphere, and the cool, clear descriptions given by the announcers brought into thousands of homes the diamond at Forbes Field, Pittsburgh." The paper might have liked Graham's Forbes Field crowd description during the seventh-inning stretch: "The vast crowd stood up to rest its collective fannies."

So WEAF did the play-by-play live and WJZ used a Western Union report. White was less than 15 seconds behind McNamee's live broadcast. The *Tribune* said, "Major White chose, quite wisely, to eliminate all attempts at imaginative coloring of the wire reports, supplying a calm, clear, and complete story of baseball as it was played at Forbes Field."

The newspaper did criticize the production of the WEAF broadcast and McNamee himself, for dramatizing the "local color." "The crowd noise came through almost too well, drowning out McNamee's words at the height of the action." Grammatical purists might also object, the *Tribune* said, to McNamee's use of slang. A sign of the times? Radio, it appears, didn't immediately accept baseball's nomenclature.

It's interesting to note how the broadcasts stacked up when juxtaposed. Stuart Hawkins, the "Pioneer," penned the radio column in the *Herald Tribune*. "For ourselves we spent most of the game swinging from WEAF to WJZ and back, trying to match the advantages of the two systems—the reportorial, WJZ, and the descriptive, WEAF. Such entertaining incidents as the lugubrious pawls of the umpire announcing the batteries were offset in WEAF's broadcast by the maddening loss of McNamee's words in a melee of crowd noise, while the sometimes overlong intermissions between Major White's reports were compensated for by the clarity of his statements. WEAF's description required constant attention for full appreciation, whereas WJZ's commanded it when things had happened on the diamond."

So how did the experts at the time compare the baseball styles of the two pioneers, McNamee and White? The respected Ben Gross, who spent decades with the *Daily News*, first as its radio critic and then its radio and television critic, wrote in 1927, "Major White's descriptions were like those of an amiable gentleman speaking leisurely from an easy chair. Complete but not exciting. McNamee's, on the other hand, was tinged with the enthusiasm and sense of drama which might be expected of a fan in the grandstand or the bleachers." Apparently, the two were as opposite in style as they were in vantage point. These were days before press boxes had all the comfortable amenities. They each had boxes in the mezzanines, Columbia between third and the plate and NBC between first and the plate.

The *Telegram* endorsed both McNamee and White in 1928, saying that "every bit of the description was terse and apt, and had just the right amount of staccato to make it vivid and real. Judicious placing of extra microphones brought the color to hard-pressed imaginations." McNamee was so popular then that not only was he inundated by autograph seekers, but requests were so great that he ran out of ink in his fountain pen. In these pre-ballpoint-pen days, he then had to turn down all autograph seekers until a good-looking young lady approached him. The suave popular announcer then borrowed a pen.

In the early years of World Series broadcasts, Commissioner Landis made broadcast decisions year by year. There were no long-term contracts with any networks and baseball itself didn't receive a penny in rights fees. There was also a haphazardness to carriage. Some stations would join a network, while others might decide to produce their own wire service report of the games.

Initially, radio also encountered turbulence from newspapers which urged Judge Landis not to permit radio to broadcast the Series for fear of a loss of circulation. There was particular trepidation on the part of evening newspapers. The immediacy of radio made the partial scores in the evening papers rather obsolete. Over a short course of time, though, the print media appreciated the synergy that radio produced. It actually created interest of new fans, folks theretofore unexposed to the sport.

McNamee was to the 1920s and early 1930s what Curt Gowdy was to the 1970s, the "voice of everything." He covered football, including the biggest gridiron event, the Rose Bowl, the heavyweight title fights, which were unsurpassed in interest, and the World Series. McNamee was a trailblazer. He provided Sports 101 for millions of the uninitiated. In the 1970s, on the other hand, Gowdy might have made fanatics of the unexposed as he blitzed into millions of homes during television's most explosive decade.

While McNamee was Red Barber's hero, he was hardly the founding father of radio baseball, albeit that he was the "voice of the World Series" 12 of the first 14 years it was on radio.

McNamee hardly mastered the sequential delivery that helps make baseball the great sport it is on radio today. He might have reported the results of each pitch but it wasn't presented with an anticipatory punch line. Today, an announcer will tell his radio listeners that the pitcher is winding up. His very tone of voice then picks up slightly as the pitch is made, "he throws." There is a pause to create a sense of urgency as the outcome of the pitch is awaited. "The batter swings!" The audience is now on the lookout. "He hits it hard to right." Will it be caught or will it be a base hit? The listener is now not only following the game as he would at the ballpark but he is also involved. These are the rudiments of baseball on radio, which for the most part were developed by Barber.

In the seventh and final game of the 1926 Series, McNamee provided the following call in the first inning:

Babe Ruth is up, taking his tremendous left stand at the plate. Here is a slow ball. One ball, a little outside to a left-handed batter. Babe Ruth settles his cap more carefully on his head, grabs hold of the wagon tongue by the end. A little bit outside—two balls. Three balls.

He drove the next one to Hornsby. St. Louis has again gone crazy. That was a ground ball, Hornsby to Bottomley.

Later, in the seventh inning, the star-emblazoned McNamee:

Combs, the head of the Yankee batting list, is up in the last half of the seventh inning. And a hit! They've now almost made another one of those wild jumping catches. He went up plenty far enough, but not straight enough to get the ball. It just touched the top of his glove, a single.

The Series ends when Ruth tries to steal second:

Babe Ruth is up. Rogers Hornsby is now talking to one of the greatest pitchers in baseball to decide what to do about Ruth. It seems that Hornsby wanted Alexander to pass Ruth, and Alexander didn't want to do it. Alexander seemed to hesitate to do what he was told. One strike. That might not have been the conversation at all. Hornsby may have been telling him to pitch to Ruth. One strike. One ball, a little outside to a left-handed batter. Here it is coming—a foul ball. Two strikes and one ball and the crowd howls with joy. So we give it to them for good sportsmanship. I'll say we will. Here is what we came to see. There is danger of a home run, tying the score. And Alexander the great is pitching to Babe Ruth. Here it is—two balls. This is a duel. There is electricity in the air. Here it is again—a ball, just outside. Ruth is again walked for the fourth time today.

One strike on Bob Meusel. Going down to second—the game is over. Babe tried to steal second and is put out, catcher to second.

The World Series of 1926—we will never say it again—is over! It has come to a close, and the championship goes west, southwest, down to the sovereign state of Missouri.

In 1926 McNamee began three straight years of Fall Classic coverage by teaming with Phillips Carlin. Carlin was to McNamee in the 1920s what Jim Simpson was to Curt Gowdy in the 1970s, NBC's number two man. And given RCA's 1926 purchase of WEAF from AT&T, the Graham and Phil team were on both WJZ and WEAF.

Fans loved Mac. On his way home from St. Louis after the Classic, he stopped in Pittsburgh to attend a radio show. He addressed a throng of 27,000. One appreciative baseball fan gave him a platinum wristwatch and another fan presented him a beautifully inscribed gold fountain pen.

White was off the 1926 Series. With the merger of WEAF and WJZ, White was busy with football, covering among other big games in October 1926 the Yale-Brown game. The moment RCA owned both stations, it created two NBC networks, the Blue and the Red. It immediately fed two football games each Saturday to its affiliates, the WEAF–NBC Red and the WJZ–NBC Blue.

McNamee wasn't afraid to criticize if he felt it was warranted. During one game in 1926, he blurted out, "This is nothing to write home about." Stuart Hawkins, "the Pioneer," reported in his October 4, 1926, column that some felt that "Mr. McNamee wasn't anything to write home about himself. His remarks were no more inspired than those of any other mortal." The Pioneer went on, "Judging from his work Saturday and Sunday, Carlin is not going to be a mere second fiddle among baseball announcers after this Series is over." As it would be, Carlin was in management by 1929 and off the air.

Fred Lieb of the *Sporting News* wrote of McNamee's shortcomings of baseball knowledge during that 1926 Series: "Before the first game, Graham asked me to bring National League president John Heydler to do an interview. I dragged him from the lower box seats at Yankee Stadium to Mac's radio perch. Heydler was given a flowery buildup.

"I have a real treat for you radio listeners, a former great pitcher, congressman, governor, and now National League president, John K. Tener," said McNamee. Graham had introduced a man who had left the league presidency in 1918, eight years before. "After mumbling a few words, the sensitive Heydler told me he was never so humiliated in his life."

The Cardinals-Yankees 1926 World Series would also be the last one to be broadcast on just one network until 1939. That's when Gillette got the rights and put the games on Mutual exclusively.

By 1927, the seventh-ever World Series broadcast, NBC had a coast-to-coast network. The older of the two webs had 43 stations hooked in, including the city-owned WNYC. Again, WEAF, the NBC flagship didn't carry Sunday games. NBC, nonetheless, estimated a listenership of 50 million. In fact, the NBC broadcast was picked up as far away as Greenland. Columbia, the fledgling radio union, had 10 affiliates, as the Series was carried on two networks for the first time.

In Pittsburgh, home of the participating Pirates, the *Pittsburgh Gazette* ran its big Play-O-Graph board and invited readers to watch the big scoreboard with the sound of McNamee and Carlin on KDKA. And many obliged. The radio broadcasts of the Series did wonders for receiver sales and batteries. Newspapers across the land were full of ads promoting both gadgets at the time of the classic. And the year that Charles Lindbergh flew the Atlantic solo, Judge Landis was still allowing stations to re-create the Series off the wires if they were unaffiliated with either NBC or Columbia. Tom Manning, who would later call the Series on NBC and work Cleveland Indians games, re-created the games in Cleveland, and as far west as Los Angeles, a wire account of the games was given by Oscar Reichow, a minor-league radio announcer in Los Angeles's Wrigley Field.

White had formed Columbia and gave NBC a run for its money. The first president of CBS did the 1927 and 1928 Classics live with Harold Totten, the established "voice of Chicago baseball."

With radio's coverage of the Series, school absenteeism increased. Students started staying home to listen to the Series. The *Times* reported how one school installed a big radio in the auditorium. It worked to a degree because fewer students played hooky. For decades to come, the World Series was played exclusively in daylight. Night games weren't tried until 1971. Until then, radios were always around schools and if a teacher didn't allow the whole class to listen as a group, some would bring little transistor radios and snake the earphone wiring clandestinely through shirt sleeves and into their ears.

Even then, in 1928, the World Series received enormous coverage. Excluding radio, 960 "men" were members of the press covering the contests, 435 reporters in the press box, 300 roving field reporters, 100 telegraphers, and 125

photographers. The telegrapher is now about as common as the elevator operator. One of those not included in these numbers was Ted Husing, who assisted
White as such, broadcasting his first World Series.

Again in 1928, the "street fans," as the *New York Times* referred to those
who kept their ears pinned to the loudspeakers at public gathering spots, drew
throngs. Interest was at a fevered pitch during game two until the Yankees exploded for four runs in the third inning. Then the crowds began to melt away,
truckmen got back on their vehicles and businessmen returned to their desks.

For White, the '28 classic was his last. He would later be exclusively in
administration before leaving CBS and the radio business in 1930. There seemed
to be little chemistry between White and boss Bill Paley. White founded the
network, and was its first president, chief cook, and bottle washer.

"My dad had little use for Paley and Paley had little use for my dad. Paley
thought CBS started and ended with him. He didn't like acknowledging my
dad's pioneering work. Dad sold his CBS stock shortly after he left. Otherwise,
I would be a millionaire today," said White's son, Blair, now living in Southern
California. The Major, who moved to the Los Angeles area in the 1940s, where
he became a clinical psychologist, did love listening to Vin Scully when the
Dodgers left Brooklyn for California in 1958.

Unlike the three New York teams, the Cubs and White Sox invited radio
into their ballparks, and Hal Totten did daily baseball in Chicago as early as
1924. While New York was deprived of local radio broadcasts, the likes of Pat
Flanagan, Johnny O'Hara, and later Bob Elson all started building their reputa-
tions doing baseball in the 1920s in the Windy City. There was no limitation on
the number of stations that carried each of the teams. In other words, there were
many broadcast perches at Wrigley Field and Comiskey Park.

Elson, a Hall of Fame broadcaster, influenced virtually every baseball
announcer who grew up in the Midwest. Milo Hamilton, a big-league announcer
since the 1950s, said, "If you sat us all down and analyzed us today, you would
find that there was a lot of Elson in all of us." Jack Brickhouse and longtime
Cubs voice Vince Lloyd would echo his sentiments. Unlike the Midwest style of
today, initiated by Brickhouse and Bert Wilson, Elson was not a cheerleader.

Elson attacked uncharted waters when he started doing baseball in
the 1920s.

He covered the White Sox for 38 years, beginning in 1930. "The Old
Commander," as he was known, only had his service broken for three years
during World War II to do Navy duty. He was a champion gin rummy player
and loved playing a "guess-the-attendance" game with his announcing associate
and engineer in the booth.

Totten was a crime reporter for the *Chicago Daily News*. He knew Al
Capone and his underworld cronies. As a young man in his 20s, he turned to
broadcasting and went to work for WMAQ. Affiliated with Columbia, Totten
and White teamed together for the two fall championships that featured the great
Yankees team of 1927 and the Yanks' 1928 revenge against the Cardinals, both
four-game sweeps. He later worked on NBC's coverage of the Series in the
1930s and teamed with McNamee on the first All-Star Game in 1933.

Totten and McNamee started broadcasting baseball at roughly the same
time but Hal, doing baseball day in and day out, was less forced in his presentation. In fact, NBC sent Graham to Chicago for the first-ever All-Star game be-

tween the National and American leagues in 1933. Mac himself was scheduled to handle play-by-play and Totten was to do color. But as game time approached, it was almost as though Mac knew better. Graham turned to Totten and asked him to do the play-by-play while he did the color.

Totten had a big warm voice and sounded like everybody's jolly uncle. His drama painting can hardly be confused for Vin Scully but remember that he didn't have any canvasses to study, either. A snippet of Totten from the 1929 World Series between the Cubs and Connie Mack's Philadelphia Athletics:

Ehmke throws and it is a strike. Ehmke has got that loose-jointed, lazy nonchalant way of working. He throws again and that one is wide across the shoulder. It is one and one for Woody. English takes the second ball, low and across the knees. It is two and one for English. Woody swings. He hits the ball, the pitcher just barely touches it, the ball is deflected to the shortstop, who gets it and throws to first, and the runner is safe. It goes as a single for English, the first hit of the Series. Hornsby is coming up.

Hornsby is standing pretty well back. Ehmke gets ready to pitch the first one to Raj. He throws, and Hornsby takes a strike.

Hornsby hits one away out in right field near the fence. Miller gets it and throws it to second base. English was almost to second.

It is two outs in the first inning for the Cubs, with Hack Wilson at bat. Wilson hits a line drive to right field. Miller comes in fast and makes another catch. It is three outs, no runs, one hit, and one man left on base for the Cubs in the first inning.

The score is nothing to nothing, end first inning.

While there was a peacefulness to Totten's style and a lot of soft crowd noise as a backdrop, there were huge gaps between pitches. There was absolutely no delving into strategy and few anecdotes. It truly sounds primitive to hear it today.

When Major White put the World Series on the air on Columbia in 1927, the network was operating on a shoestring. It was hardly in a good bargaining position. The Paley family didn't bail out the network financially until 1928. Unlike NBC which already owned several stations at that point, Columbia didn't own any. Columbia's World Series was carried by WOR from which the network leased time. The Chicago affiliate was WMAQ, whose station manager was a tough lady named Judith Waller. It appears that she insisted that Totten, her sports guy, work with White on the Series.

Totten did the 1929 Series on WMAQ alone. Ted Husing, by then Columbia's lead sportscaster, did the Classic all by himself on all his network's stations except Chicago. Neither of these two gentlemen was eager to share the microphone with anyone, so perhaps it was decided to split the broadcasts. Jimmy Dudley, a Cleveland Indians broadcast fixture who traced his roots through Chicago, knew both men. "Totten closely guarded the mike. He was like Ted Husing, who I knew in the early 1940s, and who told me when I was trying to get on the air, 'Hey, kid, you're good. I let you do a little baseball and football and the first thing you know, you'll be taking my job.'" Totten did eventually leave the booth but remained in baseball in a front-office capacity.

College football was enormously popular in 1929. In some places, it might have been followed with greater interest than the Series. NBC, working the World Series out of glass-enclosed booths, would give college football updates from key gridiron venues on Saturdays of the Series. Meanwhile, Husing was relishing his beloved role of working alone, which he did through 1931. If there was another voice interspersed, the role was a cameo. It was hardly noticed. Ted worked best this way. He might have put a writer on with him for short spurts but he was in charge, and it allowed him to have "mind, eye, ear, and tongue merge into a single unit."

The networks were growing in affiliates. CBS was up to 33 for the 1929 Chicago-Philadelphia encounter, and NBC reported 58 stations hooked in.

Going into the 1930s, the World Series broadcasts were extremely popular in New York because the three teams rarely, if ever, allowed regular-season broadcasts. Ford Frick, the future National League president and later Commissioner of Baseball, was a sportswriter for the *New York Evening Journal*. He later did sports updates, which were then popularly referred to as résumés. He was heard on WINS and WOR. Upon the few rare occasions that local baseball teams would allow stations to do a special game, Frick was one of the men involved. He writes that the greatest response he ever had in his years in the media was when he did a baseball game on WOR from Ebbets Field.

In 1930 Frick shared the spotlight with McNamee in the NBC World Series booth.

Of course, Frick will always be remembered for placing an asterisk near the name of former home-run king Roger Maris after he hit his 61st in 1961. Frick covered Babe Ruth as an announcer and as a writer. He insisted it be noted that Roger's accomplishment took 162 games while the Babe's 60 took just 154. The asterisk has since been removed.

Frick was well received. He was knowledgeable and was compared by one critic to the fast-talking and glib NBC newsman and sometime sports announcer, Floyd Gibbons. McNamee, though, it was now said, was sounding tired. Bear in mind that Graham was all-everything, and he was beginning to burn out. Not only was he covering every major sporting event, from football to regattas, he also was at political conventions, inaugurations, and special events. And this was all in addition to his role as studio staff announcer.

By 1931 George Hicks, an award-winning newsman who covered wars and presidents, was back with Mac. He worked the 1929 October hoopla, traveled with Herbert Hoover at the time of the 1930 championship, but was back doing color in 1931. He was Graham's choice. But McNamee was enduring more and more criticism. The *Chicago American*, in the hometown of Commissioner Landis, wrote its radio review early in the Cardinals-Athletics seven-game championship, "World Series static—the ever glib McNamee seems less eloquent than usual." It also criticized Husing. "Husing, 'Here 'tis, a long fly, no, a short high fly,' And so it goes. Nevertheless, our vote goes to the versatile Ted."

McNamee also caught heat for this boo-boo prior to the start of the first game. He had the Athletics taking the field instead of the Cards. He also told of a foul ball between first and third, which must have been a new one on baseball fans.

© National Baseball Hall of Fame Library, Cooperstown, N.Y.

Ford Frick

Variety, the weekly entertainment magazine, started reviewing the World Series broadcasts in the 1930s. Its 1931 criticism of the veteran broadcaster might have done him in. "Runs were scored, and Graham promptly muffed 'em. Close plays occurred, and he didn't seem to know what happened until a few minutes later. It's a good thing for both teams that Graham wasn't the umpire." This would be the last year that these two popular network correspondents, McNamee and Husing, would preside over the big October event. The winds of change were beginning to pick up in velocity.

The *New York Evening Journal* headlined this story, "World Series Broadcasts May Result in Relief Man for McNamee." The story went on to say that NBC was toying with possible changes even as quickly as the middle of the 1931 classic. "His exuberance, flair, and suavity are heavily outweighed by his inexpertness and his failure to improve." The report quickly circulated all around the country.

The *Journal* correctly predicted that Cleveland sportscaster Tommy Manning, "voice of the Indians," would be brought in to help Mac out. He was indeed added as the Series headed to Philadelphia for game three. It was an embarrassing blow for Graham.

The *Plain Dealer*, in Manning's native Cleveland, unsurprisingly hailed the choice. "Tom Manning was heard doing the detail of the World Series game yesterday during the fourth and fifth innings. Despite some nervousness, Manning did an acceptable job." He arrived for game three and did two innings of each of the remaining five games of the Classic which went the full seven. McNamee insisted that Hicks continue doing sidelight reports, which he did.

Husing's support wasn't strong, either. *Variety* termed his performance workmanlike but "he's so full of figures, percentages, and biographical data that it tends to leave the listener annoyed from the steady drone of his voice."

Doing only a handful of games made it almost impossible for McNamee and Husing to learn the game's nuances, develop a tempo, and perfect the difficult craft of calling baseball. Those who were doing it on a daily basis locally were more adept at it. The daily announcers handled what today is rudimentary. They were able to chronicle the game more proficiently and keep it more interesting.

Variety had more on Husing's 1931 broadcasts. The review not only offered detail of Husing's call but insight on the interesting way baseball was followed before the immediacy of radio. "Husing seemed to have two obstacles throughout the games, one of which he never did clear up and the second not until the last contest. Most important was that he never clearly defined a hit. Any ball driven to the outfield was either 'a line drive' or 'a fly,' and the listener had

149

to deduce for himself the chances of it falling safe until Husing recorded the movement on the bases. He could easily and immediately have designated each safe blow by crying 'a hit' and then going on from there.

"Lack of this information was not only confusing but always tended to take some of the thrill from his recounting. A long time ago an electrical scoreboard in the old Madison Square Garden (the new one then was on 50th and Eighth), used to ring a bell to register every hit while the batted ball was still on its way. It was such a tingle that the crowd would holler "Ring the Bell" when its favorites were at the plate. It was dramatic color and that being one of Husing's main objectives, he missed plenty of chances, outside of the home runs.

"The other matter which Husing never straightened out until the finish in St. Louis was his conception of a Texas leaguer. Anything to the outfield was a Texas leaguer to him for days. Not that it made much difference except to lessen his standing as an authority with the fans."

Judge Landis put his foot down after the '31 World Series. The non-day-to-day baseball announcers were out as play-by-play callers. The 1932 match featuring the Yankees and Cubs included Husing and McNamee, but both were relegated to color.

The country was now listening to baseball names on play-by-play, Manning and Totten on NBC, and Pat Flanagan and Bob Elson on CBS. Was there a Chicago connection? Absolutely. With the exception of the Indians' Manning, the other three were daily radio baseball announcers affiliated with the Chicago stations. Landis, who approved each selection, was Chicago-based and familiar with those in the Windy City. After all, both the Cubs and Sox were on the air. The Yankees, Giants, and Dodgers were still banned from doing so by their owners.

Through the '30s when the more-than-competent Elson was prominently featured on the World Series, it was always said that his friendship with the commissioner didn't hurt him in getting assignments. Landis would be exposed to Elson's work all season.

In 1932 in New York, five stations again latched on to CBS and NBC, and Gross opined in the *Daily News*: "What I can and will say about the opening broadcasts of the World Series is that they were probably the best from a technical standpoint in the history of the game. Both Graham McNamee of NBC and Ted Husing of Columbia were shoved into the background, doing only the crowd descriptions and the summaries. The play-by-play was handled by Hal Totten and Tom Manning for NBC, while Bob Elson, star announcer of WGN, and Pat Flanagan did the same for Columbia. These fellows know the fine points of the battle and proved it. But it must be admitted that none of 'em ever achieved the drama that Graham and Ted drummed up on such occasions."

It was the Series in which Babe Ruth allegedly pointed to the spot in the stands where he would hit a home run. Totten, interviewed 40 years later, said, "That was all a figment of some New York sportswriter's imagination. It became so generally accepted that I believe in the end, Babe almost believed it himself. I interviewed him on the field the next season and he told me, 'I may be a fool, but not that big a one. If I'd done that, Charlie Root [the Cubs pitcher] would have stuck that ball right in my ear, and I wouldn't be here today.'"

By the end of the 1934 fall encounter "the two great masters of fancy verbiage" were gone completely. McNamee, who had been the subject of ridicule, had little left to contribute. Husing lambasted the umpires in his color role in 1934 and didn't qualify for Landis's approval in 1935. "There is one announcer, you gentlemen know him, who isn't here, and I don't have to go into that," the czar of baseball told his gathering of 1935 World Series play-by-play men, as he went through his dos and don'ts with them before the first game. The esteemed late sportswriter Shirley Povich blasted Landis for his action. "Husing broadcast what he saw, and because he broadcast what he saw, he is penalized. He was no puppet up there in the press box to be maneuvered by the whims of baseball officials who can't stand criticism." Other scribes also felt that Landis's censorship was repugnant.

In the early years, the announcing assignments for the October championships were under the aegis of the commissioner. And despite his assigning of "baseball people," Ben Gross said, "Take my word for it. For a clear, concise, and really understandable picture of the game as a whole, nothing can take the place of a well-written account in a newspaper."

Hardly a ringing endorsement of the radio beat he covered.

In 1933 Fred Hoey, a New England baseball institution who worked long and hard for a Series assignment, got the blessings of boss Landis. But it would backfire, almost embarrassingly. Fred could imbibe. In the fourth inning of the first game at the Polo Grounds, he was working the CBS broadcast and his voice silenced. It was brushed off as a bad cold. Others knew better. He apparently had one too many drinks the night before. Some even said that he was enticed by members of rival NBC.

If that was the case, Hoey got a little revenge in 1936 when Mutual had Red Barber and Bob Elson slated to do the All-Star Game from Boston. After a fairly big buildup, the fledgling network was told by authorities that there was no space available for its broadcast crew. Mutual was forced to take a feed of the Yankee Network (which had nothing to do with the New York Yankees), featuring Hoey and Linus Travers.

The 1930s featured Ty Tyson, the "voice of the Tigers" on WWJ. When Mickey Cochrane's Tigers won the pennant in 1934, Landis wouldn't allow Ty, a Detroit broadcast fixture with the Tigers since 1927, to announce on the networks. The commissioner felt that Tyson was too much of a rooter. To overcome criticism and protest, Landis permitted Tyson to do the Series locally on WWJ. With the Tigers headed for another Series in 1935 and having obtained a petition from some 600,000 Michigan fans, the commissioner acceded. Tyson worked with Hal Totten on NBC. Tyson was beloved. Detroit Mayor Edward Jefferies proclaimed May 26, 1947, Ty Tyson Day in honor of the announcer's 25th anniversary with WWJ.

Flanagan, a Chicago legend in the 1920s on WBBM, spent his later years in Phoenix before his death in 1963. Al McCoy, the longtime "voice of the National Basketball Association's Phoenix Suns" arrived in the Valley of the Sun in the late '50s and was doing minor-league baseball. "I heard Flanagan as a kid growing up in the Midwest so I invited him to do a few innings of play-by-play with me one night. He would turn to me and whisper, 'Who is that about to bat?'"

In his prime, Flanagan had his supporters, including a fan who wrote a flowery letter published in the *Sporting News*. "Between Pat Flanagan's broadcast and that of all too many announcers is the difference between reading history from the pen of Voltaire or reading it from the encyclopedia. The story may be the same, but only Flanagan has the power to stir the imagination, warm the blood, and create the fever pitch of enthusiasm."

Voltaire might have been the right analogy. Flanagan actually was a professor of philosophy before he turned his attention to play-by-play.

Manning started with the Indians in the mid-1920s and continued as the "voice of the Tribe" until 1932 when rights shifted from WTAM to WHK. That's when ex-major-leaguer Jack Graney got the assignment. Graney later became the first ex-baseball player to do a World Series when he was teamed with France Laux on CBS in 1935. At first, there was reluctance on the part of Landis because Graney had played the game. But Jack approached Judge Landis and said, "My playing days are over. I'm now a sportscaster and should be regarded as such." The commissioner concurred.

Associated with powerhouse KMOX in St. Louis, Laux called six straight world championships, 1933–38, for CBS. He picked up the play-by-play after Ted Husing wore out his welcome with Landis. By all accounts, Laux, who influenced future broadcasters such as Merle Harmon and Bill King, was a good reporter. A nuts-and-bolts type, Laux called Browns and Cardinals games from 1929 through 1946. When the styles of flashy announcers such as Harry Caray and Dizzy Dean surfaced, Laux, according to the indomitable St. Louis scribe Bob Broeg, became "too old-timey." He was slowly eased into management.

Manning worked seven network Series between 1931 and 1938. Through his friendship with McNamee, he forged a profitable relationship with NBC where he was assigned football games and boxing matches. He returned for a year of Indians play-by-play in the mid-1950s but by then he was deaf in one ear, and the rigors of plane travel were just too much.

In 1933 six New York stations belted out the World Series, all taking feeds from either CBS or NBC. Franklin D. Roosevelt was in his first year in the White House, and a round-trip on the New York Central between Manhattan and Albany was all of $2.

In 1934 radio baseball enjoyed an influx of cash, its first major advertising sponsorship. The benefactor was the Ford Motor Company, and the automotive company got seven games out of the Cardinals-Tigers matchup. Henry Ford himself negotiated the deal with Commissioner Landis.

Coverage by three networks for the first time in World Series history occurred in 1935 with the evolution of Mutual. Landis permitted the network to join the other two webs on the eve of the Classic.

Initially, Mutual had just four affiliates but the signals presented were outstanding. WGN in Chicago and WOR in New York are 50,000 watts, WXYZ, the station in Detroit that originated *The Lone Ranger*, had a more-than-adequate stick, and WLW in Cincinnati could sometimes be heard from coast to coast back then. Its wattage in 1935 was an overpowering 500,000 watts before later being reduced to 50,000, which it still is today.

Ford re-upped in 1935 and spent $355,000 for the privilege. Of it, $100,000 went to baseball and the rest to the trio of networks. There were 194 stations in all airing the Tigers-Cubs entanglement. (NBC got $120,000, CBS $115,000, and upstart Mutual $20,000). Today, all this won't buy one spot on World Series television. The commercial plugs that year were a soft sell. There was no hyperbole about the car's power, durability, or economy. The few announcements were nonintrusive and came only between innings. They informed the audience that the new Ford models would be out a few days after the end of the October championships.

The three network crews were abiding strictly to the commandments of Landis. *Variety*'s review reflects the flavor. "Though the daily newspaper sportswriters covering the games indulged in plenty of *ifs*, *ands*, and *buts*, this type of experting was kept off the air. Mutual, as the junior web of the three, didn't get the preferred broadcast positions. Occasionally, Barber and Bob Elson had to wait before they can make a definitive call. So while Mutual was on its feet, it was staggering a bit for accreditation."

Fifty years later, Barber sat in the den of his relatively modest Tallahassee home telling one of his admirers never to complain about broadcast location or other personal problems. "Listeners don't care," a retired Barber said. In 1935 Barber, 27, was just happy to announce baseball's golden event.

So the year that the beer can was invented in Richmond, Virginia, 1935, the man who would later push Schaefer in Brooklyn made his classic debut. It would be the first of 11 October affairs that he would illuminate on the radio. Nine of the 11 would be for Mutual, two for NBC. For his partner, Elson, it would be his second of nine network classics. Quinn Ryan, whose affiliation was WGN and whose roots traced back to the 1925 Series with McNamee, joined Barber and Elson. Who was Ryan addressing when he broadcast? "I talk to the boys in the barbershop back home," he would say unabashedly.

In game one, Ryan, according to Red, stumbled along with his pre- and postgame remarks. Elson did the first three and last three innings. Red reported the middle three. John Clark, WLW's station manager raised hell with Mutual, and by game two in Detroit, Elson and Barber split the play-by-play evenly. And by the time the Series reached Chicago, Ryan was taken off the broadcasts. Barber now extemporized through the before- and after-game broadcast proceedings. What did Barber get paid for his first World Series broadcast? Nothing. He got no more than his weekly salary from WLW. That's the way it was then.

In 1936 there was a to-do over Red's services. Barber was an employee of WLW and was then the "voice of the Reds." WLW was a Mutual affiliate, and his name was submitted for approval by the Judge. Landis permitted Red to do the games on Mutual. Then a tiff of sorts developed between WLW and Mutual, and on the eve of the Yankees-Giants Series the station switched affiliation to NBC. The sponsor, Ford, had made a sponsorship commitment to Mutual on the basis of the precocious redhead announcing the games. It told the commissioner that if Barber is moved to NBC, it saw no reason to fulfill its sponsorship commitment.

Initially, it was decided that the fairest thing to do was to have Barber not work at all. It might have been fair to the networks but not to the fans. So Red, perturbed that he couldn't work the Series, proceeded to South Bend to do a Notre Dame football game.

He was so dispirited that he didn't even listen to the first game on the radio. The phone rang in his hotel room almost immediately. It was WLW telling him to report to New York. He took the next train and reported to NBC in time to do the second game. The Southerner was in New York for the first time ever. And there he was, broadcasting the first subway Series since 1923. He didn't miss much the first day. Game one was played in a downpour.

The two stadiums, the Polo Grounds and Yankee Stadium, were just a Babe Ruth blast apart. But first it was a matter of an announcers' meeting at NBC. It was in the office of network boss, John Royal, that Barber met his partners, Manning and Tyson. McNamee, missing his first Series since entering radio, was at the production conclave. At that point he served as no more than a front man and glad hander. It was nonetheless a thrill for Barber to be formally introduced to his idol for the first time. Red felt that McNamee was being blamed for trivial mistakes and that the criticism of him was much ado over nothing.

As he got set to work the broadcast, Red's feelings must have been eerie. "The great Graham was sitting only a chair's width away from the microphone, but it might as well have been an eternity." Just 28 years old

Red Barber

at the time and after a couple of innings of work at the Polo Grounds, Red got the greatest endorsement for which he could dream. Mac gave him a squeeze and said, "Kid, you've got it." It couldn't get any better for America's fair-haired baseball broadcaster.

With Red still awaiting the outcome of the NBC-Mutual dispute over his services during game one, Gross gave the nod to Mutual's Bob Elson for best job of the day. "Bob had more verve than the rest." When Red got to Yankee Stadium, he described the hordes of fans sitting on building rooftops behind the outfield wall. "They paid these landlords as much as a dollar for the privilege of the vantage point."

Barber shared the play-by-play with Manning and Tyson, but it was Red who sparkled. After Lou Gehrig battled a tough sky to catch a pop fly, Barber's words captured the moment brilliantly. "Lou twists his head wryly as though to shake tears out of his eyes."

Later in the game, baseball's pioneering broadcaster was behind the mike when Joe DiMaggio was batting. "Joe's a dirt picker-upper. He gets a handful and throws it away. Now Joe walks to the plate, cocks the bat high in the air, now behind the right ear, waiting."

Barber was a man ahead of his times. The other two were pedestrian. Manning ended sentences with "you know." "The stadium is packed today, you know," or "The weather is nice, you know." Tyson's idea of description was "a battle of two fat boys on the hill, one fat, one fatter, Hadley and Fitzsimmons."

Manning earned his first job in Cleveland when he won a yelling contest. It started with selling newspapers. "The paper had an outing for the newsboys, and one of the events was a yelling contest. Well, I had a high falsetto with unlimited carrying power and I won. A little later, I was at a boxing match, and the ring announcer failed to show up. Someone pointed to me and said, "there's the kid who won the yelling contest. He can do the announcing." Manning called Ohio State football games for more than 30 years and covered other college football games for NBC Radio.

There weren't any New York announcers assigned to the all–New York 1936 games because the New York teams still banned local broadcasts. It was another all–New York Series in 1937, and it apparently didn't impress Ford. Considering the matchup "anticlimactic," the automotive giant dropped its sponsorship of the World Series leaving the three network broadcasts self-sustaining and the commissioner responded by tightening the economic vice. As long as Ford was plucking down a $100,000 rights fee, the network announcers were given the red carpet treatment. Without the corporate support, Landis made each announcer, each technician, and anyone else associated with the production of the broadcasts, pay $6.60 per ticket per game.

When it appeared that Ford would not renew, the commissioner pitched but failed to land General Mills, makers of Wheaties. He also got close to a deal with a couple of the offspring companies of the Standard Oil Company but they too didn't materialize. As a judge before he was appointed baseball boss, Landis presided over a landmark case which caused the breakup of the oil giant.

To this point, one NBC production went out over both its Red and Blue Networks. But by 1938 NBC felt government pressure on its ownership of two networks. It was construed at the time as monopolistic, and eventually NBC would have to sell one. So as the Cubs and Yankees participated, NBC fed two separate productions for the first and only time. It meant that the Series was on an all-time high four webs. NBC now needed another announcing crew. With the Pirates in the pennant hunt, it received a petition of 15,000 signatures from loyal baseball fans in the Pittsburgh area urging the appointment of local favorite Rosey Rowswell. Although the Bucs led the National League in September, they didn't make the World Series, but Rowswell got the nod nonetheless.

Rowswell was a Pittsburgh institution, and according to his successor, the colorful Bob Prince, the progenitor of the Midwestern style of rooting. It was an infectious style that spread to the Gunner himself and to others such as Bert Wilson in Chicago, Earl Gillespie in Milwaukee, and of course, Harry Caray in St. Louis. Rowswell did the Pirates from 1936 through 1954 and earned the boundless loyalty of the fans in the tri-state region of Pennsylvania, Ohio, and West Virginia.

A Pirate home run was greeted uniquely, "Hurry up, Aunt Minnie, raise the window," or "Open the Window, Aunt Minnie, here it comes." At Forbes Field or in the studio where he would re-create road games, the signature call was always accompanied by the sound effect of glass being shattered. And Aunt Minnie was sure kept busy in Rosey's days by home run king Ralph Kiner.

The only New York announcer involved in the Series broadcast was Stan Lomax. A journalist by training, not a play-by-play man, Lomax was a WOR daily fixture for more than 40 years. He worked with Bob Elson on Mutual when the 1938 Series was being played in New York.

But the 1938 World Series broadcast was muzzled. The networks could not broadcast the clubhouse celebrations. It had already grown into a radio custom but after the Yankees' four-game sweep, fans didn't hear any champagne bottles popping on air. Manager Joe McCarthy put a ban on the extemporaneous coverage, a ban that resulted from an earlier incident when a player made a radio remark that was considered offensive.

The national audience might not have heard blaring celebrations or cacophonous screams of joy in the victorious Yankee clubhouse, but for the first time it heard the mellifluous and seductive sound of Mel Allen. The Alabama native had arrived in New York in 1937, manifesting his precocity on Manhattan College and Fordham University football broadcasts over WINS. He was hired as a staff announcer at Bill Paley's CBS to be an understudy to newsman Bob Trout and sports giant Ted Husing. In 1938 Allen did color for Bill Dyer, a Philadelphia announcer, and Laux. It would be 38 years until CBS Radio would carry another World Series broadcast. But in between he would do 7 on radio and 10 on television. Between 1947 and 1963, Allen would grace the Series microphones with his warmth and love of the game 16 of the 17 years.

In 1939, as war swept through Europe, America was still at peace militarily, but the paroxysms across the Atlantic made it almost unconscionable to be at peace of mind. Yet baseball was a wonderful diversion as it would be argued later when world war escalated. There was then a clamor to put a moratorium on organized sports in deference to the military lists, which among other things pared the major-league rosters.

It also sent announcers packing. Mel Allen, Bob Elson, Al Helfer, Bill Slater, and Marty Glickman among many others were in the military. Even Larry MacPhail, who ran the Dodgers, rejoined the Armed Forces during the war in a fairly high-echelon position and apparently was involved in pivotal clandestine military activities. By the time Allen left, he had established a name for himself. The late longtime baseball man, Frank Slocum, recalled driving to a ball game with Mel on the eve of his departure. "I hope they remember me when I get back," he cried. It was the incipience of unnecessary insecurity that would torment Mel throughout his illustrious career. Of course, all military men were assured of their jobs when they returned home.

Baseball business was churning. Without a sponsor for a couple of years after being dropped by Ford, Gillette stepped to the plate in 1939. The commissioner granted Gillette an exclusive, and not until 1960 would it relinquish any of its exclusivity. It had say over announcers, networks, and more.

There were repercussions. The sponsor made a deal with Mutual which granted it exclusive broadcast rights. CBS and both NBC's were out. It would be the first World Series to be carried on just one network since 1926. NBC and CBS, the two older webs, were furious.

Mutual was even more furious. It was running into obstacles tying up stations. It was the youngest of the three networks and had the fewest affiliates. One of its hopes in securing the rights to the Fall Classic was to increase the size of its network. After all, the Series was of great appeal nationally. The Federal Communications Commission wanted to establish whether the public interest was violated by CBS and NBC. Did they put pressure on their stations, making it difficult for them to take the Mutual feed? Did NBC and CBS take steps to exert influence on its affiliated stations not to carry the Mutual broadcast?

While CBS and NBC knew that they couldn't get carriage rights back, they also knew that Mutual assured Gillette minimum clearances for commercial purposes. Clearances are usually based on percentage of the country covered. Mutual's Fred Weber registered informal complaints with the commission of an alleged conspiracy by rivals CBS and NBC. The FCC sent out a questionnaire to suspected stations, those that might have carried the first game then dropped off the World Series network, and to others who might have considered carriage but were intimidated not to take the broadcasts.

The hubbub and Mutual's exclusivity of the World Series did dramatically increase its number of affiliates. Remember that the network was made up of just four stations when it began four years earlier in 1935. But even by 1944, when Mutual claimed 300 domestic stations and additional ones in Canada and Cuba, the network failed to clear stations in major cities such as Phoenix, Miami, and Houston.

It's hard to believe that Bill Paley was losing much sleep over the whole Mutual–World Series tiff. Net profits at CBS were more than $4 million for the first time in 1939, an increase of 40 percent over 1938.

The move to Mutual and the fact that there were holes in major markets did affect ratings.

The Yankees' four-game sweep over the Reds in 1939 did a 21 rating, far below a cumulative high of 31 when all networks were running the game in 1938. The ratings would improve to a 25 in 1940 when the championship would extend to seven contests.

Between 1939 and 1943, the Red Barber–Bob Elson team was prominent on World Series broadcasts. Elson, known as "The Commander," was in the Navy in 1942, so the two voices who would dominate radio baseball in New York through the mid-1960s paired in the booth, Mel Allen and Red Barber. In 1943 Elson was allowed a leave to come back and handle the broadcasts. A *Time* magazine article previewing the '42 Series referred to Barber as "the verse of Brooklyn" and to Allen as "the skyrocket."

From 1941 through 1946, Gillette and the lords of baseball, first Judge Landis and later Happy Chandler, who became commissioner in 1945, appointed Bill Corum to do color and commentary. Corum would do many other events on Gillette's behalf, including heavyweight championship fights and big football games. A thick voice, thickened further by years of cigarette smoking, Bill was a gifted writer and columnist for the *New York Journal American.*

In 1947 when Leo Durocher was suspended from baseball for associating with undesirables, Corum blasted Commissioner Chandler's decision. Was it then a matter of coincidence that Corum didn't work the great 1947 Yankees-Dodgers subway Series? When the owners didn't renew Chandler and the more media-friendly Ford Frick took over as baseball boss in 1951, Corum with his deep Missouri drawl was welcomed back. He eventually moved to Churchill Downs in Louisville where he ran the track that annually hosts the Kentucky Derby. It was there that he popularized the phrase "run for the roses."

Mutual was back battling a business issue in 1941. The battleground was New York where interest was heightened by an all–New York Series. Sports announcer, later turned actor, Paul Douglas told his audience to "shine up your nickels boys, it's a subway Series." (The token was then five cents, of course.) The Dodgers and Yankees were about to go at it. By that point, Muzak was in business, piping music into elevators, lounges, and restaurants. It intended to pick up Mutual's Series broadcast and make it available in its subscribing restaurants. Mutual told Muzak, wait a minute. The network wanted to protect its turf. It sought the injunction of a judge. It was adjudicated that Muzak could carry the games but it had to carry the Gillette spots and put up signs outside restaurants that the broadcasts were courtesy of Mutual and Gillette.

Did it help ratings? In 1941 the Series rating jumped to 32.8, a fantastic increase over the 25.2 the year before. The continuing growth of Mutual's affiliates helped the audience numbers grow. But by 1942, with the world at war, there was a dip to 30.1. Mutual explained the decrease was due to work in war plants and kindred activities which had reduced the number of daytime stay-at-homes.

Between 1944 and 1946 the World Series didn't include a New York team, and its radio coverage didn't include either New York staples, Barber or Allen. Mel was back from the war and reestablishing himself. Barber was sailing along in Brooklyn where the borough was eating out of his hand.

In 1944 an all–St. Louis Series matched the Browns and Cardinals. A newspaper reported that Barber made a request to Commissioner Landis that he be appointed to the radio broadcasts of the All-Star Game and World Series. Barber denied that he approached baseball's boss. As it turned out, he didn't work either of the two events. Gillette had a lot to do with this decision, and Red could not have been too happy with the razor company.

There was a sour history. Barber's relationship with Gillette was never very good. In baseball's off-season leading to the 1944 campaign, Gillette undertook a Yankees-Giants sponsorship after the clubs' dual package wasn't on at all in 1943. At that point, according to Red, Gillette made a run at him to cross boroughs and leave the Dodgers. He wouldn't, and Gillette wasn't happy. So in 1944 Bill Slater, basically a football and track announcer, and Don Dunphy, the boxing announcer, both of whom had worked the Giants-Yankees package during the regular season, would get the honors for both the All-Star Game and the Series. It would all come to a head between Red and the sponsor in 1953 when the two parties couldn't come to terms on a fee for the World Series telecast.

In 1945 the military man, Slater, back from Army responsibilities and back for another Series, joined brother Al Helfer, closely associated with Mutual. "Out of all of them, Husing, Stern, and so on," said Marty Glickman, a young announcer perfecting his craft, "Slater was one of the nicest." Slight pause and right from the diaphragm, "and a good football broadcaster," said the man who would become a pretty good one himself. Notice that it's football which is associated first with the name Bill Slater.

Jackie Robinson had just finished up his triple-A career in 1946, the year before "all hell broke loose." The Classic was again void of a New York identity. It matched the Boston Red Sox and St. Louis Cardinals, and Barber must have been bristling. After nine straight Fall Classics when reviewers and fans generally raved over his work, 1946 would be the third straight year he would be shut out of a Series spot in the booth. His stomach must have been churning.

The critics were different then than they are today. In the 1990s the newspaper people who critique the sports announcers are generally tribunes, safeguarding the public airwaves for fairness. Adequate presentation of the game itself is expected or assumed. Today's media scribes rarely grade play-by-play

Courtesy Sheila Dunphy

In a photo probably taken during the 1942 or 1943 World Series, Don Dunphy, left, known more as an announcer for boxing, interviews Judge Kenesaw Mountain Landis. Behind Landis is St. Louis manager Billy Southworth, and to his right are Yankees manager Joe McCarthy and Larry MacPhail.

talent on the rudimentary: picture painting, pausing, drama, reportorial skills, description, personality, warmth, and passion. There's more of an emphasis on announcer honesty and integrity, and serving as watchdogs for shills and for those who chronicle with a jaded eye.

Prior to the 1980s the critics could be harsher than many in the local papers today. They could be downright acerbic, lambasting the on-air correspondents who opined instead of sticking strictly to play-by-play. Report the game and the game only as you see it. Today there's more announcer opinion expected, albeit within a politically correct verbal environment.

The 1946 Cardinals-Red Sox Series was the last one not televised. There was peace on earth. The boys were back. Baseball would dominate the next score of years before a faster-paced society would espouse football and basketball.

Jim Britt and Arch McDonald were given the plum assignment. They would officiate over Mutual's microphones. And the reviewers didn't like it, clamoring for anybody but those whom they heard. "The World Series is over, but as far as radio, the sour taste lingers on," *Variety* reported almost bitterly. "Thousands of squawks by wire, postcard, letter, and phone calls thundered into network headquarters and individual stations complaining about the sub-par work of the announcers. Even the mayor of St. Louis telegraphed a squawk!" The magazine took seemingly everybody to task but primarily Commissioner Happy Chandler.

Britt was assigned the Series because he was "voice of the Sox and Braves" in Boston. But why McDonald? Were there some political undertones? Chandler was an ex-governor and a Democrat. McDonald, "voice of the Washington Senators," was running for a congressional seat in Maryland as a Democrat. The exposure couldn't hurt. (But as Red Barber said of the ex-Yankees play-by-play man, "The voters decided to keep him in the booth.")

McDonald, a laid-back announcer, was getting heat. Commissioner Chandler had to intercede. After the second game, the baseball czar tried some levity to quell the public's ire. He told the press, "I just went up to the broadcast booth and touched Arch McDonald. I touched him to see if he was still warm and breathing. He is both. As long as he stays warm and continues to breathe, he is going to announce the World Series."

Britt mistakenly referred to Dominick DiMaggio as the "eldest" of the three ballplaying brothers and had Boston right fielder Leon Culberson smacking a clean single when he wasn't even in the game. McDonald had teammates flying out to one another as he misidentified names, and the magazine reported that Arch had a batter thrown out on a close play after hitting a foul ball. Britt is also the fellow who once got so excited calling a home run that he said "it was under the fence." Bill Corum wasn't included in the uproar over the announcers. The newspaper man's contribution was primarily before and after the game. As a result of this public ordeal, Gillette was given even more say on announcers in ensuing years.

Red Barber had experimented with baseball's first telecast in 1939 at Ebbets Field. And while the first Series televised was in 1947, the networks were ready to start in 1946. NBC, CBS, and the now defunct Dumont were all trying to strike a deal that summer. The negotiations, though, reached a stalemate but it had nothing to do with technology. It was, rather, a reason that is common today.

The ballplayers were balking before there was even a product to fight over; they wanted a share of the video rights. The demand held up negotiations between baseball, Gillette (the exclusive sponsor), and the would-be network.

The television people finally struck a deal in 1947, just in time for a great subway Series. The Boys of Flatbush played the Bronx Bombers in the third straight World Series that extended the full seven games. The three tube networks NBC, CBS, and Dumont alternated coverage of the seven-game Series. NBC did the first game, Dumont the second, CBS the third, and so on.

Rheingold Beer offered to sponsor the telecasts in their entirety but Commissioner Chandler turned the brewery down. Gillette put up additional bucks for the television coverage, and Ford came in as a cosponsor. If it sounds like a big deal it wasn't. Only a small percentage of Americans had sets, and those who did had to squint their eyes because the monitors were minuscule.

Television announcing pioneer Bob Stanton did the play-by-play and color of the first-ever Series telecast. It was on NBC. He basically worked all nine innings alone. Joe Cronin served as commercial announcer, doing live spots for Gillette. He would rove between television and radio. Gillette's television spots in its World Series TV debut were hardly sophisticated. Before the game started, one of the two cameras doing the entire game focused on Cronin looking down at his script throughout the entire spot and reading it verbatim on the tube. After the first inning, Cronin ambled over to radio and read the exact same plug. "Look sharp. Be sharp. Feel sharp," said Gillette, except the commercial spots weren't sharp. Ford, meanwhile, had filmed commercials that it ran during its advertising time.

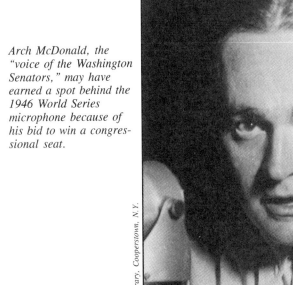

Arch McDonald, the "voice of the Washington Senators," may have earned a spot behind the 1946 World Series microphone because of his bid to win a congressional seat.

© National Baseball Hall of Fame Library, Cooperstown, N.Y.

Variety's reaction after game one tells the story. "Because of the small screen and the limited scope of the camera lens, viewers still received the impression of the field being cut off directly behind the pitcher's box. Unless a ball was hit to the outfield, the most comprehensive view furnished was one including the pitcher, batter, catcher, and umpire." There were problems with the late afternoon shadows which obscured the picture, and viewers also felt that the initial Classic telecast lacked the intimacy of radio.

But one thing that started that very first year of TV coverage hasn't changed a bit in the better than half century since. The cameras kept spotlighting the celebrities at the ballpark. There were shots of Danny Kaye, Leo Durocher (out of baseball that year), Laraine Day, and Babe Ruth. It didn't take long for the lords of baseball to figure that by showing a star-studded lineup in the crowd, women would be attracted to attend future games to just rub elbows with these highly visible personalities.

Most television-viewing back then was in bars and taverns. Attendance at matinee "women's" pictures such as *Desire Me* held steady but the Series on the tube did cause a slump of as much as 50 percent at several Broadway deluxe showcasers.

The production was so primitive that *Variety* debated whether the telecast was any improvement at all over radio where Mel Allen and Red Barber brought the October matchup to life. Together for only a second time and for the first Series in five years, the two elegant baseball voices sparkled. And when great ones, the likes of Barber and Allen, are given material, the results are memorable. A seven-game Series, a near no-hitter, and a fantastic game-saving catch, robbing Joe DiMaggio, made for an unforgettable Series.

Could it have gotten any better? The postwar economy was beginning to boom. Baseball's color barrier was broken, and the man who broke it, speedster Jackie Robinson, would steal second base in the very first Series game against the Yankees. Television, while still an embryo,

Mel Allen

© *National Baseball Hall of Fame Library, Cooperstown, N.Y.*

promised such a bright future for news, sports, and entertainment. And on radio, the two best announcers in the game, certainly from a provincial New York view, were detailing the unfolding drama with their seductive southern drawls. The setting was perfect.

The economics were good, too. Gillette willingly bankrolled the October doings for a ninth year, and affiliates were lining up, despite pressure from competitive networks. Mutual lined up 600 stations for the 1947 games. This was a dozen or so years before Castro, and they listened in English in Cuba.

Gillette was spending about $1.5 million in radio advertising in 1947. Nearly all the dollars were spent on sports advertising. *The Gillette Cavalcade of Sports* was blossoming. While Craig Smith turned into Red Barber's nemesis as the company's visible and apparently parsimonious advertising director, the man responsible for the company's coffers was its Harvard-trained president, Joseph Spang. He believed in radio and sports. Smith executed his wishes.

Many classics later, 49 to be precise, Vin Scully graced the CBS Radio microphones, covering another Yankees championship, a come-from-behind effort over Atlanta. He reminisced with partner Jeff Torborg. While banter is certainly not Scully's on-air forte, the subject of the subway series arose. Torborg brought up the names Allen and Barber, names synonymous with the postwar subway Series, and it must have struck a nerve with Scully.

The ex-manager Torborg, New Jersey-raised, recalled arguments between fans on New York street corners. The better of the two superstar announcers would be the debate. Hallowed names, Scully thought, likening the polemics to the perpetual argument of the day—who was the best clarinet player, Benny Goodman or Artie Shaw?

There was a profound contrast in styles but at least an ostensible mutual respect for one another. Red was a family man, essentially introverted, his words guarded. He considered baseball announcing a job. Mel was single, extroverted, garrulous, and thought of baseball as his life.

Longtime baseball man Frank Slocum knew both. "Barber was about himself, and Allen was about baseball," he said. Red's mission was to paint a picture of the baseball game. Mel's mark was to have fun. Barber was stern. Allen was indulgent. Yes, they were both Southern by birth. Barber was Episcopalian, from a line of American ancestry, and Allen was Jewish, the son of Russian immigrants.

Allen espoused baseball superstitions, Barber did not. And it manifested itself in the great 1947 Series. In game four, New York's Bill Bevens was pitching a no-hitter at Ebbets Field and just one out away from baseball immortality. He had to retire just one more man, Cookie Lavagetto. It was 2–1 Bombers, and the Dodgers had runners on first and second. Allen had done the first four and a half innings, Barber the last four and a half. If it was Allen's turn, listeners could have bet the mortgage that Mel would make only oblique mention of the no-hitter.

Some will say that the very quiver in Allen's voice would have heightened the suspense. Superstitious, yes. Would it temper the drama of the call? Only if the listener was truly unaware of the developing feat.

Red made plenty mention of the no-hitter and made reference to no-hitters and near no-hitters of the past. Barber thought this superstition business was nonsense. Allen cringed as he heard Red violate the sanctity of one of baseball's oldest unwritten rules.

In baseball retirement later, Red told his National Public Radio partner, Bob Edwards, "When I leaned into the mike and said that Bevens had given one run, so many walks, and no hits, the breath gurgled in Allen's throat like a country boy trying to swallow a chinaberry seed."

"Allen was of the hoodoo school, one of its staunch members," Red said of Mel. Phil Rizzuto, one who would hardly scoff at the witchcraft of play-by-play, underscores Mel's superstition. If late in a game Phil reported that a Yankees batter was three-for-three or four-for-four, Mel would cast a nefarious eye at him.

Barber's pithy call better than half a century ago would be pegged as one of baseball's greatest:

Swung on, there's a drive hit out toward the right-field corner.
Henrich is going back! He can't get it. It's off the wall for a base hit.
Here comes the tying run, and here comes the winning run!

Young budding announcers can dissect the economized description and appreciate the impact of each spoken word and the ironic eloquence of verbal condensation. By bellowing the word *hit*, fans knew immediately that Bevens' no-hitter had been broken up, and smartly, he never said "here comes Gionfriddo racing from second, here comes Miksis from first." The punch line was delivered perfectly: "Here comes the tying run, and here comes the winning run!" Barber hit the heart of the matter with unequaled drama. The beauty was in the simplicity. It was Barber at his best.

As Cookie was being mobbed by his teammates, Red:

It will take a police escort to get the Dodgers away from Lavagetto.

Stan Fischler, a prolific sports author and lifelong New Yorker, will never forget the day. "For some reason, I left our Williamsburgh house at the end of the eighth inning and started walking around the neighborhood. Usually, there was no need for a radio. Red's voice came out of cars, stoops, porches, taxi cabs, and even beauty parlors. It was eerie that day. The streets were quiet, intensely so. People stopped their activity to listen. All of a sudden, there was this tremendous roar. People poked their heads out of their windows and exulted." Were they watching on television? Astonished by the question, "Are you kidding? Who had a television then?" A Barber masterpiece, October 3, 1947.

Game six was played at Yankee Stadium. The Bums had no margin for error. They needed a win to force a seventh game. Red again had the last four and a half frames. Brooklyn led 8–5 in the sixth inning. Joe DiMaggio was up with two on. A blast ties it. Red:

Swung on, belted! It's a long one! Deep into left center. Back goes Gionfriddo. Back, back, back, back, back, back. He makes a one-handed catch against the bullpen! Oh-ho, Doctor!!

Normally impervious to emotion, this would be about as impassioned as Red Barber would get. Unforgettable!

Can you imagine, an all–New England World Series? It almost happened in 1948 when Cleveland and the Boston Braves met. But first there was a playoff game at Fenway Park where the Indians beat the Red Sox, 8–3, to qualify for the Series. That's when New Yorkers heard one of their future Knicks announcers and longtime WOR newsman, Lester Smith. He was then a Boston sportscaster, and the telecast was picked up in New York on Channel 5.

Mel Allen worked the radio broadcast with Boston's Jim Britt, who was back despite the criticism of him a couple of years earlier. Barber acquiesced to Gillette's request that he help dignify the television effort. The Redhead teamed with future Tigers announcer, then Indians telecaster, Van Patrick. Allen battled a cold throughout the championship, and Barber endured Allen as a companion on the train who spent half the time gargling with saltwater.

A sign of overcommercialization in 1948 is almost laughable today. Gillette drew the wrath of the Cleveland newspapers. "We are sure that Gillette got little good, stuffing commercials into the listeners' ears between every inning. As a last resort, the Federal Communications Commission should step in." What would those scribes say today when the commercial time between innings is more than twice as long as it was in 1948, two minutes instead of one minute, and there are drop-ins galore.

Growing pains? How about television coverage in 1948? Gillette graduated to filmed commercials but New Yorkers had to settle for the games from Boston only. Because there was no coaxial cable from Cleveland to New York, the games couldn't be fed to the Big Apple. And when televised from Boston, there were many wrinkles. On-air, Barber asked for certain shots that the network couldn't accommodate or just ignored altogether. And most views of the battery cut off the top of the pitcher's head.

Ingenuity? How about a television version of a re-created telecast? When the Indians played the Red Sox in Boston in the one-game playoff, WEWS in Cleveland couldn't pick up the game live. So Van Patrick and Tris Speaker sat in a studio with a large scoreboard bought at a downtown department store. It showed runs, hits, and errors. As each player stepped to the plate, his nameplate was shown on the scoreboard. A base hit produced a moving tract progressing down the baselines. With the use of the ticker and the gadgetry, Patrick and Speaker pulled off a television re-creation.

"It was Brooklyn against the world. They didn't think that they were part of the five boroughs. It was the working class against everybody," Mel Allen would say. In 1949 he was back in the radio booth with Red. The Bombers, in a heart-stopping pennant race, beat out the Red Sox, then took care of the Boys of Flatbush in five World Series games. Mel would have worked the radio whether or not New York advanced. He was told by Mutual about a month before the games started that the network wanted him on the broadcasts. Radio's growing competition, television, would present the Series in 27 cities (in the East and Midwest) with a total of 2 million sets in circulation.

Through 1978 the World Series broadcast booth was graced by a member of each participating club's announce team. On either television or radio, it would be a special treat each fall, sprinkling the sports broadcast landscape. The World Series was truly "world." The booth was a melting pot and from the speakers came a multicultured sound. It was Broadway on tour.

It was the return of Russ Hodges with the Giants in 1962 or the mellifluous Vin Scully with the Dodgers in 1959. Whether it was Harry Caray bellowing "Holy Cow" or Waite Hoyt broadcasting in the past tense, it was a crisp unique style of a popular regional voice. Hoyt would say, "He was out," instead of the more popular "he is out." By the time it was uttered off the lips of the play-by-play man, Hoyt would argue, the play already happened.

The 1950 Phillies-Yankees Series meant Gene Kelly, who broadcast the combination A's-Phillies package in Philadelphia. Gene will be remembered for his McCarthy slipup. Prior to a game one night, he was brought a note that Joe McCarthy had died. Kelly proceeded to tell his audience that the ex-Yankees manager had passed on and how baseball had lost a dedicated friend. It was a nice touch except that the baseball McCarthy was alive and well in Buffalo. It was the Communist-hawking senator who had died. The nonhoofer Gene Kelly had to do some serious dancing.

Kelly also had to extricate himself out of another verbal blunder. Broadcasting a late-night game back from California, it was past midnight in Philadelphia. After a double play, he said, "If you're scoring in bed, it was six, four, three."

The 1950 fall encounter would also be the first where the team's participating stations were allowed to take the Mutual feed in addition to the Mutual affiliate in the team's market. WOR, the Mutual affiliate, no longer had an exclusive when any of the three New York teams advanced. WINS, the Yankees affiliate, was on board that first year of the new decade.

In game three of the 1951 Giants-Dodgers playoff matchup, Gillette advertising boss Craig Smith stuck his head into the broadcasting booths. He told Red Barber and Russ Hodges that the announcer of the winning team would work the Series on TV. Mel Allen would join Al Helfer on radio in 1951. And because he was Mutual's lead voice on the network's *Game of the Day* broadcasts, Al Helfer handled the Series on radio the next five years.

Jack Brickhouse came East from Chicago to do his first radio Classic, working with Helfer and Corum in 1952. With his nemesis, Commissioner

Chandler, out, Corum was back in the radio booth. Jack had a distinguished career in Chicago and a wonderful relationship with the Windy City-based Commissioner Landis. But when Chandler became baseball's boss, he was concerned about Brickhouse's ties to the old administration. It took a head-to-head meeting between the two for Jack to effectively cultivate Chandler earlier.

"He told me that I wasn't for him. I told him that I didn't know what he was talking about. I said that I didn't know who would have told him that, but that I adopted a wait-and-see attitude toward his tenure as commissioner," Brickhouse recounted. "I told him that I have absolutely no apology to make for my past and my relationship with Judge Landis. At the same time I have no recollection of making any critical remark about you."

Bob Elson wasn't quite as lucky. Elson and the Judge were tight. His 1942 Series was his last. He didn't get another World Series assignment once the Judge was out of the baseball picture. When Chandler was in charge, baseball's headquarters was in Cincinnati near Happy's Kentucky home.

The 1952 World Series was the first and last time that the illustrious duo of Red Barber and Mel Allen would blend their marvelous talents on the NBC Television Network. NBC estimated that almost 70 million viewers watched it. And anybody watching or listening had to wonder about Gil Hodges, who Red once called Russ Hodges. The Dodgers' first baseman went a nightmarish 0-for-21 against Yankees pitching.

These were great New York autumns. Five of the six World Series between 1951 and 1956 were subway Series. They were all memorable to millions but in 1952 Barber was fuming over the fee that sponsor Gillette was paying him. At $200 per game, Barber was convinced that he was vastly underpaid. This was the crème de la crème, the World Series, network television's plum. He agreed to the fee but promised himself that he would have his agent negotiate his compensation next time.

The 1953 World Series was a turning point in the career of Walter Lanier Barber. When the Brooklynites advanced to play the Yankees, Gillette proudly announced that Barber had once again been appointed to work with Mel on television. The talent fee was predetermined by Gillette, and it was apparently nonnegotiable. Barber on the other hand was adamant. He told Craig Smith to work out his compensation through Bill McCaffery. Both parties were intransigent, and Red stunningly was off the telecast.

Remember that this wasn't the first run-in Red had with Gillette. According to Red, in 1944, when Gillette had the rights to the Yankees-Giants package, it made a push to have him jump ship from Brooklyn. Red refused, and the relationship between the parties was strained. At Dodgers headquarters, through all this, Branch Rickey was bought out and Walter O'Malley was in control. Red's relationship with O'Malley and the club soured, and the Dodgers didn't intercede with Gillette on his behalf.

Connie Desmond was considered Brooklyn's number two man at the time. He had already been with the ball club for 11 seasons. He was more than sufficiently talented to be a number one man in any major-league booth. But Connie was drinking, and the Dodgers and Gillette would take no chances with him on a national telecast.

When Barber informed O'Malley that he and Gillette couldn't come to terms, Walter told Red that he would nominate Scully. Vin had been in Brooklyn

Courtesy Ted Patterson

As the voice of Mutual's Game of the Day *broadcasts, Al Helfer broadcast five straight World Series beginning in 1951.*

all of four years and was just 25 years young when the '53 Series started. Unseasoned perhaps, Vin was certainly ready and drilled. When offered the assignment, there was one piece of business remaining. Whether as a courtesy or a prerequisite, he first checked with Barber. Red gave him his blessing, wished him luck, and as much as offered Scully his score book as a gesture of genuine endorsement. O'Malley did his part, too. He approached Allen, now in his third decade of Classic broadcasting, and said, "Take care of my boy, Scully."

Despite what had happened, Red felt accomplished and carried his head high. He was a principled man who effectively made a point about being paid a token sum for an esteemed and lofty task. As a "civilian" at the World Series that year, he told Yankees public relations director Red Patterson, "I own myself." While there might have been a clamor for his services, Barber would learn, as we all do at one point or another, no one is indispensable.

When all this came down, the sports world was shocked that Scully was given the gig. The sports world might have been equally as shocked with Scully's performance. He handled the exalted assignment with verbal aplomb and vocal

167

The sports world was shocked when Vin Scully, shown here in the booth with Jerry Doggett, was given the 1953 World Series TV assignment, but he handled the exalted job with verbal aplomb and vocal grace.

© National Baseball Hall of Fame Library, Cooperstown, N.Y.

grace. He was teamed with network star Mel Allen. Vin was still living with mom when "the Yankees broke the hearts of all of Brooklyn" by winning the Series in six games.

It wasn't without a few nervous moments and an uncaught violation of the commissioner's decree. The morning of game one, the Fordham prep alum threw up his mom's breakfast, by no fault of her cooking. Commissioner Ford Frick had also reminded all the radio and television talent of the "Landis Doctrine of 1935," which among other things interdicted play-by-play people from critiquing the work of the umpires. But Scully thought that Whitey Ford had tagged early on a fly ball and exclaimed as such immediately. Ford never tried to advance, and for Scully and the outcome it never became an issue.

New York's fascination with baseball in the 1950s is well documented. The Yankees were loaded. There was the pitching staff of Whitey Ford, Eddie Lopat, and Johnny Sain. There was Yogi Berra, Phil Rizzuto, and Billy Martin. Mickey Mantle was 21 in 1953. When he arrived at Ebbets Field for game three of the championship, manager Casey Stengel showed Mantle how to play the caroms off the outfield walls. Casey had played them 40 years earlier.

The Yankees and Dodgers didn't make it in 1954, but the Giants did. They would play the Cleveland Indians. The American League representative had won an enormous 111 games. The Giants were the underdogs but swept the Tribe in four. If Mickey Mantle and Duke Snider weren't there to play center field, Willie Mays was. And the Series will always be remembered for his fantastic catch in game one off the bat of slugger Vic Wertz.

The Mays catch is often replayed on radio. The audience hears the phrase "optical illusion" to describe the brilliant snare in the caverns of the Polo Grounds. But it's the audio of the television call with Jack Brickhouse and Russ Hodges that the audience hears today on radio. The '54 Series on radio was called by Jimmy Dudley and Al Helfer.

Dudley and Bob Neal were longtime partners in the Indians' booth but simply couldn't get along. Gabe Paul was running Cleveland at the time and had to separate the two. Neal was closer with Paul and survived. Dudley was let go.

Neal was part of the Series broadcast team the next three autumns. He and Al Helfer were there when "next year" finally arrived in 1955. "THIS IS NEXT YEAR" was the headline the next morning in the *Daily News*. The Dodgers had won their first World Series ever. Rookie Johnny Podres imperturbably won game seven at Yankee Stadium. He did it in grand style, shutting out the Bronxites, 2–0. Did Helfer get the goose bumps? He had worked the Dodgers with Barber their first two years on radio, 1939 and 1940.

Dodger fans were hysterical that October 4. Right after the game it was almost impossible to place a call from Manhattan to Brooklyn. Telephone officials said it was the greatest flood of calls since V-J Day in 1945. Tall chrome and glass buildings were still an architectural feat of the future. The windows of the Wall Street skyscrapers still opened in 1955, and overjoyed fans tossed home-made confetti which cascaded under brilliant sunshine onto Maiden Lane.

For Vin Scully it was also a euphoric moment. He had again worked the Series with Mel Allen on NBC Television, which lined up 185 stations for carriage. Scully did the last four and a half innings of the ultimate encounter, and at the moment of victory he was close to tears. As the crowd erupted, Scully let the pictures do the talking. He knew then as he does now, a picture is worth a thousand words. "Ladies and gentlemen, the Brooklyn Dodgers are the champions of the world." At the end of the broadcast the cordial Scully, who always maintains his equanimity, almost forgot to say goodbye to partner Allen as he left the booth overjoyed.

Brooklyn was enjoying a wave of provincial pride and unprecedented enthusiasm. But in the following morning's *New York Times*, there was an ominous note. Borough president John Cashmore ordered a survey for a new stadium in the heart of downtown Brooklyn, at Atlantic Avenue and Flatbush Avenue. The world's championship was still fresh on the mind of the community, if not the stench of celebration on its breath. "They must never leave Brooklyn," he said steadfastly, as the borough folks were still awash in emotion.

The stadium, though, was a sore subject, and the shrewd Walter O'Malley was already California dreaming. Two years later, the Dodgers' owner made the dreaded announcement. The Dodgers were headed for Los Angeles, and the golden-voiced Scully, not quite 30 at the time, was going along. Red's voice will always be remembered for echoing from stoops and tenement windows. Scully's voice would now reverberate from open vehicles and sun-drenched beaches. Barber was adored by a generation; Scully would be for two generations.

The Yankees would recapture the title the next fall when New York was treated to one last subway Series. It featured an unforgettable pitching performance. On October 8, 1956, Don Larsen made World Series history, throwing a perfect game on the hallowed grass of Yankee Stadium. To this day, the scene etched in the minds of millions is the still photograph that captured catcher Yogi Berra leaping into Larsen's arms in front of the pitcher's mound. Mel Allen worked with Vin Scully on television that day. "The only time I ever stood up and cheered was Larsen's perfect game. I didn't cheer into the microphone," the Yankee voice said.

It would be Mutual's 17th and last year of exclusive coverage of the Grand Event. The Brooklyn–New York showdown would be piped into the studios of three different radio stations—WOR, Mutual's flagship affiliate; WMGM, the Dodgers' outlet; and WINS, the home of the Yankees. Those who heard game five on one of the 800 stations hooked in will never forget where they were.

Scully and Allen would be together for their penultimate World Series on television while Bob Neal, Bill Corum, and Bob Wolff would amplify on radio. All of New York sat stiff keeping track of the nerve-tingling ninth inning. On radio, Wolff howled right through the final pitch to Dale Mitchell. The likable Wolff was at the right place at the right time. Two days later he and his partners presided over the Yankees' seventh-game victory, Mutual's final Fall Classic game, and the valedictory for the retiring pioneer, Jackie Robinson.

Milwaukee played in both the 1957 and 1958 championships. Earl Gillespie, the "voice of the Milwaukee Braves," was Midwest through and through. His idol was Chicago's Bert Wilson, and he sounded much like him. "In the '50s, Bert was making $60–70,000, and I was making in the twenties. I lived pretty well on that money back then. But he was in Chicago, and I was in Milwaukee."

When the Braves announced their move to Atlanta less than a decade later, he knew what he was doing, staying put in Brew City. In fact, he didn't even stay on to announce the team's final Milwaukee years, once it was known the Braves were lame ducks. His loyalty to the community paid off. He was a television fixture for decades, doing the sports on newscasts for years, and for 31 years called University of Wisconsin football games. Still renowned in the dairy state, Earl was bestowed the honor of leading the Badgers through the tunnel on Homecoming Day. And once he retired and left for Florida in the mid-1990s, Gillespie was brought back by a funeral home chain to do commercial spots. Part of his compensation, he chuckled, was a free funeral.

The practice then was to have the team announcer in the victorious locker room to do interviews with the winning ball club. The wild session was simulcast on both NBC Television and now NBC Radio, which secured the rights from Mutual beginning with the '57 Classic. Until recent years this was always an undertaking of complete disorganization. Champagne would pop, no one would stay put, and everybody seemed to be elbowed, pushed, and shoved.

When the Braves won the 1957 Series, Earl drew the locker room assignment and, amid the bedlam, talked to whomever he could. "When I got out, drenched, smelling of champagne, and sweaty, the first one I ran into was the daughter of manager Fred Haney. 'Oh Earl, you didn't interview my dad.' To this day, I feel terrible about it. But back then, you got whomever they threw at you."

There was no locker room assignment for Gillespie in 1958. Mel Allen was back in his glory when the Bombers won the return battle with Milwaukee, rallying back from a 3–1 deficit in games.

Jack Brickhouse

Forty-plus years after meeting Red Barber for the first time, Gillespie recalled the pioneer's suggestion. The visiting and home broadcast booths neighbored one another at County Stadium. Because Gillespie was so enthusiastic, he bellowed at full throttle throughout the game. Barber who sat right on top of the mike but never raised his voice, couldn't help but hear Earl scream all the innings he worked. Meaning well, Barber told him later, "Young man, you will burn yourself out."

In 1959, when the Chicago White Sox traveled to the Los Angeles Coliseum for the World Series, Al Lopez referred to the football stadium with its unending right field as "a freak park." What was "freaky" about the broadcast team was the glaring absence in the television or radio network broadcast booths of longtime Sox voice Bob Elson.

As the story goes, Tom Gallery, who headed up NBC Sports, had a deep dislike for the Chicago on-air institution and looked for any angle to rationalize not appointing him to the anointed position. Lindsey Nelson, then NBC's second in command to Gallery, was cognizant of his boss's dilemma. A member of the Sox announcing team had to be part of the big event's crew. He had the answer, Jack Brickhouse. The WGN Television announcer did a combined Cubs-Sox package on the independent Channel 9 and would qualify as a team representative. Elson and Gallery had apparently grown up together in the Windy City, and the animosity between the two traced its roots to their youth.

The broadcasts of baseball's last premier event in the nifty '50s caused a clamor in Chicago. The result was bizarre for the time. WCFL radio, the Sox flagship, was given special dispensation to run the games and assign its own talent. In New York and all over the country, Mel Allen and By Saam were in the radio saddle while Brickhouse and Scully graced the television booth. Elson, a Windy City icon and one of the pioneers of network World Series coverage, was constrained to Chicago.

NBC Sports chief Gallery was not one to hold back. He obviously disliked Elson but he wasn't a fan of Elson's five-time World Series partner, Red Barber, either. "I hate that Psalm-singing, sanctimonious son of a bitch," he once told Lindsey Nelson.

Saam, the longtime Phillies announcer, started his career in Philadelphia in 1938. Network radio wasn't completely void on his résumé. He had done major bowl games, dating back to the 1938 Cotton Bowl. But apparently his nerves tightened when he was given his first World Series job.

171

There were more than 90,000 at game five in Los Angeles. Many had grown accustomed to bringing their transistor radios to the Coliseum. It was about the only way to follow the balls and strikes in the oversized park. The throng and the millions of listeners, hearing Saam perhaps for the first time, must have wondered, "What's with this guy?" Mel did the first four and a half innings one game and turned it over to his Philadelphia-based partner with the usual exalting introduction. "Now to carry you along is the excellent "voice of the Phillies," By Saam." Perhaps a bit bewildered momentarily before his big moment, Saam had obviously not heard a word Mel had said. "Right you are Mel and hi everybody," an overwhelmed Saam trumpeted.

Saam's absentminded openings were hardly what earned him a spot in the Frick wing of the Hall of Fame. "Hello, By Saam, this is everybody speaking," was how this Texan hit the airwaves one day early in his career.

It's easy to get trapped in memories of baseball's past but the ironic twist to the 1960 hardball event was unforgettable. Going into the seventh game, the Yankee bats had averaged almost 13 runs in each of the team's three wins. New York batted .338 as a club for that matter in the entire Series. The Pirates' pitching staff had an inept 7.11 ERA. But maybe 7.11 was Pittsburgh's good fortune.

The Pirates, on the other hand, had just three Series home runs going into the bottom of the ninth of the seventh game. The game was tied when second baseman Bill Mazeroski ended the grueling fest by walloping a Ralph Terry pitch over the left-field wall. The Bucs were averaging not quite three runs through the first six contests but won it, 10–9.

While Maz stood waiting for the pitch that would immortalize him, Chuck Thompson was in the NBC Radio booth about to make the professional boo-boo of his on-air career. It was late in the afternoon and millions were driving around American roads listening assiduously to the dulcet-toned and pearl of a man who announced the wrong pitcher, "Art Ditmar throws . . . " Thompson erred ignominiously and forever agonizingly.

While much wasn't made of it initially, probably because of the bedlam of the moment, Anheuser-Busch played the recording as part of one of its fluffy network television commercials during the 1985 Series. Ditmar sued Anheuser-Busch for incriminating the innocent. It magnified Thompson's error but after an outstanding career he could laugh about it.

The '61 Yankees were often compared to the '27 Yankees, baseball's ultimate paragon of excellence. And how eerie. Waite Hoyt, ace of the '27 Yankee pitching staff turned Cincinnati Reds announcer, chronicled the Series on NBC Radio along with Bob Wolff.

Hoyt, a recovering alcoholic and native New Yorker, made his mends. He started his second career while in New York doing all sorts of studio work, including pre- and postgame shows on the Brooklyn broadcasts over WOR in the 1940s. He was determined to make it as a play-by-play man, and when the opportunity arose in Cincinnati in 1942, he jumped. Before he left, Hoyt consulted Red Barber on the nuances of scoring. Barber agreed to help but on one condition. Still imbibing at the time, Waite could get a bit boisterous after a few. So Red insisted that Hoyt bring his wife when they met. He did, and the two had a productive visit.

But for Hoyt, known as "the aristocrat of baseball," it wasn't his play calling that made him popular in the Queen City. It was rather his nimble wit and captivating ability as a storyteller that had Reds fans rooting for rain delays. It was then that he produced notable narrations of interesting episodes in his baseball career. After all, baseball was then played during the day, and at night he and Ruth would have "ample time to go here and there." A pallbearer at the Babe's funeral, Hoyt drew the praise of the fastidious Barber. "He went to the microphone highly intelligent, industrious, and a great storyteller." In Cincinnati one day a Reds game was rained out, so he re-created five out-of-town games off the wire simultaneously. It drew a flood of praise from fans who could have sworn that he was at each venue reporting live. It was improvised play-by-play but done so imaginatively that the broadcast flowed like a river of words.

The Hall of Fame ex-Yankees pitcher and accomplished Cincinnati baseball raconteur had a lot of pitching stories to spout, but all about the New York hurlers. They started with Whitey Ford, who didn't allow a run in 14 innings, and continued with Luis Arroyo, the star of the bullpen during the regular season who was hardly needed against the Reds. He pitched just four innings in the Yankees' five-game win.

The Cuban missile crisis made October 1962 a grim and fear-inflicting month. Signs were posted all over the country for the nearest bomb shelters, and schoolchildren didn't know what tomorrow would bring. As the Yankees and San Francisco Giants extended their Series to seven games, they had to endure a three-day weather delay in the Bay Area. Although, "endure" might be a stretch. Who would turn down three extra nights in San Francisco?

In the radio booth, history was made. It was the first and only time that baseball's crowning occasion was covered exclusively by two ex-major-leaguers. Erstwhile catcher Joe Garagiola, an alumnus of Harry Caray's Cardinals booth and then NBC personality, was united with George Kell, who played for five American League teams in the 1940s and 1950s. Down to the wire they went, right to the last out, for that matter. Kell was on the mike when Bobby Richardson snared the line drive off the bat of Willie McCovey ending the Big Show.

Bill Lyon, writing in the *Sporting News*, described Joe's approach to the broadcast booth. "He was a catcher, and he brings a catcher's personality to the job—steady, plodding, squatting in the dirt, doing all the hot, dusty work."

Garagiola would do four straight World Series on the radio, and in 1963 it was a contrast in eloquence. "How did I get on the air, I always drop my ing's," the kid from the Hill in St. Louis would say. And there he was with Ernie Harwell, baseball's poet laureate.

Together they marveled over the first-game performance of Sandy Koufax who struck out 15 Yankees. The Dodgers went on to sweep the Yankees in four games.

Garagiola, the Henny Youngman of the baseball booth, was once an aspiring comedian. "If you tie an Italian's arms, you render him mute," he would say. During that Series in Los Angeles, where everyone at the ballpark seemingly had a transistor radio, he faced one of his toughest tests. "At first I didn't know what was going on in the park. I was just doing my usual routines, and glares of laughter kept sweeping the park, distracting everyone, me included. Then I realized that everyone had a transistor in their ear."

Because of the expeditious Dodgers, battery drainage was kept to a minimum. But the pain of defeat did cause significant drainage of Mel Allen's voice in the NBC television booth. Scully had to spell Mel when his voice turned

Ex-catcher Joe Garagiola
did four straight World
Series in the early '60s.

© David J. Halberstam

hoarse and the legend had to suffer the Yankees' fate in silence. Dick Young, the great *Daily News* columnist, called it "psychosomatic laryngitis," postulating that the Yankee voice choked, witnessing the butchery and demise of his beloved team. It was the last game of the Series, and the baritone would never do another one.

Allen got the unceremonious boot in 1964 when the Yankees shocked the baseball world, eschewing Mel, or for that matter Red Barber, and inexplicably nominating Phil Rizzuto. In many circles the circumstances remain a mystery to this day. One New York paper had a picture of Mel on the porch of his Bedford Village home sitting idly during the proceedings. He appeared to be in a stupor. Shortly after the Cardinals' seventh-game win, stunned New Yorkers were told without elaboration that their beloved voice was being let go. The Yankee broadcasts would never be the same.

There would be other lasting changes. NBC insisted that it have a representative in the booth. Curt Gowdy, former Yankees and Red Sox announcer and growing network star, partook in the coverage. Broadcasters split duties for the first time, doing radio and television. Phil Rizzuto and Cards announcer Harry Caray, the two authors of baseball's "Holy Cow," alternated between radio and TV. Joe Garagiola was in the mix, too, giving New Yorkers a glimpse of what they would hear the following regular season when Joe would join the Yankees crew, replacing Allen. What they heard among other things was their broadcasters' favorite Italian dishes.

The broadcast story was being nurtured down on the field. Four future play-by-play men were in St. Louis uniforms. The Cardinals had their future longtime announcer, Mike Shannon, in the outfield. First baseman Bill White would be a Yankee broadcaster seven years hence, and Bob Uecker didn't play in the Series but was a backup catcher for the Cards. The witty thespian still calls Brewers games on radio in Milwaukee. Arguably the best of the future crop was

© National Sportscasters and Sportswriters Assn.

Harry Caray

catcher Tim McCarver, who today is still in the prime of his baseball tele-casting career, locally with the Mets and nationally on the Fox Network. Caray's sidekick, Jack Buck, wasn't nominated to work either network ra-dio or TV but paid his own fare and showed up at Yankee Stadium. When no press pass was waiting for him at the gate, Yankees longtime public re-lations man, Bob Fishel, found him a seat somewhere in the stands.

Game one of the '65 affair was on Yom Kippur and Sandy Koufax, like Hank Greenberg before him, wouldn't play, paying homage to the Jewish high holiday. Don Drysdale started and the Dodgers got rocked for six runs in the third inning. The Twins won the first two and the Dodgers the next two. On 588 radio stations, Saam and Garagiola described Willie Davis's three stolen bases in the key fifth game and the Dodgers' seven-game Series win. Koufax was the *New York Times* "Man in the News" after he shut out Minnesota in the ultimate contest. Back then the *Times* also ran employment ads separately, "men wanted" and "women wanted."

In 1966 Scully did the first of his many World Series on radio, as he alternated with Chuck Thompson, joining Gowdy on television and Bob Prince on radio. Prince, a Pittsburgh legend, was stylized, perhaps even more so than his predecessor, Rosey Rowswell. He would eat an apple and read a book while calling a game. But the O's four-game sweep didn't give the colorful "Gunner" much time to bite into too many of the new crop of Macintosh's.

Prince was adored in the Steel City, where he was an unabashed rooter. With the Bucs down a run in the ninth, he wasn't shy about his desires, "all we need is a bloop and a blast." The eloquent Bob Costas once described him as "quirky, provincial, and irreplaceable." When he was fired, fans mounted a protest. They marched on the downtown headquarters of his employer, KDKA. A truly unique character, he was told by team general manager Joe Brown to ignore incidents that didn't put the ball club in a positive light. So, when Pirate infielder Richie Hebner threw a bat angrily into the stands in Houston, the super-cilious Prince told his audience wryly, "Something just happened but I'm not going to be able to tell you about it."

Alternating with Boston announcer Ken Coleman, Harry Caray growled again in 1967. If Harry was energetic, outgoing, and inimitable, Coleman was restrained, ponderous, and prudent. Pee Wee Reese, Curt Gowdy's partner on NBC's *Game of the Week*, combined with the contrasting two local announcers for all seven games. Reese, the longtime Brooklyn shortstop and a Hall of Famer, will always be remembered for his support of teammate Jackie Robinson just after the black man broke the color barrier.

Ernie Harwell, left, joins home-run record holder Henry Aaron. Aaron holds a record of the song Move Over Babe *that was written by Harwell and Bill Slayback.*

In 1968 America seemed to pit the old against the young, long hair against short hair, pro–Vietnam War or anti-war. There was unrest on campuses and riots in American cities. Songwriter and Tigers announcer Ernie Harwell was asked by ownership to line up the singers for the three World Series games against the Cardinals at Tiger Stadium. For game five, it was a young, blind Puerto Rican, Jose Feliciano. Without the support of a band the singer strummed his guitar and sang. There he was, on national television, in dark glasses and long hair, slowly singing "The Star-Spangled Banner." It was certainly different and could easily be construed as irreverent. Many in the stadium bristled. Millions watching on network television were enraged by the rock-soul rendition and caused network switchboards to be flooded.

Unconventional? Yes. Disrespectful? Unlikely. The act was soft compared to what's heard today in arenas and stadiums. But in 1968 it was viewed as a political statement of the left at a time when the country was terribly divided on these matters. Feliciano and Harwell, who accompanied him out to center field, were jeered. The mild-mannered and distinguished Tigers play-

176

by-play announcer found himself aberrantly in the middle of a national mael-strom. Immediately after this tumult, Ernie had to go to St. Louis and join Reese for game six of the Series on network radio. When he returned, he got a mild letter of reprimand from the ownership, and there were even rumblings of Ernie's imminent firing.

When it was apparent that summer that the Cardinals might participate in baseball's shining moment, Jack Buck approached Cardinals management and suggested that the club nominate two broadcasters instead of one, Caray for television and him for radio. Harry wasn't too pleased but the club agreed. Detroit nominated Kell, its television voice, and Harwell. As such, the games in St. Louis were on NBC television with Harry and Gowdy and in Detroit with Kell and Gowdy. Buck worked radio with Pee Wee in Detroit and Harwell with Pee Wee in St. Louis. The following year, Caray fell out of favor with the Busch family and was forced off the Cardinals' broadcasts. As for Ernie, the Feliciano incident blew over and he is now a Hall of Fame announcer. As far as Feliciano, the incident helped him become a successful national figure.

No New York sports fan will forget 1969. The Jets won the Super Bowl in January, and the Mets accomplished the Impossible Dream, winning the World Series in October. The city went wild. It was the year that America landed a manned spaceship on the moon, and it was said, "If a man can walk on the moon, the Mets can win the Series." And a pint-sized hitter like Al Weis batted .455 against the Orioles!

Lindsey Nelson was the Mets' choice for television. It was a natural. He had worked at NBC for years and his college football broadcasts were renowned throughout the land. Ralph Kiner got the radio assignment and alternated with the Orioles' Bill O'Donnell. Jim Simpson would start a run of six straight World Series on radio.

How about Bob Murphy? "I just watched," he said. Was he disappointed that he wasn't assigned? "Absolutely! Folks in the commissioner's office wanted me but M. Donald Grant [the Mets' top man in the front office] didn't want me," Murphy said, still harboring some anger three decades later.

Simpson, always professional and invariably the consummate network broadcaster, was much like Chris Schenkel or to a lesser extent, Keith Jackson. Baseball wasn't their passion. Simpson was a backup, second behind Gowdy. If Curt did the number one football game on Sunday, Simpson did number two. If Gowdy did the "grand-daddy" Rose Bowl, Simpson did the lesser Orange Bowl. If Gowdy did the Series on TV, Simpson did it on radio.

Simpson was born in the Washington, D.C., area and was the ultimate jack-of-all-trades but master at none. He covered everything from the Olympics to parachute jumping. His love as a kid was the outdoors. As a young teenager, he contributed a hunting and fishing column to a magazine, becoming the young-est member of the Outdoor Writers Association of America. He was perfectly qualified to be number two man to Gowdy on the *American Sportsman*. But baseball? Such, though, was the result of the removal of the team announcer. Through it all, Bob Murphy, who suffered with the club from day one, must have wondered, "why am I not doing this?"

The well-groomed Simpson also authored 10 straight radio All-Star Games, five with Sandy Koufax. "I used to think of myself as an athlete until I started working with Koufax," the versatile broadcaster said. After retiring as an active player, the Brooklyn-born pitcher pursued a broadcast career. "His name will always remind you of strikeouts," Vin Scully would say. True. Koufax certainly felt more comfortable throwing a fastball on the mound than a curveball on the air. By 1974 he would be replaced by Maury Wills, his former Dodgers teammate.

Team announcers were part of the fall broadcasts through 1978. Monte Moore did a trio of them when the A's were cooking in the early 1970s. Moore was known as "the spy in the sky," a pipeline of sorts for absentee maverick owner Charles O. Finley. There were no satellite dishes for picking and choosing games in the comfort of one's living room. Finley, living in Chicago, and for that matter George Steinbrenner from his home in Tampa, would dial in to their team's radio stations and listen on their speaker phones. Moore was under Finley's constant microscope. The A's progress was being painted almost exclusively by Monte.

Moore was raised in the Midwest and had a style redolent of the Midwest, occasionally prone to hyperbole. But with the likes of Reggie Jackson, Bert Campaneris, and Catfish Hunter, what's there not to be impressed with? Egos are fragile, and the broadcast booth is full of them. There's also a fine line between ego and insecurity, and Moore had to be a confident man. Finley matched him in the Oakland booth with some pretty big names, Harry Caray, Bob Elson, and Al Helfer. He outsurvived all of them, spending 16 years with the ball club, starting in Kansas City and extending to the Bay Area. "Elson spent the final year of his broadcast career in Oakland. Finley grew up listening to him in Chicago and thought the world of him. It was pretty bad. He wasn't prepared and was more interested in spending time on the phone outside the booth placing bets," Monte recalled. When Moore's play-by-play days were over, he entered the radio station ownership business.

In 1973 the Mets were back in the Series and so was Kiner on network radio, and Nelson again was part of the television team. Joe Garagiola saw ex-Pirate teammate Kiner and kidded him, "Don't be nervous, Ralph. There will only be eight million people listening to you." If Murphy was around, he wouldn't have found it amusing. M. Donald Grant left him out of the booth again.

In 1974, the year that Richard Nixon, a native Californian, became the first U.S. president to resign in midterm, the state enjoyed an all-California World Series, and the country enjoyed the refreshing sound of Vin Scully drawing a masterpiece on the canvas, waxing poetically over the Dodger infield of Lopes, Russell, Garvey, and Cey. The A's got the last laugh when experience beat youth in five games. Monte Moore remembers the broadcasts. "Scully and I were to join Curt Gowdy for home games on television. We would join Jim Simpson on radio for road games. Word was out that Scully only wanted to do television. At our preproduction meeting, NBC boss Chet Simmons sat everybody down, officially handed out the assignments, and told us that if anybody was unhappy with them, there were hundreds of guys around the country capable of doing the job."

In 1975 New York City was on the brink of financial disaster. Will help come from the president in Washington? The answer was a resounding no. In bold print on the front page of the *Daily News*, the headline read "FORD TO CITY, DROP DEAD." Other things were changing. The country was learning about a new dreaded word, *inflation*. It was spiraling and often smothering.

Bob Murphy   *Ralph Kiner*

The New York City colleges were about to end their long-standing tradition of free tuition.

NBC Radio was no longer gung-ho about its baseball coverage. After 19 years, the 1975 Red Sox-Reds Series would be its last. On May 8, 1975, CBS announced it acquired the rights to baseball's national radio package beginning in 1976.

Larry Barnett, the longtime American League umpire, won't forget the Series that was NBC Radio's last. He was the umpire behind the plate in game three. In the 10th inning, when Cincinnati's Ed Armbrister got tied up with catcher Carlton Fisk, he didn't make an interference call. Hearing the strident Boston dissenters then, one would think New England was being invaded by enemy troops. Barnett got many death threats, had to change his telephone number in his Prospect, Ohio, home and blamed television announcers Curt Gowdy and Tony Kubek for enraging Sox fans. The Reds won in seven and 71 million folks saw it on NBC television.

On radio, NBC went out with a whimper. WNBC in New York didn't carry the games on its powerhouse AM facility. The Series wound up being the first and only Classic to be covered exclusively on FM radio. It didn't go without protest, either. At that time, many vehicles weren't equipped with FM receivers, depriving drivers and automobile passengers of following the controversial championship.

The CBS Radio Network started building much of its identity around news and sports. Within time, its stable would grow to include the valuable National Football League, the NCAA Final Four, and Major League Baseball. Initially, the network of Paley continued the long-standing tradition of team announcers for its first three years as rights holder. For that matter, when the Yankees ad-

Longtime radio and TV broadcaster Curty Gowdy was considered by many as the "voice of everything" for NBC.

© National Baseball Hall of Fame Library, Cooperstown, N.Y.

vanced in 1976, the Yankees' Bill White became the first black announcer to call a Series.

In the 1970s, because of their limited geographical distribution, Rheingold, Ballantine, and Schaefer couldn't advertise on the growing number of hours of network television sports. Anheuser-Busch and Miller distributed their products nationally, and network sports fit like a perfectly tailored suit. The concurrent rise of network sports programming and national brewers, Miller and Anheuser-Busch, is hardly a coincidence.

The beers put dollars in the pockets of the networks, and the networks then put dollars in the pockets of the owners. It was both synergy and a viscous cycle. The power of the webs ballooned, and they purged the October turf of the locals like Bob Prince and Harry Caray. A once-indomitable local and varied sound of baseball's Grand Event was about to be silenced by the green cash of the overpowering folks on network row.

Anheuser-Busch also penetrated the country, market by market, securing ties with almost every team and becoming the ubiquitous sponsor of local baseball. A team's bond with a local beer, Rheingold and the Mets for example, was slowly being bankrupted by the deep corporate pockets and improved technology of the national brewers. Gone, locally, were the days of the "Ballantine blast," the "Schaefer Circle of Sports," or "My beer is Rheingold, the dry beer." Wallops on local radio were greeted by "This Bud's for you."

The new television contract started in 1976, and it enabled the alternating networks, ABC and NBC, to assign their own talent. Television was about to do the blasphemous. The two behemoths eliminated the long-standing tradition of featuring the local announcer. NBC chose to do it gradually. In 1976 Phil Rizzuto appeared on television with a fur coat in the crisp chill of a New York fall night and did three innings. It was after Chris Chambliss homered in the American League Championship Series to beat Kansas City and send the Bronxites to their first postseason finale in 12 years. The World Series seemed almost anti-climactic, and the Yankees were done in four by Cincinnati.

ABC wanted no part of the Dodgers' and Yankees' broadcast talent in its play-by-play presentation when the teams renewed their autumn rivalry in 1977. It invited Scully, already a three-decade veteran of network fall baseball, to partake in a ceremonious but demeaning cameo role of running down the line-ups. Scully declined and severely criticized ABC for spurning tradition. The linguist might have remembered the words of E. H. Carr: "Change is certain. Progress is not."

Just 22 years earlier, New York had basked in the glory and the sunlight of a daytime subway Series. Allen uplifted and Scully refreshed. There was something harmonious even as the IRT screeched a cacophony on the el behind right field. Twenty-two years later, Cosell chirped contempt for baseball while rambunctious fans at Yankee Stadium carried on menacingly. Through it all, ABC cameras focused damagingly on the Bronx, repeatedly showing an arson fire burning just a few blocks from the ballpark.

In 1979 radio followed television. CBS head Dick Brescia hired Scully to become the voice of baseball's premier happening; to do all nine innings. There was an irony. Two years earlier Scully was network television's first local victim. Now, at the expense of his local brethren in Pittsburgh and Baltimore, he was network radio's first World Series centerpiece. There he was, elaborating on the marvels of 39-year-old "Pops," Willie Stargell. The Orioles' Chuck Thompson and the Pirates' Lanny Frattare had no pulpit. They were, as Scully might say, "carpenters without tools."

The master of lexicons would probably have preferred to work all alone, as he does so eloquently in Los Angeles. Brescia might even have believed that Scully alone would work gloriously. Scully is perfect by himself. His golden voice is melodious, and it doesn't grate on the listener. But networks, even radio networks, can't easily shun perceived convention. If convention dictates a color man, how about Sparky Anderson? The former Cincinnati manager, now with Detroit, teamed with Vin from 1979 through 1982. The contrast of the two was part of the pizzazz; Scully, facile with Fowler's use of the English language, and Sparky, spewing the double negatives characteristic of the baseball dugout.

Until NBC television came knocking on Scully's door in 1983, radio was his mat. "On radio you're a puncher, and on television you're a counterpuncher," this son of radio's golden age would often say. On television, there's the camera that a play-by-play man captions. On radio, it's the announcer who is the monitor, producer, director, the graphics, and the telestrator.

If "radio is a blank canvas," Vin's name is Picasso. What the brilliant painter did with his hands, the word-picture artist does with his vocal cords. Blessed with the blarney of his Irish descent, the absolute command of the English language, and, most importantly, in-depth baseball knowledge, Scully has owned October radio.

The orator spoke delicately of George Brett's 1980 bout with hemorrhoids while gushing about his great year at the plate. In 1981 George Steinbrenner lashed out in frustration at Dave Winfield. The Yankees' boss called the outfielder "Mr. May" when he went 1-for-21. All Scully would say is, "Dave is trying to break the shackles of a galling slump," remembering perhaps the punishing '52 Series of Gil Hodges. And when, in Los Angeles for game three, the Dodgers and Fernando Valenzuela led 3-0 at the end on an inning, it was "the Dodgers three and the Yankees, nada señor." If Steve Garvey slid hard into second base, "he took pieces of Dodger Stadium real estate with him."

Never at a loss for the appropriate phrase, Scully was ready for St. Louis and Milwaukee when the teams in the beer capitals met in 1982. "One thing for sure," Scully assured his listeners, "there will be no bad hops in this Series." And as Robin Yount continued to devour the Cardinals, batting a sizzling .414, "the Robin is killing the Redbird," he trumpeted. And in 1982 the local announcers were no longer left out. Each participating team was permitted to produce its own broadcast for its local constituency.

But Art Watson, fellow Fordham alum and NBC Sports boss, usurped baseball's eminent radio voice in 1983 with the allure of the bright lights of television. For the next six years Scully would glitter under the spotlight. As Hank Raymonds told the press when he was introduced as Marquette's head basketball coach following Al McGuire's retirement, "No one replaces him— they succeed him." So on radio, Brescia and company knew no one would replace Scully. Jack Buck did succeed him.

Unlike basketball or hockey announcers, baseball voices are not paid for how they describe the play. It's how they handle airtime between plays, how they handle the gaps. Good baseball announcers are entertaining, the kind whom you would like to have over to the house for dinner. They're storytellers, full of anecdotes, reminiscences, and chuckles. Buck's one of them. He's a storyteller and a good one, a man popular on the banquet circuit. The St. Louis fixture is outgoing and one who would hold court, so to speak, when among a group of people. When he was breaking in partner Mike Shannon, they were in their broadcast booth in St. Petersburg, getting ready for an exhibition game. Jack said to Mike, "Get me the umpires." Mike certainly did. About 10 minutes later, there they were. The three umpires working the game, huffing and puffing, climbed the stairs to the booth. Jack cracked up. "All I wanted were their names, knucklehead."

He's done virtually everything, almost any sport imaginable, from radio to television and from bowling to soccer. He's confident and self-assured. A spectator once kept harassing him during a soccer broadcast, questioning Jack's knowledge of the sport; so during a time-out, the announcer decked him, knocking him halfway down the bleachers.

Buck got his triple-A baseball job in Rochester when Ed Edwards, the man he succeeded, told a dirty story at a banquet and was fired on the spot by the team's general manager, Bing Divine. Buck, the New England native, got the job. He did Rochester Red Wings baseball and Rochester Royals basketball. Recreating a road game from Montreal one afternoon, Jack relied on a French-speaking Western Union operator in Montreal who couldn't communicate clearly.

Jack Buck

So until he was able to get things sorted out, Buck bought time cleverly, fabricating a batter fouling a pitch off his finger and going into the dugout for medical attention. Jack was pretty convincing. That night, the hitter's wife, who was listening to Jack's re-creation, called her husband with concern for his ailing finger.

The husky-voiced play caller spanned five decades as a Cardinals announcer. His service was separated twice, once when he was replaced in the early 1960s by Buddy Blattner and again when he left voluntarily for the failed NBC mid-1970s studio program, *Grandstand.* For years he played second fiddle to Harry Caray, getting to call just a couple of innings a game. Harry was such an emotional rooter that he would rage out of the ballpark if the Redbirds lost a close one. With two outs in the last of the ninth and St. Louis down a run, Caray would bark, "Brock off third, the tying run ninety feet away, Flood at the plate, here's the pitch, popped-up." Harry was dispirited. "Jack will be back with the recap after this," he bristled, slamming his fist against the broadcast table and storming out of the booth. The station was in a commercial break, and Harry was gone before the ball was ever caught.

Through all his popular years, Buck worked year-round at KMOX radio. At night, when atmospheric conditions are right, the St. Louis CBS affiliate can sometimes be heard from coast to coast. Bob Hyland, who passionately and lucratively ran KMOX for years, took a liking to Buck and hooked him up with the network's coverage of baseball and football.

Scully and Buck have dominated the World Series on radio since 1979. They've been the voices of October. They're also quite different. Scully is flowery, and Buck is meat and potatoes. Scully is Shakespeare, and Buck is Hemingway. Scully lives in Pacific Palisades, and Buck lives in the Midwest. Scully's leisurely moment is on the golf course, and Buck's is taking a skydive. Scully would be prim in the booth on a cruelly sweltering day, and Buck would broadcast with his feet in a bucket of ice. Scully would be publicly neutral, and Buck would introduce Bob Dole at a rally before the 1996 presidential elections.

That's a Winner is the title of Buck's autobiography and his signature stamp on a Cards win. It's what he could have said when Scott McGregor shut out Mike Schmidt (1-for-20 in the affair) and the Phillies 5–0 to win game five and the 1983 Series for the Orioles. In 1984 Sparky Anderson made history, becoming the first manager to win titles in two leagues. He left Buck in the radio booth with Brent Musburger and celebrated a five-game Tigers championship over the Padres.

Buck hardly did any celebrating in 1985. He was on the air nationally and showed great self-restraint on the CBS microphones when in game six, his Cards were about to hold off the Royals in Kansas City and capture the flag. But umpire Don Denkinger made a controversial call at first base in the bottom of the ninth, enabling the Royals to come back. The next night Bret Saberhagen shut out Whitey Herzog's team, 11–0, in game seven. Only later and off the air was Buck critical of the American League umpire.

By 1986, when the Mets and Red Sox met in a memorable classic, the team's local affiliate was allowed to carry the games with its own announcers. Thus, for the first time in 46 years, there was more than one production on New York radio, the CBS broadcast on WCBS and Bob Murphy and Gary Thorne electrifying Mets fans on flagship WHN.

Somewhere in between the two booths, Buck might have ribbed Murphy, "You little S.O.B., you beat me out for the Red Sox job in '54." But Bob was too immersed to be slighted by some good-natured kidding from his fellow National League cohort. Shunned from the World Series mike in '69 and '73 by M. Donald Grant, he was now basking in the glory of the Mets' success.

There would be an implausible twist in game six. Murph and Mets fans would be on top of the world. "Mookie Wilson up," the Oklahoman would ring with that ineradicable twang. Mets fans know the rest. They have listened to it joyously and repeatedly:

Here's the pitch by Stanley . . . and a ground ball trickling . . . it is a fair ball, gets by Buckner, rounding third Knight . . . the Mets win the ballgame. The Mets win!

New York forced a seventh game, winning 6–5 with a three-run rally in the 10th inning. By the time game seven rolled around, the Red Sox had their New England "kishkas" taken out of them and the Amazin's were champions of the world.

The CBS Radio Network continued to broadcast baseball's big October event, but in 1987 all-news WCBS, the network's owned and operated flagship station, wanted to stick to news instead of running nonlocal play-by-play. The CBS broadcasts moved to WFAN, which was born the previous summer, a result of the former WHN. Buck joined forces with the Yankees' Bill White who worked with Buck the next couple of years.

The former Cardinal sat with Jack as they reported for their radio constituency that the home team won each of the seven games of the '87 extravaganza. In the celebration of the clubhouse, "Mr. October," Reggie Jackson, interviewed former St. John's standout and Twins reliever, Frank Viola. The Twins had won their first championship ever by beating St. Louis.

One of the most memorable radio highlights of World Series history took place in Los Angeles in 1988. The Dodgers trailed in the opener 4–3 going into the bottom of the ninth. Oakland A's ace reliever Dennis Eckersley retired the first two hitters. Tommy Lasorda's team was down to its final out. But Mike Davis walked and Lasorda sent Kirk Gibson to the plate. Kirk was hurt. He wasn't even in the dugout at the time he was summoned. The former Tiger could hardly walk, he limped to the plate. Scully, working on television would say that it was Dodger Stadium's most theatrical moment ever. Gibson used the bat as a cane to walk from the dugout to the plate. He then miraculously homered into the right-field grandstand. Buck's call was from the heart and unforgettable:

Unbelievable! The Dodgers have won the game on a home run by Kirk Gibson! I don't believe what I just saw!

Dodger Stadium exploded as Gibson staggered around the bases. Up the road a year later in San Francisco, it wasn't just an explosion, it was an earthquake. Buck and partner Johnny Bench were at Candlestick Park. The quake struck during the pregame show but CBS was able to remain on the air. Buck would say later, "It lasted for twenty-two seconds which doesn't sound like a long time until you're in the middle of it." Buck's first thought was that the press box would collapse. Bench's wife was at the game and pregnant. He stormed out to be at her side. Jack kidded him later, "If you would have run like that when you played, you would never have hit into a double play."

It was Buck's last year on radio. He moved to CBS television the following year where he worked a couple of years with Tim McCarver. Television in the '90s wasn't Buck's canvas. The network told him that Tim was to be number one. He was to be no more than a mechanic, a set-up man for the former catcher. Buck wasn't happy announcing that way, and CBS didn't pick up his option after 1991.

With NBC out of the World Series and Buck on television, CBS Radio smartly rehired Scully. After Cincinnati made quick work of Oakland in 1990, the man beginning his fifth decade as a big-league announcer would say, "It just went too quickly." There were now more radio and television sports media critics than ever and invariably, from Seattle to Florida and up the coast to Maine, they were singing his praises.

It didn't go quickly in 1991. Minnesota and Atlanta went the distance. When the games are close and dramatic, Scully is at his best, and six of the seven were decided by just one run. Jack Morris was the hero of the ultimate contest, hurling a 1–0 shutout.

No announcer plays the crowd better. When Henry Aaron hit his record-setting 715th home run in 1974 against the Dodgers, Vin described it:

A long drive . . . to the track . . . to the wall . . . gone.

With the ensuing uproarious salute, Scully calmly went to the back of the booth, drank a glass of water, let the crowd noise die down, and sat back down in front of the microphone.

In October 1992, Atlanta and Toronto faced one another. Scully was there, broadcasting the grand game's first Series from Canada. He came prepared, "canvas, brushes, paints, and a palette." Vin links his words, "And I paint the broad strokes and I mix the colors, and I paint the fine lines and the shadows and delineations and eventually, at the end of the three hours, the canvas is full, and that's the best I can do for the day." Preparation is what he was taught by his mentor, the taskmaster Red Barber, whose health was failing throughout the Series. Red died as the fall drama ended and after the sixth and final game on October 24, 1992, Vin picked himself up and proceeded to Tallahassee for the funeral of his mentor.

Mel Allen, Barber's former rival and later his partner, flew to Tallahassee, too. His luggage, though, arrived in Orlando. Appropriate? Allen had the trimmings of Disney World and Barber the homespun phrases of the plain folks in the Florida panhandle.

The prominent "voice of NBC Sports," Dick Enberg, spent time in Los Angeles where he called Angels games on radio and television. Enberg had time to listen to and study Scully. "He has the patience to hold off using a note in the first inning when it might better sustain the drama of the eighth." Most importantly, Scully remembers that the game is the story. So when Joe Carter homered in the ninth inning of the sixth game in 1993 to give Toronto the crown, Scully, as usual, let the crowd paint the frenzied picture.

Scully had a difficult year in 1994. His son Michael died in a helicopter accident, and because of baseball labor strife, there was no Series that fall. Had there been one, Vin would have been in the booth and would have remembered the words of teacher Barber, "Don't bring your problems with you into the booth." In 1972 Scully had to bury his young wife who died in his arms. Not all is roses. Another fantastic Southern California announcer, Chick Hearn, has had both his children die tragically.

Baseball was back in business in 1995 when Cleveland and Atlanta went at it. And so was Scully. He had a new partner, former Dodger catcher Jeff Torborg. "Statistics are used the way a drunk uses a lamppost, for support, not illumination," Vin would tell millions on the radio when many of one team's individual numbers looked good one game but the end result didn't. And it wasn't just a hard line drive, "He lined it so hard, you can hang your hat on it."

But by 1996 the still peerless Scully was seemingly less tolerant of on-the-field blunders. When young Yankees shortstop Derek Jeter failed to field a ground ball in game five, Scully, almost sounded slighted when he said derisively, "After all, at his salary, it's not much to ask that he pick up a routine roller!" Earlier, in game four, Atlanta jumped out to a 6–0 lead. When the Yankees rallied from behind, Scully, had the appropriate word. "Until the Yankees scored three in the sixth, it appeared this thing would turn into a soporific."

At Yankee Stadium the crowd was "screaming itself weak" after a big strike-three call which ended a Braves threat. At one point, Atlanta manager Bobby Cox was furious over a strike call but couldn't catch the attention of the umpire from the dugout. So, in the din of the ecstatic throng, Scully analogized, "It's like the guy in the balcony winking at the showgirl."

By 1997 Scully had called three perfect games and 18 no-hitters, and each of his calls was distinct. When Fernando Valenzuela pitched a no-hitter in 1990, Scully captured the moment after the last pitch, "and if you have a sombrero, toss it to the sky." He once described the lean pitching ace, Ramon Martinez, as looking like "six o'clock" on the pitching mound. A team hit a certain pitcher "as if they were his wicked stepparents." Subtly, he is always selling the game. With a World Series game on the line, he extols baseball for its inherent greatness. "A team can't freeze the ball and you can't fall to one knee. A pitcher has to deliver," an impassioned Scully imparts, quickening the pulses of his listeners.

The appeal of the lefty is universal. At age 70, Scully is still exhilaratingly fresh, and his play-by-play is enjoyed at a Blarney Stone or at Four Seasons, admired equally by truck drivers or English professors. He has the warmth, the wit, the expertise, and the enthusiasm.

In Florida, for the 1997 Marlins-Indians Series, there was a tone of sarcasm to his distinguished voice when he talked about Pro Player Park, a division of Fruit of the Loom, being the only stadium named for underwear. Then again, there was pride as he talked about Cleveland outfielder Manny Ramirez who hails from the same area as Scully, Washington Heights. Scully reminisced about the old "hood." When he was there, it was 90 percent Jewish, he said. Now it's 90 percent Hispanic.

And when a mass of eager fans at Florida's first-ever World Series game clicked their cameras under the nighttime skies, creating a glitteringlike effect in the stands, Scully came up with another gem. It reminded him of Japanese fans in Los Angeles who always brought their cameras when Hideo Nomo was still pitching at Dodgers Stadium. "It's like opening a jewel box." When Florida's Gary Sheffield made a great catch scaling the stadium wall, "He goaltended it."

In September 1997, ESPN Radio announced that it had obtained the rights to the Major League package, beginning with the 1998 season. Baseball's first exclusive contract was with Mutual. It lasted 18 years beginning in 1939. NBC had it from 1957 through 1975, 19 years, and CBS's deal went the next 22.

Life's best lesson came from Scully, and it had nothing to do with language or baseball. Barry Jackson of the *Miami Herald* asked him about the prospects of the 1997 Series being his last. "You should always look at everything you do as the last one you're ever going to do." That's an unbeatable attitude for anything in life.

As it turned out, ESPN offered the maestro a cameo role in 1998. But as he had done in 1977, Scully took the high road, graciously turning down a diminshed position "to spend more time at home."

On the eve of the Yankees-Padres Series, an executive at ABC (which runs EPSN Radio) said rather matter-of-factly, "We offered him a couple of innings, but he decided to call it a day."

So the man who does the best Scully imitation, John Miller, was assigned the lofty fall task.

6

BASKETBALL

MILLING AND WEAVING
ON THE HARDWOOD

The New York metropolitan area adopted basketball almost immediately. In 1920 the best sign of acceptance was attendance. Some 10,000 fans turned out at an armory to witness New York University defeat City College.

St. John's, CCNY, Manhattan, and New York University started filling Madison Square Garden as early as December 29, 1934, when a doubleheader was introduced by Ned Irish. Initially a sportswriter and later a Garden executive, Irish promoted the twin bill featuring St. John's against Westminster and NYU facing Notre Dame. It was an instant success, drawing 16,138. Irish's eight doubleheaders that inaugural 1934–35 campaign averaged some 12,000 in attendance.

The New York teams started prospering and so did interest. Between key prizefights, and from the time the college football season ended until baseball started in the spring, it helped fill the interest of the New York sports fan.

The college game actually dominated the basketball scene until the point-shaving scandals of the 1950s. It was this unfortunate development that sparked the pro game's growth in popularity. Unlike football, boxing, or even baseball, interest in basketball was confined to a team's region. New York couldn't care less about teams in Kansas or vice versa.

Doubleheaders featuring traveling pro teams were occasionally played on the stage of the Hippodrome in the 1920s. A cryptic listing appeared in the radio

189

section of the New York papers on October 14, 1928. WPCN radio was to broadcast a "basketball description" at 10 P.M. from the Hippodrome in the heart of Manhattan.

Earl Harper, the "voice of minor-league baseball's Newark Bears" and perhaps the most popular local New York play-by-play man in the 1930s, was the first to broadcast a basketball game from Madison Square Garden when he called a college contest in the mid-1930s.

But basketball broadcasts in New York were spotty at that time. There was hardly anything ongoing. Baseball, and even football, on radio were still young in history and presentation. Basketball on the air had hardly been examined at that point.

Certainly budding sportscasters didn't aspire to broadcast basketball. If anything, they wanted to emulate the great voices of the day, pioneers such as Ted Husing and Graham McNamee, who never did a basketball game during their brilliant careers. The young and the fringe, perhaps, looking for any assignment at all, would do some. But hardly with vigor or fire and hardly capturing the rhythm of the game. They flew by the seat of their pants because there was no history on which to base their approach.

Very few had basketball experience. In addition to Harper, Don Dunphy, who broke into the business in the 1930s and later had brilliant years as the "voice of boxing," was one. Stan Lomax, a studio sports reporter who dabbled with play-by-play and would also occasionally broadcast basketball in the 1930s, was another. These three would actually do full games.

Later, Mel Allen would also report on basketball, taking air after the 11 P.M. news, summarizing results of the doubleheaders and perhaps sprinkling in some developments of the second game as it was winding down. But Mel's work was hardly basketball play-by-play as we know it today.

Basketball didn't afford the luxury that football and baseball did. It had no natural pauses. Announcers couldn't reset playing conditions for their audiences. Basketball's action was incessant and fast paced. There was constant milling and weaving and a hodgepodge of shot selection. Stations and sponsors were not convinced that radio could decipher and present basketball vividly.

While such was the case in New York, *Radio Daily* reported on April 7, 1939, that "increased interest in basketball games throughout the country has developed into a source of additional revenue for stations offering local games for sponsorship."

Indeed, a directory of broadcasters in 1933 indicated that Russ Winnie in Milwaukee enjoyed calling "the fast-paced action of basketball." He was apparently pretty good at it, too. Hilliard Gates, one of the game's early prominent voices, heard Winnie in the 1930s and considered him to be a basketball broadcast pioneer.

And that's quite a compliment, considering that Gates was selected to work with Marty Glickman on Mutual's coverage of the first NBA All-Star Game in 1951. Gates did Indiana University basketball and the Ft. Wayne Pistons for many years and perfected the craft.

The Midwest in many ways was ahead of New York in radio sports coverage. Local baseball was on the air in the 1920s, and football and basketball followed shortly. In Peoria in 1938, the venerable Jack Brickhouse was a WMBD

Curt Gowdy

broadcaster. The station, as so many other affiliates were then, was committed to network programming. At night, the CBS affiliate had Eddie Cantor and Kate Smith. So Jack kept pushing management to carry Bradley University basketball on tape.

"I was asked to conduct a poll in the center of town to see whether there was enough interest in town to listen to games on a tape delay. Eight of ten people said no. So I threw it out and concocted my own. The station gave me a one-game trial and it was a big hit. Even though fans knew the score, the response was enormous. We eventually took on the entire schedule. When we would go on the road, fans held listening parties."

Curt Gowdy was working in Oklahoma City. In nearby Stillwater, Oklahoma A&M had a national-championship-caliber team. KOMA was a network affiliate and had commitments to Jack Benny and Fred Allen. It wouldn't touch basketball. Curt, too, pushed and station management acquiesced to carry games on tape after the 10:15 news.

"We were amazed by the response. People called and asked us not to give the score. They wanted to hear the game as though it was being played live." Gowdy turned into quite a good basketball announcer. When he worked Yankees baseball games later with Mel Allen, he would spend a couple of winters filling in occasionally for Marty Glickman. He's contributed so greatly to coverage of basketball that the announcers' wing at the Basketball Hall of Fame is named in his honor. In the South, WSB carried the Southern Conference Tournament with Bill Munday in 1928.

Madison Square Garden owned a radio station, WMSG, but by the time the college doubleheaders were introduced in 1934, it had dissolved itself of it. Purchased in 1926 by promoter Tex Rickard, the station had a poor signal, and it was a time-sharing arrangement, meaning that it owned only a set number of hours during the broadcast day. When Rickard died in 1929, Madison Square Garden management eventually got tired of the red ink and pulled out of the radio business. Records show that Garden events such as hockey and boxing were initially broadcast on WMSG. But the inadequate signal was such a detriment that Rickard moved the programming to stations with better signals in town.

Bert Lee was at WMCA in the late 1930s as the station's sales manager before going over to WHN in 1939 where he was both sales manager and an on-air announcer. Among other things, Lee himself was the "voice of the Rangers" and a believer in sports programming. He would eventually be appointed station manager and it was under his helmsmanship that play-by-play and sports shows sprouted on WHN. Over the next few years, WHN would acquire the Brooklyn Dodgers, the New York Football Giants, the Rangers, the great college doubleheaders, and when they were born in 1946, the Knicks. What else was there? Lee's ability to attract sponsors and his dedication to the format enabled sports programming to flourish on the station. WHN seemed to have it all.

But basketball lacked a prominent presence on radio in New York in the late 1930s. The college doubleheaders were hardly a radio attraction at that point. Sponsors hardly supported the sport in New York and no one really convinced the major stations that the excitement of the sport was translatable on radio. The sport lacked a striking and eminent voice, something that Mel Allen and Red Barber would become for baseball. Basketball was growing but stations didn't believe that the sport deserved to be showcased on New York radio.

From a historical perspective it's important to remember that stations were not yet even carrying major-league baseball from the three New York City ballparks. And basketball was certainly not in baseball's category of support and popularity.

Marty Glickman would change this. A former New York City high school sports standout who excelled at Syracuse University in football, Glickman was a member of the U.S. track team at the 1936 Olympic Games in Berlin.

Marty's first on-air experience was in Syracuse in 1937, where as a student athlete he hosted a weekly sports program on WSYR. It was sponsored by a haberdashery which was hoping to cash in on Glickman's popularity as a star football player. "I stutter and stammer," Glickman told the sponsor but when he was told he'd be getting $15 a week, he accepted.

After he arrived in New York, Glickman played semipro football for the Jersey Giants for one season before deciding that he wanted to pursue a career in radio. As a track man, he was called upon by WMCA to cover the "stride-for-stride" of a Madison Square Garden track meet in 1940. Later Marty called upon Dick Fishell, another ex-Syracuse athlete and a sportscaster at WHN. It was there that he hooked on as a go-fer for Lee and Fishell. It was truly an apprenticeship. Marty didn't get paid a dime for a whole year. But he learned the ropes.

Through his first few years at WHN, Marty kept trying to convince Lee to undertake basketball. Bert didn't buy it. Finally, in December 1942, Marty broadcast his first basketball game, a matchup between North Carolina Pre-Flight and Long Island University. His partner was Lee himself. But that was it for a while. World War II was raging, and the next year Marty left for the Marines.

There were wartime broadcasts. Dunphy, Lomax, and Harper kept the game alive on radio while Joe Hasel also would do an occasional Army basketball game on city-owned WNYC. But generally, the broadcasts didn't capture the game's rhythm. There were players' names but no geography and little description of ball movement.

Glickman returned from the Marines in December 1945, and Lee immediately put him to work with Connie Desmond on the broadcasts of college doubleheaders. When the series actually started, Marty was still in transit, so announcer Ted Lawrence worked with Desmond until he arrived.

Glickman was an innovator looking for a niche. He knew that the popular baseball and football jobs were taken, and if his career was to progress, his basketball qualities would have to stand out.

He gave basketball its radio geography, much the way legendary voice Foster Hewitt did for hockey, situating the puck for listeners by using simple phrases such as "back of the cage" or "red line." Marty figured that basketball, too, had zonal positions: top of the key, baseline, right of the lane, and others. He incorporated these geographic points into a fast-paced delivery of ball movement. It was blended by fantastic voice inflection, reflecting the action's drama.

Each trip down the floor, his delivery was pitched perfectly so that there was special tension to his voice when a shot was taken. Players weren't just taking a shot, they were taking a hook, a set, or a runner. Marty had played the game and could talk quickly and clearly without stumbling.

Glickman might not have been the first to broadcast basketball but he might as well have been. He gave it the radio identity that Husing did for football and Barber did for baseball. In 1946 CBS initiated basketball telecasts with announcers Bob Edge and Jack O'Reilly. By December 11, 1946, *Variety* remarked, "As with boxing, basketball is well suited to video through the fact that all the action takes place in a small area."

Basketball was growing after the war, particularly in the New York City area, where the school yards were filled with kids playing the city game. Marty would exclaim "swish" when shots went through the net cleanly without touching the rim. Radio was big then and the term "swish" was echoed on the New York City basketball courts. Later, in 1947–48 when Nedick's sponsored the Knicks' basketball broadcasts, made-shots weren't just good, they were "good like Nedick's," another phrase often imitated by basketball fans all over town.

The college basketball broadcasts became so popular that they were occasionally picked up by other stations across the country on Mutual and CBS. This was college basketball's golden age. The game was a constant subject of conversation and Glickman was the voice identified with it. In 1950 CCNY became the only team in the history of the college game to win both the National Invitation Tournament and the National Collegiate Athletic Association crown in the same year. The Beavers beat Bradley in both of the title games and Marty called each one. The city was enthralled. Madison Square Garden drew 600,000 for college basketball that winter.

Unfortunately, it all came crashing down when the point-shaving scandals hit, and it was found that players at CCNY and other schools fixed games. City College, Long Island University, and New York University never really recovered. It would take some 30 years before St. John's and the Big East would restore electricity to the college game again in New York.

As a matter of record, professional basketball was hardly a dream in New York in the 1930s. The National Basketball League was around. It was formed in 1937 and it was one of the two forerunners to the National Basketball Association. But its roots were in small towns, and the NBL was really no more than an industrial league situated in places such as Akron and Dayton. It wasn't until 1946 that the Knicks were born as part of the new Basketball Association of America. The BAA then merged with the NBL to form the National Basketball Association in 1949, and professional basketball was alive.

When the Knicks were launched, there was an uncertainty whether pro basketball would make it in a major market. Even the most pollyannish of dreamers

Courtesy Marty Glickman

Marty Glickman broadcasts a basketball game from the old Madison Square Garden in 1946 on WHN.

then couldn't envision the look of the league today: television ratings of the NBA Finals rivaling those of the World Series, constant sellouts, and dominance of the newspaper pages. The start of the new league in 1946 was truly an adventure into uncharted areas.

When the Knicks were being organized for their first season in 1946, it was clear that their radio match was WHN. At that point, sports fans were certainly familiar with WHN. It had the Dodgers and the football Giants, both with Red Barber and Connie Desmond, and the Rangers with Bert Lee and Ward Wilson. There was a variety of non-play-by-play sports programming, too. And as far as the Garden was concerned, WHN had one indispensable asset—Glickman, who put radio basketball on the map in New York City.

WHN agreed to a rights fee with Ned Irish and business manager Fred Podesta in the spring of 1946 and aired Knicks games with Glickman as the principal voice through 1955. Through it all, the New York City–bred Glickman gave the pro game a colorful call, continuing to develop the nomenclature by incorporating the players' vernacular and making them household terms.

The league was basically being organized by arena owners who were hoping that basketball would add revenue on what otherwise would be dark nights.

Irish thought that the league would succeed if it could attract women. As such, he suggested that a lady be involved in the broadcasts. The answer was Sarah Palfrey Cooke, a Wimbledon and U.S. Open champion. It was a good idea but she hardly knew the rudiments of the game.

The first two Knicks games that initial season were not broadcast and it would be 41 years before all Knicks games each season would be carried live. On the train to St. Louis for the trip to the first Knicks broadcast ever, Marty explained elementary scoring rules. A field goal, he told her, was two points. When Cooke asked what's a field goal, it was obvious that this wasn't a marriage made in heaven.

Before long, Stan Lomax was summoned to take over for Cooke. Although a fixture at WOR, management then wasn't generally as restricting. It would allow talent to do work on other stations. Sponsors owned programming back then and wielded more power than stations. As an example, one night in 1945, Don Dunphy did the first game of a doubleheader on WINS and a boxing match a bit later that night for Gillette on WHN.

When he arrived in St. Louis, Glickman remembers running into the colorful Harry Caray, who was broadcasting the game for the listeners in St. Louis. Caray's son, Skip, and grandson, Chip, have since also done play-by-play of NBA games, making for three generations of Carays on the NBA airwaves. It was then November 7, 1946, the 24th birthday of the great jazzman, Al Hirt, that Marty Glickman made music of his own, equal in rhythm and beat.

Glickman's presentation was rapid-fire, and there was an infectious tension to his voice. Marty always said that when he broadcast, he felt as though he was playing, as though he was on the floor. If the ball was being moved around the perimeter so quickly that time constraints didn't allow him to identify both location and player, Marty would often give location only, sacrificing names.

In other words, a sequence may sound something like this, "Braun has it in the right corner, back of the key it's moved, now into the left corner to Vandeweghe." Marty's explanation makes sense. When watching a game from the stands or on television for that matter, fans are conscious of a gorgeous pass, the shooter, or the rebounder. On routine movement of the ball around the perimeter, ball movement and rhythm are paramount, not each player who might have touched it for a fleeting second. Location first, name second. It's radio.

During the closing moments of the first half when a team was holding for a final shot, the point guard was dribbling the ball at the middle of the floor, and the players were standing around. Marty simply said, "Hobbs dribbles in place. The players aren't moving, the clock is." One memorable Glickman description was, "Hobbs dribbles along the right sideline with those silky hands and supple wrists while his teammates are milling and weaving in and out of the lane." Brilliant!

Jim Gordon, who had a long and successful broadcast career in New York, which included some Knicks games, remembers that he was in Syracuse broadcasting the Nationals at the time the league started in 1946. In those early days, as teams hired new announcers, they all scrambled around for tapes of Glickman to hear how it was done.

What's sad is that today there are no tapes of Glickman's professional basketball. Tapes were on wire in those days and, believe it or not, they would melt and were hardly durable. They're truly a lost treasure.

In 1949 Herman Masin was sports editor of *Senior Scholastic*. He was a student, not a professional media critic. But this kid had a good feel for the business. "Unfortunately, the television masterminds now have Mel (Allen) doing the big Madison Square Garden basketball games, and what Mel knows about the game could fit into a midget's hip pocket.

"The greatest play-by-play announcer is a fellow you may never have heard of. I refer to Marty Glickman, the former Syracuse University footballer and Olympic sprinter, who now broadcasts for station WMGM. He does local basketball and football games, and anything else that comes along.

"He can't be touched for actual game announcing, especially in basketball. You know how fast a basketball game moves. Well, Marty never misses a pass or a shot. He stays on top of every play, and despite a machine-gun delivery, he rarely fluffs a line. You have to hear it to believe it."

Even the *New York Times* was complimentary of what then was an innovation, the presentation of basketball on radio. "Marty Glickman has devised a special technique in his work. His delivery is smooth and assured."

Glickman's broadcasts were so graphic and informative that if coaches were unable to get to a game, they would sometimes rely on Marty's broadcast when having to scout. Certainly, his influence on other broadcasters is well documented. Marv Albert, Johnny Most, and Spencer Ross head the list. The great Chick Hearn, a Hall of Famer himself, says that the first pro game he ever heard was announced by Marty.

AM stations were dominant. Sister FM stations that were co-owned usually simulcast AM's programming. By the late 1940s the *New York Times* listed FM programming but invariably said, "Same as AM." The exception was WFUV, which was producing the likes of Vin Scully, Charlie Osgood, and Bill O'Donnell.

Television was still the second medium. It was desperate for programming and would carry semipro basketball games in prime time. One Saturday night, Channel 4 had the New York Gothams against the Bridgeport Steelers from the Jamaica Arena.

In his Knicks days, Marty had various partners, as opposed to color commentators. They included Lomax, Desmond, and ex-player Bud Palmer. They would do some play-by-play, provide player profiles, and read commercials. The so-called analyst was still a couple of decades away. Chris Schenkel would fill in for Marty on Knicks broadcasts, too.

Desmond, a talented sportscaster who will always be linked to the Brooklyn Dodgers, had an unfortunate alcohol problem which cut his career short. Sadly, there were nights that the drinking was just too much. Before a basketball game, he would lean over the railing near the broadcast perch at the Garden and tell Marty that he simply could not work. One drink too many and he knew he wasn't up to it. Years later, this once distinguished broadcaster would come up

Johnny Most   *Chick Hearn*

to buddies he would know at various radio stations and ask for a handout. It was deflating for everyone.

In the early '50s Glickman broke in Johnny Most, who spent two seasons with the Knicks. Most had been at WVOS in the Catskills. Johnny was solid doing Knicks play-by-play. Glickman later recommended Most to Red Auerbach when the Celtics were looking for a replacement for Curt Gowdy in 1953. The Bronx-born Most was forever effusive in his praise of Glickman. Sitting in the press room at the old Boston Garden in 1988, Most was asked to compare Glickman with the accomplished Marv Albert. "Marv couldn't shine his shoes," he graveled.

Most rooted unabashedly when he got to Boston, where he had a 32-year run of Celtics distortion. But in his Knicks years, he gave excellent description. Of course, there was no one better to sit next to and learn the craft from than Glickman. After a lifetime of two packs of cigarettes a day, Most's voice was inimitably raspy. He liked to say, "According to the Surgeon General, I've been dead since 1955."

Johnny was alive and well in 1988 when he and Chick Hearn teamed on the radio broadcast of the NBA All-Star Game. Prior to the game, Hearn was thoroughly prepared and laid his papers down at the broadcast table. He then turned to Most courteously and asked, "Do you have enough room for your game notes?" Johnny responded, "What notes?"

There was a Celtics voice before Most, Curt Gowdy. Already broadcasting Red Sox games, he was asked by Celts owner Walter Brown to do the Celtics in 1951. Brown promised Gowdy a small fee which he didn't have and never paid.

He would do home games live and an occasional road game via re-creation. Yes, re-created basketball games on the radio. "Our Western Union telegrapher tried to tap out every pass but it got crazy, he couldn't do it. Things moved too quickly. Then I said, just give me the scoring. 'Jones, a hook shot; Smith a rebound; Brown, a set shot.' I'll make up the rest."

A dozen or so years later, University of Miami broadcaster Sonny Hirsch re-created Hurricanes games. At that point, it was easier. Contact lenses were popular and Rick Barry wore them. When Sonny would lose communication with the information purveyor from the road arena, he would say, "Barry has lost a contact lens and they're scurrying all over the floor trying to find it." That's how he would buy time until he reestablished communication.

A charismatic NBA announcer for the Warriors for two decades, Bill King re-created some of the club's road games their first year in the Bay Area. "We would do ten or twelve. Pro basketball wasn't greeted enthusiastically at first. It was thought of as mindless basketball and the station didn't want the added expense.

"I had done minor-league baseball re-creations and took a similar approach. It took ingenuity. I sketched a player in my mind. I had an image of each one. It wasn't unlike Red Barber who pictured a batter's physique and batting stance when he re-created baseball." It was unlike Barber, though, because King used preproduced crowd noise and some theatrics.

King had a reputation for ripping officials. "He's the paragon of ineptitude," a very literate King would carp. The officials were on scholarship when King did re-creations.

Jim McKechnie, the longtime "voice of the Syracuse Nats" and son of former baseball manager Bill McKechnie, did re-creations so well that he made plays up as he went along. Players would kid him that he knew the Syracuse offense better than they did. Jim needed some creativity. He did it without crowd noise!

Back then color commentators weren't analysts. Their comments during the action were sparse. They assisted with some play-by-play, read some promotional announcements, and filled in during the many unsold commercial breaks. Back then, of course, there was one or perhaps two sponsors, not the laundry list enjoyed today.

Color commentary on radio, where the game is hard enough to follow, can be a bit overbearing. Presenting it at every pause or on every trip down the floor can be obtrusive. Oftentimes, some color men get so technical it's hard to understand on television where diagrams can be drawn. But on radio, it's absolutely impossible.

The Knicks' first radio color man was John Andariese, who joined Marv Albert in 1972. He was economical with his comments and when he had something to add he spoke. Otherwise, he remained silent. The effect was that listeners would perk their ears to hear what he was saying. Andariese provided color commentary on Knicks cablecasts and rejoined Marv Albert on Knicks radio in 1998.

Today there's so much more to share. There are monitors in front of announcers with state-of-the-art technology that produce statistical data instantly. There are numbers galore on screens in front of announcers and they are updated continuously. Too many announcers today lean on numbers to a point where the numbers become a crutch.

Glickman recently listened to a tape of a game. At the very top of the broadcast, the announcer gave the teams' won-lost records and their records against each other. Simple, right? Marty stopped the tape immediately. Even though he had just heard the numbers, he couldn't repeat the records. The point was made. A listener has a hard time digesting numbers on radio. Yet, the double-digit wins and double-digit losses are often just the beginning of an unending numerical recital. Many play-by-play people get into the arcane on radio. It's often unwieldy.

Statistics are best left for the agate page of the newspaper where they can be studied and digested. The popular Bob Prince, the legendary "voice of the Pittsburgh Pirates," decried the announcers of today who use statistics. "They play it safe, they statistic you to death."

Glickman worked the first NBA All-Star Game in 1951 on radio and the league's first network television package on now defunct Dumont and later on NBC. His partner on TV was Lindsey Nelson. "Lindsey was cordial, warmer than Red Barber, but a very private guy. We used all sorts of gimmicks to promote the league. We miked Al Cervi, Larry Foust would dunk, and George King would dribble between his legs."

Marty was a busy sportscaster in his early days, running from one event to another. Normally, Glickman was so thorough in his preparation that he would recite from the poet Chaucer to warm up his mouth before a broadcast. One weekend though, he was away and was to return directly to Madison Square Garden to broadcast a track meet with the esteemed Ted Husing. A track star himself, Glickman felt he knew enough about the sport and didn't need to prepare much. But once on the air, Marty realized he was ill-prepared to do the broadcast. It was one of the more embarrassing moments of his young career because of the respect he had for the venerable Husing. He felt as though he let down the legendary broadcaster, and it taught him a valuable lesson.

Travel in those days was hardly simple. Not only was the means of transportation rail, often it would involve train–ground–transportation–train connections. It was a while before airplanes would become the standard mode, and it would be even longer before jet charters would be used.

In the early 1950s Glickman and Palmer were to do a game together in Syracuse. Palmer took a plane that resembled one of those concoctions that Wilbur Wright flew. Glickman traveled safely by train. Palmer, an ex-Knick, got there first, and Glickman rushed in just as they were about to tip it off. Marty can remember the maddening experience of being unable to find the broadcast location or his partner.

Conditions in the fledgling league were hardly state-of-the-art. Glickman recalls, "I did a game against the Waterloo Hawks in Waterloo, Iowa. It was heated by hot air blowers at one end. They would turn up the blowers when the Knicks were shooting fouls at that end, and it would give a knuckleball effect to the shots."

Knicks broadcasts weren't always a priority. Stations couldn't always secure sponsors and even when they did, baseball or other programming would take priority. Today each team has every game on radio although there are nine professional teams in addition to college sports in New York. There weren't as many willing radio stations, hardly enough sponsorship support, and certainly not the alternative stations that there are now.

On April 25, 1952, the NBA title was on the line when the Knicks played the Minneapolis Lakers in the seventh game of the championship series in Minneapolis. WHN wasn't scheduled to carry the game because the Dodgers were scheduled to play. There would have been no radio coverage and certainly no television coverage. Here were the Knicks in pursuit of a title and no live coverage whatsoever.

Luckily, the Dodgers were rained out that night. So at the last moment, WHN arranged for a feed of the Minneapolis broadcast. That's how New Yorkers followed the championship game, won by the Lakers, 82–65, and they had the rain—divine intervention—to thank.

Things were quite disjointed during the early years of the Knicks. Broadcasts on Monday could not run past 10 P.M. because WHN was committed to boxing. So promptly at 10 P.M., no matter the state of the basketball game, the station would put on the fights. It wasn't until the boxing was over that WHN would pick up the remainder of the basketball game.

On the collegiate side, St. John's University, the New York area's only consistent major national presence, didn't have a New York City radio home until 1982. It has flourished on radio since, boosted by excellent sponsorship support.

In 1952 St. John's advanced to the finals of the NCAA tournament against Kansas in Seattle. Again, no television, no prime-time viewing. The national title game was scheduled to begin at 12:30 A.M. eastern time. Glickman had other commitments so WHN arranged for an out-of-town pickup by West Coast announcer Rod Belcher. These may have been golden years for radio because television was at a nascent state. Yet radio coverage today, while perhaps not as salient or as glorious, is so much more reliable, except for an occasional snafu like the time in the late 1980s when St. John's played Villanova the same night that the president's State of the Union address was scheduled.

The broadcast of the game was run on an hour delay. With the matchup hanging in the balance and under a minute to go, there was a time-out. Going into the commercial break, the crowd was at a fevered pitch. There was electricity on the air. At that point, it was time for WCBS to go to the next reel of tape. But the station skipped a reel accidentally and coming out of the break, the listener heard, "Our guest on tonight's postgame show is Dick Vitale following St. John's loss to Villanova." It took about a minute for WCBS to correct the mistake.

After WHN lost the Knicks-Rangers rights to WINS at the end of the 1955 season, Marty Glickman cut down on his Knicks play-by-play. He did some Knicks games on WINS and returned for one last year in 1962–63, a season in which the Knicks were terrible, finishing in last place at 21–59. Doing one game from a broadcast location way upstairs at Cobo Hall in Detroit that season, he lamented over the poor play of the Knicks and the row upon row of empty seats beneath him. Many were still apathetic to the NBA then.

In the 1980s the basketball broadcasting pioneer finished his career by calling University of Connecticut basketball games and later Seton Hall games on WNEW.

Glickman was the first inductee into the Curt Gowdy media wing of Basketball's Hall of Fame in Springfield, Massachusetts, in 1990. He was enshrined the same night as Harry Gallatin. The "Big Horse" paid Glickman the highest praise. He related how, as a member of the Knicks, he would return from a long two-week trip and would want to tell his wife about his team's performance on the road. She would stop him immediately. "Harry, I listened to Marty and saw it on the radio."

As a player for the Miami Heat in 1997, Alonzo Mourning, a bright fellow, was injured for a while. When the team went on the road, he stayed home in Miami to rehabilitate his foot. He would regularly visit team therapist David Shea.

On this particular day, Mourning was on Shea's office table while the Heat were playing an afternoon game in Charlotte. Shea put on the radio to listen to the game so that he and "Zo" could follow the team's road game. The player told Shea that he had never heard a basketball game on the radio. Welcome to the television age.

With WINS in the Knicks' fold in 1955, the name Les Keiter became popular, and over the next half-dozen years, the Keiter-Glickman rivalry would fester and intensify. Les would do Knicks games for all or parts of six of the next eight seasons. But between 1955 and 1967, the Knicks would finish above .500 just once. Keiter had virtually nothing with which to work.

During that period, coverage was erratic. In 1955–56, the very first year WINS had the games, only eight early-season games made it on the air. They were self-sustaining broadcasts because of an inability to get a sponsor. In financial hock, the Knicks' broadcasts were canceled after the abbreviated schedule. Yet all games were on the following year, a partial schedule in 1957–58, the whole schedule in 1958–59, partial again the next year, and not on at all in 1960–61. On November 15, 1960, the Lakers' Elgin Baylor scored a record 71 points in a game against the Knicks at the old Garden. There was no radio and certainly no TV. It was hardly a dependable situation. Then in 1961–62 there were some experimental broadcasts at the end of the campaign.

It was a viscous cycle. The team was losing, the club wasn't drawing, interest levels weren't high, and stations and sponsors couldn't be relied upon. The Garden was at the mercy of WINS's ability to land a sponsor. When it did, the games were on. When it didn't, the games were off.

The *New York Times* didn't seem too interested at the time, either. When Wilt Chamberlain torched the Knicks for 100 points in a single game on March 2, 1962, in Hershey, Pennsylvania, it had only a wire service report. The *Times* didn't have its own reporter there. Today it is not uncommon for the *Times* to have two reporters with the Knicks when the team heads as far as the West Coast.

If New Yorkers say they heard the Chamberlain point explosion on radio, either they are lying or they picked up the Warriors' broadcast on the Philadelphia outlet with Bill Campbell and By Saam. The game was not carried in New York on either television or radio.

Despite having little material to work with, Keiter made his mark. He had a deep choppy voice, riveting delivery, and catchy phrases. Keiter brought warmth and a sense of urgency to the broadcasts. Marv Albert and Spencer Ross will definitely be quick to point out that they were influenced by Les.

There's hardly a New York sports fan of the 1950s who doesn't remember Keiter. He was quite visible, broadcasting hockey and football, calling fights, doing pregame shows for the Yankees' radio broadcasts, and more. WINS, for that matter, was the sports station back then. It had the Knicks, Rangers, the Yankees through the 1957 season, and the football Giants. And from 1958–60, it was the home of Keiter's re-creation of the baseball Giants' games from San Francisco.

Keiter created a whole vocabulary for basketball. Briefly, they are:

Tickling the twine	*Marty Glickman's version of "swish," no iron*
Ring-tailed howitzer	*an off-balance last-second shot*
The arithmetic reads	*the score of the game*
In the air . . . in the bucket	*a shot launched that was good*
In-again-out-again-Finnegan	*a shot that agonizingly falls out after it's halfway in*

While Glickman couldn't tolerate Keiter's clichés, Albert was quite kind in his praise of Keiter in his 1979 book, *Yess!* "I could sit in front of a radio and listen to Marty Glickman and Les Keiter doing play-by-play forever. They simply lifted the listener right out of his seat and made him feel he was sitting right there on the Knicks bench."

Glickman and Keiter were among the best-known names in New York radio sports in the 1950s, and they were arch rivals. Remember that this was before the growth of local and network television sports and way before cable. ESPN wasn't even the abbreviation of a law firm back then.

They were essentially with different radio stations. Glickman at WMGM (the call letters of 1050 AM from September 1948 to March 1962) and Keiter at WINS. Their styles were drastically different. The stations were constantly battling for rights to various sporting events and the two were fierce rivals. Keiter thought that Glickman was haughty, and Glickman felt that Keiter was full of bluster.

One can understand. The New York–reared Marty was respected at the time as "voice of the Knicks and Giants," the ultimate host of pre- and postgame baseball programming, and here comes this carpetbagger, usurping broadcast rights and making a mark for himself. From Keiter's viewpoint, Glickman simply wanted to dominate and not share.

In his 1991 autobiography, *Fifty Years Behind the Mike*, Keiter tells of the day that WINS got the rights to the football Giants. He called Glickman to ask him to be his partner on the broadcasts. According to Les, Marty was curt and told him, "Either I'm number one or I'm not on the broadcast," referring to the conversation as his "first encounter with big-league sportscasting egos."

Marty had done the Giants for seven years to that point and it would have been quite a letdown to have to do color for this Johnny-come-lately, Keiter.

Oddly enough, despite the dislike that the men had for one another, they worked together during the 1956–57 Knicks season. Often, because of other assignments, one would do the Knicks game while the other was doing unrelated programming somewhere else. Other times, Keiter and Glickman would share the game. Each would do a half. It wasn't as though there was much conversation between the two when they were on the air. The Knicks didn't have a true color commentator until John Andariese in 1972. So let's say that they worked alone together.

The blood between the two is so bad that to this day neither can recall the season of sharing the Knicks broadcasts. I remember meeting Keiter in Hawaii in 1975. Unaware of the sour relationship at the time, I proudly mentioned that I knew Marty. Les grumped, "Glickman's a difficult man."

When he wrote his book, Keiter asked Marv Albert, his one-time statistician, to do an endorsement for the jacket of the book. Reading the manuscript and of the comments Les had for Marty, the one-time understudy to both refused to do it.

In the early 1990s Marty was vacationing in Hawaii when he turned on the television in his hotel room. There was Keiter being introduced for a final time before retiring. I'm sure that Marty shed no tears to see Keiter leave the on-air sports scene. Marty's Hawaii vacation was complete.

As previously stated, Keiter dealt with hoop ineptitude in his New York days. The Gardenites featured mediocre names such as Kenny Sears, Willie Naulls, and Ray Felix. The league consisted of only eight teams and it didn't extend farther west than St. Louis. During the Keiter years, the Knicks finished higher than last place just once.

Yet, the pipe-smoking broadcaster made the games entertaining with a unique but cliché-ridden style. The man was Mr. Excitement. He made the Knicks sound like warriors and the games like World War III, with unmatched energy in his delivery and an exigency to his sound.

In those days Knicks seven-foot center Ray Felix would sign a 10-foot beam in the Keiters' living room without the help of a stepladder. The players may have been more accessible and ostensibly friendlier, but many, including Keiter, will tell you that the game was equally as physical. A veteran of many heavyweight title fights, Les said, "My years with the Knicks led to the biggest fight that I would ever see. The game was very physical with lots of bumping, elbowing, and pushing." He then went on to describe a benches-clearing brawl in Philadelphia that spilled into the stands. "I described for the listening audience the nonstop action of chairs flying, players fighting players, fans fighting fans, officials pulling at heaps of players, and bloodied noses."

Keiter was also involved in one of the most hilarious, if not embarrassing, moments in broadcast history. The ownership of WINS, for whom Keiter broadcast the Knicks' games, was rather parsimonious. If there was a way to save a penny, it knew how to save two. Back then, the only way to transmit long-form programming from out of town was via costly broadcast lines installed by the then monopolistic telephone company.

The cost for a so-called "equalized line" was based on an outrageous per-mile, per-minute tariff. This expense in fact was one reason stations were reluctant to carry many road games. With a dearth of sponsors, the economics were prohibitive. During the 1956–57 season, WINS undertook the most aggressive Knicks-Rangers package to that point, airing every game. The WINS engineering staff concocted a device which enabled the station to transmit remotes over a standard telephone line, effecting a major cost savings.

As such, all WINS would do is order a telephone at every venue, dial up the station, connect its equipment, and transmit over the phone. It saved thousands of dollars but the quality was hardly in the satellite caliber that listeners are accustomed to today. High-range notes were not picked up and too often the broadcasters sounded completely muffled. Not only were the listeners cheated but so was the phone company, which claimed illegal use of equipment. Let Keiter relate the rest of this comical experience:

"The long-distance operator kept interrupting me over the telephone line we were using for the live broadcast. I would say 'there's a pass to Kerr.' And the operator would come on and say 'what is the number you are trying to reach' and I'd say 'I'm broadcasting a basketball game' and this would go on for 10 minutes." Keiter ignored the operator and eventually was cut off the air.

In his book, *Rocking America*, the late Rick Sklar, who programmed WINS at the time and later was credited with developing WABC into the number one station in America, said that the ownership of WINS took AT&T to court, and the judge was so impressed by WINS's creativity that it had the phone company build a similar unit and make it available to radio stations for rent. Using the basic telephone line and adding what engineers called "line extenders" in later years, this piece of equipment not only improved broadcast quality but also saved stations a ton of money in the years ahead.

Keiter's last mark on Knicks broadcasts was his eight-game experiment late in the 1961–62 season. He asked listeners on-air whether there was any interest in Knicks broadcasts. Anheuser-Busch and Phillies Cigars were the sponsors. It worked to a point but not for Keiter. WINS dropped sports and there was an ownership change. Les left for Philadelphia after the season, where he became a popular sportscaster over the next eight years. Les did pro basketball and Big Five broadcasts in the City of Brotherly Love.

He spent the last 20 years of his career as the dignified "voice of sports" in Hawaii. But Knicks fans of the 1950s will never forget the name of Les Keiter. The rasp was part of the New York tapestry.

His nemesis, Marty Glickman, was the beneficiary of the so-called eight-game experiment. Although the Knicks didn't cooperate, finishing in last place at 29–51, their third straight finish in the cellar of the Eastern Division, they had a new home the next season, WCBS. The station broadcast 50 Knicks games with "original voice" Glickman and 50 Rangers games with Jim Gordon. Marty was ubiquitous. Despite covering the football Giants at the time for WNEW, Glickman was handling various assignments for WCBS including pre- and postgame shows for the station's Yankees broadcasts.

But a fourth consecutive finish in dead last meant another year off the air in 1963–64 when the Knicks would again wind up in last place. But although he coached the club to three straight dreaded last-place finishes, Eddie Donovan was retained as Knicks coach at the start of the 1964–65 campaign. Donovan, of course, would be credited years later with being the architect of the franchise's first championship team in 1969–70 as the club's general manager.

Today with $1,000 courtside seats, Donovan would have been out the front door after a few errant passes. But back then it was a different currency, the G.O. (General Organization) card. High school students got in for 50 cents. Given the economics then, there was a greater level of tolerance.

Despite the plight of the ball club, the Knicks were able to negotiate their way back on radio in 1964–65, albeit only for Saturday night games. The station was WOR and the club's attraction was rookie Willis Reed, who would lead the Knicks in scoring, averaging 19 points per game. For WOR, it was hardly disruptive—just once a week, punctuating a generally low-rated Saturday night schedule.

The Knicks were on radio 16 of their first 18 years in the NBA, with either the legendary Marty Glickman or colorful Les Keiter as their principal broadcasters. Moving to WOR meant the incorporation of the station's talent into the broadcasts, one of whom was actually part of the club's broadcast crew their very first year. Stan Lomax, the dean of New York's radio sports reporters, was to do

Courtesy WEVD Radio

Bill Mazer

color for Lester Smith, one of the most versatile broadcasters at the time. Smith was quite a talent who, among other assignments, anchored the hourly news at WOR Radio, working alongside legendary names Lyle Van and Henry Gladstone.

Smith also had a nice run on co-owned WOR Television where he hosted *New York Reports*. A strong and glib street reporter, Smith could do just about anything. He proudly points out that he covered every political convention from 1944 to 1992. .

A New Englander, Smith was a fairly accomplished sports announcer, having covered an assortment of teams including the Boston Braves with Jim Britt for two years, a gig he would lose when the National League club moved to Milwaukee in 1953. In 1957 Smith came to New York.

At the point of getting his Knicks assignment, Smith spent 20 years broadcasting college football and many basketball games. He and his partner, Lomax, were no strangers to one another. They had done seven years of Army football together for WOR.

A good "generalist," Smith lacked the passion for basketball that Glickman and Keiter brought to their broadcasts. The abbreviated schedule was hardly sufficient to produce great memories. But Smith and Lomax did provide some sort of a link, albeit limited. And, oh yes, the Knicks were back in their familiar last-place spot, completing a 31–49 campaign. That made it six straight seasons fixed at the bottom of the Eastern Division standings. It would be the addition of Baltimore to the East in 1966–67 that eventually ended the ignominious drought and lifted the New Yorkers out of last place. They finished fourth again, but this time there were five teams in the division.

Baseball and football were having a tough time securing a couple of sponsors. "Basketball?" time buyers would ask. "The Knicks?"

"The Knicks wanted us to carry the entire schedule in 1965–66," Smith said, "but station management was lukewarm on the Knicks to begin with, so that was the end of it." The Knicks did manage to maintain a radio relationship in 1965–66 but again it was a Saturday night format, this time with Bill Mazer on WNBC.

There was no compelling reason to carry the Knicks on a regular basis. These were lean times for the ball club, and the broadcast package was hardly a moneymaker. The interest in the team was limited. Basketball was hardly a ratings winner, and sponsors weren't lining up to sign advertising contracts. The Garden denizens had no alternative.

They were still in the old Garden on 50th Street and Eighth Avenue, and it had a seedy-looking marquee that hardly belied the peep-show parlors on neighboring streets.

So while the Knicks game against the St. Louis Hawks at the old Garden, scheduled for Tuesday, November 9, 1965, was canceled because of the great blackout that hit the Northeast, no broadcast was canceled because no broadcast had been scheduled at all.

The well-schooled Bill Mazer had a "friend-at-the-game" style of play-by-play. While the Knicks were preparing to play the Hawks at about 5:30 on the night the lights went out, Mazer was at the WNBC studios at Rockefeller Center doing his popular talk show. Suddenly, it was dark.

Influenced by Jack Paar, Arthur Godfrey, and Ted Husing, Mazer had come to New York from Buffalo a year earlier and introduced metropolitan area fans to sports talk radio. But he needed no introduction to New York City where he was raised. He had a brilliant mind, had attended yeshiva, and studied the Talmud. In the embryonic years of television, Mazer worked in New York doing college basketball from Madison Square Garden in the late 1940s working with Al Barlick, later a major-league baseball umpire.

Now in 1965 he was telling the story of the Knicks' unsuccessful experiment with a double post, 6-foot, 11-inch Walt Bellamy and 6-foot, 9-inch Willis Reed.

An institution in Buffalo, Mazer had broadcast the games of the "little three," St. Bonaventure, Niagara, and Canisius. But he was hardly a rapid-fire broadcaster of the likes of Glickman, either. Marty, though, had a hand in his career, recommending him for a job at a Buffalo radio station shortly after the war. "When I first heard him, I thought he would be the next Ted Husing. He had a marvelous voice, tremendously quick mind, and a great command of the language," Marty said.

He developed such an enormous popularity in Buffalo that the station for which he worked took out ads on buses that read, "Tune in the Little Three with Mr. Basketball, Bill Mazer." On a trip to Buffalo, Marty noticed the advertisements and remarked, "I wonder what Nat Holman would think," referring to the esteemed coach of CCNY, whose contribution to the game was so enormous that scribes dubbed him "Mr. Basketball."

Mazer on the air was deliberate and opinionated. "I used to coach when I would broadcast a game." Those who grew up with him, such as longtime *Sports Illustrated* writer Cory Kirkpatrick, swore by him. His warmth was infectious and he had a marvelous ability to make interviewees feel at home and at ease. "All of Buffalo was gripped by his broadcast of the famous four-overtime Canisius NCAA game. I will never forget it."

Neither will Mazer. He lost his voice and took singing lessons for voice conditioning so that it would never happen again.

But those who picked up his Buffalo basketball broadcasts in New York on WKBW would write Mazer letters asking if the game was slower there than in New York, because Glickman was going a mile a minute compared to him.

While the Knicks were bouncing around from one station to another, Chick Hearn in Los Angeles and Bill King in San Francisco were gilding their legends with the Lakers and Warriors, respectively, where they broadcast every game of each team.

The exposure at NBC headquarters led Mazer to many commercial voice-overs and a spell as host of the popular television quiz show, *Concentration*.

Marty Glickman broadcasts on cable from the new Madison Square Garden during halftime of a game in 1970.

Courtesy Marty Glickman

By 1966 the Knicks made strides by packaging more games on television over WOR-TV Channel 9, while the radio package moved for a third time in three years but this time to WHN, which beefed up its sports presence. The Garden higher-ups brought in a bright young star, Don Criqui, a Notre Dame alum who grew up in Buffalo listening to Mazer. Criqui would do both radio and television, the home games on WHN and many of the road games on Channel 9. It was obvious early that Criqui was more adept at the visual medium. And his highly successful network career has proved it.

Criqui had presided over yet another year in which the Knicks were not above .500, their 11th in 12 years. It was the last season before the Marv Albert era and Willis Reed remained a towering beacon of hope.

Although Criqui's local radio play-by-play was limited to the one year with the Knicks, he served for years as the sports anchor on *Imus in the Morning* over WNBC, where his quick wit was not only a requirement but also quite entertaining.

By the summer of 1967 there was reason to believe that years of frustration would finally end. To begin with, the Knicks were scheduled to move into a brand-new Madison Square Garden about a mile south of the old one. Two bright stars would come along who promised to change their fortunes on the court, Walt Frazier, who had electrified the old Garden the previous March with a brilliant performance for Southern Illinois at the National Invitation Tournament, and Bill Bradley, the Rhodes scholar from Princeton. These two, of course, would turn into indispensable pieces in the Knicks' first championship puzzle which blossomed into fruition in 1970.

Meanwhile, there was one other name that would join the Knicks' family during the 1967–68 season, a name that would be as synonymous with the Garden roundballers in the years ahead as any of the players. If there's one broadcaster identified with the Knicks, it's Marv Albert.

A native of Brooklyn, Marv had made his Knicks broadcast debut on January 27, 1963, at age 21, filling in for Glickman. He had been a go-fer for the Brooklyn Dodgers, a ball boy for the Knicks, a statistician for both Glickman and Keiter, and an organizer of the team's first fan club.

He had attended Syracuse where he studied broadcasting and later worked at several stations in the central New York State town. He did a variety of sports and music shows and would even occasionally host classical music shows.

If there was anyone born for play-by-play, it was Marv. If a Tiger Woods or Michael Jordan comes along only once in a generation, a Marv Albert isn't born every day. Just ask Marty Glickman, another Syracuse man who believed in Albert from day one, nurtured him from his callow teenage days, and got him gigs early in his career. During the next decade, New Yorkers would witness the epiphany of this broadcast giant-to-be.

He was born Marvin Aufrichtig, the older brother of Al and Steve, both of whom would also enjoy successful sportscasting careers in the years ahead. They all must have come from great broadcast stock, but I guess that no one will ever know. Their dad, Max, ran a grocery near the family home in Brighton Beach.

As a kid, Marv would schlepp his cumbersome reel-to-reel tape recorder to Ebbets Field where he would practice play-by-play. He was hard working, conscientious, and precocious. By 1963 Marv left Syracuse to complete his college studies at NYU and to assist Glickman.

The very fact that Glickman had him work the Knicks game on that Sunday afternoon in 1963 is quite a testimony to his young pupil's talent. Glickman got held up in Europe, and Jim Gordon had a Rangers assignment. Marty suggested to WCBS management that Marv fill in.

It's hard to believe that the Knicks were then in great demand. After all, they were stumbling along with folks such as Dave Budd, Al Butler, and Gene Conley, a two-sport player who also pitched for the Boston Red Sox. Things were so loose in those days that Conley would occasionally leave the bench in uniform to get a hot dog from the concession stand.

WCBS, the station carrying the games that year, didn't seem to believe that its audience felt there was a compelling immediacy to the Knicks-Celtics game on January 27 when Marv made his broadcast debut in Boston. The station ran the game on a tape-delayed basis so that it could carry its regularly scheduled programming, the *Texaco Philharmonic*. Tape or live, Marv would nonetheless call it "the most nervous day of my life."

Marty worked alone then, so Marv worked alone that day. There wasn't a color commentator. Al Albert, the middle brother of the three future broadcasters, made the trip with Marv to help calm his nerves and assist with statistics. After taking an all-night train out of Grand Central Station, the Brooklyn boys ran up against a crusty guard at the Boston Garden who demanded credentials. In those days the traveling media party was scant, and usually the team's public relations man didn't travel with the ball club, either. In fact, many teams had only part-time public relations people.

The security people in Boston were not convinced that the boyish-faced Marv was the Knicks' broadcaster. He knew no one with the Celtics so there was no one at the Boston Garden to vouch for him. Marv desperately opened his briefcase and flashed it at the guard. It was filled to the brim with preparatory notes. At that point the guard must have said to himself, maybe he's for real. He called around and, finally, Eddie Donovan, the Knicks' coach that season, came to Marv's rescue. So there he was on that fateful afternoon, perched on the front ledge of the upper tier of the Boston Garden balcony, knowing that he was staring opportunity right in the face. Thirty odd years later and who knows how many Knicks games later, he's a basketball broadcast Hall of Famer, enshrined with immortals Marty Glickman and the venerable Chick Hearn.

Marv would later say, "I can't believe they allowed me on the air. Here was a college kid doing what sounded like a bad impression of Marty."

As the 1963 portion of the 1962–63 campaign continued, Marv found himself getting more and more work, getting his first Rangers assignments as well as the Knicks. Glickman was in constant demand. Marv would eventually face the same hectic schedule as his star rose. But back then, he was happy to settle for the last-place Knicks playing in winter-weather paradises such as Syracuse. Yes, Marv actually goes back to the Syracuse Nats days. The Syracuse Nats didn't leave for Philadelphia, where they became the 76ers, until the end of the 1963 season.

While Marv was appointed Rangers voice in 1966, he wasn't given the Knicks job until 1967. When he was told that he had the Knicks gig, he went back to his Manhattan apartment, shut the door, and screamed. Marv Albert had achieved a lifelong dream.

There were other responsibilities. That summer WHN acquired the rights to the Yankees and Albert kept himself busy with wraparound programming. When a great American League pennant race developed that summer, Albert would re-create updates between records that the station disc jockeys were spinning. Back then baseball dominated, and Albert threw himself right into the hardball mix.

That winter he kept a busy schedule of Knicks and Rangers play-by-play and did a winter weekly hot-stove baseball show. In fact, he was so busy that when the Knicks opened the new Garden in February 1968, the game was televised. It wasn't on radio, and Marv was at the studio on another assignment.

But it was the Knicks nonetheless that was Marv's ticket to fame. He was living a boyhood dream, and his broadcasts mirrored his unrestrained enthusiasm. It was theater at its very best, compelling theater. There was boundless passion. Other broadcasters might have equaled the word picture he painted, but few matched his flair on radio. His intensity and his signature staccato were inimitable. When Marv would do a Knicks game, his whole body would shake. His concentration was unbending and as a result he rarely made a mistake. He was very prudent and had the ability to say something instantly that others would have to think about twice.

Through all his years on radio, Marv was always cognizant of the elementary requirements such as following the ball. The listener could close his eyes and see the game. In his early years of Knicks broadcasts, Marv got so excited that when he listens to some of those early tapes today, he cringes. It was the pitch of his voice then that makes him shudder today, not the exhilarating passion for his craft which continues to manifest itself. In that regard his enthusiasm hasn't waned a bit.

His basketball broadcast career has already spanned four decades and it has touched a couple of generations. He has made a smooth transition from popular radio announcer with a highly regionalized style to national basketball announcer of our generation. If Marty Glickman was the canonized creator, Marv was his apostle, propagating his teachings, spreading the germ of the Glickman doctrine.

There's an old saying, "If you're good, you're lucky, and if you're lucky, you're good." And while Marv's work was invigorating, there were four supporting circumstances.

First was the fact that when he joined the Knicks in 1967, interest started to grow. All the team's home games were basically blacked out on television. Sterling Manhattan Cable piped the games into parts of Manhattan but that was it. It was common then for bars to charge a cover fee to watch the Knicks' and Rangers' games. A ticket was getting harder and harder to secure, so unless fans got to a Manhattan bar, they were out of luck. Certainly in the outer boroughs and in the early years in the suburbs, there was no cable. Radio was it.

But there was Marv, and to many it was as good as television. They hung on his every sacred word. Many would not attend any home games at all, so the building was no more than a product of their imagination based on Albert's word picture. The Knicks, for all they knew, played in only two directions, "from the 8th Avenue end to the 7th or from the 7th to the 8th," Marv's descriptive landmarks.

Second, the radio schedule was made up of a preponderance of home games just when the young Knicks of Frazier, Bradley, and company started winning on the Garden floor. In Albert's second season the Knicks were 30–7 at home.

Thus when the Knicks scored and Marv boomed his patented "yesss," the crowd behind him roared its approval, reverberating a positive reinforcement of Marv's call. Road games were generally left for television.

Third, unlike previous seasons, the Knicks were winning and the Garden gave them their just due. No longer were they shipped off to the decrepit 69th Regiment Armory when the circus came to town during the playoffs in April. They were now a cherished tenant. The town was behind them and any announcer knows that when the team is triumphant on the floor or field and the fans feel good about their hometown team, the broadcaster can do no wrong. Such was certainly the case for Marv Albert who spent 19 glorious years in the Knicks' radio booth before moving to television full-time.

Courtesy Madison Square Garden

Realizing a lifelong dream when he was assigned to the New York Knicks radio booth, Marv Albert spent 19 seasons on the job before moving to television full-time.

Fourth, by the late 1960s Mel Allen was out and Red Barber was gone. There was plenty of room for an up-and-coming hero.

Early on, Albert's booth was up in the nosebleeds, way upstairs. He could almost touch the building's famous fan-shaped roof. Finally Madison Square Garden management had some sympathy and constructed a couple of seats above the players' ramp at courtside.

During the Knicks' first championship run in 1970, Marv did not do any of the team's road playoff games. They were televised. But the Knicks had a strange setup where a network of radio stations with a separate crew was formed. This group of stations, all outside the metropolitan area, carried all home games and all playoff games. Jim Gordon called the famous final series with the Lakers for this network. As interest picked up, WNBC ran Gordon's feed. In other words, the Knicks' pivotal overtime win at the Forum in game three was not voiced by Marv, who, of course, did do game seven, played at the Garden.

Speaking of the famous game seven, there's an often-heard tape of Marv describing Willis Reed's pregame grand entrance onto center stage at the Garden. Fans held their breath to see whether Reed was well enough to play. With a sense of urgency to his voice, Marv describes Willis's first practice shots and the crowd responds. What many don't know is that the tape is a reenactment.

The game was run by ABC Television that night in New York on a tape-delayed basis and Marv worked alone on radio as usual. It might have been radio's greatest listenership ever to a basketball game, as the Knicks were about to play a gripping game for the league title. There was no color man or pregame and postgame host.

So unlike today, where broadcasts pick up live locker-room interviews after games, there was no such hookup. Marv finished the broadcast alone and switched it to the studio where WHN ran music. The station ran music while champagne was bubbling in the locker room. Marv gathered some tape from the winners in the bedlam of the celebration and later went back on the air and told the story of the wild coronation.

While Marv's broadcasts were precise, upbeat, and virtually flawless, he started running thin due to his own success. To begin with, the Garden had him broadcasting both the Knicks and Rangers and later the Knicks on over-the-air television. Marv was doing the 6 and 11 P.M. nightly sports for WNBC-TV in 1973, the football Giants on radio, and then gigs for NBC Television, starting with college basketball and pro football. The more work, the more Marv thrived. He loved it. But due to all these commitments, Marv was missing more than just a handful of Knicks radio broadcasts.

It came to a head when, in the mid-1980s, the affable play-by-player was doing an afternoon game between the Knicks and Celtics at the Garden. The Knicks were down 25 and made a great comeback, sending the contest into overtime. Marv was cutting it close. When the first extra session started, Marv should have been on his way to Rockefeller Center to get ready for his early news sportscast. He sweated it out through the first overtime before a second one was about to begin.

At that point he simply had to leave. Bob Wolff finished the game. Right then and there, it was clear that Marv had grown into even more prestigious roles, namely television. By the end of the 1985–86 season, a change was effected. Bob Gutkowski, president of the MSG Network at the time, asked Albert to move over to the growing cable side and give up radio.

It certainly wasn't the end of his established phrase, "Yesss," which he might have picked up while in Syracuse from Syracuse Nats broadcaster Jim McKechnie. The phrase became an even more identifiable trademark on the tube.

So who was better, Glickman or Albert? It depends on who you ask. Many old-timers will swear by Glickman and some younger folks today, who unfortunately may never have heard the pioneer, can't pass judgment. In retrospect, while Marv may have been more impactful, particularly as basketball's popularity exploded, Marty was more influential. Both were broadcaster's broadcasters.

In 1992 Marv was deservedly honored by the Garden for his years of dedication. It was an unusual night. To be sure to please Albert, the Garden asked him to choose the exact date and game and to select those who would introduce him. Marv made the best of it. He asked that Marv Albert Night be held when the Bulls come to town. At that point not every Knicks game was a complete sellout, except, of course, when Michael Jordan came calling. And then the building was indeed packed. As his presenters, for good promotional measure, Marv arranged for the highly rated Mike and the Mad Dog of WFAN fame.

Courtesy David J. Halberstam

Author and former "voice of the Miami Heat" and "voice of St. John's University" David Halberstam, center, is flanked by Marty Glickman, left, and Marv Albert in 1991. Old-timers who grew up with Glickman argue he was the best, while younger fans, who may never had heard Glickman, throw their support to Albert.

While the Garden and Knicks sponsors showered him with gifts, it wasn't as though Marv's theatrical introduction brought the house down. To begin with, it was intermission. Many fans were at the concession stands.

Those who were in their seats applauded but hardly screamed themselves weak. Why? After all, for years after his resignation in 1964, the introduction of longtime Yankees voice Mel Allen produced a thunderous reception at the Stadium every Old Timer's Day.

For one thing, younger Knicks fans that night might not have remembered the heydays of Albert's emotional radio broadcasts in the early 1970s. Second, while Marv was indeed emotional about basketball, he didn't root openly. He didn't forge the "bond with blinders" as Allen, Rizzuto, or Johnny Most did with their clubs. Perhaps his journalistic integrity distanced him from the fans. They might not have felt the team blood dripping from his broadcasts. It's hard to have both the journalistic integrity and the ardent love of the fans.

The most important lesson of Marv Albert Night was that fans love players first. When Albert himself was master of ceremonies on Walt Frazier Night, he witnessed this firsthand. The response "Clyde" got was deafening, as was the case for other canonized ex-players. Announcers are not the heroes that players are.

1986 brought on a new era. Albert and partner Andariese moved over to television completely and Jim Karvellas switched over from cable to radio. Ernie Grunfeld, ex-Knicks player and one-time New York City high school standout, was brought in to do color.

Albert agreed to television but protected himself at the same time. This was when CBS still had the national television contract and before he was the "voice of the NBA" on NBC. So Marv was concerned about his role in the event that the Knicks made it to the finals. The Garden, and perhaps rightfully so, protected him. In that eventuality, Marv would have the option to do games on radio.

Karvellas had been around the league seemingly forever. He actually started with the old Chicago Zephyrs in 1962–63, not the club that was eventually led by Michael Jordan. (The Chicago Bulls were formed in 1966.) The NBA didn't have a team in Chi-

Jim Karvellas

Courtesy Madison Square Garden

cago at the start of the 1960s, an embarrassment to the league given the fact that Chicago was then the nation's second-biggest market. So in 1961–62 Chicago was awarded the Packers. Hardly successful, they changed their nickname to the Zephyrs the next season.

"Karvo," a Chicago native, got involved doing all sorts of things from handling the public address to trying to get the team on radio. He put together some sort of broadcast package on an FM station. Remember that in the early 1960s virtually all the country's listenership was on AM. FM didn't become popular until the early 1970s. FM stations were often simulcasting the programming of their sister AM facilities. My, how things have changed. Winding up on an FM back then was rather obscure.

When the Zephyrs moved to Baltimore in 1963, renamed the Bullets, the husky-voiced Karvellas went along and eventually became the club's popular radio and television broadcaster. Those who grew up with Karvo chronicling the story of Earl Monroe, Gus Johnson, Jack Marin, Wes Unseld, and others, adored him.

He was exciting and opinionated, and his broadcasts exuded warmth. Growing up a basketball nut in Brooklyn in the late 1960s, it was a pleasure to be able to dial in to Johnny Most in Boston, Andy Musser in Philadelphia, and Karvellas in Baltimore. The games and the broadcasters were memorable. There was a magic and a fascination that triggered the imagination from listening to these folks, hopping figuratively from city to city.

There was a profound contrast between Albert and Karvellas in presentation and preparation. Marv was the perfect technician, nuts and bolts and facts and figures. Karvellas was the daydreamer in the booth, reflecting, conjecturing, and pontificating. Marv was more concerned with what and when and Jim more with how and why. Albert had the informational data and Karvo the strategy.

Albert expressed with prescribed rhythm, and Karvellas would freelance haphazardly. Albert would spend little time with assistant coaches and scouts; Karvo would close the bar with them the night before at the hotel. Albert's opening remarks were sharp and rehearsed, Karvo's were a soliloquy. Albert's hairpiece was perfectly groomed, Jim's head of hair was tousled. Marv was Felix Unger, and Jim was Oscar Madison.

Unlike the Albert-Andariese team where there was an unwritten rule as to when the play-by-play announcer ends and the color commentator begins, Karvellas and Grunfeld were very informal and conversational. To the radio purist reared in New York it might have been maddening, but to still others it might have been refreshing. Karvellas knew the game and presented it in a "blue-collar" way. When the Knicks played the Rockets in a preseason game one year and the Garden was about half empty, he blurted, "Only the basketball freaks came out tonight."

He was influenced by Ed Kennedy of the Cincinnati Royals, Buddy Blattner of the St. Louis Hawks, and Bert Wilson of the Chicago Cubs. But he was hardly the rooter that these Midwest announcers were. Karvellas was unique. He would get on himself if he wasn't sharp. In Atlanta one night, it took him a few minutes to get his bearings, humorously mistaking the time-of-day clock for the game clock. Instead of brushing it under the table, he spouted, "Wake up, Jim."

By the time Grunfeld left the booth in 1989 to become an assistant coach with the club, there were a number of key developments. First, in 1987–88 Madison Square Garden gave radio a full commitment. To that point, only nontelevised games were being carried on radio. For the first time ever all Knicks and Rangers games were being carried live. Amazingly, the Knicks were the last NBA team to have every game on radio.

Second, after many mediocre seasons, there was promise. Rick Pitino was brought in to coach the club, and in his first season the New Yorkers advanced to the playoffs. It was Patrick Ewing's first appearance in the postseason. Third, by 1988 the Knicks' flagship was WFAN, the new all-sports station. While television was overwhelming, radio had a new prominence and Karvellas was its centerpiece. The broadcasts might not have had the mechanical structure inculcated by Marv but the basketball talk was so good that it drew the praise of an unlikely source. Columnist Peter Vecsey, one who's rather stingy with a compliment, sang Jim's praises in the *New York Post*.

What Karvellas lacked as a craftsman, he redeemed with warmth, honesty, and analysis.

Grunfeld had a lot of knowledge to offer, and he and Jim had good on-air chemistry. When Grunfeld left for the bench, the Garden hired a beloved link to their championship years, Walt Frazier. The Knicks' broadcasts would never be the same again.

Clyde brought a whole new dimension to the radio broadcasts. He was very opinionated and didn't hold back. If a play was asinine, Walt would use precisely that word to describe it. Frazier was a very heady player, and his approach on radio was brilliant. Basketball color commentators on radio are not afforded much time to elaborate. Radio is generally considered a play-by-play man's medium, while television is considered a color commentator's medium. Walt was challenged by the time restraints and made the best of it.

Although having to economize on his commentary, Clyde became insightful, provocative, and unique. It got to the point where Frazier was as identified with the Knicks' radio broadcasts as his play-by-play partner. There isn't a radio color commentator in the NBA today who is linked as closely to his team as Frazier is to the Knicks.

But it came at a price. The three years he spent with veteran broadcaster Karvellas were not heavenly. Karvellas wanted to lead, not be led. Frazier could be disparaging in his analysis, and Karvo was candid but couched his criticism. To the listener, it was good radio.

Frazier's colorful and rhyming descriptions have become his unique trademark. Mark Jackson didn't just spray passes, he was "swishing and dishing." Magic guard Scott Skiles wasn't just driving, he "was driving recklessly." Ewing wasn't only doing damage in the post, he was "lurking and irking, or posting and toasting." A smart player wasn't just heady, he was "sagacious." Charles Oakley wasn't just fearless, he was "intrepid." And if he was shooting well, "Oak had the stroke." Frazier would produce clever comments but Karvo rarely, if

Courtesy Madison Square Garden

Walt Frazier

ever, responded to the offbeat. There wasn't even a retort when Frazier provocatively mentioned that veteran NBA forward A. C. Green was a virgin.

For many, the best way to watch Knicks games in the Karvellas-Frazier days was with the television on and the sound down to the radio. Nothing was predictable. It was hardly the cookie-cutter approach to basketball on radio. Karvellas made up in opinion what he lacked in description, and Frazier was frank, candid, and full of verbal challenges.

One Frazier incident made for great fodder for popular morning man Don Imus. The Knicks lost a heartbreaker to Milwaukee one day at the buzzer. Frazier thought the broadcast was already in commercial break when he emoted, "Oh, shit!" It went right out on WFAN and Imus replayed it for weeks.

Imus lapped up the day in 1992 when the Knicks knocked off the Pistons to win a first-round playoff series. Karvellas started his postgame commentary by congratulating the Knicks on their triumph. Frazier interrupted and went into a fit. "For what, Jim? They should have killed these guys. There's no reason to congratulate them." The on-air polemics produced Imus material for weeks as the two battled it out on the air. It also put Frazier in the hot seat with Garden management but he weathered the storm. Ironically, at the end of the season, it was Karvellas who was not renewed.

After the 1991–92 campaign the Garden sold its rights to WFAN, giving the station some decision-making input with talent. Mike Breen was Imus's morning sports man and hosted Knicks pre- and postgame shows. He was promoted to play-by-play. Breen knew the game, had played it for a while, and at one time was an aspiring official.

While very witty and humorous as sports anchor on the *Imus in the Morning Show*, Breen was very businesslike and straight-laced in his play-by-play. He had worked at WFUV, the student station at Fordham University, where he sharpened his broadcasting skills. His style was more of the Glickman/Albert ilk, and he gave Frazier the room he needed to make his contribution. Opinionated but not controversial, off the air and on, Breen continued a hectic schedule working mornings with Imus and games at night. His day was made even longer when NBC came calling and assigned him to football and more.

One quiet day in the spring of 1997, the sports and broadcast world was stunned when Marv Albert, a 35-year broadcast veteran, New York icon, and father of grown children, was indicted in Virginia on sodomy and assault charges. The indictment stemmed from an incident with a woman in an Arlington hotel room.

Marv immediately declared his innocence and assured his employers at NBC and Madison Square Garden that the accusations were absolutely false. Publicly to that point, Marv's persona was impeccably clean. He was always considered composed and his demeanor mainstream. It hardly took a leap of faith by his two employers to allow him to continue to work while he assured them and the enthralled public that he would be completely exonerated.

While grotesque stories of Marv's sexual behavior surfaced and he became the butt of jokes on late-night television, Marv staunchly denied the allegations. In that period of time, NBC allowed him to cover the NBA playoffs, serving as the centerpiece of the network's coverage. The beleaguered announcer did an amazingly flawless job despite overwhelming pressure.

But at the trial in September, there was damaging and ignominious testimony which will forever taint Marv's once flawless reputation. There were gaudy revelations. Concerned perhaps that the prosecution was prepared to present more damaging testimony and to spare his witnessing family any further pain, Marv and his lawyers stopped the trial by agreeing to plead guilty to the lighter misdemeanor assault charge. Immediately thereafter, he was fired by NBC and resigned from the MSG Network. When the trial ended, Marv addressed the legion of media outside the courtroom, promising to "rehabilitate his personal life and his career." At 56, his true age disclosed, Marv Albert's career had been shattered.

The trial got damning headline coverage. Sadly, there was a sense at times that there was a thirst for the downfall of a public figure. Marv was the ongoing, unflattering focus of the front page of the New York tabloids. Lurid reports unmasked an unwholesome past, revelations that were particularly sobering for those who grew up idolizing this cynosure of rapid-fire sports. One couldn't help but remember the words of F. Scott Fitzgerald: "Show me a hero and I'll show you a tragedy."

Ian O'Connor, the *Daily News* columnist, wrote, "Albert went for the fences and missed, last swing of his career." Public opinion, though, seemed to be divided on whether or not he should be allowed back on the air. Marv then sought to redeem himself in the obloquy of one who had betrayed a perceived public trust. While many felt that he ought to shed the spotlight, Marv agreed to interviews on national television in the hope of evoking public sympathy.

For Albert's sake, it is hoped that time was the best healer. Inuring the sidelines after three decades of play-by-play was a difficult withdrawal process. Marv does games with an unconquerable spirit. Taking it away is like keeping a thoroughbred in the barn. And taking it away makes the sports fan the biggest loser of all.

Mike Breen was promoted to the MSG Network and Gus Johnson, already in the Garden stable of announcers, was appointed to the radio side. He became the first permanent black radio play-by-play announcer in the NBA.

In a bold move, Madison Square Garden announced in July 1998 that it had rehired Marv Albert to host *Sports Desk*, a nightly news and magazine-formatted cable television program, and to share the play-by-play on Knicks radio broadcasts. While women's groups protested Madison Square Garden's decision, New York fans were generally supportive of the home-grown Albert's return. After almost a year in punishing exile, in September 1998 Albert was back on the air again starting his broadcast career comeback in areas where he traced his roots, radio play-by-play and TV

Courtesy Madison Square Garden

Mike Breen

sports news. The shortest distance between two points is a straight line. Albert has come full circle.

The Nets were born in 1967 as charter members of the old American Basketball Association. Over the course of the next 30 years, they would have 13 different play-by-play broadcasters and one of them, Steve Albert, had two different stints. In the same period the Knicks have had just four different play-by-play announcers.

The first Nets voice was a Marty Glickman disciple, Spencer Ross. When he interviewed for the position, he was asked how he would approach the broadcasts. He said, "Like Marty Glickman." He was hired immediately. Ross grew up in Brooklyn, played high school basketball at New Utrecht, and then attended Florida State. He listened to a lot of Keiter and Glickman and swore by Marty. "Buddy Lee's, a clothier in downtown Brooklyn, sponsored Marty's broadcasts. Glickman spoke with such conviction about Buddy Lee's that I insisted my father buy me my bar-mitzvah suit there," Ross would say.

Ross has done virtually every sport on radio, but none better than basketball. He knows the game, he's very quick, and pays great attention to detail. Glickman, to this day, thinks very highly of Ross's talents. "No one could pick up speed and reverse his delivery as smoothly as Spencer." In fact, in 1995 Glickman's endorsement of Ross's candidacy for the Celtics' radio job helped land him the assignment.

The New Jersey Americans, as they were known when they were born, were coached by Max Zaslofsky and they played at an unfit facility, the Teaneck Armory. Yankees baseball star Yogi Berra threw up the first ball on October 23, 1967, and at age 27 Ross was about to do his first-ever pro game. They didn't exactly elbow their way into the facility either, Ross remembers. "There were

Courtesy Madison Square Garden

Spencer Ross

some games when we could have sent all the fans home in the same cab." But the lack of fan support didn't dishearten Ross's enthusiastic broadcasts.

The Americans had Bobby Lloyd. "We were friendly," Spencer remembers. "He spent a night in my Manhattan apartment and had his car parked on the street. The next morning we had a flight to Pittsburgh. When we got to the car, it had been broken into and Bobby's uniform was stolen. Things were so bad back then that the team didn't have an alternate jersey. Max told people Bobby couldn't play because of a sprained ankle, and he did color with me on the radio."

The Nets finally gained some respect after floundering in dilapidated facilities such as the Commack Arena and the Island Garden. They moved to the Nassau Coliseum in 1972 under owner Roy Boe. It was then that WHN, having lost the Knicks' and Rangers' package to WNBC, picked up Nets games and hired Al, the middle of the three Albert brothers, to do play-by-play. This Albert had been a hockey goalie in college but brought a radio presence to the Nets' broadcasts over the prestige of a 50,000-watt facility. Glickman was long gone from WHN but Albert borrowed his signature phrase "swish" on a successful field goal.

By the time the 1972–73 season hit, Boe had purchased the Islanders, an expansion hockey franchise, and Albert found himself broadcasting both basketball and hockey on WHN. To lighten the load a bit, Albert shared play-by-play responsibilities with Bill Mazer, who had moved over to the station to do a talk show, and with the versatile Jim Gordon, no stranger to winter sports.

Gordon, in an earlier stint with WINS and WHN, had filled in for Les Keiter and Marty Glickman on Knicks and Rangers broadcasts. Gordon could talk a mile a minute. He might have been the most rapid-fire sportscaster when the action called for it. There was a lot of ineptitude in the old American Basketball Association, and one familiar Gordon call was, "Rebound, up no good, up no good, up no good, up good." Gordon said, "I prided myself on never missing a rebound."

Albert had the privilege of working with Lou Carnesecca, who many forget actually coached the Nets for three years in the early 1970s. But by 1973–74, Al's last year with the club, Lou was back at his beloved St. John's, coaching the college game, and ex-Johnnie, Kevin Loughery, was brought in to coach the club. There was one other addition, a gravity-defying 6-foot, 7-inch forward named Julius Erving. A native Long Islander, he was now playing back home at the Nassau Coliseum. It was a young Nets team in every way. The oldest member was center Billy Paultz. This ex-St. John's star was just 25.

The Bronx-born Loughery was all of 33. The Nets won their first ABA title that season, beating the Utah Stars in the finals. WHN was carrying the Mets, though, during the 1974 campaign, forcing Albert, Mazer, and Nets fans to endure tape-delayed broadcasts of many playoff games. And back then television coverage was scant at best. After the season, the Nets' broadcasts were dropped by WHN and an independent packager, Manchester Broadcasting, took over the Nets' and Islanders' rights. It meant a new station, WMCA, and a new play-by-play announcer.

Courtesy Madison Square Garden

John Sterling

Mike DiTomasso, a one-time league referee, owned Manchester. He would do color. Dom Valentino, who had covered the Cincinnati Royals, would do play-by-play. In these pre-headset-mike days, the gravelly sounding Valentino would work with a custom-designed leather harness wrapped around his chest and a stick mike protruding toward his lips.

John Sterling, an acerbic sports talk-show host on WMCA, was dying to get a play-by-play break, although he had little experience. His play-by-play would first be heard on New York Raiders hockey broadcasts in 1972–73. The team was part of the World Hockey Association and his partner was Yankee pitcher Fritz Peterson. In the summer of 1974, when the New York Stars of the now defunct World Football League landed on WMCA, the Stars were pushed into assigning him to the broadcast. The football team didn't last the season, playing at antiquated and ill-equipped Downing Stadium.

Sterling did fill-in work for Valentino during the 1974–75 campaign. He was hardly crisp or descriptive but he was effusive and quite enthusiastic, which sat well with ownership. The one basketball line he used was "bull's eye." Jim Karvellas must have bristled when he heard it. Sterling traced his roots through Baltimore, where he did some color for Jim on Bullets broadcasts. Karvo was the first to popularize "bull's eye."

The Nets would win the 1976 ABA title with Sterling behind the mike in the last year of the league, and Sterling went out of his mind, telling his talk-show audience the day after the clincher that he was out all night with Kevin Loughery and spent the night at his house. Kevin was not only familiar with Sterling as a friend but one night he had the opportunity to hear Sterling call a Nets game. An overturned truck on the Jersey Turnpike brought traffic to a complete stop. The road was impassable for hours and there was Loughery listening to Sterling do the first quarter of the game on the radio.

Despite some terrible bouts with laryngitis which would sideline him for long stretches, Sterling would stay with the Nets for five seasons before eventually not being rehired and moving to Atlanta. Sterling would later blame columnist Pete Vecsey for his New York demise. "He ran me out of town." The acerbic Vecsey, though, had little tolerance for the broadcaster's deficiencies.

Joe Tait

The ABA folded in 1976 and the Nets were absorbed into the NBA. Reality set in quickly. To stay afloat, owner Roy Boe had to unload Erving to Philadelphia and the club won just 22 games during its first year in the established circuit.

Over the next four years a pattern of instability developed in the radio booth. The Nets went through four separate play-by-play men. But among them, in 1981–82, Nets fans were treated to a broadcaster many say is still the league's best. Unfortunately, Joe Tait spent just one season in the metropolitan area and few could enjoy him because the games were on two weak signals, WVNJ (620) and WWRL (1600).

Tait was in exile from Cleveland where he's since returned and where he's treated with much deserved reverence. He has been the beloved "voice of the Cavs" since the club's inception in 1970 except for a couple of years of exile after openly criticizing parsimonious Cavs owner Ted Stepien.

In Cleveland, when he announced that he was leaving, there was an outpouring of support. It was prior to the last game of the season. Attendance had dwindled to just a few thousand per game. But 20,000 showed up to honor Joe Tait. It made the front page of the Cleveland newspapers.

Budding broadcasters raised in Brooklyn would spend time picking up powerful WWWE to enjoy the master at work. He wouldn't miss a beat even though he keeps his own score while doing play-by-play. Tait's a broadcaster's broadcaster, today's Picasso of radio basketball. Sadly, Cleveland owner George Gund is blind but luckily he has Joe Tait whom he relies on every game. That's almost as good as seeing the game.

Of the succession of voices to have marched through New Jersey, the Nets had Mel Proctor for a couple of years. Lewis Schaffel, who once served as the Nets' chief operating officer and who had a good feel for broadcasting, said that Mel would prepare one new piece of information on each player each game just to break the monotony. Proctor spent most of his career in Washington where he called Bullets games on both radio and television for years.

When he left for San Diego in the spring of 1997, he was honored at halftime of a Bullets game and the reception was hardly emotional. Apparently, Proctor was unable to forge a bond with the constituents. Proctor was always upbeat, right on top of the action, and well prepared. While in Hawaii doing a variety of sports, the gifted Proctor had some appearances in *Hawaii Five-O*.

Neil Funk, another Syracuse man, also had a couple of years at the mike for the Nets. Funk had been around, schlepping broadcast equipment around as the Kansas City Kings' radio man. After leaving New Jersey, he did the 76ers on television. He's been with the Bulls in recent years and has been awarded with presiding over multiple NBA titles. Blessed with a dry wit, Funk would always have his play-by-play colleagues in stitches at league meetings. But his two seasons with the losing Nets were nondescript. The club was under .500 each of his two seasons and it's tough to make your mark under those settings.

Howard David came into the Nets' picture in 1987 and remained for seven years. He was sharp but had a sarcastic wit that many mistook for cockiness. David didn't have any NBA experience when he was hired, but grew into the position. A commanding voice, he left over what was ostensibly financial differences, but others later confirmed that he was pushed out for being overbearing. David can be clever, humorous, and entertaining. As someone close to the Nets organization would say later, "Howard's lines were funny nine of ten times, the other time it would be offensive." David need not worry about his critics. He was appointed to be the "voice of *Monday Night Football*" on CBS Radio in 1996 and is heard on some of the biggest stations across the country every week. David was also picked up quickly in the NBA by the Milwaukee Bucks and later the Boston Celtics.

It's quite difficult to foster any radio identity with the community when radio announcers are changing as fast as musical chairs. So David leaves and Ian Eagle arrives. Inexperienced, Eagle did so well on radio that he moved to television the next year. In came Steve Albert for a second tenure of duty after leaving the Golden State Warriors. Again, a contractual squabble ensued and Steve was gone after season's end. So in 1996 Bob Papa, the Giants' voice and ESPN boxing announcer, took over. But other commitments forced the Fordham graduate to miss games.

The one mainstay on the college side through the years nationally was Cawood Ledford, the longtime "voice of the NCAA Final Four" and popular "voice of the University of Kentucky." New Yorkers were treated to his broadcasts each spring until he retired in the early '90s. In Kentucky his popularity was so strong that a pilot who was flying over Kentucky at about three in the morning on a clear night noticed that while neighboring states were dark and folks apparently retired for the night, Kentucky was wide awake. The lights of the homes in the state were all on and it created a silhouette of the state. When the pilot asked the tower what was causing the entire state to stay up, he was told, "The Wildcats are in the finals of the Great Alaska Shootout and everybody is up listening to Cawood."

In the Glickman and Keiter years, broadcasters were accepted as part of the family. Players would be at announcers' homes and would socialize. For that matter, Glickman would work out with the Knicks in the early years. When a party was thrown for Dick McGuire's 65th birthday, Marty was an esteemed guest.

At Marv Albert's 25th wedding anniversary, his then beautiful Sands Point estate was packed with broadcasters and executives. But there weren't any players. Why? Is there anything wrong with it? Who's at fault, if anyone? Should coaches bar announcers from team charters? Should play-by-play people just call the game or be tabloid journalists? These are the issues as we reach a new millennium.

7

THE BROOKLYN
DODGERS

BREAKING THE BAN
AND POPULARIZING
THE "CATBIRD" SEAT

By the 1930s baseball broadcasts were mushrooming in the heart of the country. But the lords of the three New York teams had seats to fill. Radio, they feared, would be a deterrent. Their logic was, why should fans come to the ballpark when they could have the picture painted for them at home on the radio?

Chicago was then the citadel of baseball on the radio. Hal Totten was at one of the two stadiums every day covering either the White Sox or Cubs, whoever was at home. The ownerships of the two clubs welcomed radio with open arms. In fact, the games were carried by several radio stations at the same time. In the 1920s and 1930s, other announcers in addition to Totten would become household names across the Windy City and the Midwest—Johnny O'Hara, Pat Flanagan, and later Bob Elson.

Ty Tyson was reporting on the Detroit airwaves, reporting on the beloved Tigers. Tom Manning, "the megaphone man," told the tales of the Cleveland Indians, and France Laux was the voice from the ballpark in St. Louis. On the East Coast, New England baseball fans would develop a love affair with Fred Hoey, calling the action from the Boston ballparks.

But New York was barren. The clubs were just adamant. They believed that daily radio coverage in the three-team market would kill the gate. In the '20s the New York teams would limit their broadcasts to opening day. The loudspeakers outside radio stores would amplify the description of the proceedings at the ballpark. The throngs would assemble and cheer, inaugurating the New York baseball season, but that was basically it.

In 1928, as an example, WEAF and WOR aired the Giants-Braves opener from the Polo Grounds. WOR presented the pregame ceremonies and the sounds of the band with special announcer Alfred McCann. Then Major J. Andrew White handled the play-by-play. Graham McNamee would be mikeside for WEAF. Upon occasion the teams would acquiesce to the carriage of a series of special significance.

Ownership around the major leagues was split over the issue of radio as late as 1931. It came up at league meetings that year, and while a resolution was not reached, it was agreed that no team would extend any of its radio contracts beyond 1932. Ford Frick, then still a sportswriter with the *New York Journal* and later president of the National League, remembers, "The baseball meetings of those days frequently developed into real donnybrooks, with the battle lines closely drawn between the advocates of radio and the old-time conservatives who saw red whenever the new medium was mentioned." It basically wound up being a club matter but the New York clubs remained steadfast in their opposition.

As a result, major-league baseball, a sport perfectly suited for the audio box because of its timelessness and simplicity, wasn't on the air regularly in New York in the 1930s, the golden age of radio. The local baseball games that were carried included scintillating battles on WNYC involving the fire and police departments. Or, as was the case on June 16, 1934, WEAF, a powerhouse of a signal at 660, broadcast the high school PSAL championship baseball game between Textile and Tilden.

Fans were hungry. But the only major-league baseball New Yorkers were enjoying on the radio was the World Series, the All-Star Game, and the occasional regular-season broadcast. In 1931 Dodgers management gave four stations a one-day shot—WEAF with McNamee, WABC with Ted Husing, WMCA with Sid Loberfeld, and WOR with Frick. "It brought a flood of fan mail," Frick recalled in his book, *Games, Asterisks, and People.* Later that season the Dodgers and Cardinals played one another on the final weekend, a series that decided the pennant. Frick called it on radio. "It was a hit-or-miss production that entirely lacked the professional touch of today's presentations," he wrote after retiring as commissioner of baseball in 1965. In Frick's 1978 obituary the *New York Times* printed a quote of his, "I received more than three hundred letters and, even more amazing, all favorable."

Frick teamed with Stan Lomax, another newspaperman turned broadcaster. "I'll never forget a game we were re-creating when the Giants were in Chicago to play the Cubs," he said. A fire outside Wrigley Field disrupted the Western Union service to the New York studios. "Ford had a batter fouling off the pitch about eight times. Then he followed with a lengthy argument between the umpires and the two managers. For 10 minutes, he filled in with pure cleverness and imagination."

But even occasional broadcasts stopped shortly thereafter and by the mid-1930s, the Giants, Dodgers, and Yankees signed a formal radio ban that they all seemingly honored through 1938.

The teams were also serious about policing the ban. In October 1935 the National Exhibition Company, owner of the Polo Grounds and the New York Giants, sought an injunction to restrain alleged bootleg broadcasts of baseball games. The suit was brought against Teleflash Inc., a news organization that allegedly provided the bootlegging stations with updated information from the Polo Grounds. In July 1936 three American League teams, New York, Boston, and Philadelphia, filed a formal complaint with the Federal Communications Commission that WMCA was reproducing baseball broadcasts from their stadiums without their permission. For pirating the games they owned, these teams wanted WMCA's license revoked! The station claimed it was just broadcasting its version and never stated that the broadcasts were emanating directly from any of the stadiums. The dramatizations were running about an inning behind the actual play.

Enter Earl Roy Harper, New York's busiest and most popular play-by-play man of local sports in the 1930s. Harper became a de facto "voice of New York baseball." On December 18, 1933, the *New York Evening Journal* reported that "WINS announced a rival for pioneers Ted Husing and Graham McNamee in the person of Earl Harper, whose spectacular sports broadcasts made station WJAY the talk of Cleveland."

When the Alabama native arrived in New York in 1933, he got WINS to agree to carry baseball broadcasts and then got a sponsor to commit to bankroll it. When he was turned down by the Giants, Dodgers, and Yankees, Harper approached the Newark Bears, the Yankees' farm team. George Weiss was running the Bears for Colonel Jacob Ruppert. Initially, Weiss agreed to the broadcasts on an experimental basis. Weiss and the Bears discovered that the visibility of radio brought out new fans, especially women. The Newark broadcasts became permanent.

By 1937, when the Bears won the Little World Series, the games moved to WNEW. There was no live play-by-play of major-league baseball on radio, so Harper's ecstatic calls became popular. He was the first of New York's Southern voices who were well accepted. Mississippi-born Red Barber, Alabama-born Mel Allen, and Georgia-born Ernie Harwell would follow. In just a short period of time Harper won the admiration of baseball fans. In fact, in 1937 WNEW and the Bears held a "radio appreciation night," and it drew the largest crowd of the season, 17,816.

Harper was colorful, vivid, apt, and resourceful. "I remember the tune-in ads in the buses," said George McClelland, a longtime sports editor of the *Virginia Pilot* who grew up in Newark. "Harper was so exciting and so convincing. Then I would see those bus ads with his picture on it. 'The Bears, sponsored by Piel's, the pride of Newark.' I then just pestered my dad to take me to a Bears game at Ruppert Stadium." The Bears had a fabulous team with the likes of Charlie Keller, Bob Seeds (who once hit seven consecutive home runs), and Tommy Henrich. Willie Klein, who covered the team and was later sports editor of the *Newark Star Ledger*, said, "That team could probably beat half the major-league teams today. Harper had great material to cover. He gave the games life on the radio." Remembering back to the days when he would occasionally sit next to Harper in the booth, Klein said, "He would have you hanging onto the edge of your seat on a routine fly ball."

McClelland, now living in Florida, talked about the lasting influence of the pioneering broadcasters. "Listening to Red Barber talk about the beauty of

Florida all those springs just made me want to move down here. And the first time I went to Williamsburg, Virginia, to cover William and Mary, I looked around and saw the Roman columns and thought it looks just the way I heard Ted Husing describe it on the radio when I was a kid."

As was common then, home games were called right from the stadium and road games off the ticker. Harper had a marvelous ability to effuse a short telegraphic message into an epic tale. From a two-word message of "McQuinn fanned," Harper could make it sound real:

McQuinn comes up. Sewell is out there looking him over.

Here comes the stretch and pitch. Ball one. High and outside.

Now Sewell is set to go again. George took that one waist high, right over the inside corner.

Again the stretch and pitch, a foul ball back of third. Six fans in the stands dive for the loose ball.

It almost hit the lady in the blue dress over there.

Two strikes now. Sewell takes his windup. Here it comes. Strike three! McQuinn is plenty mad about that one. [Manager Oscar] Vitt also didn't like the decision. Abadaba had something to say about it.

All from a two-word dispatch, "McQuinn fanned."

Harper also gave the popular players and manager nicknames. Manager Vitt was "Abadaba" because he could perform Hindu tricks. Jim Gleeson was "Gee Gee" because every one of his sentences seemed to start with *gee*. "Gee, we'll win the pennant," or "Gee, wasn't that some catch in the outfield?"

Harper was busy year round. He was the first to announce pro football on a regular basis and did the first-ever college basketball broadcast from Madison Square Garden. He had such an impact that when he switched from WINS to WNEW, the club decided to move its games as well so that it could have Harper call the play-by-play.

The pioneer entered the broadcast business in New Orleans. Working for a meat-packing company, Earl wrote a letter to the station that carried the local minor-league baseball team, criticizing the play-by-play announcer. The station manager invited him to do three innings. He did and never gave up the microphone. From New Orleans he went to Cleveland where he worked for WJAY.

The Indians' rights were with a competitor. But WJAY felt that no team had the right to make its games available on an exclusive basis. When it couldn't get into the ballpark, WJAY monitored its competitor for reports and that's how Harper called Indians games, stealing the play-by-play from the other station. It ended when, as Harper said, "They faked a few plays on the air on purpose and heard us announce the same report. That ended our steal."

Harper was a strong-willed man. He was opinionated and battled with station management at several stops along the way during his five-decade broadcast career. Perhaps this explains why he wasn't selected to be a part of the Yankees' booth when the team finally aired games in 1939. After all, he was a natural. He was situated right in the Yankees' backyard handling their minor-league team, was popular, and the only local baseball broadcaster in the area.

Earl Harper was New York's busiest and most popular play-by-play man of local sports in the 1930s.

© The Sporting News

He continued to call Bears games through 1943 but it wasn't the same once the Polo Grounds, Yankee Stadium, and Ebbets Field unlocked their radio booths in 1939. After leaving the New York area in 1943, Earl spent the bulk of his remaining career in Virginia, where he covered minor-league baseball. McClelland knew Harper there. "He was a great guy but he was hotheaded. He could be his own worst enemy at times. Harper did some big-time drinking in his day. In Virginia, he used to sip buttermilk when he would do a baseball game."

Yet baseball fans of the 1930s won't forget the name Earl Harper. He was an important part of New York baseball at a time when fans were thirsting for the sound of the bat and ball on the air. Fans of that decade may also recall that in 1938 Joe Bolton—Officer Joe, as he was known later on WPIX-TV—broadcast the Jersey City Giants' games on WHN. It was the last year that minor-league ball was in the radio spotlight. For New York fans, the deprivation was about to end.

In 1938 when the Reds' Johnny Vander Meer pitched the second of his historic back-to-back no-hitters, he did it against the Dodgers. It just so happened to be that it was the first-ever night game played at Ebbets Field. (The Giants played their first in 1940, the Yankees in 1946.) But folks were truly kept in the dark. There was no communication with the fans whatsoever. Not only could New Yorkers not follow the game on radio but neither could the folks back in Cincinnati. Red Barber was still broadcasting in Cincinnati at the time and would have re-created the game. But the rules of the New York radio blackout were so strict that it even prohibited telegraphers from wiring the dots and dashes to out-of-town stations.

The general radio prohibition ended after the 1938 season but its strict enforcement and the circumstances that caused its abrogation are a matter of contention. Red Barber claims that when Larry MacPhail arrived in Brooklyn in 1938, the agreement had one year remaining. In one of the several books he penned, *The Broadcasters*, Barber clearly indicates that the aggressive and innovative MacPhail simply opted not to renew the radio restriction with his New York baseball brethren when the ban ended in 1938, opening the baseball airwaves in 1939.

But the issue may not have been that simple. To begin with, as late as 1938, Al Helfer, then a staff announcer for WOR, said he did the Braves-Giants opener from the Polo Grounds on an experimental basis. "Carl Hubbell was on the hill for the New Yorkers. I'll never forget it," the longtime sports chronicler said. "We sat right out in the crowd, up in a second-tier box."

MacPhail had been a gifted, groundbreaking, and accomplished general manager in Cincinnati. He ran the Reds brilliantly until a difference of opinion with owner Powell Crosley caused his departure.

The progenitor of the MacPhail baseball dynasty was indeed innovative. He introduced night games in 1935 despite cries of protest from fellow owners and the press that he was destroying baseball's revered traditions. Also under his domain, the Reds were the first team to travel by air. And when the plane took off, Red Barber was on it. Using special equipment, Red transmitted a live report from the plane including interviews with players who were flying for the first time.

When MacPhail arrived in Brooklyn in 1938, he openly voiced disagreement with arrangements barring broadcasts. That season he installed lights at Ebbets Field despite the fact that the three New York teams had also agreed not to schedule any night games. It appears that the night game agreement was tied to the radio ban. When MacPhail was asked in 1938 how he could schedule night games, he said that the agreement was no longer valid and that he was also considering radio broadcasts that very summer. While games weren't aired in 1938, it fueled speculation throughout the fall that Brooklyn would introduce full-time radio in 1939. At that point the three New York clubs were the only major-league teams without radio.

On November 15, 1938, the *Brooklyn Eagle*, then a daily newspaper in the borough, reported that a major sponsor had made arrangements to put Dodgers games on WOR and that a combined Giants-Yankees package would air on the CBS flagship station WABC.

Indeed, MacPhail announced from New Orleans on December 6 that all home and road games would be carried on radio the following season. A rankled Ed Barrow, the Yankees' business manager, responded immediately. "The agreement among the three clubs still has two years to run, but since MacPhail has seen fit to violate it, the other two clubs are no longer bound by it and can move as they see fit."

MacPhail still vehemently denied that he was breaking any agreements with the Giants and Yankees. Three days later, Barrow tempered his claim over the remaining length of the agreement. "All I know is that the Giants, Dodgers, and Yankees entered an agreement, signed by Mr. [Horace] Stoneham [Giants owner], the late Mr.[Stephen] McKeever [Dodgers owner], and Colonel [Jacob] Ruppert [Yankees], not to broadcast and that this agreement had another year to run." The polemics continued. MacPhail insisted that he would meet the press and reveal two letters, written the previous year, which released the Brooklyn club from the pact.

On December 13, 1938, a story in the *Daily News* ran under the headline "On the Air." It reported, "Today comes the 'Revelation,' for Larry-the-Red MacPhail, Brooklyn's comrade and general manager, promises to lay on Commissioner Landis' desk the dynamite of *written proof* that the Giants and Yankees last Summer released him from the nonbroadcasting agreement, which had another year to run." The daily also said that Leo Bundy, the Giants' treasurer, already admitted that the Dodgers had been given their release.

On December 14 the *New York Times* wrote, "In spite of the belated admission by the Giants and Yankees on the previous evening that they actually had agreed to abrogation of the treaty against broadcasting, Larry MacPhail went through with his announced intention to display the documents to the press at noon yesterday. All the writers perused the papers and were duly convinced that Roaring Red had been wronged in previous comments."

It seems that a number of would-be sponsors had showered all three teams with sponsorship proposals and that in 1938 when it was apparent that the Dodgers eventually planned to extricate themselves from the agreement and air their games, the Giants and Yankees hoped to beat them to the punch with a broadcast package of their own and took the initiative themselves to release Brooklyn from the ban. But the strategy backfired.

After the Dodgers' announcement it didn't take long for the other two clubs to react. The Giants committed to radio shortly thereafter and on December 22 the Yankees joined the other two clubs and announced that their games would be on radio. Finally major-league baseball was alive on New York radio! The Dodgers were on their own, and the Yankees and Giants partnered for joint broadcasts of home games.

While the *Journal American* reported that Stan Lomax had the inside track on broadcasting baseball, it only made sense that Red Barber who had broadcast MacPhail's games in Cincinnati would be appointed. On December 12 Barber came to New York and went with the General Mills people, the Dodgers' sponsors, to the NFL championship game between the Giants and Green Bay at the Polo Grounds. A deal was struck. Red was bound for the Dodgers and Brooklyn would never be the same again.

Al Helfer, "Brother Al" as he was called by Red, became Barber's partner. (He had worked in Pittsburgh before joining Barber in Cincinnati where they worked the Reds games together for a couple of years.) The word *partner* is used loosely. Helfer was Barber's associate but did only one inning, the fifth. It was Red's show. It was the wrong environment for Helfer's sizable ego. He lasted three seasons and would then bounce around, not staying very long with any team. WOR was the Dodgers' first station and carried the Bums through 1941. In 1939 the games were actually on both WOR and WHN.

The Manhattan and Bronx teams selected Arch McDonald as their principal announcer and it seemed that McDonald was ballyhooed by the press. *Time* magazine did a feature article on him and it angered, if not inspired, his impending competitor, Barber. The piece praised the "big, bearlike" McDonald as "Ambassador of Sports." It marveled at his following and told of the time when he was laid up in a hospital. Small boys sneaked past guards and climbed through transoms to visit Arch. The profile also raved about his colorful descriptions: "two dead birds" for a double play or "ducks on the pond" for base runners.

Meanwhile, MacPhail wasn't about to be beaten to the punch. The other two teams would not begin their broadcast schedule until the start of the regular season. Brooklyn started airing contests during spring training while the team was barnstorming its way back north. Back then, clubs would stop in one minor-league town after another for a week or two after breaking camp.

The Brooklyn broadcasts, though, didn't start auspiciously. When Barber set out trying to do his first re-creation from the studio, the telegrapher at some hamlet in South Carolina wasn't experienced and communicated in a language of his own. After the first three batters stepped to the plate, Red had the bases loaded when in actuality the side went down in order. So as the teams went to the bottom of the first, Red was still in the top of the first with no one out. He canceled the broadcast and apologized to his audience, explaining that there were some technical problems translating the wire report.

Red found a quick solution. Roscoe McGowen, the *New York Times* writer who was covering the team on its way north, had been a dot-and-dash man for the railroads. He also obviously knew baseball. Roscoe gave the Dodgers broadcasts the lift they needed until the team got home.

Back then, virtually all announcers dramatized their wire reports. The play-by-play was embellished with the hum of recorded crowd noise, enhanced further by the fabricated cries of food vendors hawking their wares or sound effects of the bat making contact with the ball. Some announcers even delayed their re-creations by an extra minute or two, so that by knowing what was about to happen they could provide more theater to their presentation. Not Barber. He was strikingly and silently different.

Red called a wire service game the way he would a live one right from the ballpark, weaving in stories and relating anecdotes but he never wanted to fool his audience by making it feel he was somewhere he wasn't. "I assumed the audience knew that this was a wire service re-creation and I broadcast it that way. The listeners were a lot brighter than these fellows [the other simulcast broadcasters] seemed to think they were." Oddly, when Vin Scully, Barber's star pupil, re-created some games during a tight pennant race in 1957, he did use crowd noise and some dramatics such as, "This is a sight to behold."

Brooklyn didn't do road games live until mid-1948. They were all done off the wire and all the listener heard were two things, the sound of the ticker and the clicking of the typewriter used by the receiving operator in the studio. Red studied each hitter's batting stance, committed to memory a thumbnail biographical sketch, and drew a picture in his mind of the interior and contour of the ballpark the Dodgers were visiting. But there were no embellishments.

"I remember Barber coming into the studios to do those re-creations. He would carry his bag, walk in unobtrusively but was hardly the warm, gregarious personality that he was on the air. He was all business," said Marty Glickman, who worked periphery pre- and postprogramming around Dodgers broadcasts and had an opportunity to witness the pioneer announcer at work. "When he would do those re-creations, I could see it now. He looked up and gazed at the ceiling as though he was imagining Ralph Kiner take his position in the batter's box. If he knew a hitter picked up dirt after every pitch, he might work it in to his description. He was masterful." While live play-by-play announcing is extemporaneous and certainly requires spontaneity, it demands less creativity than re-creations. As such, at Ebbets Field, baseball's pioneer broadcaster would work sitting down. But when working the game from the studio, he would stand up.

A fan might occasionally pull a quick one in a tavern where Barber's re-creations were always blasting. He would listen closely to the actual sound of the ticker and then bet some fans around the bar how a batter would do. People watching the exchange would be fascinated. But a telegrapher had the ear of a watchmaker and could interpret each click, detecting a home run from a strikeout. The fan was always right. The foist worked until somebody blew his cover. It was revealed that the prognosticator was a former dot-and-dash man himself!

The Brooklyn broadcasts were an immediate hit, aided to a large degree by the improvement of the ball club. MacPhail pumped money into the acquisition of players and spruced up old Ebbets Field when it needed it badly. There were several long marathons, authenticating the drama of Barber's broadcasts. One game went 19 innings, another 23. It was compelling theater and Barber captured it wonderfully. And, of course, day-to-day major-league baseball on radio was still a novelty. Red gave the fans a broadcast that they could relish every day.

His Southern drawl was refreshing and reassuring, his phrases homespun, and his descriptions colorful and smile evoking. "I didn't broadcast with a Brooklyn accent, but I did broadcast with a Brooklyn heart," he would say. Red's old team, Cincinnati, won the pennant in 1939 and 1940 but the Dodgers were third and second, respectively. By 1941 the Dodgers won the National League, their first pennant since 1920. By then Red Barber was not only the novel, soft, and serene voice, his name was synonymous with winning.

Glickman hearkens back to that golden period. "A fan didn't need a radio. Barber was echoing out of porches, car windows, and storefronts." The broadcasts were a tremendous hit. Robert Creamer, who worked with Red on his book *Rhubarb in the Catbird Seat* said, "You can thread your way through the crowd on a beach and get the game from portable radios."

In 1938 the Dodgers were third in New York attendance behind the Yankees and Giants, but by 1939 Brooklyn outdrew the other two. In a short period of time, from 1938 to 1941, the Dodgers just about doubled their attendance, going from 660,000 to more than 1.2 million.

With so many of the games played during weekday afternoon hours, many women became avid listeners and Brooklyn fans. Women listened in their kitchens while Barber taught them the rudiments. "He is a ladies' favorite. Before he came to Ebbets Field, the games resembled a For Men Only preview," wrote the *Saturday Evening Post* in 1942. "But last year, 15,000 women stormed the gates for one game and Brooklyn authorities say that the come-hither tones of Red are responsible."

The Mississippi- and Florida-reared Dodgers announcer called games with simplicity, imagination, and personality. His accent reflected his roots but Leonard Shecter wrote in the *Post*, "It does seem to some observers that Barber sounds slightly more Southern on the air than he does on the ground." Red introduced his New York constituency to homespun Southern idioms never heard before in the big metropolis. *Newsweek* printed just a few of them in 1945:

Sitting in the catbird seat .... *everything is going your way*

I'll be a suck-egg mule .... *Red is pretty concerned*

A can 'a corn .... *an easy-to-catch fly ball*

F.O.B. .... *the bases are full of Brooklyns*

The bottom of the pickle vat .... *the Bums are in bad trouble*

His voice filled the streets with an honest report, fair to both sides. He never raised his voice; he announced in a speaking level which reflected the sequential of the drama.

If anything, it was his fairness that would occasionally make the listener bristle. The year that the Dodgers won the pennant, 1941, they lost a game to the lowly Phillies, temporarily falling out of first place. A group of fans was draped around a parked taxi listening to the smooth impartial call of Red. When it ended, the radio snapped off. "That Barber, he's too fair," one listener was heard to say. One thing fans listening to Red would never complain about was getting the score frequently. Red had a well-publicized egg timer in front of him at all times. When the sand ran out, he knew to give the score.

In his book *Bums* Peter Golenbock writes, "If the Dodgers were a religion, then Red Barber was Billy Graham." The descriptions were profound, and they mixed the verses of the classics and the double negatives of the rural South. The rhythm to his delivery was mesmerizing, and the softness to his voice comforting. New York in general and Brooklyn in particular had never heard anything like it. His heralded rival McDonald was gone after just one season. Barber would be a hit for years.

The broadcasts became so popular that during the 1941 pennant race, one listener, who was hawking newspapers at a street corner, was arrested for noise pollution after the neighborhood complained he was blasting his radio. Brought in front of the magistrate, the culprit was asked by the judge, "What game was that?" The newsdealer told him.

"I remember that one very well. I hired a caddie just to carry a portable radio around so that I could listen to the broadcast. Good game, too. Case dismissed!"

Helfer spent three years with Red before the cries of war had him in the Navy, where he rose from lieutenant to commander. Helfer, robust and broad-shouldered at 6 feet, 4 inches, was almost a foot taller than Red. Every now and then, Barber and Brother Al would harmonize in off-microphone barbershop to get themselves tuned for the game. Five minutes before airtime they were relaxed and ready to go.

When he returned from the service in 1945, Helfer worked one season with Bill Slater on the Yankees-Giants package. The following year he was back in Cincinnati, out of the broadcast business and working for an ad agency. Fairly well known and a well-rounded talent, Helfer was back on the air as a reporter at the presidential conventions in 1948. When he was assigned to work the presidential train, Harry Truman's whistle stops, Helfer introduced himself to the president. The chief executive acknowledged him, "Oh yes, you're the sports announcer." It was a thrill. "I got a big kick out of that," he reminisced.

Red Barber, second from right in the first row, is joined by a veritable who's who of radio sports personalities in this publicity shot taken in the 1950s. Also shown are (first row, from left) Marty Glickman, Mel Allen, Phil Rizzuto, Barber, and Jim Gordon. Back row, disc jockey Jerry Marshall, Gussie Moran, and the morning comedy duo of Ted Brown and the Redhead.

Helfer's departure created an opening in Red's booth. Allen Hale, a former FBI man who had done broadcast work in Chicago, took over Helfer's cameo role. But after the one season, 1942, Hale headed back to his Pacific Northwest home because his wife was ill. It was there that he entered the advertising business and was never heard on the air in New York again.

As the war raged in Japan and in Europe, Barber was in his mid-30s, married, and had a child. While many of his broadcast colleagues served in the military, Red was not drafted. He did undertake a blood drive on behalf of the Red Cross. His appeals were cogent and galvanizing, luring masses to the donor centers. The very word *blood* was an anathema in radio's vocabulary then. It was considered too gaudy for mass audiences. But Barber chose to incorporate the word to inspire volunteerism.

Brooklyn continued to have the advantage over its New York neighbors. While Red was breezing along calling every Brooklyn game, the Yankees and Giants shared one broadcast outlet, in essence carrying just home games. Red would weave in marvelous stories and as he told talk-show host Art Rust in 1986, "I only used statistics when they had a bearing on the game."

Connie Desmond arrived in New York from the Midwest in 1942, a talented broadcaster reared in the industry in the days prior to specialization. Working as a staff announcer at WOR, he was equally comfortable doing play-by-play, hosting a music show, or for that matter singing in a band. He had a husky, hearty, and warm voice, soft and smooth in his baseball reporting. In 1942 Cornelius Desmond worked with Mel Allen on the Yankees-Giants package aired conveniently over WOR.

After the 1942 season the Yankees-Giants package was again in jeopardy, and Hale had left the Brooklyn broadcasts. One day at Toots Shor's, the sports hangout, Desmond sought out Red and told him of his predicament. "I don't have a contract with them. Nobody over there can tell me what day tomorrow is going to be."

At that point Red unhesitatingly rushed to the powers that be and saw to it that Desmond was hired. They worked together for 11 years. When Connie died in 1983, Barber told Bob Edwards on National Public Radio, "He was by far the best associate, the best assistant broadcaster, I was ever around. It's easy to find a good principal announcer. But to find the good associate, the assistant, is very difficult because you have to find the man who has the ability to do the work of the principal and yet is willing to step aside while the principal performs." Helfer, Barber's first aide in the booth was given just one inning of play-by-play. Desmond graduated to two, the third and sixth. Connie was indeed highly regarded and could have been a principal announcer, a number one man, elsewhere. When he joined Red in Brooklyn in 1943, the Dodgers were barred by the Giants from doing the games at the Polo Grounds because the Giants-Yankees package was off the air that year. The Giants weren't about to allow the competition to do it.

Desmond was Barber's age. Both were born in 1908. Connie was raised in Toledo, where he began his career at popular WSPD Radio. He was busy doing morning drive, a man-on-the-street program, interviewing passersby on a downtown street corner, and announcing marathon dances at the Coliseum. In sports, he called Toledo Mud Hens baseball games and Ohio State University football games. In New York the talented voice did basketball and football, including the Orange Bowl. He was one of the first sports telecasters and *Look* magazine bestowed upon Connie its first television sports award for his solo coverage of an Army-Navy football game.

The 1940s were wonderful for Barber and the Dodgers' broadcasts. He got along famously with MacPhail and wonderfully with his successor Branch Rickey. The two bosses were diametrically opposite personalities but Red had a close relationship with each of them. MacPhail was irascible, used profanities, and was a drinker. Rickey was restrained, didn't utter any vulgarities, and was a teetotaler.

By 1942 MacPhail left the Bums for a lofty executive military post at the age of 52. It ended an outstanding five-year run with the Dodgers. After serving his country, he joined the Yankees in January 1945, where he owned a piece of the team with partners Dan Topping and Del Webb. The Yankees' radio was still unsettled and muddled with the Giants. MacPhail was determined to give the Yankees a needed individual identity. He planned to put all the games on the air and do road games live.

Barber was his man, having worked for Larry in Cincinnati and Brooklyn. Red's contract was up in Brooklyn at the end of the 1945 campaign. He called Red that summer, shared his vision, and promptly offered Barber $100,000 over three years. The subway was still a nickel then. The money on the table was a heap.

The Yankees were the most successful team in sports and Red was about to accept. Barber walked into Branch Rickey's office in Brooklyn and told the parsimonious boss that MacPhail made him an irresistible offer and that he was inclined to accept it. Rickey asked him to delay his decision three days and the announcer obliged. In the ensuing 72 hours Red looked around Ebbets Field, appreciated what he had earned, and what he had. He then sat down with Rickey again and Branch offered him a contract directly with the team at $105,000. Barber stayed but the mind wonders. What would have happened had Red accepted MacPhail's offer and gone with the Bronxites in 1946? What would have happened to Mel Allen?

Red claimed that he stayed with Brooklyn because of his loyalty to the club, the borough, and to Rickey. But one wonders how fond Red was of traveling. More than once in his writing, Red insists that a man's spot at night is his home. It was something inculcated by his dad who had a great deal of influence on him. His father was a railroad locomotive engineer who did his run during the day and returned at night. The Dodgers were the last of the three New York teams to travel their road broadcasts and Red was probably one reason why.

One day Rickey confided in Barber that he planned to break baseball's color barrier and bring up Jackie Robinson. A Southerner who said he was "well taught," Barber cogitated and contemplated quitting. He wasn't quite sure that his mind would be at peace calling games of integrated baseball. The broadcaster though came to grips with the impending move that he would describe in his book, *1947—When All Hell Broke Loose in Baseball.* He realized that no one was in control of his color of skin and he also recalled Commissioner Landis's caveat to the broadcasters prior to the 1935 World Series, "Just report, leave your opinions in your hotel rooms."

After Red's death in 1992, Jack Kroll, a fine journalist, wrote, "I'll never forget listening to Barber the day Robinson batted cleanup for the first time. Barber said Jack deserved it. 'He's a tremendous ballplayer.' And there was a joy in the way he said 'tremendous,' the self-redeeming joy of a good man who had broken through some barriers of his own."

Things were humming along just nicely for the University of Florida alumnus. *Newsweek* reported that his income, which included his commercial work and his responsibilities as director of sports for CBS Radio, was $124,000. And in New York, his work continued to be a big hit. "According to surveys, 300,000 radio sets are tuned in to his easy, literate, and technically impeccable daily reports on the Dodgers, and the mail from his listeners keeps two secretaries busy."

The other big hit was plural, the big hits played by Ted Husing on the Dodgers' flagship station, WHN. In 1946 Barber had taken over for Husing as network sports head at CBS while still calling the Dodgers' games. Husing was then hired by WHN to host a bandstand. It aired six days a week, 10 A.M. to noon and 5–6:30 P.M. Husing started the program on October 15, 1946, once the baseball season was over. The show was huge, generating big dollars into the station coffers. It also poured money into Husing's pockets, a large base salary plus a talent fee for every commercial that he read live. MGM owned WHN and it decided that Husing would take precedence over the Dodgers.

In 1947, when Dodgers games approached 5:00 P.M., and most baseball then was played in the afternoon, Barber's voice was silenced by the opening

Courtesy Ted Patterson

Connie Desmond, left, who worked with Red Barber for 11 seasons, is joined by Ernie Harwell in the booth. Harwell, a Southerner like Barber, was called in to finish the 1948 season when Barber was hospitalized with a severe ulcer attack.

to *Ted Husing's Bandstand*. Red wasn't very fond of Husing to begin with, so this had to enrage him further. If the contest was hanging in the balance and it was late, the eighth or even the ninth inning, it didn't matter. The Dodgers were off and Husing was on. Fans would have to wait for Ted to report the final score.

By 1948 WHN's sister facility, WMGM–FM, carried afternoon games in their entirety so that those listening on WHN could at least switch over at 5:00. The problem though was that few had FM receivers then. By 1951 Husing acceded to the Dodgers. Speaking of Husing, there were rumors that he would have taken the Dodgers' job if Barber had jumped to the Yankees in 1946.

In mid-1947 Barber knew that the Dodgers' broadcasts had to move into the modern age. MacPhail had the Yankees' announcers on the road while he was still re-creating away games. On Yankees road games, there was the authentic roar of the crowd and the crack of the bat. Restricting the sound of his wire service reports to the rhythm of the ticker, Red might have felt that Brooklyn fans were being deprived. Even though he might have preferred not to travel, he knew that the time had come, if for no other reason than to be competitive with the Bronx. While the Giants were still re-creating, they too had plans to travel beginning in 1948.

Red visited with Rickey in mid-1947, reviewed the road broadcasts, and it was decided to bring sponsor Old Gold into the loop and seriously address the future of radio coverage of away games. When the 1948 season began, the Dodgers hadn't made a move. But in mid-season 1948 with the Yankees and now the Giants already traveling, Brooklyn agreed to do the same. In July, when Idlewild, now Kennedy Airport, opened for business, the Dodgers started traveling.

The first live road broadcasts were from Philadelphia over the Fourth of July weekend and went smoothly. But later that month when the Bums headed on their next excursion, Red had a lot on his mind. As loose and at ease as he sounded on the air, Red was apparently pretty tightly woven. The trip was to include "the West," Cincinnati, St. Louis, Chicago, and Pittsburgh. Once he got back, Barber, a homebody, was to head to London for CBS to cover the summer Olympics. He never made it.

The Dodgers' principal announcer was on the last leg of the trip in Pittsburgh, playing golf with partner Desmond and a couple of other gents. He collapsed of an ulcer attack and was quite critically ill. Word made it back to New York quickly where Mel Allen wished him well on the Yankees' broadcasts. Red was enervated and completely dispirited. He was out for six weeks and it took the urging of Rickey to get him back to work. On September 9, 1948, Red returned but didn't do any play-by-play, and Rex Barney greeted him by pitching a no-hitter against the Giants.

It was on the trip where Red fell ill that manager Leo Durocher stunningly left the Dodgers and joined the Giants. Desmond completed the trip working alone but asked Pittsburgh legend Rosey Rowswell to do a few innings to give his voice a breather.

The Dodgers acted quickly. Georgia-bred Ernie Harwell, "voice of the Atlanta Crackers," was contacted immediately. He had some conversation with the Dodgers' organization prior to the season about filling in for Barber when he would go to the Olympics. Harwell was also told by Arthur Mann, Branch Rickey's assistant, that Red might not want to travel and that he may be needed for road games. This conversation in itself was further evidence that Barber wasn't thrilled about leaving home for any length of time and perhaps why the Dodgers were indeed the last to travel.

Crackers owner Earl Mann, though, wouldn't release Harwell from his contract unless he received something from Brooklyn in return. As a result, Harwell wound up being the only announcer in history to be involved in a trade. Rickey agreed to ship Cliff Dapper, a catcher for Brooklyn's Montreal farm club, to Atlanta.

Harwell blended in nicely. He was another warm Southern voice who spoke in measured, short, and durable sentences. Wherever he's been since, listeners have found him easy to digest. His 50 years as a big-league baseball announcer have proven his durability. While Harwell has done television through his popular career, his first love is radio and it's where he has sparkled. "In radio, nothing happens until the announcer says it happens," says the gentleman who is helpful to anyone seeking his wisdom or generous to the many seeking his time. Conditions weren't too sophisticated in 1948. In Boston the broadcast would emanate directly from the regular seats way out in right field. There was no broadcast booth at Braves Field. Announcers then weren't given luxurious hotel suites. In Chicago, for example, Harwell had to double up with Barber in one room.

Connie Desmond was warm to Harwell and made him feel at home in the Brooklyn booth. Barber, though, was a taskmaster who expected nothing short of excellence from his assistants and associates. If Harwell, or later Vin Scully, came back from the dugout with the lineups and a batter was hitting fifth instead of third, it wasn't good enough. "Find out why the change was made," Barber would demand.

While Ernie didn't detect friction between Barber and his 11-year partner, Desmond, he does relate one verbal paroxysm in his autobiography, *Tuned to Baseball*. When Red was ill, a commercial script was delivered for Connie, written in Barberese, tailored to Red's speech and delivery. "Forget it," Connie shouted angrily and threw the script to the back of the booth. Ernie sensed some resentment.

Red wasn't only tough on his fellow announcers, he had little tolerance for mistakes by his statisticians. His young statistician, Bob Passoti, was responsible for bringing number one pencils for day games and number two pencils for night games. If things went wrong, Red would hurl pencils at the statistician. At least Red didn't need spotters for baseball broadcasts. When Jack Buck saw Bill Stern show up for a baseball broadcast one day with spotters, he couldn't believe it.

In 1949, once Barber was fully recovered and there were three men in the booth, Harwell's number of play-by-play innings was limited. The season was another memorable one for the Brooklyn fans. Trailing the Cardinals throughout, the Dodgers won the finale over the Phillies in 10 innings to edge out St. Louis for the pennant by 1 game. At the end of the season a job opened at the Polo Grounds and Ernie left for the Giants and the less-stringent Russ Hodges.

Barber remained the boss. He would be the one to select Harwell's replacement. Branch Rickey would do no more than rubber stamp Red's recommendation. The change that was about to occur would have a bicoastal effect, first bringing listening pleasure to fans in New York and later symphonic joy to millions in California.

Vin Scully was born in November 1927. At age eight, during the 1936 World Series, he was returning from school to his Washington Heights home. In the window of the local laundry, that day's score was posted. Observing that the Yankees licked the Giants 18–4, young Vin felt so bad that he instantly became a Giants fan.

He attended New York Catholic schools and graduated from Fordham University. He played a couple of years of collegiate baseball for the Rams and, undoubtedly, while patrolling the outfield grass would practice play-by-play to himself. He served at the school radio station and, with apologies to Charles Osgood, became its most famous alum. He called baseball, football, and basketball. But watching Georgetown and the University of Houston in the 1984 NCAA Finals, he flipped the channel. Like his mentor Barber, hoops didn't turn him on.

If one cannot detect his New York roots in his mellifluous speech, Scully says it's because he's spent his entire life trying to rid himself of it. "When I was 4 years old I was taken to Ireland for a visit, and they tell me that when I came home I had a brogue you could cut with a knife."

After graduation in 1949, he landed a replacement job at WTOP in Washington. In the fall of 1949, through Ted Church, a CBS executive who liked his work, Scully was introduced to Red Barber, then the network's sports director.

"When I met Red, he was on his way to a meeting so he had no time for me. He told me to leave my name and number and he would get back to me." About a week later, Scully came home and his mom said, "Vinnie, you will never guess who called for you. He wants you to call him—Red Skelton." Scully knew right away that it was Red Barber.

CBS needed announcers for the *College Football Roundup,* which was Red's brainchild. It featured reports from a handful of games around the country and Red was short an announcer one weekend. The bright-eyed Scully was assigned the Boston University–Maryland game at Fenway Park.

It was his big moment. "I was thrilled for two reasons. Naturally, I wanted to do a game that would be on network radio and I also knew that Boston's Fordham alumni were having a dance that same night and I would be able to attend."

One problem. Vin dressed for the dance, not for the inclement conditions at the football game. "It was a beautiful day when I left my hotel and I didn't bring my topcoat to the game." Scully thought he would have a glass enclosed booth but had to work from the stadium roof. By the second half, it was awfully cold and his hands were frozen stiff. But he never complained and did yeoman's work. Barber was impressed. A few days later, Barber got a call from the Boston people apologizing for the mix-up and for not providing an enclosed booth. Red was now doubly impressed and assigned Scully the Harvard-Yale game the following weekend.

When the Dodgers' job opened up, Barber knew he wanted a young man he could groom. "I was broadcasting baseball at $5,000 a year," Scully says. Just 22 years old when he was hired, Vin paid his dues. Some days, he might get a couple of innings. If it was a radio-only game, Scully might not do any play-by-play at all. He was third on the depth chart behind Barber and Desmond.

It was Barber who took Scully under his wing and told him to be himself. The veteran was demanding of his pupil. As an example, Red told Scully never to drink before a game. When he caught the callow broadcaster having a beer in the press room before a game, Red let him have it. Red, himself, said years later that Scully sulked for about a month afterward. Harwell remembers meeting Scully during his first season and asking him how it was going with Red. "The Ole Redhead is giving me a tough time," he answered. Ernie told the young lad, "Hang in there. He's tough but he's a great teacher. It will be worth it."

The one rap on Scully early was that he could provide too much information, a bit much for the listener to digest on radio. Scully elaborates on the man who hired him. "Barber is the most important man in my career. He taught me to slow up, shut up, and show up early at the ballpark, the most important things a broadcaster has to learn.

"The broadcast booth in Ebbets Field was directly back of the plate. One day Barber was writing a note and he just got his hand up in front of his forehead when a foul ball whistled back. The next day, they installed protective wiring," recounted the Red protégé. "Barber used to kid me about being a bachelor when we were on the air together. I used to tell him, I'm not a bachelor, just single."

While Barber bonded immediately with Branch Rickey, he had no affinity for his successor, Walter O'Malley. And O'Malley had little use for Red or his big salary. The two of them tested and probed one another until the relationship was irreparable. On the other hand, O'Malley viewed Scully as the fair-haired boy. So much so in fact, that while the Dodgers were still in Brooklyn, Scully was invited to join the Dodgers on a tour of Japan. Vin's roommate in the Far East was Walter's son Peter. Scully and the O'Malley family have had a mutually enjoyable alliance for almost 50 years.

Vin was there in 1950 when the Bums lost a heartbreaker and the pennant to Philadelphia on the final day of the season. That's the day that Barber reassured Brooklyn fans that the sun would nonetheless rise the next morning. George Vecsey, the erudite *Times* writer won't forget it. "I can remember him summing up the season, saying that it did not quite work out for the Dodgers but that it had been a good season, and that there would be another season, and it too would probably be good. He was promoting the Dodgers, selling tickets in a sense, but it sounded like prophecy to me."

In 1951 Scully witnessed the Dodgers squander what was seemingly an insurmountable first-place lead and lose to the Giants in the playoffs. He wasn't on the air the day that Bobby Thomson stuck a dagger into the Dodgers' fans' hearts. It was radio only and it was just Red and Connie. But Scully was there, painfully.

"Ralph Branca and I were very close. Before he was married, we used to double-date and spend a lot of time together. Well, when he threw the home run ball to Thomson, I didn't say to myself 'the Dodgers lost the pennant,' I just put my hands over my face and groaned to myself, 'Oh, my god, poor Ralph.'"

But Scully, who generally doesn't get close to players, keeps his broadcasts neutral. Even in Brooklyn he was quoted, "Once a guy told me that he couldn't tell from the tone of my voice whether the Dodgers were winning or losing. I considered it a compliment."

Barber made it clear immediately to O'Malley, who had a bitter dispute with Rickey, that he was Branch's guy and that O'Malley would have to live with it. Then when Barber was over in Spain, he bought a *boina*, a beret-type headpiece. O'Malley scoffed at it and asked him a number of times not to wear it. But Red insisted, almost out of a testing defiance, and wore it all season. At the end of the '53 season, when Barber was asked to do the World Series and was unwilling to work at the going rate, he leaned on O'Malley for support. The Dodgers' boss didn't give it to him.

Once Barber declined to work the Series and O'Malley nominated Scully as his replacement, Vin made sure it was OK with both Desmond and Barber. They both gave the young announcer their blessings to undertake the lofty assignment.

When the Yankees beat the Dodgers in the Classic and O'Malley didn't renew Barber's Dodgers contract, he explained the decisions to aides. He asked them to envision a length of pipe filled with peas. "You put in Vin Scully at $7,500 and at the other end, out drops Barber at $50,000." Red Barber, whose very name was as synonymous with the borough as the Brooklyn Bridge itself, was out. He was a victim of his own posturing. In retrospect it appears as though Red thought it was incumbent upon O'Malley to win him over, instead of the other way around. He learned that no one is indispensable.

The Dodgers used three announcers because virtually every home game was on television. O'Malley later regretted the aggressive television schedule. In his mind, he was giving the product away free and cutting down on attendance. With Barber out, Brooklyn had an opening in its booth going into 1954.

A number of men were considered. Frankie Frisch was one. He had done a couple of years of Giants baseball and was 55 at the time. Bill Mazer was another. "Allen Osborne of ad agency BBD&O heard me in Buffalo and liked my work. He had me meet with John Johns, the account man on the Schaefer business," Mazer recalled. Johns had a concern according to Mazer. He didn't want anyone breathing down young Scully's throat. Bill alertly told Johns, "No one has to protect Vin Scully."

Through Connie Desmond, Mazer met with O'Malley. At the interview, Walter probed, "What kind of name is Mazer?" Bill answered, "Do you mean, what is my nationality? I'm a Russian Jew." Sensing perhaps that Mazer might have been defensive about it, O'Malley said to him, "Jewish people are very critical of their own." As it turned out, Andre Baruch, himself Jewish, got the job.

A commercial announcer, hardly a play-by-play man, Baruch spent two long years in the Dodgers' booth. A native of Paris, Baruch came to the United States at the age of 14. He spent his youth studying piano and portrait painting. Baruch then attended Columbia University and Pratt Institute, earning a scholarship to study illustrating at the Beaux Arts in Paris. He spoke seven languages and became Mazer's neighbor in Westchester. He died in 1991 and "was a wonderful guy," according to Mazer.

In the 1930s his pleasing voice and keen wit added sparkle to programs such as *The Kate Smith Hour* and *The Shadow*. His athletic ability was in swimming where he was a former 50-yard backstroke champion of Europe. Dulcet toned, yes. A baseball man, apparently not. He was third on the depth chart for play-by-play but one forgettable call of Baruch's was, "He slid into second with a standup double."

Based on seniority in 1954, Desmond should have been number one in the Brooklyn booth. He was 45 and had been with the Dodgers since 1943. Scully was just 26 and beginning just his fifth year with the team. In addition to being a solid and smooth play-by-play correspondent, Desmond, according to Harwell, "had a great voice and a wonderful personality." On radio-only games, Desmond did five innings and Scully four. The *Sporting News* listed Desmond ahead of Scully indicating that Connie was considered the lead announcer.

Harwell always knew Desmond as a "social drinker" but Connie started drinking heavily. "Perhaps it was the pressure of being number one and 'replacing' the legendary Barber. He could only have dreamed of becoming what Barber described as the 'principal announcer.' Now he was it," Ernie theorized.

The Ohio native started missing games and the invariable explanation to the public was, "Connie is sick." The absences affected not only his baseball work but his basketball schedule as well, where he started missing assignments with Glickman.

By early 1955, just at the start of the regular season, O'Malley had no choice but to fire him. Al Helfer was hired for his second Dodger stint and began again on May 7, 1955. He had been the principal "voice of Mutual's *Game of the Day*"from 1950 through 1954, and the five nights a week of travel got to him. Now, at least, he had his own bed when the Dodgers were at home.

Desmond entered Alcoholics Anonymous. But booze deprived him of the Dodgers' best season ever in Brooklyn, the year the Dodgers finally beat the Yankees to win the world championship. Scully, to this day, lists the '55 championship as his number one highlight in almost half a century in the team's booth.

Scully explains the emotions of the subway Series. "The Yankees were the lordly pinstripes. The Dodgers were the ragamuffins who never won. That was the mind-set." Can a Mets-Yankees rivalry compare with the Yankees, Giants, and Dodgers of the 1950s? "I don't sense people arguing every day over the merits of Todd Hundley and Joe Girardi as catchers. I saw people actually getting into a fight over who was a better shortstop, Phil Rizzuto or Pee Wee Reese."

Baruch wasn't rehired at the end of the 1955 season, and O'Malley needed a third announcer to join Scully, by now the number one man, and Helfer, the number two man. Lindsey Nelson and Curt Gowdy pushed the Schaefer people and the Dodgers to hire Jerry Doggett, a minor-league baseball announcer in Dallas who had also done play-by-play for the defunct Liberty Network. He was hired in February and quit his work in Texas.

Desmond, married with children, asked O'Malley for a second chance. O'Malley faced a dilemma. To begin with, how reliable was Desmond, and what does he do about a commitment he had just made to Doggett?

O'Malley put his faith in Desmond and gave the longtime Brooklyn announcer a second chance. Doggett was disappointed and had to get his job back in Texas. But O'Malley's decision backfired. Connie was back on the stuff and by July he was gone for good. As fate had it, Doggett was brought up to Brooklyn from Texas on Labor Day weekend, 1956.

The minor-league veteran grew up in Iowa listening to Johnny O'Hara, a pioneer baseball announcer in Chicago and later in St. Louis. Now 39, he was finally in the major leagues. In 1996, a year before his death, Doggett said, "I had confidence. It was no more than a one-month audition in 1956 but I was back in 1957 and spent thirty-two seasons with the Dodgers."

Desmond sadly drifted into the streets and was forced to panhandle. "He would come up to the station," Marty Glickman would say. "He needed the proverbial loan. His clothing was frayed but he always looked neat. It was sad." Earl Gillespie, the Braves' announcer, remembered stepping in front of a restaurant in Chicago. "He was bumming across the country. It looked like he hadn't had a meal in a week. I bought him dinner."

In 1964 Desmond attempted a comeback of sorts. He was one of the organizers of a radio network for taxis. If Muzak served spots of public consumption with specially organized soft music, Desmond's network, under the appropriate call letters of WCAB would serve taxi passengers with music, stock quotes, news. It never quite took off, and Desmond returned to Toledo.

"Connie Desmond was like an older brother to me as Red was the father. He (Connie) was remarkably gifted and did all sports exceptionally well—great on-air personality and a warm, ingratiating laugh. Unfortunately, he had the 'problem' that ruined him. He did manage to live to be 75," Scully remembered sadly.

Scully, America's most durable and acclaimed baseball announcer, painted lovely pictures right from the beginning. When the Dodgers opened a home stand, "Pull up a chair, it's just the start of the things from Ebbets Field," he would suggest. "And it's great to be back home, although I just spilled a hot cup of coffee over a pair of pants, fresh out of the dry cleaner." A moment later, Scully, soaking wet, raved about the beauty of the Brooklyn sky. "When the lights go on and take effect at Ebbets Field, the gray skies above are nice and blue."

Courtesy Vin Scully

Vin Scully

Scully then promoted Brooklyn's next home game. It was against the Cubs at Roosevelt Stadium in Jersey City. The talented *New York Post* columnist, Jimmy Cannon, once bemoaned, "But what the hell is a Brooklyn team doing in New Jersey?" The Dodgers drew some 3,000 after they set a record for winning 10 consecutive games at the start of the season. It was a harbinger.

Vin's occasional home run call "forget it" was born in Brooklyn. "I picked up 'forget it' from the players themselves around the batting cage. If a guy gets what they judge to be a base hit, he gets another chance. Naturally, there's a lot of arguing as to whether it would have been a hit since there are no infielders during batting practice. But when it's a home run, they just say, 'forget it'." The signature caught on. Bert Lee would imitate his "forget it" call on pre- and postgame shows over WMGM. And with the innate ear of a jeweler, Scully could detect the slightest chip of a broken bat. "That's what happens when you were a terrible hitter yourself," he says, in reference to his days as an outfielder in college.

Barber and Scully have ruled the Dodgers' booth for 60 sparkling years. Both private, both cultured, Red's style was conversational, Scully's delivery is more of an oration. Both reportorial, Barber could be combative, Scully more agreeable. Scully did a World Series at age 25, Barber at 27. Barber sounded insouciant, Scully can sound brilliantly rehearsed. Both congenial, Barber was a prolific author, Scully hasn't penned a book yet. Both fastidious, Barber would often be didactic, and Scully is never obtrusive. Both generally detached emotionally, Barber disliked Walter O'Malley, Scully liked him. Both thoroughly prepared, Barber presented the game simply, Scully can be more intricate. Both excelled. Barber was fired twice, Scully has never been fired.

Through it all, the periphery programming was entertaining. Starting in 1939, when most baseball was played in daylight hours, WHN ran *Today's Baseball* every evening, a dramatized reenactment of the three local teams' games. It featured Bert Lee and Marty Glickman. Pregame shows started in 1942. They were called *Warm-Up Time* with Dick Fishell, and the postgame show with Lee was dubbed *Sports Extra*. By the mid-1950s, ex-tennis star Gussie Moran joined the station. "Gussie was cute but sports-dumb," Glickman says in his autobiography, *The Fastest Kid on the Block*. Unmistakably novel then, Moran, according to Marty, was humorous, charming, and lively.

By 1957, the Dodgers' last season in Brooklyn, the Dodgercasts featured Scully, Doggett, and Helfer. Brother Al told the *New York Post*, "I feel as secure in this business as anybody can. This, don't forget, is show business and show

243

business is never secure." Then an apparent dagger at Scully. "All they seem to want is kids," bristled the man soon to be 50. Scully was only 29 then.

In Brooklyn the Dodgers needed three announcers because of the big television commitment. In Los Angeles they needed only two. O'Malley maintained that TV was killing the Bums in Brooklyn. When they arrived in Los Angeles in 1958, the Dodgers only televised the games from San Francisco. O'Malley wasn't going to get caught in the television trap on the West Coast. He wasn't about to give away what he was trying to sell.

So, off they went. When the Los Angeles stations told O'Malley that they had announcers there, O'Malley said, "I'm bringing my two, Scully and Doggett." Helfer was left behind. According to Lindsey Nelson, Helfer demanded that O'Malley give him as many innings as Scully. It wasn't about to happen. In November the Dodgers flew their crew to Los Angeles and Brooklyn was no more than a great memory. To use a Barberism, the bases would no longer ever be "F.O.B." (full of Brooklyns).

8

THE NEW YORK YANKEES

THE BOOTH THAT MEL BUILT

In the 1920s and 1930s the Yankees, like the Giants and Dodgers, chose to deem radio an anathema. The bosses, Colonel Jacob Ruppert and General Manager Ed Barrow, essentially locked the medium out of Yankee Stadium and the Polo Grounds. There were all sorts of reenactment programs that ran following the games, but nothing live, nothing official, and nothing sanctioned.

When Don Dunphy was the sports director of WINS in the mid- to late 1930s, he had a sports update show that preceded the Yankees' game reenactments each evening. All games were played during the day. Dunphy was told by management that he could give as many scores as he would like except the Yankee score. The future boxing broadcast great was livid. Running every score but the home team Yankees was a turnoff. But the WINS Yankees reenactments with Jack Ingersoll were sponsored by Seidenberg Cigars, and to protect its listenership, the benefactor insisted that Dunphy's lead-in show cooperate. After telephone and written complaints from listeners, the sponsor and station acceded to Dunphy's pleas and allowed him to give the Yankees' score.

Live Yankees play-by-play broadcasts were a result of the action taken by Larry MacPhail of Brooklyn. He committed the Dodgers to a full schedule of radio broadcasts on December 6, 1938. At that point the Giants and Yankees bonded against MacPhail, the newest man on the block, the one they deemed a renegade. There was some thought that perhaps they would sit out the 1939 season in the hope of upping the ante from a sponsor the following year. But by December 22, 1938, both the Giants and Yankees committed to radio "after a study of the situation."

Under the aegis of Wheaties and Ivory Soap, the clubs formed a radio partnership whereby the home games of each team were broadcast. The way the schedule broke, the neighboring Giants and Yankees were never home at the same time. The initial year, CBS network flagship WABC carried the games. The sponsors hired two announcers, both of whom would shift from the Polo Grounds to Yankee Stadium, depending on which team was at home. If one was on the road when the other wasn't scheduled at all, there would be an occasional re-creation.

Arch McDonald was hired as principal announcer. He was considered top grain, earning his reputation in Washington, where he had called Senators games from 1934-38. His first-year salary in New York was a fairly whopping $25,000. Senators owner Clark Griffith had brought him up from Chattanooga where he had called the minor-league games of the single A Lookouts. His nickname was "The Old Pine Tree," because of the spin that he would put on some Washington Senators achievement, a non sequitur, "They did it again. They cut down the Old Pine Tree," words that he adopted from a country ballad he heard down South.

Born in the sporting atmosphere of Hot Springs, Arkansas, McDonald wandered out west as a young man and served as an extra in Hollywood. He then found himself working as a towel handler in Jack Dempsey's camp for the Jess Willard fight. In 1932 McDonald found his way into radio. He became so popular in the South that fans stuffed the ballot boxes with 57,960 votes, making him the *Sporting News*' Most Popular Broadcaster. The baseball junkie's bible lauded McDonald for being able to "outstrip such a notable field." Harry Hartman, who preceded Red Barber in Cincinnati, finished second with more than 52,000 votes. But way down the list were personalities such as Bob Elson, Hal Totten, Ted Husing, and Graham McNamee. McDonald won the award again in 1942 and 1945. *Newsweek* painted McDonald as having a "deep, dry voice with a home-spun personality."

New York opened its radio booths for the first time and the development got quite a bit of attention. McDonald, chosen by sponsor General Mills, was the beneficiary of a big buildup. To Red Barber's frustration, on April 17, 1939, *Time* magazine ballyhooed McDonald and ignored Barber, who was about to put Brooklyn on the air for the first time ever.

If Red Barber was Southern, Arch McDonald was almost hillbilly. If Red sounded brisk, Arch sounded sleepy. If Red's style was novel, Arch's was foreign. If Brooklyn loved Barber and Barber loved the city, McDonald never took to New York and New York never took to him.

Marty Glickman was a budding broadcaster then. After a distinguished on-air career, he now coaches sports announcers nationally. "Arch was a bust in New York. He was one of these big-voice broadcasters who don't make it in baseball. Barber and McDonald were both from the South but Red was easy to listen to, never disturbing, almost musical."

It was McDonald, the true original "voice of the Yankees," who dubbed Joe DiMaggio the "Yankee Clipper," not Mel Allen. He also came up with other catchy phrases such as "right down Broadway" (a pitch right over the plate) and "the ducks are on the pond" (men on base).

But the broadcasts lacked energy. The "Old Pine Tree" sounded lethargic. His delivery lacked any sense of urgency. Arch would announce one pitch, then amble to the cooler in the back of the booth, have a drink of water, and casually sit down again. Acknowledged as an entrancing story teller, his tales apparently were better appreciated in the nation's capital where he spent the bulk of his career. After just one season at Yankee Stadium and the Polo Grounds, he returned to Washington where he was accepted and admired. In fact, Vice President James Garner (1933–41) maintained that Arch was "the world's greatest baseball announcer."

Frankly, it's hard to believe that any announcer could fail. Fans were ravenous for baseball on radio, which New York listeners were deprived of previously because of the ban. In 1939 the Bombers won their fourth straight world championship. In the battle of who would achieve more popularity, McDonald or Barber, the Hot Springs native should have won hands down.

Anthony Lukas, writing in the *New York Times Magazine* in 1971, suggested that Arch was too folksy and that his slow, deep drawl and paucity of words earned him the nickname, "master of the pause." There is something to be said for his endurance. One day the Senators played a twin bill in Boston, and McDonald was on for seven straight hours, nonstop, all by himself, including handling the between-games show.

In a self-serving shot at McDonald, Red maintained that Arch wanted to leave New York and go back to Washington where he had no competition. In retrospect, though, Barber was on every day with the same team, the Dodgers. McDonald was an "announcer" following just the home games of two teams, the Giants and Yankees, each with different constituencies.

After an unhappy season in New York, Arch McDonald returned to Washington where he called Senators games into the 1950s and later Redskins football. And for some added spice, he did some live theater and also ran unsuccessfully for Congress. On October 16, 1960, McDonald was returning from New York, of all places, after broadcasting a 'Skins-Giants contest. He died of a heart attack on the train back to the nation's capital. After 25 years with the Senators, 7 with the Redskins football team, and 1 lonely year with the Yankees, McDonald was dead at 59.

There were those who wondered why Earl Harper wasn't appointed to the play-by-play position. Harper was quite popular at the time as "voice of the Newark Bears," the only team on the radio locally. And after all, the Bears were a minor-league team of the Yankees.

In New York, McDonald's assistant was Garnett Marks, and his prime responsibility was to read all the commercial copy. There were no taped commercials. Everything was live. Marks did baseball as far back as the 1920s in St. Louis. In New York he didn't last quite six weeks. Once he goofed ignominiously, a second time he erred disastrously. The failed words were "Ovary Soap," which the people at Proctor and Gamble who make Ivory Soap and sponsored the broadcasts didn't appreciate. "I'll tolerate any mistake, as long as it's not the same one twice," bosses will say. Marks's tenure was brief. In June 1939, the month that the Baseball Hall of Fame opened, Arch had a new assistant, Melvin Avrom Israel. On the air he borrowed his dad's middle name and would be known forever as Mel Allen. Over the next five decades, Mel Allen would become a New York phenomenon and win national acclaim.

Mel was born in Johns, Alabama. His parents were Russian immigrants. His dad was in the dry goods business and his granddad was a rabbi in the old country. "Mother's folks lived in Detroit and we visited there in the summer. I sold soda at the ballpark just one day to get in for free. They didn't ask me back because I spent my time watching the game instead of selling soda. One day I saw Babe Ruth play in Detroit. It was the only time I ever saw him play."

Blessed with a gifted mind, Allen was just 15 when he entered college at the University of Alabama. Law school followed. He got involved doing the public address at the football games and before long stumbled into the broadcast business.

Allen was asked to do football by a local radio station and was paid $5 per game. In an interview with the *New York Post* in 1957, Mel told the story of a blunder in one of the first football games he broadcast. "Somehow, I lost a down. I said second down and the scoreboard said third. So while they were in a huddle I made up a phantom play and ran it into the line for no gain."

In 1936 Mel and some of his buddies drove up north. He was in the New Jersey house of a friend, Irving Berlin Kahn, the nephew of the great songwriter. Through the Alabama station for which he was working, a CBS affiliate, Mel had made some contact with CBS in New York. He was asked to audition. A few days later, he was asked back for a second audition. Impressed, CBS offered him a job as an understudy to Robert Trout in news and Ted Husing in sports.

"My parents weren't happy about it, since I had studied to become a lawyer and passed the bar." So while Allen accepted the job in early 1937, he never expected broadcasting to be a career. The eventual great "voice of the Yankees" did a variety of work at CBS, including organ selections, signing on the network, and introducing dance bands. By the fall of 1937 Allen was selected to do local college football on WINS. His worked was praised by both fans and newspaper critics.

In 1938 CBS was one of four networks to broadcast the World Series, and Allen's first major baseball assignment was to do color for veteran France Laux. When McDonald was hired to come to New York, Allen was asked to replace him in Washington. But just as he was about to leave for the Senators, the team owner, Clark Griffith came up with a brainstorm, hiring former pitching great Walter Johnson. So it wasn't until the Marks verbal debacle that Allen got his break, joining McDonald as the "associate" announcer at Yankee Stadium and the Polo Grounds.

The baseball broadcast legend was an instant success. Mel became the lead announcer on the Giants-Yankees package when the "Old Pine Tree" ambled back to Washington in 1940. Interestingly, the first four baseball announcers New Yorkers heard were all Southerners. Harper and Allen were from Alabama, Barber was from Mississippi originally, and McDonald hailed from Arkansas. Later there were more, such as Ernie Harwell, Frank Messer, and Lindsey Nelson.

The stentorian, Allen, never married. His career was his life and his family. He would say, "I am a bachelor by circumstances rather than design. I was engaged when I went into the Army in 1942, but with all my income cut off, I let my head rule my heart. She got tired of waiting I suppose."

In 1940 Mel had separate partners, one for the Yankees, J. C. Flippin, and one for the Giants, Joe Bolton. It turns out that the Giants' ownership didn't like Flippin, so Bolton served with Allen on Polo Grounds broadcasts. Another announcer, writer Richards Vidmer, would join Mel on Giants broadcasts, too. Bolton later did all sorts of work for WPIX Television including serving as host of children's shows such as *Superman* and *The Three Stooges*.

Allen dubbed Tommy Henrich "Old Reliable" and Joe DiMaggio "Joltin Joe." He carried on with great enthusiasm, a hearty voice, and a riveting style. Ralph Waldo Emerson said, "Nothing great has ever been achieved without enthusiasm." Allen loved his job and loved baseball. The stocky 6-foot, 1-inch personality could extemporize for an hour at a time, going on and on about nothing. He had an innate ability to make something of nothing. Initially, being longwinded was viewed as an asset. But in the end it would be the bane to his career.

To baby boomers in the 1950s, Allen was synonymous with the hazy and lazy days of summer. Mel made baseball and radio blissfully compatible, and fans adored him. He sounded like anybody's easygoing storytelling uncle. It always seemed as though his voice was smiling as he spoke over the radio. He had style and personality, and he was warm and entertaining. Mel had a rich but human voice.

After a couple of years on the air, the Yankees-Giants package was not carried at all in 1941. How many times have fans heard Mel's call in which DiMaggio's 56-game hitting streak comes to an end? What they actually hear is a complete reenactment. The game in Cleveland wasn't carried live or even re-created. The Yankees were simply off the air in 1941.

So while Barber was going strong in Brooklyn, the Bombers and the Giants were off the air. Their two-year sponsorship deal with General Mills had come to an end after the 1940 season and the teams were off WABC. It wasn't until 1942 that the two clubs were back on. This time it was WOR, and Connie Desmond, a staff announcer at the station, was selected as Mel's associate.

Don Dunphy worked with Mel on the '42 broadcasts, or sort of did. Virtually every game was played in the afternoon and Dunphy did a five-minute postgame show if Allen got off the air by 5:55 P.M. At 6 P.M., WOR aired the news. The game might end at 5:30 but garrulous Mel would go on and on and on, often depriving Dunphy of doing his show.

It would be the last of the three years that Mel Allen would do the Giants-Yankees package. He left for the Army, spending most of his time at Fort Benning, Georgia, where he was asked to use his radio experience to boost the morale of the troops who were heading for the war zones.

Meanwhile, the Yankees and Giants were plagued by inconsistencies. They were off the air again in 1943 but back on in 1944 under the aegis of Gillette. The blade sponsor tried unsuccessfully to lure Red Barber, so it settled for Dunphy and Bill Slater, a track and football man. It would be Dunphy's only year of broadcasting big-league baseball. Off-again, on-again, the Yankees-Giants package was having a tough time competing against Brooklyn and the solid and steady Red Barber. By 1945 the Yankees had yet another announcing change. Slater would stay, but Al Helfer replaced Dunphy.

When Allen returned from the service, there were some major developments. First, Madison Square Garden aborted its attempt to purchase the Yankees. Larry MacPhail was now running the team. The former Dodgers boss owned a piece of the club, along with Dan Topping and Del Webb. MacPhail was to do something drastic with radio. He convinced Horace Stoneham, the Giants' owner, that the two clubs should break their partnership and that each should air all their games separately. MacPhail was also determined that the Yankees would become the first major-league team to have announcers travel and do all road contests live. His decision was made out of conviction and pragmatism. It gave the Yankees a competitive marketing gap because the other two local clubs were still re-creating. In fact, he would have made the drastic change as early as 1945 but the Giants and Yankees were locked into the second year of the Gillette deal.

Visiting with Stoneham, Allen was offered his job back and he accepted. He was set to do the Giants and not the Yankees. But two things happened. First, MacPhail hoped to hire Barber for the Yankees but was turned down, and second, Stoneham couldn't get a station. On the other hand, MacPhail was all set for 1946. He had the advertising backers and WINS. The station had been the home of the Yankees-Giants broadcasts since 1944 and would now carry a Yankees-only package. It did, in fact, do just that through 1957. Turned down by Barber, MacPhail approached Allen and made the Yankees' announcing offer to him. Allen went back to Stoneham to whom he had committed his services and asked him what to do. Horace told him that if the Yankees have a station, he should go with them. He told Allen that frankly he didn't have a station yet and couldn't make any commitments. Mel was released from his Giants agreement and accepted MacPhail's offer.

So the man with magnificent resonance and timbre to his voice started his Yankees-only career in 1946. Every game, home and away, was live play-by-play, and as MacPhail promised, there wouldn't be any re-creations. Mel Allen would be hailed in the years to come by those back from the war and later by their children.

Allen was warm and influential. He had style, humility, and personality. The man would become a household name linked to success. Over the next 19 years, the Yankees would win 15 pennants. The club was a winner and so was he. Only twice in that span would a World Series broadcast not have his signature. Barber may have been the pioneer but Allen personified spirit as the gentle cheerleader.

If Red Barber was not afraid to walk away from the greatest gem of an assignment, the World Series, Mel Allen's fear was not to be assigned one. "If I were a millionaire, I'd pay somebody to let me do the work I do," he once said. For all his wonderful talent, Mel embodied insecurity. He wanted to be liked.

Unlike Barber, who detached and distanced himself from players for fears of corrupting reportorial principles, Allen fraternized with team members. They were surrogate family. The *Post*'s Leonard Shecter wrote, "His voice, it's said, betrays the state of the game. Ebullient when the Yankees are ahead, dull when they're behind." Allen defended it. "Any fair-minded individual would know there is no prejudice, just partisanship." What's prejudice? "Seeing only one side."

Defensive and a bit sensitive to the criticism, Allen had other explanations. The voice thought that folks listened quickly and got the wrong impression. Furthermore, he explained, he talked a lot more about the Yankees because they were winners. What about the anti-Yankees fans in the 1950s? "They hated me. If I would compliment Mickey Mantle, they would say, 'what about Willie Mays, you bum?'" Writing in the *New York Times*, Stephen Jay Gould lionized Allen as "a voice of heart." He grew up with Mel, "a man of grace and integrity, a shameless huckster of charming originality."

© National Baseball Hall of Fame Library, Cooperstown, N.Y.

Mel Allen, right, is honored at a Yankee Stadium ceremony. For Allen, a bachelor, the Yankees were his family.

To many, the announcer was a salesman, pushing beer and cigars. He may have been as well known for the "Ballantine Blast" or the "White Owl Wallop" as "going, going, gone" for a home run or "how about that?" for his home-team acclamation. "People liked it. You have to do what the fans like, not some sophisticated critic." It went further. "Why, that ball was foul by the bottle of Ballantine beer," Allen would say. Gould remembers when the Yankees' ultimate salesman stopped in midsentence, "foul by no more than a bottle of Bal . . . " Then, he paused, "No, that ball was foul by the ash on a White Owl cigar." After a while Ballantine and White Owl got as much play as the Yankees and the game they were playing. Commissioner Ford Frick stepped in and asked Allen and other hucksters to tone it down.

"'How about that!' originated in 1949 just after Joe DiMaggio missed 65 games. When he came back he hit four home runs in three days. Fans were hysterical and I couldn't help showing enthusiasm as they began to climb. It was during those exciting afternoons that I would cry, 'How about that!'" He elaborated, "I did this without the slightest premeditation. It was just a natural impulse."

The other Allen expression, "going, going, gone," also emerged naturally. In 1946, when a ball kept carrying at Yankee Stadium, "I just kept saying, it's going, going, as the ball sailed out of sight."

When the broadcasts split in 1946, Allen's partner was Russ Hodges. Over the next 12 years, when radio was seemingly indispensable, Hodges would feed the listener's baseball fantasy in New York. For the first three years on the "Home of Champions Radio Network," Russ assisted Mel and did a couple of innings of play-by-play each game, the fourth and seventh. One day Mel told Russ that he had never had the opportunity to call a no-hitter. A day or two later, Bob Feller of Cleveland had a no-hitter going into the seventh inning. Mel was about to turn it over to Russ but Russ waved him off, suggesting that Allen continue. Russ was a genuinely nice man with a heart as big as his frame.

Hodges earned a football scholarship to the University of Kentucky. When he broke his ankle, he was asked to be a spotter for the radio announcer and it launched his career. Working at WCKY, a station licensed to Covington, Kentucky, but covering Cincinnati and beyond, he made all of $25 in 1932. It was there that Hodges petitioned Larry MacPhail, then the Cincinnati general manager, to allow WCKY to carry Reds games. MacPhail turned him down because the station's signal was so strong that it swept into Pittsburgh. MacPhail and Hodges quibbled over the issue and it might have left the two with a distaste for one another.

The aggressive Hodges attended law school at night and earned his degree. He worked in Chicago doing a variety of sports, the Cubs and White Sox among them. Football and basketball were part of his responsibilities as was, yes, wrestling on radio. After a stop in Charlotte re-creating Senators games, Hodges went to Washington where he assisted Arch McDonald.

Allen got a chance to hear Hodges in 1945 and liked his warm and pleasant sound. McDonald told his old partner, Allen, that Hodges didn't have a big ego. When Larry MacPhail put the stamp of approval on his hire, the Yankee booth became the only one in sports history to be an "all-lawyer booth" (Allen and Hodges). Hodges was actually surprised that MacPhail approved him after the Cincinnati incident years before.

And there was something that Hodges had in common with Red Barber. Both their fathers were railroad men. "People in my family have been railroaders for years. Good, solid people who go off with the lunch pail every day. My going into radio was a real upheaval for them. They have never understood why I don't settle down." Despite the similar stock, Barber and Hodges didn't get along. They weren't cut of the same cloth. Working a football game together, Red did the first quarter and turned it over to "Russ Hughes." Without losing a beat, Russ said, "Thank you, Red Baker."

Hodges was easygoing, a regular kind of guy. He may not have been as prepared in the booth as Mel. "It's a game," was his attitude. "Let's not make life or death of it." He liked broadcasting baseball so much that he emoted, "I'd rather be doing what I am than be president. I'm one of the happiest guys in the business." While working for Dan Topping's Yankees, he was also asked to broadcast the New York Yankees of the All-America Football Conference in the fall of 1946.

Russ was a straight shooter, not afraid to rib himself after a blunder. While broadcasting a pivotal Illinois football game that had Rose Bowl implications on network radio, he said, "On the key play of the game, I had the wrong guy throwing the pass and the wrong guy intercepting it and scoring the touchdown. It's true it was foggy and a little hard to read the numbers but that's no excuse. I just blew it." This broad and pleasant man tells the upshot. "When I called home that night, my daughter tells me 'Daddy, you really blew one that time, didn't you?' My own daughter!"

Allen and Hodges had quick-thinking minds. The duo was vibrant and entertainingly bubbly at a time when the Yankees' dominance was at its incipience. Hodges was first to bring an upbeat emotional patter to the baseball booth. The excitement in his voice manifested itself in his throaty delivery, when announcing purists dug deep into their diaphragms for greater resonance. They were a terrific match.

They also had their moments. On Saturday, April 24, 1948, the two of them had to leave the air for 30 minutes because of a sudden burst of obscenities. A cross-connection of wires apparently permitted the utterances of some irate caller to leak into the programming channel. The incident caused a flood of protests from listeners for several hours.

When the season ended, Hodges took the leap across the Harlem River, becoming the number one "voice of the New York Giants." Jack Slocum, who was helpful to the Yankees in the Hodges search, worked on behalf of sponsor Wheaties. In his travels through the Southwest, he got a chance to listen to Curt Gowdy who was broadcasting minor-league baseball in Oklahoma City. Slocum liked Gowdy's work and "relaxed style" and recommended him to Mel Allen and the Yankees' brass. Allen, the ensconced voice in the Bronx, had a great deal of influence on who would be hired. After all, the new employee would be Mel's assistant.

Allen, General Manager George Weiss, and Trevor Adams, the Yankees' broadcast director at the time, had to be pretty impressed with the 29-year-old broadcaster. When asked, Gowdy told the Bronx-based club that he had seen only one major-league baseball game in his life, as a youngster traveling from his native Wyoming to Chicago with a softball team. Yet the eventual network sports giant had such impressive tapes and credentials that he earned the biggest break of his life. In 1949 he became the Yankees' number two man behind the burgeoning Allen. The games continued at WINS although there were plans for a new owner to come in and reformat the programming to foreign language. The ownership change never materialized.

When the umpire cried "play ball" at Yankee Stadium in April, there was Gowdy on an overcast day, sitting near Mel Allen, about to call his first-ever major-league game. "I was scared to death. I was nervous and tense, but everyone on the Yankees was wonderful. They had class, real class." Curt credits Mel with teaching him much, from naturally weaving in commercials to paying attention to detail. They would sit down and talk, review almost each broadcast, and see where they could improve.

"Mel liked to talk back and forth on the air, which I had never done before. And I didn't have any clever answers. I would just sit there. In a couple of months though, I loosened up and built my confidence," said Gowdy, who spends much of his retirement time in Palm Beach.

Gowdy got into broadcasting by accident. He had played basketball for the University of Wyoming, but hurt his back. After he underwent spinal surgery, he had a call from a Cheyenne, Wyoming, radio station. "The manager wanted to know if I would like to do a football game. I told him that I had never broadcast, and he said, 'it's either you, or my wife and I will have to, and neither of us has ever seen a football game.'"

"The Cowboy" started announcing football and basketball regularly, and a short number of years later was recruited to Oklahoma City, where he fostered a relationship with Bud Wilkinson, broadcasting his nationally prominent football teams at the University of Oklahoma, and with Hank Iba, calling the games of his powerful Oklahoma A&M basketball teams. Within time, it was Oklahoma City Indians baseball of the Texas League.

After a couple of years under Mel's wing, he correctly envisioned a limited future in the number one man's shadow. The Red Sox, who had broadcast jointly with the Boston Braves, went out on their own, and Gowdy was hired as their first lead announcer. "Funny, the first two games were at Yankee Stadium. I started getting hate mail. Sox fans called me a Yankee lover." Gowdy, interestingly, points out that although he had a year remaining on his Yankees contract and despite the fierce on-the-field rivalry between the two teams, the Yankees released him from his commitment. "The front offices had a good working relationship," the legendary announcer-sportsman pointed out.

In New England, he had to learn not to butcher the pronunciations of New England towns. Narragansett Beer was the sponsor. Its treasurer, Carl Haffenreff, told Gowdy, "You've got to learn some New England English. Guys in bars are complaining to our distributors that you're murdering the names of their hometowns." After 14 years Curt left for NBC where his very voice was a signal of the importance of the event itself. It didn't matter, the World Series, the Super Bowl, the NCAA Final Four, or the Rose Bowl, he was equally adept at all of them. In the 1970s he was as big a name on network television sports as anyone before or anyone since. But for two years Gowdy graced New York with his never-rushed sound and his always-at-ease storytelling.

In 1951 Allen was on the prowl again for an assistant. The search took a different twist this time. And it went back to Curt Gowdy's first day on the Yankees' job. General Manager George Weiss had thrown a party for the press and Gowdy bumped into the new manager, Casey Stengel, in the bathroom. Unaware that Gowdy was a rookie broadcaster, Stengel said, "I want you to do something for me. There's a fellow on the West Coast who broadcast my games last year who's a great baseball man. He deserves a shot at the big leagues." The man turned out to be Art Gleeson, and in 1951 he became Mel's assistant in the radio booth.

Something quite unusual was done between 1948 and 1951. White Owl and Ballantine would alternately sponsor the Yankees' telecasts. When it was the beer, Mel would simulcast. His radio broadcast would serve as television's audio. During that period, Dizzy Dean, who would colorfully butcher the English language, was brought in to work Yankees telecasts. Because he was doing a radio play-by-play on television, Mel would often blame those years for his admitted verbosity.

By the mid-1950s the *New York Post*'s Leonard Shecter wrote, "He likes to talk. He talks on radio, he talks on television, he talks in restaurants. He'll talk to anybody who will listen. He has been roundly condemned for talking too much on television, where his critics say the picture should do the talking." Mel would defend himself, pointing to the fact that a fly ball, as an example, can't be seen on the screen. It must be described. He also felt that he had an obligation to educate new fans about baseball. A number of years after the simulcasts ended, the Yankees' announcer said, "We did a simulcast and I got little criticism from the fans. I talk less now than I did a year or two ago but I think silence lessens the drama."

Like Allen, Gleeson never married. The two bachelors were a team in 1951, and when Bill Crowley came along for a year in 1952, it was a trio in the booth. Both Gleeson and Crowley were gone at the end of the 1952 season, another one which ended when the Yankees beat Brooklyn in the Series. The club wanted to recast its play-by-play crew, with the ever-popular Mel, of course, remaining as anchor.

Gleeson went to work for Mutual and was one of its *Game of the Day* announcers. Through Gowdy, he hooked on as a Red Sox announcer in 1960 when Mutual's package was about to end. The man he replaced was Bob Murphy. On October 1, 1961, Gleeson sat near Ned Martin in the Sox booth when Tracy Stallard delivered a pitch that Roger Maris slugged into the right-field seats for his historic 61st home run. After five seasons with Gowdy, he suffered an untimely death in November 1964. Crowley, who had done some television with Dean, also did three years of Red Sox broadcasting before becoming the Bostonian's publicity director.

One of those interested in joining the Yankees in 1953 was Lindsey Nelson. While Mel Allen was quite interested in him and two announcers were added, Lindsey wasn't one of them. The main play-by-play addition to Allen would be Jim Woods. Born in Kansas City in 1916, Woods had been a minor-league announcer in the South. He attended the University of Missouri but not for very long. "I was working for the college radio station and I was told that if I wanted to be in radio I was wasting my time in college. So I quit."

After selling war bonds in Idaho and Montana from 1942–45, his first gig was in Mason City, Iowa. He did minor-league baseball there and then went to Atlanta, handling major-league re-creations. It would be 20 years before Atlanta had a major-league team of its own. But in 1948, when Ernie Harwell, the likable "voice of the Atlanta Crackers," was summoned to Brooklyn to take over for the ailing Red Barber, Woods succeeded him.

Five years later Woods got the biggest break of his professional career, a microphone in the House that Ruth built. In 1975 Woods, by that point a number two announcer for 22 years, told *Sports Illustrated* that he knew he was in the big time when he walked into the booth and Allen was on the telephone talking with Joe DiMaggio about Marilyn Monroe. As was the case with his two Allen-assistant predecessors, Hodges and Gowdy, Mel would pick each broadcast apart in an attempt to perfect the presentation.

Allen called Nelson during spring training in 1953 from St. Petersburg to tell him that Woods got the number two job but that he was still being considered for the pre- and postgame assignment on television. Shortly thereafter though, New York hired Joe E. Brown, a movie star whose son would later be the longtime general manager of the Pittsburgh Pirates. (While still in Oklahoma City, Gowdy took his future wife, Jerre, on a date. They saw a road company, starring Brown, in Harvey. Little did they know then, either the man in the stands or the man on stage, that they would both later end up being Mel Allen's assistant in the Yankees' booth.) Of the selection, Lindsey said, "For Joe E. Brown, a fan, it was just a pleasant way for him to spend the day at the ballpark." But it wasn't a walk in the park. By June he was taken off play-by-play. Allen and Woods would finish the season without him.

Now came the shocking changes. Barber had turned down Gillette and the 1953 World Series television. He knew that his contract was up in Brooklyn and that Walter O'Malley was in no hurry to bring him back. A civilian, so to speak, he bought

Jim Woods

his own World Series tickets. Barber had worn out his welcome in Brooklyn and with just Allen and Woods in saddle, the Yankees' brass did the blasphemous. During the Classic, they hired the Ole Redhead to come to the Bronx. By then, Larry MacPhail, for whom he worked in Cincinnati and Brooklyn, was gone. Dan Topping was the head honcho and Weiss was his general manager. They brought Barber over from Brooklyn.

Barber's primary responsibility was to host the pre- and postgame telecasts in addition to a few innings of play-by-play on radio and television at home games only. Barber didn't travel. Long baseball trips were against his grain. Red preferred to travel only for football where the trips were generally just one night.

For the next three years the Yankees' booth was anchored by Allen, Woods, and Barber. For Red, it was a new experience. In Brooklyn, he was in charge of the booth, assigned the innings, and evaluated his associates' performances. In the Bronx, he would be no more than an associate.

Barber's hearing in his left ear had been deteriorating. He was 46 when he took the Yankees job and went in for advanced surgery in January 1954. Unfortunately, the surgery was a total failure. He came out completely deaf in the left "auricle," a term Ted Husing once used on the air to refer to an ear. It was depressing. With only one good ear, among many other punishing limitations, it's impossible to detect the direction of sound. The proud man started staying at home and had it not been for his wife, Lylah, he would have become a hermit.

In Barber's humble estimate, the trio of Barber, Woods, and Allen "were the best baseball broadcasting trio in history. Unless it was Desmond, Scully, and Barber—anyhow both teams worked together, we knew how to do it, we did it." Barber, who used Woods freely and confidently on the *CBS Football Roundup*, credits him with uniting the trio, helping keep the peace. "Mel and I never had a coolness between us, and Jim helped what could have been a sticky situation."

In retrospect, what were Topping's reasons for bringing Barber aboard? After all, the Yankees' owner had some bad history with Barber, stemming from an alleged breach of services contract covering the Brooklyn Dodgers' NFL broadcasts in the 1940s. Topping owned the Dodgers football team at the time. The key reason was Barber's talent and image. The booth was now star-studded with sparkling voices. Topping had several run-ins with Allen, too, and threatened to fire him several times. With two superstars sharing the mike, perhaps he thought he would keep both men's large egos in check. Woods liked to tell the story about the time when Red was with the Dodgers. Walter O'Malley and Topping were having a few pops one night when they both started ripping their own announcers. Half-kidding, they suggested a trade, Allen to Brooklyn and Barber to the Bronx.

Red spent 13 years in the Bronx, two fewer than he did with the Dodgers. In Brooklyn, he was the pioneer, the boss, the principal, and there every game, the voice of the upstart Dodgers. In the Bronx, he generally didn't do road games, he was heard half the time, he wasn't the boss, he was an associate. Barber wasn't the same man physically either. He had half his stomach removed after the 1948 ulcer attack and now his hearing was terribly limited. According to Ernie Harwell, his voice wasn't as strong, either.

Through it all though, his relationship with Allen was cordial. They weren't close but there was a sense of mutual respect. The styles contrasted profoundly. But the men didn't seem to get in each other's way in the booth. Of course, Barber stayed at home when the team was on the road, so it was difficult for the men to get into each other's hair. The *New York Times* referred to the two aptly: fire and ice. Allen was effulgent, extroverted, and a perfectionist. Barber was reserved, individualistic, and pedantic. They were the first inductees into the Ford Frick wing of baseball's Hall of Fame, jointly in 1978.

When he jumped from the Dodgers, he found himself having to do live endorsements for new and competitive sponsors. One day he was telling everybody about Old Gold, now it was Camel. But he was almost defensive about it. "I won't work for a sponsor I can't believe in. I've got faith in the sponsors. I bank at Bankers Trust and I insure my autos at State Farm Insurance and I smoke Camels and Winstons." But to the general public it was somewhat curious that Barber, at the drop of a hat, could go from singing the praises of one cigarette to doing the same for another.

And there was the Redhead in 1957, 49 years old, broadcasting Yankees games on WINS, a station that was playing early rock 'n roll. Asked about his music preferences, Red said he had a good collection of classical records. "I also like Belafonte and Burl Ives. But not rock 'n roll, that isn't music." Not one to mince words, the Columbus, Mississippi, native was kinder to the medium of radio. "The broadcaster is the whole show on radio. When you are at the microphone you describe the whole thing. But on TV you are the servant of the monitor. You can't tell a story because you'll never get to finish it. You are a broadcaster on radio and a narrator on TV. Radio is more creative. Television is more mechanical."

In 1956 the Yankees, looking for a veteran to help them win another pennant, wanted to sign 40-year-old Enos "Country" Slaughter, who had been waived by Kansas City. The odd man out was shortstop Phil Rizzuto, a month shy of his 39th birthday. The Yankees weren't thinking public relations, though, when releasing the popular longtime shortstop unceremoniously on August 25, Old Timer's Day. But in the waning months of his playing career, the New York native began to contemplate plans for the time he would put away his magical glove for the final time. "You weren't set like the ballplayers today. You didn't have a nest egg. Those days it was like the end of the world."

"The Scooter" took a liking to broadcasting. "In the last two or three years, Casey Stengel would rest me from time to time, and now and then Mel Allen would ask me up to the radio booth to give the play-by-play for a half-inning. That got me excited and I never missed when Mel asked me upstairs. I began dreaming that maybe somebody who thought I might have a chance to be a broadcaster would hear me." It might almost sound unimaginable, but the same man who would later leave a game early to beat the traffic worked diligently to prepare himself for his second career. He would watch the other New York teams, the Giants and Dodgers, on television with the sound down and call the games to himself. Phil also had a chance to fill in for Frankie Frisch who was doing Giants postgame shows on television.

There was talk that Rizzuto would become a fourth man in the Yankees' booth, doing only home games. The Giants also had an interest in putting Rizzuto behind the microphone. And the Baltimore Orioles, along with their beer sponsor, offered the now retired star shortstop a $30,000 salary to join their broadcast booth.

Mel Allen said it best in his 1963 book *You Can't Beat the Hours*. It's a highly coveted job. So when the job you love disappears, it hurts. And when the job you love disappears for no apparent reason, it's painful and frustrating. In 1956 Jim Woods was completing his fourth year and the trio of Allen, Barber, and Woods was sailing through another model season chronicling another Yankees march to a world championship.

In the fall George Weiss called Woods into his office and told him he was ordered by sponsor Ballantine to replace him with Rizzuto. As a player, Rizzuto had hobnobbed with Ballantine executives and the regional beer felt Rizzuto's warm personality would be a big plus to their marketing efforts in the community. The Yankees' general manager told Woods that he was doing something he never had to do, fire somebody who had done a good job. On December 18, 1956, the announcement was made that Rizzuto would replace Woods in a three-man booth. "When I first started as a broadcaster, Howard Cosell told me, 'You'll never last. You look like George Burns and sound like Groucho Marx,'" Rizzuto chuckled.

"They promised him [Rizzuto] a job in the organization, if he wanted it," remembered Mel Allen, who was asked to sharpen the broadcast rookie's skills. Shortly after his firing, Woods said, "It was a political thing, somebody had to go," adding, "it's a family business and these things happen." Ballantine, it is said, also didn't want to lose the popular Rizzuto to Baltimore and a competitive beer.

Through his career as an associate, Woods worked for six different big-league ball clubs, backing up big names. In addition to Allen and Barber, Woods teamed with Bob Prince in Pittsburgh, Jack Buck in St. Louis, Russ Hodges in

Phil Rizzuto

New York, and Monte Moore in Oakland. "You won't get a more loyal number two man," Moore said of Woods, who spent 22 years in the majors. "He just enjoyed being there, getting on the plane and going to the next city, and after a win, he would just say, 'let the good times roll.' There was never a cross word with any of the big names he assisted."

In his first season, Rizzuto was very uneasy and very uncomfortable the first few weeks. Working for taskmasters was exceedingly demanding. Allen and Barber might have resented Rizzuto. He was the first ex-ballplayer to encroach upon their august booth. Twenty years after he retired as a ballplayer, Phil shared a first-season spring training announcing experience with *The Sporting News*. "The Yankees and Cardinals were about to get one started when the rain came. I started to get up when Mel said, 'I'm gonna get a hot dog with Red. We'll be right back. You take it.'

"So now they force-fed me. They didn't come back for fifteen minutes. I mean, they were off in a corner where they could see and hear me, but they made me fill that dead air unassisted."

On the eve of his 80th birthday in 1997, the beloved Scooter told the *New York Post*, "When I began as a broadcaster, it was difficult. They (Barber and Allen) resented me as a former player. I was one of the early ones to invade their domain. They were professionals, I wasn't, and they let me know I wasn't. But they came around. I got along with everyone I worked with. I really did." In Curt Smith's *Voices of the Game*, for that matter, Woods went a step further, pontificating that the Rizzuto appointment created negative common ground for Allen and Barber. Phil, Woods said, would counter by going down to the dugout where he was still viewed by the players as one of their comrades, get some personal dope, and purposely not share it with Mel and Red.

But in the long run, he benefited by his apprenticeship. If Phil would say "foul ball back in the stands," Mel would whisper, "back where?" Red, though, wouldn't whisper, and Scooter won't forget it. "He'd find out what the natural rock is for the state of Michigan, or how many states are on the Nevada border," the Scooter said of Red who asked Phil these questions on the air. "Now, how was I supposed to answer that?" Barber, a stickler for grammar, would pounce on Phil's syntax. "If I would say that I had a pizza pie before the ballgame, he would say that it was redundant. 'Pizza,' Barber said, 'means pie.' I'm very weak with the Italian language." Many years later Phil would kid partner Bobby Murcer. "Red used to tell me that I was in 'sartorial splendor,' I had no idea what he meant."

From the time that he started in 1957 until the Yankees hired a fourth announcer, Jerry Coleman in 1963, Rizzuto put in a hard and long day's work. During that time, Barber was generally not traveling. For six years, only Allen and Rizzuto would go on the road. And when games were televised back to New York, each would have to work nine innings without the benefit of a color commentator. There were some long pauses back then, even on television.

Giving birthday greetings on the air, a Rizzuto signature, started early in Phil's broadcast career. "I was used to the network stuff on CBS. You just don't do that kind of thing. It was his own style. The game was primary. To Phil, the game was secondary. That's not criticism on my part. I just mean that is his style," Allen would say. Despite it, though, Scooter strayed less in his early years and could be quite descriptive. In a 1960 game between the Yankees and White Sox:

Big Ted Kluszewski turns and looks at umpire Larry Napp. If he looked at me like that, I'd run right out of the ballpark.

By Rizzuto's second year in broadcasting, 1958, the Yankees left WINS, their station of 14 years, and went to WMGM, a station deserted by the Dodgers. With it came the pre- and postgame crew of the Dodgers, starring Glickman and Gussie Moran. Although he was the "voice of the Celtics," Johnny Most would do work then for WMGM. In fact, in 1959 Don Gillis filled in for Most on a Celtics game so that Johnny could do a Yankees postgame show. While Most was on the air in New York, Gillis told the Boston audience that Johnny couldn't make it because he had laryngitis!

Fans connected with Rizzuto. He was warm, the guy next door. He had a magnetizing personality and an infectious enthusiasm. He called the Yankees' pennant clincher in 1960 against Boston on September 25, "The Yankees win the pennant! The twenty-fifth pennant in the Yankees' career!" In 1961 the Yankees moved their games to WCBS and the Scooter was there as Roger Maris made history with his 61st home run of the year:

Here's the windup. Fastball. Hit deep to right. This could be it, way back there. Holy Cow! He did it!

Barber, unmoved, called it on television with a matter-of-fact reportorial voice cadence. If Red's pants were burning, he wouldn't have yelled "fire!" either. Allen later re-created the historic moment for a highlight record album.

In the Yankee Stadium booth, Coleman helped preside over a couple of Yankees pennants in 1963 and 1964, and then the team's precipitous demise. In 1963 he was a rookie play-by-play man and needed a pat on the back. What he got from one fan was a record that had jungle sounds. There was a note attached: "If you want to hear what you sound like, listen to this."

The native Californian, who grew up in San Francisco, had a distinguished career on the ball fields and battlefields before embarking upon a broadcasting career. World War II summoned just after he was offered a basketball and baseball scholarship to the University of Southern California.

"My education wound up being preflight training and the eighteen months it took me to get my wings. We all wanted to be heroes. I had to wait until I was eighteen to do what I wanted in the Naval aviation program."

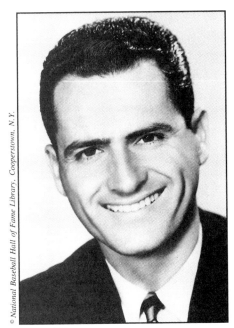

National Baseball Hall of Fame Library, Cooperstown, N.Y.

Jerry Coleman

Coleman entered the military with the same alacrity that he did the infield or the broadcast booth. He flew dive-bombing missions in the Solomon Islands and the Philippines during the war, and then later interrupted his playing career to serve in Korea. By the time he retired from the military, Coleman was decorated with two Distinguished Flying Crosses, 13 Air Medals, and three Navy Citations.

Jerry was Rookie of the Year in 1949 and MVP of the 1950 World Series. But Korea shattered his playing career when he returned in 1954 after two years out of baseball. He never regained his earlier sharpness, and guys like Gil McDougald, Billy Martin, and Bobby Richardson made it more difficult for Coleman to recapture his pre-Korea status.

"They took me off the field and offered me the job of Assistant Director of Player Personnel," Coleman recounted. "I loved the work. But it was too much travel. In 1959, I was gone for 223 days," said the man who had a family at the time. He quit to take a position with Van Husen Clothing in its sales department before undertaking some spot on-air duty for CBS Radio. He took a liking to the on-air work, and when the Yankees and Ballantine were interested in adding a man to their crew, he was hired. According to Barber, the brass wanted to add the former Yankees second baseman in 1962. To work it into their budget, the beer company asked Red to take a salary cut. He refused. So the addition waited until 1963.

Coleman and his brassy voice were always upbeat and enthusiastic. While Barber and Rizzuto didn't enjoy traveling, Coleman was a trained pilot. While Rizzuto's "Holy Cow" irritated Harry Caray, who claimed a patent on it, Coleman's exclamation "Oh, Doctor" didn't seem to ruffle partner Barber, who made it famous long before Jerry ever put on big-league cleats. "I could prove I said Holy Cow first," Caray, who died in 1998, once bristled. "I did it in a game that Rizzuto was playing in."

Over three decades as a big-league broadcaster, the affable Coleman has enjoyed a career best characterized by casual optimism, spoonerisms, and malapropisms. Writer Don Freeman once wrote, "It's a charming coincidence that Jerry's old manager, Casey Stengel, also had his curious locutions known as 'Stengelese.' I suspect ol' Case would have been greatly entertained by Jerry's 'Colemanisms.'"

There have been more than just a host of tongue entanglements attributed to Coleman:

He's throwing up in the bullpen.

Smith's on first base and he's always a threat to grow.

The way he's swinging a bat, he won't get a hit until the 20th century.

Leaping up to make one of those diving stops only he can make.

We're all sad to see Glenn Beckert leave. Before he goes, though, I hope he stops by so we can kiss him goodbye. He's that kind of guy.

That could be an omen about things to come.

They have seven innings to catch up but they better hurry.

Winfield's going back, back, his head hits the wall, it's rolling toward second base.

The former Yankees second baseman transcended the Allen-Barber era, the Allen firing, the Barber firing, the post-two-legends era, the Garagiola tenure, and Rizzuto. He's now an institution himself in San Diego, where he's broadcast for more than a quarter century and where one newspaper said, "He has become like an unusual sculpture in a city square." And for more than 20 years the country had a chance to tune him in on the CBS *Game of the Week* and postseason broadcasts.

By the early 1960s Mel Allen was getting more verbose. He would slur his words, ramble on, belabor the obvious, and become a bit overbearing. As Anthony Lukas said in a *New York Times Magazine* article in 1971, "At times, Allen showed an unfortunate fondness for meaningless alliteration, a weakness for bad puns, and a penchant for the high-sounding clichés. As Allen got older, he grew increasingly prolix."

Initially, in the 1950s, networks found his ability to talk forever about so little to be a plus; later it was his vexation. In 1964, Mel's last year, the Verrazano Narrows Bridge opened, hailed as a triumph of "simplicity and restraint." According to Topping, Allen had neither verbal simplicity nor verbal restraint.

To this day, the Yankees have never elaborated on the reasons for Mel's abrupt and stunning dismissal. The news broke in a couple of waves. First the Yankees nominated Phil Rizzuto to do the Yankees-Cardinals World Series on NBC instead of Allen, a perennial Fall Classic voice. Then came word that Allen was being fired. The mighty man had fallen. Barber witnessed part of it. Topping told him the afternoon following the September 1964 morning when he fired Allen. He swore Red to secrecy, telling him that they were allowing Mel to make his announcement during the off-season. Mel, who according to Barber, would usually come into the booth at the last second, was ready well in advance of airtime of the next game. The big voice was just gazing out on the field. If the legend would have been hit with a feather, he would have fallen off his chair. "He was the saddest looking man I have ever seen. He was in a nightmare. His look was not frantic, not wild—just sad, numb, deserted. He just couldn't believe it. He was desolate, stricken," Barber wrote.

The undisclosed reasons for Mel's firing have been cloaked in secrecy for years. Ralph Houk was the team's general manager in 1964 and was in the room with Topping when Mel was let go. "All I'll say is that it wasn't my decision, but I won't get into it. I know Mel's brother, Larry, and his sister in Connecticut, and although Mel's passed on, I won't talk about it." The very firmness of

Houk's commitment to silence 33 years after the fact adds further intrigue to what many still consider a mystery.

In retrospect it appears to be a confluence of developments that caused the stinging change. First, although it was Topping who hired him in 1946, he wore out his welcome with the Yankees' boss. When Topping told Barber that Mel had been fired, he said, "I'm tired of him popping off." Apparently, Mel had become bothersome to Topping. The Yankees' boss threatened to fire him several times, including once when, according to Lindsey Nelson, he took Mickey Mantle on an unauthorized visit to his own personal physician. Second, sponsor Ballantine had grown weary of him. Third, his skills were eroding and he couldn't stop talking, particularly on television. In addition, he had lost his luster with the networks, being unable to keep a production "tight." The 1963 World Series was also fairly fresh on everyone's mind. It was then that he had lost his voice. Some said it was mental laryngitis. Finally, the Yankees were about to be bought by CBS. Was the bachelor Allen its image? This was 1964.

Mel never came back to full-time play-by-play. He did some television briefly for the Braves and Indians. On Channel 9 the cantankerous Clure Mosher cracked inflammatorily, "Mel's feeling sorry for himself." But it took him many years to move on with his life. He was single, had been married to the Yankees, and there wasn't a family to serve as a pillar of support. For years Mel tried to figure out why he was banished from the Stadium. If anything, he would tell people he thought it was the sponsor, Ballantine, which was suffering financially and was looking to make cuts. Although Houk said little, he eliminated Ballantine. "He was employed by Ballantine, but it wasn't their decision," said Houk, now retired in Florida.

The legend would do some games for SportsChannel on cable. The voice was there. So was the resonance and timbre. But he was more garrulous than ever and was losing his sharpness. Some who knew him were afraid to start a conversation with him because he would chew their ear off.

His professional resurrection was *This Week in Baseball*, a weekly syndicated television program that started in 1977. Until then, according to the producers of the show, "he seemed directionless." Allen hosted the show for 17 years, and as late as 1990, six years before his death, the *Sporting News* wrote, "Mel Allen may be 78, but his voice is resonant, mellifluous, and invigorating as ever." For the first 10 years after its inception, the program was essentially an outlet for highlights. It later became entertainment, things off the beaten path such as "baseball funnies." Mel Allen's vibrant voice was the show's signature. To many too young to have experienced his play-by-play, Allen will be remembered as the narrator who gave baseball life and a few nonscripted rings of "How about that!" on *This Week in Baseball*.

To many, Mel Allen *was* baseball. The "Ballantine Blast" might have died in 1964 but it could still shatter glass in the memories of Yankees fans today. Mel's voice was so strong that it carried as far as Mickey Mantle's third-deck home runs and his deep resonance could stir excitement in the least emotional fan. "Going, going, gone" even thrilled my dad, a physicist to whom a baseball was no more than a composition of atoms and molecules.

After the Allen firing, Barber was given the indication by Topping and Houk that he would assume the number one spot in the booth. But when Perry Smith was brought in as director of broadcasting, the Yankees hired Joe Garagiola to succeed Allen. Smith and Garagiola worked together at NBC. It would be the beginning of the end for the Ole Redhead. He disrespected Rizzuto, feuded with Garagiola, and never cared for ex-players invading the booth.

Garagiola grew up a neighbor of Yogi Berra in the Italian St. Louis neighborhood known as The Hill. As a major-league catcher, Joe had an un-distinguished career which was ham-pered by a shoulder injury. As he sat around recovering, he would listen to Harry Caray's inimitable broadcasts and later broke in under him in the St. Louis booth.

By 1960 Joe had written a book of baseball anecdotes, *Baseball is a Funny Game*, which sold some 500,000 copies. His inexhaustible re-source of one-liners caught the atten-tion of television network executives, and by the early 1960s he was han-

Mel Allen

dling a variety of assignments for NBC including *The Today Show* in 1962.

At NBC in the early 1960s the quipster also called the *Game of the Week*, which then was going to non-major-league cities. But after 1964 the peacock network lost the package to ABC, and Garagiola was uneasy with the thought of not doing baseball the following spring. In mid-December 1964 he called the Yankees to express his interest in their opening and was hired. In the winter of 1965, oddly enough, Garagiola was anchoring the NBC Radio show *Monitor* when Allen was doing sports. But when spring training hit, Joe was off to Ft. Lauderdale and Allen stayed home. The whole thing was sort of incongruous to the ear and alien to the senses.

When asked what it would be like to team with Rizzuto, Garagiola said, "It's the Mafia's answer to Huntley and Brinkley [the popular NBC Television news duo]." And there was some light humor from Howard Cosell, who said that despite stories to the contrary, he assured fans the games would not be broadcast in Italian. But there was little to laugh about for Garagiola. In St. Louis he ended up not being on speaking terms with both Caray and slugger Stan Musial, and in New York he clashed with Barber, who felt that he was butting in on his innings. It was an intractable environment in the booth.

Garagiola was taking over for a legend in Allen, and while he admitted he was a little nervous before his first season, he brought a catcher's perspective with a constant sprinkling of wit to the broadcast. His approach was fast, breezy, and sometimes irreverent. "That home run traveled through four different time zones, and where it landed is a $4.80 cab ride." Double plays "were always a pitcher's best friend" and a bunt hit "was a line drive in the morning paper." If he suspected a pitcher was throwing a spitter, it was "because the pitch created its own rainbow." And this anecdote about neighbor Yogi: "When we had to wait in line at a popular restaurant, Yogi got a bit impatient and snapped, 'no wonder no one comes here, it's always packed.'"

These were hard times for the Yankees. Their popularity was plummeting and the Stadium was losing its appeal. Garagiola chronicled three terrible years. In 1965, after five straight years in the Series, the team finished under .500 for the first time since 1925. Even an October 1965 visit by Pope Paul to Yankee Stadium didn't help. In 1966 the Yankees needed more than divine intervention, finishing in 10th and last place. By the end of the 1967 season Garagiola left day-to-day baseball to become a full-time co-host on NBC's *Today Show*. In November 1988, after 27 years with the network, many of them spent doing its *Game of the Week* and postseason broadcasts, he resigned. He was making a reported $800,000 a year.

Meanwhile it was becoming apparent that Barber would be the odd man out after the 1966 season when it was rumored that the booth would be pared from four to three. Admitting that he missed the control of the booth that he enjoyed for years in Brooklyn, Barber was becoming increasingly bossy and surly. He resented Rizzuto's casual broadcast preparation ("Phil has never become the professional broadcaster he should be because he won't do the professional preparation.") and Garagiola's intrusion into his innings ("Joe was so self-centered I don't think he ever once paused to consider anybody else."). Red even criticized Coleman in his book, saying that he worked hard "but his voice and temperament didn't blend into the mike."

It didn't help that the Yankees were staggering. The four announcers were getting memos from management to enliven the broadcasts. Topping sent a memo to Smith, "We have the best broadcast crew in baseball; however, of late all four have been horrible . . . and it has gotten so bad that I am tired of answering all the letters of complaint . . . The club is coming out of its slump; tell the other four to get going, too." On one occasion Smith "dressed down" Barber in the press room for talking too much on the telecasts. When Red went to Houk for guidance, support, and perhaps counseling, he got none.

In late September the Yankees, dreadfully detached from any pennant race, played a meaningless game in the rain at the Stadium against the White Sox. Only 413 fans attended. Working the early part of the game on television, Barber asked the director to show all the empty seats in the cavernous park. He felt that the attendance was the story. The director, with Perry Smith at his side, refused.

Shortly afterward, Barber met with Mike Burke, who was put in charge of the Yankees by CBS, the team's new owner. Expecting a contract renewal, he was fired. After 28 years in the Bronx and Brooklyn, Barber's voice was silenced. The Yankees had a weekend series remaining in Washington. They were to be Red's last broadcasts. He never got on the air. All the games there were rained out.

While it's a popular belief that the attendance incident alone led to Red's downfall, there was more to it. Burke claimed that the decision to fire Barber had been made a couple of weeks before he took administrative control. "I fired Barber personally because he was giving us a terrible time in the broadcast booth, squabbling with Rizzuto, going out of his way to embarrass Garagiola on the air and make him look stupid." Burke felt that Barber resented the ex-athletes so much "that he couldn't resist the temptation to make them look bad."

"Red Barber makes such a 'brouhaha' about wanting to get cameras to show the empty seats and all that propaganda that he pulls out. I said (on the air) 'There are more people going to confession at St. Patrick's than there are people at the ballpark.' And that's a pretty good put-down. Mike Burke never said a word," Garagiola said.

Red never got back into daily play-by-play. While he turned down an opportunity to work with Jack Buck in St. Louis after Harry Caray was let go in 1970, Red never fully retired, either, writing, doing radio and television sports reports, and eventually a weekly program with National Public Radio. The Yankees' firing never quite humbled Red. He said his father taught him, "Don't ever let a man make you afraid of your job, make you believe that the job you have is the only job you will ever have." He claimed the firing gave him his life back, that it was a blessing in disguise. The great broadcasters, Scully, Allen, Glickman, and Cosell, are or were all well read and well rounded. Barber had other interests and moved on. He put play-by-play behind him.

Barber was cordial but could be ice cold with visitors. On business in Tallahassee in February 1985, I asked the general manager of a local radio station to arrange for me to spend a half hour with him. I had tons of things to ask. Just as I was warming up, he politely picked himself up off his chair, extended his hand, and thanked me for coming. The 30 minutes were up. The egg timer had run out. That was it.

People who knew him say he was a complicated man. Could be. But then again, so many accomplished and gifted people are. I would like to remember Red as the trailblazing baseball announcer who touched millions in New York when radio was the game.

After the 1966 season the Yankees were abandoned by their flagship station and sister division, WCBS Radio. In 1967 the station launched an all-news format and the games would then be heard on WHN. The Yankees also lost Ballantine Beer, its major sponsor since 1947. The loss of revenue resulted in Barber not being replaced at all. The Yankees were down to three announcers, all ex-major-leaguers, Garagiola, Coleman, and Rizzuto. The only nonathlete involved in the broadcasts was Marv Albert, who handled pre- and postgame shows plus winter hot-stove league shows.

When Garagiola left at the end of the 1967 season, the Yankees were urged by their well-respected public relations director, Bob Fishel, to bring in a professional balls-and-strikes baseball announcer. The club felt that it needed a bona fide play-by-play announcer. His name was Frank Messer and beginning in 1968, for the next 18 years, he would anchor the Yankee Stadium booth and serve the ball club loyally.

A native of Asheville, North Carolina, Messer got the broadcast bug as a youngster. He would spend summers with his mom at his grandparents' home in Buffalo, New York. His mom would later tell him that he would walk around imitating the play-by-play announcer. Messer paid his dues. He worked minor-league games, culminating with triple-A baseball in Richmond, Virginia, for about a decade.

In 1964 he got his call. Frank Cashen, then the general manager of the Orioles, hired him to work in the Baltimore booth with the silky-voiced Chuck Thompson, and, beginning in 1966, with Fordham alum Bill O'Donnell. Messer was solid, no shtick, just baseball. Simple play-by-play, an occasional story, and hawking team wares from tickets to merchandise. Four years with the O's, including their world title team in 1966, was sufficiently convincing. He would do what was asked of him.

Having dealt with announcers who have egos, who pontificate, shirk, or are verbose, voices who are irreverent or are comedians, the Yankees needed purity, piety, clarity, and simplicity. Frank Messer was that man. "Manifest plainness, embrace simplicity, reduce selfishness, have few desires." Messer was another refreshing Southern voice, his accent, though, not as pronounced, following in the footsteps of a Harper, McDonald, Barber, Allen, and Harwell. "Good golly, Miss Molly," was certainly not born in Brooklyn.

The *Times* praised Messer for being "exceptionally alert, his eyes roving the field, looking for scraps of information he can turn to some use." But Messer was always selling, as ordered by his bosses. At a time when football was outdistancing baseball in popularity, Frank pointed to some turnouts in excess of 30,000 and blurted, "So, who said baseball is not our national sport?"

If Rizzuto was taking the game lightly, Messer was taking it seriously. If Rizzuto didn't know the name of the Red Sox pitching coach, Messer knew the name of the equipment manager. If Rizzuto was casual, Messer was meticulous. If Rizzuto was unready, Messer was prepared. If Rizzuto was spontaneous, Messer was conscientious. Rizzuto found statistics boring, Messer kept his own assiduously. As Anthony Lukas wrote in the *New York Times*, "He compensates for his lack of verbal style or dramatic flair with lots of hard work and attention to detail."

For 18 years Messer was the straight man, not particularly assertive, colorful, or one who would emote. He provided the game, did so reliably and accurately. He was like an old comfortable pair of shoes.

And if the Yankees' brass was angry with the announcers, he was always an easy target. After all, they certainly weren't going to mess with Rizzuto. "One day, we had a rain delay and it was John Sterling's job to fill time at the studio. He was our pre- and postgame host but he wasn't there. We tried his beeper but he wasn't wearing it. I ended up having to do it. It was one of those situations where everyone knows the game would be called but league rules dictated that we wait an hour. There was no one around and no one to round anyone up. For one hour, I talked to our batting practice coach, Tony Ferrara. It was hardly a probing interview but he was the only one around. The next day Bob Fishel was upset. 'You should have come to me,' the Yankees vice president said. 'Where were you?' I said. It was about the closest I ever came to a cross word."

After the 1969 season Coleman's picture appeared in the *New York Post*. He was leaving after seven years, heading back west, going to work for Golden West Broadcasting doing a variety of things both in the studio and out. Veteran baseball writer Joe Trimble in the *Daily News* reported that the Yankees front office became "disenchanted" with Coleman and "dropped him." In the fall of 1971 he agreed to employ his voice in San Diego.

So the year after the United States first landed men on the moon, the Yankees wanted a young announcer on his way up. That was fine, but after just one season, 1970, it was apparent that Bob Gamere was no Vin Scully. The word at the time was that Gamere was being paid $15,000 for his services. His skimpy résumé lacked major-league baseball experience.

Gamere had announced in Worcester, Massachusetts, covering Holy Cross football and basketball. He came from obscurity and lacked maturity. Mike Burke, who hired and fired him, later said that Bob "was inexperienced and lacked judgment in dealing with players." Burke wanted his announcers "to aim to transport the television and radio fans into the ballpark." Apparently, Gamere didn't do the job that was expected. He moved up to Boston and did television sports and Harvard football.

Courtesy New York Yankees

The Yankees received more than 200 tapes from applicants interested in replacing Gamere. At the urging of Howard Cosell, the Bronx-based team hired Bill White, who became the first black broadcaster in major-league history. "I had lunch with Mike Burke and told him he

Bill White

should not overlook Bill White," Cosell said at the time. The ex-first baseman had played 14 years (Giants, Cardinals, Phillies) and had one year of non-play-by-play broadcasting experience in Philadelphia. He was born in 1934 and grew up near Cleveland.

Oddly enough, about 10 years later, the irascible Cosell and White wouldn't talk. White told Art Adler, the Yankees' executive producer, "That man is impossible. I know I wouldn't be here if it weren't for his recommendation and guidance. But you won't believe this. He's been cold-shouldering me for a year."

White confronted Cosell. "He claims somebody told him he heard Rizzuto relate a silly story about Howard on the air and that this person heard me giggle in the background. Would you believe it? Cold-shouldering me for a year over thirdhand information." Adler said that the two never regained their friendship.

At the time of White's hiring in 1971 it was said that the Yankees were hoping to expunge their stodgy image and appeal to minorities. White remembered, "I said I didn't really want to be hired because of that (being black). The [Yankees] executive explained that baseball had an obligation to the country, that the Yankees were one of the best-known teams, and in the Bronx, he felt it would be great for young black kids to turn on the TV and see one of their own as the best spokesman."

White became an outstanding announcer. He combined technique, warmth, knowledge, and enthusiasm. He received a warm reception from his fellow booth mates, Rizzuto and Messer, and for the next 16 years the disarming former first baseman lit up the airwaves with yarns, description, humor, candor, and professionalism. As the team headed into the 1971 season, it also had a new radio station, WMCA, and an invigorating new broadcaster, White.

Messer won't forget White's first broadcast. The Yankees were playing the Orioles in an exhibition game in Miami. "Bill had a previous commitment in Philadelphia and arrived in the second inning. Rizzuto was on the air alone and I was watching the game from the other end of the press box. White walks into the booth. He had never done play-by-play, and Rizzuto introduced him and welcomed him to the Yankees family. With the corner of his eye, Phil sees DiMaggio. He jumps out of the booth and leaves White there all alone. The poor guy had just arrived, he must have been real nervous, and there he was trying to do something he's never done without any support." White meshed well, though, with the straight-shooting Messer and made for good banter with the Scooter, who rarely called him Bill. "Hey White!" he would bark.

Almost immediately, White added insight in what the *Times* described as an "easy colloquial style studded with nuggets of pithy description." When Bill Rigney managed the Twins, he was out talking with the umpire. "Rigney used to have lots of trouble with umpires. So now the first thing he does when he gets out there is put his hands in his pockets." After a fine stop by the shortstop, "He sure can pick it." And when Brooks Robinson handled a difficult ground ball, "Brooksie has soft hands." It was White who didn't have soft hands that first year. Reaching for a foul ball heading toward the booth at the old Stadium, he broke his wrist watch.

At spring training White checked out Rizzuto with Elston Howard (the Yankees' first black player). "Everything he said was positive." White leaned on Scooter that first year. "Phil would help me with some of the techniques and timing and differences in the leagues." White attested to the solid relationship between the cohabitants in the Yankees' booth. "A lot of the broadcasters are jealous of each other and don't even speak to each other except when they're in the booth. That never happened in the Yankees booth. There were no egos in the Yankees booth while we were there." One reason could have been diverse interests. Rizzuto liked golf and White liked fishing.

Rizzuto and White had a lot of fun together including the time that Rizzuto went on the air and introduced himself as Phil White. And when one day Rizzuto recited one happy birthday wish after another, Bill said, "Hey, Phil, don't you have a name on there that doesn't end in a vowel?" White was clever. He knew how to play foil to Rizzuto, a darling of Yankees fans. Stan Isaacs of *Newsday* once wrote, "Rizzuto's ebullience and White's sly needling combined for a good team."

White was highly regarded as a broadcaster. He was rarely criticized. Isaacs might occasionally take issue with him for only wanting to talk about what's happening between the lines. The Yankees have been fraught with controversy outside the lines. White, though, distanced himself from it as did his club-paid partners, Rizzuto, Messer, and company.

Rizzuto was so emotional that he couldn't stand watching the Yankees lose. There was a classic game in 1972, the nightcap of a twin bill from Chicago. It wasn't being televised. Not every game was then. The Yankees were ahead by a run in the last of the ninth. The Sox had a runner on base and reliever Sparky Lyle was facing the potential winning run, Dick Allen. "Power against power," the Scooter said bravely. But two words and one sigh later, Rizzuto was just too heartbroken to continue. "The pitch . . . awww." He didn't have to say another word. The crack of the bat, the scoreboard erupting, and the fireworks at Comiskey

Courtesy New York Yankees

Frank Messer, Phil Rizzuto, and Bill White (left to right) broadcast Yankees games together for 15 seasons.

Park said enough. Phil was too painfully dejected to even provide an out-cue to the break. Out of the din came a taped commercial followed by Frank Messer's wrap-up. Rizzuto was in a cab to the airport the moment Allen completed his home-run swing.

For all the ribbing that Rizzuto took for finding excuses to leave early ("I've got the fewest complete games," Rizzuto admits.), Messer says, "If I would have one game, Rizzuto would be the man. He sees everything on the field." And for all his rooting, the Scooter isn't afraid to gently criticize. In the 1970s when third baseman Danny Cater let a perfectly hit double-play ball go through his legs, Scooter said, "A little bit of indecision on Danny's part." And then there was the day that big Frank Howard was wearing a girdle. Scooter, "There's slim, trim Frank Howard. I wonder what kind of diet he's on, Bill?" White said it wasn't a diet. "Oh, you mean he's wearing one of those things."

The Yankees' broadcast package was running into financial problems. In the early 1970s there was one season when WMCA was making more money on its overnight talk show than it did on late-night games from California, and some West Coast games were not carried. In 1975 Manchester Broadcasting acquired the rights and absorbed all financial responsibilities. It added Dom Valentino, a raspy sounding import from Cincinnati. Gabe Paul, the Yankees' general manager, allowed him to do just the middle innings. He was a rapid-fire type trying to adjust to the untimed pace of baseball. At one point Paul suggested that he slow down when delivering the lineups. "Let people digest them, repeat each name twice," Paul said to him. Unfortunately, Valentino suffered a heart attack in midseason when the club was in Minneapolis and never returned to the airwaves.

In 1976 the Yankees were improving and won their first pennant in 12 years. White and Rizzuto were having a blast. Bill had just completed interviewing George Steinbrenner. Now Rizzuto would interview Billy Martin. In the middle of the conversation, Martin pulled out a rubber snake and Phil started backing off, getting all entangled in the wires. It was a wild sight.

It was conventional knowledge that Phil was not enamored with flying and ran at the sight of lightning. But how about this? One night Rizzuto was sitting on the top of the back of the chair, his feet on the seat of the chair and his pant cuffs wrapped tightly around his legs. It turns out that someone told him that there was a squirrel in the booth. Scooter was deathly afraid that the critter would run up his leg. Everyone in the press box was laughing uproariously.

Scooter was broadcasting a game from Seattle and he told his audience that the Yankees were staying in a new hotel, one that had round rooms. "My wife, Cora, isn't with me on this trip. But if she was, there would be no conquering Cora tonight." Yankees management had conniptions.

Rizzuto had emollient powers. His eccentricities and idiosyncrasies reassured all of us that frailties are part of human existence on earth. His stream-of-consciousness delivery was disarming and his unpretentious on-air personality loosened up the sternest of listeners.

Art Adler, who helped revolutionize the business side of radio sports, had taken over the Yankees' broadcasts and turned them into a financial bonanza. He was also the executive producer. The team feuded with WMCA, which had one interest in carrying the games: dollar bills. Its owner, the Strauss family, carried the games as a necessary evil. It would have preferred to run talk shows. With the Yankees now prospering on the field and the radio broadcasts off the field, Adler turned to highly rated WINS, an all-news station. The club bought the time, and for the next three seasons each broadcast was interrupted twice each game for news updates between designated innings. By 1980 though, it was apparent that there was a clash between Yankees baseball and the immediacy of news. During the two weeks of political conventions in 1980, the games moved to WABC, its eventual longtime home.

Reggie Jackson was a pivotal part of the Yankees' championship teams of the 1970s. He was tight with retiring catcher Fran Healy, and in midseason 1978 the slugger helped convince Steinbrenner to put Healy in the booth. Through the 1981 season Healy and Rizzuto would develop an entertaining rapport. Vic Ziegel, the distinguished New York sportswriter writing in *New York Magazine* in 1982, said, "The Rizzuto-Healy exchanges, four years of nonsense with a few pitches thrown in, were kind of a golden age of chatter."

One day the Yanks were playing the White Sox, and the Scooter left the booth and came back a few minutes later. Healy greeted him, "Here's Scooter, back from the men's room." Rizzuto responded, "Healy, you Huckleberry, you're not supposed to tell people that. Tell them that I went to see Bill Veeck [the White Sox president]. Besides, Healy, I've been drinking coffee all day. You

know what happens when you drink
coffee all day." Healy: "What's that?"
Rizzuto: "You go see Bill Veeck."

Adler and Steinbrenner eventually let Healy go, probably because
Fran was in Jackson's camp and
Reggie was battling with the boss.
Ostensibly, Adler said that Healy
didn't improve his play-by-play and
"couldn't evolve a positive relationship
with Messer and White, and that was
six innings of the broadcast." Healy
moved on to Mets broadcasts.

Messer was the straight man, the
pennant waver, the old pro. By November he would be hosting a func-
tion or banquet, spreading the Yankees' goodwill. The other guys were
constantly clowning around, he was
just plodding along. Where did he fit
in? Did the Yankees feel that he fit in?
One off-season he was debating
whether or not to return. It was late at

Courtesy New York Mets

Fran Healy

night and he was on his way back to his New Jersey home from a Yankees
community assignment. A cab pulled up alongside and spotted him. "Hey, Messer,
you're doing a great job." It inspired him to continue, to keep plugging.

In 1982 John Gordon replaced Healy and started the first of four seasons
behind the Yankees' microphones. He came up the ranks, having worked minor-
league games in Columbus and some television in Baltimore. Adler admitted that
Gordon retained "a little of that minor-league promotional voice, the tendency to
try to make a game more interesting than it is. When you're in a booth by
yourself, the silence can be deafening. He had to learn that if he had nothing to
say, it was OK to let six seconds go by."

"I've heard people say I'm not as good as Fran Healy was with Phil. I'm
not, I shouldn't be. That's not my role," the straight-laced announcer said. One
broadcast veteran said, "Gordon always sounds like he's shilling. He seems to
be reaching out to tell you that Thursday night is Cow-Milking Night, a carryover
from his minor-league days." Gordon was eventually demoted to pre- and postgame shows before leaving the organization. He's since had a long and successful stay as Herb Carneal's number two man in the Minnesota Twins' radio booth.

On July 4, 1983, Yankees pitcher Dave Righetti threw a no-hitter against
the Boston Red Sox and Messer called it dramatically. "It was Fan Appreciation
Day and Phil and I were on the field most of the day for giveaways between
innings. White did the whole game. I came back upstairs in the ninth inning and
he said to me, 'you're the senior guy, you call the ninth inning.' He insisted. It
was a class act."

By 1985 Messer was taken off the television side and, like his counterpart
Bob Murphy at Shea Stadium, was doing radio exclusively. The games were on
WABC and there were those who felt his home-run call was a reach, "A. B. C.

you later!" The television booth, though, was getting crowded. There was a cable crew and an over-the-air crew. Once, it was just three men covering both radio and television. By 1990 the Bombers had as many as 10 different announcers. "One day I walk into the press room during the game, I see Phil watching the game on television. 'Why aren't you in the booth?' I asked. 'I tried, I got spiked.' The booths were just overrun with announcers." It was the beginning of the end for Messer who was dismissed at the end of the year after a good 18-year run.

He moved to the White Sox, where he had a short stay before retiring to his Florida home. He still emcees Old Timer's Day and in the early '90s he introduced old partner Phil Rizzuto. The beloved Scooter addressed the Yankee Stadium throng and took the opportunity to blare an impromptu endorsement on Frank's behalf. "You huckleberries should hire Messer, he's great." Rizzuto had his day on August 4, 1985. In front of a crowd of 54,032, a cow kicked him during the ceremony and Tom Seaver, pitching for the Chicago White Sox, recorded his 300th win.

Reflecting in 1997, Messer said, "One of the greatest compliments I ever had was recently when the *New York Times* wondered about the crowded Yankees TV booth dominated by ex-players. 'What happened to the days of play-by-play guys like Mel Allen and Frank Messer?' it wrote."

In 1987 White and Rizzuto moved over to television exclusively, and in 1989 White left the booth completely to become president of the National League. In his role as an administrator that first spring, he attended an exhibition game between the Mets and the Yankees and was asked if he missed the booth. "I looked up at the booth and thought I can be up there right now *B-S*-ing." A private man, he shunned the public spotlight of his new position. A principled man, he battled with the head of the umpires and dared the owners and commissioner to back him. He eventually didn't seek a renewal of his contract. The disciple of Henry David Thoreau is now retired and does what he loves most, fishing and spending quiet time in New Zealand and Australia.

When it was all said and done, Phil Rizzuto spent 30 colorful and unforgettable years in the radio booth. He would continue doing some television after his radio days were over at the end of the 1986 season. Only Bob Murphy has had a longer radio baseball life in New York than Phil Rizzuto.

In 1987 Bobby Murcer and Spencer Ross were brought in. Each did just one season of radio. Murcer learned quickly what pressure was like. He came up with the Yankees in 1965 at the age of 19 but never lived up to lofty expectations. He enjoyed a good playing career but not a great one. A center fielder, he followed legends Joe DiMaggio and Mickey Mantle. Like Mickey, Murcer was from Oklahoma. Unlike Mickey, Bobby didn't hit 536 home runs, but did hit 252.

In the booth, he had a laid-back style. He enjoyed Rizzuto. "Working with Phil is a hoot, you never know what will happen," he said. Bobby was generally understated and had a dry wit. Although he worked for the Yankees, he was angered when WABC General Manager Jim Haviland compensated him for handling an assignment by giving him a cruise for two that expired by the time the season ended. Murcer was furious. By the time that August and September rolled around, Murcer kept telling his audience that he planned to enjoy a cruise in the fall, courtesy of Jim Hanlon. The next day, it was courtesy of Jim Harlin, the day after it was courtesy of Jim Howell, and so on.

Spencer Ross, left, spent one season in the Yankees' radio booth. In 1991 at a reunion of the 1961 Yankees, Ross was invited to join the team picture. Next to Ross are Ralph Houk, Mickey Mantle, Yogi Berra, and Whitey Ford.

Ross is a solid broadcaster who can do virtually any sport and do it well. He's smart, a quick learner, and genuinely curious. Either full time or in a substitute's role, Ross has done radio play-by-play for the Yankees, Jets, Knicks, Nets, Rangers, and Devils. He's comfortable at any game. Invent a sport that's never been done on radio and Ross will find a way to describe it. Spencer was never given a chance to grow in the Yankees' booth. In all, he was a Yankees announcer for three years, one season on radio, one season on cable, and one season on WPIX Television.

By 1987 the Yankees sold their radio broadcasts to WABC outright. Rizzuto and White would remain exclusively on television. For the next 10 years the station would hire the talent and sell the advertising. Program manager Mark Mason signed Hank Greenwald, imported from San Francisco, where he had done the Giants since 1979, and Tommy Hutton, an ex-major-leaguer who had done Blue Jays broadcasts. Hank was understated and Hutton was solid and had little shtick. Neither was overbearing and the two developed a nice rapport. Mason was pleased with his selections, "They're acquired taste."

Greenwald liked to play the crowd. Coming back from a commercial break, Hank would wait a second or two before speaking again. He feels that even this small fraction of time creates a relaxing, unpressured backdrop for the listener. After just a couple of seasons at Yankee Stadium he left. The upstate native and Syracuse University alum returned to San Francisco where he was revered.

In 1996, at the age of 61, and tired of the enervating travel, he retired. As far as his two seasons in New York, he told a San Francisco magazine, "[George] Steinbrenner is everything you've heard, maybe worse. Sometimes the team bus was late because Steinbrenner was reaming out the manager. The man yells at the little people, which may be his worst trait. I would walk through the Yankees offices and I could tell if he was in town or not from the fear level of the office workers."

WABC was losing a ton of money on its Yankees package and in 1989 relieved both high earners Greenwald and Hutton. It was the beginning of the John Sterling era. His partner for the first couple of years would be Jay Johnstone, the "Moon Man," who played for a handful of big-league teams in an undistinguished career. He had gained a reputation as a prankster but seemed to have problems conveying the humor and expressing his thoughts in the Yankee Stadium booth. As a member of Tommy Lasorda's Dodgers, Johnstone had an elfish charm. He was a clown of sorts. National television would show him in the Los Angeles dugout with grossly oversized sunglasses, getting a chuckle from those around him.

The Yankees' undertaking was bleeding red. To stabilize rights fees, procure Yankees programming long term, and create the mechanism for potential profitability, WABC extended its rights deal. Negotiating financial incentives, General Manager Fred Weinhaus stretched the station's rights with the Yankees through 1996 in the hope that the station would eventually end its financial bath.

In the interim, WABC would run any commercial contest that produced revenue. WFAN's Mets broadcasts were providing stiff competition. Commercial sponsorship packages on the Yankees' broadcasts were made available at deeply discounted prices. One particular Yankees advertiser sponsored a contest every game when Johnstone would read a new contestant's name and his or her hometown.

One day Johnstone was handed a sheet with the contestant's name: Barry Smith-Wilton Conn. Jay had no idea. In an uncertain tone, Johnstone says, "Today we have two contestants but we haven't been given their hometowns. They are Barry Smith and Wilton Conn. A moment later, the station calls the booth in a panic. "Hey Johnstone, there's only one contestant. It's Barry Smith of Wilton, Connecticut." The funny sequel to this story is that Johnstone was born in Manchester, Connecticut. Johnstone wasn't rehired at the end of the 1990 season.

John Sterling came to New York in 1971 to do a sports talk show on WMCA Radio. He listened carefully to Bob Grant, then a star on the station. The opinionated Grant was generally controversial and argumentative, harsh and strident, and would spend hours lambasting callers. Sterling adopted Grant's no-nonsense approach, hosting his program in a bold, rude, and brash manner. "Give it a rest," Sterling would denigrate in no uncertain terms. He had a following. In the early 1970s Sterling's show was quite popular. Times were different. It was before cable made significant inroads and before the birth of all-sports radio.

After he left New York in the late 1970s, Sterling drifted to Atlanta where he did a talk show, started broadcasting Hawks basketball games, and later hooked up with the Superstation WTBS on Braves telecasts. The radio broadcasts in Atlanta were unique. They were replete with opinions and stories which came at the expense of fluid play-by-play and description.

Historically, when popular announcers are fired, there's often a flood of protest. Way back in the 1930s when Fred Hoey was fired in Boston, the public protest was sufficient enough to restore his job. When the legendary Bob Prince was canned in Pittsburgh, fans marched on the Westinghouse Building downtown.

John Sterling, left, entered the Yankees' booth in 1989. He was joined by Michael Kay, right, in 1992.

In Atlanta the twist was the opposite. There were fans who clamored for Sterling's firing. In July 1985 Joanne Todd, in conjunction with the Atlanta chapter of the American Cancer Society, organized a poll of sorts, suggesting that fans seeking his banishment from the Braves' booth send a $1 contribution to the charity. Mrs. Todd added, "John is just too wordy. Some people say he's gotten better, but I just don't know. He won't let you savor the moment. He has to jump in there every play and overanalyze."

Fans were irked by Sterling's condescension and haughtiness. He was eventually fired from the Braves' booth in 1987, but continued to broadcast basketball. One of his partners in Atlanta was Walt Frazier, who wasn't given his due airtime by Sterling. The *Atlanta Constitution* reported that when Sterling accepted the Yankees' job in 1989, he didn't notify then TBS chief of sports Bob Wussler, and as such lost his Hawks job, too, for the 1989–90 season. It was a rough year for Sterling, then 51, having just lost his sister to cancer.

After a couple of seasons in the Bronx with Jay Johnstone, there was talk that Ernie Harwell, then 73 and recently deposed in Detroit, would join Sterling in the Bronx. It didn't eventuate. WABC brought in Joe Angel, a solid and traditional play-by-play broadcaster whose style clashed terribly with Sterling's. The two hardly spoke and when Angel left New York, he would mimic Sterling unflatteringly. Angel was a longtime number two broadcaster, perfectly quali-fied to be a number one. He had bounced around before joining Sterling, work-ing in San Francisco, Minnesota, and Baltimore. In 1992, after just one year in New York, he returned to Baltimore before he was hired to be the number one voice of the expansion Florida Marlins in 1993.

A baseball play-by-play job is hardly secure. So between gigs, Angel got his real-estate license in Northern California just in case. Jerry Doggett, the longtime Dodgers announcer, had retired while Angel was out of baseball work. When he was looking for a home in Northern California, Angel was his agent. It was Angel's only sale.

Angel's quick wit, storytelling, and understated play-by-play has earned him the adoration of Marlins fans. His signature call after Florida victories, "It's in the win column!," has become part of the verbal tapestry of the Miami sports community.

A talk-show host, inexperienced in play-by-play, Sterling never had the opportunity to learn the fundamentals of picture painting. He sat near Jim Karvellas doing basketball and later near Skip Caray doing baseball. His on-air play-by-play cadence was a mixture of the two, but lacked the tempo that's the beauty of baseball on radio or the rhythm that's synonymous with a lazy baseball summer afternoon. Many feel that his husky voice is best suited for a studio where he can opine, debate, and slam receivers on listeners.

Never has there been a play-by-play broadcaster in New York more criticized than John Sterling. Yet, after 10 years, Sterling is living proof that only one person needs to like a broadcaster's work—the one who signs his checks. In the case of John Sterling, it's Yankees boss George Steinbrenner who has endorsed Sterling all these years. As far as Sterling is concerned it's all that counts. Interestingly, Stan Kasten, president of both the Braves and Hawks, always liked Sterling's enthusiastic approach but apparently such wasn't the popular opinion in Atlanta.

Big John would be criticized for anything from digressing on baseball broadcasts by talking for innings at a time about other sports to putting himself ahead of the game to chasing other broadcaster's jobs. Sterling seems to have hit a trifecta, being unpopular among his peers, being constantly decried by media critics, and being seemingly unpopular among fans.

Sterling had his eyes on a combined Braves-Hawks radio job when there was a rights change in the mid-1990s. He considered the announcers he wanted to have removed, good friends. But he called regularly, assuring the club and the station that he would help sell seats and increase ratings.

In 1997 Phil Mushnick wrote in the *New York Post* that Sterling places "self-promotion over accuracy" and Bob Raissman in the *Daily News* wrote, "We've come to learn—but will never accept the fact—that Sterling puts himself ahead of the game." Richard Sandomir writing in the *New York Times* called Sterling "so unlistenable."

Mushnick made reference to a patent that Sterling had filed for his home-run call, "It is high, it is far, it is gone." The patent was filed with the intent of selling T-shirts and sweatshirts. The call, which many consider affected, "begins," according to Phil, on all sorts of occasions, "doubles off the wall, fly-ball outs, line drives that barely clear the wall, and the occasional home run that actually meets Sterling's description."

Occasionally, he will even croon on the air. One letter to the editor in the *New York Post* read, "Lately, he (Sterling) has gotten into the habit of singing lines from songs, usually off key. I consider his loquacity and off-key singing noise pollution. Why do we fans have to hear this?"

When the Yankees went into the Skydome in Toronto for the first time, Sterling attempted to describe the state-of-the-art facility and the hotel that overlooks the outfield. But he gave up in the middle by telling his listeners, "You'll get a chance to see it." It was hardly in the "word-picture" spirit of Barber, Scully, or Glickman.

For all the criticism, John's unique approach can be quite entertaining and has drawn the praise of WFAN sports-talk hosts Mike and the Mad Dog. He can tell funny stories and provide interesting insight. He works at his task. Interviewed on WQEW in the summer of 1997, Sterling was asked, "Do you see and tell when you're on the road?" His answer, "Did Mel Allen tell on Mickey Mantle? No. But neither did Mantle tell on Mel Allen." During the same interview, he advocated a new West Side Stadium for the Yankees, suggesting it be called "Yankee Stadium–Empire Center" which would attract Super Bowls and Final Fours.

In 1992 Sterling had a new partner, Michael Kay. A newspaper man with the instincts of a good reporter, Kay learned the ropes and has not been afraid to ask tough questions. He worked at WFUV, the Fordham student station, and later became a reporter for the *Daily News*. He has a good nose for the story line and has grown as a play-by-play man. His development has been lauded by Mike Lupica, the *Daily News* columnist, who suggests that Kay be given more than a meager two innings. But that seems unlikely until George Steinbrenner blows the whistle on Sterling. Kay always remembers what the late Mel Allen told him: "When you're on the air, make believe that you're talking to just one person."

Kay gives opinions and is quite descriptive, while at the same time conversing with his partner Sterling. To many, he's made John more tolerable. In his Christmas Gab Bag column, Raissman suggested that Kay get "a sharp object to puncture Sterling when he puffs up with condescension."

In 1998 Sterling was lauded by Lupica and others for suppressing any personal agenda and describing pitcher David Wells' perfect game with breathtaking and memorable drama.

Through it all, there's redemption. It's the stately sound of Yankee Stadium public address announcer Bob Sheppard, dignified and restrained and whose syllables are perfectly enunciated. The echo of the octogenarian's voice is part of the Stadium's lore and has been the backdrop of Yankee broadcasts for five decades.

9

THE NEW YORK
BASEBALL GIANTS

THE PLANK
AT THE POLO GROUNDS

As has been discussed in the two previous chapters, when Larry MacPhail took administrative charge of the Yankees in 1945, he informed Giants owner Horace Stoneham that in the best interest of both ball clubs, the Yankees and Giants should split their joint broadcasts beginning in 1946. The two were already locked into a joint package for 1945. The Dodger broadcasts were more popular. Every Brooklyn game was on radio. Basically, only the Yankees' and Giants' home games were on radio; MacPhail's Yankees and the Giants had ground to make up. They agreed to split.

When Mel Allen returned from military service, Stoneham offered Mel the Giants job. Allen had, of course, done the joint Giants-Yankees package before leaving for wartime duty. At the same time, MacPhail attempted to lure Barber from Brooklyn to the Bronx. But when he couldn't, he offered Allen the Yankees. Meanwhile, the Giants' immediate broadcast future was uncertain. While the Yankees were all set with sponsors and WINS, the Giants were having trouble nailing down station commitments. Unsure whether he would be able to deliver a job to Allen, Stoneham encouraged Mel to accept the Yankees' offer, extricating him from the commitment to the Giants.

So while the Dodgers' and Yankees' plans were all detailed early, the Giants were scrambling around as the 1946 season approached. At the 11th hour they made a deal with Pabst and WMCA. The station agreed to carry home games live and the road games via the ticker. As would be the case with WMCA in all its years owned by the Strauss family (it became a Christian station in 1989), sports were a necessary evil, a revenue stream. Ownership's programming heart was elsewhere.

Jack Brickhouse had first applied for the number two job in the Bronx with Mel in 1946 but didn't get it. Through Pabst and its Milwaukee-stationed advertising manager, Nate Perlstein, the Chicago-based Brickhouse was hired by the Giants. He had started his broadcast career in Peoria and graduated to Chicago where he covered the Cubs and White Sox on WGN Radio from 1940–43 and the Sox again on WJJD radio in 1945. When his mentor, Bob Elson, returned from the Navy after the 1945 season and got his Sox job back, Brickhouse was out of work. Although his roots were entirely Midwest, he ventured east to the Polo Grounds to get work.

Brickhouse, who would later become a Chicago institution, was teamed with Steve Ellis, whom he detested. To clear time on WMCA, the Giants had to acquiesce to having Ellis, the station's sports director, share the play-by-play. Ellis was his stage name. He was born Armand Yussem and, according to Don Dunphy, it was through "connections" that Ellis landed in the Polo Grounds booth. Not only was he endorsed by WMCA but Steve had latched on to Art Flynn, an advertising man who was well-known in the business. Flynn and Horace Stoneham were very close and he urged the Giants' owner to hire Ellis. The announcer had a fine voice and an excellent delivery but his best work, according to most, was in the studio. He later did disc-jockey work, televised boxing, and closed-circuit fights, including Ali-Liston in 1964.

"The only unpleasant experience I ever had was with my partner that year, Steve Ellis," Brickhouse once wrote. "Ellis hadn't done as much as one inning his entire life, not even Little League." Jack told Ellis immediately that he didn't endorse him getting the job because of his glaring lack of baseball experience. "He used so many clichés and slang expressions that tears came to my eyes," the broadcast Hall of Famer added. Brickhouse told Ellis, "I will teach you." But Ellis apparently resented the approach.

The adversaries cohabitated the Polo Grounds booth for home games and the WMCA studios for road games, covering a bad baseball team that finished 61–83 in eighth and last place in the National League. Brickhouse must have winced one day when he read Walter Winchell's column: "Steve Ellis hits a home run as the Giants' broadcaster."

Yet even back then, Brickhouse, who was known for his years of exclaiming "hey-hey" when the Cubs would do anything positive, rooted openly on the New York airwaves. When Mel Ott's team did beat the Dodgers one day, he emoted, "Oh, we beat those Bums!" Through the years, New York has generally been devoid of announcers who root openly or refer to the team they're covering as "we."

At the end of the season Brickhouse thought he ridded himself of Ellis. He hoped that he would be teamed on the 1947 broadcasts with the "Fordham Flash," Frankie Frisch. When he went in for contract renegotiations, he was told that it took a large financial commitment to get Frisch. Brickhouse couldn't come to terms with the club and sponsor, so he packed his microphone and headed back to Chicago. "I enjoyed the New York experience but this wasn't one of the

Frankie Frisch

things that I cherished." He immediately began a 35-year run broadcasting Cubs and White Sox baseball on Chicago television.

On January 30, 1947, at the Waldorf Astoria Hotel, the Giants announced that Frisch would broadcast their games on WMCA Radio. Walter Johnson, Jack Graney, Waite Hoyt, and Gabby Street had gone from the field to the broadcast booth. Now the former member of the Gas House Gang would become the first ex-player in a New York booth at a salary of $20,000. In 1939 Frisch had done Red Sox games, taking over for the indomitable Fred Hoey, who was worshipped by fans all over New England. The Flash was on the job there for just one season. Taking over for a legend was apparently a bit much to ask from a broadcast rookie. He had done other shows since, including programs with the ex-pitcher Johnson. Now, according to owner Stoneham, Frankie Frisch "is a man in the Giant tradition and one who will help us to carry it forward." An ex-Giant and former Cardinals captain, the colorful Frisch was a writer's favorite when he was a player.

When Brickhouse moved on, Ellis, who was to be demoted to doing only a pregame show, shared game announcing responsibilities with Frisch, who would constantly refer to him as "partner." At the beginning of his tenure, Frisch labored with road games off the ticker. "It's when I'm doing the out-of-town games at the studio that I still feel a little tense," he admitted. Critics felt that Frisch could sometimes get lost "in a flurry of excitement." The husky, silver-haired ex-skipper was compared by the *Times* to the gravelly voiced Clem McCarthy who had "exciting undertones." His famous and reverberated cry was, "Oh those bases on balls!"

In 1948 Ellis was replaced by Maury Farrell and for the first time, the Giants joined the Yankees and started doing away games live. No longer did Frisch have to extemporize off the ticker. But Farrell, a disc jockey from Birmingham, didn't even finish the year. By September he was gone and a number of substitutes completed the season. Martin Block, a New York radio legend who started in the 1930s and created the *Make Believe Ballroom* on WNEW, was one of those to fill in.

It was apparent that the Bronx-born Frisch missed the field. He moved around restlessly in the broadcast booth and was heard to say, "There's nothing like being down there on the field." With the Giants now under the helmsmanship of Leo Durocher, Frisch was invited to join the Lip's coaching staff.

As the 1949 season approached, the Giants and their sponsor had two openings in the booth. The sponsor was Liggett & Myers, makers of Chesterfield cigarettes. Russ Hodges had built a nice name for himself. The Dayton, Tennessee, native was personable, well-liked, and exuded warmth on the air. Hodges had just completed his third year with Mel Allen at Yankee Stadium but had been a Giants fan since he was a kid. When the tobacco company approached Russ and offered him the job, it was a dream come true. Horace Stoneham, though, had to approve it, and it would take a bit of time until the deal was done.

In the intervening time, word leaked that the Yankees' announcer, Hodges, was going to the Polo Grounds. When asked by the press, Stoneham denied it, saying he knew nothing about it. When this made the papers, it jeopardized Hodges' Yankees job and he still didn't have the Giants' assignment. It got tense and he almost wound up unemployed completely. Finally, all the pieces were put together and Hodges was bound for the Giants.

Marty Glickman was developing a reputation for himself on basketball, football, and pre- and postbaseball programming. Marty was a young announcer on the way up, and Chesterfield was interested in hiring him to be Hodges' partner. But Marty had a young family and had just purchased a home. The dollars Chesterfield was offering weren't good enough, and he had to turn it down. One other who was also considered for the Giants' job in 1949 was Curt Gowdy, but he ended up replacing Hodges at Yankee Stadium.

Al Helfer got the job as Russ's partner. Brother Al had left the on-air side some three years earlier to go into the advertising agency business but now had the itch to get back behind the microphone. He ended up being only one of two announcers to call all three New York baseball teams at one time or another. Helfer had earlier had a stint with Red Barber and the Dodgers, and in 1945 the Giants-Yankees package with Bill Slater. Connie Desmond was the only other to do all three. His one year with Mel Allen on the Giants-Yankees package in 1942 was followed by 14 with the Dodgers.

When the seasons started, Helfer did three innings on radio-only games (all home games were televised), but was cut to two in the middle of the season. After a year at the Polo Grounds, Helfer found an opportunity with Mutual, which in 1950 started a game-of-the-day series. It commissioned him to travel from one city to the next, five to seven days a week during the baseball season. He would head back to his Westchester County home, throw his laundry into the washer, and go back out on the road. Mutual's live broadcasts were carried only in non-major-league cities. But in 1950 it meant that games were broadcast in all but 10 American cities. Every day another ball game from another venue. The travel eventually got to the big-framed man. In 1955 he joined the Dodgers for their final three years in Brooklyn. In 1962 he worked with Gene Elston on the Houston Colt .45s' broadcasts, and the A's first two seasons in Oakland in 1968 and 1969, teaming with Monte Moore.

"We found him doing news in Denver. He had a wonderful voice and he was the first guy I had ever heard do a big-league game when I grew up in Oklahoma," Moore said. He was a big guy and he would lumber from one city to the next. "We would go out on the road and into fine restaurants, and this big fellow would tell the waitress to just give him raw meat, 'warm it up a little, but not too much.'"

Helfer was getting older then and had apparently started having problems seeing. "We had this system that if a deep fly was caught, I would touch him on

Courtesy Pat Hodges

When Russ Hodges was offered the job of broadcasting Giants games, it was a dream come true.

the arm," Moore said. What kind of broadcaster was Helfer? "Al was very generic, accurate but not very colorful." Did he ever talk about his days back East? "I don't know why, but he had some bad memories of those days. Maybe he didn't feel he was given his fair share," said Moore, who later successfully built a stable of small-market radio stations. Helfer was the longtime master of ceremonies of the Heisman Trophy dinner and one of the few persons ever to receive an honorary Heisman trophy. After leaving the A's, he joined radio station KRAK in Sacramento as head of the news department.

With the Yankees Hodges deferred to Allen. When he assumed the number one post across the Harlem River, Hodges became more emotional. "I sure as hell am a fan," Russ said about the Giants. "I bleed inwardly for them," he explained. "When you travel with a club, you know the personal lives of the players, you know their families. You want to see them do well."

After Hodges' first season in 1949, he was doing Columbia University football games. Through exposure to the cold, he was struck with a disease called Bell's palsy. It threatened his career, and there were rumors in the winter of 1950 that he wouldn't return to the Giants. Bell's palsy affects the nerves of the face and alters speech ability. Yet, after rest and rehabilitation in Florida, he was ready to open spring training with the Giants in Phoenix.

Hodges had another physical scare one night. In 1953 he called the Jake LaMotta–Danny Nardico fight on television. After LaMotta got knocked down for the first time in his career, Hodges wanted to go into the ring. "With the microphone in my left hand, I grabbed the metal ring post with my right hand. Well, it seems the power for the ring lights went through the pole and it hadn't been properly grounded. I was the perfect ground—5,000 volts. I got knocked galley west—and on television!"

Hodges got a new partner in 1950 when the venerable Ernie Harwell took Helfer's place.

"I took the job because the dollars were better and it would be two instead of three," said Harwell, explaining his move from Brooklyn to the Giants. "There were three of us in Ebbets Field. At the Polo Grounds, it was just Russ and me. I had an opportunity to do more innings. Russ was more relaxed, easygoing, and less of a perfectionist than Red. 'I want you to have fun over here,' was his first greeting to me." Hodges knew how stern Barber was about rules in the booth.

The mild and modest Harwell tells the story of the cramped Polo Grounds booth that had no toilet. "To alleviate our relief problems, we would urinate into paper cups and then put the cups on the floor of the booth. One day a visitor to the booth kicked over one of the cups. The amber fluid leaked through the boards onto the box seat patrons down below.

"The head usher appeared in our booth. He said, 'We're getting complaints from those people in the box seats. They said for you to quit spilling beer on 'em.' I told him, 'if it's beer, it's used beer.'"

The mellow Georgian who presents the game simply and rhythmically has turned into an institution in Detroit, where he's covered the Tigers since 1960. A gas station owner in a small Michigan town says that he works "from 7:30 in the morning till five minutes to Ernie." And it's Ernie who has a love affair with radio. "Radio is to TV as a book is to a movie. With the radio and the book the listener and reader uses his imagination."

Russ Hodges, of course, is a name that will always remind baseball fans of the "shot heard 'round the world," Bobby Thomson's home run in the 1951 playoffs that enabled the Giants to beat the Dodgers and win the National League pennant. The WMCA call was classic and it has been replayed thousands of times.

The Giants trailed the Dodgers by 13½ games on August 12, but battled back to tie Brooklyn at the end of the regular season. The neighborhood rivals met in a three-game playoff. The teams split the first two contests. The third and decisive game was played at the Polo Grounds on October 3. Before 34,320, Brooklyn was up 4–1 going into the bottom of the ninth. Leo Durocher's Giants rallied. Whitey Lockman knocked in a run to cut the lead to 4–2. With runners

Courtesy Ernie Harwell

Ernie Harwell, left, became Russ Hodges's partner on Giants broadcasts in 1950. Here he is interviewing Ted Williams in Atlanta in 1942.

on second and third and one out, Dodgers manager Chuck Dressen took out Don Newcombe and brought in Ralph Branca. Thomson was due up. In the booth Hodges was about to make an indelible call:

> *So don't go away. Light up that Chesterfield. Stay with us and we'll see how Ralph Branca will fare against Bobby Thomson . . . Thomson against the Brooklyn club has a lot of long ones this year. He has seven home runs.*
>
> *Branca pitches and Bobby takes a strike called, on the inside corner . . . Branca throws, there's a long fly . . . it's gonna be . . . I believe . . . the Giants win the pennant . . . the Giants win the pennant . . . the Giants win the pennant . . . the Giants win the pennant . . . the Giants win the pennant. Bobby Thomson hits it into the lower deck of the left-field stands . . . The Giants win the pennant and they're going crazy!*

The printed word doesn't do the emotional call justice. Hodges went berserk and Red Barber would later say, it was an "unprofessional call." Now it's common for announcers to rant and scream. Back then announcers may have been less critical but would have never erupted the way Hodges did then.

Pat Hodges, Russ's son, remembers the emotional grinder his dad went through the summer of 1951. "As the Giants were making their fantastic comeback, my dad would wear the same shirt every day. He had this yellow shirt and it had to be washed every day."

Russ wasn't the only one who made the call. His partner, Harwell, called it on the Giants' telecast which was picked up nationally. Red Barber did it for

Brooklyn on WMGM with ostensible indifference. When Branca was warming up, Connie Desmond gave listeners a rundown on the pitcher's background. Gordon McLendon, the "Old Scotchman," was on the Liberty Network and Harry Caray was sent by KMOX in St. Louis to cover the playoff.

"They wanted to carry the game and asked if we could set Harry Caray up in the booth," Hodges remembered. There was so little room that "we ended up putting Caray in the same booth with us, and putting a blanket between his microphone and ours." In addition, Bob Prince, the Pirates' announcer was in town and the guest of Hodges in the booth.

After Thomson's home run, Hodges had to run to the locker room, which was in center field at the Polo Grounds. Harwell was on television, so Russ needed someone to fill until he made the wild dash across the field. He just threw the microphone to Prince and asked him to take over.

Curt Gowdy listened to Thomson's home run. "I was driving on a highway in Massachusetts and I drove off the road! Russ captured the emotion. It was one of the glorious moments in baseball history," the Hall of Fame broadcaster said.

Unlike today, broadcasts weren't routinely taped. WMCA didn't record the game. "There's a fellow in Brooklyn named Lawrence Goldberg to whom I am forever indebted," Hodges said. "The next day he called me and offered it to me. It was the only one in existence. It's been copied a thousand times since." People have said that Goldberg was a Dodgers fan hoping to send Russ a tape of the broadcast where he cries in his soup, so to speak. "Whenever I feel down or blue, I turn it on. It perks me right up. It brings back the greatest thrill of my broadcasting career," Russ said.

Larry King, once the king of nighttime radio and now a prominent television interviewer, grew up in Brooklyn when baseball dominated. "The Yankees were Mel Allen, whom we hated. We argued who was best. Russ Hodges versus Mel Allen versus Red Barber. Barber was to us a class act. He never rooted for the Dodgers. And he taught us a lot more about baseball than Mel ever taught anyone. Red was the best, because you learned the game from Red."

When Harwell's contract was not renewed at the end of the 1953 season, he became the first "voice of the Baltimore Orioles" and was replaced at the Polo Grounds by Bob DeLaney. "All the Elmira DeLaneys just thought it would be nice to have a different spelling," said the man who would later do some work for WPIX Television in the 1960s. He had been working in Boston with Curt Gowdy doing the Red Sox games for Chesterfield and was transferred to New York when Hodges needed a new partner in 1954. When he joined Gowdy in 1951, he had little play-by-play experience but sponsors seemed to appreciate his ability to cogently sell their products. DeLaney wasn't picked up for his baseball knowledge or passion for the game, rather for his reputation as a strong commercial announcer. The Elmira, New York, native was one of the early sports announcers who attended Syracuse University's School of Speech and Dramatic Arts.

"Baseball broadcasting is the first thing I've come up against that I couldn't do well. I dislike being mediocre. I thing I'm capable of doing better, and that's what I'm trying to do all the time," DeLaney said. But he didn't seem to have his heart in it. It was the commercial aspects of broadcasting where he excelled. "That's what I do well." When the Giants moved to California, his work was restricted to the studio or commercial announcements. Bob DeLaney never returned to baseball play-by-play.

The 1954 Giants won it all, sweeping the heavily favored Cleveland Indians in the World Series. It was the last glorious achievement for the franchise that would head to San Francisco at the end of the 1957 season. It was the year that Hodges authored his home-run call, "bye-bye baby." The signature call later became quite popular in San Francisco. "It's a battle cry which any western follower of the Giants instantly recognizes and now we even have a song based on it," Hodges said in his 1963 book, *My Giants*. "But New Yorkers never adopted it. To them, it was just another pet expression by a sports announcer."

It was during that 1954 season that the personable Hodges held a midseason party at his home and one of the attendees was Giants owner Horace Stoneham. Known to enjoy a drink every now and then, Stoneham announced to those assembled that he planned to fire Leo Durocher. Hodges interceded on Leo's behalf which prompted the team boss to tell Hodges to stay out of it or be fired, too. The Lip ended up winning the Series that year.

Meanwhile, the Giants were suffering at the gate. There was talk that the Dodgers were heading for Los Angeles. "All the gossip was about the Dodgers. Nobody mentioned the Giants," Hodges said. "Sometimes all we heard was the sound of our voices. There were times when the place was so quiet, we had to speak softly to keep from interfering with each other, because the television and radio booths were side by side." Attendance dropped to less than 600,000, the lowest in the National League.

The Giants were on WMCA through all their years in New York, and in 1954 and 1955 their pre- and postgame shows were aptly named *Johnny on the Spot*. The hosts were ex-Giant and Yankee Johnny Mize and the raspy-voiced Johnny Most.

In 1957, the Giants' last year in New York, the club added a third announcer, Jim Woods, who had just been let go by the Yankees. A career number two man in the baseball booth, Woods enjoyed the praise of all those with whom he worked. "Before we hired him in Oakland, I called Jack Buck who, like everybody else, kept saying how loyal a man he is. He just liked getting on those planes, going from one stadium to the next and being a part of it. He was a real solid guy," said Monte Moore, the longtime A's broadcaster. "I thought he should be able to broadcast at least one game of the World Series when we made it in the 1970s. He deserved it. I was willing to give up a game. Charles Finley said OK but NBC turned it down."

The next-to-last game at the Polo Grounds drew only 2,768 people. The final game on September 29, 1957, drew 11,606. Woods closed the radio broadcast. His last words were, "God bless you." The Giants were headed to San Francisco.

Hodges' memories were of Eddie Brannick, the team secretary who had been with the club for 52 years. He was 65 years old and brought up in Hell's Kitchen on Manhattan's west side. He, too, was going to San Francisco.

Russ went to San Francisco but KSFO there wanted his partner to have local roots. As such, Lon Simmons was hired. Woods was in the hunt again. He landed with the Pirates where he had a long stay teaming with Bob Prince.

For Hodges, the next-door kind of guy, the thrills of following Willie Mays continued. "For thrills, there can never be anything to match Bobby

Thomson's pennant-winning home run in one game, but for excitement for some twenty years now, there can be no one to match Willie Mays," Russ said in 1971 shortly before his death. He had broadcast Giants games from 1949 through 1970. There was a forced retirement, prompted to a degree by one of the major sponsors. He died in April 1971 of a broken heart.

But in 1958 the Giants still had a following in New York, and fueling the fire was Les Keiter. His station, WINS, had the Yankees through 1957 but lost the games to WMGM in 1958. Keiter, who had done pre- and postgame shows around the Yankees, discussed the baseball void with general manager J. Elroy McCaw. It was decided that the station would re-create games from the West Coast. Keiter, the station's sports director, was asked which of the two departed teams the station should cover. He told McCaw that the Dodgers were getting older and that the Giants had a promising future. McCaw set up a three-year deal with the Giants, and from 1958 through 1960 Keiter and WINS were New York's link to National League baseball.

Rick Sklar remembers the re-creations. "Les Keiter wore Bermuda shorts under a Hawaiian print, open sports shirt and had a baseball cap pulled low on his forehead. Hunched over the microphone, he would eat popcorn while he described the game." Engineers would mix sound from two turntables, balancing any effects from "a low murmur to the bedlam that follows a grand slam. When a batter hit a ball, Keiter would tap a small hollow sounding box with a drumstick to simulate the crack of the bat." Marv Albert, then a budding announcer, ate it up. "He had all the works and was quite entertaining."

In these pre-expanded days of television sports and before the birth of cable television, Keiter had a huge following. Les was quite creative. When the Western Union wire was interrupted, Keiter told the audience the game was being suspended for rain and had a mythical ground crew roll out the tarpaulin. An anachronism today, Keiter's re-creations were entertaining. When Willie Mays would get an infield hit, he would shout in that inimitable gravelly voice, "he beat the ball, he beat the ball, he beat the ball!" And even though the information off the ticker was bare bone, a double or triple could be "a long drive to right, *boom*, it hits the wall."

By 1961 the re-creations were a thing of the past and the town was left exclusively to the Yankees.

10

THE NEW YORK METS

JACKETS, MALAPROPS, AND "HAPPY RECAPS" GLITTERED

When the Dodgers and Giants bolted New York for California in 1958, there was still a craving for National League baseball. In addition to Les Keiter's re-creations of Giants games on WINS from 1958 through 1960, television hoped to cash in. Al Helfer and former Brooklyn pitcher Rex Barney did some Phillies games back to New York, and under the aegis of Anheuser-Busch, Cardinals games against the Dodgers and Giants were carried on Channel 13, then a regular commercial television station. Jack Buck was the broadcaster. When Jack missed a game because his child had a life-threatening accident, Joe Garagiola, then a Cardinals announcer, filled in. It was the ex-catcher's first New York television exposure in what would become a very successful broadcast career. The imported telecasts lasted only one year after the Yankees threatened to send their games to St. Louis and Philadelphia.

While the Giants' games were on radio (about 90 a year), the Dodgers' schedule was not. The Dodgers fed an out-of-town network for years with a separate announcer. The Dodgers' network transcended Brooklyn and Los Angeles but never cleared New York City. The web essentially sprinkled the South and the play-by-play was re-created by Nat Allbright, who claimed that among the 100 stations that carried the Dodgers at its peak, the outlet in Washington did a better rating than the Senators. What does that say for Clark Griffith's perennial losers?

The old Dodgers station, WMGM, picked up the Yankees once Brooklyn was out of the borough. If WINS, which had the Yankees, was to take the Dodgers, it would have had to run Allbright's feed. The Giants didn't have a re-creation network à la Allbright's, so Horace Stoneham allowed WINS and Keiter to re-create the San Francisco games back East.

The National League's glaring hole in New York precipitated a succession of events. Mayor Robert Wagner immediately appointed William Shea, a prominent attorney, to restore National League baseball. A former athlete who earned a basketball scholarship to New York University, Shea was a one-time law partner of Dodgers owner Walter O'Malley. An attempt to move one of the existing franchises such as the Pirates or Reds failed.

Shea then contacted Branch Rickey, retired and 77 at the time, to cultivate supporters and doers. Wealthy backers were cultivated. They included Joan Payson, who had a minority interest in the New York Giants and whose financial adviser, M. Donald Grant, was the lone stockholder to cast a dissenting ballot when the Giants' board voted to approve the move to San Francisco. Unable to expand Major League Baseball, as it was structured then, Payson, Jack Kent Cooke, and others formed a rival loop, the Continental League. Rickey was appointed its president and initial franchises were to be situated in New York, Houston, Denver, Minneapolis, and Toronto. Atlanta, Buffalo, and Dallas were also considered for franchises.

The Continental hoped to become a third conglomeration in addition to the National and American leagues under the major-league umbrella. But baseball was unwilling to expand drastically and share its wealth significantly. Fearing that the influential organizers of the Continental would force a congressional investigation into its antitrust status, Major League Baseball reached a compromise.

The Majors agreed to expand by four teams. Los Angeles got an American League team, Clark Griffith was permitted to move his Washington franchise to Minneapolis, and the Senators would be replaced by a new team in the nation's capital. The National League was to swell to Houston and New York. Each league would now have 10 teams. The American League got a jump start, expanding to 10 in 1961. The senior circuit would wait until 1962. Payson would own the New York team, named the Metropolitans or the Mets. Funding was also approved for a new stadium in Flushing Meadow. The Mets were in business and after five years without representation in its confines, New York once again had National League baseball in 1962.

On November 10, 1961, the Mets sold their broadcast rights to Liebmann Brewing, makers of Rheingold Beer. The F&M Schaefer Brewing Company reportedly had the Mets' rights all but nailed down but were outbid at the very last moment. The *New York Times* reported that Liebmann paid $1.2 million over a five-year period. In addition, it committed to purchase 10,000 tickets to Mets games.

"One day I got a call and was asked to attend a luncheon at Luchow's, not a popular advertising hangout," said Norm Varney, who was responsible for sports programming at J. Walter Thompson, Rheingold's agency. "Phil Liebmann announced to the assembled that Rheingold secured the rights to the Mets broadcasts. As prime sponsor and rights holder, it was Liebmann's responsibility to cut the deals with the stations and hire the announcers." The telecasts went to WOR-TV, Channel 9, and the radio broadcasts to powerhouse WABC with its 50,000-watt omnipotent signal.

Through the course of the negotiation between potential sponsors and the Mets, it seemed to be a foregone conclusion that Schaefer would wind up with the rights. The Brooklyn-based brewery was fairly well committed to sports programming and had a relationship with the Dodgers when they were in Brooklyn. Tom Villante was head of sports and syndicated programming for Schaefer's agency, BBD&O. "Schaefer bid what it considered the package deal to be worth," said Villante, a former Yankee batboy. "This evaluation was based on what Ballantine beer has paid to the Yankees. Then Rheingold came along with so many dollars that we dropped out. We didn't think it was a legitimate price. If Rheingold wants it that badly, they can have it."

One fellow who was absolutely devastated when Schaefer took itself out of the sweepstakes was Les Keiter. Villante was high on Keiter. Had Schaefer made the deal for the Mets, Les would have gotten the assignment and Ralph Branca would have been his partner. In fact, Dick Young in the *Daily News* reported it. Keiter's name surfaced as early as November. But with Schaefer out, Rheingold and Varney were in charge with the club getting approval rights over the announcers. Later, in February, The Brown & Williamson Corporation signed a five-year contract to cosponsor the Mets on radio and television, promoting Viceroy, Kool, and Sir Walter Raleigh cigarettes.

Varney set upon the task of securing the talent. "We agreed with George Weiss and the Mets that our lead play-by-play man would be popular and network caliber. My first thought was Russ Hodges. He was popular in New York, having done the Giants, and had done network sports. He also worked for Weiss on Yankees broadcasts in the 1940s. Hodges and Varney met at Duke University, Varney's alma mater. Hodges had called the school's football games, and Varney had spotted for him. George and I had agreed that Russ would be a natural." Nearly 35 baseball seasons later and about a year before his death, Varney continued, from his Connecticut home, "I called Russ and he was genuinely interested but had just re-signed with the Giants in San Francisco and couldn't pursue it. He did have a suggestion. 'There's a guy at NBC who does the baseball game of the week that airs in non-major-league cities. He's very visible with his football broadcasts and would be a great choice. It's Lindsey Nelson.'"

Varney reviewed Hodges' suggestion with Weiss and they agreed to approach Nelson. "I called Lindsey immediately. He was heading out to Green Bay to call a football game. So I asked whether I can drop by the NBC building. I will never forget it. When I arrived, the lights flickered and went out. It got completely dark. I shouted 'Lindsey'. He uttered 'Norm'. We made contact, the lights went on, we sat down, and Lindsey was interested in the job." Talks progressed.

Nelson was in Los Angeles for the Pro Bowl. He and Chuck Thompson were set to work the telecast of the football game, and Keiter and veteran Van Patrick were to work radio. Although Schaefer was out, Keiter thought he was still in the running for the job because the Mets liked his audition tape.

The Friday before the Pro Bowl, January 12, 1962, Varney called Nelson in Los Angeles. Lindsey recalled the conversation. "He said it was all set, that he

SPORTS ON NEW YORK RADIO

had approval from everyone concerned, forty-five thousand dollars per year for two years, with an additional three-year option at fifty thousand dollars a year. I said OK and we agreed to make the announcement with a press luncheon at Mamma Leone's." As a frame of reference, Paul Richards of the Baltimore Orioles was reportedly the highest-paid manager in baseball at the time, making all of $50,000.

The stories vary slightly from here. Rumors were swirling. Nelson said he was sworn to secrecy until the announcement. To begin with, Keiter said he did the Pro Bowl on television and Nelson did it on radio. In reality, it was the other way around. According to Lindsey, Keiter approached him and questioned him. Sworn to secrecy, Lindsey said, "Where did you ever hear a thing like that?" Les's story is different. Under the impression that he was getting the job imminently, Keiter spotted Nelson and approached him to "give him some of the background information on my new job. Lindsey suddenly took a deep breath and speaking just above a whisper said 'Les, I guess you haven't heard. The Mets officially announced their plans about an hour ago. They've offered me a three-year deal to do the play-by-play. I thought the job was yours, everybody did. And I want you to know I didn't have anything to do with it. I'm sorry.'" In 1996 Varney didn't remember Keiter being considered when he and Weiss cut down the list of candidates.

No matter how it came down, Keiter was distraught. "I was devastated. I could hardly do the football game. I knew Lindsey had nothing to do with the change in broadcasters. On reflection, it had been a gutsy thing for him to tell me himself. But my disappointment overwhelmed me. I flew back to New York that night to tell Lila [Les's wife]. She was in shock after hearing the news. It was the lowest point of my career." From that point Keiter could only have wistful thoughts about lost opportunities, one he had with Brooklyn in the mid-1950s when he was told that he wasn't ready and now the thwarted Mets expectations.

With the Tennessee native in the fold, Varney and Weiss talked about the next hire. Lindsey had never traveled with a baseball team. He was a network man about to assume a local role. George wanted someone who had experienced the rigors of day-to-day baseball broadcasts. Varney was overrun with audition tapes.

Bob Murphy had been Curt Gowdy's associate in Boston from 1954 through 1959 and joined the Orioles' broadcasts in 1960, working with Herb Carneal for two seasons. The Birds' chief sponsor, Hamm's Beer, had lost the broadcast rights and Murphy was in the job market. Lindsey Nelson bumped into Bob's brother, Jack Murphy, a distinguished San Diego sports columnist. Jack told Lindsey that Bob was looking for work. The orator promised to keep his eye open for him. Whether or not Lindsey had any influence in Bob's hiring is a matter of conjecture.

"I was told that the tape that won the Mets job for me was my call of Roger Maris's 60th home run in 1961. He hit it against the Orioles off Jack Fisher," Murphy recalled. "Exactly why they picked me, I'm not sure. Maybe they liked my voice in the commercials." With eight years under his belt in the majors, Murphy, then 37, got the nod from Varney and Weiss. "Norm wanted a player of renown, that was Ralph [Kiner], a broadcaster with a national reputation, that was Lindsey, and he selected me as the third man. I'll always be grateful to Norm."

Courtesy New York Mets

Bob Murphy, Lindsey Nelson, and Ralph Kiner (from left) were the first to broadcast Mets games when the team began play in 1962, and they stayed together through 1978. Murphy is still a member of the Mets' radio crew, while Kiner does television.

But not so fast. "Initially, Weiss wanted us to hire just two announcers. He needed to be convinced that we needed three. But we made a pretty big commitment to the number of television games and he went along with a trio of broadcasters. Ralph is interesting," Varney continued about the events that led to the establishment of the Mets' only announcers until 1979.

A slugger who had retired in 1955 after a distinguished career with the Pirates, Cubs, and Indians, Ralph Kiner had been a minor-league administrator in his home state of California. In 1949 the slugger had a chance to pad his 54 homers going into the final weekend of the season. His manager, Billy Meyer, offered to bat him leadoff to boost his total. Kiner said, "Whatever mark I make, I want it to be honest, skipper." In 1960 he visited Pittsburgh where he was considered a hero for all his successful years with the Pirates. "The Bucs were in the World Series and I was asked to do a television show following each game of the World Series," said the man who was born in New Mexico in 1922 and grew up in California. In 1961 he joined the legendary Bob Elson and Milo Hamilton on White Sox radio broadcasts. It was how the slugger broke into play-by-play. "And that in turn was responsible for the assignment that would change my life," Kiner said in his autobiography, *Kiner's Korner*.

It was January 1962 and Ralph had been asked to do interviews with golfers at the Bing Crosby National Pro-Am. On the eve of the tourney, Kiner got a call from George Weiss, the Mets' first president. He asked Ralph whether he would have any interest in joining the Mets' broadcast team. The affable 6-foot, 2-inch Hall of Famer gave Weiss an unequivocal yes. Weiss told Kiner that he and Varney would be watching his performance on the national telecast of the Pro-Am.

What followed was comedic, if not frightful. Ralph was about to do his last segment. He was about to interview Gay Brewer and Phil Harris, a bandleader and comedian. Turning to Harris, Kiner said, "Phil, you know Gay Brewer, don't you?" Harris responded, "Gay Brewer? I thought he was a fag winemaker from Modesto."

Kiner was stunned but didn't stagger. He handled it very smoothly and completed his segment unruffled. But he thought it was over. The Mets would never consider him after this ugly incident. Varney remembers. "He didn't panic, didn't get flustered, he handled it very professionally. We were all impressed. If he could handle this, he could do a ball game." Other than Kiner, Varney said that he and the Mets were also looking at Pee Wee Reese and Bobby Thomson as possible men who could fill the role of the ex-player.

While the three announcers hired to call Mets games were all told that they were equal with one another and the work was generally split evenly, there's no question, according to Art Friedman, that it was Lindsey's booth. Friedman was the broadcaster's statistician and information purveyor. "If there were ever any immediate decisions needed to be made, Lindsey would take charge. From rain delay interviews to handling a delicate matter, Lindsey would take the lead."

Nelson, Kiner, and Murphy together outlived eight Mets managers from Casey Stengel who rings a bell with everyone to Joe Frazier who rings a bell with no one. For the next 17 years these three announcers were unshakable. They grouped their wares with an indistinguishable difference in work philosophy. "We never had a cross word," Nelson would proudly say later. Together they broadcast more than 3,000 games and did so impervious to extraneous influences. Over the same 17 years the Yankees' booth had 10 different announcers and more guests than the Grand Hyatt. "None of us believed in that. Lindsey was very much against it," Murphy said, suggesting that the distractions vitiate the presentation of the summer game.

The Mets' booth those 17 years was structured and predictable. Kiner clutched his cigar, Murphy smoked his cigarette, and Nelson held a pencil or some other inanimate object. Each of the three did his play-by-play with seductive charm. In the Yankees' booth Barber pontificated, Allen instructed, Rizzuto enlightened, and Garagiola blamed the Yankees' demise on "termites in the bat rack." "We didn't have to be funny," would be Nelson's retort. "Our jokes were on the field." In the Mets' booth, Murphy kept score assiduously, while in the Yankees' booth, Rizzuto used the initials "ww" (wasn't watching) when he drifted off. It led Lindsey to say, "Scoring is like religion, everybody does it differently."

Born in Columbia, Tennessee, Lindsey Nelson attended the University of Tennessee where he "devoted every waking moment to thoughts of the Vol fortunes on the gridiron." He tutored scholarship athletes in freshman English, spotted for the radio announcer, and was a stringer for newspaper reporters. In 1940, when the University of Tennessee played in the Rose Bowl, he was given $25 to serve as spotter for the famed Bill Stern. Nelson considered himself a protégé of Stern's and his style was influenced by the broadcast legend. During World War II he served in the Army for four years from North Africa to Sicily and Europe. His assignment was as a public relations officer. He was fascinated by the military, and military books accompanied him on the Mets' bus.

After the war Lindsey returned to Knoxville, where he broadcast minor-league baseball, the University of Tennessee games for three years, originated the statewide Vol Network, and developed a close relationship with legendary football coach Bob Neyland. In 1951 Nelson went to work for the Liberty Network. Based in Dallas, it primarily re-created baseball games, feeding them to non-major-league cities. When Liberty began in 1948, it was the first time regular-season big-league games were available in towns off the beaten path.

Working for the colorful Gordon McLendon, the "Old Scotchman," Nelson once re-created 62 games in 30 days. "It was an experience I wouldn't have traded for anything. After that, live games were duck soup." McLendon demanded that his announcers get excited. The studio was set up so that there were four turntables with crowd noise for every occasion. To make the broadcasts sound authentic, McLendon had an engineer in every ballpark record crowd noise and other music played there. The production was real theater. To make the re-creations sound real, McLendon even had a second announcer in a booth pretending to be a public address announcer. Yet, in the interest of honesty, the announcers would never say, "here in Washington," when, of course, they were in Dallas. They would simply say, "Washington, D. C., the cherry blossoms are beautiful this time of year."

Liberty eventually went out of business in 1952, after it had been told by many teams it could no longer re-create their games. It also lost its major sponsor, Falstaff Brewing. Mutual, though, did do a *Game of the Day* live through 1960 into non-major-league cities. Out of work, Nelson was introduced to NBC Sports Director Tom Gallery, who hired him as his assistant. Nelson's salary then was $7,500, and he was essentially in an administrative role, not doing on-air work.

One thing led to another, and Nelson began doing college football and, in 1957, baseball's game of the week to minor-league cities. In New York, where his baseball work was blacked out, he was known primarily for his college football play-by-play. As a network football announcer, Lindsey covered many events—the Rose Bowl, Sugar Bowl, and 25 Cotton Bowls. He also did NBC's *NBA Game of the Week*. Nelson is a member of the Ford Frick wing of Baseball's Hall of Fame and also a recipient of the Pete Rozelle Radio-Television Award given by the Pro Football Hall of Fame.

When Nelson took over the Mets' gig, he hadn't done radio baseball in many years. He had done the re-creations for Liberty in the early 1950s but few of them were live. Yet he adapted quickly, enjoyed it, and exuded warmth on the radio beginning with the early spring-training broadcasts from St. Petersburg in 1962. "On television, you are simply writing cutlines for the pictures. On radio, you paint the whole canvas with words, pace and intonation. You are the listener's eyes," said the man who would teach broadcasting at his alma mater after his retirement. At the University of Tennessee, the baseball stadium on campus is in fact named in Lindsey Nelson's honor.

On television, Nelson and the Mets were an immediate hit. Longtime sports radio and television personality Bill Mazer observed that the crowd shots helped make the Mets a draw on television. "Fans at home felt involved. They were products of their time. Jack Simon was a very creative director," Mazer said. The club, its colorful manager, Casey Stengel, and its collection of castoffs became the rage of New York.

Nelson's strength was television, where he perfected his skills at NBC. He was also quite creative and sought a niche on the telecasts. When he learned that the club planned 120 games on the tube, he started wearing multicolored jackets as a way to draw attention from the crosstown rival Yankees. "I went into a clothing store and asked the clerk to show me all the sports jackets he couldn't sell. People didn't always recognize me, but they knew my outfit." At one point, he owned 335 of those trademark psychedelic sport coats.

When Lindsey was inducted into the Hall of Fame, spokesman Bill Guilfoile said of the jackets, "They clashed with his soft, Southern drawl." When the popular announcer completed his short speech the day he was honored in Cooperstown, he took off the blindingly colorful jacket he was wearing and left it as a gift for the Hall. When he did, the crowd laughed and cheered.

The unshakable trio had to be entertaining, tolerant, and patient. The 1962 Mets lost 120 games. For that matter, during Lindsey's 17 seasons, the Mets averaged 91 losses a year. To Nelson, the Mets represented the "last age of innocence. They played for fun. They weren't capable of playing for anything else."

New York missed National League baseball and the Mets were an instant success. On Memorial Day, 1962, the Dodgers made their first visit to New York since leaving Brooklyn. The Polo Grounds was mobbed. Most of the cheers were for the Mets. A few days later it was the Giants, and Willie Mays was back stalking center field.

On June 30, the Mets played in Los Angeles at brand new Dodger Stadium. Sandy Koufax was on the hill and would pitch his first career no-hitter that evening. During the game, the camera took a shot of Lindsey in the booth. "We have somebody who would like to say hello," Nelson told his audience on the opposite coast. He then opened a sliding opaque window behind him. Visible through it was Vin Scully who waved to his old admiring New York constituency.

The upbeat salutation, "This is Lindsey Nelson with Bob Murphy and Ralph Kiner," was always an endorsement of New York summers no matter where the Mets played. When the team played in the Astrodome for the first time in 1965, he daringly crawled a catwalk to the apex of "the eighth wonder of the world." He was 20 flights directly above second base, describing the eerie site of a game played some 208 feet below. "I was in fair territory but I was safe," Lindsey would say of the experience. His only form of communication was a walkie-talkie which got mixed up with a local taxi company's two-way radio.

Lindsey always delivered the punch line dramatically, whether it was from Pittsburgh "at the confluence of the Allegheny, Ohio, and Monongahela rivers" or from "windblown Candlestick Park in the city by the bay." And how many times would this lover of poetry recite *Casey at the Bat* on the air? He was the consummate professional who would play hurt. There was the day during spring training when the Mets played the Yankees in Ft. Lauderdale and a heavy metal door slammed on his fingers. He was taken to a hospital, actually lost a piece of one finger, but returned to finish his broadcast.

The communicator was there the improbable day that the Mets won the World Series. It was Lindsey's most memorable baseball day, October 16, 1969. "Baseball is theater. It has all the elements—drama, tragedy, and comedy," said the man Bob Costas called a "cheerful chronicler."

In 1973 Lindsey's wife, Mickie, died suddenly in their winter home in Spain. "It devastated him," boothmate and statistician Art Friedman said. "Lindsey couldn't handle booze. He had been on the wagon for 20 years. But when Mickie passed on, he was off the wagon for a while. He would have one drink and he was out. We would have to take him up to his room or make sure that he didn't fall over any tables in restaurants. Lindsey wouldn't get loud or obnoxious. He was a very private man, a very proud man, and one of the most generous men I knew. Lindsey would always take care of the people that he trusted and those who helped him. I miss him. He was so cultured. We would be around a pianist and he knew the words to every Broadway show song. He was special and the broadcasts reflected it. What a professional."

How did the durable three get along? "We had very few disagreements. Like a good marriage that runs for seventeen seasons, the relationship will never be flawless," he wrote in his autobiography, *Hello Everybody, I'm Lindsey Nelson*. There were differences of opinion and all three went through personal and professional hardships in that span. Yet Nelson, Kiner, and Murphy were good friends and remained so, even after Lindsey left following the 1978 campaign.

When the man with the pronounced sing-song moved on, it surprised his partners. "As friendly as we were, I never felt I really knew him," Kiner would write. "It caught me by surprise." Ralph remembers Lindsey fondly. "For a man of his reputation, he had no ego. He never pulled rank."

In 1979, with the Mets going nowhere, Nelson joined the Giants where he worked for three years. He had always wanted to live in San Francisco. This was the opportunity. The Giants had a rights change and a station change. Lon Simmons, one of the club's original voices, was out. When Nelson arrived at Candlestick on opening day, he told the attendant that he didn't have a press credential but that he was the team's announcer. "Funny, you don't look like Lon Simmons," the attendant said to him. "That was a continuing problem for me. I didn't look like Lon Simmons and I didn't sound like him, either," Lindsey wrote. Or, as he told a writer after his three short seasons there, "I have been a stranger in a strange land."

Mets fans' first real hero was Tom Seaver, the ace of the pitching staff. Lindsey called his first win in 1967 and although he had retired from broadcasting baseball, the Yankees brought him back to call the last pitch of the Californian's 300th win in 1985.

Ralph Kiner worked at his craft. He may not have been as smooth as partners Murphy and Nelson but had a pleasant voice, shared game insights, wore well, wasn't intrusive, and could spin a tale with the best of them. "The Dodgers had a player named Babe Herman," he would say. "One day he got on base on a ground ball to the infield. The official scorer ruled it a base hit making him two-for-four for the day. The next morning the paper shows him as having gone one-for-four. When he gets to the ballpark the next day, he confronts the official scorer. 'That was a clean base hit,' he tells him. The scorer says, 'You're right. It must have been a typographical error.' Still steaming, Herman tells him 'Typographical error, bull, it was a clean hit!'" Friedman has heard the inexhaustible supply of tales. "They're great," he says, poking fun at a man he admires. "And we all kid him. He may tell the same story twice in a game, but they're all great."

While other play-by-play men inculcate numbers, Kiner imparts substance. In Chicago, "It's not called the Windy City because of the velocity of the wind but because of its windy politics." And even well into his 70s, Kiner is current. He may be a bit forgetful but not anymore so than he was 30 years ago. "It's funny," Friedman says, "Sometimes, say, he's scheduled to do the third and fourth innings and turn it over to Gary Thorne in the top of the fifth. He will come back from the commercial break at the end of the fourth and just keeps doing the play-by-play. He just forgets. We all chuckle. That's Ralph. He'll smoke his cigar, have a drink, and talk baseball."

Kiner drew praise from Red Barber, not a fan of ex-athletes in the booth. "Kiner anchors the booth at Shea Stadium," Barber wrote. It's rare to hear an unkind word about Ralph unless it's umpires. "Kiner is unfair to umpires. All he does is second-guess. He's the worst and he doesn't come down to talk to us to get our side of things," umpire Bruce Froemming said in 1988, and equally unflattering comments were echoed by fellow umpires, Dick Stello and Terry Tata.

It must have been difficult in those early years with the Mets. Nelson and Murphy were almost infallible and Kiner, well, he was Ralph. Trying to sound as smooth as his partners, he would gloss over mistakes. "Ground ball to the shortstop, who's standing near the second baseman who picks it up and throws to first." Or, "The score at the end of seven innings, the New York Giants . . . who moved to San Francisco . . . 4, and the Mets 3."

In 1963 pitcher Roger Craig lost 18 straight games for the Mets. The club finished with 51 wins, 11 more than it did in its inaugural year. Craig and Kiner teamed one night at flagship radio station WABC to re-create a game that affected the National League pennant race. Howard Cosell was doing the radio pre- and postgame shows with Ralph Branca, or as Howard would refer to him, "Big Ralph—Number 13—Branca, and the wrap-up edition of *Clubhouse Journal.*" Cosell introduced the Craig-Kiner re-creation. "There will be no crowd noise or other fabrications," said the man "who told it like it is."

"I don't think Howard was happy a day in his life," Lindsey Nelson said of Cosell. "I think he always wanted to do something else." In his pre- and postgame programming, Cosell would not be afraid to take shots at manager Casey Stengel. When the Mets switched to WHN in 1964, some said that the club didn't want to put up with Cosell's pontificating and diatribes. In actuality, WABC found baseball programming disruptive as it was becoming a successful rock 'n roll radio station. At WHN, the Mets' pre- and postgame programs were eventually done by Marv Albert, but in the mid-'60s it was boxing's Don Dunphy.

In their new digs at Shea Stadium in 1964, there was the Phillies' Jim Bunning's perfect game in the first of a twin bill on Father's Day. There was the big event on the other side of the viaduct. The New York City Transit Authority hoped it would increase subway ridership. It advertised, "It's the World's Fair and the subway special takes you there." A writer told Casey Stengel that the traffic at the Fair would help attendance at Mets games. After a few sellouts at Shea in the early season, Stengel told the same writer. "I see where we've sold out four games already and the World's Fair hasn't sold out once yet."

When the Mets accomplished the "Impossible Dream" in 1969, one of Kiner's dreams was fulfilled. He never played in a Classic, but as he said when he was hired in 1962, "My next biggest thrill to being in a World Series would be to broadcast one." That season, a Mets game wasn't complete until Tom Seaver dripped in perspiration on the postgame TV show *Kiner's Korner* and until Bob Murphy did the "happy recap."

While Nelson did leave, Kiner almost did, too, in the mid-1970s. When a third man was to be added to the Dodgers' booth, he applied. He would have joined Vin Scully and Jerry Doggett. He grew up in California and spends his winters in nearby Palm Springs. It made sense. The club pared down its list of candidates to two. Ross Porter got the job. Ralph says that pursuing the opportunity would not have occurred to him had the Mets not been in such "dire straits." After winning the pennant in 1973, the club took a nosedive.

Of course, Ralph Kiner, the broadcaster, is best known for his "Kinerisms." And there are a ton. From pronunciations to spoonerisms, Kiner has had some beauties. In the book *Baseball: A Laughing Matter* by Warner Fusselle with Rick Wolff and Brian Zevnik, some are listed:

Tony Gwynn was named player of the year for April.

The Hall of Fame ceremonies are on the 31st and 32nd of July.

The Pirates won 8 of their 102 losses against the Mets last year.

That's the great thing about baseball, you never know what's going on.

The name fluffs are too innumerable to list. But let's start with calling himself Ralph Korner. He's called the national anthem the New York anthem, Milt May was Mel Ott, Gary Carter was Gary Cooper, and Vince Coleman was Gary Coleman. Ralph also was the first to cheer the name change of Mets long-time sponsor, Manufacturers Hanover to Chemical. No matter how many times he would try over a course of 20 years, he would find some creative way to entertainingly butcher the bank's pronunciation. After the 1981 season, when general manager Frank Cashen split the radio and television booths, Ralph was assigned to television full time. Radio listeners miss him.

Now it's only on television where viewers will hear, "With the large salaries, if Branch Rickey was alive today, he'd be spinning in his grave." In his annual gift bag column, the *Daily News*'s Bob Raissman suggested Ralph get "royalties for his malaprops."

Bob Murphy's tenure with the Mets has transcended subway strikes, two power blackouts, the repeal of the death penalty and its reinstatement, eight United States presidents, two Germanys, the Seattle Pilots, and Washington Senators. He's pushed Rheingold Beer, Schaefer Beer, and Budweiser. He's been heard on six different flagship stations, including one of them for three separate stretches. Bob Murphy has been the "voice of summer" since 1962. Hearing his very Oklahoma twang on the air has meant that spring is in the air.

After being discharged from the U.S. Marine Corps, where he served during World War II, the Oklahoma native attended the University of Tulsa, where he majored in petroleum engineering. At the urging of his late brother, Jack, he entered sportscasting in Oklahoma. His first regular job was covering hockey, the Tulsa Ice Oilers. Murph's first baseball assignment was with the Muskogee Reds in the Class C Western Association. "I was going to school during the day and did the games at night for $45 a week," he recollected 50 years later.

It was followed by play-by-play for a season with the Tulsa Oilers in the Texas League and then to Oklahoma City, where he expanded his responsibilities. "If you've ever done a minor-league game, you'll know what a thrill the majors are." Former longtime A's voice Monte Moore is also from Oklahoma and heard a lot of Murphy in his formative Southwest years. "He's absolutely solid and does all sports with the same rhythm."

In addition to Texas League baseball, the effusive announcer called Bud Wilkinson's Oklahoma University football team and Hank Iba's Oklahoma A&M basketball team. Murph was there through the great years when the football Sooners won 31 straight games. It was in Oklahoma that he befriended Curt Gowdy, who was gilding his early image covering all sports in the same state.

Established in Boston, where he had arrived in 1951, Gowdy brought Murphy to Boston in 1954. His salary his first season was all of $10,000. He supplemented his income, broadcasting, among other things, the *New England College Football Game of the Week*. He was building a big family. The Murphys, Bob and his first wife Mary Jean, had five children—three girls and two boys.

It was under Gowdy's tutelage that Murphy grew professionally. "Gowdy told me, let's announce like we're friends just talking to each other. He steered me through, allowing me to adopt a conversational style. He taught me to project a warmth, a camaraderie. I was a typical young announcer, a motor mouth, nonstop. Curt taught me the art of pausing, of taking a deep breath. He was the most influential teacher in my career," Bob said one steamy South Florida day before a Mets-Marlins game. "We did all the radio and television, and Curt helped me clean up my Southwestern twang. Now folks think I'm from the Midwest."

In 1960, after six seasons at Fenway, Murphy went to Baltimore replacing Ernie Harwell, who left for Detroit. "I had a chance to work with the Birds and Paul Richards. Baseball was a chore, though, in Baltimore. Everything was the Colts." There were changes at the end of the 1961 season, when the O's won 95 games but finished third, 14 games behind the Yankees who won 109. Hamm's Beer was replaced by National, and Murphy was out of work. His Baltimore partner, Herb Carneal, ended up in Minnesota where he still does Twins games.

In 1962 the Mets carried every spring-training game back to New York. The WABC broadcasts served as an effective promotional vehicle for the club about to compete with the Yankees. The Bronxites, meanwhile, couldn't clear their Florida games on WCBS. They were carried on WCBS-FM in times when the majority of listeners didn't have FM reception. Murphy, Kiner, and Nelson were given a head start of sorts.

When Casey's misfits opened for real in St. Louis on April 11, 1962, Murphy delivered the first pitch on New York radio. It must have been eerie because he grew up a Cardinals fan in Oklahoma. Murphy promoted the first home game against the Pirates at the Polo Grounds, telling his audience that Pittsburgh was also the last team there in 1957 for the final game against the New York Giants. Murph encouraged fans to buy box seats. They were $3.50 at the time and were available at Howard Clothes, long since out of business. Then, of course, "you won't want to miss the welcome-home dinner, a perfect way to greet National League baseball back in New York."

Gus Bell would get the Mets' first hit. Thirty-four years later, the man who described it, Murphy, would still be there, still sounding fresh, now talking about Bell's grandson David, an infielder for the Cardinals. There were fewer commercial breaks in 1962. (Rheingold was the lead sponsor. "My beer is Rheingold, the dry beer. It's not bitter, not sweet, it's the right beer.") Games didn't take quite as long and the announcers had more opportunities to inject personality. Perhaps it was nerves but Kiner sounded less laid-back in 1962. Murph also introduced Lindsey, who came along in the seventh inning that first night. Everyone sounded bubbly. "If we're not having a good time, how can our audience?" says Murphy, a man who has spent more years broadcasting baseball on New York radio than anyone in history.

Little has changed about Murphy's style in 35 years. Jonathan Schwartz, music aficionado and baseball fan, says it softly but poignantly, "Murphy, no better, no worse." The "treasure," book contributor Dick Barhold, says that the only thing that Murphy has altered is how he lines up the defense. In the early years, he started at third and went to first. Now he starts at first and goes to third. Otherwise, he's the same. Yet it's the sameness and predictability that's so reassuring, a quality New Yorkers look forward to each frosty winter night.

It's memories of the Mets' youth, the staggering Mets. "Al Jackson . . . born on Christmas Day in Waco, Texas." Oddities, in 1963, "Carl Willey retires the Alou brothers." In 1964 Jim Davenport breaks up a 23-inning game for the Giants in the second of an afternoon twin bill that stretched until 11:25 at night. And how many times was the transistor under the pillow when the Mets were playing a summer night game at Candlestick? Perennially quoting Twain, "The coldest night I ever spent was a summer's night in San Francisco." It was all Murphy.

The squat announcer had his detractors. Those who carped thought he talked too much on television or was simply too repetitive. "How many times can we hear 'baseball is a game of redeeming features'?" they would ask. The powerful columnist, Dick Young, claimed that most of the negative mail he received on Mets announcers in the early years focused on Murphy. Years later, Bob himself admitted he got letters from fans asking him to economize verbally on television. Despite the television complaints, when Channel 9 needed a host for its locally produced *Bowling for Dollars*, Murphy got the nod. There he was each night in our living rooms.

There were those Mets fans who quivered when he would extol the virtues of an opponent. "Ollie 'Downtown' Brown, is up. They call him 'Downtown' because he can occasionally hit them that far." Boom, he would hit one against the Mets. "Richie Allen is wielding a heavy bat." Boom, he would tag one against the Mets. One fan said that he can even kiss off the weather. The twang rang, "A beautiful day for baseball." In an hour it would be pouring.

M. Donald Grant wasn't a Murphy fan. Grant was the financial caretaker and influenced the operation of the ball club. He eventually took over entirely and wasn't terribly popular after trading "the franchise," Tom Seaver. "Grant was enamored with big names. He liked Lindsey and Ralph," Friedman said, "and gave Murph a hard time." Bob felt uneasy about the situation. In 1965 he had an opportunity to take a spot in the Red Sox booth at Fenway Park.

"I visited with general manager George Weiss and he didn't want me to go anywhere. He called the owner, Mrs. Joan Payson, and offered me a new contract." The throaty voice stayed put. Thirty-plus years later he continues to grace the New York airwaves. In a city as busy as the Big Apple, Murphy is as identified with the Mets as Ed Kranepool or Jerry Koosman.

The 1969 Mets were "my boys of summer," he says. "You'll never enjoy a year any more than covering the '69 Mets." They included some of his favorite players: Tom Seaver, Jerry Koosman, and Tug McGraw. "Koosman might be the best guy I've ever been around. And I enjoyed being with Gil Hodges as much as anybody."

So while the attitude in the Yankees' booth was less restrained, the Mets trio meant business. "It's a big thing of mine, to run a clean store. I don't say hello to this guy, happy birthday to that guy. Lindsey was very adamant about this, that we run as clean a broadcast as we possibly could." Murphy remembers other Nelson influences. Lindsey didn't like the conversational style, which Bob had developed with Gowdy in Boston. "Curt told me that the broadcast should be like two guys sitting at the ballpark, enjoying the game, having a good time. Lindsey preferred the monologue."

In 1967 the Mets were dropped by WHN, which picked up the Yankees from WCBS. The radio landscape had changed. The Mets had no choice but to move to a regional type setup. There was a New Jersey station, WJRZ, which barely covered the five boroughs, and WGLI on Long Island to cover the area east of Queens. It was inadequate. There were just too many holes where Mets broadcasts couldn't be heard. But those who could hear WJRZ (now WWDJ-AM 970) listened to Bob Brown host the pre- and postgame programming. He was soft and warm and gave away manager Gil Hodges' book if a listener was able to answer complicated questions such as how many outs there are in an inning. The Mets were able to clear WABC-FM to cover the signal holes of their poor AM setup.

In 1972 the Mets were able to get back onto a station with a decent signal. They were back on WHN where Bill Mazer was now doing a nightly interview program. They were there when the club won the pennant in 1973 with Tug McGraw's rally cry, "You Gotta Believe!" That's when manager Yogi Berra told his team, "It ain't over till it's over." The team lost to the Oakland A's in the Fall Classic, which Kiner and Nelson called on radio and television, respectively. Murphy watched, enjoying it as a baseball fan, but bristling that, again, he was shut out of the booth.

The team took a quick turn for the worse in 1975. Berra was fired and Roy McMillan was hired on an interim basis. The Mets labored through years of gloom in the 1970s, but Bob remained forever positive in the booth. The subway viaduct would be filling up late in a game when the Mets were certain to lose again. But Murphy's expectations were chimerical. "The potential tying run is in the dugout," he would be capable of saying with sincerity.

One night, Randy Tate, a 22-year-old Mets rookie pitcher, was close to throwing a no-hitter against the Expos. From the old school, Murph didn't want to jinx the youngster. He found all sorts of ways to avoid saying the dreaded words "no-hitter." The listener could feel the tension in his quivering voice. But by the eighth inning, he couldn't hold back anymore. "Randy Tate," he baritoned with that deliberate, twangy delivery, "should he pitch a no-hitter, he would become the first Met ever to do so!" There was a pause. Murph must have wondered what price he will pay for blasphemously violating the unwritten rule of the booth. "Now here's Jimmy Lyttle, a tough, line-drive hitter." To hear the man pronounce the word *line* is alone worth the effort of putting on the radio. The stretch of the vowel in the word is unending, unintentional but inimitable. A split second later, "The pitch, a *liiine*-drive base hit." Murphy fans in the neighborhood talked about it for days. It was a classic Murph kiss-off!

WHN went out of the sports business temporarily and Thornton Geary, the Mets' broadcast director and Dick Young's son-in-law, made a deal with

WNEW in 1975. The station ran show tunes and musical classics. It wouldn't tinker with its afternoon format. So weekday games were bumped, first to WRVR-FM, then a struggling jazz station and now the thriving LITE at 106.7, and later noncommercial WNYC-AM. By 1978 Geary made a reluctant deal with WMCA, a station with an inferior signal and one with a reputation for being terribly greedy. There were no alternatives. The Mets' field performance was hardly a testimonial. Joe Torre's team finished last in 1978 and the future looked so discouraging that Nelson left after the season. It ended 17 unforgettable years of stability, serenity, and structure. Murphy, Kiner, and Lindsey, they were an ineradicable part of the New York summer tapestry.

When Lindsey's departure broke up the unwavering threesome, the Mets' stock was in decline. It needed help. There was a sense that the broadcasts needed an infusion of youth and fresh enthusiasm. Meanwhile, Murphy and Kiner were both gentlemanly and obliquely lobbying for the top spot. When the 1979 season started, one new announcer would be hired and each of the new trio would remain equal. The new man was Steve Albert, one of a famed trio himself, comprised of older brothers Marv and Al.

Basketball and hockey were growing. Baseball wasn't. Mets management hoped to cash in on Steve's experience with the rapid-fire sports. It was thought that he might be able to attract younger listeners, viewers, and fans. But he wasn't a baseball man. He didn't have the experience of broadcasting the summer game day to day. Could it be nurtured? Steve Albert is likable, personable, and a professional announcer. And after all, after doing tennis on radio, baseball should be a breeze. "Tennis on radio made me a man," the Brooklyn-born Albert said some 17 years later.

"I tried to fit in. I had my moments. I was best once the pitch was delivered. The experience helped reinforce that I was better suited for the fast-action sports." And, indeed, he has excelled at basketball, hockey, and boxing. "I learned a lot. They were a bizarre three years of my career. Yet it was beneficial because I realized what I wanted to do." One wondered whether timing, circumstances, expectations, and partnerships would have improved Steve Albert's chances of baseball longevity.

There was a laugh along the way. Kiner, Murphy, and Steve were all together in the booth on a radio-only game. "Kiner is doing the play-by-play, smoking a cigar. He's calling a fly ball to the outfield when in the middle of it he bellows this scream of pain and Murph had to finish the description. Ralph had been dropping his ashes on the heap of ticker tape of out-of-town scores under his chair. The papers caught fire and he got a hot seat. We laughed for days."

In 1981 former Met Art Shamsky was added to the Mets' broadcasts. That season, baseball was hit by a crippling strike. On the radio, the Yankees were enjoying their first year on WABC. The powerhouse replayed old baseball classics, including one game of the 1936 World Series with Red Barber, Ty Tyson, and Tom Manning. On television, the Mets sent Albert and Shamsky to Japan to cover baseball in the Far East. The whole crew also went to Norfolk, Virginia, to cover their minor-league Tidewater Tides. "It was fun," Steve remembered. "I went from a team in last to a team in first. And Tidewater had a star named Ronald McDonald!" Murphy went with the alacrity of a Tides player destined for Flushing. Gary Rajsich somehow "has a world of power!" and Gil Flores, "when he hits 'em they go!"

At the end of Albert's short tenure, the Mets made some stinging changes. Frank Cashen assigned Kiner to full-time television and Murphy to full-time radio. Albert and Shamsky were let go. "Maybe I was fired because I said they made 130 errors in 105 games but I don't think anybody could have made the Mets sound or look good last year," said Shamsky, the former outfielder who was fired after just one year.

The demotion hurt Bob Murphy. "He was bitter. You can tell from his voice," Friedman said. Years later, Murph wouldn't deny it. "I can't lie, I was pretty disappointed that first year. Frank said I was a better radio guy than TV guy and in New York, television increases your exposure and enhances your opportunity to make money."

Bob Murphy's first radio-only partner in 1982 was Steve LaMar. When the game was on, he delivered with the tempo of a maestro. LaMar was brought up to the bigs after some brief minor-league experience. His voice was mellifluous, a delight to the ear. Not harsh, not thin, perfect. His descriptions were fine but there was no depth of knowledge. This would be obvious his first year when Murphy attempted to engage him in on-air baseball conversation. It just wasn't there. Vic Ziegel in *New York* magazine wrote, "Steve LaMar seems to agree with everything Murphy says on radio." Baseball is the one sport where an announcer can't get away with a lack of knowledge. There are too many lulls to fill and too many strategic decisions to ponder inning by inning. Baseball announcers are paid for what they say between pitches.

By 1983, when the club broadcast from Florida, they were back on WHN for the third time in franchise history. Al Harazin, then in charge of business affairs for the Mets, said that it was a great pleasure to be able to politely tell intransigent WMCA that the Mets didn't need them anymore. During spring training, Phil Mushnick wrote in the *Post*, "Steve LaMar has a smooth style and a pleasant voice, but he should spend spring training learning to identify different kinds of pitches, an absolute must for radio." He didn't. By his third season, LaMar was still reading from the press guide. "LaMar wouldn't go down to the field," Murphy explained. Steve LaMar's contract wasn't renewed after the 1984 campaign.

In 1985 Murphy had a new partner. Harazin hired Gary Thorne. In the footsteps of Mel Allen, Bill Munday, Russ Hodges, and Howard Cosell, Thorne had legal training. He was a practicing Maine attorney who also found the time to do play-by-play for the University of Maine hockey team and Triple-A baseball for the Maine Guides, a team he co-owned. Distinguished baseball writer Peter Gammons gave Thorne a plug that opened the door to Harazin, who saw him after Thorne nudged him at the winter meetings in Houston. He won the audition and got the nod. Bright and eager, Thorne made the best of the opportunity. "Knowing the players is absolutely necessary," he said with conviction. It was this dictum that made the attorney spend time on the field, getting familiar with personalities. But, "A high fly that will be caught by Strawberry," makes Bill Mazer wonder, "How does he know?"

The Mets were now showing signs of promise. By 1985, Davey Johnson's team finished just three games behind the Cardinals in second place. The team finished with 98 wins. The club's success and Thorne's effulgence seemed to energize Murphy to new heights. Together, there was chemistry. Gary was assertive and bubbly but deferential. Murphy didn't find him threatening. The

Courtesy New York Mets

Gary Thorne

lawyer was hard working, even using the 1985 All-Star break to take part in a tax hearing in his last active case.

In the booth the ebullience was infectious. Cable television penetrated New York significantly but unlike radio it wasn't ubiquitous. "Radio can identify so beautifully with baseball," Murphy intoned. And quickly, the Mets' success was being echoed on radios throughout the metropolitan area. Murphy and Thorne were an instant success. *New York* magazine even named the 37-year-old newcomer its Rookie of the Year.

Gary Thorne's presentation oozes with warmth, confidence, style, and vitality. It's sprinkled with an unrestrained hearty laugh. His ex-partner, Murphy, doesn't hesitate to applaud his four-year full-time mate. "He's a number one announcer today, he's got everything it takes." There was no sophomore jinx for this play-by-play man on the rise. The 1986 Mets won the World Series, and through it all, he was Murphy's talented sidekick. The broadcasts were heaped with praise.

Bob Murphy has broadcast more than 7,000 major-league games. His favorite of them all was in 1986, the famous 16-inning affair. It was the sixth game of the National League Championship Series at Houston. The game took so many strange twists. The Mets resourcefully battled back from a 3–0 deficit in the ninth to tie it. The Mets took the lead in the 14th but the Astros tied it. The Mets went on top again in the 16th and with Houston threatening in the home half, Jesse Orosco struck out Kevin Bass to give the Mets the pennant. "I think that's the best baseball game ever played," the longtime veteran said of the game that put the New Yorkers in the World Series. The Major League contract allowed the two to broadcast the Red Sox–Mets Classic on WHN and Murph finally did his first World Series.

There was a confluence of developments that helped lift Murphy's image to icon status. The play on the field by the Mets, the synergy produced with partner Thorne, cable's reach wasn't quite full yet, and later in 1987, the emergence of WFAN. Could the Mets have asked for any better lead-in programming? Night and day, sports and sports talk was a natural environment for a team on the rise. Initially, as WFAN tried to find itself, Mets play-by-play was the only programming that had a track record of success. For Murph, the additional exposure was a valued windfall. The call of the famed Bill Buckner error in the Series has been replayed a thousand times as have so many other of his highlights. One New Year's eve WFAN even ran the first Mets game in 1962 in its entirety. It was another link, bonding Murphy, the Mets, and the New York sports fan. Could it get any better? It did. In 1988 WFAN moved to 660, arguably the most powerful dial position in New York. At night it can be picked up in almost half the country.

The exposure afforded Thorne great dividends, too. The opportunities knocked. The Devils wanted him to do television. It would have meant absences from some Mets games. After the 1988 campaign Thorne couldn't reach a compromise with Cashen over his future hockey broadcasts. He gave up the Mets for the Devils. Why? "It was a matter of working and not working," he said. He took a stand and he let his standards and qualifications be his best testimonial. The networks beckoned, ABC and ESPN. And even when he left the Mets over the disagreement, he made sure to do so amicably. It, too, paid off. In 1994 he was back, paired with Tim McCarver and Ralph Kiner on Mets telecasts on WWOR Channel 9. He also does occasional fill work on Mets radio broadcasts.

Gary Cohen

The squabble opened a position for Gary Cohen and in 1989 the Queens native was hired. A dean's list student at Columbia University, the versatile announcer worked his way through the ranks quickly. Cohen earned his due. The apprenticeship was thorough. It included stops in Spartanburg in the Class A South Atlantic League in 1983–84. In 1986, it was Durham where he did the famed Bulls team in Class A of the Carolina League.

By 1987 Cohen graduated to Triple-A baseball, broadcasting the Pawtucket games in the International League. It was in Rhode Island that he hooked on with Providence College, ably handling the Friars basketball and hockey broadcasts. At the age of 30, he was more than ready.

"Technically, he's as good as they come," says Bob Murphy, whom Cohen grew up listening to as a kid. Can he be a number one man in a baseball booth? "He can," says Murph, always the gentleman, always prudent with his comments. What's it take? Bob explains succinctly, "To convey baseball is a family game."

It was clear from the beginning that Gary Cohen was bright. He wouldn't have earned his Ivy League stripes if he wasn't. He's well-read, has studied the game, and understands the strategic nuances of baseball. A Mets fan tuned to Gary's baseball broadcasts can listen assured that the game will be reported accurately, intelligently, and thoroughly. The action will be described as well as anybody. In fact, CBS radio has been impressed for a number of years and has used him on its national baseball broadcasts and its Olympic hockey coverage. He's equally facile with both.

Murphy, the dean of New York baseball play-by-play men, explains that there are two facets to play-by-play—information and entertainment. Did Thorne's departure leave the associate's role with a void for storytelling or for a contagious laugh? Has Murph laughed as much since Thorne left him in 1988?

"Gary Cohen is very businesslike. He doesn't have the natural and warm laugh that Thorne and McCarver have," says Art Friedman, a childhood friend of Marv Albert and longtime observer of play-by-play men. "But don't get me wrong, he's very good at what he does." Does Cohen provide so much that it's too difficult to digest all of it on radio? Not according to the *Daily News*'s Raissman who gave him a grade of "A" in his 1997 review because he "produced precise play-by-play with genuine emotion." In his "B" grade of Murphy, he made reference to a lack of chemistry between the two in the booth.

In 1996 the Mets played the San Diego Padres in Mexico. Murph didn't make the trip. The intelligent and capable Howie Rose did. Cohen and Rose talked about the poor lighting in the stadium. Cohen showed his quick wit, "Is that why a lot of shady characters have come to hide here through the years?"

But as one seasoned announcer said about Cohen, "There's a deluge of data and he spews it brilliantly with computerlike precision. But do all the stats and facts make the fan enjoy the broadcast? He's a bright guy, but a cross between Mister Rogers and a robot." Some from the noncomputer age feel that many play-by-play men on radio today generally have an agenda. They come with more notes than Senator Joe McCarthy had on Alger Hiss, and they have to get them all in.

In 1994 Murphy was paid the highest accolade a baseball announcer can earn, receiving the Ford Frick Award, and he was enshrined at Hall of Fame ceremonies. It was unquestionably his "happiest recap." By 1997 there were 11 winners of the coveted honor who trace their roots through New York. The Hall established it in 1978, and eight of the first nine worked New York teams— Allen, Barber, Hodges, Harwell, Scully, Brickhouse, Gowdy, and Buck Canel, the longtime Spanish "voice of the Yankees." Only Bob Elson of Chicago didn't. Later, Lindsey Nelson, Joe Garagiola, and Murphy were honored.

Now in his 70s, still sharp, poised, assertive, intense, stylized, and focused, Bob Murphy works a reduced schedule. Ed Coleman of WFAN, limited in his play-by-play experience, was assigned a permanent third-man position in the booth beginning in 1998.

It's all part of a summer day in New York.

11

THE BUSINESS OF
RADIO SPORTS

IT'S ALL ABOUT MONEY

Micky Arison, who bought management control of the NBA's Miami Heat in 1995, once said that sports ownership is the most difficult business he's ever experienced. This comment came from a man who has owned a cruise business, an airline, and several other intricate enterprises. That's quite a testimony.

The whole sports marketing business has exploded in recent years. Teams have chief marketing officers. They have research resources, organizational charts, corporate sales staffs, packaging equations, and yield management formulas. Branch Rickey, Walter O'Malley, and Larry MacPhail would think franchise owners have gone berserk. Then again, they would probably turn over in their graves if they knew what players' salaries are today. A once simple mom 'n pop organization that worked years ago is no longer adequate. Marketing expectations are just too high. The cost of running a franchise is so enormous that it demands a sophisticated group of specialists and professionals.

It may sound implausible today when there are as many as 50 different advertisers in a game broadcast, but through the first 20 years or so of radio, team broadcasts had one sponsor at best. It may have been expanded to two in the 1950s and three as late as the 1960s. The sponsor was truly synonymous with the team then. It wasn't uncommon for a preteen Mets fan to insist that his dad bring back only Rheingold. If his dad already brought back Ballantine, he would say, "Dad, I will be embarrassed if my friends see that we have that Yankees beer in a Mets house."

With fewer sponsors then, baseball games also took less time to complete. Only one minute of advertising was run between innings and even so, commercials weren't run every inning. Often, the time was spent just talking about the game, giving scores, or softly promoting an upcoming home stand.

In the early years, the sponsor, not the team, held the broadcast rights and employed the announcers. For years, Red Barber didn't work for the Dodgers but for General Mills or, later, Old Gold. Mel Allen got his paycheck from Ballantine. All the years of the great fight broadcasts, Don Dunphy was under contract to Gillette. As a result, announcers could not work for a competing advertiser.

For example, several times, Harry Wismer did only one half of a football game in the 1950s, the half sponsored by Pontiac, the company with which he was affiliated. The sponsor of the other half insisted upon its own broadcaster. When United Artists sponsored the Patterson-Johanssen heavyweight title fight in 1959, it insisted that the stars of the movie it was promoting, *The Horse Soldiers*, be involved in the broadcast commentary. As such, Howard Cosell's time was cut down. He had to share the mike with John Wayne and William Holden.

When Red Barber switched from the Dodgers to the Yankees in 1954 and promoted Camel instead of Lucky Strike, fans actually were impressed. "Wow, Red Barber not only changed teams he switched the cigarette brands that he's smoking." I guess they also believed he also suddenly switched the beer he was drinking from Schaefer to Ballantine.

The way sponsorships broke down in the early years is depicted in the chart at the top of the next page.

The demand today is so great and the economics so rich that no one advertiser can afford to own an exclusive sponsorship of a team's broadcasts. It's impossible. Gillette actually held an exclusive on the World Series from 1939 through 1959. Gillette was generally the only commercial spot that listeners or viewers heard or saw. By 1960 Gillette could afford only half the game. General Motors bought the other half. Until that point, Gillette was involved in hiring the talent and making production decisions.

Radio sports was hardly a lucrative business in the early years. The paucity of advertisers sometimes made the situation very unsettling. Teams sometimes couldn't get on the air. With fragile sponsor support, stations were reluctant to make play-by-play commitments. Even the Mets and Yankees struggled in 1971 when cigarette makers were no longer allowed to advertise on radio or television, eliminating a major revenue source. It was the only season when neither team was on a 50,000-watt station.

Art Adler and Herb Salzman would change things in 1976, when they were brought in by the Yankees as turnaround specialists. The team had been losing money on its radio broadcasts through the 1970s and desperately needed to increase sponsorship sales. For the first time, personnel were dedicated to the radio advertising sales of one team. It was no longer handled by the station's sales staff that was also responsible for general program advertising.

Sales picked up dramatically. After Salzman left to purchase a radio station, Adler built the Yankees' radio coffers. Yankees radio became Adler's life,

Teams and Principal Sponsors

Brooklyn Dodgers.................. Wheaties (1939–42), Ivory Soap (1939), Le-
ver Brothers (1940–41), Old Gold (1942–
48), Post Cereal (1947–1950), Schaefer
(1949–57), Lucky Strike (1952–57)

New York Baseball Giants .... Wheaties, Ivory Soap (1939), Wheaties, Camel (1940), Wheaties, R. H. Macy (1942),
Gillette (1944–45), Pabst, Hoffman Sodas
(1946–47), Chesterfield (1948–55), Knicker-
bocker (1956–57)

New York Yankees................. Wheaties, Ivory Soap (1939), Wheaties,
Camel (1940), Wheaties, R. H. Macy (1942),
Gillette (1944–45,) Pabst, White Owl (1946),
Ballantine, White Owl (1947–55), Ballantine,
Camel (1956–66)

New York Knicks.................. unsponsored (1946), Nedicks, Old Gold
(1947, 1948)

New York Football Giants .... Wheaties (1939), Pabst (1941), Old Gold
(1942–47), Schaefer (1948), Pabst (1949),
Adler Shoes (1950), Miller (1950–55)

livelihood, and obsession. He understood the nuances of selling sponsorships, knocking on the right doors, and how to package programs attractively. He didn't stop at reluctant ad agencies. He went to the advertisers directly. Incorporating tickets, trips, and sales incentives, the doer hit the right buttons and made the cash register click. Art Adler was a trailblazer of sorts, responsible for the explosion of the radio sports business.

The entrepreneur also got lucky. The Yankees started winning and sponsors always want to be associated with a winner. The team went from having just two or three advertisers in a season to 40 or 50 in less than 10 years. With more money in the till, Adler convinced the club to buy the time from a better station. The Yankees did just that when they moved to WINS in 1978. Adler then moved the package to powerhouse WABC in 1981. The sponsorship activity was brisk, and the broadcasts were heard up and down the East Coast.

Adler's success had a ripple effect. The national broadcast sales representatives and advertising agencies soon formed their own sports divisions to respond to the increased activity of selling and buying sponsorships. Sports marketing companies sprouted all across the country. By the mid- to late 1980s the broadcasts of most local professional teams enjoyed plenty of sponsorship support.

In the 1980s the economics of radio play-by-play also got a major lift from Anheuser-Busch, which determined that it wanted to have a presence in all major local sporting events. It didn't want to play a secondary role to Miller in local sports visibility. The brewer of Budweiser gobbled up virtually everything it could. The strategy worked. Anheuser-Busch became far and away the number one brewery in the United States.

By 1987 WABC felt it would fare better if it held the rights to the Yankees as opposed to simply being the carrier of the broadcasts. It thus put Adler out of business by buying the rights directly from the club. But WABC was terribly unsuccessful trying to recoup the big rights fees it paid, and it lost tons of money on the Yankees' package. In 1997 WABC was bailed out by Madison Square Garden, which bought the rights directly from the Yankees.

More money invested in radio sports resulted in higher rights fees and an expansion of inventory. Basketball for many years would allocate just one minute of advertising at time-outs. The demand for inventory expanded the break to a minute and a half. Baseball went to two-minute breaks between innings.

In the late 1970s and early 1980s, when the domestic automobile companies suffered for the lack of an efficient product, the Japanese automakers started buying sports sponsorships. Other new categories would mushroom every year. Cellular telephones, bottled water, and computer manufacturers were just a few.

One interesting story developed in Detroit during the upswing years in foreign car sales. Because of the painful domestic auto sales slump, there was rampant unemployment in Detroit. The WJR Tigers broadcasts couldn't get a car sponsor. At the same time, Nissan sales were rocketing, and it looked at a proposed Tigers sponsorship package.

Nissan's USA headquarters in California was about to approve the idea. But it wondered whether it would be rubbing it in the face of the Detroit constituency? After all, the success of the foreign car companies was causing layoffs. Many owners of foreign vehicles in Detroit had their cars stoned. Would Nissan leave itself vulnerable? California decided to let its Japanese headquarters make the decision. Japan did, and prudently turned down the opportunity because it anticipated a public relations backlash.

Today there are three different ways radio broadcasts are packaged. Two are common, the third uncommon. The first is when the station purchases the rights directly from the team. It then hires the announcers, sells the sponsorships, and retains all revenue. It's a simple transaction. The second approach is when a team buys the block of time from a station, produces its own broadcasts, and sells its own sponsorships. The team then retains all the advertising revenue. The third procedure is when a third party owns the rights.

The radio rights to local National Football League teams are usually sold directly to a station. Because football's once-a-week schedule is not disruptive, all stations, including many FM outlets, find the rights attractive. They can run uninterrupted programming all week and still link with a popular local NFL franchise on Sundays. From a team standpoint, the rights fees are enormous, and it avoids having to assume the responsibility of producing the broadcasts or selling sponsorships. Prior to the 1973 lifting of the NFL television blackout of home games, radio was indispensable. Now virtually every game is on local television. Yet rights fees still seem to escalate every year because of the promotional and identity value of the NFL.

Baseball is split. Many teams retain their own rights, while others sell their rights. When a team retains its own rights, which is done commonly in basketball and hockey, it pays the talent and the cost of production and generally buys the block of time from the flagship. The flagship benefits by having the play-by-play programming without taking a financial risk. Teams can then package their in-stadium signage, ticket plans, corporate suites, and other elements along with their radio inventory.

Madison Square Garden was one of the first to take broadcasts in-house. It was initially done out of necessity when the Knicks and Rangers couldn't get themselves on either radio or television in the 1960s. The Garden smartly set up its own radio and television department, bought time from radio and television stations, and set up its own production and sales staffs. Now Madison Square Garden has a whole network of programming on television and radio.

As far as the sponsor is concerned, each system has its advantages and disadvantages. When the station has the rights, advertisers can negotiate bonus spots and bulk up with more media for their investment. When teams own the rights, advertisers will have an easier time negotiating more team promotions.

When a third party purchases the rights, it does its own station clearances, its own advertising sales, and its own hiring of announcers. For instance, Madison Square Garden owns Yankees radio rights and then buys a block of time from a radio station. In the 1970s Manchester Broadcasting owned the rights to the Nets, Islanders, and Yankees. Way back in the 1950s, Liberty Broadcasting, a Dallas-based network, owned the rights to the New York Yanks of the NFL.

So in this growing age of television, how does radio position itself for an advertiser?

- Unlike television, radio carries every game. The television schedule is often split between cable, network, pay, and local over-the-air. On radio, advertisers have a consistent link with the team through every game. The advertiser's message is inculcated game after game.

- By linking with a local radio broadcast, the advertiser is forging a bond with the announcer who's tied to the ball club. It's almost an implicit endorsement that provides instant credibility.

- The medium of radio is indigenous to promotion. As an example, an auto company can sponsor a baseball team's broadcast and then lure would-be customers to its dealerships by filling a car full of baseballs and having fans guess the number of baseballs in the vehicle. The radio station promotes it throughout the broadcast day, benefiting all involved.

- Stations can run tune-in announcements to further hammer home the identity. "Tune in Mets baseball sponsored by The Wiz."

- Sports are clean. Commercial messages run when attentiveness levels are high and when potential customers are thinking positively. Unlike when the news is on, there aren't any stunning atrocities or tragedies to taint the program environment.

- Sports enables an advertiser to bond with an entire marketplace. For example, when advertisers buy commercial time on a country music station, the message reaches just the segment of the market that enjoys country music. Sports, though, are supported by the community at large.

- It's a great way for corporations to support the channel of distribution. The merchandising programs that generally come with a sponsorship package on radio include tickets, parties, contests, and trips to road games. They can be used as effective sales incentives.

- On radio there's no zapping during commercial breaks. Listeners generally stay put.

313

The explosion of sports marketing has resulted in the creation of many more sales-related positions. And while effective sports salespeople can make a good living, it isn't an easy sell. Advertisers have to commit budgets far in advance and for a long period of time. They have to buy spots that for their pure comparative media value are less efficient than other radio programming. Because of these deviations, the entire process can be exasperating. Unlike television, radio is not rated on a program-by-program basis, making the determination of numbers a matter of interpretation and difficult negotiation.

It takes the patience of a saint to stomach the hardships and frustrations that go with the daily territory. The seller has to be able to handle rejection, telephone calls that are not returned, and pressure from management. The radio-sports seller has to be hungry. The attitude has to be "where is my next meal coming from?"

For all its success, play-by-play broadcasts have an alarmingly small stable of sponsors. To add new ones, the buying hierarchy of each prospect must be penetrated diligently and perseveringly. There is no book of leads. The only sport that has a book of leads is the college game. The alumni of any school are a great place to start. St. John's University basketball has done astonishingly well, for example. The school's loyal throng of graduates has been successful in various fields of business and helpful in sponsorship support. It has enabled the Red Storm to thrive financially on radio.

12

TALK RADIO

MAKING EVERYONE'S
OPINION COUNT

Radio today is generally tightly formatted. Stations have defined programming missions. Each maintains a sense of consistency. For the most part, AM radio provides information and FM entertainment. Music, once the domain of AM, has exploded on FM, enabling the record and radio industries to grow synergistically. AM has filled the void by widening its concentration from only news to news and views, and from analysis to advice. AM radio has produced opinion mongers, political demagogues, holistic health advocates, and scam artists.

And there are niches within formats on both bands. Years ago stations simply played rock 'n roll. Today FM stations program light music, oldies, a mix, contemporary, dance, and more. New York today has AM stations of a variety of formats, from all news to all talk and from religion to foreign language. In 1998 one all-news facility, WINS, gears its coverage to stories of local interest, fires, shootings, and police scandals. Another, WCBS, uses its rich network resource to stock upscale features for timely airing and to carry the latest national and international developments. WBBR, a third news station that evolved out of a business format, still has a discernible financial sound to it.

In radio's early years, when stations first sprouted, there was less consistency. To begin with, AM stations served as a source of both information and entertainment. Each evening, families would gather around radios in their homes and absorb orchestras, comedies, and staged drama that crackled through the airwaves.

To survive financially in the early years, stations sold blocks of time, not commercial minutes as they do now. If they were unsuccessful in selling blocks, programs were "sustaining," a dirty word back then. At first, commercial announcements were unwieldy. They were woven in and extemporized. It was well before advertisers produced prerecorded spots and before the development of research to help advertisers match program audiences with targeted customers.

Programming was dominated by the networks which put entertainers under exclusive contracts. The big names, Rudy Vallee, Ed Wynn, and Jack Pearl, were all associated with one web and were usually under the aegis of one advertiser. Just as is the case on television today, network-affiliated stations in every market were then most prominent. They had the prestige and the popular shows. The unaffiliated stations were considered secondary. It wasn't until television became America's prime source of nightly entertainment in the 1950s that radio networks slowly gave up long-form programming. The network orchestras and quiz shows slowly disappeared. While doomsayers predicted its ultimate death, radio not only survived, it eventually flourished. Radio evolved into a true local medium, giving rise to the nonaffiliated stations that were able to carve a piece of the audience.

AM stations produced local music and variety shows. Local personalities emerged. John Gambling on WOR, Gene Klavan on WNEW, and Jack Sterling on WCBS developed large followings. When AM radio was the only popular band, many stations became "middle of the road," formatting a programming service that appealed to everyone, mixing entertainment and information, music, and news.

On-air sports programs were generally limited to play-by-play, game re-enactments, and popular résumés. Up until the 1960s there was only a sprinkling of interview and sports dialogue shows. Boxing broadcast legend Sam Taub, as an example, had a popular Sunday morning show, *The Hour of Champions*. From Joe DiMaggio to Jack Dempsey, personalities appeared happily and gratis. The questions posed were hardly probing. Those who were accomplished on the playing field were invariably presented in a positive light. Controversial issues or shameful behavior by athletes was generally not raised.

The technology that is required to run live actualities and immediate player reactions was not available yet. News conferences held immediately after games when coaches spoke candidly or angrily or when players spewed knee-jerk diatribes hardly ever made it on the air. It was easier to think of sports heroes as pure. They weren't exposed, they were almost never presented in an unrehearsed or noncontrolled environment.

If there was an equivalent to ESPN *SportsCenter*, it was Stan Lomax, a New York fixture and favorite for five decades. He was at WOR from 1931 to 1977. When baseball was played during the day, Lomax was on each evening with a thorough 15-minute sports recap. This was before the immediacy of the Internet, cable television, or even over-the-air television. Each evening, and for most years at 6:45 P.M., the Pittsburgh native hit the air with a thorough recap of what occurred and what was scheduled. There weren't any taped interviews, play-by-play cuts, or opinions. It was 15 minutes of well-delivered and beautifully written sports news. If Lomax said it, the news was official. School kids and adult sports fans were tuned in after dinner, before dinner, or during dinner.

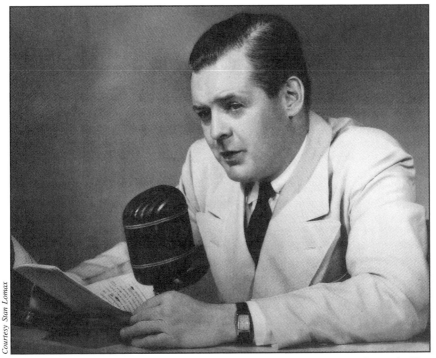

Courtesy Stan Lomax

Stan Lomax, who started his career as a sportswriter, was an on-air fixture in New York for more than 45 years.

Later in the evening, until all-news radio arrived in 1965, it could be quite difficult to get late out-of-town scores of games played at night.

Lomax started as a writer at the old *New York Journal*, teaming with Ford Frick. They shared writing assignments and, later, on-air duties. Both eventually left the newspaper side, Frick to embark upon a baseball career that would lead him to become commissioner and Lomax to concentrate on radio exclusively. Because of his writing background, Lomax, a Cornell alumnus, would avoid using the same word twice on air. If he had to refer to football a second time in a sportscast, it would be gridiron, and a third time, it would be tundra and so on.

"The first time I ever went on the air, it was on Stan Lomax's show. His show was big. I was a high school athlete at Madison and it was my first on-air experience," said Marty Glickman, who had a decorated broadcast career of his own. "Stan was like your warm uncle. You couldn't help but love him. There wasn't a sports fan in town who didn't know who he was."

With the luxury of a lengthy 15-minute sportscast and a love for amateur athletics, Lomax devoted time on each of his shows to provide results and news of relatively obscure college sports programs. It wasn't uncommon to hear Stan not only give the final score of a Concordia College baseball game but also the batteries of the winning and losing teams. Even after a forced exit from WOR in 1977 at the age of 77, Lomax continued by volunteering his air services at the city-owned WNYC. At the age of 80 he even did color on a football game from a parked car at Brooklyn College. The field didn't have an enclosed press box so he and his play-by-play announcer, Barry Kipnis, took shelter during a down-pour calling the game from an automobile at ground level.

The 15-minute local radio sportscasts have gone the way of the dinosaur. With the advent of all-news and other tight formats, capsulated sports reports have become ubiquitous. Time is confined and sports anchors are given 90 or 120 seconds to tell it all. Ed Ingles, a popular morning-drive sports anchor for 25 years, did groundbreaking work in molding the concise time-constrained up-dates. Each morning on WCBS he provided a mouthful with marvelous preci-sion. Restricted to precious seconds, Ingles edited and weeded out anything re-motely extraneous. He was really the father of the sports capsules now heard regularly on many stations across America, including those that are all sports.

But through it all, there wasn't the daily forum of sports talk radio to rehash games, analyze athletes, and assess team management. There weren't hosts taking calls and serving as sounding boards for emotional rooters. To begin with, the technology wasn't in place yet. Full-time general telephone talk radio, not sports, began in California on KLAC, the Metromedia station. The first host to take listeners' calls in New York was Barry Gray in the 1950s. Engineers spliced pieces of tape creating the "seven-second delay." It enabled hosts and producers to expunge listeners' profanities from the air-waves if necessary.

Non-play-by-play shows were limited to 15 minutes or half an hour. In 1947, as an example, WNBC (660) ran the *White Owl Sports Smoker*. The show was on the air for all of 15 minutes on Friday nights. It was run during the baseball off-season and might include football predictions and interviews. The closest listeners might get to going on the air was by participating in a contest with the hosts, Mel Allen and Russ Hodges. Voices of athletes were on air so irregularly then that the two hosts would engage mystery guests in conversation. The first listener to correctly guess the mystery guest by calling the producer at the studio would win a prize. Athletes' voices are immediately recognizable to-day because they are on regularly. It wasn't so then.

Shortly afterward in the late 1940s on WHN, Marty Glickman ran the first one-way talk show. Technically impossible to put the caller's voice on the air, Glickman invited listeners to call in questions to the studio. Marty would then repeat them, saying something like, "Joe from the Bronx would like to know how the Dodgers' pitching staff will do this year." Marty would then respond and move on to the next caller.

Journalism on radio might have started with something as simple as sec-ond-guessing. On *Sports Extra* over WHN, Glickman and Bert Lee would en-gage in lively conversation and Lee might be critical of Dodgers manager Chuck Dressen's moves.

The father of broadcast journalism, of course, was Howard Cosell, an attorney-turned-sports broadcaster. He began local interview programs on WABC in the mid-1950s. His approach was initially refreshing. Cosell would readily criticize. It would start with manager Casey Stengel. Howard didn't agree with the platoon system that Casey might employ. It all sounds soft today but in the 1950s, when newspaper columnists were rather benign, radio personalities were even softer. As such, when Cosell later accused Stengel of falling asleep in the Mets' dugout, the comments were viewed as radical. Howard, of course, later accelerated his journalistic style, challenging fans to examine issues beyond their surface. In the 1960s he was openly critical of coach Weeb Ewbank although he hosted the Jets' pregame show on WABC radio. An accepted practice today, Cosell's frankness then was eye-popping.

Sports talk radio was born in New York in 1964. The Big Apple's founding father of sports talk radio was Bill Mazer. Raised in New York City and a veteran of World War II, Mazer was working in Buffalo, where he gilded his legend, doing anything and everything in sports including wrestling matches on radio. He did studio work, minor-league baseball, pro football in the All-American Conference, and college basketball. By the 1960s Mazer was hoping his career would turn to a bigger market. "The people were great but I just prayed that I wouldn't die there."

"I was working at WGR when one day the general manager called me into his office. He said 'Bill, I want you to meet Mike Joseph. He's consulting our station.' We talked and I end up offering him a lift to the airport. So we get into my car and Joseph proceeds to tell me that he's recommending WGR change formats. So here I am, giving a lift to a guy who's recommending that my station fire me because they won't need me anymore. 'But you're good,' he says."

A short time later, Joseph was consulting WNBC, the 50,000-watt New York City powerhouse, and recommended to its management that it introduce telephone sports talk in afternoon drive and that Mazer be the host. So in 1964 the encyclopedic-minded Mazer arrived in New York and introduced the market to its first-ever telephone sports talk show.

"In the beginning, I would hang around Toots Shor's, which was right across the street and wonder if anyone was listening," said the man who started his career in Grand Rapids, succeeding the legendary Mike Wallace at WOOD. "But I got kids involved and then their moms would call in. It was the friendliness with kids that made the program. It wasn't the diatribe that you might hear today," said the versatile stentorian whose warmth has permeated the New York airwaves for four decades.

"We ran this contest where we challenged listeners to stump me on a piece of trivia. If they did, they would win a prize. I always won and the goody closet was brimming with prizes that we never gave away. One day, the manager came in and told me to take a dive for the good of the sponsors. Everything was just in good and clean fun." The show ran daily through 1968. By the late 1960s WNBC tinkered with its format again. Mazer was off radio but the NBC television folks put Mazer to work on quiz shows.

In the late 1960s, before FM receivers were widely distributed, the two rock 'n roll stations in New York were WABC and WMCA. Eventually, the former devoured the latter which threw in the music towel and introduced a talk format. In 1970 Jack Spector, one of the carryover WMCA jocks, or "good guys" as they referred to themselves, hosted a telephone sports talk show each evening. Spector wasn't contentious, his callers weren't confrontational, and the discussions were rather innocuous if not uninspiring. The Brooklyn native presided over the program into 1972 before going back to his first love, music, hosting morning drive at WHN. It was then that John Sterling first hit the New York airwaves.

John was New York's first opinionated, unyielding, and bullheaded sports talk-show host. He may not have realized it himself but his work, in retrospect, was groundbreaking. Sterling's time slot followed provocative host Bob Grant, who had little tolerance for callers who questioned his right-wing politics. Sterling emulated the man he followed on the air every day and introduced New York to its first, sometimes acrimonious, sports talk show.

Sterling was often unintentionally hilarious. He would have no patience for callers whom he didn't deem worthy or intelligent. If a caller was inarticulate and started spewing non sequiturs, Sterling would sometimes let him ramble while ignoring him. Over the somewhat faint voice of the strident caller, Sterling began salivating over the cuisine at a French restaurant that sponsored the program. It was an unpaid and unrehearsed endorsement. When he had enough, he would tell the caller to "give it a rest!" and cut him off.

Because Sterling was irascible, there were those who called just with the intention of having him snap. One evening a listener phoned in and asked, "John?" "This is John," Sterling responded. "John?" the caller asked a second time. "How can I help you?" Sterling wanted to know. "John?" the cantankerous caller persisted. Sterling then paused ominously. "Let me get him," Sterling told the caller before raising his voice as though trying to reach someone vocally on the other side of the room. "John, John, you have a call." Slight pause. "John's coming," he told the caller. Sterling then used his hands to simulate the rhythmic sound of a man's footsteps rushing to the phone. With a panting sound and acting out of breath, "John, here," he tells the caller. Sterling was either loved or hated, but he had a significant impact on New York sports radio in the 1970s.

"John is a piece of work," says TNT announcer Bob Neal. "He's got a great voice in the studio and when he got to Atlanta in the 1980s, John certainly made his mark doing telephone talk." Neal chuckled recalling the day that he worked a football game with him. They were staying on the same floor of a hotel and the two were scheduled to meet at a prescribed time in the lobby. On his way down the hallway to the elevator, Neal noticed that the door to Sterling's room was open. He knocked on his door, entered the room, and thought they might go downstairs together. Sterling was dressed, standing, and talking on the telephone. Not wanting to disturb him, Neal motioned to Sterling that he would meet him downstairs. "Hold on, I'll go with you," Sterling snapped abruptly, unflinchingly hanging up the telephone. "I didn't mean to cut short your conversation," the gentlemanly Neal tells John. "Oh, don't worry about it. I wasn't talking to anyone, I was just practicing my voice." Neal thought he had heard it all. Sterling might be the only sportscaster who talks to himself on the telephone.

In the 1970s the play-by-play announcers still had great prestige in New York. Glickman, Albert, Rizzuto, and Nelson were names that were immediately recognizable. Talk shows were fledgling and first starting to carve a niche. Sterling wanted a play-by-play pulpit.

Sterling eventually left to do the Nets games and was followed briefly on WMCA by Art Rust, the city's first black sports talk-show host who dominated the decade of the 1980s when he moved to powerhouse WABC. The only sports forum on the air at the time (except for a weekly show on Fordham University's WFUV), Rust was an icon through the 1980s, a period that preceded the introduction of New York's first all-sports radio station. Art had instant recall on facts and figures of old-time baseball and boxing. Rust was smart enough to bring on guests and let them dominate segments when dealing with subjects

Courtesy WNYC Radio

Art Rust

where he didn't feel comfortable with his own knowledge. Rust could also be brusque, unafraid to make strong statements, especially about perceived racial discrimination.

Mark Mason had a strong hand in molding sports talk in his role as programming executive first at WMCA, later at WABC, and eventually at WFAN, the nation's first all-sports station. "Art was the only sports talk show in town," Mason said. "He was strong in every male demographic. He set the table for what's to come by demonstrating that sports talk is commercially viable. Guys would drive home and listen after a stressful day. It was a concentrated period. Art was very confident, very definitive, and always very alive. There didn't seem to be a dull moment. He was the king.

"Art's downfall was competition. Slowly other stations began programming sports at night, WNBC and WNEW and of course, later WFAN. Rust was mired in the past and sports talk became news driven. If a caller wanted to know the latest on the Knicks' attempt to sign a Kiki Vandeweghe, he was better off calling another show.

"For a while, I brought him back at WFAN on weekends, thinking that there was room for a 'nostalgic type show.' But the trained audience was caught in the spirit of the moment. While we were catering to an audience of eighteen plus, the average listener was under forty. I was disappointed. It was a throwback that didn't work."

WHN had a fabled history of sports coverage. Starting with the New York Rangers in 1939 and the Brooklyn Dodgers in the 1940s, it was the home to the great Glickman and the colorful Lee. It was the station that carried the first Knicks team in 1946, the football Giants in the 1950s, the City College double championship team in 1950, and the Yankees in the late '50s and '60s. The 1050 dial position was Marv Albert's first lectern and where Rangers fans followed the 1940 Stanley Cup and their many subsequent years of hockey futility. If call letters were to give birth to an all-sports station, WHN was it. In New York there couldn't be a more traditional and more suited spot on the dial than 1050.

The great irony was that the pioneering all-sports radio protagonist had Midwest roots and that he presided over a format that initially was very unlike New York in culture—country and western music. Jeff Smulyan was and is a Hoosier. A practicing attorney, Smulyan bought a radio station in his home state of Indiana. Successful and ambitious, he and his partners expanded. They slowly built a stable of stations and when the opportunity presented itself, Smulyan's group, Emmis Broadcasting, now Emmis Communications, bought an FM-AM combination in New York from Doubleday. The AM was a sputtering WHN. It had the rights to the Mets, who were on their way up. But otherwise Emmis was saddled with a financially fruitless format.

"We were an FM group. We saw FM as the future and were successful in building FM audiences. We had specific goals for our New York FM. I knew there was no hope for country on AM. I had this wild idea about all-sports as a college student some twenty years earlier. But each time, I raised the thought as a format for WHN, our management team almost got annoyed. We all knew that there was no hope for country. We needed information," said Smulyan, 10 years after the gutsy format change.

An all-sports format is very labor intensive, very costly, and there was no proven record of success. If

Courtesy Emmis Communications

Jeff Smulyan

anything, there was failure. In 1981 Enterprise Radio launched a full-time national all-sports network that lasted only months. Weak-signaled WWRL 1600 was its New York home and the ratings were nil.

Emmis was a successful company but a young one. It hardly had the resources of CBS. "We couldn't get consensus and I thought that the sports idea is dead. But the underlings felt bad. This is Jeff's idea.

"Joel Hollander was then the sales manager of WHN. He believed in the all-sports idea and correctly thought that it had a future. I'll never forget an informal meeting we had at a coffee shop on Seventh Avenue. It must have been early winter 1987. Steve Crane and Doyle Rose of our team were there. We talked about it again. We knew we had to do something. We also knew that we had the Mets and that in an all-sports environment, baseball would be critical. We decided to go for it."

Howie Rose transcended the old and the new. He was with WHN as its sports director when it ran country and an integral member of its air team when it went all sports. "I well remember the day in the spring of 1987. It was announced at Toots Shor's. 'We are launching a nationwide talent search,' they said. At that point, I knew we were screwed. We were heading down the wrong path. Radio is a local medium. The format needed a New York sound. It was a misguided and a suicidal approach."

Emmis hired John Chanin, a veteran ABC executive, who had been lobbying for an all-sports station with anyone who would listen. His general tenets included not carrying play-by-play (feeling it would interfere with any consistency of information), tackle national issues, and hire big names. "His wife came up with the name FAN," Smulyan recalls. On July 1, 1987, Emmis turned WHN into WFAN, and the sports radio landscape was forever changed.

By John Filo, © CBS

In 1996, four years after it acquired WFAN from Emmis, Infinity Broadcasting merged with CBS Radio making its chief, Mel Karmazin, the most powerful man in radio.

Rose recalls, "Emmis had blind faith in Chanin. We didn't talk New York. College football is huge in many parts of the country but it's not the subject of conversation in New York. We didn't have an appealing local sound and furthermore, we were not worthy of trust! Jim Lampley and Greg Gumbel were fine. But there wasn't a New York sound to it. Even when a New York issue was raised, there wasn't the believability."

Chanin seemed to be impervious to the gushing of red ink. He would fly talent in from all over the country to do simple updates. The station was overrun with people, many of whom had no idea what tomorrow would bring. "There were no rules," says Mark Boyle, then an update person on the overnight shift and now the "voice of the Indiana Pacers." "We just wondered whether we would have a job the next day."

In the summer of 1988 WFAN 1050, hit rock bottom. Lou Boda, who had worked for ABC television, was one of Chanin's "name" update people. Boda always seemed to be on the fringe at the network but never reached the top echelon. He was now being paid handsomely to do updates on the fledgling all-sports station. "He was a bitter sort of guy," Howie Rose surmised. "He was bumped aside for guys like Frank Gifford and never felt that he was given his just due." When cuts were instituted at WFAN, Boda was given notice that he was being let go. Resentful, Boda stung his employer on his parting sportscast. His final words will live in infamy. "If this is the 'sports authority,' [WFAN's slogan] I'm going to sing in Carnegie Hall." It was an ignominious moment for the fledgling radio station.

"Yes, we struggled early. Chanin had a network approach. He built a great little bureaucracy but it turned into the Vietnam War of Emmis," Smulyan remembers. "We were losing money and I told Hollander that we needed more revenue. 'It will happen,' he kept saying. Joel was the one guy who was behind it throughout. He always believed in it, even in the worst of times. Quite frankly, we were going to get out of it." Hollander and his sales staff faced a monumental task. The programming didn't have any history. WFAN wasn't getting any early ratings and advertisers had to be swayed to commit on good faith. Advertisers had moneys set aside for stations with substantiated audiences. Hollander had to ask these marketers to redirect their dollars to an unproved commodity. It was like trying to persuade a man to divorce his wife for another woman whose picture he couldn't even display. Meanwhile, Chanin was spending Emmis's money profusely. It was turning into a financial quagmire. "The station lost $4 million the first year and $2 million the next," Mason approximates.

Audiences take time to develop. Formats don't explode overnight. News and talk stations struggled when first inaugurated. In the long run, each was financially viable. Greg Gumbel, primarily a television personality, was doing morning drive, and Jim Lampley, a national television figure, was on middays. Much of the time, Lampley did his program from Los Angeles where it was mighty difficult for him to feel the pulse of the New York sports fan.

WFAN's first centerpiece was Pete Franklin, an acerbic talk-show host who excelled in Cleveland. But the station was dealt an immediate setback when Franklin took ill just before his New York debut. The station had to shuffle personnel until Franklin was sufficiently recovered to undertake his new role. There hardly seemed to be any stability. Competition made it even more challenging. Rust was still on WABC, while WNEW (1130) and WNBC (660) started running sports at night.

In 1988 the winds of change were blowing. Historically, it will be remembered as the year that WFAN took its most pivotal step in achieving lasting prosperity. When NBC divested itself of its radio division, Emmis, attracted primarily by the established broadcaster's out-of-town FM facilities, bought some of NBC's key stations in a number of major markets. One of the stations that Emmis acquired was an overpowering AM, 66 WNBC. On October 7, 1988, WFAN moved down the dial to 66. It almost guaranteed success for these reasons:

■ At 660 on the dial, WFAN was on arguably the most powerful signal in New York.

■ Don Imus would host morning drive, radio's most listened-to day-part. Imus was an established ratings winner and would give WFAN immediate credibility.

■ By moving WFAN to 660 from 1050, Emmis silenced its previous WNBC 66 sports competition. Furthermore, a short time later, WABC and WNEW would give up their nighttime sports programming. As such, before long, WFAN didn't have any sports competition.

■ By acquiring WNBC, WFAN inherited the rights to the Knicks' and Rangers' broadcasts. With the Mets, WFAN now had year-round local play-by-play.

Emmis hired Mark Mason in 1988 to program the station. The company ridded itself of the free-spending Chanin and his unworkable network approach to local radio. Mason concentrated on three areas: maximizing Imus's morning drive presence, improving afternoon drive, and generally giving the station a local sound. "Early research indicated that 80 percent of fans seeking scores turned to either WCBS or WINS. A year later we started turning it around. Listeners were coming to WFAN," Smulyan recollects. "Mark and Scott Maier [WFAN's first general manager] did a great job."

The Imus-Emmis marriage was a godsend for both parties. Mason presided over it. "Imus was discouraged by the neglect of NBC management to radio overall. Through his long tenure at 66 under NBC's ownership, the format kept changing. One day it was oldies, the next day talk. His ratings were down. He had been in and out of rehab. It was almost as though the acquisition by Emmis provided him with an infusion of enthusiasm. Imus was reenergized. He

Courtesy WFAN Radio

Don Imus

worked hard at making the show succeed and his image was back. Imus brought a name brand to WFAN, which was still lacking an identification in 1989."

Mason was asked how hard it was for Imus to blend into WFAN. "Remember, Imus didn't have to make any changes. It was almost as though WFAN came to Imus, not the other way around. The station moved to Imus's house. And let me add that the station's sports niche programming would never have had a large audience until Imus was part of it. Suddenly, he had focus and comedy. Early on, he might have had witty Don Criqui do sports and later it was Mike Breen. In the beginning, Imus might have goofed on Frank Cashen and George Steinbrenner. Later it was the politicians. He's changed through the years but so have we. One of the things we put back immediately to capture the old and give the station some of Imus's old identification was the duck (quack-quack)."

Current WFAN programming boss Mark Chernoff concurs. "Imus has reinvented himself. He's become a political pundit. He continues to be entertaining and engaging. He's now a national figure through syndication."

The New York radio programming veteran, Mason, was also the man to match the long-running, popular afternoon-drive team of Mike and the Mad Dog. But at the time of his arrival Mason inherited Pete Franklin. "Emmis needed attention when it first introduced all sports at 1050. The company believed in the single star. WFAN was going up against Bob Grant. Franklin had the image of 'nasty.' He sounded older, was crusty, and insulting. He would call listeners 'a scum bag.'"

When WFAN moved down to 66, Franklin and Imus were on the same facility. "I just didn't think that Franklin would recycle Imus's audience. It wasn't the same fit. It wasn't in keeping with the overall mission demographically." When Franklin left in 1989 after a brief two-year stay, Mason faced his biggest programming decision. Who would host afternoon drive?

Chris Russo, a strident-sounding New Yorker who can screech and be disarming at the same time, went to college at Central Florida, worked at a radio station in Orlando, and surfaced in New York at WMCA. Mike Francesa, a St. John's man, had a brilliant grasp of sports and encyclopedic recall of facts and figures. For years he wallowed behind the scenes as the brains for visible network stars such as a Brent Musburger. After pleading for a position on WFAN when it was first born, Francesa started on weekends and was later teamed with Ed Coleman in middays. The consensus was that Russo had the personality and Francesa had the knowledge.

"We wanted to put together a station for guys," said Mason, one of the key architects in the building of WFAN. "With one host, the station is limited to callers and guests. With two hosts, there are different points of view. It's more provocative and more stimulating. It cumulatively yields more entertainment. Mike was super knowledgeable and Chris was one who had a goofy little show on weekends."

Mason and WFAN went with the duo, and together they will always be known as Mike and the Mad Dog. "I would drive home at night wondering, 'Will this ever work?' The early days were rocky. We had sales problems. Russo shrilled and squealed a mile a minute and advertisers complained that they couldn't understand him when he read their spots."

In the beginning the duo would fight constantly. Mason assesses: "Through the years, the relationship has been up and down like a marriage. For the most part, they have had the maturity to work together. Both had to travel to the middle. These were fairly obscure people driven into celebrity status. Each of the two's presence made the other better. Mike became more entertaining and Chris more knowledgeable. Each inspired the next."

The duo became the Abbott and Costello of sports. Their popularity swelled and ratings grew. In recent years, according to Chernoff, the *Mike and the Mad Dog Show* has been a steady number one in the important advertising demographic of men 25–54. But in New York, there's hardly a sports fan unaware of Mike and the Mad Dog. Before a big game, they would offer insight and emotion. After a big game or small, the two personalities provided their candid, and often cynical, exegesis. Phil Mushnick, the *New York Post* sports tribune and media critic, went so far as to say that Francesa has become the "voice of sports in New York." And it's hardly hyperbole. Consider that in the heyday of Mel Allen, Red Barber, and Marty Glickman, there weren't any highly rated afternoon-drive sports talk shows. It was the play-by-play men who were canonized and glorified. Today, with virtually every game televised and so many New York teams in existence, most fans couldn't even name each team's radio play-by-play announcer. Yet they all know Mike and the Mad Dog.

By 1997, ten years after it went on the air, Chernoff says that WFAN reaches 1.3 million people each week. "It all starts with Imus. We need a general market show in morning drive. Imus is perfectly compatible and he turns over 50 percent of the audience to the rest of the radio station." In the interim Smulyan bought the Seattle Mariners baseball team. It was a cash drain and by 1992 he had to sell WFAN, by then a valuable asset, to Infinity Broadcasting. Maier was replaced by Joel Hollander, a WFAN original, as general manager.

Through the the first 10 years of WFAN, Hollander would be the station's external protaganist and internal crisis solver. First as sales manager and later as general manager, he would build the station into a $50-million-a-year gold mine. As a deal-maker, he would grow the number of local franchises in WFAN's stable to six (Knicks, Rangers, Mets, Giants, Jets, and St. John's). By its 10th anniversary, the all-sports trail blazer was the envy of America's station operators.

How does the play-by-play affect ratings? Chernoff: "The nighttime numbers are a reflection of each team's success. In the early years, the station was driven by the Mets. When the Mets suffer so do our nighttime numbers. When the Knicks and Rangers made their run in 1994, our nighttime book was excellent." Said Eric Spitz, a WFAN production executive who was there in year one

Courtesy WFAN Radio *Courtesy WFAN Radio*

Mike Francesa, left, and Chris Russo have teamed up to form the popular duo Mike and the Mad Dog on New York's WFAN Radio.

and takes pride in the station's growth, "It's funny, early the Mets carried us. Now, it's almost as though we carry them."

The availability of sports news on radio through the years has made tremendous strides. From no reliably steady source for scores and news, there was first the twice hourly scores and updates of the all-news stations starting in the 1960s. The emergence of WFAN enabled radio to strike instantly. News conferences are covered live and who can forget the Christmas night in 1989 when Howie Rose broke the tragic news of Billy Martin's death in an automobile accident?

As a constant sports forum, the enormity of WFAN has had a profound effect on sports management and the durability of coaches. It has almost deputized fans, giving them a voice, making teams quasi-public institutions. The constant stream of opinions makes it incumbent upon ownership to consider the sentiments of the fans. The station reflects the pulse of the sports fan. Team owners, dependent upon the support of the city's corporate fathers and the general ticket-buying community, must now weigh the views of WFAN's free-spoken hosts and open-hearted listeners. And if the airwaves of WFAN aren't enough, the views and responses of the WFAN hosts, 24 hours a day, are constant fodder for the radio and television sports critics in the local papers, which among other things afford WFAN incessant free promotion.

There was the day when the pen was mightier than the throat, when powerful columnist Dick Young could influence the thinking of fans and team management. Then Howard Cosell came along. While it was easy for team management to ignore just one outspoken voice, Young might have appreciated the incipience of the power that radio hosts such as Cosell represented. As such, he used every opportunity to decry "Howie."

The confluence of cacophony on WFAN might be drowning the sound of the rational columnist. Bob Ryan, the erudite columnist of the *Boston Globe*, doesn't pull any punches. "It's poisoned the atmosphere between the legitimate press and players. The athletes lump talk radio hosts, callers, and writers under a general umbrella of 'the media.' It creates a 'bigger wall.' There's no accountability. They don't have to face anyone. There's certainly no accountability for callers who disappear into the ozone."

Chernoff disagrees. "A host is like a columnist. He states an opinion." Frank Cashen, the ex-Mets president now in retirement on the Maryland shore, had his battles with WFAN and categorizes talk radio as tabloid. "They will say anything for a response. And there's no denying that it creates controversy," Cashen said.

Howie Rose ran a frank pre- and postgame show around Mets broadcasts. He wasn't always charitable, and it didn't sit well with Cashen and the Mets' brass. His questions of Buddy Harrelson on the *Mets Extra Show* were candid and undeviating. During troubled times for the ball club, they would often put Buddy on the spot and the tenor of the program was less rosy and more probing. It didn't please the Mets' management of Cashen and General Manager Al Harazin, and Harrelson quit doing the show.

"The Mets felt I should be a cheerleader. I told Buddy that on WFAN I had to treat the show as a journalist, as an unbiased beat writer. Had this been WHN, I could have played ball with them a bit." The whole episode strained the relationship between the club and the station and underscored the power of sports talk radio. Even if he wanted to, Rose couldn't accede to the Mets' requests that he use his emollient powers flatteringly and obsequiously.

In 1995 Pat Riley left New York after serving as the head coach of the Knicks for four years. "When I left New York, I issued my release and because I wouldn't go on the air with WFAN, they lynched me on the air," Riley said two and a half years after his hasty New York departure. "It became very personal."

Riley says he ignores a lot of talk radio. "Management has to show restraint. It can't go with impulses." He feels it's different for players. "They are more sensitive. I explain to them, 'take your hits.' Let it roll off your shoulders. Take the good with the bad." The accomplished coach, though, is adamant when he hears incorrect facts. "I'll call them on the air and correct them."

"The good hosts have strong analytical opinions. It's not based on rumor. The more opinions, the bigger celebrities the hosts become. Some have agendas, not a sense of objectivity. It can get vitriolic. It's all about ratings. Unfortunately, opinions become facts in people's minds."

Riley says it's different dealing with newspaper beat writers. "They can't make up stories. They have to face you the next day. They have to interview you again for the next day's newspaper. The talk show hosts move on to the next story. They don't have the obligation to face you the next day."

When WFAN launched the all-sports format in 1987, there was much skepticism. Few thought it could work. The late Rick Sklar, a radio programming guru at the time, said, "You can bet that if it works, you will see fifty of them around the country, including a second in New York City." Sklar was wrong. It did work, but more than 50 have sprouted all over America. Most of them try to emulate WFAN. Imitation is the best form of flattery.

13

MAKING UNWANTED HISTORY

STEPPING OVER THE LINE

It was one of those cherished seasons, a broadcaster's dream. Pat Riley's 1996–97 Miami Heat were in the midst of an implausible 60-win season, finishing a remarkable 61–21. Implausible because the summer prior to the season a free-agent signing of star forward Juwaan Howard was nixed by league officials for violation of complex salary cap rules. Implausible because the franchise had to that point never won more than 42 games. On paper, the Heat were mediocre at best.

The Heat were led by two determined superstars, Tim Hardaway and Alonzo Mourning. Riley had won four titles in Los Angeles in the 1980s. Yet many felt that he was doing his best job of coaching with this Miami team, a group still noticeably limited in talent.

Yes, there was St. John's, and I had been its broadcaster for 14 of its 30 straight years without a losing season. And 1985 was indeed colorful. Lou Carnesecca coached his Johnnies to the Final Four and New York was in a frenzy. Louie's lucky but ugly chevron-shaped sweater was as visible in the tabloids as Mayor Ed Koch. The run in the NCAA tournament that year was riveting but the '97 Heat were gripping and excelling at the very best level of basketball.

The Heat ended up in first place, beating out the Knicks to win the Atlantic Division. Professional basketball in South Florida was catching on like the beloved sun. Eventually, the group of overachievers would advance all the way to the Eastern Conference finals. This was virgin territory for the team and uncharted for the riveted community. Pat Riley was the Heat's president and coach. He will always be synonymous with coaching perfection and impeccable fashion. Riley was different than the other coaches I had been around. Among other things, he distanced himself from the media, including his own broadcasters, although they actually worked directly for him. Our group of announcers—Jose Paneda, the team's Spanish broadcaster; Eric Reid, the television play-by-play man; and Hall of Famer Jack Ramsay, the popularly stylized television color commentator—wasn't allowed on the team charter. Our contact with players was very limited because we didn't travel with them and because Riley dogmatically kept his practices closed to anyone other than team members. He instituted this closed-door policy in New York where he coached the Knicks before breaking a contract and leaving as a pariah.

Even though we were together for 90 games and traveled, albeit separately, to every corner of the country, we often wondered if the players even knew our names.

From the day of my arrival in South Florida in 1992, I worked Heat games alone. In New York, where I worked for almost 20 years, I always had a color man for both the hundreds of college games and the 50 or so Knicks games that I had broadcast. The NBA game is fast paced and demands an attentive listener. Unlike baseball, one cannot follow the game adequately with half an ear. There's a geography to the court and there's something to say for an uninterrupted flow, for a simple presentation of the game. Present basketball simply and descriptively on radio, and it can satisfy the fan with a passing interest as well as the aficionado. Too many statistics and too many interludes for arcane strategy are often overbearing on radio. The beauty of radio is its simplicity and the theater created by a listener's imagination.

Initially, when I arrived in Florida, I went through a difficult indoctrination. Fans didn't take to my style or to the solo broadcast. But, thankfully, after a couple of seasons they warmed up to me, my descriptive approach, and my storytelling. A nonabrasive presentation generally ages nicely on the air. After a while listeners feel as though they're stepping into an old pair of comfortable shoes. I wasn't blessed with Ted Husing's dulcet voice or Vin Scully's eloquence, but in time things worked out.

For me, 1996–97 was the most glorious and fulfilling NBA season I had ever experienced. Now it was mid-March and the wins were almost getting predictably giddy. On March 19 the Golden State Warriors, who were mired in another losing season, were making their only appearance of the year at the Miami Arena.

Early in a radio basketball broadcast, particularly when a dominant team is playing a weak one, it's a challenge to keep it interesting. As such, I like threading stories into the broadcast:

Dan Majerle comes right, he's letting his hair grow, now to Keith Askins in the right corner, he's shaved his head.

Dennis Scott is in three-point range . . . Scott owns a restaurant here

in downtown Orlando. Scott's defended by P. J. Brown . . . P.J.
doesn't own a restaurant anywhere.
Hardaway is running the point. He has it at the middle of the floor.
Timmy's a happy man today . . . Hardaway comes right. Tim's
college coach, Don Haskins, was elected to the Hall of Fame today.
Tim comes left . . . Haskins won a national title in 1966 . . .
Hardaway gets it right for Brown . . . Texas Western beat Kentucky in
the '66 title game . . . Brown gets it over to Lenard . . . Pat Riley
played for that Kentucky team.

In midseason 1996–97 Pat Riley signed John Crotty, a guard from the University of Virginia. A marginal NBA player, Crotty was bright, scrappy, friendly, and a budding coach. Even when he wasn't in the game, Crotty would strain his ear to glean what he could during a Pat Riley huddle. He was a bit different than his teammates and it made for interesting radio anecdotes.

So on this fateful night I suffered a near professional disaster. And forever, the name John Crotty will be linked to mine inextricably. I'll never forget his name and I'm sure that he won't forget mine.

Midway through the first half, John Crotty checked into the game. "Crotty works it into the frontcourt . . . He attended the University of Virginia, a school founded by President Thomas Jefferson." A few sequences later Crotty made a gorgeous pass and the hometown crowd erupted. So I added, "Jefferson would have been proud of that pass by Crotty." Had I only stopped there. Had I only!

I can't quite remember exactly what entered my consciousness at the time or what led me to elaborate further, but my big mouth led me to say something that made me teeter on the brink of play-by-play extinction.

"Basketball wasn't invented at the time of President Jefferson but those slaves on his farm, I'm sure they would have made good basketball players."

At the time I made the comment, my mind was also concentrating on following the ball so I couldn't fully measure the impact of my comment. I knew immediately that I had said something provocative but I certainly didn't realize that I might have crossed the dreaded line. Because I meant no harm, I didn't really give it a second thought immediately. But our radio statistician, Bettina Krugler, a sensitive soul, kept shaking her head and finally dropped it to the table. When we reached the next time-out and went to our next commercial break, she just gave me a troubled look. At that moment my pulse started quickening a bit and I turned to our engineer, T. C. Fenederson, who I had worked with for years and who, incidentally, is black.

It just so happened that at the time of my comment, T.C. was either attending to a production or technical matter and had wandered off mentally. I anxiously told him what I said and he started laughing. When I asked him why he was laughing, he said "because I know you and you didn't mean anything by it."

When we came out of our commercial cluster, the game action started again and I picked up the play-by-play. Then at our next break our flagship station informed me that it had gotten one phone call complaining about my comment. At that point I started wondering. Do I explain what I meant? I thought about it briefly and decided not to do so because I had such a strong conviction that I had meant no harm and that an explanation would only dignify a flippant comment. My mistake at the point was not realizing the sensitivities; that the comment could be misconstrued or that some would be offended by it. If I had been quick enough to anticipate, I would have explained my thinking and apologized unhesitatingly to those taking umbrage to what I thought was an innocent comment.

I was tense throughout halftime and, quite frankly, I didn't know what to expect. We've all made dumb and regrettable comments on the air. Somehow though I was hoping it would go away. It didn't.

At one of the early breaks in the third period, I noticed that a WSVN-TV, Channel 7, cameraman was taking a close-up shot of me. I asked T.C. to check it out but he couldn't establish contact with the cameraman. I knew that WSVN was a tabloid-minded television news station and that it wasn't suddenly and coincidentally doing a positive profile feature on me.

The play-by-play became an afterthought as I kept wondering what repercussions I would face. Early on the score was the incipience of a blowout. But it turned into a dandy. The Heat trailed by 20, bounced back and won in overtime. It was hard to concentrate but thankfully, having done basketball for almost a quarter of a century, I learned that in an emergency I could do play-by-play on semicruise control. In that situation, my on-air emotions had to be factitious. My mind kept straying from the action.

After I wrapped up the game broadcast, there was a hush near the broadcast table. I guess word had gotten out that I had made an inflammatory comment. At that point, T.C. had confirmed to me that Channel 7 (WSVN) had picked up what I said and would report on it. I left the building with great trepidation, fearing the worst. Somehow when this happens, it's easy to get very defensive. I was sure that anybody who looked at me funny on my way out of the Miami Arena had heard what I said. At that early point, though, very few of those inside the arena had.

As I was about to get in the car, Dr. Jack Ramsay sees me approaching. He was getting into his automobile a short distance away. "So what did you say?" Now what am I going to tell the esteemed coach and my traveling partner? "About what, Coach?," I said. "About the game, of course." Usually, these were cherished moments. Ramsay taught me so much about the game and life as a whole. I kept our conversation short and never mentioned anything about the comment. I couldn't wait to get into my car to be by myself, digest the developments, and collect my thoughts.

On the way home I listened to postgame programming and as the host took each call, I cringed, hoping that the incident wouldn't be raised. Thankfully, not a word. The Heat game was on WIOD, and the all-sports station WQAM fielded calls about the game but my comment was never raised there, either.

When I got home, my wife Donna was half-asleep and my seven-year-old, Mollie, had fallen asleep next to her. It was usually my job to carry Mollie to her room. I did and then woke up Donna and told her that I was in trouble. After grumbling at me for waking her, I convinced her to listen to the tape. She did and provided some emollient reassurances. Unfortunately I knew better. If I slept an hour that night, it was a lot.

That night I remembered a fable. The King needed lioness's milk to save his life and offered a courageous citizen a tremendously huge fortune to brave the jungle, tackle the deadly beast, and bring back the life-salvaging potion. A bold hero accepted the challenge and was just about to accomplish his mission. As he was about to escape the jungle, he nodded off in a cave where he had a dream. His various limbs were arguing among themselves as to which one was indispensable. The arms said that without them the milk couldn't be retrieved. The legs argued that without them he wouldn't have gotten there. The mouth argued, without explanation, that it was most pivotal in the mission. The mouth?

When the king's hero arrived at the foot of his majesty's throne, he excitedly and gleefully exclaimed, "Here's the goat's milk." Hearing "goat," the king was infuriated and was certain that a hoax had been foisted. He angrily ordered the milk retriever into the dungeon. It was there that he had another dream. The mouth reinforced its importance. Everything might work perfectly but with a slip of the mouth, one's life and dreams can come to an abrupt end.

The first thing the next morning I called the Heat offices and asked for Steve Watson, the team's vice president who was responsible for broadcasting and communications. He was aware of the incident and aware that Channel 7 was going to run with a story that evening on all their news reports at 5, 6, and 10 P.M. What he didn't know was that they would lead with the story. We did two things immediately.

First, I issued an apology, followed by the team. Second, we cooperated with WSVN, who was in search of an audiotape of my faux pas for its telecast. As the Heat office convened on how to deal with this potential crisis, the telephone receptionist got two or three calls of protest through the course of the entire day. I wondered how big a deal could the public make of this?

I had no idea what to expect and wondered whether I would even make it to the next game, a Friday night encounter with the Los Angeles Lakers at Miami Arena.

WSVN indeed led with the story on its evening news, as my wife and I watched apprehensively and uneasily. We sheltered the kids from the program, not to alarm them. WSVN, in typical yellow journalism, equated my comments to those of Al Campanis and Jimmy the Greek, who had both made racial remarks. Campanis, a Dodgers executive, and Jimmy, a CBS announcer, both lost their jobs. After running interviews of fans on the street who were generally apologetic, the Channel 7 story closed ominously, mentioning that Jimmy the Greek died several years after his comment. I turned to Donna and said "I guess that I don't have that long to live."

The local newspapers were next and my name, unfortunately, got prominent and unwanted attention. Initially, the papers reported just the facts: the comments that I made, the apologies made by the team and by me. The talk shows came next and the slew of phone calls by listeners. To a man, the hosts were greatly supportive, starting with the king of late-night sports talk, Ed Kaplan, continuing with market legend Hank Goldberg, and lastly by talk-show generalist and guru Neil Rogers, the highest-rated host in town. The preponderance of callers urged the acceptance of my apology and the hosts invariably expressed great anger with Channel 7's lack of journalistic prudence in handling this story. Kaplan vowed never to watch the WSVN newscasts again.

The next night the Lakers were in town and by now, regrettably, I was the subject of conversation in the concourses and in the press room. Now a marketwide story, the writers were questioning the Heat players for their response in the pregame locker room. Photographers of the three local papers and cameramen of the other television stations in town were preparing to shoot my on-air apology at the start of that night's broadcast. This media spotlight was nerve-racking.

Underestimating the response to my innocuous comment, I mistakenly never approached the players first. In retrospect, this was wrong. To begin with, because Riley had brought in pretty much an entire new group of new players in the off-season and inasmuch as we didn't travel with the team, I wasn't close with any of the players.

They expressed anger and disappointment with me. The harshest comment in the next day's paper came from reserve forward Keith Askins, which troubled and perplexed me greatly. Keith had been with the team longer than I. He was there when we still traveled the team charter. We sat near one another on buses, did some soul-searching on the long trips, and developed a genuine liking for one another. Keith told reporters that my comment suggests "there's something there. Why would he bring it up?" He told the media that the subject of slavery touches a nerve with him.

As game time approached, photographers and television camerapeople gathered around me. Thankfully, I had the strength and confidence to get through it. I apologized and focused on the game. When I wrapped up the broadcast, the media circus wasn't over. The columnists came calling and Donna stayed close to me. The next day, a Saturday, the *Sentinel* did a column that was fairly critical of me and intimated that there was justification for the club to fire me. It was truly disheartening.

But in the NBA, life goes on. On Saturday we had a four-hour flight to Minneapolis for a Sunday matchup with the Timberwolves. Criticized severely and unsure of what the immediate future would bring, it wasn't easy for me to leave a supportive wife and three children on a weekend afternoon to go on the road. By the time I left for Minneapolis, word had spread nationally of this incident and the Associated Press put out a story on the wire. By Sunday morning, when I opened my hotel room door and picked up the *Minneapolis Tribune*, there was a story on page two of the sports section. The nationally syndicated radio and television sports programs such as ESPN were reporting it. This wasn't the ideal way to wake up on the road, believe me.

I did get an early morning call in the hotel room from Donna to tell me that Dan LeBatard, a prominent *Miami Herald* columnist, did a favorable story, suggesting among other things that the sensitivity issue had gotten out of control and that those not familiar with my style—which he characterized as a "stream of consciousness"—could easily misinterpret the intent of my comments. It lifted my spirits. Now I was prepared to tackle the players' angst before the game and arrived particularly early at the Target Center.

When I arrived, I went into the press room to get the latest game notes and a bite of food before having some difficult conversations. The team had just arrived from the hotel. Of all people, coach Riley, who almost never leaves the sanctum of his desk in the locker room, was getting a cup of coffee in there at the same time. It was a good thing and the first time I had an opportunity to see him since the occurrence. The first thing I did was apologize to him. Riley is one of the most focused people I had ever gotten to know. He eschews anything extraneous. Now all of a sudden, Riley had to deal with this and deal with me.

We talked briefly. Riley is not one for small talk. He asked me how I was holding up and I told him that this whole thing was difficult for my family. When I explained that I was about to talk to the players, he asked me to hold off. Not one to mince words, the coach made it clear that there were some players who wanted "more than a slap on the wrist." He said that he was cognizant "of the ground swell of support" and promised to get back to me. I obliged and didn't go into the room.

Riley was a brilliant tactician. During the next couple of days, from what I was able to glean, he polled and lobbied his players with unmatched mitigating powers. On Tuesday I was told to be ready to address the team, as a group, prior to the shoot-around the next morning, Wednesday, at 9:30. The Heat and Sacramento Kings were scheduled for a Miami Arena encounter that night.

Between Sunday and Tuesday, though, there was a related development that did not augur well for me. Word started spreading of a racial invective on the part of Nets first-year head coach John Calipari. He apparently called *Newark Star Ledger* reporter Dan Garcia "a Mexican idiot." The National Basketball Association suddenly faced two potential improprieties.

Occurring in the media's backyard, New York City, the New York tabloids lambasted Calipari and, unfortunately, my comment was lumped with his. I was pained more by those who equated my comment with those of Jimmy the Greek and Campanis. Mine, while terribly regrettable and unfortunately insensitive, was flippant and judged out of context. It ate my heart out.

On Wednesday I arrived at the Arena and checked in with coach Riley who told me it would be a few minutes before I would talk to the team. The players were in the process of taking the annual team photo. I gathered my thoughts and waited to be called. The players hardly knew me and the key point that I wanted to get across is my racially impeccable background. But I kept debating whether to delve into my dad's experiences as an Auschwitz survivor and the gassing of his entire family there. It was too personal and I wasn't sure if it was the right setting. I had debated it for several days and was still thinking about it when assistant coach Tony Fiorentino bumped into me in the hallway. The one thing he suggested was to tell the players about my personal experiences growing up as a Jew. I decided then that I would tell them.

Riley called for me and we went to the area near the locker room. He asked me to wait while he talked to the team first. After a couple of minutes, the door opened and Riley motioned me in.

It had been a week since my inflammatory remark and I didn't know what to expect. But I knew this was my best shot to heal a deep wound. There was a hush as I walked through the door. If a pair of socks would have fallen out of one of the cubbies, it would have sounded like an explosion. The players were all sitting in front of their lockers on low shelves.

The silence was eerie if not anomalous. After so many victories during this very special year, it was a room synonymous with celebration, not one that had the sound of a library and the mood of a wake.

There was no eye contact as I sheepishly walked through the door. Riley took a seat behind me. The players sat in front of their lockers, arms on knees, glancing ahead or toward the floor. It wasn't as though they had rolled out the red carpet in anticipation of my arrival. It was my moment to be heard.

As I started speaking my voice quivered. I didn't talk long. I went through my background in the game, the relationship that I had established with black players through the years, and the years of broadcasting college basketball at the Division III level in an urban setting. I expressed the love I had for the Heat and my bone-deep desire to see the team succeed. I then went through the horrors my dad's family suffered at the hands of the Nazis and finished by imploring for their understanding and forgiveness. When I concluded, Keith Askins spoke on behalf of the group.

A native of Alabama, Keith experienced racial discriminations that a white person could probably not understand. He talked about seeing groups in white hoods and witnessing other racial atrocities. He apparently was speaking on behalf of the group in saying that he would forgive me. But there was an ominous epilogue. He said that he could not control players not interviewing with me on the radio after games. At that point I was happy to hear the word *forgive* and didn't give any thought to player appearances on the postgame show that I hosted. I left the room feeling a bit relieved.

After the sapping emotions of addressing the team that Wednesday morning, I picked up the national edition of the *New York Times* on my way home. Just when I had hoped that talk of the subject would subside, columnist Bill Rhoden was critical of Commissioner David Stern, pointing out that the league was quick to take action against players and coaches for head butting or publicly criticizing referees. But the league showed remiss discipline by standing pat when a coach and broadcaster were guilty of indecorous remarks off the court. David Stern is a bright New York City–raised attorney. I'm sure he reads the *Times* religiously, especially a column dealing with him.

As I returned home, the Heat office called. I was told that Deputy Commissioner Russ Granik wanted to have a discussion with me on the phone. Jay Cross, the team's president of business operations, would join in on the conference call.

Granik asked me what took place. I explained what I said, what I meant, my flawless background racially, the apology I issued, and the meeting I had with the team. Cross told me he thought the call went well and that the league would not act.

When I arrived at the arena, I went through the usual routine, reviewing the game notes, preparing my game sheets, and talking to some coaches and scouts. About an hour or so before the game, I was talking with assistant coach Scotty Robertson when Riley spotted me. Usually imperturbable before a game, he stopped to glance at me. I told him of my discussion with Granik and that I thought it went well. He stopped me and asked that I come into his office where he told me that the league took action, fining me $2,500. I told him that I hoped this wouldn't ruin my career. He said it wouldn't.

Although he never said it, I got the feeling that Riley didn't agree with the league's action. After all, if he, as the team's president, felt that I deserved a fine, wouldn't the team have levied one? I later asked myself what would have happened if Calipari wouldn't have erupted, would the league have acted? Probably not.

What a day it had been already and it hadn't even begun. Now I had to sit down for the game broadcast. I started wondering when the media would be told that a fine was levied. I prepared a statement, in case I would be asked for one.

At halftime, after the writers were informed of the league's action, I was asked for a reaction. I told the scribes that I would pay the fine out of my own pocket, that I didn't plan to appeal it or ask the club to pay it for me. I wanted to use the opportunity to again apologize to those offended.

As a historian of radio sports, I unintentionally and unfortunately made history on my own. I remembered that in 1935 Commissioner Kenesaw Landis had taken the legendary Ted Husing off the World Series broadcast on the CBS Radio Network after he was critical of the umpires. But never had the commissioner of any sport fined a broadcaster.

I heard from friends and fellow broadcasters alike. I even heard from broadcasters whom I didn't know. Each of the broadcasters told me how they've said things that they later regretted. When I traveled into Detroit, Vinnie Johnson, the ex-Pistons guard, asked me if the team paid the fine. I told him that after the ignominy I subjected the Heat to, I wouldn't dream of asking. I was just happy to still be calling the games. Later in the season, when Curt Gowdy was at a Heat game, he sought me out to tell me how this whole thing got blown out of proportion.

Unfortunately, there's a double standard set for radio broadcasters. Talk-show hosts get away with virtually any flagrant remark and it's just brushed off as shock radio. Yet should a play-by-play person digress in an untraditional manner it's decried as having gone above the line. I guess a team announcer represents the club and has to be particularly circumspect about anything potentially provocative.

As an epilogue, whether this incident influenced his decision or not, Riley and the Heat decided not to renew my contract at the end of the 1997–98 season. I've accepted it as his prerogative, wished the Heat well, and moved on.

REFERENCES

THE BEGINNINGS

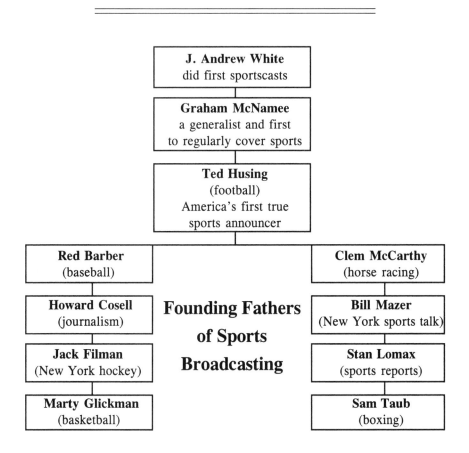

J. Andrew White
did first sportscasts

Graham McNamee
a generalist and first
to regularly cover sports

Ted Husing
(football)
America's first true
sports announcer

Red Barber
(baseball)

Clem McCarthy
(horse racing)

Howard Cosell
(journalism)

Founding Fathers

Bill Mazer
(New York sports talk)

of Sports

Jack Filman
(New York hockey)

Broadcasting

Stan Lomax
(sports reports)

Marty Glickman
(basketball)

Sam Taub
(boxing)

THE FOUNDING FATHERS

Founding Father	Category	Contribution
Red Barber	Baseball	There were others around the country, mainly in the Midwest, who first did baseball regularly. Barber was the first in New York. He assimilated the sequential ingredients of baseball and reported it on radio with rhythmic delight.
Howard Cosell	Journalism	Surfacing on New York radio in the 1950s, he was the first broadcaster to probe athletes, question news makers, and provoke fans to examine, scrutinize, and dissect.
Jack Filman	Hockey	Filman didn't have the consistent pulpit nor did he get the acclaim enjoyed by Toronto's Foster Hewitt. Yet Jack was New York's first hockey announcer and he spewed in rapid-fire fashion. His broadcasts began immediately as Madison Square Garden introduced hockey in the mid-1920s.
Marty Glickman	Basketball	America's pioneering basketball announcer gave the game an identity and a melodic adaptation on radio. He was the first voice of the Knicks, influenced generations of budding play-by-play announcers, and was the first broadcaster enshrined in Basketball's Hall of Fame.
Ted Husing	Football and other live events of interest	Beginning in the 1920s, Husing introduced a methodology to sports on radio, particularly football. The interviewing process with coaches and players prior to a broadcast, objectivity in play-by-play and varying voice intonations are the rudimentary ingredients that Husing conceived. Through the "golden age of radio," there was no bigger name associated with sports broadcasting.
Stan Lomax	Sports Reports	For 45 years, beginning in 1931, Lomax hosted a nightly program with "the day's doings in the world of sports." Before all-news radio stations, cable television, and when baseball was played primarily during the day, Lomax was New York's most popular sports reporter.
Bill Mazer	Sports Talk	Arriving in 1964, the well-informed Mazer hosted New York's first listener call-in sports talk show. Over 50,000-watt killer 66 WNBC, Mazer's show ran in afternoon drive from 1964–68.

Founding Father	Category	Contribution
Clem McCarthy	Horse Racing	When the popularity of horse racing was at its height, American presidents would cut short press conferences to listen to this pioneer's raspy and inimitable call from America's top racetracks. McCarthy was so captivating that he was perennially among the country's most popular sports announcers.
Graham McNamee	First Popular Announcer	From 1923 through the mid-1930s, radio's formative years, McNamee dominated the medium. It was before the advent of the sports specialist, so Mac described any big event, sports or otherwise, from title fights to the Rose Bowl and the World Series. McNamee's galvanizing calls helped usher in the decade of the '20s, considered by many "the golden age of sports."
Sam Taub	Boxing	When radio sets sprouted in the 1920s, boxing was the craze of the sports constituency. It was then that Taub initiated regular blow-by-blow broadcasts that were spiced with verve and laced with exuberance. In a colorful span of some 20 years, Sam covered 7,500 tussles on radio.
J. Andrew White	Pioneer Sports Announcer	In radio's nascent years of the late teens and early '20s, White had the vision to foresee sports as a means to turn the masses onto the medium. This founding father arranged for and called the first-ever sporting event on radio, the heralded Carpentier-Dempsey fight. He continued on air through much of the 1920s, a time in which he also helped found what is today CBS.

SPORT-BY-SPORT AND FORMAT PIONEERS

BASEBALL—RED BARBER

In the 1920s Chicago was the cradle of baseball announcing. The owners of the White Sox and Cubs allowed radio broadcasts from their ballparks about 15 years before regular radio play-by-play was introduced in New York. As such, the early baseball announcers were Windy City names such as Hal Totten, Johnny O'Hara, Pat Flanagan, Quinn Ryan, and Bob Elson.

In New York, Red Barber was the pioneer. The Southern-raised Barber was the first baseball announcer associated with any of the three local teams. There were a host of ephemeral broadcasts locally, but the lords of the three local teams banned full-season radio broadcasts for fear of a diminishing gate. When Larry MacPhail broke the tradition in 1939 and broadcast all Dodgers games, he sought out Barber whom he had hired in 1935 in Cincinnati. Barber was an instant success, developing the rhythm and flow that have been passed on gently through the generations. His soft and warm Southern drawl was perfect for the timeless game of baseball. New Yorkers, afforded an opportunity to listen to daily major-league baseball broadcasts for the first time, embraced the Redhead. Barber called the summer game on radio from 1939–66. On his broadcasts he taught the rudiments and nuances of the game, painted colorful pictures, wove in entertaining stories between pitches and used homespun expressions that were refreshingly novel to hard-nosed New Yorkers. His motto was "preparation and execution." The Old Redhead approached a game meticulously and set the standards for baseball on radio.

Mel Allen debuted slightly after Red in midseason 1939. While Red was building a gigantic following between 1939 and 1945, Mel was not on regularly, serving in the armed forces during World War II. Mel might have been the more popular among many, particularly Yankees fans, but Red developed the blueprint and the technique still in use today.

BASKETBALL—MARTY GLICKMAN

Mel Allen, Earl Harper, Don Dunphy, and others did some basketball on radio. Allen would join a college doubleheader at 11 P.M. and broadcast the last few minutes of the second game from Madison Square Garden. But they never really provided more than a score and a few of the high scorers, and certainly did little to stay on top of the fast-moving action. The broadcasts were generally haphazard, without an ebb and flow and with little rhythm. Perhaps nothing more was expected then. The sport was relatively new. Baseball and football were kings on radio and the game of basketball itself was first beginning to gain popularity.

Marty Glickman (second from left), sits down to dinner with some of the greatest athletes in the world. From the left are Olympic swimming champion and actor Buster Crabbe, Glickman, world indoor mile record holder the Rev. Gil Dobbs, and world mile record holder Glenn Cunningham.

Marty Glickman formulated the language and he had the God-given gift of being able to talk a mile a minute without tripping over his own tongue. He studied the game under the great coaches and employed the lingo of the players and teachers of the game. Marty gave the court a radio geography that enabled his listeners to follow the action on an easily followed grid. Whether it was college basketball or later the Knicks, the broadcasts were gripping, vivid, and pioneering. He inspired many, including two understudies, who themselves grew to legendary status—Johnny Most and Marv Albert.

When the action was fast, the speed of his voice would pick up. When the ball was walked up the floor, his voice would slow down to a deliberate delivery. No matter the speed, even when he went a mile a minute, every letter was clear and distinct. A listener could close his eyes and through the crackling on the radio, the position of the ball was as clear as a swish of a perfectly tossed field goal.

When the NBA was formed in 1946, the broadcasters, hired by the teams across the country, scrambled for tapes of Glickman's work to study for the task of broadcasting NBA basketball.

BOXING—SAM TAUB

Boxing was king in the early days of radio. There were prizefights virtually every night in every weight classification, and they were held in every corner of the city. Each New York daily newspaper was filled with boxing stories every day.

The ring played a pivotal role in the early history of radio. When New York City's first radio station, WJZ, went on the air in 1921, it carried the Dempsey-Carpentier tussle from Jersey City. The awareness it created prompted many to buy radio sets for the first time. Boxing was clearly radio's top sports draw and would remain so for more than two decades.

Sam Taub, a sportswriter with the *Daily Telegraph*, was a fight devotee. In 1926, when Madison Square Garden put WMSG on the air, Taub was asked to describe fights on the air. A command performance, he proceeded to create the language that is referred to today as blow-by-blow. With a thick New York accent, Taub broadcast very emotionally and from all corners of town. After WMSG, he called fights on WMCA and continued to set the standards for blow-by-blow coverage. Throughout his broadcasting career, Taub called a staggering 7,500 fights.

Because the big heavyweight fights were the showcase of NBC from 1926 until 1941, the network used its big-name talent at ringside, first Graham McNamee, then Clem McCarthy. It wasn't until 1938 that Taub made his network debut. Under the aegis of Adam Hats, Taub captivated a nation calling 12 heavyweight scraps until the rights went to Gillette in 1941 and the boxing baton was passed along to Don Dunphy.

FOOTBALL—TED HUSING

While those who followed him perfected his breakthrough contributions, Husing's football broadcasts were epic, riveting a nation from the 1930s through the 1940s. He established the fundamentals, the conceptual and verbal framework, with which football is broadcast on radio. Husing's voice was impeccable and his delivery dramatic. While Graham McNamee was the first broadcaster to do football regularly including the Rose Bowl, he was essentially radio's first general assignment reporter, and covered many remote assignments, sports and nonsports.

Husing was personable, had a marvelous on-air presence, and his work was truly captivating. His career began shortly after McNamee's. He chose sports as his broadcast niche, covering baseball, including the World Series; tennis; golf; and regattas.

Football, though, was the sport at which he excelled. He organized his staff of spotters, statisticians, and assistants, developed a routine for his task, and unlike his predecessor, McNamee, did not fly by the seat of his pants. Husing spent time with football coaches, learned the rules of the game, and set up depth charts for his broadcasts. Husing is generally considered the first to do so. In fact, he was so intent to learn the game of football, that at the urging of his mentor, Major Andrew White, he played football in one of the New York Catholic leagues. White suggested that he even have his nose broken so that he can feel the physical toughness of the game. Husing broadcast football through the 1930s, 1940s, and into the early 1950s, all on radio. He broadcast the first Orange Bowl from Miami. Husing's popular broadcasts of those early Orange Bowl games on the CBS Radio Network helped solidify the New Year's Day event as an annual affair. In New York, Marty Glickman, who worked one Giants season with Husing, is generally accepted as Mr. Radio Football. Yet Husing was first and developed the art that Glickman perfected.

HOCKEY—JACK FILMAN

The New York Americans of the National Hockey League were born one year ahead of the Rangers, in 1925. The schedules were shorter and, much like today, hockey had a niche interest. In the sport's early years, folks attending hockey games would do so in formal wear. It was treated by attendees much the way as the theater was on Broadway. Boxing was the first sport on radio, followed by football and baseball. In addition to the sport's limited interest, hockey with its fast-paced incessant action was considered indescribable on radio. How would a broadcaster assimilate the furious activity and present an intelligible word picture? It was considered an impossible task.

Foster Hewitt, though, brought popularity to the sport in Canada and is generally considered the founding father of hockey on radio. But Hewitt was never heard broadcasting in New York. Ask Marty Glickman about the approach he took as a trailblazing basketball broadcaster and he will tell you that he listened to Hewitt's legendary broadcasts, observed his geographic approach to hockey on radio, adopted many of the corresponding terms, and applied the same to basketball.

But fans of the Rangers and Americans in the 1920s and 1930s, had only one link to their teams other than Madison Square Garden itself. It was the pioneering radio broadcasts of Jack Filman, a one-time lacrosse coach at Yale who covered hockey on radio in the 1920s and 1930s. But hockey was hardly covered the way it is today, from the opening face-off to the final horn. Between 1926 and 1938, Filman was New York's voice of hockey covering both the Rangers and the Americans. Most often, only the third period or the end of the game was broadcast. Believe it or not, only one-half or three-quarters of an hour was presented. Yet Filman spoke crisply and a mile a minute and presented hockey scientifically, descriptively and captivatingly.

SPORTS REPORTS—STAN LOMAX

From the early 1930s this radio sports icon provided daily sports reports over highly rated WOR. Remember, television was still a dream, FM radios weren't in use yet, and getting the latest scores or sports developments meant Stan Lomax. For over half a century, Lomax would open his report with a warm and husky, "This is Stan Lomax with the day's doings in the world of sports."

Lomax started his professional career as a sportswriter working alongside the legendary Ford Frick, who would later become commissioner of baseball. While he did some play-by-play and color work on, among other things, the World Series and Army football, his forte was his reports. Before the advent of all-news radio (WINS in 1965) Lomax was the key late-afternoon source. He announced like a writer, never—or at least it seemed so—repeating the same word twice in a story. His shows were 15 minutes and he was afforded the luxury of time to detail stories and add non-opinionated but colorful insights. Today if Lomax was limited to 90 seconds or two minutes as is the case on all-news radio, his style would be inappropriate.

TALK RADIO—BILL MAZER

Sports talk radio is essentially the last sports programming format in place. It's amazing. Today, hosts Francesa and Russo can be at the Super Bowl in

Arizona, have a guest on the show who might be in Chicago, and still field calls from listeners in New York. Somehow it all proceeds smoothly and effortlessly.

Sports talk has come a long way. Marty Glickman attempted talk radio, if you want to call it that, in the early 1950s on WHN. The technology wasn't available. It was, as described earlier, one-way talk. Callers would ask questions that only Glickman could hear. He would have to repeat the question for his audience before replying.

Enter the bright, intelligent Bill Mazer, who truly introduced sports talk to New York in 1964 each afternoon over WNBC radio. Bill was the first to do so and the program, aired on the powerhouse at 660, was enormously popular. Bill was the perfect man to inaugurate this format in the Big Apple. He was versatile, opinionated, bright, terribly articulate, and warm with listeners and callers. Bill could do anything called for on radio, from interviews, to bantering with fans, to occasionally doing play-by-play. While Mazer moved successfully into television, where he excelled for years, his roots were radio and sports talk.

Later, of course, all-sports radio stations were born and with them different personalities, some brasher and some softer, some funnier and some more opinionated. Sports talk is still relatively young, unlike play-by-play which has been on radio since the 1920s, so diverging styles are born every day.

A SNAPSHOT OF NEW YORK'S AM RADIO LANDSCAPE

MAJOR STATIONS

1926		1935		1940	
WNYC	570	WMCA	570	WMCA	570
WEAF	610	WEAF	660	WEAF	660
WJZ	660	WOR	710	WOR	710
WBBR	720	WJZ	760	WJZ	760
WOR	740	WNYC	810	WNYC	810
WHN	830	WABC	860	WABC	860
WMCA	880	WHN	1010	WINS	1000
WGBS	950	WOV	1130	WHN	1010
WMSG	1410	WINS	1180	WOV	1100
		WNEW	1250	WNEW	1250
		WBBR*	1300	WEVD	1300
		WEVD*	1300	WWRL	1500
		WWRL	1500		

1945		1955		1965	
WMCA	570	WMCA	570	WMCA	570
WEAF	660	WVNJ	620	WVNJ	620
WOR	710	WRCA	660	WNBC	660
WJZ	770	WOR	710	WOR	710
WNYC	830	WABC	770	WABC	770
WABC	880	WNYC	830	WNYC	830
WPAT	930	WCBS	880	WCBS	880
WAAT	970	WPAT	930	WPAT	930
WINS	1010	WAAT	970	WJRZ	970
WHN	1050	WINS	1010	WINS	1010
WNEW	1130	WMGM	1050	WHN	1050
WOV	1280	WNEW	1130	WNEW	1130
WEVD	1330	WOV	1280	WADO	1280
WWRL	1600	WEVD	1330	WEVD	1330
		WWRL	1600	WWRL	1600

1975		1985		1998	
WMCA	570	WMCA	570	WMCA	570
WVNJ	620	WVNJ	620	WJWR	620
WNBC	660	WNBC	660	WFAN	660
WOR	710	WOR	710	WOR	710
WABC	770	WABC	770	WABC	770
WNYC	830	WNYC	830	WNYC	820
WCBS	880	WCBS	880	WCBS	880
WPAT	930	WPAT	930	WPAT	930
WWDJ	970	WWDJ	970	WWDJ	970
WINS	1010	WINS	1010	WINS	1010
WHN	1050	WHN	1050	WEVD	1050
WNEW	1130	WNEW	1130	WBBR	1130
WADO	1280	WADO	1280	WADO	1280
WEVD	1330	WWRL	1600	WWRL	1600
WWRL	1600				

* time share

FIRST BROADCASTS

BASEBALL

Team	Year	Station	Freq.	Announcer(s)
New York Yankees (with Giants)	1939	WABC	860	Arch McDonald Garnett Marks
New York Yankees (alone)	1946	WINS	1010	Mel Allen Russ Hodges
Brooklyn Dodgers	1939	WOR and WHN	710 1010	Red Barber Al Helfer
New York Giants (with Yankees)	1939	WABC	860	Arch McDonald Garnett Marks
New York Giants (alone)	1946	WMCA	570	Jack Brickhouse Steve Ellis
New York Mets	1962	WABC	770	Bob Murphy Lindsey Nelson Ralph Kiner

FOOTBALL

Team	Year	Station	Freq.	Announcer(s)
New York Giants	1934	WINS	1180	Earl Harper
New York Jets (as Titans)	1960	WMGM	1050	Tom Moorehead Frank Leahy
New York Jets (as Jets)	1962	WABC	770	Bob Murphy Jim Crowley

HOCKEY

Team	Year	Station	Freq.	Announcer(s)
New York Rangers	1926	WMSG	1350	Jack Filman
New York Islanders	1972	WHN	1050	Al Albert Jim Gordon Jack Decelles
New Jersey Devils	1982	WVNJ	620	Larry Hirsch Fred Shero

BASKETBALL

Team	Year	Station	Freq.	Announcer(s)
New York Knicks	1946	WHN	1050	Marty Glickman Sarah Palfrey
New Jersey Nets	1967	WJRZ	970	Spencer Ross

YEARS OF
NEW YORK
INFLUENCE

PIONEERS, LEGENDS, AND MAINSTAYS

	1920s	1930s	1940s	1950s	1960s	1970s	1980s	1990s

Marv Albert

Mel Allen

Red Barber

Jack Buck

Jerry Coleman

Howard Cosell

Connie Desmond

Don Dunphy

Win Elliot

Jack Filman

Mike Francesa

Joe Garagiola

Marty Glickman

Jim Gordon

Merle Harmon

Earl Harper

Ernie Harwell

Al Helfer

Russ Hodges

Ted Husing

Ed Ingles

Jim Karvellas

Les Keiter

Ralph Kiner

REFERENCES

	1920s	1930s	1940s	1950s	1960s	1970s	1980s	1990s
Bert Lee			▬					
Stan Lomax		▬▬▬▬▬▬▬▬▬▬▬						
Bill Mazer					▬▬▬▬▬▬▬▬▬▬▬			
Clem McCarthy	▬▬▬▬▬▬							
Graham McNamee	▬▬▬▬							
Frank Messer					▬▬▬▬▬▬▬			
Bob Murphy					▬▬▬▬▬▬▬▬▬			
Lindsey Nelson					▬▬▬▬▬▬▬			
Phil Rizzuto				▬▬▬▬▬▬▬▬▬				
Chris Russo							▬▬▬	
Art Rust					▬▬▬▬▬			
Vin Scully				▬▬		▬▬▬▬▬▬		
Bill Slater		▬▬▬▬						
John Sterling						▬ ▬		
Bill Stern		▬▬▬▬▬▬						
Sam Taub	▬▬▬▬							
Bill White						▬▬▬▬▬		
J. Andrew White	▬							
Harry Wismer			▬▬▬					

351

BAKER'S DOZEN OF MOST DRAMATIC CALLS IN NEW YORK RADIO HISTORY

	Year	Announcer	Sport	On-Line
1)	1991	Jim Gordon	Football	Scott Norwood of Buffalo missed a field goal attempt which would have given the Bills a Super Bowl win over the New York Giants.
2)	1927	Graham McNamee	Boxing	Gene Tunney defended his title, beating Jack Dempsey in the fight known for its controversial "long count."
3)	1960	Chuck Thompson	Baseball	Pittsburgh's Bill Mazeroski's home run in the last of the ninth inning of game seven gave the Pirates a World Series win over the Yankees.
4)	1986*	Bob Murphy and Jack Buck	Baseball	Bill Buckner booted a slow roller hit by Mookie Wilson that gave the Mets a win in game six of the World Series, tying the games at three apiece.
5)	1951*	Russ Hodges and Red Barber	Baseball	Bobby Thomson's home run in the last of the ninth inning won the pennant for the Giants over the Brooklyn Dodgers.
6)	1938	Clem McCarthy	Boxing	Joe Louis beats Max Schmeling for the heavyweight title in a fight that had racial and political undertones.
7)	1958*	Les Keiter and Bill McCallgen	Football	Alan Ameche's one-yard plunge gave the Colts an overtime win over the Giants in the NFL title game.
8)	1961	Phil Rizzuto	Baseball	Roger Maris hit his record-setting 61st home run in the final game of the regular season.
9)	1956	Bob Wolff	Baseball	Don Larsen of the Yankees struck out Dale Mitchell of the Dodgers to complete the first-ever perfect game in the World Series.
10)	1947	Red Barber	Baseball	Cookie Lavagetto broke up the no-hitter of the Yankees' Bill Bevens in the last of the ninth inning of game four to tie the World Series at two games apiece.

* Two separate broadcasts were heard in New York.

11)	1940	Bert Lee	Hockey	Bryan Hextall's overtime goal in the sixth game of the finals gave the Rangers the Stanley Cup championship.
12)	1976	Bill White	Baseball	Chris Chambliss's home run in the bottom of the ninth inning in the fifth, and deciding, playoff game against Kansas City propelled the Yankees to their first World Series in 12 years.
13)	1978	Frank Messer	Baseball	Bucky Dent's seventh-inning home run in a one-game playoff propels the Yankees to a Fenway Park win over the Red Sox for the Eastern Division championship.

TEN MOST POPULAR PHRASES

Author | **Phrase**

Mel Allen .... "It's going, going, gone!"
signature home-run call

Marv Albert .... "Yesss!"
for a made Knicks basket

Mel Allen .... "How about that!"
anything astonishing

Phil Rizzuto....................... "Holy Cow!"
anything from Roger Maris's 61st home run to traffic on the George Washington Bridge

Marty Glickman .... "Swish!"
a shot that went right through the cords without hitting iron

Bob Murphy .... "We'll be back with the happy recap"
going into a commercial break after a Mets win

Marty Glickman .... "It's good . . . like Nedicks!"
a basket by the home team (Nedick's sponsored broadcasts)

Marty Glickman .... "It's high enough, it's deep enough, it's through there!"
a made field goal on the gridiron

Les Keiter .... "In again, out again, finningan"
a shot on the hardwood that pin-balled in and out

Marv Albert .... "Kick save and a beauty!"
great save by the goalie in hockey

THE FIVE MOST DRAMATIC TALENT DECISIONS

1946

After starting his baseball career broadcasting the combined Yankees-Giants package, Mel Allen opts for Yankees when the teams split their package. Through their glorious 1940s, 1950s, and early 1960s, Mel was as identified with the Yankees as Whitey Ford and Mickey Mantle.

1954

After 15 years as the first and indelible "voice of Brooklyn," Red Barber joins the Yankees in the "House that Ruth built," joining rival Allen in the booth in the Bronx.

1964

Allen is unceremoniously and mysteriously fired as "voice of the Yankees." The Yankees nominated Phil Rizzuto to represent them on the World Series broadcast team in 1964, an augury of the broadcast upheaval which shocked the baseball world.

1966

Barber is released by the Yankees after a steadily worsening relationship with his booth mates and club officials.

1973

Marty Glickman, as much a part of the Giants' family as Y. A. Tittle, bolts for the Jets, uprooting the football broadcast landscape in New York. Marty was the link to the glorious championship days of the 1960s and blackout Sundays. Glickman replaced the Jets' Merle Harmon, who himself enjoyed nine fine years with the Shea Stadium denizens and whose voice electrified the 1969 Super Bowl radio broadcast.

THE SEVEN BEST AND WORST MOMENTS OF RADIO SPORTS

THE SEVEN BEST

1939 .... The New York baseball teams end their ban on radio.

1946 .... All three New York baseball teams broadcast every game.

1948 .... The Brooklyn Dodgers are the last of the three New York baseball teams to broadcast all road games, live from the ballpark, officially ending re-creations.

1964 .... New York gets its first telephone sports talk show, hosted by Bill Mazer on WNBC.

1965 .... New York gets its first-ever all-news radio station, WINS. It provides fans with sports news and scores every half hour.

1987 .... WFAN, New York's first all-sports station, signs on.

1987 .... The Knicks and Rangers become the last of the pro teams in New York to broadcast every one of their games live.

THE SEVEN WORST

1935 .... Ted Husing is taken off World Series broadcasts by Commissioner Landis for criticizing the umpires during the previous series.

1941 .... Fans can't follow Joe DiMaggio's record-setting hitting streak because Yankees games are not carried on radio.

1947 .... Brooklyn Dodgers games running past 5 P.M. would be dropped in midbroadcast so WHN can run Ted Husing's music shows.

1956 .... The first two New York football Giants games are not carried because WINS can't find sponsors. Les Keiter asks listeners on-air to call him with sales leads.

1962 .... Wilt Chamberlain scores 100 points against Knicks. But fans couldn't follow game because team didn't have radio or TV home.

1962 .... Marty Glickman's WNEW broadcast of the NFL championship game between Green Bay and the Giants was canceled because of an engineering strike. Since games were blacked out on television, fans had to resort to the network radio broadcast on WNBC.

1979 .... CBS Radio, rights holder to the World Series, removes the local announcers from its national coverage, ending a generation-long tradition of listening to the participating team announcers handle play-by-play of the Fall Classic.

THE DOZEN LEGENDARY VOICES

MARV ALBERT

Hoop broadcasts were never more popular than when Marv Albert, the long-time voice of the Knicks, enthralled listeners with pulsating play-by-play. From the late 1960s through the 1970s, he made basketball fans out of those previously nonplused and riveted those already hooked. He was as synonymous with the Knicks and Rangers as Walt Frazier and Rod Gilbert. With a flair to his staccato and a stylized beat to his animated delivery, the Brooklyn-born Albert became a New York institution. When the Knicks scored, Marv bellowed "yes" with such an unmatched passion that it became a signature echoed ubiquitously in the New York school yards.

MEL ALLEN

The postwar generation reaped the joys of prosperity and from the mid-1940s to the mid-1960s no sports franchise was as successful as the New York Yankees. The team's very name will always trigger thoughts of royalty, power, leadership, and wealth. Mel Allen, forever the "voice of the Yankees," presented all these qualities. Accomplished but warm, dominant but soft, and triumphant but modest, Allen arrived from Alabama and presided in the hallowed stadium booth with unequaled mastery. The Hall of Fame announcer developed a kinship with his audience through a deliberate speech cadence, a caring husky sound and an infectious love of the game. Mel's listeners were engrossed, became addicted, and endorsed the game and him forever.

RED BARBER

Red was first. In 1939 he brought daily major-league baseball to the New York airwaves, forever setting the broadcast standards. His voice was everywhere. Just walk down a street and his matter-of-fact drawl would waft from radios on porches and storefronts like a soft gentle breeze. Using homespun Southern phrases, he delivered with the equanimity of an unbiased reporter and enjoyed a 28-year New York run, 1939–66. He and Mel Allen were the first two announcers inducted into the broadcast wing of baseball's Hall of Fame.

DON DUNPHY

When the Gillette Company purchased the rights to the highly rated boxing broadcasts in 1941, the New York–raised Dunphy won an audition and was assigned as blow-by-blow announcer. Dunphy was the sport's radio kingpin for a score of golden years into the 1960s. While boxing matches on radio are now generally an anachronism, the fight broadcasts then attracted enormous ratings and there was hardly a big fight that didn't have Dunphy's radio signature. By the time he retired, the one-time Manhattan College track star called 22 heavyweight championship fights on network radio.

MARTY GLICKMAN

Marty's contributions to New York play-by-play are endless. College basketball fans of the 1940s and 1950s remember his gripping calls of City College's double championship. Early Knicks fans won't forget the cries of "swish" crackling the airwaves. Fans of the 1960s swear by Marty's riveting play-by-play of great football Giants teams at a time when all home games were blacked out on television. Jets fans of the 1970s, late 1980s, and early 1990s also absorbed his graphic and robust play calling. Glickman has influenced the careers of so many, including Johnny Most, Marv Albert, Spencer Ross, and Dick Stockton.

TED HUSING

From 1928–46, America's first sports announcer riveted a nation on the CBS Radio Network. The gifted Husing brought structure and organization to sports reporting and defined the principal requirements for play-by-play. From preparation to execution, Husing laid the groundwork, developing the process of gathering the facts, reporting them fairly, and describing them with a sense of genuine theater. He influenced many. Marty Glickman, Bill Mazer, and Mel Allen were just some who trace the roots of their styles to the legendary Husing.

Courtesy Sheila Dunphy

Don Dunphy, right, was a popular personality in New York. Here he joins actor Kirk Douglas, left, and Ed Sullivan in a fund-raising telethon.

STAN LOMAX

New York's number one radio sports reporter, Lomax dominated the airwaves with his nightly résumés for almost half a century. He began in 1931 on WOR, where he spent some 45 years. Each night Lomax would provide a thorough 15-minute review of the day's happenings which he would open with his familiar, "Good evening everyone, this is Stan Lomax with the day's doings in the world of sports." Lomax provided thorough coverage of all sports at all levels from the popular to the esoteric, from the major leagues to the sandlot. Lomax's show was as popular then as ESPN's *SportsCenter* is today.

GRAHAM MCNAMEE

There were no roots to study and no predecessors to follow. The popular Mac was first. When radio hit the airwaves in the 1920s, McNamee embarked upon uncharted waters. He fashioned the lingo to describe baseball, football, boxing, and other sporting events. McNamee's enthusiastic broadcasts captivated a nation and lifted the popularity of sports to unprecedented heights. His groundbreaking work and great success spawned many others to follow, to improve, and to perfect.

BOB MURPHY

Bob Murphy has broadcast more baseball games on New York radio than anyone else. The Oklahoma native is now the indisputable "voice of summer." No New York sportscaster has been associated with one team on radio as long as Murphy has been with the Mets. He hit the airwaves when the Mets went to bat for the first time in April 1962 and there have since been eight U.S. presidents and many "happy recaps." Inducted into the broadcast wing of baseball's Hall of Fame, Murph has become like an old pair of shoes. Step into them and feel comfortable.

PHIL RIZZUTO

Beginning in the 1950s when he was flanked by two aversive taskmasters, Allen and Barber, Rizzuto ushered in a refreshing and popular broadcast style of neighborly warmth. Down-to-earth even in the 1950s, when on-air informality wasn't in vogue, the Scooter spent 30 years in the Yankees' radio booth, 1957–86. By the adulation heaped upon him by an adoring public, the Scooter will always be enshrined in the annals of baseball broadcasting for simply being himself and for giving announcers license to break convention and protocol.

VIN SCULLY

Just as Louie Armstrong was a jazz man's jazz man or Albert Einstein was a physicist's physicist, Vin Scully is a baseball announcer's baseball announcer. More than any of his peers, he's enriched the cultural vitality of baseball on radio with a dulcet voice, rich description, keen knowledge, and an inexhaustible reservoir of anecdotes. For almost 50 years, 8 of those in Brooklyn, Scully has enlightened and illuminated. Since leaving Brooklyn for Los Angeles in 1958, New Yorkers have cherished his masterful and mesmerizing World Series broadcasts which have made him an unofficial but cogent and eloquent ambassador of the game.

BILL STERN

There wasn't a sports fan in America from the mid-1930s through the 1950s unfamiliar with the name Bill Stern. When network programming dominated radio, he was the sports director of NBC, the biggest of the networks. On the *Colgate Sports Reel* (1939–51) Stern dramatized anecdotes about the nation's sports heroes with the captivating ability of a Hollywood actor. Bill Stern also presented football play-by-play melodramatically and did the Rose Bowl for 10 years when the game was equivalent in popularity to the Super Bowl today. Colorful and provocative, Stern was also involved in coverage of prizefighting and horse racing's triple crown. He inspired many, including Lindsey Nelson.

WHO'S WHO OF THOSE WHO AFFECTED RADIO SPORTS IN NEW YORK

ART ADLER

Adler served as executive producer of the Yankees' radio broadcasts from 1976–86. His commercial reformatting and aggressive sales effort salvaged the Yankees' broadcasts from a financial exigency. Adler's success set new industry standards that revolutionized the radio sports business. During his tenure, rights fees increased considerably and sponsor commitments grew to unprecedented highs.

AL ALBERT

The middle of the three Albert brothers (Marv and Steve), made his New York debut as radio "voice of the New York Nets in 1971. He was later the first "voice of the Islanders" when they were born in 1972.

MARV ALBERT

One of the most impactful and popular play–by–play announcers in the history of New York radio, Marv Albert captivated fans with his stylized coverage of Knicks basketball (1967–86) including two Knicks titles in '70 and '73 and Rangers hockey (1965–1997) including a Stanley Cup in '94. A veteran of four Giants radio football seasons (1973–76), two NBA All–Star Games on national radio (1974 and 1989), he also did sports reports and talk shows for WHN in the '60s and WNBC in the '70s. In 1997 his career came crashing down when he pleaded guilty to an assault charge in Virginia. He was rehired by Madison Square Garden and began Knicks radio broadcasts in 1998.

STEVE ALBERT

The youngest of the Albert brothers holds the distinction of being the only radio play-by-play person in New York to do baseball (Mets '79-81), football (Jets '85), hockey (Islanders '78-80) and basketball (Nets '80-81 and '95-96).

MEL ALLEN

The legendary "voice of the Yankees" alone (1946-64) and original Giants-Yankees package (1939-40 and '42) Allen and Red Barber were the first broadcast inductees into the Baseball Hall of Fame. Allen also did Giants football ('39 and '60) and bowl games. The Alabama native did 8 World Series on radio (between '38 and '59) and 12 All-Star Games (between '39 and '51). One of the most popular broadcasters in New York history, Mel's unexplained firing by the Yankees in 1964 remains one of the profession's unsolved mysteries.

JOHN ANDARIESE

A longtime on-air partner of Marv Albert, Andariese had three stints as a radio color commentator with the Knicks (1972-76, 1982-86, and again beginning in 1998).

RED BARBER

Considered by many as the pioneering "voice of baseball," the Ol' Redhead was the first "voice of the Brooklyn Dodgers" (1939-53), was part of the Yankees' air team (1954-66), did 11

359

World Series and 11 All-Star Games. On radio, the baseball Hall of Famer also did six seasons of Giants football, the Orange Bowl, and the Rose Bowl. In '46 he started a stint as sports director of the CBS Radio Network.

MIKE BREEN

Breen has been a sports mainstay of the *Imus in the Morning* program. He made his commercial New York radio sports debut handling sports talk on WNBC. In 1992 Breen got his biggest play-by-play break when he was named radio "voice of the Knicks," working with Walt Frazier. In 1997 he moved to Knicks television.

JACK BRICKHOUSE

The Chicago television sports broadcast pioneer was the first "voice of the Giants" when the Giants-Yankees package was split in 1946. In addition to his one year at the Polo Grounds, Brickhouse did one World Series, one All-Star Game, and heavyweight title fights on radio.

JACK BUCK

A St. Louis fixture since the 1950s, Buck chronicled 8 World Series and an enormous 17 Super Bowls. He was the voice of CBS Radio's *Monday Night Football* from 1978 through 1985 and from 1988-96.

BILL CHADWICK

A colorful Hall of Fame hockey referee, Chadwick was Marv Albert's first Rangers color commentator, serving radio listeners for five years.

CHIP CIPOLLA

A color man on the football Giants' broadcast crew, Cipolla assisted Marty Glickman and later Marv Albert, working from 1967 through 1975. Through much of the '60s and '70s, Cipolla was the afternoon sports anchor on WNEW.

GARY COHEN

A versatile play-by-play man, Cohen has called Mets games, St. John's basketball, and has filled in on Rangers radio broadcasts. He's also been assigned Olympic hockey games for CBS and been a part of the network's *Game of the Week* baseball broadcasts.

JERRY COLEMAN

A longtime "voice of the San Diego Padres," Coleman was a member of the Yankees' broadcast crew from 1963 through 1969, participated in CBS Radio's *Baseball Game of the Week*, and the network's coverage of nine All-Star Games.

HOWARD COSELL

A trailblazing network journalist, Cosell broke in on radio, doing commentary on WABC in the 1950s. He later hosted a long-running Sunday night national radio show, *Speaking of Everything*, which more often than not dealt with sports issues. Cosell did the Mets' pre- and postgame shows on WABC in 1962 and 1963, and participated in seven heavyweight championship radio broadcasts from 1959 through 1965.

TOMMY COWAN

Later a longtime staff announcer with WNYC, Cowan was a pioneer broadcaster with WJZ when it first went on the air. He relayed the developments of the first-ever World Series broadcast in 1921.

BILL CORUM

An influential sports columnist, Corum covered key events for Gillette, including 9 World Series, 3 All-Star Games, and 14 heavyweight title fights.

DON CRIQUI

Criqui spent many years as a morning sports anchor, first for WOR on the *John Gambling Show* and later with WNBC on the *Imus in the Morning* program. He did one year of Knicks games on radio (1966–67) and was selected as principal announcer (1986–87) of NBC Radio's NFL package, covering two Super Bowls.

HOWARD DAVID

David broadcast New Jersey Nets basketball from 1987–94 and was a member of CBS Radio's football play-by-play team before being appointed its lead NFL announcer in 1996. His first Super Bowl was 1997. In 1998 he was named "voice of the Jets" on WFAN.

SAM DELUCA

An ex-Jet, Deluca was color commentator on Jets broadcasts from 1968–72 and 1979–86. Sam worked with Merle Harmon on the improbable Jets Super Bowl win in 1969 and was with WABC-FM in the late '60s doing Mets pregame and postgame shows when the station was part of the New York Mets' network.

AL DEROGATIS

"Dero" teamed with Marty Glickman on Giants broadcasts from 1961–1967 when all the team's home games at Yankee Stadium were blacked out on television.

CONNIE DESMOND

Desmond and Mel Allen called the combined Giants-Yankees package over WOR in 1942. In 1943 he joined the Dodgers, where he spent 14 years before alcoholism ended his stay in 1956. Connie also did college football for the CBS Radio Network, did six Giants football seasons, college basketball, and one season of Knicks basketball.

PAUL DOUGLAS

Later a successful actor, Douglas did a daily sports show on New York radio in the 1930s over CBS-owned WABC. He also did play-by-play of local college football, two World Series, and one All-Star Game.

JACK DREES

A Chicago-based sportscaster for years, Drees's radio distinction is having done the first Super Bowl in 1967 for CBS, teaming with Tom Hedrick. He also did the final three National Football League championship games (1964–66), two heavyweight championship fights, the 1959 Orange Bowl, and the 1965 Cotton Bowl.

DON DUNPHY

Dunphy followed Sam Taub as the country's leading boxing announcer, working the blow-by-blow of 22 heavyweight championship fights heard on New York radio. Don served as sports director of WINS for 10 years beginning in 1936. He later did one year of baseball, the 1944 Giants-Yankees package, All-Star Game, and World Series, plus three Cotton Bowls.

WIN ELLIOT

A versatile sports and entertainment broadcaster, Elliot did four seasons of Rangers hockey on radio, joined Dunphy covering four heavyweight title fights, hosted the CBS *Weekend Sports Roundup*, and anchored the network's coverage of the World Series.

STEVE ELLIS

Over WMCA, Ellis did the Giants' baseball package for two seasons when it separated from the Yankees in 1946. He was also assigned three heavyweight title fights.

JACK FILMAN

A man ahead of his time, Filman was New York's first "voice of hockey." When the New York Americans were born in 1925 he covered their games, and the following season, with the birth of the Rangers, Filman provided what was referred to then as "skate-by-skate" coverage.

DICK FISHELL

Fishell was first heard on New York radio in the early 1930s, primarily with studio reports on WMCA as well as college football play-by-play. In 1938 he moved to WHN where, beginning in 1939, he did three seasons of Giants football and Rangers hockey. In 1939 he was also a part of the original broadcast team that did the long-running program *Today's Baseball.*

MIKE FRANCESA

Recognized for his encyclopedic depth of sports knowledge, Francesa exploded onto the New York radio scene in 1988 shortly after the birth of all-sports radio WFAN. He worked weekends at first before being teamed with Chris Russo in 1989. Together they've broadcast thousands of highly rated *Mike and the Mad Dog* shows in afternoon drive.

WALT FRAZIER

A basketball Hall of Famer, Frazier became the Knicks' radio color commentator in 1989 bringing an irreverent, refreshing, and rhyming style, spiced with frank commentary.

FORD FRICK

The eventual baseball commissioner did sports reports over WOR and WINS in the early 1930s. Frick worked with Graham McNamee on the 1930 World Series for NBC and did a Columbia University football package for WINS in 1933.

JOE GARAGIOLA

Garagiola did four straight World Series on radio from 1962–65. During his long tenure with NBC, he was often heard on the NBC Radio Network's *Monitor* program from 1965–70. *Monitor* aired on weekends. In 1965 Garagiola replaced the dismissed Mel Allen in the Yankees' booth, where he remained for three seasons.

MARTY GLICKMAN

The founding father of basketball on radio, Glickman was on the New York airwaves for six decades from the 1940s into the 1990s. He originated Knicks radio broadcasts in 1946, called CCNY's historic NIT and NCAA title games in 1950, and the first NBA All–Star game in 1951 over Mutual. Glickman also did Giants football for 19 years (one season of color) and the Jets for 12. The 1936 Olympian did two years of Rangers color, pre– and postgame shows for the Dodgers and Yankees, and a telephone sports talk show on WNEW in 1971.

JIM GORDON

A New York sportscaster for five decades, Gordon did Rangers hockey and Knicks basketball. He also filled in on the Islanders. On radio, the native New Yorker is most identified with his football Giants play-by-play, which he delivered for a record–setting 18 straight years from 1977 through 1994.

CURT GOWDY

Gowdy traces his New York roots through two seasons with Mel Allen in the Yankees' booth beginning in 1949. The dominant network broadcaster of the 1970s did the 1975 World Series on radio plus four Cotton Bowls, 1954–57; the 1959 Sugar Bowl; and the 1961 Rose Bowl. Curt also filled in on Knicks radio broadcasts.

Marty Glickman   *Ernie Harwell*

MONTY HALL

The man famous for his years of deal-making on the long-running network television program *Let's Make a Deal*, Monty Hall did the 1959-60 season of Rangers color on WINS.

MERLE HARMON

A Midwesterner, Harmon spent nine seasons as "voice of the Jets," including the Super Bowl-winning season in 1968 and the Super Bowl itself on January 12, 1969, for WABC.

EARL HARPER

An Alabama native, Harper called Newark Bears minor-league baseball games on New York radio beginning in 1934. He started when the three major-league baseball teams banned radio, so Harper was the so-called "voice of summer." Harper was the first "voice of the football" Giants in 1934 and did the first-ever college basketball broadcast from Madison Square Garden.

ERNIE HARWELL

A Hall of Famer, Harwell joined the Brooklyn Dodgers in 1948 when Red Barber fell ill. He remained until 1950 when he teamed with Russ Hodges on Giants baseball broadcasts. An institution in Detroit, Harwell has done World Series, All-Star Games, and postseason playoffs for both NBC and CBS. In 1951 he also teamed with Marty Glickman, providing color on football Giants broadcasts over WMGM.

AL HELFER

A Pennsylvanian, Helfer had two stints with Brooklyn, one with the Yankees-Giants combined package and one with the Giants-only package. The beefy and accomplished broadcaster did six World Series on radio, seven Rose Bowls, and an Orange Bowl.

LARRY HIRSCH

An emotional broadcaster, Hirsch was the first "voice of the New Jersey Devils" when the club came east from Colorado in 1982. Hirsch teamed with the late coach Fred Shero for the first four years of the franchise's existence. At first, the broadcasts were carried by WVNJ. Later they were heard on WMCA.

RUSS HODGES

A Hall of Fame broadcaster, Hodges worked the Yankees games from 1946 through 1948, the baseball New York Giants from 1949–57, and Columbia University football in the 1940s. He covered the 1959 All-Star Game for NBC Radio and the blow-by-blow of five heavyweight title fights.

WAITE HOYT

Hoyt started broadcasting during the off-season in New York while still a pitcher for the Yankees. In 1940 and 1941 Hoyt hosted pre- and postgame shows around the Dodgers' broadcasts, then did Reds games for 24 years. In 1961 he broadcast the World Series on WNBC and the NBC Radio Network.

TED HUSING

America's first true sports announcer, Husing was sports director of the CBS Radio Network from 1928–46. During that period, Husing made a science of football on radio and covered virtually any sport of interest to the American public, including regattas, tennis, track, and golf. Husing was the first "voice of the Orange Bowl," serving for 10 years beginning in 1937, and did seven World Series for CBS Radio. The legend also did one year of Giants football.

ED INGLES

Ingles was sports director of all-news WCBS through much of the 1970s, 1980s, and 1990s. He was the first to shape the economized sports report, necessary under a tightly compressed format. He was also the radio "voice of the 1976 Super Bowl" on CBS Radio.

DAVE JENNINGS

A punter for both the New York Giants and later the Jets, Jennings became the Jets' color commentator in 1988. After five years with Marty Glickman at WCBS, he moved with the package to WFAN.

GUS JOHNSON

Johnson was assigned the Knicks play-by-play job in 1997, succeeding Mike Breen and becoming the first black announcer to call games of an NBA team on radio.

JIM KARVELLAS

The first and longtime broadcaster of the Baltimore, later Washington, Bullets, Karvellas called Knicks games from 1986 through 1992 and New York Cosmos soccer from 1977–83.

LES KEITER

A popular New York sportscaster from 1954 through 1962, Keiter called Giants football, the Knicks and Rangers intermittently, as well as doing reports from the WINS studio. He also did pre- and postgame shows around Yankees broadcasts and dramatically re-created Giants baseball from San Francisco on WINS from 1958 through 1960. The colorful Keiter also did eight heavyweight championship fights.

RALPH KINER

A Hall of Fame slugger, Kiner did Mets radio from 1962 through 1981, serving as one of the unshakable trio with Bob Murphy and Lindsey Nelson through 1978. Kiner also did the 1969 and 1973 World Series on NBC Radio.

BARRY LANDERS

A City College graduate, Landers was radio "voice of the Islanders" from 1981 through 1997. Landers also did the New York Golden Blades of the World Hockey Association in 1973 and had filled in on Nets and Rangers radio broadcasts in the 1970s.

CAWOOD LEDFORD

The "voice of the University of Kentucky" basketball team for four decades, Ledford was the "voice of the Final Four" from 1979 until his retirement in 1992. He also did several Kentucky Derbys in the late 1970s.

BERT LEE

Bertram Lebhar off the air and Bert Lee on the air, he chronicled Rangers hockey, did color on Giants football, lively baseball pre- and postgame shows, and reenactments in the 1940s and 1950s. Lebhar also managed WHN through much of the '40s and was responsible for bringing sports to the station.

STAN LOMAX

The dean of New York sportscasters, Lomax transcended generations of New Yorkers, beginning his radio work in 1931 with WOR. His popular nightly sports résumé aired for some 45 years. After leaving WOR and still in his 80s, Lomax continued on-air, doing commentary, news, and even color on football broadcasts, chiefly for city-owned WNYC. Lomax participated in the 1938 World Series broadcast on WOR and Mutual, did Giants and Army football, and Knicks basketball.

DICK LYNCH

A mainstay of the stingy football Giants defense in the 1960s, Dick Lynch has been the Giants' radio color commentator since 1975, transcending an assortment of coaches, quarterbacks, lows, and highs, including two Super Bowl championships.

GARNETT MARKS

In 1939, when the three New York baseball teams ended their ban on radio, Marks and Arch McDonald were appointed the first broadcasters of the combined Yankees-Giants package on WABC. Marks was replaced by Mel Allen in June of that year after Marks mispronounced Ivory Soap as "ovary soap" for a second time.

BILL MAZER

New York's founding father of sports talk radio, Mazer arrived in New York in 1964 to host New York's first-ever listener–participant sports show on 50,000–watt WNBC. He also did play-by-play of Knicks games in 1965–66, and Nets and Islanders games on WHN in 1973–74. After many years on television, Mazer returned to radio in the late 1980s on WFAN and early 1990s on WEVD.

CLEM MCCARTHY

The founding father of horse racing on radio, McCarthy was on NBC Radio's staff from 1928-48 when he covered virtually every major race and triple crown. He also called many boxing matches including four heavyweight titles, all of which involved Joe Louis. In 1938 McCarthy did the blow-by-blow for the famous Louis-Schmeling encounter, a radio broadcast that received an all-time high 63 rating.

ARCH MCDONALD

McDonald spent just one season in New York. But as first principal voice of the Yankees-Giants joint package in 1939, he will forever be ingrained in broadcast lore. An institution in Washington, the "Old Pine Tree" covered the 1936 and 1937 All-Star Games for CBS Radio as well as the 1946 World Series for Mutual.

GORDON MCLENDON

McLendon founded the colorful Liberty Network (1948-52) which re-created regular-season baseball games for non-major-league cities. McLendon himself covered the New York Yanks football team in 1950 over WINS and in 1951 over WMCA.

A tennis star, Gussie Moran, second from right, was the first lady of New York radio sports on WMGM from 1955 through 1960. Joining her is Marty Glickman, far right.

GRAHAM MCNAMEE

The nation's first national radio announcer, McNamee was a generalist who covered sports. Mac covered 12 World Series from 1923-34. In 1927 he did the Rose Bowl, the first-ever sporting event carried nationally. Graham described the blow-by-blow of eight heavyweight title bouts including both Dempsey-Tunney fights in 1926 and 1927. While he was phased out of his sports assignments in the mid-1930s, McNamee remained with NBC until his death in 1942.

LARRY MACPHAIL

Never an on-air personality himself, MacPhail, general manager of the Brooklyn Dodgers, had a lasting impact on the radio coverage of baseball when he ended the broadcast ban in 1939 and hired Red Barber. In 1946, when he was with the Yankees, MacPhail pulled the Yankees from their combined Yankees-Giants package, hired Mel Allen, and put all 154 games on live. The Bronxites became the first team to end re-creations and do all road games live.

FRANK MESSER

Messer replaced Joe Garagiola in the Yankees' booth in 1968. For the next 18 seasons, Messer was part of the Yankees' broadcast crew, the first 17 doing radio and television, and in 1985 doing radio only.

SAL MESSINA

Having started in 1973-74, Sal Messina has covered more Rangers games than any announcer in team history. With the continuing procession of permanent and substitute play-by-play announcers into the Rangers' booth, the popular Messina has remained a pillar of consistency.

GERTRUDE (GUSSIE) MORAN

A tennis star, Moran was the first lady of New York radio sports, participating in Dodgers and Yankees pre- and postgame shows on WMGM from 1955 through 1960.

JOHNNY MOST

The legendary Celtics announcer worked with Marty Glickman two seasons broadcasting Knicks games (1951-53) and Giants games (1953-54). In 1988 Most and longtime Lakers voice Chick Hearn worked the NBA All-Star Game for the NBA-ABC Radio Network (heard on WNBC).

BILL MUNDAY

In the late 1920s and early 1930s, Bill Munday exploded onto the radio sports scene doing numerous sporting events for NBC. Munday called the 1929 Rose Bowl when Roy Reigels ran the wrong way. Alcohol damaged this brilliant talent's career in the mid–'30s.

BOB MURPHY

A New York institution since 1962, Bob Murphy has called more baseball games on New York radio than any play-by-play voice ever. The Hall of Fame announcer has also broadcast the Liberty and Orange Bowls, and the New York Jets (1962–1963). Murphy was first heard on New York radio over WMGM in the early 1950s covering college basketball for the long-defunct Liberty Network.

BRENT MUSBURGER

Primarily a television personality, the talented Musburger started broadcasting the NBA Finals for ESPN Radio in 1996. During his visible career with CBS Sports, Musburger called eight baseball All-Star Games on the radio, color on one World Series, and did regularly scheduled stylized commentaries.

LINDSEY NELSON

Nelson was with the Mets for the first 17 seasons of the club's existence (1962–78), all of which time, he, Ralph Kiner, and Bob Murphy worked together on radio and television. Nationally on radio, the Bill Stern protégé did one All-Star Game, four seasons of *Monday Night Football* for Mutual, the Cotton Bowl, and later the NFL for CBS Radio.

PAUL OLDEN

Olden became the first black to broadcast play-by-play of pro football on New York radio when WFAN hired him in 1992 after it acquired the rights to the Jets. He did the games through 1996.

VAN PATRICK

A football voice for decades, Patrick broadcast radio's first Monday Night NFL package over Mutual beginning in 1972 until his death in September 1974. The broadcasts were heard in New York on WMCA. He also called Army games and Notre Dame football for Mutual.

PHIL RIZZUTO

A Hall of Fame shortstop with the Yankees, Rizzuto joined Mel Allen and Red Barber in the Stadium's booth in 1957, working 30 years of radio through 1986. For many years the Scooter also hosted *It's Sports Time*, a nightly sports show on the CBS Radio Network, and in 1964 the World Series on NBC Radio.

TONY ROBERTS

A Mutual fixture since the 1970s where he's covered college football and basketball games, Roberts has been the network's "voice of the Notre Dame Fighting Irish since 1980.

HOWIE ROSE

A Queens College graduate, Rose has done Rangers play-by-play, backed up on the Mets, and was with WHN when it turned all-sports under the call letters of WFAN. At the studio, he hosted talk shows as well as anchoring frank pre- and postgame shows on Mets broadcasts.

SPENCER ROSS

Ross was first heard in 1967 on the broadcasts of the New Jersey Americans, then a charter member of the American Basketball Association (now the Nets of the NBA). The versatile Ross has since been with the Yankees and Jets, and has intermittently filled in on

Rangers, Islanders, and Devils broadcasts. In the late 1980s Ross also hosted a midday sports talk show on WFAN.

CHRIS RUSSO

One half of the *Mike and the Mad Dog* sports talk show on WFAN, Russo was teamed with Mike Francesa in 1989. The duo have dominated sports talk. His earlier New York experience had been on WMCA where he hosted sports talk in the mid-1980s.

ART RUST

A provocative sports talk-show host, Rust dominated sports talk in the 1980s until the advent of WFAN. Before joining WABC, Rust had done sports talk for WMCA and other stations. The opinionated Rust's area of specialty was baseball and boxing.

VIN SCULLY

The Fordham University alum joined the Dodgers in 1950 at the age of 22, spending eight years in Brooklyn. By the end of the 1998 season the Hall of Famer had been with the Dodgers 49 seasons, covered a radio record 13 World Series, and 6 All-Star Games.

JIM SIMPSON

The longtime NBC staff man covered four Super Bowls, including the first in 1967. He also anchored 6 World Series (1969–74) and 10 All-Star Games (1966–75).

BILL SLATER

Slater emerged in 1933 broadcasting the Army-Navy game for CBS Radio. He did play-by-play football through the 1930s and most of the 1940s. Later employed by CBS, NBC, Mutual, and others, he anchored NBC's coverage of the 1936 Berlin Olympics, two years of the Yankees-Giants package, two World Series, one All-Star Game, the 1937 Sugar Bowl, and the 1945 Cotton Bowl.

LESTER SMITH

The versatile Smith was heard on news and sports. From 1958–64 he and Stan Lomax did Army football. Smith also was play-by-play man for the Knicks on WOR in 1964–65 and filled in for Marty Glickman on the Jets in 1974.

JEFF SMULYAN

In 1987 Smulyan, the chief executive officer of Emmis Broadcasting, turned WHN into an all-sports station and changed its call letters to WFAN. America's first all-sports station, it forever changed the radio landscape. This pioneer then moved the format to the enormously powerful 660 which Emmis bought from NBC. It enabled WFAN to establish an invincible presence.

JOHN STERLING

Sterling did sports talk each evening on WMCA beginning in 1972, and he did play-by-play for the New York Raiders of the World Hockey Association in 1972–1973. In 1974 Sterling did play-by-play for the New York Stars of the World Football League and was later appointed to do the Islanders and Nets. In 1989, after nine years in Atlanta, he was selected to do Yankees broadcasts on WABC.

BILL STERN

Stern surfaced at NBC in 1934. From the mid-1930s through the early 1950s, Stern was the number one play-by-play announcer at NBC, broadcasting college football each Saturday. Stern called the 1938 Sugar Bowl, each Rose Bowl from 1939 through 1948, and the Cotton Bowl from 1950–52. He hosted Kentucky Derbys, did heavyweight championship fights, anchored the melodramatic *Colgate Sports Reel*, and later did mornings on WINS in 1957. His career was blemished by drug abuse.

HANK STRAM

The ex-NFL coach joined Jack Buck on *Monday Night Football* broadcasts for 16 years from 1979 through 1996. The duo teamed for 16 Super Bowls, 15 of which were heard in New York.

SAM TAUB

The founding father of boxing on radio, Taub broadcast some 7,500 fights of all weight classifications in a 25-year span that earned him the title "the voice of boxing." Starting on Madison Square Garden's WMSG in 1926, Taub did his first heavyweight title fight for network radio in 1938, one of 13 overall that he would do. From the 1930s to the 1950s, Taub also hosted *The Hour of Champions*, which included headliners from Joe DiMaggio to Jack Dempsey.

GARY THORNE

A four-year member of the Mets' radio crew (1985–88), Thorne, an attorney, broadcast the memorable 1986 World Series alongside Bob Murphy on WHN.

SUZYN WALDMAN

A New Englander, Suzyn Waldman's voice was the first ever heard on WFAN when it went on the air in July 1987. Doing pioneer work, she covers the Yankees and Knicks beats for the station as well as sports talk shows.

BILL WHITE

Bill White became the first black announcer in baseball history when he joined the Yankees' broadcasts in 1971. White enjoyed a 15-year radio stay in the Yankees' booth. His national assignments included four World Series. He later became president of the National League.

J. ANDREW WHITE

Major J. Andrew White did the first-ever live sportscast, broadcasting the Dempsey-Carpentier heavyweight scrap in 1921 over WJZ, the city's first radio station. He also shared the microphone with Graham McNamee on the Dempsey-Tunney fight of 1926, did three World Series live, and re-created two others. White was one of the founders of CBS in 1927 and its first president.

WARD WILSON

Wilson worked on the New York Rangers' radio broadcasts from 1944–56, did college football on WMCA in the late 1930s, and at WHN-WMGM participated in the popular pre- and postgame programming around the Brooklyn Dodgers' broadcasts.

HARRY WISMER

Wismer did 11 NFL championships from 1939–51, 10 straight Sugar Bowls from 1943–52, and key Army-Navy and Army-Notre Dame tilts in the 1940s. Wismer later owned the New York Titans which folded and later became the New York Jets.

BOB WOLFF

Although best known in New York for his television work with Madison Square Garden, Wolff called three World Series on radio including Don Larsen's perfect game in 1956. He also served as a dependable fill-in announcer on Knicks broadcasts into the 1980s and later received the Frick Award from the Baseball Hall of Fame.

JIM WOODS

A career play-by-play "associate," Woods worked two New York teams, the Yankees and Giants. In 1954 he worked with Mel Allen and Red Barber at Yankee Stadium and joined Russ Hodges and Bob DeLaney in the Giants' final year in New York, 1957. Woods continued his baseball work with Pittsburgh, St. Louis, Boston, and Oakland.

RADIO SPORTS
IN NEW YORK
A YEAR-BY-YEAR REVIEW

1920 The first live play-by-play was broadcast on Thanksgiving Day in College Station, Texas, over radio station WTAW. It was a football game between Texas and Texas A&M. It did not feature a live voice, rather Morse code.

1921 On July 2 Major J. Andrew White did the blow-by-blow of the heavyweight championship fight between Dempsey and Carpentier in Jersey City. It was the first live sporting event ever broadcast in New York and it was carried by WJZ, the city's first radio station.

Tommy Cowan provides the first-ever radio coverage of a World Series, over WJZ.

1922 Renowned *New York Tribune* sports editor Grantland Rice announces the entire World Series over WJZ.

1923 On September 14 Major White broadcasts the heavyweight championship fight between Dempsey and Firpo over WJZ.

The legendary Graham McNamee broadcasts his first World Series, assisting noted sports columnist Bill McGheehan on WEAF. For the first time, two out-of-town stations also hook up, WMAF in South Dartmouth, Massachusetts, and WCAP in Washington. White and Rice broadcast the Series on WJZ.

1924 McNamee broadcasts his first World Series alone and it is now carried by eight stations in the Northeast.

1925 While McNamee and Quinn Ryan broadcast the World Series live on WEAF, other New York stations re-create the Series. Major White, re-creating on WJZ, was said to be only 15 seconds behind McNamee, using wire services for information.

Football broadcasts are now carried regularly with broadcasters White, McNamee, and Phillips Carlin.

1926 Madison Square Garden invests in a radio station, WMSG. Garden boss Tex Rickard arranges for the broadcast of boxing and other events over this facility. The transmitter is built on the roof of the Garden on 50th Street and Eighth Avenue.

Jack Filman becomes the first "voice of the Rangers" on WMSG, broadcasting what the newspapers term "skate-by-skate" coverage. In reality, the game was picked up in progress and only a portion of it was covered.

Sam Taub becomes a popular New York boxing announcer, broadcasting fights from the Garden and other boxing halls all over town.

On September 23, the first Dempsey-Tunney encounter is broadcast from Philadelphia. McNamee and White share the blow-by-blow on the newly formed NBC Radio Network. The *New York Times* runs a verbatim report of the broadcast in its next morning editions.

1927 The beginning of a dramatic radio sports year starts with the first-ever national broadcast of the Rose Bowl on NBC with Graham McNamee.

White, now the president of the newly formed CBS, attempts in September to broadcast the second Dempsey-Tunney showdown from Chicago. He challenges the right of the fight's promoter, Tex Rickard, to give Graham McNamee and NBC an exclusive broadcast. On the morning of the fight, a Chicago judge refused to issue an injunction against the exclusive broadcast. As such, CBS was not allowed to transmit the fight and the fledgling network was badly criticized by the print media for failing to fulfill a commitment to its affiliates and listeners. It marked the first-ever show-down between NBC and CBS and the first time that a court of law determined that broadcast rights are an equity.

For the first time in World Series history, two radio networks broadcast the games. NBC uses McNamee and Phillips Carlin while CBS uses White and Hal Totten, a pioneer Chicago baseball broadcaster. In New York CBS leases time from WOR which serves as its affiliate.

1928   While daily broadcasts sprout in Chicago, Cleveland, Detroit, and elsewhere, New York owners limit coverage for fear of the effect at the gate. Only the season-openers are carried. The loudspeakers at retail outlets all over town attract crowds to hear Graham McNamee over WEAF and Alfred McCann over WOR broadcast the Giants–Boston Braves game from the Polo Grounds.

Ted Husing begins his air work over CBS, broadcasting football and assisting Major White on the World Series.

Clem McCarthy, the founding father of horse racing on radio and later a popular prize-fight commentator, begins his colorful 20-year NBC career.

1929   Bill Munday, who exploded onto the national scene over NBC, calls Roy Riegels' wrong-way run in the Rose Bowl.

Ted Husing becomes the lead World Series announcer for CBS.

1930   The Rose Bowl "bans" eastern radio announcers after McNamee misidentifies the San Gabriel mountains and promotes Pasadena for its gorgeous weather while it was actu-ally raining.

Ford Frick, a New York sportswriter who would later become commissioner of baseball, works with McNamee on the NBC broadcast of the World Series.

1931   Tom Manning, a popular Cleveland Indians baseball announcer, is brought in to the NBC World Series broadcast smack in the middle of the Classic when it is felt that McNamee needs help. Judge Landis, the commissioner of baseball, is beginning to take greater control of World Series radio broadcast talent.

The venerable Ted Husing is banned from Harvard football games after referring to Crimson quarterback Barry Wood as "putrid." The suspension would be lifted in 1933.

The legendary Stan Lomax begins his daily sports reports on WOR radio. Lomax would transcend three generations of New Yorkers, broadcasting into the 1980s.

1932   After apparently pointing to the precise spot in the outfield stands as though predicting exactly where he would hit it, Babe Ruth homers for the Yankees in a World Series game at Wrigley Field. It is reported on NBC by Hal Totten, Tom Manning, and Gra-ham McNamee, and on CBS by Pat Flanagan, Bob Elson, and Ted Husing.

1933   The three New York baseball teams agree to ban broadcasting in their ballparks.

The first baseball All-Star Game is played in Chicago and it is carried on WEAF with NBC broadcasters Graham McNamee and Hal Totten, and on WABC with CBS broad-casters Pat Flanagan and Johnny O'Hara. College football broadcasts fill the New York airwaves in the fall, including WINS's coverage of Columbia University with future baseball commissioner Ford Frick. Bill Slater does his first national broadcast, covering Princeton-Yale game for CBS. Slater's voice would be prominent in sports-casts for more than 10 years.

CBS and NBC are criticized for overlapping coverage of the same college football games on Saturday afternoons.

1934   Sam Taub broadcasts his first heavyweight championship fight, doing blow-by-blow of Carnera's win over Loughran on WMCA from Miami Beach.

Ted Husing does his seventh and final World Series after he is critical of umpires working the Fall Classic. Husing is banned the following year by Commissioner Landis.

The football Giants enjoy their first year of regular radio coverage when Earl Harper calls the action over WINS, including the famous "sneaker" game for the NFL championship. Harper becomes popular as the radio voice of the Newark Bears minor-league baseball team.

In the fall, Bill Stern debuts over NBC as a football broadcaster. He would later have an ugly and fierce rivalry with Husing of CBS.

The Detroit Lions' game on Thanksgiving Day is the first-ever NFL game carried on national radio. The announcers are Graham McNamee and Don Wilson.

1935 Graham McNamee covers his eighth and last heavyweight championship fight in Braddock's victory over Baer in New York.

The Mutual Broadcasting System, linking stations in New York, Detroit, Chicago, and Cincinnati, is born. It rivals CBS and NBC. Mutual's inaugural sports broadcast is Major League Baseball's first-ever night game from Cincinnati. WOR is Mutual's New York affiliate. Red Barber, a Cincinnati Reds announcer, makes his New York broadcast debut, assigned to Mutual's Series coverage.

For the first time ever, the World Series is covered by three networks, CBS, NBC, and fledgling, Mutual.

1936 The Berlin Olympics are covered on CBS by Ted Husing and on NBC by Bill Slater, who had previously been at CBS. Slater later leaves NBC after a disagreement arises over his Olympic expense report. Stern becomes the lead sportscaster for NBC.

New York's local sportscasters include Don Dunphy on WINS, Dick Fishell on WMCA, Ray Saunders on WHN, and Lomax on WOR.

1937 Ted Husing and CBS broadcast their first Orange Bowl. Husing's lead-in reports from Miami prior to the game each year would help secure the long-term future of the annual classic.

Clem McCarthy calls his first heavyweight title bout for NBC in June from Chicago. It turns out to be the beginning of Joe Louis's reign when Louis defeats Braddock for the heavyweight crown.

Mel Allen is first heard on the New York airwaves, voicing Fordham University and Manhattan College football on WINS.

1938 McCarthy's broadcast of the famous Louis-Schmeling fight gets an incredible 63 rating and is broadcast to 146 stations nationwide, including NBC's two New York stations, WEAF (660) and WJZ (760).

For the first and only time, four networks cover the World Series: CBS, Mutual, and both NBC networks, the Red and Blue.

Mel Allen covers his first World Series, working with France Laux and Bill Dyer on CBS.

1939 NBC, which had broadcast every Rose Bowl since 1927, uses Bill Stern on play-by-play for the first time. Rose Bowl officials agreed to end an unofficial ban of eastern announcers.

The major-league baseball teams end their radio ban. Red Barber and Al Helfer call the Brooklyn games which are carried by both WOR (710) and WHN (1010). The Yankees and Giants do home games only over WABC (860), initially with Arch McDonald and Garnett Marks. Later in the season, Mel Allen replaces Marks.

Gillette sponsors the World Series and it is carried exclusively on Mutual throughout the country and WOR in New York.

1940 Bert Lee and Dick Fishell complete their first season covering Rangers hockey on WHN. The club cooperates by winning the Stanley Cup in Toronto.

1941 The Yankees and Giants are off radio again and Joe DiMaggio's 56-game hitting streak is not covered live.

Sam Taub broadcasts his last-ever heavyweight championship on radio, doing Joe Louis's win over Max Baer in May in Washington.

The Don Dunphy era begins when Gillette gets rights to the fights and Dunphy begins teaming with sports columnist Bill Corum covering the Louis-Conn title bout at the Polo Grounds in June.

1942 Pioneer broadcaster Graham McNamee dies at age 54.

Harry Wismer, who would later own the now defunct New York Titans, broadcasts the first of 10 NFL title games.

1943 After spending one season working with Mel Allen calling the combined Yankees-Giants package, Connie Desmond joins Red Barber in Brooklyn. It marks the first of 11 years together for the popular twosome and the first of 14 seasons in Brooklyn for Desmond.

1944 Mel Allen joins the Armed Forces and the Yankees-Giants package is covered by Don Dunphy and Bill Slater. The duo joins Bill Corum to broadcast the World Series.

1945 Basketball broadcast pioneer Marty Glickman starts his regular play-by-play coverage of college games on WHN.

1946 Ted Husing broadcasts his last Orange Bowl.

The Yankees and Giants split their combined baseball packages. The Giants put all their games on WMCA, albeit re-creations from the road. Jack Brickhouse and Steve Ellis were the announcers. The Yankees assigned all games to WINS, doing road contests live. Mel Allen and Russ Hodges were the Yankees' voices.

The Knicks begin their inaugural season and Marty Glickman becomes the team's first voice over WHN.

1947 Ballantine begins its first year of Yankees sponsorship.

Legendary race caller Clem McCarthy calls the wrong horse as the winner of the Preakness on the national broadcast over NBC radio. It creates a hubbub.

Red Barber, broadcasting the World Series on radio, calls Cookie Lavagetto's famous ninth-inning breakup of Bill Bevens' no-hitter in game four.

1948 Bill Stern broadcasts his last Rose Bowl over WNBC and NBC Radio.

The baseball Giants and Dodgers join the Yankees, broadcasting all road games live. Re-creations are now generally over.

Red Barber suffers an ulcer attack while the Dodgers are on the road. Ernie Harwell joins Connie Desmond in the booth, beginning a long and distinguished baseball broadcasting career.

1949 Russ Hodges jumps to the Giants. Curt Gowdy replaces him at the Stadium as Mel Allen's associate announcer. Together, the two tell the story of the great Red Sox–Yankees pennant chase over WINS.

Red Barber and Mel Allen work their last World Series together on radio over WOR.

Notre Dame breaks away from the three-network coverage of occasional games and sets up its own network to cover all games.

Marty Glickman broadcasts his first season of Giants football on WHN.

1950 Vin Scully begins his illustrious baseball broadcasting career when, at age 22, he's selected by Red Barber to join Connie Desmond and him in the Brooklyn booth.

Bert Lee and Ward Wilson follow the Rangers on WHN through their loss in the Stanley Cup finals to Detroit.

On WMGM Marty Glickman calls City College's historic double championship of the NCAA and the NIT titles.

Over WCBS Russ Hodges calls the first of four heavyweight title fights when Ezzard Charles knocks out Joe Louis in New York.

Ted Husing broadcasts his only season of NFL football, working the Giants' games over WMGM.

1951 The NBA plays its first All-Star Game in Boston; it is carried on WMGM and Mutual with Marty Glickman and Hilliard Gates.

Bobby Thomson hits the shot "heard 'round the world" to propel the Giants over the Dodgers in the National League playoffs. Russ Hodges emotes over WMCA and Red Barber is collected over WMGM.

Johnny Most, who would later become the legendary "voice of the Celtics," begins a two-year apprenticeship under Marty Glickman working Knicks games on WMGM.

1952 St. John's advances to the NCAA finals against Kansas in Seattle. WMGM picks up a local Seattle broadcast that aired live at midnight with Rod Belcher.

Jack Brickhouse broadcasts his only World Series on radio, the Yankees and Dodgers over WINS and WOR.

1953 Red Barber, the "voice of Brooklyn" since 1939, cannot agree to contractual terms for his play-by-play services to broadcast the World Series on television, then leaves the Dodgers after the season.

Covering Army football, the venerable Ted Husing does his last season of play-by-play.

1954 Red Barber moves to the Yankees and joins Mel Allen and Jim Woods over WINS. In his book, *The Broadcasters*, Barber implies that this threesome is the best in baseball broadcast history.

The World Series is broadcast in Spanish for the first time and is carried by WLIB.

Jimmy Dudley and Al Helfer call Willie Mays's great catch of Vic Wertz's wallop to center field in the Polo Grounds over WMCA and WOR.

Win Elliot does the first of four nonconsecutive seasons of Rangers hockey over WMGM and WINS. Elliot also joins Don Dunphy on heavyweight championship fight broadcasts.

1955 Al Helfer and Bob Neal describe Brooklyn's first-ever World Series championship on WMGM and WOR.

WINS gets Knicks and Rangers rights and Les Keiter begins his New York play-by-play work.

1956 Bill Stern has breakdown at the Sugar Bowl; it is later revealed that the legendary sportscaster is addicted to drugs.

Alcohol addiction forces Connie Desmond to "retire." Jerry Doggett, a longtime baseball and football announcer in Dallas, replaces him and begins his long association in the booth with Vin Scully.

Bob Neal, Bob Wolff, and Bill Corum call Don Larsen's perfect game over WOR, WMGM, and WINS.

Popular game-show host Bill Cullen joins Marty Glickman broadcasting Army football over WRCA.

Although Les Keiter broadcasts the entire season of Giants football on WINS, rival Marty Glickman does Giants' NFL title game win over Bears. A sponsor conflict developed whereby Keiter couldn't work.

1957 Phil Rizzuto begins his 30-year career as a member of the Yankees' radio crew, joining broadcast legends Mel Allen and Red Barber.

Jim Woods joins Russ Hodges at the Polo Grounds. Together they do the Giants' final year in New York over WMCA. Woods closed out the final broadcast wishing listeners a warm, "God bless you." Hodges would move with the club to San Francisco, Woods would go to Pittsburgh.

Vin Scully completes his final year in Brooklyn. He and Doggett would continue in Los Angeles.

After 19 years on Mutual, NBC acquires the exclusive rights to the World Series.

1958   Les Keiter keeps the National League alive in New York with popular re-creations of Giants baseball games from San Francisco over WINS.

The game that historians claim "made" the National Football League, Baltimore's over-time win over the Giants at Yankee Stadium, is called by Les Keiter on WCBS.

1959   Howard Cosell broadcasts his first heavyweight title fight when he joins Les Keiter on Ingemar Johansson's KO of Floyd Patterson in Yankee Stadium. Keiter and Cosell would cover five heavyweight tittle bouts together.

Monty Hall, a Canadian who later gained fame as host of TV's *Let's Make A Deal*, does his only season of color on Rangers radio broadcasts, joining Jim Gordon on WINS.

Mel Allen does his last-ever World Series on radio, joining By Saam on WNBC and NBC radio for the Dodgers–White Sox matchup.

1960   On WNBC, WHN, and NBC Radio Network, Chuck Thompson misidentifies pitcher Ralph Terry as Art Ditmar in calling Bill Mazeroski's World Series–winning home run in the ninth inning of the seventh game of Pittsburgh's victory over the Yankees. It would later result in a lawsuit by Ditmar.

1961   The Yankees' radio broadcasts move to WCBS and Phil Rizzuto calls Roger Maris's record-setting 61st home run on the final day of the season.

The Giants move to WNEW, beginning a record-setting 32-year association with the station. Marty Glickman rejoins the broadcasts and is teamed up with Al DeRogatis, creating local radio football's most popular broadcast duo ever.

1962   The deaths of broadcast pioneers Ted Husing and Clem McCarthy.

Wilt Chamberlain of the Philadelphia Warriors scores a record 100 points in a single game against the New York Knicks. Sadly, the game is neither on radio or television in New York.

George Kell and Joe Garagiola team to cover the 1962 World Series on NBC. It's the only time that the World Series radio booth is made up exclusively of ex-major-leaguers.

The Mets are formed and the trio of Lindsey Nelson, Bob Murphy, and Ralph Kiner are hired as broadcasters. They would be together for 17 seasons. WABC becomes the Mets' first station.

The football Giants advance to the NFL championship game against Green Bay, but due to an engineering strike at WNEW, the Glickman-DeRogatis broadcast is canceled.

1963   Over WCBS radio, 21-year-old Marv Albert makes his New York Knicks debut, filling in for Marty Glickman on Knicks-Celtics game, and on Rangers-Detroit game, substituting for Jim Gordon. It would be Glickman's 11th and final season with the Knicks.

1964   Bill Mazer arrives from Buffalo, introducing New York to sports talk on WNBC radio.

The Knicks once again complete a season of not being on radio at all.

Mel Allen is fired mysteriously at the end of the baseball season, ending an indelible 22-year tenure as "voice of the Yankees."

With Les Keiter, Howard Cosell, and football great Jim Brown broadcasting on WABC and throughout the country, Cassius Clay knocks out Sonny Liston in Miami Beach to become heavyweight champion of the world.

1965   WINS goes all news, giving sports fans scores and updates every half hour, 24 hours a day.

Joe Garagiola replaces Mel Allen at Yankee Stadium.

Russ Hodges travels to Lewiston, Maine, and calls Clay's knock out in his rematch with Liston. It was Hodges' last title fight.

Lindsey Nelson broadcasts play-by-play from the very apex of the newly opened Astro-dome when the Mets visit Houston.

Marv Albert is appointed "voice of the Rangers" on WHN Radio.

1966   Major J. Andrew White, pioneer broadcaster, who described the first-ever live sporting event, dies in California.

Jim Simpson broadcasts the first of 10 straight baseball All-Star Games on WNBC and the NBC Radio Network.

The Yankees finish in last place and interest in the team dwindles considerably. Red Barber is fired after the season, ending 32 years as a major-league baseball broadcaster.

Vin Scully does his first-ever World Series on radio.

1967   WCBS becomes an all-news station providing fans with another option to obtain up-to-date sports information.

The first Super Bowl is played and it is carried by both CBS and NBC Radio. Jack Drees and Tom Hedrick are heard over WCBS and Jim Simpson and George Ratterman call the game on WNBC.

The American Basketball Association starts. The area franchise, the New Jersey Americans, has its games on WJRZ with Spencer Ross.

1968   Joe Garagiola goes to work full time for NBC and he's replaced in the Yankees' booth by Frank Messer, who would serve for 18 years.

Merle Harmon and Sam DeLuca call the Jets' Super Bowl season on WABC.

1969   The Mets' trio of announcers, Lindsey Nelson, Bob Murphy, and Ralph Kiner call the team's miracle season. Nelson would participate in the Series' telecast and Kiner in the national radio broadcast, which was heard on WNBC and WJRZ. Murphy would not be included in any World Series broadcast.

1970   Marv Albert thrills New Yorkers with his broadcasts of the Knicks' championship season on WHN Radio.

1971   Broadcast giant Bill Stern dies.

Bill White is hired by the Yankees as a broadcaster, becoming the first black in a local baseball booth. He joins Phil Rizzuto and Frank Messer.

For the first time since 1945, not all Yankees games are on radio. The team's new station, WMCA, would not broadcast all West Coast night games.

The first of Marv Albert's brothers is heard when Al is hired as play-by-play announcer for the New York Nets' basketball broadcasts on WHN.

1972   After having its games carried on the weak signal of WJRZ/WWDJ (970), the Mets are back on a 50,000-watt radio station when an agreement is made with WHN.

Marty Glickman does his last season of Giants football.

Merle Harmon does his last season of Jets football.

Al Albert becomes the first voice of the newly born New York Islanders on WHN.

1973   In a shocking move, Marty Glickman, synonymous with the football Giants, moves over to broadcast the play-by-play of the Jets on WOR Radio.

Marv Albert, popular voice of the Knicks and Rangers, is selected as "voice of the Giants" on WNEW Radio.

Albert and John Andariese call the Knicks' second-ever NBA championship.

The Mets win the National League pennant with Nelson, Murphy, and Kiner presiding over the airwaves. Nelson is again involved in the telecast of the Series while Kiner is on WNBC, WHN, and NBC Radio. Murphy is on the sidelines.

1974   The World Football League is formed to compete with the established National Football League. John Sterling calls the games of the New York Stars on WMCA until the team folds in midseason.

Al Albert and Bill Mazer call the first of the Nets' two ABA titles on WHN.

1975   The Mets switch stations to WNEW which agrees to carry all games except those played on weekday afternoons. These games are farmed out to noncommercial WNYC, the city-owned radio station.

The 1975 World Series is aired in New York on FM only, WNBC-FM. Since the first Series on radio in 1921, it's the first not to be carried on a New York AM station.

1976   John Sterling calls the Nets' second and last ABA championship over WMCA.

CBS gets the rights to the World Series from NBC. WCBS and WMCA carry the Yankees-Cincinnati matchup called by Bill White, Marty Brennaman, and Win Elliot.

Marv Albert broadcasts his fourth and final year of Giants football on radio.

1977   Stan Lomax's 45-year career at WOR ends. At age 78, Lomax begins doing features on WNYC.

Jim Gordon takes over Giants play-by-play, the first of 18 consecutive seasons with the football team.

1978   The inseparable trio of Lindsey Nelson, Bob Murphy, and Ralph Kiner are together for the final season. Nelson leaves following the season for the San Francisco Giants.

The Yankees move to WINS for the first of three seasons.

The Nets and Islanders are no longer dually owned. Under separate ownership, the teams split stations and, for the first time, each team is able to run every game, home and away. The Islanders stay on WMCA and the Nets move to WVNJ.

1979   Steve Albert is selected by the Mets to replace Lindsey Nelson. Albert had no major-league baseball experience.

Jack Buck and Hank Stram broadcast the first of 16 Super Bowls together for CBS radio.

Sam Taub, the founding father of boxing on radio, dies.

CBS radio, rights holder to the World Series, completely eliminates the teams' local announcers on World Series broadcasts.

1980   A decade of greater commercialism begins as rights fees begin to increase considerably. One-and-a-half-minute breaks between innings and during time-outs of football and basketball games become common.

On WMCA Bob Lawrence calls the first of the Islanders' four straight Stanley Cup championships.

With nightly shows over WABC, Art Rust begins his dominance as the decade's most-listened-to sports talk host on New York radio.

While still a part of Rangers radio broadcasts, Marv Albert misses an increasing number of broadcasts because of other swelling commitments.

1981   The Yankees begin the longest association with any radio station they have ever had when the games move to WABC.

Ralph Kiner broadcasts his final year of Mets baseball on radio.

Enterprise Radio takes the air as a national 24-hour sports network. The venture would fail after nine months. WWRL (1600) is the New York affiliate.

1982   The Mets' broadcast landscape is uprooted when the announcer assignments are split between radio and television. Ralph Kiner goes to television exclusively, and after working television as well as radio for 20 years, Bob Murphy works radio only. Steve LaMar becomes Murphy's first associate in the booth.

Colorado's National Hockey League franchise moves to New Jersey and is named the Devils. Larry Hirsch and Fred Shero team together for the first four years of the new franchise. The team is on WVNJ the first year.

1983   The United States Football League attempts to rival the National Football League. The New Jersey Generals, later owned by real estate tycoon Donald Trump, enter into an agreement with WOR and Charley Steiner handles the play-by-play.

Barry Landers and Jean Potvin describe the Islanders' fourth straight Stanley Cup over WOR radio.

1984   For the first time ever, a 50,000-watt radio station makes a commitment to carry one college basketball team exclusively when WCBS begins to broadcast all the games of the St. John's University Redmen.

1985   Marv Albert begins his last season broadcasting Knicks games on radio.

Steve Albert broadcasts Jets games on WABC, becoming the only announcer ever to be the radio voice of a New York baseball team (the Mets), a basketball team (the Nets), a hockey team (the Islanders), and now a football team (the Jets).

The esteemed boxing commentator Don Dunphy calls his last heavyweight fight ever, Spinks over Holmes, on WNBC Radio. He did one round of blow-by-blow.

NBC Radio gets the NFL national package and keeps it for two years before it's reacquired by CBS. Don Criqui and Bob Trumpy call the action.

1986   The Mets galvanize New York winning the World Series from the Boston Red Sox. Bob Murphy calls his first Series on the team's local outlet, WHN, joining colleague Gary Thorne.

The Giants' march to their first Super Bowl championship begins with Jim Gordon and Dick Lynch calling the kicks, passes, and rushes over WNEW.

Jim Karvellas, who had worked Knicks games on cable, is moved to radio succeeding Marv Albert, now assigned both cable and Knicks telecasts. Karvellas, spending the first of six radio seasons with the Knicks is teamed with Ernie Grunfeld.

Phil Rizzuto broadcasts his final year of Yankees radio.

1987   All-sports radio is born in New York when Emmis Broadcasting, owners of country-formatted WHN, turns the station into sports news and play-by-play 24 hours a day. The station's call letters are, appropriately, WFAN.

For the first time ever, all Knicks and Rangers games are carried live on radio. The primary station is WNBC with Knicks conflicts moving to WFAN and Rangers conflicts going to WEVD-FM.

Stan Lomax, a New York radio sports mainstay for almost 50 years, dies.

1988   Emmis buys radio stations owned by NBC, including powerhouse WNBC and moves its all-sports format to the clear-channel signal at 660 on the AM dial. In combining sports with popular morning host Don Imus, the station is an instant success.

As described by veteran announcer Jack Buck, an almost-lame Kirk Gibson hits a home run in the last of the ninth inning to give the Dodgers a World Series win over the Oakland A's.

1989   WFAN program director Mark Mason pairs Mike Francesa and Chris Russo in afternoon drive. The two would become New York's most highly rated sports talk radio team ever.

Jack Buck and Johnny Bench call the San Francisco–Oakland World Series on WFAN radio when Candlestick Park is rocked by an earthquake.

1990   Marty Glickman begins his sixth decade of broadcasting sports on New York radio.

After serving as NBC's top baseball announcer on television, Vin Scully returns to WFAN and CBS radio to broadcast the World Series.

1991   The Giants win the Super Bowl on WNEW with Jim Gordon, Karl Nelson, and Dick Lynch.

A bond is formed between WFAN and WEVD, a 50,000-watt station at 1050 on the AM dial, whereby WEVD airs "conflict" broadcasts of Mets, Knicks, Rangers, and St. John's games. This FAN II type concept provides unprecedented play-by-play coverage for metropolitan-area fans.

1992   The Knicks defeat the Detroit Pistons in the first round of the playoffs and the team's two radio announcers, Jim Karvellas and Walt Frazier, get into an on-air verbal spat over the merits of the achievement.

The esteemed Red Barber dies.

After the completion of the Jets' football season and after a long and distinguished career, Marty Glickman retires from on-air broadcasting.

ESPN Radio is born and is heard over WFAN on weekends. Programming is long form featuring chatty hosts and news-maker interviews.

Cawood Ledford, the longtime "voice of the NCAA Final Four" championships retires. He's replaced by John Rooney.

1993 WFAN acquires rights to the Jets, and its stable now includes Mets, Knicks, Rangers, St. John's, Jets, the World Series, and the Super Bowl.

1994 At last the Rangers win the Stanley Cup as described by Marv Albert, Howie Rose, and Sal Messina on WFAN.

For the first time since 1920, there is no World Series on radio because it was cancelled due to a players' lockout.

The second generation of Alberts hits the New York airwaves when Marv's son, Kenny, is assigned to the Rangers' radio team.

1995 Mike Miller and Sherry Ross call the Devils' games on WABC as they win the Stanley Cup for the first time.

Howard Cosell, who pioneered sports broadcast journalism on radio in the 1950s, dies.

Lindsey Nelson, a Mets voice for 17 years and longtime radio football broadcaster, dies.

1996 Jack Buck and Hank Stram broadcast their last Super Bowl together. The popular duo retire.

The "voice of baseball," Mel Allen, dies.

1997 Madison Square Garden acquires rights to Yankees radio broadcasts. Games are kept on WABC.

A second all-sports station is born in New York, WJWR, 620 on the AM dial.

Barry Landers is dropped unceremoniously as voice of Islanders.

ESPN Radio announces that it acquired rights to Major League Baseball broadcasts from CBS beginning in 1998.

The broadcast and sports worlds are shocked when play-by-play icon Marv Albert is indicted on sodomy and assault charges. He later pleads guilty to the assault charge, is fired by NBC television, and resigns from the MSG Network.

1998 Beth Mowins becomes first woman to broadcast play-by-play of NBA games when she calls a Seattle–Los Angeles game nationally on ESPN Radio.

Marv Albert is appointed to the radio booth of the New York Knicks.

Broadcasters Harry Caray, Jack Brickhouse, Don Dunphy, and Win Elliot die.

HEAVENLY VOICES

Birth and Death Years of Radio Sports Personalities

Mel Allen .... (1913–96)	Win Elliot .... (1915–98)	Graham McNamee (1888–1942)
Andre Baruch .... (1908–91)	Jack Filman .... (1897–40)	Johnny Most .... (1923–1993)
Red Barber .... (1908–92)	Ford Frick .... (1894–1978)	Bill Munday .... (1903–1965)
Jack Brickhouse ...... (1916–98)	Earl Harper .... (1903–68)	Lindsey Nelson .... (1919–95)
Harry Caray .... (1916–98)	Al Helfer .... (1912–75)	Van Patrick .... (1916–1974)
Chip Cipolla .... (1930–94)	Russ Hodges .... (1911–71)	Bill Slater .... (1903–1965)
Bill Corum .... (1893–1958)	Waite Hoyt .... (1899–1985)	Bill Stern .... (1907–1971)
Howard Cosell .... (1918–95)	Ted Husing .... (1901–62)	Sam Taub .... (1887–1979)
Al DeRogatis .... (1927–95)	Bert Lee .... (1904–72)	J. Andrew White .. (1889–1966)
Connie Desmond ..... (1908–83)	Stan Lomax .... (1899–1987)	Harry Wismer .... (1911–67)
Jerry Doggett .... (1916–97)	Clem McCarthy ... (1882–1962)	Jim Woods .... (1916–88)
Paul Douglas .... (1907–59)	Arch McDonald ..... (1901–60)	
Don Dunphy .... (1908–98)	Gordon McLendon .. (1921–86)	

WFAN STARTING LINEUP 1987

Monday through Friday

6–10 A.M. .... Greg Gumbel	3–7 P.M. .... Pete Franklin
10 A.M.–1 P.M. .... Jim Lampley	7–Midnight .... Howie Rose
1–3 P.M. .... Art Shamsky	Midnight–6 A.M. .... Steve Somers

PRE-1987 RADIO SPORTS-TALK SHOWS

1948–53	WMGM (1050)	Marty Glickman, Bert Lee, and Bud Greenspan host a one-way listener talk show. Technology was not in place yet to put listeners on the air. Hosts would repeat the listener's question that only they could hear.
1964–68	WNBC (660)	First conventional two-way sports talk radio show, hosted by Bill Mazer in afternoon drive.
1965–67	WCBS (880)	Starting with Pat Summerall, then Win Elliot, *SportsLine* is on Monday through Friday evenings.
1965	WHN (1050)	Benny the Fan was host. His real name was Benny Levine from Baltimore.
1970–72	WMCA (570)	Jack Spector hosts show and takes calls from listeners.
1971	WNEW (1130)	Marty Glickman hosts daily late-night sports-talk show.
1971–73	WNBC (660)	Marv Albert hosts nightly sports-talk show. Program is eventually replaced by disc-jockey guru Wolfman Jack.
1972–78	WMCA (570)	John Sterling becomes the first acerbic talk-show host who has low tolerance level for unyielding callers.
1978–80	WMCA (570)	Art Rust does weekend sports-talk show.
1981–87	WABC (770)	Art Rust dominates sports talk in New York, doing nightly sports-talk show. Steve Malzberg occasionally fills in.
1985	WNBC (660)	Jack Spector does a little of everything, takes sports calls, plays music, and converses about entertainment.
1986–88	WNBC (660)	Dave Sims hosts nightly sports-talk show.
1981–88	WMCA (570)	Bill Daughtry hosts weekend shows.
1987–88	WMCA (570)	Chris Russo hosts weekend shows.
1987–88	WNEW (1130)	Richard Neer is mild-mannered host, doing nightly shows.

TEAMS
AND EVENTS

YEAR-BY-YEAR LISTINGS

BROOKLYN DODGERS

Season	Station	Freq.	Announcers	Season	Station	Freq.	Announcers
1939	WOR and WHN	710 1010	Red Barber Al Helfer	1950	WMGM	1050	Red Barber Connie Desmond Vin Scully
1940	WOR	710	Red Barber Al Helfer	1951	WMGM	1050	Red Barber Connie Desmond Vin Scully
1941	WOR	710	Red Barber Al Helfer	1952	WMGM	1050	Red Barber Connie Desmond Vin Scully
1942	WHN	1050	Red Barber Allen Hale	1953	WMGM	1050	Red Barber Connie Desmond Vin Scully
1943	WHN	1050	Red Barber Connie Desmond	1954	WMGM	1050	Vin Scully Connie Desmond Andre Baruch
1944	WHN	1050	Red Barber Connie Desmond	1955	WMGM	1050	Vin Scully Connie Desmond Al Helfer Andre Baruch
1945	WHN	1050	Red Barber Connie Desmond				
1946	WHN	1050	Red Barber Connie Desmond				
1947	WHN	1050	Red Barber Connie Desmond	1956	WMGM	1050	Vin Scully Connie Desmond Al Helfer Jerry Doggett
1948	WHN later WMGM	1050 1050	Red Barber Connie Desmond Ernie Harwell	1957	WMGM	1050	Vin Scully Al Helfer Jerry Doggett
1949	WMGM	1050	Red Barber Connie Desmond Ernie Harwell				

NEW YORK GIANTS BASEBALL

Season	Station	Freq.	Announcers
1939	WABC*	860	Arch McDonald
			Garnett Marks
			Mel Allen
1940	WABC*	860	Mel Allen
			Richards Vidmer
			Joe Bolton
1941	No Recorded Broadcasts		
1942		710	Mel Allen
			Connie Desmond
1943	No Recorded Broadcasts		
1944	WINS*	1010	Don Dunphy
			Bill Slater
1945	WINS*	1010	Al Helfer
			Bill Slater
1946	WMCA	570	Jack Brickhouse
			Steve Ellis
1947	WMCA	570	Steve Ellis
			Frankie Frisch
1948	WMCA	570	Frankie Frisch
			Maury Farrell
1949	WMCA	570	Russ Hodges
			Al Helfer

Season	Station	Freq.	Announcers
1950	WMCA	570	Russ Hodges
			Ernie Harwell
1951	WMCA	570	Russ Hodges
			Ernie Harwell
1952	WMCA	570	Russ Hodges
			Ernie Harwell
1953	WMCA	570	Russ Hodges
			Ernie Harwell
1954	WMCA	570	Russ Hodges
			Bob DeLaney
1955	WMCA	570	Russ Hodges
			Bob DeLaney
1956	WMCA	570	Russ Hodges
			Bob DeLaney
1957	WMCA	570	Russ Hodges
			Bob DeLaney
			Jim Woods
1958	WINS*	1010	Les Keiter†
1959	WINS*	1010	Les Keiter†
1960	WINS*	1010	Les Keiter†

* Partial Schedule
† Re-creations

NEW YORK METS

Season	Station	Freq.	Announcers	Season	Station	Freq.	Announcers
1962	WABC	770	Bob Murphy Lindsey Nelson Ralph Kiner	1979	WMCA	570	Bob Murphy Ralph Kiner Steve Albert
1963	WABC	770	Bob Murphy Lindsey Nelson Ralph Kiner	1980	WMCA	570	Bob Murphy Ralph Kiner Steve Albert
1964	WHN	1050	Bob Murphy Lindsey Nelson Ralph Kiner	1981	WMCA	570	Bob Murphy Ralph Kiner Steve Albert Art Shamsky
1965	WHN	1050	Bob Murphy Lindsey Nelson Ralph Kiner	1982	WMCA	570	Bob Murphy Steve LaMar
1966	WHN	1050	Bob Murphy Lindsey Nelson Ralph Kiner	1983	WHN	1050	Bob Murphy Steve LaMar
1967	WJRZ	970	Bob Murphy Lindsey Nelson Ralph Kiner	1984	WHN	1050	Bob Murphy Steve LaMar
1968	WJRZ	970	Bob Murphy Lindsey Nelson Ralph Kiner	1985	WHN	1050	Bob Murphy Gary Thorne
1969	WJRZ	970	Bob Murphy Lindsey Nelson Ralph Kiner	1986	WHN	1050	Bob Murphy Gary Thorne
1970	WJRZ	970	Bob Murphy Lindsey Nelson Ralph Kiner	1987	WHN then WFAN	1050 1050	Bob Murphy Gary Thorne
1971	WWDJ	970	Bob Murphy Lindsey Nelson Ralph Kiner	1988	WFAN	1050 then 660	Bob Murphy Gary Thorne
1972	WHN	1050	Bob Murphy Lindsey Nelson Ralph Kiner	1989	WFAN	660	Bob Murphy Gary Cohen
1973	WHN	1050	Bob Murphy Lindsey Nelson Ralph Kiner	1990	WFAN	660	Bob Murphy Gary Cohen
1974	WHN	1050	Bob Murphy Lindsey Nelson Ralph Kiner	1991	WFAN	660	Bob Murphy Gary Cohen
1975	WNEW	1130	Bob Murphy Lindsey Nelson Ralph Kiner	1992	WFAN	660	Bob Murphy Gary Cohen
1976	WNEW	1130	Bob Murphy Lindsey Nelson Ralph Kiner	1993	WFAN	660	Bob Murphy Gary Cohen
1977	WNEW	1130	Bob Murphy Lindsey Nelson Ralph Kiner	1994	WFAN	660	Bob Murphy Gary Cohen
1978	WMCA	570	Bob Murphy Lindsey Nelson Ralph Kiner	1995	WFAN	660	Bob Murphy Gary Cohen
				1996	WFAN	660	Bob Murphy Gary Cohen
				1997	WFAN	660	Bob Murphy Gary Cohen
				1998	WFAN	660	Bob Murphy Gary Cohen Ed Coleman

NEW YORK YANKEES

Season	Station	Freq.	Announcers	Season	Station	Freq.	Announcers
1939	WABC*	860	Garnett Marks Arch McDonald Mel Allen	1958	WMGM	1050	Mel Allen Red Barber Phil Rizzuto
1940	WABC*	860	Mel Allen J. C. Flippen	1959	WMGM	1050	Mel Allen Red Barber Phil Rizzuto
1941	Not on Air						
1942	WOR*	710	Mel Allen Connie Desmond	1960	WMGM	1050	Mel Allen Red Barber Phil Rizzuto
1943	Not on Air			1961	WCBS	880	Mel Allen Red Barber Phil Rizzuto
1944	WINS*	1000	Don Dunphy Bill Slater				
1945	WINS*	1000	Bill Slater Al Helfer	1962	WCBS	880	Mel Allen Red Barber Phil Rizzuto
1946	WINS	1010	Mel Allen Russ Hodges	1963	WCBS	880	Mel Allen Red Barber Phil Rizzuto Jerry Coleman
1947	WINS	1010	Mel Allen Russ Hodges				
1948	WINS	1010	Mel Allen Russ Hodges	1964	WCBS	880	Mel Allen Red Barber Phil Rizzuto Jerry Coleman
1949	WINS	1010	Mel Allen Curt Gowdy				
1950	WINS	1010	Mel Allen Curt Gowdy	1965	WCBS	880	Red Barber Phil Rizzuto Joe Garagiola Jerry Coleman
1951	WINS	1010	Mel Allen Art Gleeson				
1952	WINS	1010	Mel Allen Art Gleeson Bill Crowley	1966	WCBS	880	Red Barber Phil Rizzuto Joe Garagiola Jerry Coleman
1953	WINS	1010	Mel Allen Jim Woods Joe Brown	1967	WHN	1050	Phil Rizzuto Jerry Coleman Joe Garagiola
1954	WINS	1010	Mel Allen Red Barber Jim Woods	1968	WHN	1050	Phil Rizzuto Jerry Coleman Frank Messer
1955	WINS	1010	Mel Allen Red Barber Jim Woods	1969	WHN	1050	Phil Rizzuto Jerry Coleman Frank Messer
1956	WINS	1010	Mel Allen Red Barber Jim Woods	1970	WHN	1050	Phil Rizzuto Frank Messer Bob Gamere
1957	WINS	1010	Mel Allen Red Barber Phil Rizzuto	1971	WMCA	570†	Phil Rizzuto Frank Messer Bill White

Season	Station	Freq.	Announcers
1972	WMCA	570	Phil Rizzuto
			Frank Messer
			Bill White
1973	WMCA	570	Phil Rizzuto
			Frank Messer
			Bill White
1974	WMCA	570	Phil Rizzuto
			Frank Messer
			Bill White
1975	WMCA	570	Phil Rizzuto
			Frank Messer
			Bill White
			Dom Valentino
1976	WMCA	570	Phil Rizzuto
			Frank Messer
			Bill White
1977	WMCA	570	Phil Rizzuto
			Frank Messer
			Bill White
1978	WINS	1010	Phil Rizzuto
			Frank Messer
			Bill White
			Fran Healy
1979	WINS	1010	Phil Rizzuto
			Frank Messer
			Bill White
			Fran Healy
1980	WINS	1010	Phil Rizzuto
			Frank Messer
			Bill White
			Fran Healy
1981	WABC	770	Phil Rizzuto
			Frank Messer
			Bill White
			Fran Healy
1982	WABC	770	Phil Rizzuto
			Frank Messer
			Bill White
			John Gordon
1983	WABC	770	Phil Rizzuto
			Frank Messer
			Bill White
			John Gordon

Season	Station	Freq.	Announcers
1984	WABC	770	Phil Rizzuto
			Frank Messer
			Bill White
			John Gordon
1985	WABC	770	Phil Rizzuto
			Frank Messer
			Bill White
			John Gordon
1986	WABC	770	Phil Rizzuto
			Bill White
			Bobby Murcer
			Spencer Ross
1987	WABC	770	Hank Greenwald
			Tommy Hutton
1988	WABC	770	Hank Greenwald
			Tommy Hutton
1989	WABC	770	John Sterling
			Jay Johnstone
1990	WABC	770	John Sterling
			Jay Johnstone
1991	WABC	770	John Sterling
			Joe Angel
1992	WABC	770	John Sterling
			Michael Kay
1993	WABC	770	John Sterling
			Michael Kay
1994	WABC	770	John Sterling
			Michael Kay
1995	WABC	770	John Sterling
			Michael Kay
1996	WABC	770	John Sterling
			Michael Kay
1997	WABC	770	John Sterling
			Michael Kay
1998	WABC	770	John Sterling
			Michael Kay

*Partial Schedule
†Some West Coast night games not broadcast

BASEBALL
ALL-STAR GAMES

Year	Site/Winner	Station	Network	Freq.	Announcers
1933	Chicago/AL	WEAF	NBC	660	Graham McNamee Hal Totten
		WABC	CBS	860	Pat Flanagan Johnny O'Hara
1934	New York/AL	WJZ	NBC	660	Graham McNamee Tom Manning Ford Bond
		WABC	CBS	860	Ted Husing France Laux
1935	Cleveland/AL	WEAF	NBC	660	Graham McNamee
		WJZ	NBC	760	Tom Manning
		WABC	CBS	860	Jack Graney France Laux
		WOR	Mutual	710	Bob Elson Eddie Vander Pyl
1936	Boston/NL	WEAF	NBC	660	Tom Manning
		WJZ	NBC	760	Hal Totten
		WABC	CBS	860	Arch McDonald France Laux
		WOR	Mutual	710	Fred Hoey Linus Travers
1937	Washington/AL	WEAF	NBC	660	Tom Manning
		WJZ	NBC	760	Warren Brown
		WNYC	NBC	810	
		WABC	CBS	860	Arch McDonald
		WNEW	CBS	1250	France Laux
		WINS	CBS	1180	
		WOR	Mutual	710	Bob Elson Tony Wakeman
1938	Cincinnati/NL	WJZ	NBC	760	Tom Manning Red Barber
		WABC	CBS	860	Bill Dyer France Laux
		WOR	Mutual	710	Bob Elson Dick Bray
1939	New York/AL	WJZ	NBC	760	Tom Manning Paul Douglas Warren Brown
		WABC	CBS	860	Mel Allen France Laux
		WOR	Mutual	710	Red Barber Bob Elson
1940	St. Louis/NL	WJZ	NBC	760	Tom Manning Ray Schmidt
		WABC	CBS	860	Mel Allen France Laux
		WOR	Mutual	710	Red Barber Bob Elson

Year	Site/Winner	Station	Network	Freq.	Announcers
1941	Detroit/AL	WABC	CBS	880	Mel Allen France Laux Jim Stevenson
		WOR	Mutual	710	Red Barber Bob Elson
1942(1)	New York/AL	WOR	Mutual	710	Mel Allen Jim Britt Bob Elson
1942(2)	Cleveland/AL (for war effort)	WOR	Mutual	710	Bob Elson Jack Graney Waite Hoyt
1943	Philadelphia/AL	WABC	Mutual	880	Mel Allen Red Barber Bill Corum
1944	Pittsburgh/NL	WABC	Mutual	880	Don Dunphy Bill Slater Bill Corum
1945	No game due to World War II				
1946	Boston/AL	WOR	Mutual	710	Mel Allen Jim Britt Bill Corum
1947	Chicago/AL	WOR	Mutual	710	Mel Allen Jim Britt
1948	St. Louis/AL	WOR	Mutual	710	Mel Allen Jim Britt
1949	Brooklyn/AL	WOR	Mutual	710	Mel Allen Jim Britt
1950	Chicago/NL	WOR	Mutual	710	Mel Allen Jim Britt
1951	Detroit/NL	WOR	Mutual	710	Mel Allen Al Helfer
1952	Philadelphia/NL	WOR	Mutual	710	Gene Kelly Al Helfer
1953	Cincinnati/NL	WOR	Mutual	710	Waite Hoyt Al Helfer
1954	Cleveland/AL	WOR	Mutual	710	Jimmy Dudley Al Helfer
1955	Milwaukee/NL	WOR	Mutual	710	Earl Gillespie Bob Neal
1956	Washington/NL	WOR	Mutual	710	Bob Wolff Bob Neal
1957	St. Louis/AL	WRCA	NBC	660	Harry Caray Bob Neal
1958	Baltimore/AL	WRCA	NBC	660	Ernie Harwell Bob Neal
1959(1)	Pittsburgh/NL	WNBC	NBC	660	Bob Prince Jack Brickhouse
1959(2)	Los Angeles/AL	WNBC	NBC	660	Russ Hodges Bob Neal
1960(1)	Kansas City/NL	WNBC	NBC	660	Merle Harmon Jack Quinlan
1960(2)	New York/NL	WNBC	NBC	660	Bob Elson Waite Hoyt
1961(1)	San Francisco/NL	WNBC	NBC	660	Jimmy Dudley Jerry Doggett
1961(2)	Boston/tie	WNBC	NBC	660	Ernie Harwell Blaine Walsh

Year	Site/Winner	Station	Network	Freq.	Announcers
1962(1)	Washington/NL	WNBC	NBC	660	Lindsey Nelson John MacLean
1962(2)	Chicago/AL	WNBC	NBC	660	Jack Quinlan George Kell
1963	Cleveland/NL	WNBC	NBC	660	Bob Neal George Bryson
1964	New York/NL	WNBC	NBC	660	Dan Daniels Blaine Walsh
1965	Minnesota/NL	WNBC	NBC	660	Herb Carneal Bob Prince
1966	St. Louis/NL	WNBC	NBC	660	Jim Simpson Tony Kubek
1967	Anaheim/NL	WNBC	NBC	660	Jim Simpson Tony Kubek Buddy Blattner
1968	Houston/NL	WNBC	NBC	660	Jim Simpson Tony Kubek Gene Elston
1969	Washington/NL	WNBC	NBC	660	Jim Simpson Sandy Koufax
1970	Cincinnati/NL	WNBC	NBC	660	Jim Simpson Sandy Koufax
1971	Detroit/AL	WNBC	NBC	660	Jim Simpson Sandy Koufax
1972	Atlanta/NL	WNBC	NBC	660	Jim Simpson Sandy Koufax
1973	Kansas City/NL	WNBC	NBC	660	Jim Simpson Sandy Koufax
1974	Pittsburgh/NL	WNBC	NBC	660	Jim Simpson Maury Wills
1975	Milwaukee/NL	WMCA	NBC	570	Jim Simpson Maury Wills
1976	Philadelphia/NL	WCBS	CBS	880	Jack Buck Brent Musburger
1977	New York/NL	WCBS	CBS	880	Vin Scully Brent Musburger
1978	San Diego/NL	WCBS	CBS	880	Vin Scully Brent Musburger
1979	Seattle/NL	WCBS	CBS	880	Vin Scully Brent Musburger
1980	Los Angeles/NL	WCBS	CBS	880	Vin Scully Brent Musburger
1981	Cleveland/NL	WCBS	CBS	880	Vin Scully Herb Score
1982	Montreal/NL	WCBS	CBS	880	Vin Scully Brent Musburger
1983	Chicago/AL	WCBS	CBS	880	Brent Musburger Brooks Robinson Duke Snider
1984	San Francisco/NL	WCBS	CBS	880	Brent Musburger Johnny Bench
1985	Minnesota/NL	WCBS	CBS	880	Brent Musburger Johnny Bench
1986	Houston/AL	WCBS	CBS	880	Brent Musburger Johnny Bench
1987	Oakland/NL	WNEW	CBS	1130	Brent Musburger Johnny Bench

Year	Site/Winner	Station	Network	Freq.	Announcers
1988	Cincinnati/AL	WFAN	CBS	1050	Brent Musburger Johnny Bench
1989	Anaheim/AL	WFAN	CBS	660	Brent Musburger Johnny Bench
1990	Chicago/AL	WFAN	CBS	660	John Rooney Johnny Bench Jerry Coleman
1991	Toronto/AL	WFAN	CBS	660	John Rooney Jerry Coleman
1992	San Diego/AL	WFAN	CBS	660	John Rooney Jerry Coleman
1993	Baltimore/AL	WFAN	CBS	660	John Rooney Jerry Coleman
1994	Pittsburgh/NL	WFAN	CBS	660	John Rooney Jerry Coleman Jeff Torborg
1995	Texas/NL	WFAN	CBS	660	John Rooney Jerry Coleman Jeff Torborg
1996	Philadelphia/NL	WFAN	CBS	660	John Rooney Jerry Coleman Jeff Torborg
1997	Cleveland/AL	WFAN	CBS	660	John Rooney Jerry Coleman Jeff Torborg
1998	Denver/AL	WFAN	ESPN	660	Charley Steiner Kevin Kennedy

WORLD SERIES

Year	Station	Freq.	Network	Series Results	Announcers
1921	WJZ	833		Giants over Yankees 4–3	Tommy Cowan
1922	WJZ	833		Giants over Yankees 4–0	Grantland Rice
1923	WEAF	610		Yankees over Giants 4–2	Bill McGeehan Graham McNamee
	WJZ	660			J. Andrew White Grantland Rice
1924	WEAF WNYC	610 570		Washington over Giants 4–3	Graham McNamee
1925	WEAF	610		Pittsburgh over Washington 4–3	Graham McNamee Quinn Ryan
1926	WEAF WJZ	610 660	NBC NBC	Cards over Yankees 4–3	Graham McNamee Phillips Carlin
1927	WEAF WJZ WNYC	610 660 570	NBC NBC NBC	Yankees over Pittsburgh 4–0	Graham McNamee Phillips Carlin
	WOR	710	CBS		J. Andrew White Hal Totten

Year	Station	Freq.	Network	Series Results	Announcers
1928	WEAF	610	NBC	Yankees over Cards 4–0	Graham McNamee
	WJZ	660	NBC		Phillips Carlin
	WNYC	570	NBC		
	WABC	970	CBS		J. Andrew White, Hal
	WOR	710	CBS		Totten, Ted Husing
1929	WEAF	660	NBC	Philadelphia over Cubs 4–1	Graham McNamee
	WJZ	760	NBC		George Hicks
					Gene Rouse
	WABC	860	CBS		Ted Husing
1930	WEAF	660	NBC	Philadelphia over Cards 4–2	Graham McNamee
	WJZ	760	NBC		Ford Frick
	WABC	860	CBS		Ted Husing
					Les Quailey
1931	WEAF	660	NBC	Cards over Philadelphia 4–3	Graham McNamee
	WJZ	760	NBC		George Hicks
					Tom Manning
	WABC	860	CBS		Ted Husing
					Les Quailey
1932	WEAF	660	NBC	Yankees over Cubs 4–0	Graham McNamee
	WJZ	760	NBC		Tom Manning
					Hal Totten
	WABC	860	CBS		Ted Husing, Bob Elson,
					Pat Flanagan
1933	WEAF	660	NBC	Giants over Washington 4–1	Graham McNamee
					Tom Manning
	WJZ	760	NBC		Hal Totten
	WNYC	570	NBC		Ford Bond
	WABC	860	CBS		Ted Husing, Fred
					Hoey, France
	WINS	1180	CBS		Laux, Gunnar Wiig,
	WRNY	1010	CBS		Roger Baker
1934	WEAF	660	NBC	Cards over Detroit 4–3	Graham McNamee
	WJZ	760	NBC		Tom Manning
					Ford Bond
	WABC	860	CBS		Ted Husing
					Pat Flanagan
					France Laux
1935	WEAF	660	NBC	Detroit over Cubs 4–2	Ty Tyson, Hal Totten,
	WJZ	760	NBC		Boake Carter
	WABC	860	CBS		France Laux
					Jack Graney
	WINS	1180	CBS		Truman Bradley
	WOR	710	Mutual		Red Barber, Bob Elson,
					Quinn Ryan
1936	WEAF	660	NBC	Yankees over Giants 4–2	Red Barber, Tom
	WJZ	760	NBC		Manning,Ty
					Tyson, Warren Brown
	WABC	860	CBS		France Laux, Bill Dyer,
	WINS	1180	CBS		Boake Carter
	WOR	710	Mutual		Bob Elson, Tony Wakeman,
	WHN	1010	Mutual		Gabriel Heatter
1937	WEAF	660	NBC	Yankees over Giants 4–1	Tom Manning
	WJZ	760	NBC		Red Barber
					Warren Brown

Year	Station	Freq.	Network	Series Results	Announcers
	WABC	860	CBS		France Laux, Paul Douglas,
	WHN	1010	CBS		Bill Dyer
	WINS	1180	CBS		
	WNEW	1250	CBS		
	WOR	710	Mutual		Bob Elson, Dave Driscoll, Johnny O'Hara
1938	WEAF	660	NBC–R	Yankees over Cubs 4–0	Red Barber, Tom Manning, George Hicks, Paul Douglas
	WJZ	760	NBC–B		George Higgins, Johnny O'Hara, Rosey Rowswell
	WOR	710	Mutual		Bob Elson, Dave Driscoll, Stan Lomax
	WABC	860	CBS		France Laux, Bill Dyer, Mel Allen
1939	WOR	710	Mutual	Yankees over Cincinnati 4–0	Red Barber Bob Elson
1940	WOR	710	Mutual	Cincinnati over Detroit 4–3	Red Barber Bob Elson
1941	WOR	710	Mutual	Yankees over Brooklyn 4–1	Red Barber, Bob Elson, Bill Corum
1942	WOR	710	Mutual	Cards over Yankees 4–1	Red Barber, Mel Allen, Bill Corum
1943	WOR	710	Mutual	Yankees over Cards 4–1	Red Barber, Bob Elson, Bill Corum
1944	WOR	710	Mutual	Cards over Browns 4–2	Don Dunphy, Bill Slater, Bill Corum
1945	WOR	710	Mutual	Detroit over Cubs 4–3	Al Helfer, Bill Slater, Bill Corum
1946	WOR	710	Mutual	Cards over Red Sox 4–3	Jim Britt, Arch McDonald, Bill Corum
1947	WOR	710	Mutual	Yankees over Brooklyn 4–3	Red Barber, Mel Allen
1948	WOR	710	Mutual	Cleveland over Braves 4–2	Mel Allen, Jim Britt
1949	WOR	710	Mutual	Yankees over Brooklyn 4–1	Red Barber, Mel Allen
1950	WOR	710	Mutual	Yankees over Philadelphia 4–0	Mel Allen, Gene Kelly
	WINS	1010	Mutual		
1951	WOR	710	Mutual	Yankees over Giants 4–2	Mel Allen, Al Helfer
	WINS	1010	Mutual		
	WMCA	570	Mutual		
1952	WOR	710	Mutual	Yankees over Brooklyn 4–2	Jack Brickhouse, Al Helfer, Bill Corum
	WINS	1010	Mutual		
1953	WOR	710	Mutual	Yankees over Brooklyn 4–2	Gene Kelly, Al Helfer, Bill Corum
	WINS	1010	Mutual		
	WMGM	1050	Mutual		
1954	WOR	710	Mutual	Giants over Cleveland 4–0	Jimmy Dudley Al Helfer
	WMCA	570	Mutual		
1955	WOR	710	Mutual	Brooklyn over Yankees 4–3	Al Helfer Bob Neal
	WINS	1010	Mutual		
	WMGM	1050	Mutual		
1956	WOR	710	Mutual	Yankees over Brooklyn 4–3	Bob Neal, Bob Wolff, Bill Corum
	WINS	1010	Mutual		
	WMGM	1050	Mutual		

Year	Station	Freq.	Network	Series Results	Announcers
1957	WRCA WINS	660 1010	NBC NBC	Milwaukee over Yankees 4–3	Earl Gillespie, Bob Neal, Bill Corum
1958	WNBC WMGM	660 1050	NBC NBC	Yankees over Milwaukee 4–3	Earl Gillespie Bob Wolff
1959	WNBC	660	NBC	L.A. over White Sox 4–2	Mel Allen Byrum Saam
1960	WNBC WMGM	660 1050	NBC NBC	Pittsburgh over Yankees 4–3	Chuck Thompson Jack Quinlan
1961	WNBC WCBS	660 880	NBC NBC	Yankees over Cincinnati 4–1	Waite Hoyt Bob Wolff
1962	WNBC WCBS	660 880	NBC NBC	Yankees over San Francisco 4–3	George Kell Joe Garagiola
1963	WNBC WCBS	660 880	NBC NBC	L.A. over Yankees 4–0	Ernie Harwell Joe Garagiola
1964	WNBC WCBS	660 880	NBC NBC	St. Louis over Yankees 4–3	Curt Gowdy and Harry Caray (in New York) Phil Rizzuto and Joe Garagiola (in St. Louis)
1965	WNBC	660	NBC	L.A. over Minnesota 4–3	Byrum Saam Joe Garagiola
1966	WNBC	660	NBC	Baltimore over L.A. 4–0	Bob Prince and Chuck Thompson (in Los Angeles) Bob Prince and Vin Scully (in Baltimore)
1967	WNBC	660	NBC	Boston over St. Louis 4–3	Pee Wee Reese and Harry Caray (in Boston) Reese and Ken Coleman (in St. Louis)
1968	WNBC	660	NBC	Detroit over St. Louis 4–3	Pee Wee Reese and Jack Buck (in Detroit) Reese and Ernie Harwell (in St.Louis)
1969	WNBC WJRZ	660 970	NBC NBC	Mets over Baltimore 4–1	Jim Simpson and Ralph Kiner (in Baltimore) Simpson, Bill O'Donnell (in New York)
1970	WNBC	660	NBC	Baltimore over Cincinnati 4–1	Jim Simpson and Jim McIntyre (in Baltimore) Simpson, Chuck Thompson (in Cincinnati)
1971	WNBC	660	NBC	Pittsburgh over Baltimore 4–3	Jim Simpson and Bob Prince (in Baltimore) Simpson, Bill O'Donnell (in Pittsburgh)
1972	WNBC	660	NBC	Oakland over Cincinnati 4–3	Jim Simpson and Al Michaels (in Oakland) Simpson, Monte Moore (in Cincinnati)
1973	WNBC WHN	660 1050	NBC NBC	Oakland over Mets 4–3	Jim Simpson, Ralph Kiner (in Oakland) Simpson, Monte Moore (in New York)
1974	WNBC	660	NBC	Oakland over L.A. 4–1	Jim Simpson and Vin Scully (in Oakland) Simpson, Monte Moore (in L.A.)
1975	WNBC-FM	97.1	NBC	Cincinnati over Boston 4–3	(five split series on radio and TV): Curt Gowdy, Joe Garagiola, Ned Martin, Dick Stockton, and Marty Brennaman

Year	Station	Freq.	Network	Series Results	Announcers
1976	WCBS	880	CBS	Cincinnati over Yankees 4-0	Bill White, Marty
	WMCA	570	CBS		Brennaman, Win Elliot
1977	WCBS	880	CBS	Yankees over L.A. 4-2	Bill White, Ross Porter,
	WMCA	570	CBS		Win Elliot
1978	WCBS	880	CBS	Yankees over L.A. 4-2	Bill White, Ross Porter,
	WINS	1010	CBS		Win Elliot
1979	WCBS	880	CBS	Pittsburgh over Baltimore 4-3	Vin Scully
					Sparky Anderson
1980	WCBS	880	CBS	Philadelphia over Kan. City 4-2	Vin Scully
					Sparky Anderson
1981	WCBS	880	CBS	L.A. over Yankees 4-2	Vin Scully
	WABC	770	CBS		Sparky Anderson
1982	WCBS	880	CBS	St. Louis over Milwaukee 4-3	Vin Scully
					Sparky Anderson
1983	WCBS	880	CBS	Baltimore over Philadelphia 4-1	Jack Buck
					Sparky Anderson
1984	WCBS	880	CBS	Detroit over San Diego 4-1	Jack Buck
					Brent Musburger
1985	WCBS	880	CBS	Kansas City over St. Louis 4-3	Jack Buck
					Sparky Anderson
1986	WHN	1050		Mets over Boston 4-3	Bob Murphy
					Gary Thorne
	WCBS	880	CBS		Jack Buck
					Sparky Anderson
1987	WFAN	1050	CBS	Minnesota over St. Louis 4-3	Jack Buck, Bill White
1988	WFAN	660	CBS	L.A. over Oakland 4-1	Jack Buck, Bill White
1989	WFAN	660	CBS	Oakland over San Francisco 4-0	Jack Buck
					Johnny Bench
1990	WFAN	660	CBS	Cincinnati over Oakland 4-0	Vin Scully
					Johnny Bench
1991	WFAN	660	CBS	Minnesota over Atlanta 4-3	Vin Scully
					Johnny Bench
1992	WFAN	660	CBS	Toronto over Atlanta 4-2	Vin Scully
					Johnny Bench
1993	WFAN	660	CBS	Toronto over Philadelphia 4-2	Vin Scully
					Johnny Bench
1994				*No World Series*	
1995	WFAN	660	CBS	Atlanta over Cleveland 4-2	Vin Scully, Jeff Torborg
1996	WFAN	660	CBS	Yankees over Atlanta 4-2	Vin Scully, Jeff Torborg
	WABC	770			John Sterling, Michael Kay
1997	WFAN	660	CBS	Florida over Cleveland 4-3	Vin Scully*, Jeff Torborg
1998	WFAN	660	ESPN	Yankees over Padres 4-0	John Miller, Joe Morgan
	WABC	770			John Sterling, Michael Kay

*Scully does record 13th World Series on radio, surpassing Graham McNamee's 12.

NEW YORK KNICKS

Season	Station	Freq.	Schedule	Announcers
1946–47	WHN	1050	Partial	Marty Glickman and Stan Lomax
1947–48	WHN	1050	Partial	Marty Glickman and Stan Lomax
1948–49	WMGM	1050	Partial	Marty Glickman and Connie Desmond
1949–50	WMGM	1050	Partial	Marty Glickman and Bud Palmer
1950–51	WMGM	1050	Partial	Marty Glickman and Bud Palmer
1951–52	WMGM	1050	Partial	Marty Glickman and Johnny Most
1952–53	WMGM	1050	Partial	Marty Glickman and Johnny Most
1953–54	WMGM	1050	Partial	Marty Glickman and Bert Lee Jr.
1954–55	WMGM	1050	Partial	Marty Glickman and Jim Gordon
1955–56	WINS	1010	Fraction	Les Keiter and Jim Gordon
1956–57	WINS	1010	Full	Les Keiter and Marty Glickman
1957–58	WINS	1010	Partial	Les Keiter and Jim Gordon
1958–59	WINS	1010	Full	Les Keiter and Jim Gordon
1959–60	WINS	1010	Partial	Les Keiter and John Condon
1960–61	No Recorded Broadcasts			
1961–62	WINS	1010	Fraction	Les Keiter
1962–63	WCBS	880	Partial	Marty Glickman
1963–64	No Recorded Broadcasts			
1964–65	WOR	710	Partial	Lester Smith and Stan Lomax
1965–66	WNBC	660	Partial	Bill Mazer
1966–67	WHN	1050	Partial	Don Criqui
1967–68	WHN	1050	Partial	Marv Albert
1968–69	WHN	1050	Partial	Marv Albert
1969–70	WHN	1050	Partial	Marv Albert
1970–71	WNBC	660	Partial	Marv Albert
1971–72	WNBC	660	Partial	Marv Albert
1972–73	WNBC	660	Partial	Marv Albert and John Andariese
1973–74	WNBC	660	Partial	Marv Albert and John Andariese
1974–75	WNEW	1130	Partial	Marv Albert and John Andariese
1975–76	WNEW	1130	Partial	Marv Albert and John Andariese
1976–77	WNEW	1130	Partial	Marv Albert and Richie Guerin
1977–78	WNEW	1130	Partial	Marv Albert and Richie Guerin
1978–79	WNEW	1130	Partial	Marv Albert and Richie Guerin
1979–80	WNEW	1130	Partial	Marv Albert and Richie Guerin
1980–81	WNEW	1130	Partial	Marv Albert and Richie Guerin
1981–82	WNEW	1130	Partial	Marv Albert and Richie Guerin
1982–83	WNEW	1130	Partial	Marv Albert and John Andariese
1983–84	WNEW	1130	Partial	Marv Albert and John Andariese
1984–85	WPAT	930	Partial	Marv Albert and John Andariese
1985–86	WNBC	660	Partial	Marv Albert and John Andariese
1986–87	WNBC	660	Partial	Jim Karvellas and Ernie Grunfeld
1987–88	WNBC	660	Full	Jim Karvellas and Ernie Grunfeld
	or			
	WFAN	1050		
1988–89	WFAN	660	Full	Jim Karvellas and Ernie Grunfeld
	or			
	WMCA	570		
1989–90	WFAN	660	Full	Jim Karvellas and Walt Frazier
	or			
	WPAT	930		
1990–91	WFAN	660	Full	Jim Karvellas and Walt Frazier
	or			
	WPAT	930		

Season	Station	Freq.	Schedule	Announcers
1991–92	WFAN	660	Full	Jim Karvellas and Walt Frazier
	or			
	WEVD	1050		
1992–93	WFAN	660	Full	Mike Breen and Walt Frazier
	or			
	WEVD	1050		
1993–94	WFAN	660	Full	Mike Breen and Walt Frazier
	or			
	WEVD	1050		
1994–95	WFAN	660	Full	Mike Breen and Walt Frazier
	or			
	WEVD	1050		
1995–96	WFAN	660	Full	Mike Breen and Walt Frazier
	or			
	WEVD	1050		
1996–97	WFAN	660	Full	Mike Breen and Walt Frazier
	or			
	WEVD	1050		
1997–98	WFAN	660	Full	Gus Johnson and Walt Frazier
	or			
	WEVD	1050		

NEW JERSEY NETS

Season	Station	Freq.	Schedule	Announcers
1967–68	WJRZ	970	Virtually Full	Spencer Ross
1968–69	WBAB	1440	Partial	Spencer Ross
1969–70	WGBB	1240	Partial	Spencer Ross
1970–71	WGBB	1240	Partial	Bob Lawrence
1971–72	WHN	1050	Partial	Al Albert
1972–73	WHN	1050	Partial	Al Albert
1973–74	WHN	1050	Partial	Al Albert and Bill Mazer
1974–75	WMCA	570	Partial	Dom Valentino and Mike DiTomasso
1975–76	WMCA	570	Partial	John Sterling and Mike DiTomasso
1976–77	WMCA	570	Partial	John Sterling and Mike DiTomasso
1977–78	WMCA	570	Partial	John Sterling and Mike DiTomasso
1978–79	WVNJ	620	Full Schedule	John Sterling and Mike DiTomasso
1979–80	WVNJ	620	Full Schedule	John Sterling and Mike DiTomasso
1980–81	WVNJ	620	Full Schedule	Steve Albert and
	WWRL	1600		Mike DiTomasso
1981–82	WVNJ	620	Full Schedule	Joe Tait and
	WWRL	1600		Al Menendez
1982–83	WVNJ	620	Full Schedule	Mike Zimet and Mike DiTomasso
1983–84	WNBC	660	Full Schedule	Mel Proctor and Mike DiTomasso
1984–85	WNBC	660	Full Schedule	Mel Proctor
1985–86	WNBC	660	Full Schedule	Neil Funk
1986–87	WNEW	1130	Full Schedule	Neil Funk and Mike DiTomasso
1987–88	WNEW	1130	Full Schedule	Howard David and Jim Spanarkel
1988–89	WNEW	1130	Full Schedule	Howard David and Jim Spanarkel
1989–90	WNEW	1130	Full Schedule	Howard David and Jim Spanarkel
1990–91	WNEW	1130	Full Schedule	Howard David and Jim Spanarkel
1991–92	WNEW	1130	Full Schedule	Howard David and Jim Spanarkel
1992–93	WQEW	1560	Full Schedule	Howard David and Mike O'Korren
1993–94	WQEW	1560	Full Schedule	Howard David and Mike O'Korren
1994–95	WQEW	1560	Full Schedule	Ian Eagle and Mike O'Korren
1995–96	WQEW	1560	Full Schedule	Steve Albert and Mike O'Korren
1996–97	WOR	710	Full Schedule	Bob Papa and Mike O'Korren
1997–98	WOR	710	Full Schedule	Bob Papa and Mike O'Korren

HEAVYWEIGHT CHAMPIONSHIP FIGHTS ON RADIO

Date	Station (Freq.)	Contestants	Site	Announcers
July 2, 1921	WJZ (833)	Dempsey over Carpentier	Jersey City	Andrew White
Sep. 14, 1923	WJZ (660)	Dempsey over Firpo	New York	Andrew White
Sep. 23, 1926	WEAF (610)	Tunney over Dempsey	Philadelphia	Graham McNamee
	WJZ (660)			Andrew White
Sep. 22, 1927	WEAF (610)	Tunney over Dempsey	Chicago	Graham McNamee
	WJZ (660)			Phillips Carlin
July 26, 1928	WEAF (610)	Tunney over Heeney	New York	Graham McNamee
	WJZ (660)			Phillips Carlin
June 12, 1930	WEAF (660)	Schmeling over Sharkey	New York	Graham McNamee
				Carmen Ogden
July 3, 1931	WEAF (660)	Schmeling over Stribling	Cleveland	Graham McNamee
				Floyd Gibbons
June 21, 1932	WEAF (660)	Sharkey over Schmeling	New York	Graham McNamee
				Charles Francis Coe
Mar. 1, 1934	WMCA (570)	Carnera over Loughran	Miami	Sam Taub
				Angelo Palange
June 14, 1934	WEAF (660)	Baer over Carnera	New York	Graham McNamee
	WJZ (760)			Ford Bond
June 13, 1935	WEAF (660)	Braddock over Baer	New York	Graham McNamee
	WJZ (760)			Ford Bond
June 22, 1937	WEAF (660)	Louis over Braddock	Chicago	Clem McCarthy
	WJZ (760)			Edwin C. Hill
Aug. 30, 1937	WEAF (660)	Louis over Farr	New York	Clem McCarthy
	WJZ (760)			Edwin C. Hill
Feb. 23, 1938	WJZ (760)	Louis over Mann	New York	Sam Taub
April 1, 1938	WJZ (760)	Louis over Thomas	New York	Sam Taub
				Hal Totten
June 22, 1938	WEAF ((660)	Louis over Schmeling	New York	Clem McCarthy
	WJZ (760)			Ed Thorgersen
Jan. 25, 1939	WJZ (760)	Louis over Lewis	New York	Clem McCarthy
				Edwin C. Hill
Apr. 17, 1939	WEAF (660)	Louis over Roper	Los Angeles	Mark Kelly
	WJZ (760)			Bing Crosby
June 28, 1939	WJZ (760)	Louis over Galento	New York	Bill Stern
				Gabriel Heater
Sep. 20, 1939	WJZ (760)	Louis over Pastor	Detroit	Sam Taub
				Bill Stern
Feb. 9, 1940	WJZ (760)	Louis over Godoy	New York	Sam Taub
				Bill Stern
Mar. 29, 1940	WJZ (760)	Louis over Paycheck	New York	Sam Taub
				Bill Stern
June 20, 1940	WJZ (760)	Louis over Godoy	New York	Sam Taub
				Bill Stern

Date	Station (Freq.)	Contestants	Site	Announcers
Dec. 16, 1940	WJZ (760)	Louis over McCoy	Boston	Sam Taub
				Bill Stern
Jan. 31, 1941	WJZ (760)	Louis over Burman	New York	Sam Taub
				Bill Stern
Feb. 17, 1941	WJZ (760)	Louis over Dorzaio	Philadelphia	Sam Taub
				Bill Stern
Mar. 21, 1941	WJZ (760)	Louis over Simon	Detroit	Sam Taub
				Bill Stern
April 8, 1941	WJZ (770)	Louis over Musto	St. Louis	Sam Taub
				Bill Stern
May 23, 1941	WJZ (770)	Louis over Baer	Washington	Sam Taub
				Bill Stern
June 18, 1941	WOR (710)	Louis over Conn	New York	Don Dunphy
				Bill Corum
Sep. 29, 1941	WOR (710)	Louis over Nova	New York	Don Dunphy
				Bill Corum
Jan. 9, 1942	WOR (710)	Louis over Baer	New York	Don Dunphy
				Bill Corum
Mar. 27, 1942	WOR (710)	Louis over Simon	New York	Don Dunphy
				Bill Corum
June 19, 1946	WJZ (770)	Louis over Conn	New York	Don Dunphy
				Bill Corum
Sep. 18, 1946	WJZ (770)	Louis over Mauriello	New York	Don Dunphy
				Bill Corum
Dec. 5, 1947	WJZ (770)	Louis over Walcott	New York	Don Dunphy
				Bill Corum
June 25, 1948	WJZ (770)	Louis over Walcott	New York	Don Dunphy
				Bill Corum
June 22, 1949	WJZ (770)	Charles over Walcott	Chicago	Don Dunphy
				Bill Corum
Aug. 10, 1949	WJZ (770)	Charles over Lesnevich	New York	Don Dunphy
				Bill Corum
Oct. 14, 1949	WJZ (770)	Charles over Valentino	San Francisco	Don Dunphy
				Bill Corum
Sep. 27, 1950	WCBS (880)	Charles over Louis	New York	Russ Hodges
				Jack Brickhouse
Jan. 12, 1951	WJZ (770)	Charles over Oma	New York	Don Dunphy
				Bill Corum
Mar. 7, 1951	WCBS (880)	Charles over Walcott	Detroit	Jack Brickhouse
				Jack Drees
May 30, 1951	WCBS (880)	Charles over Maxim	Chicago	Steve Ellis
July 18, 1951	WCBS (880)	Walcott over Charles	Pittsburgh	Steve Ellis
				Lester Bromberg
June 5, 1952	WJZ (770)	Walcott over Charles	Philadelphia	Don Dunphy
				Bill Corum
May 15, 1953	WABC (770)	Marciano over Walcott	Chicago	Don Dunphy
				Bill Corum
June 17, 1954	WABC (770)	Marciano over Charles	New York	Don Dunphy
				Win Elliot
Sep. 17, 1954	WCBS (880)	Marciano over Charles	New York	Russ Hodges
				Jack Drees
May 16, 1955	WRCA (660)	Marciano over Cockell	San Francisco	Don Dunphy
				Win Elliot
Sep. 21, 1955	WABC (770)	Marciano over Moore	New York	Russ Hodges
				Steve Ellis

Date	Station (Freq.)	Contestants	Site	Announcers
Nov. 30, 1956	WRCA (660)	Patterson over Moore	Chicago	Don Dunphy
				Win Elliot
July 29, 1957	WRCA (660)	Patterson over Jackson	New York	Russ Hodges
				Tommy Loughran
May 1, 1959	WNBC (660)	Patterson over London	Indianapolis	Don Dunphy
				Win Elliot
June 26, 1959	WABC (770)	Johansson over Patterson	New York	Les Keiter
				Howard Cosell
				John Wayne
				William Holden
June 20, 1960	WABC (770)	Patterson over Johansson	New York	Les Keiter
				Howard Cosell
Mar. 13, 1961	WABC (770)	Patterson over Johansson	Miami Beach	Les Keiter
				Howard Cosell
Sep. 25, 1962	WABC (770)	Liston over Patterson	Chicago	Jack Drees
				Howard Cosell
July 22, 1963	WABC (770)	Liston over Patterson	Las Vegas	Les Keiter
				Howard Cosell
Feb. 25, 1964	WABC (770)	Clay over Liston	Miami Beach	Les Keiter
				Howard Cosell
				Jim Brown
May 25, 1965	WHN (1050)	Clay over Liston	Lewiston, Mn.	Russ Hodges
				Van Patrick
				Bill Stern
Nov. 11, 1965	WABC (770)	Clay over Patterson	Las Vegas	Chris Schenkel
				Howard Cosell
May 21, 1966	WHN (1050)	Clay over Cooper	London	Edmund Andrews
Aug. 6, 1966	WHN (1050)	Clay over London	London	Les Keiter
				Van Patrick
				Bill Stern
Nov. 14, 1966	WHN (1050)	Clay over Williams	Houston	Les Keiter
				Van Patrick
Feb. 6, 1967	WHN (1050)	Clay over Terrell	Houston	Les Keiter
				Van Patrick
Feb. 16, 1970	WHN (1050)	Frazier over Ellis	New York	Don Dunphy
				Van Patrick
Feb. 15, 1978	WCBS (880)	Spinks over Ali	Las Vegas	Don Dunphy
				Win Elliot
Sep. 15, 1978	WOR (710)	Ali over Spinks	New Orleans	Don Dunphy
				Lou Boda
Sep. 21, 1985	WNBC (660)	Spinks over Holmes	Las Vegas	Don Dunphy
				Sam Nova
				Lou Boda

ROSE BOWL

Year	Announcer	Year	Announcer
1927–28	Graham McNamee	1940	Bill Stern (on NBC)
1929	Bill Munday		Sam Balter
	Carl Haverlin		Mike Frankovitch (on Mutual)
	Graham McNamee	1941–48	Bill Stern
1930	Lloyd Yoder	1949	Mel Allen
	Carl Haverlin	1950–51	Red Barber
1931	Bill Munday	1952–58	Al Helfer
	C. L. Lantry		
1932	Don Wilson		
	Don Thompson	Others since include:	
1933	Don Wilson	Don Kline	Bud Foster
	Don Thompson	Curt Gowdy	Bob Buck
1934	Don Thompson	Chick Hearn	Bob Costas
	Ken Carpenter	Fred Hessler	Marty Glickman
1935	Don Wilson	Mike Walden	Mel Proctor
	Don Thompson	Tom Kelly	Joel Myers
1936–38	Don Wilson	Bob Wolff	Wayne Larrivee
	Ken Carpenter	Bob Reynolds	Hilliard Gates
1939	Bill Stern	Tom Hanlon	Don Kramer

ORANGE BOWL

Year	Announcer	Year	Announcer
1937–46	Ted Husing	1957	Jim Gibbons and Jim McKay
1947–49	Red Barber	1958	Joe Boland and Herman Hickman
1950–51	Mel Allen		
1952	Red Barber	Others since include:	
1953	Jack Brickhouse	Jack Drees	Bill McCallgen
1954	Bob Neal	Charlie Jones	Jay Randolph
1955–56	Red Barber	Bob Murphy	Tony Roberts

COTTON BOWL

Year	Announcer	Year	Announcer
1938	By Saam	1953	Lindsey Nelson
1939	No Recorded Broadcast	1954–57	Curt Gowdy
1940	No Recorded Broadcast	1958–60	Harry Caray
1941	Bob Elson	1961	Bill McCallgen
1942–43	Don Dunphy	1962–64	Harry Caray
1944	Don Dunphy	1965	Jack Drees
	Earl Harper		
1945	Bill Slater	Others since include:	
1946–47	Jim Britt	Jack Buck	Connie Alexander
1948	By Saam	Rick Weaver	Chuck Cooperstein
1949	Al Helfer	Tony Roberts	Brad Sham
1950–52	Bill Stern	Tom Hedrick	John Rooney

SUGAR BOWL

Year	Announcer	Year	Announcer
1936	Cy Leland and Bill Pringle	1949–51	Harry Wismer and Jim Britt
1937	Bill Slater	1952	Harry Wismer
1938	Bill Stern	1953–57	Bob Finigan
1939	Jim Britt	1958	Ray Scott and Jerry Doggett
1940	Red Barber	1959	Curt Gowdy
1941	Fort Pearson	1960	John Ferguson
1942	Fort Pearson and Jim Britt		
1943	Fort Pearson and Harry Wismer	Others since include:	
1944–47	Harry Wismer and Bill Brengo	Harry Kalas	Jay Randolph
1948	Harry Wismer and Mel Allen	Tony Roberts	Marty Glickman

NEW YORK RANGERS

Year	Stn.	Freq.	Sched.	Announcers
1926–27	WMSG	1410	Partial	Jack Filman
1927–28	WMSG	1270	Partial	Jack Filman
1928–29	WMSG	1350	Partial	Jack Filman
1929–30	WMSG	1350	Partial	Jack Filman
1930–31	WMCA	570	Partial	Jack Filman
1931–32	WMCA	570	Partial	Jack Filman
1932–33	WMCA	570	Partial	Jack Filman
1933–34	WMCA	570	Partial	Jack Filman
1934–35	WMCA	570	Partial	Jack Filman
1935–36	WMCA	570	Partial	Jack Filman
1936–37	No Recorded Broadcasts			
1937–38	WMCA	570	Partial	Jack Filman
1938–39	No Recorded Broadcasts			
1939–40	WHN	1010	Partial	Bert Lee and Dick Fishell
1940–41	WHN	1010	Partial	Bert Lee and Dick Fishell
1941–42	WHN	1050	Partial	Bert Lee and Dick Fishell
1942–43	WHN	1050	Partial	Bert Lee and Marty Glickman
1943–44	WHN	1050	Partial	Bert Lee and Marty Glickman
1944–45	WHN	1050	Partial	Bert Lee and Ward Wilson
1945–46	WHN	1050	Partial	Bert Lee and Ward Wilson
1946–47	WHN	1050	Partial	Bert Lee and Ward Wilson
1947–48	WHN	1050	Partial	Bert Lee and Ward Wilson
1948–49	WMGM	1050	Partial	Bert Lee and Ward Wilson
1949–50	WMGM	1050	Partial	Bert Lee and Ward Wilson
1950–51	WMGM	1050	Partial	Bert Lee and Ward Wilson
1951–52	WMGM	1050	Partial	Bert Lee and Ward Wilson
1952–53	WMGM	1050	Partial	Bert Lee and Ward Wilson
1953–54	WMGM	1050	Partial	Bert Lee and Ward Wilson
1954–55	WMGM	1050	Partial	Win Elliot, Ward Wilson
1955–56	WINS	1010	Partial	Bert Lee and Ward Wilson
1956–57	WINS	1010		No Recorded Broadcasts
1957–58	No Recorded Broadcasts			
1958–59	WINS	1010	All	Win Elliot, Bud Palmer
1959–60	WINS	1010	Partial	Jim Gordon and Monty Hall
1960–61	No Recorded Broadcasts			
1961–62	WINS	1010	Fraction	Les Keiter and Jim Gordon
1962–63	WCBS	880	Partial	Jim Gordon and Marty Glickman
1963–64	WCBS	880	Handful	Win Elliot
1964–65	WCBS	880	Partial	Win Elliot
1965–66	WHN	1050	Partial	Marv Albert
1966–67	WHN	1050	Partial	Marv Albert
1967–68	WHN	1050	Partial	Marv Albert and Bill Chadwick
1968–69	WHN	1050	Partial	Marv Albert and Bill Chadwick
1969–70	WHN	1050	Partial	Marv Albert and Bill Chadwick
1970–71	WNBC	660	Partial	Marv Albert and Bill Chadwick
1971–72	WNBC	660	Partial	Marv Albert and Bill Chadwick
1972–73	WNBC	660	Partial	Marv Albert Gene Stuart
1973–74	WNBC	660	Partial	Marv Albert or Spencer Ross and Sal Messina
1974–75	WNEW	1130	Partial	Marv Albert or Spencer Ross and Sal Messina
1975–76	WNEW	1130	Partial	Marv Albert or Spencer Ross and Sal Messina
1976–77	WNEW	1130	Partial	Marv Albert or Spencer Ross and Sal Messina
1977–78	WNEW	1130	Partial	Marv Albert or Sam Rosen and Sal Messina
1978–79	WNEW	1130	Partial	Marv Albert or Sam Rosen and Sal Messina
1979–80	WNEW	1130	Partial	Marv Albert or Sam Rosen and Sal Messina
1980–81	WNEW	1130	Partial	Marv Albert or Sam Rosen and Sal Messina
1981–82	WNEW	1130	Partial	Marv Albert or Sam Rosen and Sal Messina
1982–83	WNEW	1130	Partial	Marv Albert or Sam Rosen and Sal Messina

Year	Stn.	Freq.	Sched.	Announcers	Year	Stn.	Freq.	Sched.	Announcers
1983–84	WNEW	1130	Partial	Marv Albert or Mike Emrick and Sal Messina	1991–92	WFAN	660	All	Marv Albert or Howie Rose and Sal Messina
1984–85	WPAT	930	Partial	Marv Albert or Mike Emrick and Sal Messina		WEVD	1050		
1985–86	WNBC	660	Partial	Marv Albert or Mike Emrick and Sal Messina	1992–93	WFAN	660	All	Marv Albert or Howie Rose and Sal Messina
1986–87	WNBC	660	Partial	Marv Albert or Mike Emrick and Sal Messina		WEVD	1050		
					1993–94	WFAN	660	All	Marv Albert or Howie Rose and Sal Messina
1987–88	WNBC	660	All	Marv Albert or Mike Emrick and Sal Messina		WEVD	1050		
	WEVD	97.9 FM			1994–95	WFAN	660	All	Marv Albert or Howie Rose and Sal Messina
1988–89	WFAN	660	All	Marv Albert or John Kelly and Sal Messina		WEVD	1050		
	WMCA	570			1995–96	WFAN	660	All	Marv Albert or Kenny Albert and Sal Mesina
1989–90	WFAN	660	All	Marv Albert or Howie Rose and Sal Messina		WEVD	1050		
	WPAT	930			1996–97	WFAN	660	All	Marv Albert or Kenny Albert and Sal Messina
1990–91	WFAN	660	All	Marv Albert or Howie Rose and Sal Messina		WEVD	1050		
	WPAT	930			1997–98	WFAN	660	All	Kenny Albert or Spencer Ross and Sal Messina
						WEVD	1050		

NEW JERSEY DEVILS

Year	Station	Freq.	Announcers	Year	Station	Freq.	Announcers
1982–83	WVNJ	620	Larry Hirsch Fred Shero	1990–91	WABC	770	Chris Moore Larry Brooks
1983–84	WMCA	570	Larry Hirsch Fred Shero	1991–92	WABC	770	Chris Moore Sherry Ross
1984–85	WMCA	570	Larry Hirsch Fred Shero	1992–93	WABC	770	Chris Moore Sherry Ross
1985–86	WMCA	570	Larry Hirsch Fred Shero	1993–94	WABC	770	Mike Miller Sherry Ross
1986–87	WMCA	570	Dale Arnold Fred Shero	1994–95	WABC	770	Mike Miller Sherry Ross
1987–88	WMCA	570	Dale Arnold Larry Brooks	1995–96	WABC	770	Mike Miller Randy Velischek
1988–89	WABC	770	Chris Moore Larry Brooks	1996–97	WABC	770	Mike Miller Randy Velischek
1989–90	WABC	770	Chris Moore Larry Brooks	1997–98	WABC	770	Mike Miller Randy Velischek

NEW YORK ISLANDERS

Year	Station	Freq.	Announcers
1972–73*	WHN	1050	Al Albert, Jim Gordon, Jack Decelles
1973–74*	WHN	1050	Al Albert, Bill Mazer
1974–75*	WMCA	570	Dom Valentino, Jim Garvey
1975–76*	WMCA	570	John Sterling, Bob Lawrence
1976–77*	WMCA	570	John Sterling, Bob Lawrence
1977–78*	WMCA	570	John Sterling, Bob Lawrence
1978–79	WMCA	570	Tim Ryan, Steve Albert, Ed Giacomin
1979–80	WMCA	570	Bob Lawrence, Steve Albert, Jean Potvin, Ed Westfall
1980–81	WMCA	570	Jiggs McDonald, Jean Potvin, Ed Westfall
1981–82	WMCA	570	Barry Landers, Jean Potvin
1982–83	WMCA	570	Barry Landers, Jean Potvin
1983–84	WOR	710	Barry Landers, Jean Potvin
1984–85	WOR	710	Barry Landers, Jean Potvin
1985–86	WOR	710	Barry Landers, Jean Potvin
1986–87	WOR	710	Barry Landers, Jean Potvin
1987–88	WOR	710	Barry Landers, Jean Potvin
1988–89	WEVD	97.9†	Barry Landers, Jean Potvin
1989–90 midseason	WEVD switch to WEVD	97.9† 1050	Barry Landers, Bobby Nystrom
1990–91	WEVD	1050	Barry Landers, Bobby Nystrom
1991–92	WPAT	930	Barry Landers, Bobby Nystrom
1992–93	WPAT	930	Barry Landers, Bobby Nystrom
1993–94	WPAT	930	Barry Landers, Bobby Nystrom
1994–95	WRCN	103.9†	Barry Landers, Bobby Nystrom
1995–96	WRCN	103.9†	Barry Landers, Bobby Nystrom
1996–97	WDRE	92.7†	Barry Landers, Bobby Nystrom
1997–98	WDRE	92.7†	Jim Cerny, Chris Botta

* Partial Schedule Broadcast
† FM

NFL CHAMPIONSHIP

Year	Station (Freq.)	Announcers	Teams
1934	WINS (1180)	Earl Harper	New York–Chicago
1935	WINS (1180)	Earl Harper	New York–Detroit
1936	WOR (710)	Cas Adams	Boston–Green Bay
1937	WOR (710)	Tony Wakeman	Chicago-Washington
1938	No broadcast listed		New York–Green Bay
1939	WOR (710)	Red Barber Harry Wismer Dick Fishell	New York–Green Bay
1940	WOR (710)	Red Barber	Washington-Chicago
1941	WOR (710)	Red Barber Bob Elson	New York–Chicago
	WHN (1050)	Dick Fishell Bert Lee	
1942	WOR (710)	Harry Wismer Jack Drees Russ Hodges	Washington-Chicago
1943	WNEW (1130)	Harry Wismer Guy Savage	Washington-Chicago
1944	WJZ (770)	Harry Wismer Guy Savage	New York–Green Bay
	WHN (1050)	Red Barber Connie Desmond	
1945	WJZ (770)	Harry Wismer Johnny Niblett	Washington-Cleveland
1946	WJZ (770)	Harry Wismer Red Grange	New York–Chicago
	WHN (1050)	Red Barber Connie Desmond	
1947	WJZ (770)	Harry Wismer Red Grange	Philadelphia-Chicago
1948	WJZ (770)	Harry Wismer Red Grange	Philadelphia-Chicago
1949	WJZ (770)	Harry Wismer Red Grange	Philadelphia–Los Angeles
1950	WJZ (770)	Harry Wismer Red Grange	Los Angeles–Cleveland
1951	WMGM (1050)	Harry Wismer Earl Gillespie	Cleveland–Los Angeles
1952	WOR (710)	Earl Gillespie Chris Schenkel	Detroit-Cleveland
1953	WOR(710)	Earl Gillespie Chris Schenkel	Cleveland-Detroit
1954	WOR (710)	Earl Gillespie Chris Schenkel	Detroit-Cleveland
1955	WRCA (660)	Ken Coleman Bill McCallgen	Cleveland–Los Angeles

Year	Station (Freq.)	Announcers	Teams
1956	WRCA (660)	Ken Coleman	Chicago–New York
		Joe Tucker	
	WINS (1010)	Marty Glickman	
		Tom Henrich	
1957	WRCA (660)	Ray Scott	Cleveland-Detroit
		Bill McCallgen	
1958	WNBC (660)	Joe Boland	Baltimore–New York
		Bill McCallgen	
	WCBS (880)	Les Keiter	
		Bob Cooke	
1959	WNBC (660)	Van Patrick	New York–Baltimore
		By Saam	
	WINS (1010)	Les Keiter	
		Bob Cooke	
1960	WNBC (660)	Blaine Walsh	Green Bay–Philadelphia
		Jack Whitaker	
1961	WNBC (660)	Ray Scott	New York–Green Bay
		Jim Lamey	
	WNEW (1130)	Marty Glickman	
		Al DeRogatis	
1962	WNBC (660)	Ken Coleman	Green Bay–New York
		Ted Moore	
1963	WNBC (660)	Jim Gibbons	New York–Chicago
		Pat Summerall	
	WNEW (1130)	Marty Glickman	
		Al DeRogatis	
1964	WCBS (880)	Jack Drees	Baltimore-Cleveland
		Jim Morse	
1965	WCBS (880)	Jack Drees	Cleveland–Green Bay
		Jim Morse	
1966	WCBS (880)	Jack Drees	Dallas–Green Bay
		Jim Morse	

SUPER BOWL

Year	Station (Freq.)	Announcers	Teams
1967	WCBS (880)	Jack Drees	
		Tom Hedrick	
	WNBC (660)	Jim Simpson	
		George Ratterman	Kansas City–Green Bay
1968	WCBS (880)	Jack Drees	
		Tom Hedrick	Green Bay–Oakland
1969	WNBC (660)	Charlie Jones	
		George Ratterman	
		Pat Summerall	
	WABC (770)	Merle Harmon	
		Sam DeLuca	Jets-Baltimore
1970	WOR (710)	Bob Reynolds	
		Tom Hedrick	Minnesota–Kansas City
1971	WNBC (660)	Jay Randolph	
		Al DeRogatis	Baltimore-Dallas

Year	Station (Freq.)	Announcers	Teams
1972	WCBS (880)	Andy Musser Ray Gerace	Dallas-Miami
1973	WNBC (660)	Jim Simpson Kyle Rote	Miami-Washington
1974	WCBS (880)	Andy Musser Bob Tucker	Miami-Minnesota
1975	WNBC (660)	Jim Simpson John Brody	Pittsburgh-Minnesota
1976	WCBS (880)	Ed Ingles Jim Kelly	Pittsburgh-Dallas
1977	WNBC (660)	Jim Simpson John Brodie	Oakland-Minnesota
1978	WCBS (880)	Jack Buck Jim Kelly	Dallas-Denver
1979	WCBS (880)	Jack Buck Hank Stram Pat Sumerall	Dallas-Pittsburgh
1980	WCBS (880)	Jack Buck Hank Stram	Pittsburgh-Rams
1981	WCBS (880)	Jack Buck Hank Stram	Philadelphia-Oakland
1982	WCBS (880)	Jack Buck Hank Stram	Cincinnati–San Francisco
1983	WCBS (880)	Jack Buck Hank Stram	Miami-Washington
1984	WCBS (880)	Jack Buck Hank Stram	Raiders-Washington
1985	WCBS (880)	Jack Buck Hank Stram	Miami–San Francisco
1986	WNBC (660)	Don Criqui Bob Trumpy	New England–Chicago
1987	WNEW (1130)	Jim Gordon Dick Lynch	Giants-Denver
1988	WNEW (1130)	Jack Buck Hank Stram	Washington-Denver
1989	WFAN (660)	Jack Buck Hank Stram	San Francisco–Cincinnati
1990	WFAN (660)	Jack Buck Hank Stram	San Francisco–Denver
1991	WNEW (1130)	Jim Gordon Dick Lynch Karl Nelson	Giants-Buffalo
1992	WFAN (660)	Jack Buck Hank Stram	Washington-Buffalo
1993	WFAN (660)	Jack Buck Hank Stram	Dallas-Buffalo
1994	WFAN (660)	Jack Buck Hank Stram	Dallas-Buffalo
1995	WFAN (660)	Jack Buck Hank Stram	San Diego–San Francisco
1996	WFAN (660)	Jack Buck Hank Stram	Dallas-Pittsburgh
1997	WFAN (660)	Howard David Matt Millen	Green Bay–New England
1998	WFAN (660)	Howard David Matt Millen	Green Bay–Denver

MONDAY NIGHT FOOTBALL

Season	Network	Announcers	Season	Network	Announcers
1972	Mutual	Van Patrick Al Wester	1985	CBS	Jack Buck Hank Stram
1973	Mutual	Van Patrick Al Wester	1986	NBC	Don Criqui Bob Trumpy
1974	Mutual	Lindsey Nelson Dave Martin	1987	NBC	Don Criqui Bob Trumpy
1975	Mutual	Lindsey Nelson Al Wester	1988	CBS	Jack Buck Hank Stram
1976	Mutual	Lindsey Nelson Tony Roberts	1989	CBS	Jack Buck Hank Stram
1977	Mutual	Lindsey Nelson Al Wester	1990	CBS	Jack Buck Hank Stram
1978	CBS	Jack Buck Jim Kelly	1991	CBS	Jack Buck Hank Stram
1979	CBS	Jack Buck Hank Stram	1992	CBS	Jack Buck Hank Stram
1980	CBS	Jack Buck Hank Stram	1993	CBS	Jack Buck Hank Stram
1981	CBS	Jack Buck Hank Stram	1994	CBS	Jack Buck Hank Stram
1982	CBS	Jack Buck Hank Stram	1995	CBS	Jack Buck Hank Stram
1983	CBS	Jack Buck Hank Stram	1996	CBS	Howard David Matt Millen
1984	CBS	Jack Buck Hank Stram	1997	CBS	Howard David Matt Millen
			1998	CBS	Howard David Matt Millen

NEW YORK GIANTS FOOTBALL

Year	Station	Freq.	Announcers	Year	Station	Freq.	Announcers
1934	WINS*	1180	Earl Harper	1942	WHN	1050	Red Barber
1935	WINS*	1180	Earl Harper				Allen Hale
1936	WOR*	710	Stan Lomax	1943	WHN	1050	Red Barber
1937	WOR*	710	Stan Lomax				Connie Desmond
1938	Not on the Air			1944	WHN	1050	Red Barber
1939	WABC	860	Mel Allen				Connie Desmond
	or			1945	WHN	1050	Red Barber
	WHN	1010	Dick Fishell				Connie Desmond
	or			1946	WHN	1050	Red Barber
	WOR	710	Red Barber				Connie Desmond
			Dick Fishell	1947	WHN	1050	Connie Desmond
1940	WHN	1010	Dick Fishell				Stan Lomax
			Bert Lee	1948	WMGM	1050	Connie Desmond
1941	WHN	1050	Dick Fishell				Bert Lee
			Bert Lee	*Partial Schedule			

Year	Station	Freq.	Announcers	Year	Station	Freq.	Announcers
1949	WMGM	1050	Marty Glickman Harold Holtz	1975	WNEW	1130	Marv Albert Chip Cipolla Dick Lynch
1950	WMGM	1050	Ted Husing Marty Glickman	1976	WNEW	1130	Marv Albert Dick Lynch
1951	WMGM	1050	Marty Glickman Ernie Harwell	1977	WNEW	1130	Jim Gordon Dick Lynch
1952	WMGM	1050	Marty Glickman Chris Schenkel	1978	WNEW	1130	Jim Gordon Dick Lynch
1953	WMGM	1050	Marty Glickman Chris Schenkel	1979	WNEW	1130	Jim Gordon Dick Lynch
1954	WMGM	1050	Marty Glickman Johnny Most	1980	WNEW	1130	Jim Gordon Dick Lynch
1955	WMGM	1050	Marty Glickman Johnny Most	1981	WNEW	1130	Jim Gordon Dick Lynch
1956	WINS*	1010	Les Keiter Tommy Henrich	1982	WNEW	1130	Jim Gordon Dick Lynch
1957	WINS	1010	Les Keiter John Condon	1983	WNEW	1130	Jim Gordon Dick Lynch
1958	WCBS	880	Les Keiter Jack Drees	1984	WNEW	1130	Jim Gordon Dick Lynch
1959	WCBS	880	Les Keiter Tom Dowd	1985	WNEW	1130	Jim Gordon Dick Lynch
1960	WCBS	880	Mel Allen	1986	WNEW	1130	Jim Gordon Dick Lynch
1961	WNEW	1130	Marty Glickman Al DeRogatis Joe Hasel	1987	WNEW	1130	Jim Gordon Dick Lynch
1962	WNEW	1130	Marty Glickman Al DeRogatis	1988	WNEW	1130	Jim Gordon Dick Lynch Karl Nelson
1963	WNEW	1130	Marty Glickman Al DeRogatis	1989	WNEW	1130	Jim Gordon Dick Lynch Karl Nelson
1964	WNEW	1130	Marty Glickman Al DeRogatis Kyle Rote	1990	WNEW	1130	Jim Gordon Dick Lynch Karl Nelson
1965	WNEW	1130	Marty Glickman Al DeRogatis Kyle Rote	1991	WNEW	1130	Jim Gordon Dick Lynch Karl Nelson
1966	WNEW	1130	Marty Glickman Al DeRogatis Kyle Rote	1992	WNEW later WBBR	1130 1130	Jim Gordon Dick Lynch Karl Nelson
1967	WNEW	1130	Marty Glickman Al DeRogatis Chip Cipolla	1993	WOR	710	Jim Gordon Dick Lynch Karl Nelson
1968	WNEW	1130	Marty Glickman Chip Cipolla Chuck (Charlie) Conerly	1994	WOR	710	Jim Gordon Dick Lynch Karl Nelson
1969	WNEW	1130	Marty Glickman Chip Cipolla	1995	WOR	710	Bob Papa Dick Lynch
1970	WNEW	1130	Marty Glickman Chip Cipolla	1996	WOR and WFAN*	710 660	Bob Papa Dick Lynch
1971	WNEW	1130	Marty Glickman Chip Cipolla	1997	WNEW and WFAN*	102.7 FM 660	Bob Papa Dick Lynch Ottis Anderson
1972	WNEW	1130	Marty Glickman Chip Cipolla Sam Huff	1998	WNEW and WFAN*	102.7 FM 660	Bob Papa Dick Lynch Billy Taylor
1973	WNEW	1130	Marv Albert Chip Cipolla Sam Huff				
1974	WNEW	1130	Marv Albert Chip Cipolla Sam Huff				

*Partial Schedule

409

NEW YORK JETS

Year	Station	Freq.	Announcers
1960	WMGM*	1050	Tom Moorehead / Frank Leahy
1961	Not on the Air		
1962	WABC	770	Bob Murphy / Jim Crowley
1963†	WHN	1050	Bob Murphy / Monte Irvin
1964	WABC	770	Merle Harmon / Otto Graham
1965	WABC	770	Merle Harmon / Otto Graham
1966	WABC	770	Merle Harmon / Dick Young
1967	WABC	770	Merle Harmon / Dick Young
1968	WABC	770	Merle Harmon / Sam DeLuca
1969	WABC	770	Merle Harmon / Sam DeLuca
1970	WABC	770	Merle Harmon / Sam DeLuca
1971	WOR	710	Merle Harmon / Sam DeLuca
1972	WOR	710	Merle Harmon / Sam DeLuca
1973	WOR	710	Marty Glickman / Larry Grantham
1974	WOR	710	Marty Glickman / Dave Herman
1975	WOR	710	Marty Glickman / Dave Herman
1976	WOR	710	Marty Glickman / Dave Herman
1977	WOR	710	Marty Glickman / Dave Herman
1978	WOR	710	Marty Glickman / Dave Herman
1979	WCBS	880	Spencer Ross / Sam DeLuca / Ed Ingles
1980	WCBS	880	Spencer Ross / Sam DeLuca / Ed Ingles
1981	WCBS	880	Spencer Ross / Sam DeLuca / Ed Ingles

Year	Station	Freq.	Announcers
1982	WCBS	880	Spencer Ross / Sam DeLuca / Ed Ingles
1983	WCBS	880	Spencer Ross / Sam DeLuca / Ed Ingles
1984	WABC or WMCA	770 / 570	Spencer Ross / Sam DeLuca / Randy Rasmussen
1985	WABC or WMCA	770 / 570	Steve Albert / Sam DeLuca / Randy Rasmussen
1986	WABC or WMCA	770 / 660	Charley Steiner / Sam DeLuca / Randy Rasmussen
1987	WABC or WNBC	770 / 660	Charley Steiner / Randy Rasmussen
1988	WCBS	880	Marty Glickman / Dave Jennings
1989	WCBS	880	Marty Glickman / Dave Jennings
1990	WCBS	880	Marty Glickman / Dave Jennings
1991	WCBS	880	Marty Glickman / Dave Jennings
1992	WCBS	880	Marty Glickman / Dave Jennings
1993	WFAN or WXRK	660 / 92.3 FM	Paul Olden / Dave Jennings
1994	WFAN or WXRK	660 / 92.3 FM	Paul Olden / Dave Jennings
1995	WFAN or WXRK	660 / 92.3 FM	Paul Olden / Dave Jennings
1996	WFAN or WXRK	660 / 92.3 FM	Paul Olden / Dave Jennings
1997	WFAN or WXRK	660 / 92.3 FM	Ian Eagle / Dave Jennings
1998	WFAN or WXRK	660 / 92.3FM	Howard David / Dave Jennings

*Partial Schedule
†Were Titans until 1963

BIBLIOGRAPHY

Albert, Marv, *I'd Love to But I Have a Game,* with Rick Riley, New York, Doubleday, 1993

Albert, Marv, *Yesss!,* with Hal Bock, New York, New American Library, 1979

Allen, Maury, *Voices of Sport,* New York, Grosset & Dunlop, 1971

Allen, Mel, and Ed Fitzgerald, *You Can't Beat the Hours,* New York, Harper and Row, 1963

Barber, Red, *Rhubarb in the Catbird Seat,* with Robert Creamer, Garden City, New York, Doubleday, 1968

Barber, Red, *The Broadcasters,* New York, Dial Press, 1970

Barnouw, Erik, *A Tower in Babel, A History of Broadcasting in the United States,* Volume I, New York, Oxford University Press, 1966

Brickhouse, Jack, with Jack Rosenberg and Ned Colletti, *Thanks for Listening,* South Bend, Indiana, Diamond Communications, 1986

Broeg, Bob, *Memories of a Hall of Fame Sportswriter,* Champaign, Illinois, Sagamore Publishing, 1995

Buck, Jack, Rob Rains, and Bob Broeg, *That's a Winner,* Champaign, Illinois, Sagamore Publishing, 1997

Douglas, George H., *The Early Days of Radio Broadcasting,* Jefferson, North Carolina, McFarland & Company, 1987

Dunphy, Don, *Don Dunphy at Ringside,* New York, Henry Holt and Company, 1988

Durso, Joseph, *Madison Square Garden, 100 Years of History,* New York, Simon & Schuster, 1979

Edwards, Bob, *Fridays with Red,* New York, Simon & Schuster, 1993

Frick, Ford, *Games, Asterisks and People,* New York, Crown, 1973

Fusselle, Warner, with Rick Wolff and Brian Zevnick, *Baseball . . . A Laughing Matter,* St. Louis, The Sporting News Publishing Company, 1987

Gleason, Archer, *History of Radio to 1926,* New York, The American Historical Society, 1938

Glickman, Marty, with Stan Isaacs, *The Fastest Kid on the Block,* Syracuse, New York, Syracuse University Press, 1996

Golenback, Peter, *Bums,* New York, G. P. Putnam's Sons, 1984

Gowdy, Curt, *A Cowboy at the Mike,* Garden City, New York, Doubleday, 1966

Gowdy, Curt, *Seasons to Remember,* with John Powers, New York, HarperCollins, 1993

Greenfield, Thomas Allen, *Radio, A Reference Guide,* New York, Greenwood Press, 1989

Gross, Ben, *I Looked and Listened,* New York, Random House, 1954

Harwell, Ernie, *The Babe Signed My Shoe,* South Bend, Indiana, Diamond Communications, 1994

Harwell, Ernie, *Tuned to Baseball,* South Bend, Indiana, Diamond Communications, 1985

Heimer, Mel, *The Long Count,* New York, Kingsport Press, 1969

Hibner, John Charles, *The Rose Bowl,* Jefferson City, North Carolina, McFarland & Company, 1993

Hirshberg, Don, *Phil Rizzuto, A Yankee Tradition,* Champaign, Illinois, Sagamore Publishing, 1993

Hodges, Russ, *My Giants,* Garden City, New York, Doubleday, 1963

Husing, Ted, *My Eyes Are in My Heart,* New York, Bernard Geis, 1959

Husing, Ted, *Ten Years Before the Mike,* New York, Farrar & Rinehart, 1935

Isaacs, Neil D., *Vintage NBA*, Indianapolis, Masters Press, 1996

Jackson, Kenneth T., *Encyclopedia/New York City*, New Haven, Connecticut, Yale University Press, 1995

Keiter, Les, *Fifty Years Behind the Microphone*, with Dennis Christianson, Honolulu, Hawaii, University of Hawaii Press, 1991

Kiner, Ralph, and Joe Gergen, *Kiner's Korner*, New York, Arbor House, 1987

Landry, Robert J., *This Fascinating Radio Business*, New York, Bobbs-Merrill Company, 1946

Mayer, Ronald, *The 1937 Newark Bears, A Baseball Legend*, New York, Viking Press, 1980

McNamee, Graham, and Robert Gordon Anderson, *You're on the Air*, New York, Harper and Brothers, 1926

McNeil, Alex, *Total Television*, New York, Penguin Books, 1980

Neft, David S., and Richard M. Cohen, *The Sports Encyclopedia: Baseball*, New York, St. Martin's Press, 1996

Neft, David S., and Richard M. Cohen, *The Sports Encyclopedia: Pro Basketball*, New York, St. Martin's Press, 1992

Neft, David S., Richard M. Cohen, and Rick Korch, *The Football Encyclopedia*, New York, St. Martin's Press, 1990

Nelson, Lindsey, and Al Hirshberg, *Backstage at the Mets*, New York, The Viking Press, 1966

Nelson, Lindsey, *Hello Everybody, I'm Lindsey Nelson*, New York, William Morrow, 1985

Paley, William, *As It Happened*, Garden City, New York, Doubleday, 1979

Rothafel, Samuel L., and Raymond Francis Yates, *Broadcasting Its New Day*, New York, The Century Company, 1925

Settel, Irving, *A Pictorial History of Radio*, New York, Grosset and Dunlop, 1960

Sklar, Rick, *Rocking America*, New York, St. Martin's Press, 1984

Slate, Sam J., and Joe Cook, *It Sounds Impossible*, New York, Macmillan, 1963

Smith, Curt, *The Storytellers*, New York, Macmillan, 1995

Smith, Curt, *Voices of the Game*, South Bend, Indiana, Diamond Communications, 1987

Stern, Bill, *The Taste of Ashes*, New York, Holt, 1959

Wimmer, Dick, *The Sandlot Game*, Indianapolis, Masters Press, 1997

Wismer, Harry, *The Public Calls It Sports*, Prentice Hall, Englewood Cliffs, New Jersey, 1965

INDEX

Numbers in italics include photos. "References" and "Teams and Events: Year-by-Year listings"
are not included in index.

413